LET'S LEARN ABOUT AGING

Old age can be a time of opportunity, rather than one of decline and despair. Yet our attitudes toward aging are almost universally negative. This remarkable collection of articles offers constructive ways to deal with the facts of aging, and explores subjects neglected or deemed taboo until now.

How do people's personalities and self-images change when everyone they encounter treats them as children?

By artificially sustaining the lives of severely debilitated patients, are doctors "promoting health and relieving suffering" — or are they doing precisely the opposite?

What are the implications for our society if, in a few decades, the average national life expectancy is 96 years?

A multitude of other questions and points of view are presented in this important new work, a work that gives the reader a clearly written, nontechnical introduction to the field of social gerontology.

The Editors of this wide-ranging volume pull together a fascinating array of articles, both professional and popular, that illuminate the scandalously unexplored field of aging. "We can no longer pretend to close our eyes," they write, "to what for many is one-third of their life span."

People must understand the physiological, psychological, and social processes of aging before they can handle sensibly the problems and needs of the aged. Free from technical jargon, this volume delves into basic concerns of the elderly: sex, money, retirement, death and dying. **Let's Learn About Aging** brushes aside the many taboos about discussing old age and tackles issues head-on. It is designed for students of social gerontology and, more broadly, for professionals and students in psychology, health, social work, sociology, and political science — with or without technical background in the field. The unusually broad spectrum of concerns about aging covered in this provocative collection ensures it a place as a foundation-work in the emerging field of social gerontology.

LET'S LEARN ABOUT

AGING

A BOOK OF READINGS

Edited by
[John R. Barry
and
C. Ray Wingrove]

SCHENKMAN PUBLISHING COMPANY, INC.

Halsted Press Division

John Wiley and Sons

New York   London   Sydney   Toronto

Copyright © 1977

Schenkman Publishing Company, Inc.
3 Mt. Auburn Place
Cambridge, Massachusetts 02138

*Distributed solely by Halsted Press, a Division of John Wiley & Sons, Inc.,
New York, New York.*

Library of Congress Cataloging in Publication Data
Main entry under title:

Let's learn about aging.

   1. Gerontology — Addresses, essays, lectures.
2. Aging — Addresses, essays, lectures. I. Barry, John Regan.
II. Wingrove, C. Ray.
HQ 1061.L46   301.43'5   76-45168
ISBN 0-470-98965-3
ISBN 0-470-98967-X pbk.

Printed in the United States of America

*Dedicated to
our friend and colleague,
Raymond Payne, 1919 – 1971*

CONTENTS

Introduction and overview.

LET'S LEARN ABOUT AGING

Introduction and Overview

The selections in this volume are intended to introduce the reader to the breadth of social gerontology in a relatively simple and intelligible way. The numbers of older citizens are increasing world wide, and the United States is no exception. Even though today approximately 10 percent of our population is 65 or older, it was not until very recently that students in the behavioral and biological sciences included this segment of our population in their studies. The folly of this neglect has become apparent at last. We can no longer pretend to understand or to be students of human behavior and at the same time close our eyes to what for many is one-third of their life spans. Governmental as well as individual efforts to help older persons live out their lives in satisfactory and meaningful ways have resulted in widespread demands for information about this age group. These readings are meant as a response to such needs.

The last decade has witnessed rapid growth of research and knowledge in the field of aging. Thus, while the coverage in the book is broad, it presents only a selected sample of works within the major areas of aging. Following a general overview of social gerontology in Section I, Section II deals with three basic processes of aging, viz., physiological, psychological, and social as developed through the research and writings of various authors in the field. Having established somewhat of a foundation of knowledge of the aging processes, the reader should then be in a better position to empathize with the aged and their concerns, three of which — sex, retirement, death and dying — are presented in Section III of our book. Finally, through selected readings in housing and institutional care, social services, and treatment approaches, we hope to show how needs of the elderly are being dealt with in contemporary America. The organizational structure of this book is not arbitrary, but presents what we believe to be a logical sequence of readings for the newcomer to social gerontology.

Coverage in this book of readings is varied, not only in content, but in the styles and sources of articles presented. Contradictory results of gerontological research show differing interpretations which continue to stimulate research. There are original papers and published articles from both scientific and popular magazines. Interviews and summaries of new developments by reporters provide a change of pace which should interest the reader.

1

The audience toward whom these readings are directed is almost as varied as the readings themselves. Undergraduates at all levels and from all settings, be they community colleges, junior colleges or traditional four year colleges and universities, hopefully will find this a useful introduction to social gerontology. Since a great deal of technical background is *not* required to understand the materials gathered here, any intelligent lay person interested in the field of aging should also find this a suitable introductory resource. As a matter of fact, the intelligibility and complexity of the material are intentionally focused to appeal to these groups. However, trial use of the manuscript also revealed the book to be useful as collateral reading for more advanced students who were uninformed about some specific area such as physiology, religion, retirement, etc.

The initial planning for this volume was begun in the late 1960s by a group of University of Georgia teachers who had searched for materials to use as collateral readings in a training program for managers and other housing personnel concerned with a better understanding of the aged. The training program was developed by Dr. H. R. Smith. The initial selection of readings was made by Drs. Raymond Payne, C. Ray Wingrove, Ruth E. Weber, John R. Barry and Mr. Donald Brewer. Dr. Payne was the central figure in the initial planning of the book of readings. After his untimely death, the present editors picked up the project and have made extensive revisions. Many of the original readings were dropped and others were added as a result of reader input. Eight different groups of students have used and reacted to different combinations of selections. The present volume, then, has profited from the initial planning of Dr. Payne and his collaborators, as well as the necessary synthesis by a smaller number of people, the present editors.

The development of this volume was supported in part by an Administration on Aging Training Managers Grant 23-42-RE348-002 to the University of Georgia. Responsibility for all materials in this collection rests entirely with the editors and does *not* reflect the policies or views of the Administration on Aging.

I
SOCIAL GERONTOLOGY

1

SOCIAL GERONTOLOGY

A STUDY OF THE AGED

Any informed student of social gerontology must have some appreciation and understanding of the demographic and ecological characteristics of the elderly as compared to the rest of the population. Likewise, knowledge of variability in basic psychological characteristics of the elderly is essential as a rudimentary grasp of the special problems in research and work with the aging. These are the topics dealt with in Section I as we attempt to help the reader build a foundation upon which to construct a more detailed and thorough understanding of the aged population.

Based primarily upon 1970 U.S. census data, Hanns Pieper presents a profile of the aged as a growing minority in the United States. His presentation includes facts, figures, and interpretations on such topics as the growth of the older population, sex ratios at different ages, and income, mortality rates, family composition, and employment status of those 65 and over.

The second reading in this section, "Status of Research in Applied Social Gerontology," by Robert Havighurst also provides a summary of facts about America's aged population. Although there is some overlap between the first part of this article and the preceeding one by Pieper, Havighurst's summary is much more succinct and in some ways more inclusive. In addition, he points up the variety and complexity of research questions still begging in this area.

Carl Eisdorfer's article gives a broad description of some of the frontiers of knowledge (as well as of ignorance) concerning psychological aspects of aging. He presents theories and demolishes many of the myths prevalent regarding the psychological functioning of the aged. The reader should find his imagination stirred and his stereotypes disappearing as Dr. Eisdorfer emphasizes that variability in almost all aspects of life increases with age. A review of compensatory behaviors which accompany age related changes rounds out this excellent presentation.

Finally, Naomi Brill points out that the basic methods of understanding and working with people are very much the same regardless of age. However, she does discuss the growing body of specific knowledge being developed in the behavioral sciences which is particularly useful in work with the aged. More specifically, she explores principles and ramifications of ego psychology, the concept of the developmental stages of life, and crisis intervention as they relate to working with older citizens. This selection should be of particular interest to those who possess a social work orientation.

These four selections, if read as a unit of material, should provide the reader a springboard from which to plunge into the more detailed analysis of age related concerns which comprises the remainder of the book.

1. Aged Americans: A Profile of A Growing Minority*

HANNS G. PIEPER**
University of Georgia

INTRODUCTION

In 1900 four out of every one hundred persons living in the United States were 65 or older. By 1970, this number had increased to almost ten out of every hundred persons. With the life style prevalent in the United States today, many people who are fortunate enough to survive longer find that they must spend their aged years with less income, fewer opportunities to contribute to society, and a family unit frequently altered due to death or mobility of former household members. It seems, then, that while advances in biological knowledge have made it possible for many more persons to reach older ages, society has not yet come to grips with their psychological, economic, and sociological needs.

The needs of the aged are related to many demographic and socioeconomic characteristics. Among the demographic factors are the number of males per females, mortality, marital status, family composition, and the mobility and geographic location of the aged. Socioeconomic variables which have direct bearing on the physical and psychological well-being of the aged include employment and income. It is the purpose of this article to discuss these characteristics in relation to the aged population of the United States. 1970 census data are utilized and are presented whenever possible for the age groups 65-69, 70-74, 80-84, and 85 and over.

Each of these age groups is associated with unique social backgrounds reflecting different needs and desires.

*Original paper written for this book.

**Mr. Pieper is a doctoral candidate specializing in demography in the Department of Sociology, at The University of Georgia, and is currently a teaching assistant there.

7

The Size of the Aged Population

In 1970 there were 20,065,502 Americans 65 and older living in the United States, comprising almost 10 percent of the total population. Due largely to trends in declining mortality at all ages, and partially to early foreign immigration, the aged population has been increasing more rapidly than the rest of the population throughout the century. Moreover, this trend is expected to continue until at least 1990. By that year, it is projected that the aged population will be about 38 percent higher than it was in 1970, and by the turn of the next century, there will be an estimated twenty-nine million aged Americans.

TABLE 1
*Number of Persons Aged 65 and Over
United States, 1900-2000*

Year	Age Groups 65-69	70-74	75+	Total 65+	Percent 65+
1900	1,304*	885	895	3,084	4.0
1910	1,682	1,115	1,157	3,954	4.3
1920	2,072	1,397	1,471	4,940	4.7
1930	2,776	1,953	1,916	6,645	5.4
1940	3,815	2,574	2,647	9,036	6.8
1950	5,013	3,419	3,862	12,295	8.2
1960	6,258	4,739	5,563	16,560	9.2
1970	6,992	5,444	7,630	20,066	9.9
1980**	8,228	6,452	9,371	24,051	10.8
1990	9,332	7,437	10,999	27,768	11.3
2000	8,532	7,759	12,551	28,842	10.8

* All numbers X 1,000.
** Based on Series E projections.
Source: Table 53, General Population Characteristics, U.S. Summary, 1970 U.S. Census.
Table 2, *Projections of the Population of the United States by Age and Sex, 1972-2020.*
Series P-25, No. 493.

Increases in the aged population are due less to increases in the overall life span than to the fact that more persons attain an age which was reached by relatively few in earlier years. In 1900 about 29 percent of the aged population was over 75 years of age, as compared with 39 percent in 1970. It is projected that by the year 2000 almost 44 percent of the aged population will be in this category. As a result of the increasingly large number of persons representing each age cohort, the aged population will be even more heterogeneous then than it is now. This added dimension of greater variability in the aged population will make planning for the needs of this group more difficult in the years to come.

TABLE 2
Population Aged 65 and Over by Race.
United States, 1920-1970

Year	Age Group 65-69	70-74	75+	Total 65+	Percent 65+
WHITE					
1920	1,926*	1,299	1,361	4,586	4.8
1930	2,609	1,847	1,789	6,245	5.7
1940	3,502	2,402	2,481	8,385	7.1
1950	4,589	3,184	3,609	11,382	8.4
1960	5,739	4,391	5,173	15,303	9.6
1970	6,299	4,982	7,049	18,330	10.3
NONWHITE					
1920	146	97	110	353	3.2
1930	167	106	127	400	3.1
1940	314	172	165	651	4.7
1950	424	236	253	913	5.6
1960	519	348	389	1,256	6.1
1970	693	462	581	1,736	6.8

* All numbers X 1,000.
Source: Table 53, General Population Characteristics, U.S. Summary, 1970 U.S. Census.

TABLE 3
*Aged Population of United States
By Race or Ethnic Status: 1970*

Age Group	Black	Spanish	Indian	Japanese	Chinese
65-69	633*	160	17	15	11
70-74	422	99	11	13	8
75-79	262	63	7	8	4
80-84	148	35	4	7	2
85+	121	26	4	4	1
Total					
65+	1,586	383	43	47	26
Percent					
65+	7.0	4.1	5.7	8.0	6.0

*All numbers X 1,000.
Source: Table 190, Detailed Characteristics, U. S. Summary, 1970 U. S. Census

As is shown in Tables 2 and 3, racial and ethnic differences exist among the elderly. The white population has a greater proportion of aged persons at present than the nonwhite population. A larger proportion of the white population also continues to attain the older ages above 75. In 1970, over 38 percent of the aged white population was in this category, while 33 percent of the nonwhite aged was over 75.

Concerning ethnic groups in the United States, the Japanese had the highest proportion of aged in their population. This reflects both the generally low mortality rates of Japanese-Americans, and the large number of Japanese immigrants in the early 1900s. The lowest percentage of aged persons was found among those of Spanish and Indian heritage.

MORTALITY OF THE AGED POPULATION

Death and its associated personal and social problems are more imminent for the aged population than for any other group. Fortunately, due to general advances in the level of living, older ages are being reached by more Americans before death and related problems become a reality. It has already been noted that a growing percentage of the aged population is over 75. Another indicator of the longer life expectancy is the declining mortality rate for certain age groups.* The number of deaths among the aged per 1000 aged population are presented by age, sex, and race, for 1955 and 1968 in Table 4. It can be seen that there are distinct differences in mortality for the age groups by sex and by race.

For the white population, mortality rates declined from 1955 to 1968 for the groups aged 65-86. The rate of mortality for persons over 85 increased during the same period. For white males there were declines in mortality for the age groups 65-69 and 75-84, and increases for the age groups 70-74 and 85 and over. Among white females there were substantial declines in mortality in the age groups 65-84, and an increase in the group over 85.

TABLE 4
Mortality Rates of the Aged Population By Age,
Race and Sex: 1955 and 1968

Age Group	Both Sexes		Male		Female	
	1955	1968	1955	1968	1955	1968
WHITE						
65-69	32.3*	29.6	41.1	41.0	24.2	20.2
70-74	46.9	46.1	58.1	62.9	37.1	33.5
75-79	75.0	68.1	88.2	86.9	64.3	54.9
80-84	120.5	104.7	133.9	123.5	110.1	92.3
85+	195.3	205.9	200.6	215.6	191.6	200.1
BLACK						
65-69	50.5	51.5	56.7	59.8	44.1	44.0
70-74	58.0	67.0	66.6	85.9	50.4	52.6
75-79	63.6	66.1	71.7	82.0	56.0	54.6
80-84	89.3	80.2	99.3	90.4	79.9	72.2
85+	96.2	111.5	103.3	115.6	90.8	109.9

*Deaths per 1,000 population.
Source: Vital Statistics of the United States, Table BJ, 1955;
    Vital Statistics of the United States, Table 1-8, 1968.

In contrast, the mortality rates for the black aged declined only for those in the age group 80-84. However, much of the increase in the rates for the black aged in the other age groups was due to increases in the rates for aged black males which increased for all groups with the exception of the group aged 80-84. Mortality for the aged black

*Data for 1968 were used rather than 1970, because 1968 was the latest year for which this information was available.

females declined in all but two age groups, those 70-74 and those over 85 years of age. The increases in mortality rates in the age category 85 and over for both races and sexes could be expected because of the decrease in mortality in the younger age groups, and the fact that the group 85 and over contains the remainder of the population and all remaining mortality.

In discussing mortality of the aged, mention should be made of the primary causes of death. In 1968, cardiovascular diseases continued to be a major cause of death among both the white and black elderly, even though mortality from this cause has declined somewhat since 1955. Malignancies were another major cause of death among the elderly and accounted for slightly higher mortality among the white elderly than among the black. The mortality rates associated with malignant neoplasms increased from 1955 to 1968 for both the black and the white aged. Mortality due to conditions related to diabetes also increased in this time period for both the white and the black aged, the largest increases being found in the group aged 85 and over.

The longer life of a large proportion of the aged population has not been without its price. Brotman reports that the cost of health services for those over 65 is three and a half times the cost for persons under that age. Even with government aid programs and other help programs, the elderly must still pay around one-third of their medical costs themselves (Brotman, 1971, 10). This occurs at a point in life when incomes have been greatly reduced.

SEX RATIO OF THE AGED POPULATION

As previously noted, many more women reach ages beyond 65 than men. In fact, the sex ratios for those over 65 (number of males per 100 females) have been declining steadily since 1940 and are expected to continue to decline. The sex ratios also decline sharply with increasing age. In 1940 there were about 99 males aged 65-69 for every 100 females in that age bracket. By 1970 there were only 81 males aged 65-69 per 100 females aged 65-69. For the age group 75 and over, there were only 64 males per 100 females in 1970.

Rural areas of the United States have more balanced sex ratios than do urban centers. This urban-rural difference becomes even more apparent with increasing age. For the age group 65-69, the 1970 rural sex ratio of 96.5 is almost 29 percent higher than the urban sex ratio of 75.3. For the age group 80-84, the rural sex ratio of 78.2 is just over 37 percent higher than the urban sex ratio of 57.0.

TABLE 5
Sex Ratios of the Aged Population:
United States, 1940-2000

Age Group	1940	1950	1960	1970	1980	1990	2000
Total Population	100.8*	98.7	97.1	94.8	95.1	95.3	95.9
65-69	99.4	94.1	88.1	80.7	79.1	77.2	78.4
70-74	98.0	91.5	85.6	74.0	71.8	70.3	70.8
75+	88.4	82.7	75.2	64.0	56.4	55.9	56.6

*Males per 100 females.

Source: Table 53, General Population Characteristics, U.S. Summary, 1970 U. S. Census. Table 2, *Projections of the Population of the United States by Age and Sex, 1972-2020*. Series P-25, No. 493.

MARITAL STATUS OF THE AGED POPULATION

The sex ratio of a given population can have pervading socioeconomic effects on its social system. Not the least of these is the potential for family formation, and the companionship of members of the opposite sex. Because of the low sex ratios at the older ages, females who wish to marry or remarry have only a very small number of potential mates from which to choose.

TABLE 6
Marital Status of the United States'
Aged Population, 1970

Age Group	Single		Married		Widowed		Divorced	
	Male	Female	Male	Female	Male	Female	Male	Female
65-69	7.1*	7.4	80.6	52.0	8.8	36.5	3.5	4.1
70-74	7.3	7.8	75.8	40.0	13.8	49.0	3.1	3.3
75-79	7.3	8.4	68.8	27.9	21.2	61.1	2.7	2.7
80-84	7.6	8.8	58.0	17.2	32.0	71.9	2.4	2.1
85+	10.8	10.7	43.4	10.7	43.4	76.9	2.4	1.7

*Percent of total population in given age-sex group.

Source: Table 203, Detailed Characteristics, U. S. Summary, 1970 U. S. Census.

As is shown in Table 6, the percent of aged who are single (never married) in any given age group does not vary greatly with increasing age. However, the percent who are married at a given time declines rapidly with increasing age, accompanied by an increase in the percent of widowed persons. The sex differentials are also apparent. At age 80-84, for example, almost 60 percent of the males were married in 1970 as contrasted to just over 17 percent of the females. If males continue to die much earlier than females and the projected sex ratios materialize, the incidence of widowhood would also continue to increase in the future.

FAMILY AND HOUSEHOLD CHARACTERISTICS
OF THE AGED POPULATION

Nearly all of the elderly live in some form of family or small household setting. Almost sixty-seven out of every hundred aged persons

TABLE 7
Household and Family Composition
of the Aged Population: 1970

Characteristic	Total	Urban	Rural
Persons 65	20,065,502	14,631,115	5,434,387
Male head of family	30.2%	28.5%	34.8%
Female head of family	5.2	5.4	4.8
Wife of head	19.1	18.2	21.5
Other family members	12.5	13.0	11.1
Not Related to head	1.9	2.0	1.5
Male primary individual	6.1	5.9	6.6
Female primary individual	19.5	21.1	15.2
Inmate of institution or other group quarter	5.5	5.9	4.5

Source: Table 54, General Population Characteristics, U. S. Summary, 1970 U. S. Census.

live with other family members. Just over twenty-seven out of every hundred live by themselves or with non-relatives, leaving just under six out of every hundred to live in institutions.

The composition of households and families varies with the residence of the aged. Those in the urban areas are more likely to live by themselves or in institutions than those in rural areas. Twenty-nine percent of the urban aged either live by themselves or with a non-relative. This is in contrast to only 23.3 percent of the rural aged. In the urban areas 5.9 percent of the aged are living in institutions or other group quarters as opposed to only 4.5 percent in the rural areas.

However, the aged comprise a disproportionately large part of the total number of persons in institutions or other group quarters. Excluding military barracks and college dormitories, over three million persons lived in institutions or group quarters in 1970. About 36.4 percent of these were 65 or over. Aged persons, who comprised 9.9 percent of the total population, made up 12.6 percent of the persons living in boarding houses, 26.1 percent of those living in mental hospitals, and 85.8 percent of those living in homes for the aged.

GEOGRAPHIC DISTRIBUTION AND MOBILITY OF THE AGED POPULATION

In the United States, 9.9 percent of the population is 65 or over. However, the aged population is not distributed evenly throughout the country. The distribution varies considerably by region of the country. The Northeastern United States with 5,200,000 aged persons has the

TABLE 8
Percent of Total Population of Region,
Aged 65 and Over, By Region: 1970

Age Group	Northeast	North Central	South	West
65-69	3.7	3.4	3.5	3.1
70-74	2.9	2.7	2.6	2.4
75-79	2.0	2.0	1.8	1.7
80-84	1.2	1.2	1.0	1.0
85+	0.8	0.8	0.7	0.7

Source: Table 57, General Population Characteristics, U. S. Summary, 1970 U. S. Census.

highest percentage (10.6 percent) of persons over 65. The second largest percentage of aged persons (10.1 percent) is found in the North Central region. The states in this region were home for 5,700,000 aged Americans. The southern states, while being the place of residence for the largest absolute number of aged persons (6,000,000), had the third highest percentage of persons over the age of 65, about 9.6 percent. The aged population of the western states was the smallest of any of the regions (3,000,000) and comprised the smallest proportion of the population, only 8.9 percent.

The variations in the distribution of the aged population are even greater at the state level. Twenty-seven states have lower percentages of aged persons while twenty-two have percentages which are higher. Only Montana has the same proportion of aged persons as the United States as a whole. Florida (14.6 percent), Arkansas, Nebraska, Iowa (12.4 percent), and Kansas (11.8 percent) are the states with the highest percentage of aged persons. Hawaii (5.7 percent) and Alaska (2.3 percent) are those containing the lowest percentage of aged persons.

There are also urban-rural differentials in the distribution of the aged. For the United States as a whole, almost 73 percent of the aged persons live in the urban centers of the United States.

The differences in distribution of the aged population can be due to many factors, such as differentials in past birth and death rates and the consequent age and sex structures of the population. Another influential factor is migration. Americans as a whole are a very mobile group throughout their life cycles. The aged population, while having the lowest rate of migration, nevertheless is fairly mobile. Data dealing with the mobility of families whose head is 65 and over are presented in Table 9. Actually, these data underestimate the mobility of aged families, since they deal only with two points in time, 1965 and 1970. It is quite possible that a considerable number of unrecorded moves were completed within that five year period. These data also do not include elderly persons living by themselves and the mobility of this group is not included here.

About 20 percent of the aged family heads moved at least once between 1965 and 1970. Of those 1,332,439 aged families that lived in a different house in 1965 and 1970, 63 percent moved within the boundaries of the same county, and another 19 percent remained in the same state. Five percent of the movers migrated to a bordering state, while the remaining 13 percent moved to a state which was not bordering. Black family heads, while having the same overall level of mobility, usually moved much shorter distances. Only 7 percent of the aged black family heads who lived in a different house in 1965 and 1970 moved to a house in another state.

TABLE 9
Percent of Families Living in Same House
in 1965 and 1970: Age of Head 65+

Family Characteristics	Total Families	Living in Owner Occupied Housing	Living in Renter Occupied Housing
TOTAL POPULATION			
All Families	79.0	85.0	58.0
Husband-Wife	78.0	84.0	57.0
Female Head	81.0	90.0	61.0
BLACK POPULATION			
All Families	80.0	88.0	64.0
Husband-Wife	80.0	88.0	65.0
Female Head	79.0	90.0	64.0

Source: Table 20, Mobility for States and Nation, 1970 U. S. Census.

EMPLOYMENT OF THE AGED POPULATION

The economic aspects of life are of concern to all once the initial years of dependence are over, but the problems of meeting the basic needs of life become magnified for many Americans later in life. Economic well-being is directly dependent upon a source of income. As is shown in Table 10, labor force participation (those who are employed or who are actively seeking employment) for men declines rapidly after age 65. In the age group 60-64, seventy-three out of every one hundred males were still in the labor force. This number dropped to thirty-nine out of every one hundred for males aged 65-69. This is a reduction in labor force participation of almost 47 percent.

The percent of persons participating in the labor force continues to decline with increasing age. What is perhaps surprising is that so many aged persons are still either employed or looking for employment. Even at ages above 85, ten out of every hundred males are in the labor force.

TABLE 10
Employment Status of the Aged
Population by Sex: 1970

Age Group	Percent in Labor Force	Persons in Labor Force	
		Percent Employed Full-time	Percent Employed Part-time
MALES			
60-64	73.0	80.7	12.2
65-69	38.9	61.2	30.2
70-74	22.4	50.2	41.5
75-79	14.2	49.3	42.0
80-84	9.0	49.6	41.2
85+	10.0	64.6	26.1
FEMALES			
60-64	36.1	65.1	27.7
65-69	17.2	49.4	41.9
70-74	9.1	44.0	46.3
75-79	5.5	46.7	42.0
80-84	3.5	50.8	35.9
85+	4.6	58.8	28.5

Source: Table 215, Detailed Characteristics, U. S. Summary, 1970 U. S. Census.

For those males in the labor force, the percentage fully employed declines to about age 79, but even at that age half of the males in the labor force still have full-time employment. It is interesting to note that almost sixty-five males out of every one hundred over 85 participating in the labor force still consider themselves to be employed full-time. Similar trends in labor force participation were noted for females but labor force participation rates were considerably lower for females than for males.

INCOME OF THE AGED POPULATION

Despite the fact that both labor force participation and full-time employment declined sharply after age 65, there was a slight increase in the percent of persons with some source of income. This is probably due to the onset of sources of income such as Social Security payments and pensions. As is shown in Table 11, the percentage of males with income declines slightly after age 65, while those for females increase slightly with increasing age. This may be in part due to widows receiving benefits after the deaths of their husbands. However, the percentage of aged females with some source of income was lower than that for aged males in all age groups.

While the percentage of persons with incomes may increase after 65, the amount of that income decreases markedly. The median income for males aged 65-69 was $3,037 less or almost 46 percent lower than the median income ($6,653) of males aged 60-64. The median income at ages above 75 was $4,513 less or almost 68 percent lower than the income at age 60-64.

The median income for females did not drop off quite so sharply with age as did the male median income, but the income levels were

TABLE 11
Income of the Aged Population: 1969

Age Group	Total Persons	Percent with Income	Median Income For those With Income
MALES			
60-64	4,043,919	96.9	$6,653
65-69	3,113,144	97.4	3,616
70-74	2,319,748	97.1	2,779
75+	3,004,738	96.1	2,140
FEMALES			
60-64	4,607,335	71.4	$2,373
65-69	3,878,119	85.2	1,558
70-74	3,128,667	86.7	1,489
75+	4,657,458	88.5	1,335

Source: Table 245, Detailed Characteristics, U. S. Summary, 1970 U. S. Census.

much lower for females at all age levels. These differences become particularly important at the older ages when widowed females become dependent solely on their own sources of income. These low incomes are probably offset to some degree by help from relatives, but it is clear that the present levels of income of senior citizens are hardly adequate to provide for an independent livelihood.

Another measure which has been developed as an indicator of economic well-being is the poverty level concept; that is, the delineation of a level of income which is considered necessary to maintain a minimum acceptable standard of living. A considerably greater percentage of families with heads over 65 fall below the poverty level than is true of all families.

In 1969 just over 19 percent of the families headed by persons 65 and over had incomes below the poverty level, contrasted with almost 11 percent of all families in the United States. As is shown in Table 12, the percentage of families with incomes below poverty level declines as educational attainment increases, but at all levels of education there is a greater percentage of families with heads 65 and over living on incomes below poverty level.

TABLE 12
*Poverty Status of Families by Age
and Education of Head: 1970*

Education (Years)	All Families	
	Total	65+
0-7	25.7	29.7
8	14.2	18.4
9-11	12.1	14.1
12	6.6	10.9
13-15	5.2	8.7
16	3.0	6.2
17+	2.3	4.2

Source: Table 263, Detailed Characteristics, U. S. Summary 1970 U. S. Census.

CONCLUSION

In an effort to identify characteristics of the aged, this population has been described here demographically and economically, using five-year age groups as units of analysis. By this means, it has become evident that for most variables, large differences exist between age groups, especially those at the extreme ends of the age continuum. The use of this method results in a more individual analysis than is possible if all people aged 65 and over are treated as a single category. However, the aged, as any other age group, continue to be composed of persons with diverse ideas, thoughts, aims, and goals. Therefore, any programs, plans, or policies which are devised for this group should go even beyond the five-year groups, and deal with these people as individuals whenever possible.

REFERENCES

Brotman, Herman B., *Facts and Figures on Older Americans*, U. S. Department of Health, Education and Welfare, Social and Rehabilitation Service, 1971.

U.S. Department of Commerce, *Projections of the Population of the United States, by Age and Sex: 1972 to 2020.* Current Population Reports, Series P-25, No. 493.

U. S. Bureau of the Census, *Detailed Characteristics*, United States Summary, February, 1973.

U. S. Bureau of the Census, *General Population Characteristics*, United States Summary, 1970 U. S. Census.

U.S. Bureau of the Census, *Mobility for States and Nation*, 1970 U.S. Census.

U. S. Department of Health, Education and Welfare, *Vital Statistics of the United States, 1968*, Volume II — Mortality, Part A, 1972.

U. S. Department of Health, Education and Welfare, *Vital Statistics of the United States, 1955*, Volume I, 1957.

2. Status of Research in Applied Social Gerontology*

ROBERT J. HAVIGHURST**

Old age in America may represent for many the triumph of technique over purpose. In the last 70 years, changes in medical care, food production and distribution, income distribution, housing patterns, and labor-saving machinery have contributed to longer life for more and more people. The prospect of old age for the vast majority of Americans has come about without much thought given to what old age should be, or might be for most older Americans. If, for most elderly people, old age is a time when energy is low, the circle of family and friends diminished, and income reduced, what is the reasonable expectation for life satisfaction in the retirement years? What is an older person's role once his family-rearing and economically productive years are past? Are these questions for a small number of individuals, or are they relevant for a sufficiently large number and large proportion of the elderly to warrant attention as problems of society deserving analysis?

Despite the accumulation of considerable data and some particular inquiries of very high standard concerning the status of the older American, it is clear that the formulation of social policies to assure his well-being does *not* proceed today from anything but a crude data base. The elementary data, however, may suggest clues to further inquiry. They prompt speculation about some of the current trends and what they may mean to old and young Americans alike.

What are some of the salient facts about old people in America today?

1. There are almost 20 million individuals who have passed their 65th birthday. Half are under 73; more than a million, 85 or over. It is estimated that by the year 2000 there will be in the population 28.2 million people who are over 65.[1]

2. The elderly population is a changing group. While in the course of a year there is a net increase of only 300,000, 1.4 million are newcomers to this group. By the year 2000, between 45 and 50 million middle-aged adults will have reached their 65th birthday.

3. The numbers of the very old, that is, those 75 and over, will continue to increase at about twice the rate of the over-65 group as a whole, and at more than twice the rate of the total population.

*Reprinted from *The Gerontologist*, Vol. 9, Winter 1969, pages 5-9 by permission of the author and the Gerontological Society.
**Dr. Havighurst is Professor of Education and Human Development at the University of Chicago.

4. Widowhood is apparently a normal attribute of a woman's old age. By the year 2000 there may be as many as 9 million aged widows.

5. Women significantly outnumber men in old age. Today there are 134 older women for every 100 older men. By the year 2000 the 65-and-over group will have at least 150 women for every 100 men.

6. Life expectancy at age 65 is presently about 15 years. We can expect this figure to rise significantly if cancer, stroke, heart disease, and major cardiovascular renal disease are significantly controlled or eliminated. If major breakthroughs do occur in these areas, we can anticipate an increase in average life expectancy of 16 years over and above the present 15. In other words, average life expectancy at age 65 might be 31 years.

7. The elderly tend to be economically poorer than the young. In 1966 half of the families headed by persons 65 and over had incomes of less than $3,645, or less than half of the median income attained by younger families of $7,922. Older people living alone were the worst off. The median income for this group of 5 million was $1,443 in 1967. Of the 7 million elderly families, about two out of five had incomes of less than $3,000 a year, while half of these latter had less than $2,000 a year. About 5 million older Americans, comprising 30% of the 65 group living outside of an institution, fall below the poverty level. In contrast, about 10% of the elderly families had income of at least $10,000 and less than 1% (a total of 75,000 families) had $25,000 a year or more.

8. While the largest single source of the $45 billion that comprises the income of the elderly is from earnings from employment, this represents a source for only about 20% of aged individuals. Regular retirement programs contributed about 40% of total income, with 30% coming from Social Security, 6% from railroad retirement and Civil Service, and 3% from private pension plans. In addition, about 40% came from veteran's benefits and 5% from public assistance. In other words, almost half (45%) of the total income of our aged population comes from retirement payments of one sort or another.

9. Private pensions will undoubtedly cover more elderly people as time goes by, but only a small number will be able to rely on this type of income.[2]

10. While there seems to be some emphasis at the present time on attempting to enlist elderly people in the labor market, the trends seem to run in favor of retirement. One of the major social decisions of the next 20 years will be to determine what proportion of people over 65 should be in the labor force by the year 2000.

11. Educational attainment and adjustment in old age may have a direct relationship. In the near future, the educational attainment of the elderly will rise significantly. About 20% of today's older population are

foreign born and received some or all education in other countries. Changes in the immigration laws since 1920 will undoubtedly reduce this proportion of foreign born elderly in the population. Similarly, the effective extension of compulsory public education to age 16 will change the picture on educational attainment that currently exists. Fifty percent of today's over-65 group never went beyond elementary school. A million elderly never went to school at all. It is estimated that about one-sixth of the elderly are functionally illiterate. Only 5% are college graduates.

12. Persons over 65 have one chance in seven of requiring short-term hospital care and one in 25 of requiring long-term care in any one year. The chances for long-term care increase with age. While only one in 50 of those between 65 and 72 requires long-term care, one in 15 of those 73 and over requires this care.[3]

13. Older people suffer more disabilities than the general population, visit their physicians more often, and, as one might expect, spend more time in the hospital. Yet about five-sixths of the elderly get along on their own.

14. The political power of the elderly has the potential for significant growth. At the present time they represent about 15% of the eligible voters. In the future they will approximate 25%, even if the improvements in life expectancy as a result of conquering major killers does not come about.

15. Older people will increasingly become more urbanized, like the rest of the population. It is anticipated that between 75 and 85% of the population will eventually live in the metropolitan communities of America. There will be increasing reliance on automobiles or other systems of transportation, which may produce special problems for those who cannot afford, or, because of physical limitation, cannot manage conventional forms of transportation.[4]

16. While only 1.3 million, or just under 10%, of the farm population is 65 and over, elderly people form a growing proportion of rural folk because of the relatively faster exodus of younger persons from farm areas.

17. Elderly people will probably form a growing proportion of those living in the central city, not because of convenience, but rather because the central city will become more and more the locus for the poor.

The shifts, changes, and trends in medical knowledge, methods of production, transportation, economic management, and other factors will occur at an even more rapid rate than they have in the recent past. The impact of changing knowledge and techniques upon society as the aged know it and encounter it has not been carefully considered.

Despite the phenomenal burgeoning of reports, studies, investigations, articles, and volumes on social gerontology, and despite improved financing from federal, state, and private foundation sources, the goals for research have yet to be identified. This is not to say that many competent investigators have not identified some of the research questions. They have. There is, however, no research policy at any level that represents a degree of agreement about goal and purpose that compares with that which lay behind the effort expended, for example, in achieving a lunar landing. This is not to say that there have been no comments about the direction research in social gerontology should take. A broad review of research needs in social gerontology has been prepared by Tibbitts. He has defined the goals of social gerontology as achieving an understanding of the manner in which time-related biological and psychological changes and environmental and cultural factors influence the development of personality and behavior of older adults, their roles, status, and collective behavior. He has suggested that the impact of our changing economy and the transition to an automated, cybernetic production system are major areas for study, even more important than the impact of changing birth rates, migrations, distributions and other population characteristics. He has raised three basic questions: (*a*) What is the position of old people in advanced society? (*b*) What are the roles for old people and can more acceptable roles be found? (*c*) Can old people respond to efforts to integrate them into a society characterized by rapid advances in knowledge and social and technological change? [7] Related questions include the general one about the impact of large numbers of older people on structured institutions of society. [7]

Is the meaning of "work" substantially altered by large numbers of "non-producing" persons? What is the meaning of retirement to the elderly and to the young?

Several investigators in social gerontology have raised important questions relative to the value system and its components. How do values change? How are they influenced? To what extent is the condition of the older American today a result of the wishes and ideas of all Americans? Can those national aspirations and values which impinge upon the life situation of the elderly be altered? To what extent do these values affect the self-image of the elderly and hence their behaviors and expectations?

If Shock is correct in saying that we must build up "a backlog of answers to the small specific detailed questions," then it would seem that it will be necessary for us to accumulate vast amounts of information about the elderly themselves and about those approaching old age.

While the field of public health has long pursued an epidemiological approach to information acquisition, there has been less attention given in the area of social disorder. In the field of aging the application of epidemiological approaches might be suggested through *(a)* definition of conditions and events affecting individuals; *(b)* development of systems for determining prevalence and incidence; and *(c)* determination of gross characteristics of those affected, such as age, sex, marital status, economic status, and geographical location. There is little information about the combination of problems most likely to occur, or concerning the circumstances under which older people incur social or physical disabilities.

Empirical observation has demonstrated that increasing disability and limited energy restricts the natural life space of the elderly. To be sure, architects have taken into account some of the physical problems of the elderly. However, there has been relatively little exploration of the social factors related to health of older people, such as relationships with family, friends, and neighbors, social institutions, real life space, protective care and services, and mental disability. Little has been done to further our understanding of the "new" population of moderately and severely retarded and severely physically handicapped persons who today, for the first time, are surviving into old age. The conditions promoting health and social adjustment have been little explored by social gerontologists.

Unless we examine younger groups in our population as well as the aged, we will have difficulty in developing either preventive or early identification measures suitable for this problem-prone population. Ethel Shanas, who is one of the few persons who has surveyed large numbers of the elderly, has indicated that research on characteristics and needs of the elderly can have substantial impact on social policy. The absence of data about the characteristics of elderly people has led to an imbalance in research. Concentration has been upon institutional development rather than upon community services. If we are to order the allocation of resources in behalf of elderly people on some logical basis it would appear that it should be done in terms of their real needs and real characteristics.[8]

In a more general vein, one cannot overlook what all writers concerned with research in aging have pointed out: the need for more longitudinal research. Hopefully, longitudinal studies may be able to give us clues as to the predisposing factors toward success or failure to achieve social adjustment and contentment in old age.

To be sure, a good deal of research must be directed toward the accumulation of basic information on the characteristics of the elderly, on the value systems of our society, on the characteristics of younger populations who are to be the elderly of the future, as well as on trends in economic conditions, housing, population, transportation, labor force composition, and education.

Nevertheless, social gerontology has a special obligation to contribute material useful for the formation of social policy, particularly when such a large segment of the population is involved. To that end, five steps seem essential.

1. *We must articulate with some degree of care objectives for life in old age.* Social planning might be taken to mean the effort to plan for the fate of a whole society. However, that fate must be expressed in objective terms. We must be prepared to come up with objectives that can be quantified: Income necessary to provide goods and services; housing of specified quality; health care; effective social centers; and so on.

The framing of objectives must encompass both the long and short range. Goals, that is, must be formulated for today's older American, as well as for the older American of the year 2000. The language of objectives must distinguish between *activities* and the *outcomes* of activities.

The social planners must attain the precision of the social researchers in developing statements of objectives. Without such precision it will not be possible to indicate what the research goals in social gerontology are for society. White House Conferences, in the traditional sense, are not adequate for this task, nor are the activities in which health and welfare councils indulge themselves.

2. *We must distinguish among those human conditions which are fit objects for change through applied social policy and those which are not.* Some elements of human wretchedness can be affected by social action, but not all — particularly if we eschew the conditioning of Huxley's *Brave New World.* There is legitimate social policy which leaves some problems to the individual to solve. This is particularly true in the society which seeks to meet the twin conditions of providing care yet maintaining independent choice.

3. *We must assess the value system in general and the value systems of the very old, the old, the newly retired, and those facing old age.* What do each seek in their old age and what do they expect? An assessment of the value system will take into account conflicting values and may make easier for us understanding what the trade-offs are. For example, we have produced an old age and survivors insurance system which is based on a contributory principle. This principle has high value, but, having been tried, it has been found to produce a model that can condemn the old to

poverty, a money-giving system which embraces virtually no services.

4. *We must assess the state of knowledge relative to life in old age and identify the gaps in some organized way.* What are the key researches yet to be done, and what systematic approach can we suggest for identifying the gaps and the questions that are of importance in the formation of social policy? In this respect, we would call upon the Administration on Aging, or, indeed, the Department of Health, Education and Welfare itself, to give leadership to such examination by financing an effort to identify these gaps.

5. *We must establish a method and system for understanding research in line with social policy and the gaps that we have identified.* Funding should follow this kind of priority scheme; and federal funding, which, after all, constitutes the major portion of funding in social gerontological research, must follow some kind of well-understood system that has meaning to all in the field.

It is time for a national idea about aging, a new approach to social policy; indeed, a new social policy itself.

REFERENCES

1. The facts summarized in the following pages have been taken from:
   a. Brotman, H. B. Every tenth American. Paper presented at the State Conference of the Iowa Commission on the Aging, Des Moines, October 2, 1968. (multilith)
   b. Administration on Aging. Memoranda. *Useful facts No. 15. National population trends as of July 1, 1966 (analytical tables)*, Table 1, and *Useful facts No. 16. Year-end statistical round-up.* Washington: U. S. Dept. of Health, Education, and Welfare, Jan. 6, 1967.
2. Epstein, L. Income of the aged in 1962: First Findings of the 1963 Survey of the Aged, *Social Security Bulletin, 27,* No. 3, Washington: U.S. Dept. of Health, Education, and Welfare.
3. Rice, D. Health insurance coverage of the aged and their hospital utilization in 1962, findings of the 1963 survey of the Aged, *Social Security Bulletin, 27,* No. 7, Washington: U.S. Dept. of Health, Education, and Welfare.

4. Grier, G. Goals and objectives in aging. Paper presented at the Annual Conference of State Executives on Aging, Washington, April 24, 1964. (multilith)
5. Shock, N. *Trends in Gerontology*, (2nd Ed.). Stanford, Calif.: Stanford Univ. Press: 1957, pp. 114-115.
6. Riley, M. W., Foner, A., & associates. *Aging and society*, Vol. 1; *An inventory of research findings*. New York: Russell Sage Foundation, 1968.
7. Tibbitts, C. Middle aged and older people in American society, Pamphlet OA, No. 227. Washington: U. S. Govt. Printing Off., 1965.
8. Viewpoint and interview with Ethel Shanas. *Geriatrics*, 1966, 21, No. 4, p. 110.

3. Alternatives for the Aging*

CARL EISDORFER**

The title of my remarks stems from a reply attributed to a white-haired Samuel Clemens who was asked how it felt to be whatever age he was at the time. "It isn't too bad considering the alternative," was the reply.

Classically, age, like weather, is something you live with which has very few alternatives. But viable alternatives already exist.

I find that the concept of age is very little understood. The first misconception, I think, is one of time. Traditionally we follow what I call the single trajectory theory of aging. I'm going to give you an example of this, in a pair of relatives, Mr. John and Mr. Joe, both born April 16, 1919.

This morning one of them got out of bed and while bending over to tie his shoelaces had an accident, a vascular accident, and expired. The other man tied his shoelaces, went to work and did whatever he was supposed to be doing that day, then celebrated his 50th birthday.

The survivor is taken by a similar accident fifty years from now, April 16, 2019, and obviously he's reached the ripe old age of a hundred.

By that time we probably don't have shoelaces so he dies pulling on his slip-on magnetic shoes. How old are Mr. John and Mr Joe this morning? Well, this morning they both were 50, but one of them was only 50 percent old. The other, in fact, was a hundred percent old. So the traditional concept of simple age or old age, based on the single trajectory, the date of birth, has to be rethought.

This concept has led to some fascinating statistical artifacts in our understanding of aging.

AGING RESEARCH MISLEADING

You know that little adage that says it's not that figures lie, it's just that liars figure. This is not quite what we are saying but there is, of course, a research methodology which is unique to a given set of events and so far as aging is concerned I think we have been using by and large the wrong kind of methodology — we've been doing the wrong kind of research.

*Reprinted from *The Torch*, Vol. 42, 1969, pages 35-40 by permission of the author and *The Torch*.
**Dr. Eisdorfer, is Professor and Chairman of the Department of Psychiatry and Behavioral Sciences at the University of Washington in Seattle. When this paper was written, he was Professor of Psychiatry and Director of Training and Research at the Center for the Study of Aging and Human Development at Duke University.

31

The process of aging really has three basic components. They consist of a biological phenomenon, a psychological phenomenon, and a social phenomenon. However, the correlation between the biological, the psychological and the social is not perfect. In attempting to understand the psychology of the aging, the application of the biological age is not enough.

Roughly 10 percent of the population, or 20 million people, in the United States have reached the age of 65 today. They commonly are defined as the aging group but not by people over 65, and not necessarily by me. This group is increasing at a slow but steady rate but not as rapidly as children below the age of 25. The other group in the middle who are working, with earned income is, of course, decreasing in relative proportion to the population at large. This says something about the tax base, but that's another story.

So, we have a problem of a considerable proportion of the population being defined by government and social systems as aging. What, in fact, is aging from a biological point of view?

As near as we can figure, the best correlate of aging is cell loss. The cell population is changing in most bodies, except those in the nervous and similar type systems.

Older persons presumably have fewer cells than younger persons and most of about nine or ten theories all seek to explain why cells are lost.

About the Radiation Theory

One of the biological theories that was pretty exciting a while back had a kind of social relevancy — it was a radiation theory. This said that the background radiation that we all live with has certain effects on the internal structure, essentially the chemical structure of the cell.

There has been some evidence, which now is questionable, that radiologists were dying about five years earlier than physicians at large, but from the same kinds of ailments as other physicians. There also is some evidence that intensively radiated animals died younger. So, there was a question of whether radiation did, in fact, shorten life.

Well, enough of it certainly will, and a lot of it received in a short period of time has rather disastrous effects. The question of background radiation now has waned somewhat in biological circles although it still receives a certain amount of credence.

The red hot theory today is something called the free radical theory and it has to do with electrons spinning off from a radical, and I won't give you a quick course in chemistry, except to say that if this is right, there are alternatives. There are ways of inhibiting free radical spin.

There is biochemistry work going on in Nebraska today which is suggesting that this may be a real possibility, so that if the free radical theory is right, which means that if you leave a group of chemicals around every so often there will be spin-off, and with time, enough of the spin-off to decompose the chemical, well, you can prevent that.

Some of the more interesting biological theories also involve what had best be called the intracellular sludge theory. Like Ivory Soap, cells are probably 99 and 44/100 percent efficient.

Their function is to get nutrients in, to metabolize them, and to get waste products out. Eventually you are going to have a garbage disposal problem. Anyone in New York during the garbage strike will understand the intracellular sludge theory.

WHAT ABOUT THE CAPILLARIES?

On a slightly different level there's the intensive study of capillaries. Everybody gets ecstatic about arteries and veins because they're large and easy to study. But capillaries, unfortunately, have come in for little attention except perhaps by dermatologists.

They really, in one sense, are the working end of the whole cardiovascular system. That is to say it's at the capillaries that all this big exchange is going on — it's a sort of truck depot, train depot, and airport. Things are moving back and forth via the single cell wall of the capillary, which is a single cell wrapped around itself.

The theory is that the capillaries themselves somehow are dying because they're not nourishing themselves in some peculiar way, maybe because of this sludge problem, maybe they are a little more susceptible, perhaps because they get layered with thin layers of fat or just abraded. When the capillaries go, obviously all the cells in the area will go. In certain areas, such as the brain, the heart, and so on, this can be rather traumatic.

Another nice and interesting theory coming from a very aesthetically pretty finding is the collagen theory. Collagen is an elastic substance that is the glue of the body and is very stringy. It has been discovered that collagen gets less stringy with time, so this is one of the few time-locked theories, but not much use at the time.

An interesting thing about collagen is that it's a kind of sludge, except that it's solid. The pretty part of the investigation is that collagen, which has a very pretty fluorescent effect under certain conditions in the heart, seems to increase with age. On the other hand, it doesn't seem to effect the efficiency of the heart especially. Although it is age-related, we really don't know for the moment whether it impairs us or not.

BOURBON IS BETTER

I'll throw in another biological theory which used to be very popular and in some circles still is. I call it the juice theory, but in truth it is the endocrine theory. An enormous amount of money is spent every year on various kinds of juices supposed to rejuvenate failing glands.

The idea is that the original good juices, the vital juices, have been sacked down with time so we replace them. My own flip attitude toward this is that pineapple juice is about as effective as monkey glands, and a lot cheaper, and that bourbon is best because it feels more effective.

The genetic mutation cell theory also is interesting. We used to think genetic mutations were important only in production of the next generation. Obviously this is not quite the case.

We're reproducing every day — cells are being born — and the genetic substrate is being used. Mistakes can happen in the reduplication of the genetic material.

Reproduction of the genetic substrate in our cells, like skin, for example, is vulnerable to certain kinds of mistakes like twins — they occur maybe one out of every 70 times. Well, if there's one turnover, the probability of mistakes is small, but by the time you get to 25 or 35 turnovers, the probability has of course gone up, and so the process is time- and metabolism-related.

GRADUAL INCAPACITATION?

I'm quite interested in a last theory and have begun work on it. It is the auto-immune theory. This is related to, for many of us, a whole new class of disease. The diseases are the same, we just understand them a little differently now. Diseases like rheumatic heart disease, arthritis, kidney ailments of various kinds, seem to be related to an interesting capacity of the body to produce antibodies.

Ordinarily when we get an infection, there's a mechanism to fight the infection. We're discovering that sometimes the ability of the body to discriminate between an outside infectious agent and its own tissue becomes a little confused.

For example, in attempting to fight off streptococci, the body will produce a substance that will cause heart muscle to change or will create a so-called thin basement membrane in the kidneys.

The auto-immune concept of aging reasons that our protein always doesn't reproduce perfectly, so we produce imperfect little pieces. As a result these imperfect little pieces are not recognized by the body which immediately responds as to an outside source and produces an antibody which picks up this stray protein but also affects the body itself.

It's a kind of suicidal theory, if you will, in which we gradually incapacitate ourselves. The auto-immune theory has promise, because we're learning an enormous amount concerning treatment of immune diseases. So, if aging is an auto-immune disease, this really throws it into kind of a wild ballpark where the real possibility of therapeutic intervention is not fantasy. As a matter of fact, it then is a high probability.

Although biology is interesting and the disease process is fascinating to the physician, it's not necessarily what we think of as aging, and we turn to psychological implications. We have talked to hundreds of individuals and asked them, "What does aging mean to you?" The answers tend to range into three general categories.

One is the perceptual loss. You know, "My eyes went and I needed glasses." And another is the intellectual decline — "Well, you know, I'm not as sharp as I used to be." The third is what I call learning and memory which is a little different, and is represented by "I can't pick up new things anymore, as readily as I did."

Perceptual loss clearly is related to chronologic age. Vision and audition both decline; deafness is nine times more common in the group over 60 than in the group between 20 and 40.

The important thing from my point of view is what do you do with this? Okay, so you've got visual loss and hearing loss, but visual loss doesn't appear to impair anybody. On the other hand, hearing loss appears to result in psychological characteristics that are best described as rigid, isolated, very hard to get along with. These reactions are characterized by "What do you mean?" or "Why did you say that?" or "How come they're always talking about me?" kind of comments.

There is a particular variant, which is "Why are you always yelling at me?", "How come you never talk to me in a normal tone of voice?" This is tied to an interesting phenomenon where there is about 20 percent of hearing loss by older people and the base threshold rises. If talk is normal, it can't be heard. Talk in a loud, really sustained voice gets heard, and heard accurately.

And so aged people have had a lot of trouble with their middle-aged youngsters and vice-versa.

I remember a professor whose face shone when I presented him this material. "Well, that's great," he said, "now I understand mother." It developed that he had not taken his mother with him anywhere for about two years, because when he replied to her questions in places like railroad stations or airports, she'd yell back at him, "Why don't you answer me?" This manifestation has nothing to do with old age, it has to do with hearing loss.

Anyone who wears glasses knows he has had visual loss. Take off your glasses. Try to read. Try to look at a platform.

But, if your hearing is bad, how do you know it? Well, because people shout at you. Sometimes you can't even hear them shout, but you can see them shout. So you may feel a little suspicious and a little, as my younger friends might put it, up tight, and a little defensive, and a little "Well, I better not move from where I am right now."

FALSE STIGMA ABOUT DEAFNESS

This feeling mostly is curable by a hearing aid. Frighteningly though, hearing aids somehow carry a stigma and so we disguise them in eyeglasses which very often have no lenses, because it's all right to have visual loss, but it's not right to have hearing loss.

The alternative here is pretty clear. I think we probably can knock ten years off psychologically by giving some people hearing aids or applying surgical intervention.

Hard of hearing men are much more affected than women, and high tone deafness is the prevalent hearing loss in men. So wives should remember that if he claims he really doesn't hear you, it may be because that band of his hearing spectrum has been somewhat modified. On the other hand, he may prefer not to hear you!

The biggest absurdity in the aging thing is belief that older people have an intellectual decline. One expert, using cross-sectional research, first said that intelligence peaked at about 17, but then the expert got older and it peaked at 23, and he got older again and at last word it peaked at about 28.

Longitudinal research is a very important concept for those of us attempting research on the aging, and it has some very serious practical problems. Essentially, it consists of comparing various age groups and usually shows a growth curve and a decline curve, which looks something like your golf score, I guess, if you haven't practiced for a while.

The upshot of this is that intelligence has pretty much been defined in the same way, with the curve a so-called bow, which rises or peaks, depending on age, and then drops.

The interesting thing about this is that it's not true. A small group of us are pretty sure it hasn't been true. In fact, we've known recently that it hasn't been true forever, rather than just learned it hasn't been true recently.

Our longitudinal data has been generated by watching people for a ten year period. The studies involve the same group of people starting at age 60, or 70, or 80 — a group in New York, a longitudinal study of twins, a group at the New England age center in Boston which deals primarily with brighter older persons, and a group in Kansas City.

At a meeting in San Francisco we pulled out data, looked at it and discovered that what all of us had been suspecting probably was true. We looked at the same individual from 60 to 70 and he showed virtually no decline. We looked at another group of individuals from 70 to 80, and they showed virtually no decline.

EDUCATION THE KEY

But, there was difference between the group that started out at 60 and the group that started out at 70. This is not surprising when you consider, for example, the change in education. If we make up a hypothetical average man — he must be somebody somewhere in the country — and his compatriot younger or older, we find that their bow-shaped curve of intelligence might look very much like what their educational background had been. Our group of people in their sixties right now had only about five years education. The group of people in their thirties had much more like nine or ten years of education.

This pretty bow-shaped curve which is supposed to represent a kind of innate biological process must have very serious heart attacks in terms of what the world was like when the 40-year-old was ten years old and when the 50-year-old was ten years old and so on.

There's another spin-off of this. Some rather detailed analyses of the medical status of our older persons brings what I think is an even more fascinating finding: that there is a group of individuals who decline.

We didn't think up this idea, other people had thought it up. One person suggested that there seemed to be a preterminal drop in intelligence, that a year or two before death, intelligence seemed to decline.

We have looked this over carefully and I can say that, from our data, and unequivocally, that persons with hypertension and high blood pressure, which is untreated and lasts for more than a couple of years and is associated with certain other abnormalities, have a significant decline in intelligence over a ten year period.

This contrasts to a study of a normal group and a borderline group who showed no decline at all, so it's got to be significant hypertension.

Some study done on air pilots suggests that they're even more sensitive to this drop. So that when you are very bright it may be that physical disease, if untreated, does result in what I guess I have to call premature aging. I'm calling it premature because anything that doesn't have to be is premature. The drop in intelligence, then, may be a result of poor medical treatment.

About Learning and Memory

The third point in the psychology of the aging is learning and memory, and that's particularly interesting. College professors are particularly vulnerable on this point because professors meet a lot of people and many say, "Well, I never remember my students anymore."

I have mostly decided by myself that these are the professors who never remember students anyway.

One of the things we do find, and one of the few truisms about aging, is that it tends to increase individual differences. Aging people tend to get less and less like each other. They are becoming a kind of agism. This is not a term I coined; it's like racism, there is an agism. And agism is rampant in the country today.

When you look at learning and memory I think you have to conceptualize in terms of what pieces go into it. The first thing needed in the process of learning is to perceive. You've got to hear, or see, or feel, so you've got a perceptual problem.

Now, as I already have indicated, visual and auditory loss are more prevalent. A set of studies in England have demonstrated beautifully, for example, that you can teach new skills to aged persons if you develop a working model which is twice the normal size.

It sounds like an idiotically simple thing to do, but it was done in teaching new skills on the assembly line to groups of women 60 years old and older.

The size of the model was doubled, then cut down a quarter and then three weeks later the apparatus itself was substituted. Having gone from the oversize model to the regular size model, the women got beautiful learning . . . like reading the *New York Times* in large print.

It behooves us to be aware of a perceptual problem a lot of us would like to deny. Denial of hearing loss is unbelievably extensive in this country. There is also a mild denial of visual loss, except when it's acuity. When it's brightness loss, we need more light to see as we get older. There's a lot of denial of this, and a lot of you are trying to read with inadequate bulbs.

Then there is the so-called short-term memory problem. It turns out that we don't remember things immediately, and permanently: Memory goes through a kind of filter stage. Information is put into what is being called a short-term memory storage bank and it stays there for periods of from half an hour to an hour. Any of you who have had the misfortune of knowing someone with a serious car accident will remember that they couldn't remember what happened during the accident.

They have a kind of retrograde amnesia—the period of time ranging from five, ten, or fifteen minutes before the accident is obliterated.

The transfer from the short-term bank into the long-term bank requires a period of consolidation. Older persons have trouble consolidating. If they try to do too many things at one time, they can't consolidate. Well, here's another way of presenting an alternative. Give yourself appropriate time to make the consolidation.

There has been a lot of discussion about whether long-term memory is impaired in older persons. I'm of the opinion that it may be a lot less than people think, because I'm hanging my bets on my next point, which is the output. In order for me to know that you learn something, I've got to have an output.

We've been doing a lot of work at Duke on the output phenomenon and discovered that older persons, unlike aged canines, can be taught lots of new tricks. The trick to trick teaching is time. And we give longer periods of time to old persons than to young persons. Young persons won't improve very much after a while, but old persons will continue to improve.

We thought originally that this was a neural transit thing, the train is slower, it seems to take more time until the process seems to get to the neurons, which are, after all, rather long. We discovered, to our surprise, that it had nothing to do with this biological phenomenon. When we gave older persons much more time than young, they were more likely to make a response. And when they made their response, they were always correct.

We were discovering the failure of the old person to exhibit learning. That's a very key word — exhibit his learning — a failure to respond. And I think now we are coming to a new concept — a failure to exhibit ignorance, a *fear* of exhibiting ignorance.

The Fear of Ignorance

Essentially, everyone in this audience is an (N) achiever because you have to be to be a member of the Torch club. An (N) achiever is a concept developed by McClellan of Harvard. N in parentheses stands for need. Need achievers are people who need to achieve.

The (N) achievement concept has to do with why people operate the way they do. It's a motivational concept. What (N) achievement purports to explain is the desire on the part of a lot of us, in what has been called Western culture, to achieve, to achieve a variety of things, not just financially, but in any situation where we are motivated toward success.

Now you may say, "Well, yes, isn't everybody?" Well, no, everybody isn't. One of the great problems of Far Eastern culture is that this is not an (N) achieving, a need achieving culture. The emphasis on family is much stronger than the emphasis on self. Many authorities have attributed to this kind of nepotism, the fall and the destruction of the Chinese Republic to the communists because there was so much more concern with the family than with success.

We are a success-oriented group, this group of Americans and Europeans. Given an alternative, when we come up to an ambiguous situation, we will always strike out with the hope of succeeding. And this is crucial to what I'm about to say. Because if we are interested in success, we will act. We'll take chances. Now let me present an alternative.

The alternative is fear of failure. Now fear of failure is a very respectable and legitimate concept. Nobody likes to fail. However, if we are in an ambiguous situation, if we're need achievers, we act. If we're fear-of-failure dominated, what do we do? Obviously, we do nothing. The fearful individual is the one who's afraid to expose himself because he's less interested in winning than he is concerned about losing.

Essentially, I think we are finding that older persons won't respond under the same conditions as younger persons. The probability of success has to be much higher for the average aged individual, than for the average younger individual.

A Matter of Culture

It may be because the younger person has been reared in a different culture than the people who are 65 to 80, the group we have been working with. On the other hand, it may be that as you get along in years, you begin to pile up failure experiences. If you've been burned once, you keep away from the stove. If you've been burned three or four times, you may stay out of the kitchen.

This is what we found about the learning of older persons. When we could encourage them to respond, they invariably did right, they did learn, and under certain circumstances they learned better than the young persons.

The social aspect of aging is even more complicated than either the biological or the psychological phases which are only mildly related in some instances.

One of the primary concepts in sociology is the role concept, the role that we play in life. Each of us has any number of them. We acquire them as we get along in life and maturity really is the acquisition of an increasing number of roles, involving boyfriends and girlfriends, and spouses and spice.

Then we become parents and we become employees and employers, and members of a fraternity or a lodge or a social organization or a church and so on. Each one of these activities carries with it its own defined set of characteristics, and each one, from the sociologist's point of view, is a role.

Role Relationships Change

Role change is one of the things that characterizes human beings. Certain people shift roles very easily and other persons don't. One of the major problems of today's culture is the rapid shifting of roles. Everytime you pull up stakes and move somewhere you have to change role relationships.

One of the problems in aging, which I guess is a social-psychological problem, is that some of the roles are changed for us, independent of anything we want to do about it. And they change in two ways.

One is rather clearly a biological phenomenon — as we get older, the probability of losing certain people who are important to us becomes heightened, so this cuts off certain role relationships, and each one causes a certain amount of attrition. You get scarred. Psychological scars are less visible, but no less traumatic, than physical scars.

Then there is what I call societally programmed role change. Society has done some very interesting things for its own needs.

We've institutionalized retirement programs; a fantastically great idea. When we shifted from an agrarian to a cash culture, we had to have retirement programs. We no longer had the family farms to retire to while junior took care of his kids.

However, if you try to get a new job, and are 45 or older, you really get traumatized by discovering that those retirement programs make it impossible for you to get work. The programs are geared so that you've got to plug in before the age of 43, in many cases, in order to collect benefits, and no one wants to permit you to "waive the rights."

THE GENERATION GAP AGAIN

There is an interesting aspect of retirement which goes hand in hand with the figure 65 and the aging process. If I were to ask a hundred people of any age when aging begins, 90 of them would say 65. A few would say 60, a few would say 75, but 65 is the age that most people identify. This is interesting because stereotypes about aging actually begin to be formed on the part of young people toward old people by about the age of 45.

The curve is pretty flat at 25 to 35 years, then starts to shoot up in a 45 degree angle so that between 35 and 45, the talk begins about rigid, hard to get along with, loss of ability and so on. If you've got any kids in college you know where the generation gap begins.

Sixty-five is the present so-called retirement age, but it really isn't. Structural economics holds that what man accomplishes in an ordinary work life now, by 1985 will be accomplished so that retirement could occur by age 39.

This says that we are producing a lot more per man, but it also is frightening. If you think it doesn't have dramatic consequences, let me recall for you that the United Auto Workers Union already has instituted a voluntary retirement program until age 55, where UAW pensions will replace your income at age 62 and then they pull back and you live on Social Security.

So, if retirement defines aging, will it define it when it moves ahead to age 55, and 45, and 39? We used to think that retirement was predicated on serious interpersonal crisis, serious loss of health and so on. That's another myth that's been exploded.

Most people get healthier after they retire and the psychological assaults, the trauma, occur among the highest level of the retired, characterized by managerial and professional folk. It doesn't occur in the middle, and it occurs not at all in the so-called blue collar workers

PROFESSIONALS ADAPT BETTER

But what happens a couple of years later is an interesting phenomenon. The managerial-professional class makes a good adaption to retirement, shifting a lot of interests. It's the group in the middle and at the bottom that have trouble. The trouble seems to be related to a fascinating psychological phenomenon that's called money.

The psychology of money may be a whole new area for study because it turns out that you can predict almost perfectly how well people will do in retirement on the basis of how adequately their income matches their needs.

One of the most critical areas in aging, of course, is the relationship between health and age. There has been enormous confusion.

Older people are, on a probability basis, statistically more likely to be sick than younger people, except for infants, who are the most susceptible of all.

By age 65 about 38 per cent of all adults have cardiovascular ailments. They are more likely to have a disease than not. This somehow has become programmed in people's heads like the bow-shaped curve of intelligence, described earlier, to imply that old age means illness and has resulted in disastrous consequences.

At the University of Illinois 900 aged men in the community were studied in terms of what *they* thought about their health and how often they saw physicians, and then were examined. The men were on welfare so that medical care for them really was free.

The examination revealed that 15 to 20 percent of the men said they were sick, that 80 percent of them were in fact sick, and 55 percent were moderately to severely sick.

So, this indicates that fallacious nature of the notion that older people are crocks, a kind of technical-medical term meaning they are kind of a pain, and shopping around between one doctor and another.

Sickness Tied to Acceptance

The aged are in fact accepting illness as part of being old with the result that they are getting sick. No physician in his right mind would dispute my comment that the best treatment is prevention. And the best way to stop disease is to get it early, and I'm not just talking about cancer, I'm talking about any disease.

Yet we are having a real problem because the patients won't come to the doctors since they think they're supposed to be immobile.

There's one other difficulty in being old and having a doctor. Usually the doctor is younger, and this is not a simple problem. I think all of us have to get back into the business of developing for ourselves sets of relationships whether they're with doctors, friends, or with the people we love.

So, I think some clear alternatives are available to the aging who can experience the most exciting part of their life. It's the time when you have achieved.

It's the time when you have really completed many of the chores. It's a time you can shift responsibilities and pay society back in a way in which you've never had the chance to do before. I think the potential contribution of 20 million people who are working in the interest of better community relations and more involvement in better relations with one another could really change the nature of our society. I think this is the alternative.

4. Basic Knowledge for Work with the Aging*

How old is "old?" When we speak of work with the "aging" — where do we put the starting point of this process? In our rapidly changing culture, such definition is difficult. Laws, business, and insurance policies tend to fix a point somewhere around age 65, and yet an increasing number of families contain representatives of two generations 65 and over. People can find themselves at retirement with continuing responsibility for both parents and children.

Perhaps if we approach it from the point of view of that constellation of factors which often accompanies an accumulation of years and creates special problems in living, we might achieve a more dynamic definition.

Increasing years often bring decreasing income. They may be accompanied by a loss of physical and mental vigor and by the onset of chronic illness, a gradual narrowing and lessening of social contacts and a real or felt loss of status and frequent concomitants. Supportive family ties may be severed by death or geographical distance. Widowhood, remarriage, increasing dependency — all make demands for emotional adjustments that are, at best, difficult.

And yet, in spite of the specific problems of aging, we find that the basic methods of understanding and working with people are very much the same regardless of whether they are 6, 16, 26, or 66. In each instance we are faced with the need to develop a meaningful, helping relationship; to evaluate together with our client the problem situation and decide the point at which it can be tackled most effectively; to consider the various alternative solutions and select the one that seems the most acceptable and hopeful in terms of the reality needs and capacities of the client, physical, mental, and emotional; and finally, the need to decide what each of us shall do and then act.

With this as the basic framework applicable to all problem solving, let us look at some of the specific knowledge being developed in the

*Reprinted from *The Gerontologist,* Vol. 9, 1969, pages 197-203 with permission of the author and the Gerontological Society.
**Ms. Brill is Associate Professor in the Graduate School of Social Work at the University of Nebraska in Lincoln.

behavioral sciences that is of particular usefulness to work with the aged. I would like to make reference here to three trends that seem particularly meaningful.

The first is the development of our knowledge of *ego psychology and its application to social work*. During the Second World War, Anna Freud (1946), daughter of Sigmund Freud and a skilled therapist in her own right, was working with English children who had been separated from their families and displaced by the bombing of Britain. Out of this experience and based on the work of her father and other pioneer psychiatrists of the period, application of the concepts of ego psychology developed. These were carried further by many thinkers, among them Hartman (1958), the psychiatrist, as well as Perlman (1957), and other social workers who saw their usefulness for social work.

In essence, the ego was seen as that capacity of the individual which enables him to adjust to the external reality. In a sense it acts as a mediator between the individual and his needs on the one hand and the social reality and its demands on the other. Just as the children Anna Freud worked with were able to adapt to destruction of home and loss of parents, people adapt to physical handicaps, inadequate parents, loss of income, destructive attitudes of society, and so on — the list is endless. Perlman developed this idea further when she spoke of life itself as a "problem-solving process," starting with the problem of survival for the infant who must begin to breathe air and continuing throughout his life. As the individual learns to master the problems of living, he develops a unique coping ability which, to a large extent, constitutes the individual pattern of living for him.

What does this mean to us in work with the aging? The fact that a person has survived to become the aged client generally means that the person has developed capacities to cope with the demands of living that have worked very well for him in his unique situation. These patterns may constitute strengths that the aged persons can call upon in the problem of adapting to the new tasks that being old present to him. Each person is unique and adjusts in his own unique fashion.

It is well to remember here that coping patterns, while they work for the client or they would not be developed and maintained, are not always necessarily constructive. Clients from varying cultures, for instance, are often caught in the situation where the coping mechanisms they have developed to meet the demands of living in their own particular familial or cultural group do not work in other cultures or other settings.

Let me illustrate these last two points by contrasting two elderly women in a nursing home.

Miss Minnie is 83, a widow of a coal miner, a little dumpy woman with no legs below the knees. She lived all her life in a mountain county — had never been to the town 150 miles away where the nursing home is located until brought there in an ambulance after her husband's death. As she tells it, "the Red Cross nurse cum to see me one day an' cried an' said, 'Miss Minnie, they're gonna take you away an' I don't know where' and I said, "Hit don't make no difference where I be" an' the nurse said, "I wish they wuz all like you, Miss Minnie."

She is "on welfare" — gets $2 a month spending money — is totally alone. She was having her hair done when I met her — it costs her $1 for each hairdo — she was friendly, outgoing, talkative and the girls and the attendants in the shop spoke warmly to and of her. She managed her own wheel chair and wriggled nimbly in and out of the chair under the dryer without help.

She was like a friendly puppy, reaching out with warmth and love to those around her, dependent as she had to be, but independent as far as able and "making the best of things." For her the red carpet was rolled out, her life-time coping mechanisms worked.

Miss Annie was an old friend. She was 90, has lived in the home for three years since the death of the daughter who cared for her. The youngest and only girl in a well-to-do family of five, she was pampered and petted and developed into a dissatisfied, demanding woman. Miss Annie's picture on her honeymoon at Niagara Falls around the turn of the century showed beautiful furs, picture hat, handsome husband and a petulant, unhappy face. Financially secure, she has many acquaintances — a large family — none of whom will live with her. She is dissatisfied, lonely, demands to be taken home and complains constantly.

The contrast between these two women is marked and serves to illustrate our point well. Each is coping with the demands of aging and adjusting to life in a nursing home as she coped with living throughout her lifetime. Each adopted her pattern because it worked for her. Miss Minnie's pattern continues to work effectively; Miss Annie's is causing her trouble.

This, then, is our first principle, that each *individual has his own coping ability developed through a lifetime of problem solving that is applied to the unique tasks of aging.*

This leads us quite naturally to the second of the three knowledge areas we are considering, the concept of the developmental stages of life and the tasks which are involved in each stage. Knowledge stands on the shoulders of other knowledge and many people have worked on the development of this idea. Erikson (1959), Havighurst (1953), and Duvall (1957) are three whose work I have found particularly helpful. The basic idea is that in his lifetime the individual goes through a series of developmental "crises," each of which carries with it the demand for certain tasks which must be learned and performed satisfactorily in order for that person to progress to the next stage. Havighurst has said a developmental task is "one which arises at or about a certain period in the life of the individual, successful achievement of which leads to his happiness and to success with later tasks, while failure leads to unhappiness in the individual, disapproval by the society, and difficulty with later tasks."

Thus birth, infancy, childhood, adolescence, marriage, parenthood, middle age, aging, and death can each be seen as a different crisis in life, each of which carries with it certain problems to be coped with, certain tasks to be performed, each of which is dependent in a sense on what has gone before. One writer has likened inadequate learning of how to cope in an early crisis as a "small time bomb" that goes off in a later one when problems may be more acute.

What are these tasks that living demands of us all? I've divided them into four groups to organize our thinking.

First is that of *supplying the basic material needs without which life cannot be sustained —food, clothing, shelter, and enough money to secure them*. While these needs are present throughout life, for the aged person they have special meaning. They must be geared to increasing physical and mental limitations and decreasing earning power. Often it is beyond the capacity of the aged person to meet adequately these needs himself and he must adopt a dependent role.

Second is the task of *acquiring the essential knowledge of the resources that exist within our very complex society to help in coping with the demands of life and thinking and planning in a sufficiently orderly fashion to make the maximum use of this acquired knowledge*. At any point in modern life, this is a task that is becoming increasingly difficult. The sociological and technological changes within one lifetime stagger the imagination; the demand for specialized knowledge is greater than ever before and poses a bigger and more bewildering problem for older citizens. Any one of you who has helped steer an aged client through the complexities of application for medical aid can testify to this.

Third is the task of *adjusting to the changes in the human situation that accompany each developmental stage*, those within the individual himself

— physical, intellectual, and emotional — within the family and within the society. In aging there are certain special changes. Weiss (1964) calls these changes "the progressive losses of aging" and lists them as "the loss of physical capacities, the loss of status, the loss of significant object relationships and the loss of discharge moods for drives."

It is unfortunate that we often tend to see the changes that accompany aging as loss rather than as growth because it colors our whole attitude toward the process and this attitude is communicated to the people with whom we are working. Aging is a natural process. It and death are the culmination of life. We move inevitably toward it from the moment of conception and in a sense are aging from that time on. I stress this point because it significantly affects our ability to establish meaningful relationships and communication with old people. How do you see them? — as people whose life is over and who are waiting to die? Or as people who are living through one of the stages of life using the skills, the knowledge, and the ability developed through all the other stages in order to cope effectively with its tasks?

Browning's (1931) *Rabbi Ben Ezra* starts out,

> Grow old along with me!
> The best is yet to be,
> The last of life for which the first was made.

If those of us who work with the aged could understand and accept what Browning was saying and see these changes as natural and desirable, and not mirror the customary contemporary attitude of the high status of "the lively set" in the tooth paste ads, some of the problems in adjusting to the changes in the human situation that accompany aging might be minimized.

The fourth and last developmental task is that of *finding ways to satisfy the basic emotional needs that are with us throughout our lifetime* — the need to be secure and loved, the need to utilize our potential for growth, the need to relate meaningfully to others (Josselyn, 1948). These basic needs are present fully as strongly in the aged person as in the young but their satisfaction has to be on a different level than for an adolescent. The provision of food, comfort, and affection must be geared to the capacity of the old person to receive and use. The provision of opportunities for growth and enrichment of life must take into consideration what the person can do, whether it be relearning to comb his own hair after a stroke or mastering the ability to polish rocks. In the rock museum at the San Diego Zoo I once saw half a dozen aged people polishing rocks which they had collected in the hills and, as someone has said, "their faces were like little suns."

Meeting the need to relate to others again must be in keeping with the individual capacity and desire of the client. Some old people respond happily to group situations, others prefer less socialization. Sometimes it seems that in our current society we think all our problems can be solved if we join a group. This is not necessarily so.

We have talked about ego psychology, we have talked about the developmental stages with their accompanying tasks; the third and final knowledge area I see as particularly meaningful for work with the aged that we will consider today is that of *crisis intervention*.

Out of research in public health and work with people who survived traumatic experiences, two men, Caplan (1964) and Lindeman (1944), contributed heavily to this concept. Rappaport (1965), Parad (1965), and others have adapted it to use in social work, and we are finding it more and more useful in all areas of work, particularly with the aged. In brief, this theory says that we as individuals exist in a state of balance both internally and externally. Critical events in our life experience can create a feeling of crisis within us, the internal balance is upset, and the individual strives to achieve a new adjustment or balance. Research in this area has indicated several interesting facts that are pertinent to our work.

First, a state of crisis is time-limited. In about 6 weeks we tend to achieve a new balance.

Second, the changes, the adaptations, that come out of a crisis may be either constructive or destructive.

Third, an individual is more amenable to change in a state of crisis than when the balance of his life is steady and he is fairly comfortable.

Finally, when in crisis, the old scars of past traumatic experiences tend to hurt again and we have to deal anew with problems and feelings from the past.

What does this say to us in our work with the aging? *(a)* We must be so available to them, so much a part of their life experience, that we can enter into the situation at the time of crisis, which is often the point at which the social worker becomes involved; *(b)* we must move quickly and actively to help them achieve a constructive new balance and to get maximum advantage from the impetus to change; *(c)* in our activity we must remember that there must be time and opportunity to rework some of the old hurts.

I can recall a situation I discussed with a public assistance worker of Mrs. L., a recently widowed client, who was trying in a rather numb way to qualify for financial assistance. She seemed disorganized, almost paralyzed, unable to move or plan constructively and with great need to discuss the other losses in her life — her parents, a stillborn child, a son in the war, and now her husband. She felt lonely, deserted, and unloved. With time to discuss these feelings, with emotional support, with understanding, with concrete direction, she was able to move forward again.

We have here briefly touched upon four knowledge areas that are meaningful in work with the aged: *(a)* the scientific method that we use in approaching the solution of problems; *(b)* the concepts of ego psychology and adaptive patterns; *(c)* the theories of developmental stages and the tasks accompanying each stage, and finally, *(d)* the learnings from crisis intervention theory. How then, can we put this knowledge into operation?

A number of years ago I had a colleague who used to liken social work to a three-ring circus — everything happens at the same time and the social worker has to be conscious of what is going on in all the rings. Thus, beginning at the point of initial discussion with the client, the worker is at one and the same time trying to relate to him in a meaningful way, to study and understand his problem, and to help him reach a solution. While I will divide our work into three areas, we must keep in mind that these cannot be separated — they occur simultaneously and are so interrelated that it is impossible to separate them in practice. The three words that I would like to use to describe what we do are *(a) communication, (b) assessment, (c) change*.

Today, as never before, we are aware of the problems in communication that face people. We know that people can converse and have no effective communication — we see this in dysfunctional families all the time. We know that of equal importance to communication by word is that non-verbal communication of attitudes and feelings that takes place when people meet. We know that it is extremely difficult to actually "hear" what another person is saying and understand it.

How do we achieve that meaningful communication with our aged clients without which a helping relationship cannot be established? Of basic importance is the fact that communication is a two-way street, that worker and client are both participants and that there is a constant giving and receiving between them. Earlier I referred to the importance of the workers' attitude toward aging with its attendant problems and I would like to mention this again. In our society, the aged, particularly the aged poor, have little status, in contrast to some cultures where the old person is revered and respected and occupies a place all his own. There are many reasons for this which we will not go into at this time. The important thing is that the worker who reflects this attitude to his client will have a hard time establishing a meaningful relationship.

Equally rocky will be his road if he thinks of old people as children. I remember the aged mother of a friend, who, as we talked, commented sadly but without self-pity, "I should have died when I had pneumonia ten years ago. No one talks with the real me any longer. They speak to me as if I were a child."

Old people are not children. They are at the other end of the continuum of life. They have had experiences, they have learning, they have memories. Why do we tend to react to them as if they did not? Part of the answer probably lies in the fact that at some point in the aging process most of us tend to become dependent again to a greater or lesser degree, a state that is generally associated with childhood and which, when observed in adults, tends to bring attitudes of scorn and resentment. A certain amount of dependency is an essential adaptation to the aging process and one that the aging person needs to be able to use. When he can no longer do for himself, he must be able to accept help from others.

This dependency not only can create problems for the old person, it can also create problems for the members of his family and for the worker because it demands a reversal of customary roles which all may find difficulty in accepting. The old person must move from being provider and planner to being provided and planned for. The children must move into what has been the parental role. The worker has had parents too and has developed attitudes and accustomed role behavior with older people that can create difficulties.

Along with this goes that thing about which we are hearing so much nowadays and that is "the generation gap" that so often exists between worker and client. The classic suggestion that "if you would understand another man, walk in his moccasins for a moon" can hardly apply here because most of us have not yet reached the final stages of aging. It is very difficult for us, engrossed as we are in our own generational tasks and our own feelings, to refrain from imputing these feelings to our clients. This can create a myopia that prevents us from seeing clearly and understanding.

This generation gap, when it exists between worker and aged client, may serve to accentuate the cultural differences that can create barriers to effective communication. What is significant to one generation and one culture may be of little importance to another.

One of my colleagues tells the story of old Mrs. Z. Born a peasant woman in central Europe, she and her family emigrated to America when she was a young mother. At 75 her children, with the help of the old age assistance worker, found a home for her and went about their busy lives. The nursing home operator called the social worker a couple weeks later. Mrs. Z sat and cried quietly and constantly. The operator tried to talk with her but got only more tears and depression. Only with considerable effort was the worker able to learn that the problem was the loss of Mrs. Z's babushka, the little head scarf, the like of which she had worn indoors and out since she was a young girl. The attendants had taken it because it was dirty. It had not been returned or replaced.

This was a point in her life in which Mrs. Z could be self-determining. The reality was that she had to go to the nursing home whether she wanted to or not, but the matter of the all important babushka was one that she could decide. The worker who could approach Mrs. Z with an open mind, striving for understanding of a person who was different and unique as all people are different and unique, convinced of the importance of involving her in the decision making and respecting her right to make decisions in matters concerning her own welfare, so far as was possible, could achieve good communication in spite of a language barrier and a generation gap.

The final point that I would like to make in this matter of communication is the need for the worker to strive for clarity and reality of perception, not only perception of himself and perception of the client, but awareness of how the client perceives him.

This latter point was beautifully but sadly illustrated in the Koerner report of the Commission on Civil Disorders (1968) where the "brittle relationship between welfare workers and the poor" was commented on and social workers were found to be second to the police in unpopularity. Social workers were not too surprised but shocked, in a sense, by these findings. We perceive ourselves as being, in the main, people sincerely motivated to help and doing the best we can with the tools we have at hand. Our clients, in this instance, perceived us quite differently.

How do the old people with whom we work perceive us? How do we perceive them? How do we perceive ourselves in our helping role and how do they perceive themselves in their role of being helped?

Clarity of perception and communication are greatly facilitated when the worker is able to approach her aging client with a sound value base involving conviction of the worth of the aged person, of his basic right to a place in our society, and of his capacity for growth and change. This latter, a belief in the capacity for growth and change in old people, not only affords the philosophic rationale for all our efforts — it also gives the worker the basic conviction that there *can* be a successful outcome to her undertaking. Research indicates that the optimism of the worker and the expectation of success play an important role in helping people change and achieve, but it must be optimism that is reality based, based on *sound* assessment of *all* the factors involved.

This brings us to the second worker skill, the process of *assessment*. We spoke of communication as being a two-way street with worker and client bringing to it responsibility for different roles, that of the helper and that of the person being helped. Equally, assessment needs must be a joint undertaking, an undertaking in which the situation with which the client needs help is evaluated, the various alternative solutions viewed, and a decision reached as to what action shall be taken.

The research division of the University of Chicago has published results of a study which indicates that *if* a client has the motivation to be helped, *if* he has the capacity — physical, mental, and emotional — to use help, and *if* the type of help he needs is available, he can change his situation (Ripple & Alexander, 1964). This is an "iffy" statement, but I think it outlines the worker's responsibility in assessment. How motivated is the client and how can you help develop motivation? What capacity for change does he have? Realistically, what is he able to do? What resources do you have to call upon to meet his need, both within yourself as a skilled and knowledgeable worker, within his family, and within the community?

Let's look at these three things separately for a moment. What determines motivation for desired change? Discomfort in the client, a crisis situation that produces discomfort, along with the hope that change for the better is possible, are strongly motivating forces. The degree to which the client is supported and encouraged to participate in deciding what change and the manner in which it will be effected — in other words, to participate in making decisions that affect his own welfare, is also a big part of motivation.

Finally the nature of the reward that can be expected for changing can be presented honestly and realistically to the client as a part of the assessment process, with full recognition that while the process of change may be difficult, and with older people it is often more so than with younger, the rewards in the long run will be more satisfying.

Nowhere is this process more clearly illustrated than in the work we do in helping old people find new living situations suited to their particular limitations and capacities. Often a crisis situation forces the move — urban development, departure of family, ill health, financial need, increasing feebleness, inability to care for self — and it is fraught with emotional significance for the client. The worker can help his client express the feelings involved, explore with him the various alternative solutions, and assist him in finding and moving to a situation that will better meet his need at this time and in the future — and the "future" orientation of the person working with the aged is of tremendous importance.

The third and last aspect of the helping process is that of bringing about change in the client's situation. (Too often social workers have tended to stop after the assessment stage.) While there is danger in being too active, in taking over and doing the work for the client, with older people particularly there is often appropriate need for considerable activity on the part of the worker. In our thinking and writing about social work, we have tended to divide our efforts into two categories — those where we work directly with the client and those where we work in the environment in the interests of the client. Unless our client is totally helpless, it is almost impossible to divide these two. Overton in the Casework Notebook (1946) from the St. Paul Study speaks of "standing with" your client and "establishing a partnership," and "assigning homework." There are few old people so handicapped that they cannot participate at all in the process of solving their own problems. They, as all clients, need to be viewed on a continuum. On one end is the client who can assume little or no responsibility for planning, making decisions, and carrying them out, for whom the worker must do all. On the other, is the client who is almost totally self-sufficient, who needs only a little additional knowledge, a little help to move out on his own. In between are all the varying degrees of ability to be self-motivating and independent. There is need for skills in differential diagnosis, for development of ability to see the client as an individual with his own unique combination of strengths and weaknesses, and for realistic assessment of what the client can do for himself.

In this whole area of encouraging the client to know and do for himself that which he is able we often need to work very closely with family members whose perception of the capacity of the older person may be erroneous, often due to their own emotional involvement.

In one case, I got a picture of an anxious couple, devoted to each other and their own way of life, greatly concerned about Mrs. John's mother and perhaps a little guilt ridden because their late marriage had left her alone. But when I asked how the mother felt about being alone, how much had she socialized before she moved, did she enjoy the demands of managing property, what did she do with her time, was she satisfied in her new living arrangement — they did not know the answers. They perceived her through their own eyes, using their own system of values instead of striving to see her as she was.

In this paper we have been concerned mainly with problem solving, but social work has an additional responsibility in working toward the enrichment of life for its clients, in helping people reach their potential for achievement and happiness. People are born with the capacity for growth, or perhaps I should say with a tremendous drive for growth that the conditions of life often thwart and distort. The aged, each in his own way, still have this need and capacity to grow as do we all.

REFERENCES

Browning, R. *Rabbi Ben Ezra*. Vol. 11. *English masterpieces*. New York: Narlon, 1931.

Caplan, G. Principles of preventive psychiatry. New York: Basic Book, 1964.

Duvall, E. M. *Family development*. New York: J. B. Lippincott, 1957.

Erikson, E. *Identity and the life cycle*. Vol. 1. *Psychological issues*, No. 1. New York: International Universities Press, 1959.

Freud, A. *Ego and the mechanisms of defense*. New York: International Universities Press, 1946.

Hartman, H. *Ego psychology and the problems of adaptation*. New York: International Universities Press, 1958.

Havighurst, R. J. *Human development and education*. New York: David McKay, 1953.

Josselyn, I. *Psychological development of children.*. New York: Family Service Association of America, 1948.

Koerner, O. (Ed.) *Report of the National Advisory Commission on Civil Disorder*. New York: Bantam Books, 1968.

Lindemann, S. Symptomology and management of active grief. *American Journal of Psychiatry*, 1944, 101.

Overton, A. *Casework notebook of the St. Paul Family Centered Project*. St. Paul: Greater St. Paul Community Chest and Council, 1946.

Parad, H. *Crisis intervention — selected readings*. New York: Family Service of America, 1965.

Perlman, H. *Social casework, a problem solving process*. Chicago: University of Chicago Press, 1957.

Rappaport, L. *The state of crisis — some theoretical considerations*. Crisis Intervention, FSAA, 1965.

Ripple, L., & Alexander, E. *Motivation, capacity and opportunity as related to casework service*. Chicago: University of Chicago Press, 1964.

Weiss, H. J. Changes in physical and mental health as related to family life. Paper presented at the University of Michigan 17th Annual Conference on Aging, Ann Arbor, June, 1964.

II
BASIC PROCESSES
OF AGING

PHYSIOLOGICAL, PSYCHOLOGICAL, AND SOCIAL ASPECTS

An understanding of aging calls for consideration of all the life processes and experiences of living. The intricate and infinite combinations of basic processes and life experiences result in the individuality or uniqueness which we observe in each person, old or young. In this section we present readings regarding the bases of aging in physiological, psychological, and social areas.

We consider physiological aspects first because these both enable and limit human behavior. Good physiology is necessary for good functioning at any age. All aging has a physiological basis. That is, the physiology and health of an individual facilitate and limit what he can and will do in all stages of life. When a person grows old, some of the physiological processes may begin to break down. However, compensations are possible which enable many elderly to function in a very satisfactory manner. Psychological functioning is very dependent upon physiological health. Both of these aspects influence how the older person interacts with his environment and how others regard him. Readings related to these latter aspects of living are grouped together under the heading, Social Aspects.

A.   PHYSIOLOGICAL ASPECTS

The first reading in this section by Nathan Shock stresses that aging begins at birth and continues throughout life. The older person does not suddenly begin to change at some prescribed time such as on his 65th birthday. Rather, the various biological functions and processes change gradually throughout one's life span. In the study of aging we look particularly at the change and decline of bodily functions in the later years. Shock suggests that the loss of body cells is a major causal factor in this change.

In the next reading, Bertram Moss describes *normal* physiological age related changes and how they differ from the changes which accompany disease. His focus is on health and, therefore, changes in the healthy older person. He discusses what is known about the normal and natural physiological modifications in the various parts of the aging organism.

In the next reading, Alexander Leaf describes his visits to the three communities in the world where there are unusually large numbers of active older people, especially beyond the age of one hundred. He discusses different rates of aging and some of the hypotheses which might account for these differences.

Finally, Alex Comfort discusses the possibility of extended productive life in future generations. He speculates concerning the present causes of death and longevity and argues that we presently, or soon will, have the medical technology to enable people to live much longer. In later sections of this book, problems in the productive use of this extended time by older citizens will be discussed.

5. The Physiology of Aging*

NATHAN W. SHOCK**

The processes of aging operate during all of adult life. The decline in function that accompanies these processes is apparently due to the progressive loss of body cells.

With the virtual conquest of want and infectious disease in technologically advanced countries, men and women in increasing numbers are living out the promised Biblical life span of three score years and ten. The diseases of age and the fundamental process of aging are moving to the center of interest in the practice of medicine and in medical research. Few people die of old age. Mortality increases rapidly with age — in precise logarithmic ratio to age in the population as a whole — because the elderly become more susceptible to diseases that kill, such as cancer and cardiovascular disease. The diseases of old age are the province of the relatively new medical specialty known as geriatrics. A still younger discipline called gerontology deals with the process of aging itself.

Gerontology is still in the descriptive stage. Investigators have only recently developed objective standards for measurement of the decline in the performance and capacity of the body and its organ systems, and they have just begun to make such measurements on statistically significant samples of the population. The first general finding in gerontology is that the body dies a little every day. Decline in capacity and function over the years correlates directly with a progressive loss of body tissue. The loss of tissue has been shown to be associated in turn with the disappearance of cells from the muscles, the nervous system and many vital organs. To get at the causes of death in the cell gerontology has entered the realm of cellular physiology and chemistry.

The ideal way to study the aging of the human body would be to apply the same battery of tests to a large group of people at repeated intervals throughout their lives. Such a program would require dedicated subjects and a scientific staff organized for continuity of operation over a period of perhaps 50 years. Obviously some compromise must be made. Instead of starting observations on a group of subjects at age 30 and following them for 50 years, it is possible to begin with

*Reprinted from *The Scientific American,* Vol. 206, 1962, pages 100-110, by permission of the author and *The Scientific American.*
**Dr. Shock is Chief of the Gerontology Research Center, National Institutes of Child Health and Human Development in Baltimore.

subjects of various ages and follow them for 20 years. At our laboratories in the Gerontology Branch of the Baltimore City Hospitals we started such a study on 400 men in 1958. Until this and similar undertakings have had time to yield results, gerontologists must rely on data accumulated from one-time tests of rather large numbers of different individuals ranging in age from 20 or 30 up to 80 or 90. Although subjects of any specific age differ widely, the average values for many physiological characteristics show a gradual but definite reduction between the ages of 30 and 90. Individual differences become quite apparent, for example, in studies of the amount of blood flowing through the kidneys. Whereas this function generally declines markedly with age, it is the same in some 80-year-old men as it is in the average 50-year-old man.

One of the most obvious manifestations of aging is the decline in the ability to exercise and do work. In order to measure the extent of the change it is necessary to set up laboratory experiments in which the rate of output and the amount of work done can be precisely determined along with the responses of various organ systems. Subjects may be put to walking a treadmill or climbing a certain number of steps at a specified rate. In our laboratory the subject lies on his back and turns the crank of an ergometer, an apparatus for measuring the work done. When our purpose is to measure the subject's maximum output in a given time, the crank can be adjusted to turn more stiffly or more easily. With the subject lying supine it is easier to make the necessary measurements of blood pressure, heart rate and heart output (blood pumped) and to collect the respiratory gases through a face mask for the measurement of oxygen consumption and carbon dioxide production. These measurements are customarily made before, during and after exertion in order to establish the subject's norms, his capacity and the rate at which vital functions recover their normal or resting rates.

As a common denominator of capacity, we seek to determine the maximum amount of work a subject can do and have his heart return to normal within two minutes after he stops working. Men 30 years old achieve an output of 500 kilogram-meters per minute (the equivalent of lifting 500 kilograms one meter in one minute), whereas 70-year-old men on the average reach only 350 kilogram-meters per minute. Thus at age 70 a man's physical capacity as defined by this test has declined by 30 percent. Over the years from 35 to 80 the maximum work rate for short bursts of crank-turning falls almost 60 per cent, from about 1,850 kilogram-meters per minute for young men to 750 kilogram-meters for the 80-year-old.

Physical performance, of course, reflects the combined capacity of the different organ systems of the body working together. The ability to do work depends on the strength of the muscles, the co-ordination of movement by the nervous system, the effectiveness of the heart in propelling blood from the lungs to the working muscles, the rate at which air moves in and out of the lungs, the efficiency of the lung in its gas-exchange function, the response of the kidneys to the task of removing excess waste materials from the blood, the synchronization of metabolic processes by the endocrine glands and, finally, the constancy with which the buffer systems in the blood maintain the chemical environment of the body. In order to determine the causes of the decline in overall capacity, it is necessary to assess the effects of aging on each of the organ systems.

Tests of the strength of the hand serve in our laboratory to isolate one aspect of muscle function. The subject simply squeezes a grip-measuring device as hard as he can for a moment. In a group of 604 men the strength of the dominant hand dropped from about 44 kilograms of pressure at age 35 to 23 kilograms at age 90. Although the dominant hand is stronger at all ages, it loses more of its strength over the years than the subordinate hand. Endurance, measured by the average grip pressure exerted for one minute, drops from 28 kilograms at age 20 to 20 kilograms at age 75. That muscle performance is not the only factor involved in maximum work rates is indicated by the fact that the decrease in muscular strength over the years is less than the decline in work rates.

 1. Brain Weight (56)
 2 Memory Loss
 3 Slower Speed of Response
 4 Blood Flow to Brain (80)
 5 Speed of Return to Equilibrium of Blood Acidity (17)
 6 Cardiac Output (at rest) (70)
 7 Number of Glomeruli in Kidney (56)
 8 Glomerular Filtration Rate (69)
 9 Kidney Plasma Flow (50)
10 Number of Nerve Trunk Fibers (63)
11 Nerve Conduction Velocity (90)
12 Number of Taste Buds (36)
13 Maximum Oxygen Uptake (during exercise) (40)
14 Maximum Ventilation Volume (during exercise) (53)
15 Maximum Breathing Capacity (voluntary) (43)

16 Vital Capacity (56)
17 Less Adrenal Activity
18 Less Gonadal Activity
19 Hand Grip (55)
20 Maximum Work Rate (70)
21 Maximum Work Rate for Short Burst (40)
22 Basal Metabolic Rate (84)
23 Body Water Content (82)
24 Body Weight for Males (88)

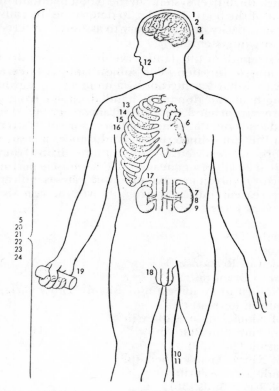

PHYSIOLOGICAL DECLINE ACCOMPANYING AGE appears in many measurements throughout the body. Changes are great in some cases, small in others. The figures in brackets following most of the labels in the key are the approximate percentages of functions or tissue, remaining to the average 75-year-old man taking the value found for the average 30-year-old as 100 percent.

The nerve fibers that connect directly with the muscles show little decline in function with age. The speed of nerve impulses along single fibers in elderly people is only 10 to 15 per cent less than it is in young people. Simple neurological functions involving only a few connections in the spinal cord also remain virtually unimpaired. It is in the central nervous system, where complex connections are made, that aging takes its toll. Memory loss, particularly for recent events, often plagues the elderly. The older person requires substantially more time for choosing between a number of possible responses to a situation, although with enough time he arrives at the correct decision. Certain routine mental activities, on the other hand, hardly change with age. Vocabulary comprehension, for example, remains strong in most people. Experienced proofreaders maintain a high degree of accuracy even at advanced ages.

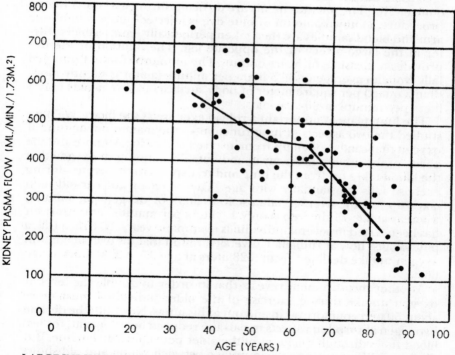

LARGE INDIVIDUAL DIFFERENCES in aging show up when, for example, the rate of flow of blood plasma through the kidney is plotted against age for some 70 men. The plasma flow is measured in milliliters per minute per 1.73 square meters of body-surface area.

Because muscles engaged in sustained exercise require extra oxygen and other nutrients and produce more waste to be carried away, the heart must work harder to move more blood through the system. During exercise the heart pumps more blood at each stroke, at a faster rate and at higher pressure. Although the resting blood pressure in healthy individuals increases only slightly with age, a given amount of exercise will raise the heart rate and blood pressure in old people more than it will in young. And when subjects exert themselves to the maximum, the heart of the older person cannot achieve as great an increase in rate as that of the younger. During exercise, therefore, the cardiac output, or amount of blood pumped per minute, is less in the old than it is in the young. This, of course, imposes limits on the amount of work the elderly can do.

Cardiac output can be measured directly and, in subjects at rest, quite easily. (The measurements are difficult during exercise.) In one procedure a known amount of blue dye is injected into a vein of one arm and blood samples are then taken periodically from a small catheter in the large artery of the opposite leg. The dilution of the dye provides a measure of heart output. The amount of blood pumped falls from an average of 3.75 liters per minute (a liter is slightly more than a quart) per square meter of body surface in 20-year-olds to two liters per minute in 90-year-olds.

The lung plays as important a role in exercise as the heart. We have studied the two aspects of lung function — the maximum amount of oxygen that can be taken up from inspired air during exercise and the ability of the lung to move air in and out. The amount of oxygen that the blood takes up from the lung and transports to the tissues during exercise falls substantially with age. The blood of 20-year-old men takes up, on the average, almost four liters of oxygen per minute, whereas at age 75 the rate is only 1.5 liters per minute. This function has been tested in several individuals over many years. D. Bruce Dill, a physiologist now at Indiana University, found that his own maximum oxygen uptake declined from 3.28 liters at age 37 to 2.80 liters at age 66.

Another measurement reveals that in order to double the level of oxygen uptake during exercise of the older individual must move about 50 percent more air in and out of his lungs. No doubt the decline in oxygen absorption reflects in part the reduced heart output, for less blood flows through the lungs of the older person in a given time. But the great difference in oxygen uptake between young and old shows that the lung tissue too has changed.

The decline in respiratory function also reflects a loss in simple mechanical efficiency. In normal respiration less air turns over and the amount of dead air space in the lungs increases, although total lung volume remains almost unchanged. Even the "vital capacity" (the amount of air that can be forcibly expired from the lung) diminishes with age. The nature of this impairment becomes clear when one measures the subject's maximum breathing capacity — the amount of air he can move through his lungs in 15 seconds. The chart for this test shows a decline of about 40 percent between the ages of 20 and 80. Since the older person expels about as much air at each breath as the younger person does, it is clear that his capacity is less because he cannot maintain as fast a rate of breathing. The impairment is an expression of the general decline in neuromuscular capacity.

Exercise produces acids and other metabolic waste products that are excreted primarily by the kidney. Because the heart pumps less blood with advancing age, less blood flows through the kidney in a given time. Changes within the kidney itself further reduce the flow of blood as well as the efficiency with which the kidney processes the wastes. The kidney puts the blood through a delicate, multistaged process. First it filters the blood, flushing the waste products out of the bloodstream in a filtrate from which it withholds the red cells and larger molecules; then it processes this filtrate, recovering the smaller useful molecules, such as those of glucose, that get through the filter; and finally the kidney actively excretes waste molecules, some of them too large to pass through the filter. The active functions take place in the tubular lining of the nephrons, the functional units of the kidney. A full test of kidney performance involves measurement of the amount of filtrate formed per minute, the quantity of blood plasma (the liquid portion of the blood) passing through the kidney per minute and the maximum excretory capacity of the nephrons. The measurements are made by infusing the blood with substances that the kidney removes in different ways; one substance, the metabolically inert polysacharide inulin, goes out through the filter, whereas para-aminohippuric acid must be actively excreted. Analysis of blood samples and urine during the infusion shows how efficiently the kidney is working. Such tests show that between the age of 35 and 80 the flow of blood plasma through the kidney declines by 55 percent. The filtration rate and maximum excretory capacity, as well as glucose reabsorption, decline to the same extent.

Intravenous administration of the substance pyrogen increases the flow of blood through the kidney in young and old. Apparently reduction in blood flow through the kidney is an adaptive mechanism of the aging body. It seems to result from constriction of kidney blood vessels, which makes more blood available to other organs. Because the kidney of the older person has less blood to work on it cleanses the blood of waste more slowly; given enough time, however, it will do the job.

The endocrine glands regulate a wide variety of physiological processes, ranging from cellular metabolism to regulation of the diameter of small blood vessels and consequently the amount of blood reaching various tissues. At the center of the endocrine system is the pituitary gland, which secretes hormones that stimulate the adrenal glands, the thyroid, the ovaries, the testes and other glands to release their hormones. There is no way to test the performance of the master gland in human subjects, but the responsiveness of other endocrine glands can be tested by administering the appropriate pituitary hormone. Sometimes the level of activity of a given gland can be estimated from the amount of its hormone or of the breakdown products of the hormone that appear in the urine. Adrenal activity is customarily measured by this means and shows a decline with age. Administration of the pituitary hormone that stimulates the cortex of the adrenals produces a smaller elevation of adrenal activity in older people. Since the adrenal hormones are the "stress" hormones, this indicates a reduction in the capacity to respond to stress. On the other hand, the pituitary hormone that stimulates the thyroid gland produces the same result in the old as it does in the young. Even at advanced ages the thyroid retains its ability to manufacture and release thyroxine, which regulates the basal metabolism, or the rate at which the resting subject consumes oxygen.

Normal function in the cells of the body requires that the chemical composition of the fluids surrounding them be closely regulated. Because the intercellular fluids cannot be sampled directly, estimates of the internal environment must come from analyses of the blood. Such factors as total blood value, acidity, osmotic pressure, protein content and sugar content remain constant in both young and old subjects at rest. But when these variables are deliberately altered, the older person needs a much longer time to recover internal chemical equilibrium. The acidity of the blood, for example, can be increased by oral administration of ammonium chloride; a younger subject recovers normal acidity within six to eight hours, whereas the 70-year-old requires 36 to 48 hours to recover.

Although the average blood-sugar level remains quite constant even into advanced age, the rate at which the system removes extra glucose drops significantly in older people. Insulin, normally secreted by glands in the pancreas, greatly accelerates the removal of sugar from the blood. When we administer insulin intravenously along with extra glucose, the glucose disappears from the blood of the young person at a much higher rate than it does from the old.

It may well be that subtle changes in the chemical composition of the blood and other body fluids account for certain physiological changes in the elderly. So far as the gross chemical characteristics go, however, the old animal or human easily maintains a constant, normal internal environment when completely at rest. But increasing age is accompanied by a definite reduction in the capacity to readjust to changes that accompany the stresses even of daily living. In other words, a key characteristic of aging is a reduction in the reserve capacities of the body — the capacities to return to normal quickly after disturbance in the equilibrium.

Another important element in the aging process shows up in those functions and activities that involve a high degree of co-ordination among organ systems. Co-ordination breaks down, in the first place, because the different organ systems age at different rates. Conduction of the nerve impulse, for instance, hardly slows with age, whereas cardiac output and breathing capacity decline considerably. Thus in those functions that involve the simultaneous output of several organ systems — sustained physical exercise, for example — the performance of the body shows marked impairment. Most of the debilities of age apparently result from a loss of tissue, particularly through the death and disappearance of cells from the tissues. The wrinkled and flabby skin so apparent in elderly people offers mute testimony to this loss. Body weight declines, especially after middle age. In a large sample of the male population of Canada average weight showed a decline from 167 pounds at ages 35 to 44 to an average of 155 pounds for men 65 and over. A sample of men in the U.S., all of them 70 inches tall, averaged 168 pounds in weight at ages 65 to 69 and 148 pounds at ages 90 to 94. Women 65 inches tall weighed, on the average, 148 pounds at ages 65 to 69 and 129 pounds at ages 90 to 94.

Individual organs also lose weight after middle age. For example, the average weight of the brain at autopsy falls from 1,375 grams (3.03 pounds) to 1,232 grams (2.72 pounds) between ages 30 and 90. The same striking loss in total weight and in the weight of specific organs shows up also in the senile rat: the total weight of certain muscle groups drops 30 percent.

The microscope shows that in many tissues a decrease in the number of cells accompanies the weight loss. Connective tissue replaces the lost cells in some cases, so that the loss of cells is even greater than the reduction in weight would indicate. In the senile rat the muscle fibers show degenerative changes with replacement by connective tissue and

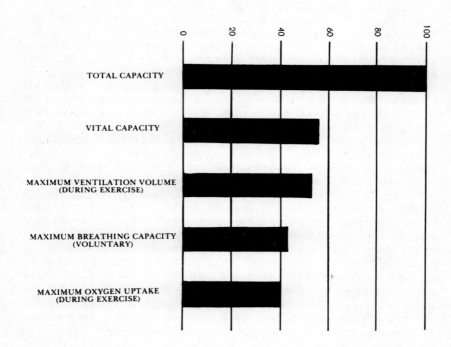

FUNCTION REMAINING (PER CENT) AT AGE 75

FUNCTIONS OF THE LUNG in man show marked decline with age. Total capacity is the amount of air lungs can hold; it does not decrease. Vital capacity is amount of air forcibly expelled in one breath. Maximum ventilation volume during exercise represents

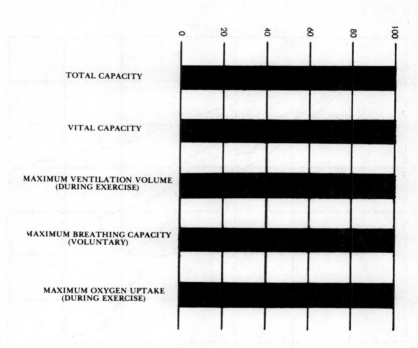

FUNCTION REMAINING (PER CENT) AT AGE 30

involuntary movement of air. Maximum breathing capacity is the amount of air that can be moved in and out of the lungs voluntarily in 15 seconds. Oxygen uptake is the quantity of oxygen absorbed by the blood from the lungs for transportation to the body cells.

PERCENTAGE CHANGES WITH AGE for nine different physiological functions are shown in these two diagrams. The average value for each function at age 30 is taken as 100 percent. Small drop in basal metabolism (1) is probably due simply to loss of cells.

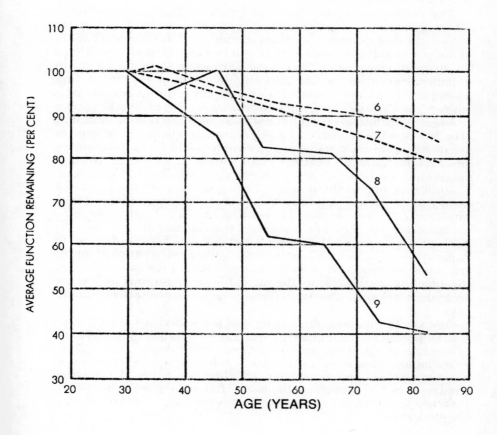

1 Basal Metabolic Rate
2 Work Rate
3 Cardiac Output (at rest)
4 Vital Capacity of Lungs
5 Maximum Breathing Capacity (voluntary)
6 Nerve Conduction Velocity
7 Body Water Content
8 Filtration Rate of Kidney
9 Kidney Plasma Flow

an increase in the spaces between fibers. Such loss of muscle fibers no doubt accounts in large measure for the lower muscular strength of elderly humans as well.

The nervous system shows a similar decline. The number of nerve fibers in a nerve trunk decreases by 27 percent at advanced ages. In the kidney the disappearance of cells is accompanied by a reduction in the number of nephrons. According to counts made by Robert A. Moore of the State University of New York Downstate Medical Center, the number drops over the life span from 800,000 to 450,000. A final example: The number of taste buds per papilla of the tongue falls from an average of 245 in young adults to 88 in subjects aged 70 to 85 years.

In early life the body is endowed with tremendous reserve capacities. The loss of a few hundred or a few thousand cells hardly affects the performance of an organ. As age advances and losses accumulate, however, impairments develop; eventually the stress of daily living or disease imposes demands beyond the reserve capacity of the organism.

Understanding of the process of aging will ultimately require discovery of the factors that cause the death and disappearance of individual cells. It may be that the death of individual cells is merely a chance event that occurs on a statistical basis in most tissues. It is more likely that changes in the internal metabolism of a cell damage its capacity for self-repair and reproduction. Biochemical study of the life processes in tissue cells is in its infancy. Within the past few years investigation of tissues from the rat and lower organisms such as the hydra have begun to reveal the effects of age on enzyme activity in body cells.

One key to understanding aging and particularly to taking action that might extend the human life span can be found in the differences in the rate of aging observed in different individuals. These differences indicate that many factors play a role in aging. When we know why some people age less rapidly than others, we may be able to create conditions that will minimize the loss of functioning cells and tissues, thereby enabling many more people to live as long as those who live longest today.

6. Normal Aging*

BERTRAM B. MOSS**

Different parts of the body resist aging more than others and various abilities fade at different rates. Clinical gerontology is most adequate in describing characteristics of the elderly. It is least adequate, however, in separating those characteristics that should be attributed to cultural or general factors from those that might be attributed to the hypothetical process of "pure aging."

Determining which aging factor is primary and which is contributory or secondary is rarely possible. Most age-related diseases are degenerative and lack a distinct dominant cause. The most common of age-related diseases in old people are the defects of the cardiovascular system, which eventually affect other body systems.

The health status of the elderly should *not* be rated according to the established mean values for young adults. If we do this, then all old people have to be considered as ill. Aging brings only quantitative rather than qualitative changes in performance. What we consider as "well" in a 40-year-old person cannot apply to what we consider as "well" in one who is 80 years old. In rating the health status of old people, we need to define our terms. The term SICK is defined as the presence of an emotional or physical illness that looks as if it will have a short-term fatal outcome, regardless of the presence or absence of treatment, or one in which the usual modes of treatments are unsuccessful. The term POOR HEALTH implies an illness in which there is major disability or discomfort and does not imply the possibility of immediate death. GOOD HEALTH among the aged means that there is no illness that produces more than a moderate degree of disability or discomfort with any immediate implication of mortality. In dealing with the aged we also need to define *their* terms. What do they really mean by CONSTIPATION? How do they truly define PAIN ALL OVER? What is their meaning of NEVER SLEEPING?

*Reprinted from *Nursing Homes,* Vol. 19, Nov. 1970, pages 33-35, with permission of the author and *Nursing Homes.*
**Dr. Moss is Chief of the Geriatric Program Development, Office of Health Facilities and Quality of Care, State of Illinois Department of Public Health. At the time the paper was written Dr. Moss was head of the Division of Geriatrics of the University of Chicago Medical School.

THE EFFECTS OF AGING

Here is a partial list of the effects of aging, and where percentages are shown, they represent a comparison of the healthy average 75-year-old with the average 30-year-old person, as reported by Dr. Nathan Shock, chief of the National Institute of Health's gerontology branch. For example, the body water content of the older man is NORMALLY 82% of that in the younger man.

Hair: Hair becomes less abundant, brittle, dull, and gray. There may be more hair in the nostrils, ears, and eybrows. The hair on the upper lip and chin of women may grow thicker and longer.

Skin: Progressive loss of elastic tissue and of the fatty layer immediately under the skin's surface leads to wrinkling. There is an increase in sensitivity to changes in temperature. Every bit of fresh air becomes a "draft." A decrease in oil secretion and sweat gland activity results in dryness and scaling, especially with frequent bathing.

Eyes: Few people over 60 see well without glasses as the result of accumulated damage to the eye, degeneration of fibers within the optic nerve, and the onset of glaucoma and cataract. The depth of the eyeball shortens and may lead to farsightedness — or the *curing* of nearsightedness. Color perception and the eye's power to adjust quickly to different levels of light and dark are reduced. About 95% of the elderly retain their vision with the aid of glasses and about two-thirds never get cataracts. Some of them with cataracts have little if any interference with normal vision.

Hearing: By age 65, the ability to hear high pitched sounds is usually lost, but this doesn't interfere with the perception of normal conversation. This often leads to Grandma being accused of hearing only what she wants to hear. Most people over the age of 65 hear adequately even though there is a degeneration of fibers within the auditory nerve.

Smell and Taste: The acuteness of these interrelated senses begins to decline at about the age of 60. The mucous membrane lining of the nose is thinned out, and the number of taste buds is down to 36% of those in the younger group.

Breasts: A woman's breast gland tissue is replaced by fibrous cells. The loss of fat tissue causes the breasts to flatten out and sag. The ligaments holding up the breast become lax.

Bone: A decrease in calcium content makes bones more fragile. The bone marrow is diminished. As the cartilage between the segments of the spinal column decreases, the vertebrae come closer together, resulting in a loss of height. This is especially so when the normal curvature of the spine becomes distorted.

Ligaments: These tend to contract and harden so that the unnatural bend of the spinal cord produces the familiar hunched-over appearance.

Joints: The cartilage between the joints wears thin and irregular. There is a decrease in the fluid that lubricates their inner surface. Arthritis superimposed on these changes potentiates the distress.

Blood vessels: The arterial walls thicken and fibrous cells replace the elastic tissue. As the walls lose their smooth surface, deposits form on the rough lining, producing rigidity and hardening. The valves in the veins that help return the blood to the heart may weaken.

Muscles: These begin to lose their strength in the middle years and become flabby, fat-filled, dehydrated, smaller, and fibrous ridden. This process can be offset to some extent by exercise or, on the other hand, worsened by joint and nerve malfunction.

Nerves: There is little functional change although there is a gradual replacement of nerve tissue by fibrous cells. Slower reaction and reflex timing results. The number of nerve trunk fibers diminish 63% and nerve impulse rate diminishes 90%. There are many mental and neurological changes which occur normally with advancing age. Neurological examination of the normal, well old person reveals impairment of the mental status, cranial nerve functions, coordination, motor system, reflexes, and sensation. The mental changes expected in healthy old age include memory impairment (particularly for recent events), slowness in problem solving, weakness of creative imagination, restlessness, and sleep disturbances. Intelligence, as measured by standard tests, diminishes, with performance items more affected than verbal ones. On cranial nerve testing, pupillary responses are found to diminish with age, to the point of disappearing completely in two-thirds of those over the age of 85. Uncertainty of gait is characterized by small steps, often with a broad-based stance. Finger-to-nose tests of coordination frequently reveal dysmetria. Deep tendon reflexes diminish and ankle jerks are often absent. Vibratory sensation is generally decreased in the feet and toes and usually completely lost by the age of 80. Although these NORMAL changes of aging involve many areas of the oldster's neurological functioning, they tend to follow a distinct pattern: deterioration is slow and occurs over long periods of time; the changes are usually diffuse and often symmetrical, with the ultimate incapacity usually moderate.

Brain: The folds of the brain flatten out and this may result in decreased circulation of blood within the brain. There may be a decrease in the total number of cells, but the brain functions normally unless its blood supply is even briefly blocked. The neurons of the brain are progressively lost throughout life and never replaced. The mentally retarded and those born with brain deficits seem to age more rapidly than normal and die at an earlier age.

Endocrine glands: There is some replacement by fibrous tissue. These glands usually function at close-to-normal rates throughout life. The thyroid, however, is usually smaller, resulting in a lower rate of basal metabolism. The body burns its fuel efficiently but less rapidly, and so less fuel is used and less needs to be taken in. The basic metabolism rate diminishes by 85%. If we use only the fasting blood sugar as a criterion for diagnosis, we would have to say that half of the people over the age of 65 have diabetes, whereas it is present only in 7 to 9% of the total population. If we believe our protein-bound-iodine determinations, then, there should also be a lot of thyroid diseases among the elderly. What is said about diabetes and thyroid disease is also comparable to kidney diseases. We must have new definitions for health and disease in the aged or we will face greater problems.

Lungs: Some functioning air sac membrane is replaced by fibrous tissue, interfering with the exchange of gases within the lungs. Maximum usable lung capacity is 56% and the breathing capacity is 43%. The amount of oxygen the blood can absorb from the lungs falls from 4 liters a minute at age 20 to 1.5 liters at age 75. The amount of air that can be moved through the lungs in fifteen seconds decreases about 40% between the ages of 20 and 80.

Heart: Muscle and valve tissue becomes replaced by fibrous cells, reducing the heart's efficiency. The older person pumps about 70% as much blood at rest as that of the younger man. Like other muscles, the heart muscle becomes weaker with age, and extreme physical effort burns up food and oxygen faster than the blood can deliver them in later years. This, as most oldsters know, limits the amount of physical work they can do. Among the life-threatening diseases, the most striking are the manifestations of coronary heart disease. About 45% probably have had myocardial infarcts and have survived. There is a great deal of peripheral vascular disease. Nearly one-third of the women over 65 have varicose veins. There is a high percentage of "strokes" of all kinds.

Stomach: The stomach secretes less acid and fewer of the enzymes which aid digestion. Truly gastric symptoms shouldn't improve by taking of antacids.

Intestines: The intestines secrete fewer digestive enzymes. The walls of the intestine become pocked and lose some of their absorptive power. The weakening of the large bowel and anal muscles may lead to evacuation problems.

Kidneys: The kidneys lose up to half their filtering ability but, if not obstructed by stones, maintain a reasonable function with almost 70% loss. The blood flow to the kidney also decreases by 50%, with damage caused by insufficient blood supply possibly leading to hypertension. Each kidney needs only 25% of its healthy tissue to function normally. All functions of the kidney decline as aging progresses. There is evidence that some of the nephrons of the kidney eventally lose their function. The adrenal hormones are the so-called stress hormones and the ability of oldsters to react quickly to stress may be reduced because of a decrease in adrenal activity.

Body weight and height: These decrease to 88% of those of younger persons. After middle age, general weight loss often sets in. A comparison of autopsied brains shows an average weight drop from 3.03 to 2.72 lb. between the ages of 30 and 90. Muscle fibers also shrink, and their place is taken by connective tissues which grow stiffer as the years pass. In 1968, Dr. Shock cited studies on American men 5 ft. 10 in. tall. The survey disclosed their weight averaged 168 lb. between the ages of 65 and 69. From age 90 to 94, that average had dropped to 148 lb.

CAUSES OF SENESCENCE

We encounter difficulty in distinguishing between biological and pathological aging. We also cannot always distinguish between pathological aging and disease. We have many descriptive effects on changes that come with aging. No one has as yet ascertained if these are biological, pathological, or a combination of either or both. Because gerontology, as a science, is in its infancy, the research results it has produced so far have been mostly descriptive. Gerontologists can say what an aging body is like, but they are still far from certain about the causes of senescence or about the reasons for which wide individual variations do occur.

7. Getting Old*

ALEXANDER LEAF**

Everyone ages, but some seem to age less quickly than others. In search of clues to the phenomenon the author visits three communities where vigorous oldsters are remarkable numerous.

"The patient, Mr. X, is 81 years old. A resident of the Dunhill Nursing Home, he has had two strokes, the first three years ago and the second a year ago. Since the last stroke he has been bedridden, incontinent and senile. He no longer recognizes members of his own family. For the past two months he has been eating poorly and failing generally. He was brought in last night by ambulance to our Emergency Service, where we found pulmonary congestion from a failing artereosclerotic heart and pneumonia."

I listen to this familiar story related by my intern at the Massachusetts General Hospital and mentally fill in the remainder of the picture. Sometimes the patient is 65, sometimes 70 or 90. Sometimes there is an underlying cancer. Usually, however, cardiovascular or respiratory problems dominate the clinical situation but are superimposed on a substrate of debility, wasting and senility. In the past pneumonia usually terminated such stories with some degree of dignity. Today modern medicine, with its antibiotics, intravenous infusions, cardiac pacemakers, respirators, diuretics and the like can often resolve the immediate problem (pneumonia and congestive heart failure in this instance) and return the patient to his nursing home again.

In a large metropolitan teaching hospital some 40 percent of the medical (as opposed to surgical) beds are occupied by patients over 65, many of them in a condition similar to Mr. X's. More than 20 million citizens are 65 or older in the U.S. today. They are the major reservoir of illness and medical needs. When I chose a career in medicine 35 years ago, I did so with the conviction that regardless of my eventual specialization my work would promote health and relieve human suffering. Today I contemplate Mr. X and wonder if my initial conviction was right. Of course, medicine does more than treat Mr. X's, but are we doing the best we can for contemporary society? The proportion of the population over 65 is between 10 and 11 percent now and will come close to 15 percent in the next few decades. What is medicine doing

*Reprinted from *The Scientific American,* Vol. 229, Sept. 1973, pages 44-52 with permission of *The Scientific American.*
**Dr. Alexander Leaf is Chief of Medical Services at Massachusetts General Hospital in Boston.

81

about it? Are we applying our resources wisely? Should we devote proportionately more of our efforts to trying to learn how we can prevent the infirmities of old age?

In the U. S. in 1969 the life expectancy at birth for white males was 67.8 years and for white females 75.1 years. That is some 23 years longer than life expectancy was in 1900. However, an adult who had reached 65 at the turn of the century could expect to live another 13 years and an adult who reaches 65 today can expect to live another 15 years, or only two years longer than in 1900. The seemingly large increase in life expectancy at birth actually reflects the great reduction in infant mortality. Little progress has been made in controlling the major causes of death in adults: heart disease, cancer and stroke. Accidents, of which nearly half are caused by motor vehicles, are a fourth major cause of adult deaths.

At the Ninth International Congress of Gerontology in July, 1972, M. Vacek of Czechoslovakia discussed the increase in mean age and the rising proportion of old people in the population. He pointed out the fact that the rise in the number of people over 65 toward 15 percent in the populations of stable, industrial countries, could be attributed to a falling birthrate. When at the conclusion of his remarks someone in the audience timidly asked if the achievements of the medical sciences had played a role in the rise in mean age, he responded that indeed they had, but that the simultaneous deterioration of the environment had canceled out any positive effect from medicine.

Mere length of life, however, may be a poor concern on which to focus. Most would agree that the quality of life, rather than its duration, should be the prime issue. The active life, so warmly espoused by Theodore Roosevelt, has been the American model. If one can extend the period of productive activity as did Verdi and Churchill, so much the better.

Most students of the field would agree with the statement of Frederic Verzá, the Swiss dean of gerontologists, "Old age is not an illness," says Verzá. "It is a continuation of life with decreasing capacities for adaptation." The main crippler and killer, arteriosclerosis, is not a necessary accompaniment of aging but a disease state that increases in incidence with age; the same is true of cancer. If we could prevent artereosclerosis, hypertension and cancer, the life-span could be pushed back closer to the biological limit, if such a limit in fact exists.

In order to observe aged individuals who are free of debilitating illness I recently visited three remote parts of the world where the existence of such individuals was rumored. These were the village of Vilcabamba in Ecuador, the small principality of Hunza in West Pakistan and the highlands of Georgia in the Soviet Caucasus.

A census of Vilcabamba taken in 1971 by Ecuador's National Institute of Statistics recorded a total population of 819 in this remote Andean village. Nine of the 819 were over 100 years old. The proportion of the population in this small village over 60 is 16.4 percent, as contrasted with a figure of 6.4 percent for rural Ecuador in general. The valley that shelters Vilcabamba is at an altitude of some 4,500 feet. Its vegetation appears quite lush. The people live by farming, but the methods are so primitive that only a bare subsistence is extracted from the land.

A team of physicians and scientists from Quito under the direction of Miguel Salvador has been studying this unique population. Guillermo Vela of the University of Quito, the nutritionist in the group finds that the average daily caloric intake of an elderly Vilcabamba adult is 1,200 calories. Protein provided 35 to 38 grams and fat only 12 to 19 grams; 200 to 250 grams of carbohydrate completed the diet. The contribution of animal protein and animal fat to the diet is very low.

The villagers of Vilcabamba, like most inhabitants of underdeveloped countries, live without benefit of modern sanitation, cleanliness and medical care. Cleanliness is evidently not a prerequisite for longevity. A small river skirts the village and provides water for drinking, washing and bathing. When we asked various villagers how long it had been since they had last bathed, the responses showed that many had not done so for two years. (The record was 10 years.) The villagers live in mud huts with dirt floors; chickens and pigs share their quarters. As one might expect in such surroundings, infant mortality is high, but so is the proportion of aged individuals. By extrapolation it stands at 1,100 per 100,000, compared with three per 100,000 in the U.S. Statistically, of course, such an extrapolation from so small a number is unwarranted; nonetheless, it shows how unusual the age distribution is in this little village.

The old people of Vilcabamba all appeared to be of European rather than Indian descent. We were able to validate the reported ages of almost all the elderly individuals from baptismal records kept in the local Catholic church. Miguel Carpio, aged 121, was the oldest person in the village when we were there. Jose Toledo's picture has appeared in newspapers around the world with captions that have proclaimed his extreme old age; actually he is only 109. All the old people were born locally, so that what is sometimes called the Miami Beach phenomenon, that is, an ingathering of the elderly, cannot account for the age distribution.

Both tobacco and sugarcane are grown in the valley, and a local rum drink, *zuhmir*, is produced. We did not, however, witness any drunkenness, and although most villagers smoke, there is disagreement among visiting physicians about how many of them inhale. The villagers work hard to scratch a livelihood from the soil, and the mountainous terrain demands continuous and vigorous physical activity. These circumstances are hardly unique to Vilcabamba, and one leaves this Andean valley with the strong suspicion that genetic factors must be playing an important role in the longevity of this small enclave of elderly people of European stock.

The impression that genetic factors are important in longevity was reinforced by what we saw in Hunza. This small independent state is ruled over by a hereditary line of leaders known as Mirs. In 1891 the Mir of that day surrendered control over defense, communications and foreign affairs to the British when they conquered his country. In 1948, after the partition of Pakistan and India, the present Mir yielded the same right to Pakistan. Hunza is hidden among the towering peaks of the Karakorum Range on Pakistan's border with China and Afghanistan and is one of the most inaccessible places on the earth. After a day's travel from Gilgit, first by jeep and then on foot from the point where a rockslide had cut the mountain road, we found ourselves in a valley surrounded on all sides by peaks more than 20,000 feet high, blocked at the far end by Mount Rokaposhi, which rises to 25,500 feet in snow-clad splendor.

The valley is arid, but a system of irrigation canals built over the past 800 years carries water from the high surrounding glaciers, converting the valley into a terraced garden. The inhabitants work their fields by primitive agricultural methods, and the harvests are not quite sufficient to prevent a period of real privation each winter. According to S. Maqsood Ali, a Pakistani nutritionist who has surveyed the diet of 55 adult males in Hunza, the daily diet averages 1,923 calories: 50 grams are protein, 36 grams fat and 354 grams carbohydrate. Meat and dairy products accounted for only 1 percent of the total. Land is too precious to be used to support dairy herds; the few animals that are kept by the people are killed for meat only during the winter or on festive occasions.

As in Vilcabamba, everyone in Hunza works hard to wrest a living from the rocky hills. One sees an unusual number of vigorous people who, although elderly in appearance, agilely climb up and down the steep slopes of the valley. Their language is an unwritten one, so that no documentary records of birth dates are available. In religion the Hunzakuts are Ismaili Moslems, followers of the Agha Khan. Their education is quite limited. Thus, although a number of nonscientific accounts have attributed remarkable longevity and robust health to these people, no documentation substantiates the reports.

In Soviet Georgia, one of three widely separated parts of the world visited by the author, a 105 year old man has the place of honor (*at head of table, left*) at a party held near the village of Gurjanni. The centenarian was the oldest guest but the man and the two women on his left are all over 80. The average diet of those over 80 in the Caucasus is relatively rich in proteins (70 to 80 grams a day) and fats (40 to 60 grams), but the daily caloric intake, 1,700 to 1,900 calories, is barely half the U.S. average.

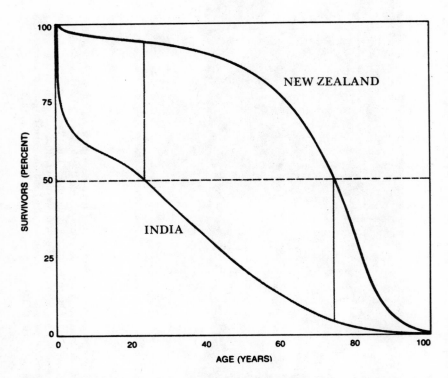

Few live to grow old in underdeveloped nations, whereas the opposite is true in the developed nations. For example, half of the women who died in India from 1921 to 1930 were 24 or younger; only 5 percent of the women who died in New Zealand from 1934 to 1938 were that young. Half of the New Zealand women who died in the same period were 74 or older. In India only 5 percent of women's deaths were in this age group.

Unfortunately there is no known means of distinguishing chronological age from physiological age in humans. When we asked elderly Hunzakuts how old they were and what they remembered of the British invasion of their country in 1891, their answers did little to validate their supposed age. If, however, they are as old as both they and their Mir, a well-educated and worldly man, maintain, then there are a remarkable number of aged but lean and fit-looking Hunzakuts who can climb the steep slopes of their valley with far greater ease than we could. Putatively the oldest citizen was one Tulah Beg, who said he was 110; the next oldest, also a male, said he was 105.

In addition to their low-calorie diet, which is also low in animal fats, and their intense physical activity, the Hunzakuts have a record of genetic isolation that must be nearly unique. Now, there do not seem to be "good" genes that favor longevity but only "bad" genes that increase the probability of acquiring a fatal illness. One may therefore speculate that a small number of individuals, singularly lacking such "bad" genes, settled this mountain valley centuries ago and that their isolation has prevented a subsequent admixture with "bad" genes. This, of course, is mere speculation.

The possible role of genetic factors in longevity seemed of less importance in the Caucasus. In Abkhasia on the shores of the Black Sea and in the adjoining Caucasus one encounters many people over 100 who are not only Georgian but also Russian, Jewish, Armenian and Turkish. The Caucasus is a land bridge that has been traveled for centuries by conquerors from both the east and the west, and its population can scarcely have maintained any significant degree of genetic isolation. At the same time, when one speaks to the numerous centenarians in the area, one invariably discovers that each of them has parents or siblings who have similarly attained great age. The genetic aspect of longevity therefore cannot be entirely dismissed.

In contrast to the isolated valleys of Vilcabamba and Hunza, the Caucasus is an extensive area that includes three Soviet republics: Georgia, Azerbaijan and Armenia. The climate varies from the humid and subtropical (as at Sukhumi on the Black Sea, with an annual rainfall of 1,100 to 1,400 millimeters) to drier continental conditions, marked by extremes of summer heat and winter cold. The population extends from sea-level settlements along the Black and Caspian seas to mountain villages at altitudes of 1,000 to 1,500 meters. More old people are found in the mountainous regions than at sea level, and the incidence of atherosclerosis among those who live in the mountains is only half that in the sea-level villages. G. Z. Pitzkhelauri, head of the Gerontological Center in the Republic of Georgia, told me that the 1970 census placed the number of centenarians for the entire Caucasus at between 4,500 and 5,000. Of these, 1,844, or an average of 39 per 100,000, live in Georgia. In Azerbaijan there are 2,500 more, or 63 per 100,000. Perhaps of more pertinence to my study was the record of activity among the elderly of the Caucasus. Of 15,000 individuals over 80 whose records were kept by Pitzkhelauri, more than 70 percent continue to lead very active lives. Sixty percent of them were still working on state or collective farms.

I returned from my three surveys convinced that a vigorous, active life involving physical activity (sexual activity included) was possible for at least 100 years and in some instances for even longer.

Longevity is clearly a multifactorial matter. First are the genetic factors; all who have studied longevity are convinced of their importance. It is generally accepted that the offspring of long-lived parents live longer than others. Yet a long life extends beyond the period of fertility, at least in women, so that length of life can have no direct evolutionary advantage. It has been suggested that living organisms are like clocks: their life-span ends when the initial endowment of energy is expended, just as the clock stops when its spring becomes unwound. L. V. Heilbrunn estimated in the 1900's that the heart of a mouse, which beats 520 to 780 times per minute, would contract 1.11 billion times during the 3.5 years of the mouse's normal life-span. The heart of an elephant, which beats 25 to 28 times per minute, would have beaten 1.021 billion times during the elephant's normal life-span of 70 years. The similarity between these two figures seems to suggest some initial equal potential that is gradually dissipated over the animal's life-span. Such calculations, however, are probably more entertaining than explanatory of longevity.

As I have mentioned, genes evidently influence longevity only in a negative way by predisposing the organism to specific fatal diseases. Alex Comfort of University College London has pointed out the possible role of heterosis, or "hybrid vigor." The crossbreeding of two inbred strains — each with limited growth, size, resistance to disease and longevity — can improve these characteristics in the progeny. This vigor has been manifested in a wide variety of species, both plant and animal, but its significance in human longevity is not known.

Next are the factors associated with nutrition. Since we are composed of what we eat and drink, it is not surprising that students of longevity have emphasized the importance of dietary factors. Indeed, the only demonstrable means of extending the life-span of an experimental animal has been the manipulation of diet. The classic studies of Clive M. McCay of Cornell University in the 1930's showed that the life-span of albino rats could be increased as much as 40 percent by the restriction of caloric intake early in life. Rats fed a diet otherwise balanced but deficient in calories showed delayed growth and maturation until the caloric intake was increased. At the same time their life-span was extended. The significance of these experiments with respect to human longevity is not known, but they raise questions about the current tendency to overfeed children.

The role of specific dietary factors in promoting longevity remains unsettled. When the old people we visited were asked to what they attributed their long life, credit was usually given to the local alcoholic beverage, but this response generally came from the more vocal and chauvinistic males. Much publicity is given today to the possible role of animal fats in the development of arteriosclerosis. Saturated fatty acids and cholesterol have also been suggested as the causal agents of coronary atherosclerosis. Since the atheromas themselves — the deposits that narrow and occlude the blood vessels of the heart, the brain and other organs — contain cholesterol, the suspicion of complicity comes easily. It is also well documented that the level of cholesterol in the blood serum has a positive prognostic relation to the likelihood of heart attacks.

Since the diet of affluent societies has a high content of animal fats, which are rich in cholesterol and saturated fatty acids, the suspicion further arises that these dietary constituents are contributing to the increase in the number of heart attacks affecting young adult males. The marked individual variability in tolerance to the quantity of fat and cholesterol in the diet, however, makes it difficult to ascribe prime importance to this single factor. We have seen that in both Vilcabamba and Hunza the diet was not only low in calories but also low in animal fats. In the Caucasus an active dairy economy allows cheese and milk products to be served with every meal. Perhaps it is significant that in this area the cheese is low in fat content and the total fat intake is only some 40 to 60 grams per day. This level is in sharp contrast to figures from a recent U.S. Department of Agriculture report stating that the average daily fat intake for Americans of all ages is 157 grams. The best-informed medical opinion today generally agrees that the Americans' average daily intake of 3,300 calories, including substantial quantities of fat, is excessive and conducive neither to optimal health nor to longevity.

Let us now consider physical activity. There is increasing awareness that early heart disease is a price we are paying for our largely sedentary existence. In the three areas I visited physical fitness was an inevitable consequence of the active life led by the inhabitants. My initial speculation that their isolated lives protect them from the ravages of infectious disease and from acquiring "bad" genes is probably

incorrect. A simpler explanation for their fitness is that their mountainous terrain demands a high level of physical activity simply to get
through the day.

A number of studies have examined the effects of physical activity on
the incidence and severity of heart attacks among various sample
populations. For example, among British postal workers it was found
that those who delivered the mail had a lower incidence of heart attacks
and, when attacks did occur, a lower mortality rate than their colleagues who worked at sedentary jobs. This same study also compared
the relative incidence of heart attacks among London bus drivers and
conductors. The conductors, who spent their working hours climbing
up and down the double-deck buses collecting fares, had less heart
trouble than the sedentary drivers. It has been reported recently that
the weekend athlete who engages in vigorous physical activity is only
one-third as prone to heart disease as his age-matched sedentary
neighbor. It is well known that exercise increases the oxygenation of
the blood and improves the circulation. Exercise will also improve the
collateral circulation of blood to the heart muscle. When the exercises
are carefully graded and performed under appropriate supervision,
they are undoubtedly the best means of rehabilitating the heart muscle
after a heart attack.

Exercise improves circulation to nearly all parts of the body. Circulation is increased to the brain as well as to the heart and skeletal muscles.
Recently it has been asserted that improvement in the oxygen supply to
the brain will actually improve thinking. In a resting sedentary individual, however, the blood supplied to the brain contains more oxygen
than the brain is able to extract. It is difficult to explain how an added
overabundance of a constitutent that is normally not a rate-limiting
factor in cerebral function would enhance that function. It may
nonetheless be that the sense of well-being that the exercising individual enjoys is likely to increase self-confidence and as a result improve both social and intellectual effectiveness.

Finally, physical activity helps to burn off excess calories and dispose
of ingested fats. Exercise may thus counteract the deleterious effects of
a diet that includes too many calories and too much fat. Indeed, it may
well be one factor that helps to account for the great individual differences in tolerance for dietary factors.

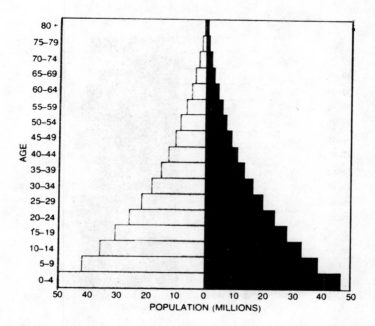

Exaggerated pyramid appears when the males (left) and females (right) of a population with a high growth rate are counted in ascending five-year steps. The graph shows the 1970 population of India; many more Indians are below the age of 20 than are above that age. In such an expanding population the elderly, although numerous, comprise a small percentage of the total.

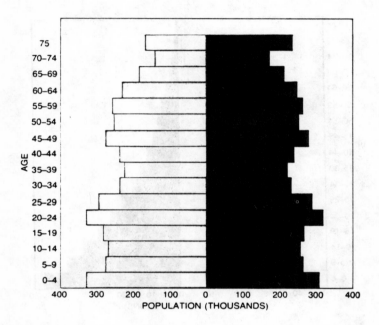

Uneven column, rather than a pyramid, appears when the number of males (left) and females (right) in a slow-growing population are similarly displayed. The graph shows the population of Sweden in 1970; about as many Swedes are above the age of 35 as are below that age. In this population, noted for its low birthrate, the elderly comprise an increasingly large percentage of the total.

Psychological factors must also be considered. It is characteristic of each of the areas I visited that the old people continue to be contributing, productive members of their society. The economy in all three areas is agrarian, there is no fixed retirement age and the elderly make themselves useful doing many necessary tasks around the farm or the home. Moreover, increased age is accompanied by increased social status. The old people, with their accumulated experience of life, are expected to be wise, and they respond accordingly. In Hunza the Mir rules his small state with the advice of a council of elders, who sit on the ground in a circle at his feet and help him with his decisions and pronouncements. When we met Temur Tarba in the Caucasus just three weeks after his 100th birthday, it was clear from his manner that he was delighted to have at last "arrived." He proudly displayed his Hero of Labor medal, the highest civilian award of the U.S.S.R. He had won it only seven years earlier for his work in hybridizing corn. The cheerful centenarian still picked tea leaves, rode his horse and worked on a collective farm.

People who no longer have a necessary role to play in the social and economic life of their society generally deteriorate rapidly. The pattern of increasingly early retirement in our own society takes a heavy toll of our older citizens. They also find that their offspring generally have neither any room nor any use for them in their urban apartment. These are economic determinants that cannot be reversed in our culture today. Their devastating effect on the happiness and life-span of the elderly could be countered at least in part by educational programs to awaken other interests or avocations to which these people could turn with zest when their contribution to the industrial economy is no longer needed. The trend toward shorter working hours and earlier retirement makes the need for such education urgent. It seems a corruption of the very purpose of an economy that instead of freeing us from drudgery and need and allowing us to enjoy a better life, it holds us slaves to its dictates even though affluence is at hand.

In their remote farms and villages the old people I visited live oblivious to the pressures and strains of modern life. Such American controversies as the fighting in Southeast Asia, conflict in the Middle East, environmental pollution, the energy crisis and the like that fill our news media were unknown to them. Of course, most of the stresses and tensions to which mankind is subject arise from more personal social interactions, such as a quarrel with a spouse or misbehavior by an offspring. As a result it is impossible for any social group to entirely escape mental stress and tensions. Nonetheless, in societies that are less competitive and less aggressive even these personal stresses can be less exhausting than they are in our own. The old people I met abroad showed equanimity and optimism. In the Caucasus I asked Gabriel Chapnian, aged 117, what he thought of young people, of his government and of the state of the world in general. When he repeatedly responded "Fine, fine," I asked with some annoyance, "Isn't there anything today that disturbs you?" He replied cheerfully, "Oh, yes, there are a number of things that are not the way I would want them to be, but since I can't change them I don't worry about them."

One cannot discuss the quality of life at advanced age without considering sexual activity. In most societies the combination of male boasting about sexual prowess and taboos against discussing the subject makes it difficult to collect reliable information about sexual activity in the elderly. Women's ovaries stop functioning at menopause, usually in the late 40's or early 50's, but this has little influence on the libido. Similarly, aging is associated with a gradual decrease in the number of cells in certain organs, including the male testes. The cells that produce sperm are the first to be affected, but later the cells that produce the male hormone testosterone may also diminish in number and activity. Sexual potency in the male and libido in the female may nonetheless persist in advanced old age. Herman Brotman of the Department of Health, Education, and Welfare reports that each year there are some 3,500 marriages among the 20 million Americans over the age of 65, and that sexual activity is cited along with companionship as one reason for these late unions.

Research on aging is proceeding in two general directions. One aims at a better understanding of those disease states that, although they are not an integral part of the aging process, nevertheless increase in incidence with age and constitute the major cripplers of the aged. Here both arteriosclerosis and cancer are prominent. Knowledge of the causes and prevention of these diseases is still very limited, and much more work is necessary before there can be sufficient understanding to allow prevention of either. If both arteriosclerosis and cancer could be prevented, it should be possible to extend man's life-span close to its as yet undetermined biological limit.

There is reason to believe that a limit does exist. Even if one could erase the cumulative wear and tear that affects the aging organism, it seems probable that the cells themselves are not programmed for perpetual activity. The differences in the life-spans of various animals suggest some such natural limit. The changes that are observed in the tissues of animals that undergo metamorphosis — for example insects — are indicative of the programmed extinction of certain tissues. So is the failure of the human ovaries at menopause, long before other vital organs give out. Leonard Hayflick of the Stanford University School of Medicine has reported that the cells in cultures of human embryonic connective tissue will divide some 50 times and then die. If growth is interrupted by plunging the culture into liquid nitrogen, the cells will resume growth on thawing, continue through the remainder of their 50 divisions and then die. Although one may question whether the cells are not affected by adverse environmental influences, Hayflick's studies support the notion of programmed death. Only cancer cells seem capable of eternal life in culture. One familiar line of cancer cells, the "HeLa" strain, has often been the subject of cell-culture studies; it originated as a cervical cancer 21 years ago and has been maintained in culture ever since.

As investigations and speculations seek an answer to the question of the natural limits of life, other workers have noted that the giant molecules of living matter themselves age. Collagen, the main protein of connective tissue, constitutes approximately 30 percent of all the protein in the human body. With advancing age collagen molecules show a spontaneous increase in the cross-linking of their subunits, a process that increases their rigidity and reduces their solubility. Such a stiffening of this important structural component of our bodies might underlie such classic features of aging as rigidity of blood vessels, resistance to blood flow, reduced delivery of blood through hardened arteries and, as a final consequence, the loss of cells and of function. Other giant molecules, including the DNA molecule that stores the genetic information and the RNA molecule that reads out the stored message, may also be subject to spontaneous cross-linking that would eventually prevent the normal self-renewal of tissues.

A new area in aging research appears to be opening up in studies on the immune system of the body. In addition to providing antibodies against bacteria or foreign substances introduced into the body, the immune system recognizes and destroys abnormal or foreign cells. When these functions of the immune system diminish, as happens with advancing age, there may be errors in the system that result in antibodies that attack and destroy normal body cells or impair their function. The net result of this disturbed activity of the immune system, like the cross-linking of collagen, would be what is recognized as the aging process.

Takashi Makinodan of the Baltimore City Hospitals thinks that methods of rejuvenating the immune system are possible. The hope that some medicine will be discovered that can block the fundamental process of aging, however, seems to me very remote until the nature of the aging process is far better understood. Much research is needed

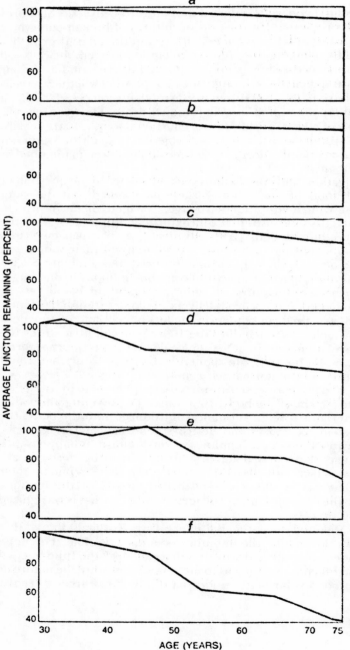

Loss of function with increasing age does not occur at the same rate in all organs and systems. Graphs (*right*) show loss as a percentage, with the level of function at age 30 representing 100 percent. Thus brain weight (*a*) has diminished to 92 percent of its age-30 value by age 75 and nerve-conduction velocity (*b*) to about 90 percent. The basal metabolic rate (*c*) has diminished to 84 percent, cardiac output at rest (*d*) to 70 percent, filtration rate of the kidneys (*e*) to 69 percent and maximum breathing capacity (*f*) to 43 percent. Diseases, however, rather than gradual diminution of function, are at present the chief barrier to extended longevity.

before such an understanding can be attained. It is nonetheless encouraging that aging research is finding increased interest and support in several countries. It is also encouraging to perceive a parallel interest in the aged among scientists, physicians, economists, politicians and others. To consider any extension of the human life-span without a serious effort to anticipate and plan for the impact of increased longevity on society would be entirely irresponsible.

8. To Be Continued*

*The prospects for multiplying our years of
youthful vigor are bright and imminent.*

However successfully we dodge the misfortunes of life, however cautious, heroic or lucky we may be, the mere passage of time kills us. And before doing so, it impairs us, which is worse. Our chief defense against the awareness of death is that it can be put forward in time — it will happen, but not yet. Some time limit and the defenses crumble — which is why cancer, the best-known terminal disease, inspires such horror in modern man. It is the most recognizable counterpart of that unpleasant skeleton that taps king, merchant and reveler on the shoulder in medieval paintings of the dance of death. The rarity of untimely death, thanks to modern medicine, sharpens our awareness of our other enemy, aging.

Aging means that we can name a year in which we shall no longer be alive. And there is another date, perhaps 15 or 20 years sooner, when, if things stay as they are, we shall be alive, but not fully. Death is bad enough, but before death there is, as Yeats puts it:

> *the death of friends, or death of every brilliant eye
> that make a catch in the breath.*

This death before death will begin, for most of us, around 65 and will continue until it kills us. It's not strictly a disease; one may hope to avoid diseases. But age we cannot avoid. It's the only disease we've all got, and, like cancer patients, we know roughly when we may expect to fail and die of it.

If, that is, things stay as they are; and that depends largely on decisions now being made. Adults alive today between the ages of 20 and 50 are the first humans to stand a fighting chance of seeing science begin to bring the process of aging under control. If this happens, as it easily could, within the next 10 to 15 years, they may share that benefit.

*Reprinted from *Playboy Magazine,* Vol. 18, Nov. 1971, pages 112, 114, 209-210, and 212, with permission of the author and *Playboy.* Copyright ©1971 by *Playboy.*
**Dr. Comfort is in the Department of Zoology, University Hospital, London, England; he has been a Distinguished Fellow at the Center for the Study of Democratic Institutions in Santa Barbara, California.

A relatively small investment now could make the accomplishment nearly certain. What amazes workers in this field of medical biology is that so few of the beneficiaries — and, indeed, so few scientists realize how close we are to this achievement.

In his article *The Immortalist* [Playboy, May 1969], Alan Harrington rightly interpreted the mood of our culture: The present generation cannot, in fact, be immortal, but it is not prepared to go on being mortal on the present time scale. If Harrington's view seems brash at first, it still represents a ground swell of feeling that is about to be implemented in science. We can now begin to offer hard predictions, both as to what is possible in the prolonging of life and as to when developments will take place.

Speed in attaining a scientific possibility and minimal disturbance of society by it depend on technological forecasts. In 1938, Hahn and Strassmann demonstrated uranium fission and showed, though they didn't know it, that atomic energy was a feasible project. The first atomic bomb was used in warfare only seven years later. In 1961, John F. Kennedy was advised that, in the present state of the art, an American could be put on the moon by 1970, given enough Government support. That this was technically possible had been known since before the first Sputnik. All that was needed was the decision to go ahead.

Students of the future call the moment at which a major possibility is seen to be practicable the Hahn-Strassmann point. Often it passes unnoticed, except by the men on the job. This has happened with the control of human aging, less dramatically than with nuclear fission but just as definitely, over the past decade. We know that human aging can almost certainly be slowed and we know how to set about trying. The necessary research, moreover, is cheap by AEC and NASA standards. The whole project would probably cost as much as one Saturn rocket or one big-dish antenna. The prestige for the achievement of a "first" would be, in political terms, not far short of a moon landing. One can infer from this that even if aging research is not promoted as a priority, it will happen, and if it is so promoted, it will happen fast. With the present research investment, it is likely to happen in America, with a fundamental backup from world science.

Science has two ways of making people live longer. It can stop their dying before their time or it can try to slow down the figurative clock that controls aging, so that old age and death take longer to arrive. So far, it has done the first, and brilliantly. Now, with some Governmental funding, but with strikingly little public awareness of what's afoot, it is about to tackle the second.

In any of the privileged countries, you can *expect* to become old. This in itself is new — one generation back, your chances of doing this would have been far less secure. Medicine and surgery, prosperity and welfare, have ensured that — war, accident, pollution, suicide and bad luck aside — most of us can hope to die of old age. We shall not, that is, die as young adults of appendicitis or tuberculosis, or as mature adults of pneumonia or childbirth infection. We are most likely, in fact, to die of heart and vessel disease or of cancer. When we do, unless we overeat, smoke cigarettes or inherit a bad hand of genetic cards, we shall also be old. In spite of modern technology and medicine, we shall get old at the same age Moses and Pharaoh did. The human life span has probably not changed throughout history. What has happened through science is that most of us now reach the end of it.

The meaning of old age hasn't changed, either. Though some are harder hit by it than others, and though there are Bertrand Russells and Artur Rubinsteins, who keep the zest for living into their 80s, aging is still loss. At 50 we become stouter and slower; at 60 we tire more easily. Then the skin wrinkles, the muscles weaken, and by 70 our strength is on the average what it was at 14 or so. The mind may or may not stay clear; but if it does, the body cannot match it. And all the time, the mortality from disease steadily climbs. Old age and death are the two great intolerables and, of these, the first is probably less bearable, because we have to live through it. We say that age has its compensations, but we don't speak of compensation unless we've been injured, and few of our notions of compensation survive an open-eyed visit to an old-folks' home.

The truth is that having assured that most of us reach 70, conventional medicine has just about reached the point of diminishing returns. Cure of the two present leading causes of death — cancer and heart and vessel disease — would add about seven years to the total life expectancy, but mainly by helping those unlucky enough to contract these diseases young. At 65, the gain would be under two years; we should simply die a few months later of something else, for aging involves a steady increase in the number and variety of our infirmities. We could improve the quality of life to some extent — for example, by treating our old people decently — but this wouldn't be much of an improvement. The men in old-folks' homes were once vigorous, the women beautiful, or at least young. The only reason we don't follow Yeats and Dylan Thomas' advice and recognize the enormity of what is going to happen to us is that so far, it has looked inevitable.

If aging on the present time scale is really inevitable, we had probably better accept it with dignity. But all the scientific evidence is that it is not. Over the past 20 years, and almost unnoticed even by the general scientific community, an international campaign has been mounted to find out exactly what aging is and whether — and, if so, how — its rate can be slowed. At present, we still don't know exactly what it is, though we have several plausible theories. We do know that the rate of aging can be altered in rats and mice by relatively simple manipulations. In the next five to ten years, there will be experiments on man, to see whether the same techniques can be used clinically. If they can, then from rat and mouse experiments, we could reasonably expect a 20-40 percent increase in the period of adult vigor — the time, that is, before manifest aging changes set in. Insofar as any scientific prediction is safe, we can now say that the length of time before we do this and the number of adults alive today who will be able to benefit from it depend quite simply on the amount of money and energy we put into the project.

Aging is, in biological terms, the increasing inability of the body to maintain itself and perform the operations it once did. Most current theories assume that this results from a loss of information at the cell level. Mammals have basically two kinds of cells — those that are constantly renewed (skin cells, blood) and those that live as long as their owner and never divide (brain cells, muscle cells). Both types carry the basic instructions for their orderly behavior in the form of blueprint molecules of deoxyribonucleic acid (DNA).

DNA is the key to most of modern biology. It consists of a long spiral molecule, rather like a computer tape. The chromosomes of each cell contain a number of these molecules, on which are stored, in coded form, all the information needed to turn that cell into a complicated organism — and to determine whether the organism will be a man, a rabbit or a peach tree. This molecule is Jim Watson and Francis Crick's "double helix," which won them a share of the Nobel Prize in 1962; we are just beginning to be able to read the language of its code, which is composed of a series of three "letter" combinations.

DNA is like a master blueprint for the body and its maintenance. What happens is that from an identical blueprint file in every body cell, copies are taken, and these copies, in turn, are used to specify chemical machine tools, called enzymes. Since a baby differs from a man, and a muscle cell from a blood cell, the body clearly has an elaborate program for transcribing parts of this stored information at one time and ignoring, or switching off, others. If we had a full set of plans for a Saturn rocket, we would need to make one set of jigs and tools for the workshop that builds the engines and another for the guidance-system shop. If some of the blueprints were locked up as soon as the patterns were made, the life of that workshop would be limited to the life span of its now-irreplaceable tools.

Unlike engineering, in which parts are checked and rechecked, biological toolmaking is never 100 percent accurate. In old nematode worms, Israel's Dr. David Gershon has found that all the necessary chemical tools of certain kinds are there, but about half are not working properly. It seems highly probable that at some point in the chain, errors enter the manufacturing process. They may be in the original DNA blueprints, which become smudged or switched off in some or all of the cells with wear and the passing of time. They may be in the copying process or, more probably, in the machine tools, the enzymes. The mischief may be of many kinds. One kind is the injection of "noise," in the communication sense. Random scratches on a negative, wormholes in punch cards, nicks in a phonograph record are noise of this sort; they confuse the original message. Or it may be that since muscle cells and blood cells must clearly use different parts of their original, total blueprint file, some of the blueprints they possess may become unavailable to them and some parts of the system may not be renewable if damaged. The damage could affect nondividing cells so that they ceased to function properly, or it could affect dividing cells so that new cells formed by an old man differ from those of a baby, becoming impaired or foreign.

Luckily, we don't have to find out which of these mechanisms is instrumental in aging. We can alter its rate without knowing. In fact, we are most likely to pinpoint the kind of information loss that's occurring by seeing what tends to counteract it. Basically, we have one big choice: If we're dealing with a phonograph record that is scratched with use until it's unplayable, we need to slow down the rate at which scratches accumulate — for example, by cleaning the stylus and excluding grit and dust. If we're dealing with a record that can be played once only and not restarted, we might conceivably find ways of running it more slowly — but not so much so as to distort the music. Either of these procedures would prolong the performance.

In rats and mice, we already know of several maneuvers that will prolong life. The oldest and simplest of these is food restriction. The life span of mice can be doubled, both by gross calorie restriction, which keeps them juvenile, and by feeding them only two days out of three. Besides postponing aging, this regime virtually eliminates tumors in some strains of mice. The lack of excess calories may slow down copying generally or cut the rate of noise injection or conserve irreplaceable machine-tool molecules. It may retard some built-in program in the body. It may even work simply as a challenge that makes the natural control machinery work better. Starved mice have big adrenal glands, and there are some adrenal hormones that can by themselves double longevity in long-lived mouse strains, probably by controlling copying processes or by preventing the rejection of divergent cells. Whether the technique of food restriction would work in man, and particularly whether it would work when started in adult life, we can find out only by trial.

Another group of approaches is based on an area of research that made great strides in the Sixties: immunology. Biologists are trying to understand and control the body's defenses against foreign cells so as to ensure the success of transplant surgery. They are unraveling the machinery that prevents grafts from taking and, in so doing, are finding more and more instances in which the body appears to react against or reject its own tissues. These conditions become commoner with age, and it seems almost certain that self-rejection plays a part, perhaps a leading part, in age changes. Either our cells alter and become criminals or our bodily policeman alter and start attacking law-abiding citizens. Drugs and hormones of the kind given to cover transplant operations are already being tried with some success as anti-aging agents in mice; and in some strains of old mice, removal of the spleen — an important organ in the rejection process — makes them survive to great ages.

Yet another approach is based directly on the error-in-copying idea. Large man-made molecules, and molecules in organic materials such as margarine or leather, perish with time through attack by chemical agents known as free radicals. A free radical has been likened to a convention delegate away from his wife: it's a highly reactive chemical agent that will combine with anything suitable that's around. Chemists protect such things as chicken feed, cornflakes and automobile tires by adding to them substances known as anti-oxidants, which mop up these unwanted agents and slow down the perishing process. The body contains both free radicals and long-lived molecules — among them, the fibers that keep our skin elastic and the blueprint molecules of DNA. If any such perishing reactions occur with aging, it ought to be possible to slow all of them down by administering some of the non-poisonous antioxidants now added to groceries, but in far bigger doses, without waiting to find out exactly where the damaging processes are located.

A position paper on the practical side of age slowing in animals in 1971 would run roughly like this: (1) We now have perhaps half a dozen ways of slowing down aging or lengthening life or both in rats and mice. (2) The exact way these methods fit together, the nature of the aging clock and whether there is one clock or more are unanswered questions, but we should be close to an answer within five years. (3) It's not certain that any of the known age-slowing methods would work in man. (4) Whether they would and whether they would work in adult life, can be found only by trying them. (5) If they don't, then it's likely that similar and equally simple methods will. (6) Human experiments will be started within the next three to five years, probably at more than one center.

The reason these techniques haven't already been tried in man has nothing to do with ethics; it's simply that, because the investigators age as well as their subjects, 70-to-80-year experiments are, for practical and psychological reasons, no go. As long as we could measure aging only by following lifelong mortality figures, as insurance agencies do, experiments on anti-aging agents were confined to rats and mice, which live but a few years. But we can now move into human studies, because greater knowledge of age changes and the advent of automated clinical laboratories and computers make it possible to measure the rate of aging in the short run.

The new strategy is to choose a battery of measurements — chemical, psychological and clinical — that change with age and follow them over a period of, say, five years, starting at a given age, such as 50. The measures are picked to be so varied that any factor that slows the rate of change in all of them would be likely to act by slowing down aging in general. This approach reduces the problem of how to retard aging in man to the size of an ordinary medical experiment, using some 500 volunteers over three to five years, like the assessment of low-cholesterol diets in heart disease.

Battery tests for aging are one of the few beneficent spin-offs from the bomb. They were developed at the Brookhaven nuclear-research laboratories to measure the rate of aging in Hiroshima survivors. (Reassuringly, the survivors didn't age faster.) Equipment like that which would be needed to carry out such tests on normal people already exists in many U.S. centers, such as the Kaiser-Permanente Medical Centers in San Francisco, Oakland and Walnut Creek, California. We could start human experiments next week, measuring such things as hair graying, skin elasticity, change in body chemicals, hearing and mental agility as indexes of the speed at which aging is progressing.

Age control will hit American business and social-service planning within months as a contingency and within a few years as a fact. Until now, the fixed human life span of threescore and ten has been one of the few facts that planners have been able to depend upon. Forecasters in all fields seem unaware of how close we are to having this hitherto solid basis demolished. In spite of efforts to foresee technological changes, it's almost certain that age control will take everyone by surprise.

Similarly, the aging public seems unaware that a little informed lobbying now could get them longer life. There is a bill before Congress to set up a National Institute of Gerontology, which could be the biological counterpart of NASA. So if anyone asks, "What can I do today to slow down my own aging?" the answer is, not jogging, not taking antioxidants, not living on lettuce alone. It is, rather, backing this kind of initiative, so that we know in time what to do. There's no point in wasting our time on advertised strums and Continental professors who are rumored to rejuvenate Popes and the wives of millionaires. These can only rejuvenate someone else's bank balance. We had better put our money on hardnosed science, and as soon as possible.

Gerontologists today face problems similar to those the rocket men had in the Thirties: they are a little better funded but no more fully appreciated at top decision-making levels. Probably, only a few million dollars stand between these men and historic results. Without the money, they will get there but too late to benefit many of us.

The aim of what we're doing is clear enough. We're looking for some agent that can be applied as late in life as possible and that will slow down all symptoms of aging. Success will neither abolish old age nor prolong it — nor, in all probability — shorten it. It will simply make it occur later. For a ten-year gain, a man of 60 who has been treated will be as he would have been, untreated, at 50, with the same vigor and the same diseases. At 80, he will be the man he would have been at 70. If we can tamper with the taximeter to give us more miles for our dollar, the journey will be longer, but it will be substantially the same, in that we shall still age and die, but we won't have to spend so big a fraction of life in so comfortless an anteroom, nor enter it so soon. We aim to create for the 1970s and 1980s a new medicine based on control of the rates at which things happen and grounded on the view that it's easier to alter a rate than rewrite a program. On this principle it should be far easier to make cancer or heart disease occur ten years later than it would otherwise have done than to prevent or cure it altogether.

What we're *not* trying to do is equally clear. We're not trying to prolong old age by keeping people alive beyond their years of vigor;

medicine is doing that now, which is why gerontology is so urgent a study. Nor are we envisaging longer life by prolonging childhood. This is probably feasible and might be easier, but it would be far from ideal. Nor are we contemplating the spinning out of a fixed amount of life by taking it in sections, punctuated by periods of hibernation. That, too, is probably feasible, but it's a different project, of interest chiefly to astronauts and to the historically inquisitive.

Prediction in science is difficult, but we can make a few reasonable guesses about what we can accomplish. Among these are the following: By the year 1990, we will know of an experimentally tested way of slowing down age changes in man that offers an increase of 20 percent in life span. We will know whether it works only when all the subjects have died; but judging by the tests we now have, we should not be far off in our predictions. The agents involved will be simple and cheap — dietary tricks or maintenance chemicals, not transplants, intensive-care units nor tailor-made serums that would be available only to the wealthy and to VIPs.

Direct application of the results will be possible world wide, at about the same rate as, and probably more cheaply than, antibiotics since 1940. All countries will elect to use them, or at least will be unable — as with the pill in Catholic Italy — to prevent their use. How widely people choose to use them will depend, no doubt, on what sorts of agents are available. If longevity requires tiresome and lifelong diet restriction, the model of cigarettes and high-cholesterol foods suggests that most of the Western public doesn't value longevity highly enough to make itself uncomfortable. All that will happen in this case is that application will be delayed until we find a painless method of getting around our self-indulgence.

Who will benefit can be seen only by trial. At the moment, the odds seem fair that a man or a woman of 50 today can expect some benefit, provided we waste no time; while a man or a woman of 20 certainly can look forward to extra years of vigor. Bearing in mind the rate of growth in biology and the intensification of the research effort that would surely follow the first and minimal human demonstration, one bonus could lead to others. We are now contemplating a 20 percent gain — 15 extra years before aging sets in. It could be more or less. Probably, we're wise to set our sights low. The point is that in the long run, it's the first step that counts. That step could be five percent, but it could as well be ten percent, and there is nothing but the analogy from mice to help us guess.

Will people want to live longer? Obviously, when it seems really possible, they will. At the moment, they are coy about saying so, partly for fear it may not happen and partly because they think of longer life as it is now — meaning longer infirmity. Ask a 40-year-old if he would like to stay as he is for another 15 years and the answer will be different.

This 20 percent prediction is based on research by those in the field. It jibes fairly will, however, with studies by the RAND Corporation and the drug firm of Smith Kline and French, scientific predictions of the future, based on a series of questions answered by numerous scientists and experts in other fields. RAND put the middle date for "significant extension" of human life at 2023, Smith Kline at 1993 — though this does not allow for the treated subjects to age and be counted. From these studies, the 10 to 20 percent increase should not be far behind, for example, the chemical or immunologic control of cancer.

If this, rather than immortalism or hopeful predictions of 200-to-300-year live spans, is a realistic model, it still leaves us with some thinking to do. For a start, our society is geared to a 70-year life span as our houses are to people between five and six feet tall. A life span with an upward limit around 70 to 80 has been the one certain factor on which insurance, promotion prospects, pensions and politics have been based. A 20 percent gain could be absorbed — but the first artificial breakthrough will knock the floor at one blow from under all these calculations and from under all past actuarial experience, because there is no knowing, for planning purposes, where it will stop. To some of the questions this will provoke from citizens who find science worrisome, if not dangerous, we can only reply with more questions.

Population is already one of our leading panics, and a justifiable one. Longer life, if it comes as one increment only, will mean greater numbers. This will be adjusted by time, but only if it's a once-and-for-all bonus, and then the bulge will fall when population problems are beginning to hit hard. On the other hand, the gain will be wholly in the productive and (unless we stick rigidly to already obsolete retirement practices) nondependent years. This, in fact, could be a gain. Today our preproductive dependency lasts about 20 years and our post-productive about 10, leaving a working life of only 40 years. In 1990, the number of Americans over 65 will be over 27,000,000 compared with about 20,000,000 now. More years of vigor will mean that many of these can still be "young." More years will also mean more sex, but not necessarily more children. At the moment, sexual activity declines with age, not for physiological reasons but through the cultural fiction that it ought to do so and because older people tend to play the age roles convention assigns. Longer life would give us the option, perhaps, of effectively living two different, consecutive lives — as we are starting to do today, but more effectively. Longer youth and adulthood would even out the discrepancy in the opportunity to do this that now exists between men and women, who are harder hit in taking up that option than are males. Women, it has been quipped, have a menopause, but men have no womenopause. Two separate lives, one fertile, the other companionate? It seems possible. Against the demographic objectors, it can be said that the population explosion will destroy us in any event, unless it is controlled, and abstaining from the application of gerontology will not prevent this. Like air pollution and the arms race, it must be dealt with now as a condition of survival.

Sheer turnover of human beings is another anxiety point. People are by nature rigid: The science and politics of today are already dictated by what their exponents learned 40 years ago, in a society that's changing so fast that the young are practically out of sight. Can we afford a 20 percent increase in life span, if that means a 40 percent increase in the tenure of professors, Senators and company presidents? Nobody knows. What is clear is that even a slight breach in the primeval human certainty that we will die between the ages of 70 and 90 will produce vast changes in our self-estimate. Show once that aging can be pushed back and, like the generation that has lived with the pill, we shall never be able to go back to the old attitudes. Admit that aging and death are not only intolerable but postponable and nothing, including our life style and our willingness to update ourselves, can ever be the same. In fact, if the rigidity attributed to the elderly is due to aging at the biological level, it will probably be postponed along with wrinkles and cancer. If it's a social convention, it will have to be unlearned. Since it needs unlearning urgently today, we hardly stand to lose.

I am as worried as anyone about the idiotic misuse of technology. But the potential misuse of aging research doesn't keep me awake at night. If it did, I wouldn't devote my time to it. Partial control of human aging is something that's going to happen. Unless we are slothful or overcome by disaster, it's probably going to happen within our own lifetime, and some of us will be the beneficiaries. Morally, it should be beneficial. Every gain in our ability to stave off death increases our respect for life — our own and others'.

This will not be luxury medicine; it will almost certainly not be abusable by restriction to wealthy, prominent or powerful people. In fact, rate-control concepts in public health will supersede, more economically, a great deal of the luxury medicine that, by its diminishing returns in quality of life, now raises embarrassing priority issues.

The only big questions are how soon it will happen, how large the gain will be and whether it will catch us unprepared to iron out preventable personal and economic side effects. So far, I have seen only one pension policy that writes in a waiver in the event of a science-based change in the normal life span: The insurance companies should be worrying about that, not about the litigatory possibilities of shenanigans based on cryogenic suspension through deep-freezing annuitants. The thing that really matters is that all of us should know what's going on and how it may shortly affect us. If we're willing to back the workers in the field with public awareness — and with money — we can hope to roll back our own old age, as well as our children's. The next five years will settle whether or not we do.

B. PSYCHOLOGICAL ASPECTS

In the first reading in this section, John Barry reviews age-related changes in behavior. While psychological changes associated with age are rooted in the physiology, such changes are affected by social factors, by what has been learned, and by a variety of other non-physiological influences. Sensory changes, changes in psychomotor behavior, and intellectual and cognitive changes are briefly discussed. He describes how these changes in psychological behavior result in changes in some of the more complex responses and reactions to life situations which are presented later in the book. The selection, then, provides a brief review of age-related changes in psychological behavior.

In the next reading Paul Baltes and Warner Schaie describe in some detail changes in intellectual behavior with age. Early research comparing different groups at different ages had led many to believe that all intellectual functions declined gradually but inevitably as people grew older. However, as a result of more sophisticated ways of studying these issues, scientists now believe that for large numbers of people many intellectual functions do *not* decline until immediately prior to death. There is even evidence that in some individuals selected intellectual abilities improve throughout the life span. This view of the intellectual functioning of older people is certainly more encouraging for the continued independent living of the older person than were earlier beliefs.

People respond to and are affected by the messages they receive from others about themselves. Consequently, when any group is devalued by almost *everyone* they meet, this effects that group's perception of themselves. Research on this by Boaz Kahana is briefly summarized to show how negatively the elderly are perceived by the young and the old alike. The almost universally negative attitudes in society toward the aged cannot help but contribute to a devaluation by the aged of themselves.

The last two readings in this section are on personality and aging. Robert Havighurst reviews research which produced a major controversial theory of aging, viz., the disengagement theory. In his first paper, Havighurst presents two contrasting theories of successful aging, the activity theory and the disengagement theory. He then discusses findings from several research programs and arrives at patterns of personality characteristics and lifestyles which describe significant numbers of older people.

In the second Havighurst paper, the process of adaptation and the life history of a person are related to the personality patterns described in the immediately preceding paper. After discussing adaptation throughout life in some detail, he describes adaptation patterns for people in different age groups. Adaptation to the problems of aging is not only necessary but a healthy thing. Here Havighurst describes hallmarks of healthy adaptation as they relate to the life history of the aged person. Havighurst emphasizes that the actual forms of adaptation can be called patterns of aging. There seem to be a finite number of these patterns which can be agreed upon by observers of the aging process. By examining closely and in detail the personality adjustment of people as they grow older, we can better understand these processes, and, thus, better serve the needs of the aged.

9. The Psychology of Aging*

JOHN R. BARRY**

How do older people behave? What are they like? How do they differ from other people? How do they differ from each other?

As interest in the growing numbers of elderly people has increased in recent years, studies of the behavior of these people have also increased. Most of the early behavioral studies of the aged were based on samples of elderly people who were institutionalized or available for study for other peculiar reasons. Thus, the picture emerging from these early studies of age-related behavior change tended to exaggerate pathology.

More recently *non*-institutionalized samples of elderly people have been studied and a much happier picture has emerged. As has been found in other areas of psychological study, there seems to be an interaction between institutionalization and decline in behavioral functioning. Very often people are institutionalized because they develop certain deficits which interfere with their taking care of themselves. Among the elderly, institutionalization may not be for the purpose of rehabilitation, but for warehousing and terminal care. Institutionalization almost always fosters dependency. Dependencies may develop which are never overcome and, thus, further behavioral deficits appear. Studies of the non-institutionalized aged now enable us to point to strengths as well as deficits among the aged.

Another methodological advance in recent years was our willingness to invest the large amount of effort necessary to study the aged longitudinally. That is, the life cycles of groups of people were studied from their early years on through their later years. This repeated and continual observation of people over time has yielded a far different picture of aging from that obtained in the earlier studies. We now find that most elderly people maintain many of their behavioral capacities through their later years and up until their death. Any decline tends to be more rapid and occurs more immediately prior to death, than we had earlier thought. Whereas the earlier picture had been one of an inevitable and gradual decline in all functioning starting around 55 or 60, it now appears that this decline is far less pervasive and may start much later than we had originally thought (Botwinick, 1973).

*Original paper written for this book.
**Dr. Barry is a Professor of Psychology at The University of Georgia and is one of the editors of this book.

113

Variability among people, that is differences among them when any specific psychological function such as memory is measured, increases with age. Also variability in the efficiency of different behavioral functions in any one person increases with age. Thus, the efficiency of different kinds of memory become more diverse and harder to predict from a knowledge of age alone as a person grows older. A young person's memory for recent events and his memory for events long past are likely to be equally good. However, as he grows older, his memory for past events may remain relatively unchanged while his memory for recent events may become far less efficient. Because variablility increases with age, the older a person becomes, the less likely are we to be able to predict his effective functioning solely by knowing his chronological age.

The rest of this chapter will deal with age-related changes in specific psychological behavior and functions. An understanding of such changes should enable us to see the kinds of problems faced by the aged and suggest possible solutions to these problems.

SENSORY BEHAVIOR

Psychologists and physiologists have long studied the responses of the sense organs to a variety of stimuli. Underlying and limiting such sensory responses is the physiological functioning of a person. If this is poor, the sensory response to stimuli will be impaired. On the other hand, if the physiology or bodily health can be maintained, there is less likelihood that sensory deficits will appear. Earlier papers in this book describe age-related changes in physiological functioning.

Vision

We come to know our world by seeing. The eye is one of our most important sense organs. With age the eye muscles tend to become less flexible, and various parts of the eye function less effectively. In general, vision, like the other senses, becomes less sharp with age. Discrimination between similar stimuli becomes more difficult. In particular, dark and light adaptation (the amount of time it takes to recover from sudden changes in the light stimulus) takes much longer even among middle aged persons. This is especially noticeable when driving a car at night into the headlights of another car. The slow response to sudden changes in the intensity of light results in temporary blindness.

Color vision becomes less good as one grows older. The lens of the eye gradually yellows with age. This filters out the blue, green, and violet colors toward the dark end of the color spectrum. Since thresholds for these colors increase with age, it is easier for older people to see yellow, red, and orange than the darker colors. As with all such phenomena, there are major individual differences.

Hearing

Hearing acuity also declines with age. Fine discriminations between similar sounds, pitches, and frequencies, become harder to make. Thresholds increase with age. That is, the absolute amount of a sound which is needed for it to be perceived increases with age. We are talking here about different kinds and degrees of deafness. Among the aged, high frequencies become more difficult to perceive with increasing age. This is especially true for men.

As people grow older, it becomes harder for them to hear high-pitched sounds and those at low intensity. After the age of 55, men experience greater hearing problems than women. It should be noted that a person can often compensate for sensory losses. If his vision holds up, he may learn to read lips. He may use a hearing aid or glasses to help him see. However, if both hearing and seeing are impaired by age, the older person's adjustment becomes increasingly difficult.

Other Senses

The senses of smell, taste, touch, balance, and the perception of pain respond in a very similar way to the senses described above. As a person grows older, acuity becomes more dull, thresholds rise, and discrimination becomes more difficult. For example, salt sensitivity decreases with age and the older person may ask for more salt and other seasoning on his food.

Another sense, kinethesis or balance, enables us to perceive changes in body position and orientation in space. This perception tends to become less accurate with age and may contribute to the increased likelihood of an older person falling. This is especially true when several of the senses become less efficient.

At least a part of these changes can be explained physiologically. As the sense organs age, they appear to become less sensitive to small differences in the stimuli presented to them. Also the sense organs follow a pattern similar to that of the rest of the body. One theory is that the body parts wear out with age from over-use. A second theory relates to disuse and exercise. As the sensory apparatus is used less or is exposed to a smaller variety of stimuli, it appears to become less flexible and sensitive. It follows from this then, that exercise may restore and maintain sensory functioning when it has not been completely lost, and if it is not diseased. It is less clear whether functions which have been completely lost through inactivity can be renewed or revived by exercise. This seems to depend upon the overall health and well being of the aged person, and on the degree to which the functioning was actually lost.

PSYCHOMOTOR BEHAVIOR

Generally, a person loses strength and agility as he grows older. Pressure for speed may make an older person anxious and tends to increase his inefficiency. Locomotion, getting around in the world, may become more difficult with age. Falling may become more frequent and accident rates increase among the very old (Carp, 1973).

Speed of Reaction Time

One of the most noticeable age related changes in behavior is in the speed at which a response is made by the older person. As early as 45 for some people, the ability to quickly respond to any stimulus begins to decline. This slowing in the speed of response appears to occur in both complex and simple responses. The slowing happens both to conditioned or learned responses and to intentional or planned responses.

An example of this slowing can be noticed among drivers of autos. The middle aged and elderly persons will anticipate and begin to respond to changing traffic conditions much earlier than the younger person. Both will make the response, but the older person knows that he will respond more slowly and so he compensates by beginning his response earlier (for example, stopping at a stop light).

Gross and Fine Motor Movement

Other psychomotor activities include various fine finger manipulations (e.g., setting a watch) as well as large body movements (e.g., throwing a ball). All of the psychomotor responses have a physiological base, the muscles and neurones. Body movement is limited by the physiology of the body and the changes in that physiology with age. These changes have been discussed in some detail in earlier chapters. Exercise will maintain such psychomotor functioning, and among the middle aged will help to renew functioning which may appear to have been lost. It is less clear whether exercise can bring back functions which appear to have atrophied through disuse over a long period of time. Since it is difficult to determine how long a function has been dormant, the elderly person should be encouraged to try to exercise, even though in some instances hope for recovery of initial mobility is not great.

Intelligence

Intellectual functions are among the most frequently measured behaviors. A wide variety of types and kinds of intellectual functions can be measured. Some of these measures may be grouped together to yield an indication of overall intellectual functioning, commonly called the IQ.

Most intellectual functions develop relatively rapidly through adolescence and into the twenties, after which they seem to level out or hit a plateau. In the later years certain functions appear to become less efficient, sometimes through a lack of use and sometimes due to physiological factors. A few weeks prior to death intellectual functioning seems to begin to show marked decreases (Kleemeier, 1962; Riegel, 1971).

In general those intellectual functions which are most often used tend to be maintained and sometimes even improve slightly throughout the life span (for example, word knowledge). In general, variability in intellectual functioning increases with age. This is true when the intellectual functioning of a number of people are compared or when the many intellectual functions of a single person are compared with each other.

More specifically, verbal skills, word fluency, understanding, and memory for events long past tend to be maintained throughout the life span. Problem solving, memory for recent events, abstract reasoning, and any kind of work with unfamiliar symbol systems tend to become less efficient as people grow older. It cannot be emphasized enough that there are great individual differences among all of these behaviors, and that the differences are likely to increase with age, especially after age sixty.

Learning

Learning occurs throughout the life span of the individual. Our culture is geared to learning first from one's parents and then from the parental surrogates in schools and other social institutions. When one goes to work, he again learns what to do and how to do it. Learning is not something that occurs in school alone. Rather, we learn continually throughout our lives.

A particular kind of learning is called conditioning. Here a specific stimulus becomes the signal for a specific response. Repetition and reinforcement of this stimulus-response pattern helps it to become automatic. For example, we become conditioned to make certain responses when we are driving an automobile. We do not stop to think about them, but rather the stimulus becomes a signal to respond immediately. Thus, with practice, we learn to stop at red lights and stop signs, almost without thinking about it.

The older person learns most readily when allowed to proceed at his own rate. Working under pressure, as contrasted to self-pacing, increases the difficulty of any task, including learning, especially for the aged. Learning performance may be improved among the elderly by allowing them to proceed at their own speed and when they feel ready.

All learning, including conditioning, appears to occur more slowly after the middle years. Such a generalization must be made with some caution. The motivation or purpose of a person is very difficult to measure and certainly affects his behavior (e.g., his speed of learning) very directly. Children are oriented in schools towards learning and may not be concerned with *why* they are learning. As people grow older and leave school, they may fall out of the habit of learning something because it is there. While incidental learning continues throughout life, the importance of interest and motivation to the learner increases with age. Older people, having been exposed to more and more, become somewhat more selective in their interests and, thus, in their willingness to learn. It is often difficult for an observer to distinguish between the inability of an older person to do something and his disinterest or lack of motivation.

PERSONALITY

A great many personality characteristics, attitudes, and psychosocial behaviors have been studied among the aged. Many of these studies are referred to in other parts of this book and hence will not be dealt with here. Theories or notions about the personality functioning of the aged include disengagement, activity, and utility theories. The first two are discussed by Youmans, Havighurst and others in subsequent papers in this book. Utility theory emphasizes the need of all people, including the aged, to feel that there is some reason, some purpose, or some use for what they do. If people can define goals or purposes and move toward these goals, they will be happier, healthier, and more effective (Hamlin, 1967).

SUMMARY

This brief description of psychological changes with age has emphasized the increasing variability in most functions as people grow older. Since this variablility is so pervasive and extensive among the aged, it is especially important when dealing with this group to take the time to know each person. While we always should attend to the individuality and uniqueness of a person, this is even more necessary when working with the elderly because of the variability in their behavior mentioned throughout this paper.

A second major emphasis in this paper concerns our new knowledge about the rate and generality of the decline of psychological functioning with age. As our methods of study have improved and as new knowledge has accumulated, it is increasingly apparent that in many aged, many of the psychological functions do not begin their decline at fifty-five or sixty but rather persist throughout the life span. Older people do not necessarily become markedly impaired in all spheres beginning at age sixty. The picture now emerging from most research is far more positive.

For a more extensive discussion of any of the matters in this chapter, see Birren (1964) or Botwinick (1973).

REFERENCES

Birren, J. E. *The psychology of aging.* Englewood Cliffs, N.J.: Prentice-Hall, 1964.

Botwinick, J. *Aging and behavior.* New York: Springer 1973.

Carp, F. M. The psychology of aging. Chapter 8 in R. R. Boyd and C. G. Oakes (Eds.), *Foundations of practical gerontology,* 2nd edition, Columbia, S.C.: University of South Carolina Press, 1973, 106-122.

Hamlin, R. M. A utility theory of old age. *The Gerontologist,* 1967, 7, 37-45 (Part II).

Kleemeier, R. W. Intellectual changes in the senium. *Proceedings of the social statistics section of the American Statistical Association,* 1962, 290-295.

Riegel, K. F. The prediction of death and longevity in longitudinal research. In E. Palmore and F. C. Jeffers (Eds.),*Prediction of life span.* Lexington, Mass: D. C. Heath, 1971, 139-152.

10. Aging and IQ: The Myth of the Twilight Years*

Paul B. Baltes and Warner Schaie**

Intelligence does not slide downhill from adulthood through old age. By many measures, it increases as time goes by.

In our opinion, general intellectual decline in old age is largely a myth. During the last 10 years, we and our colleagues, (particularly G.V. Labouvie and J.R. Nesselroade) have worked to gain a better understanding of intelligence in the aged. Our findings challenge the stereotyped view, and promote a more optimistic one. We have discovered that the old man's boast, "I'm just as good as I ever was," may be true, after all.

The Data on Decline. For a long time, the textbook view coincided with the everyday notion that as far as intelligence is concerned, what goes up must come down. The research that supported this view was cross-sectional in nature. The investigator administered intelligence tests to people of various ages at a given point in time, and compared the performance levels of the different age groups. Numerous studies of this type conducted during the '30s, '40s and '50s led researchers to believe that intelligence increases up to early adulthood, reaches a plateau that lasts for about 10 years, and begins to decline in a regular fashion around the fourth decade of life.

The first doubts arose when the results of longitudinal studies began to be available. In this type of study, the researcher observes a single group of subjects for a period of time, often extending over many years, and examines their peformance at different ages. Early lon-

*Reprinted from *Psychology Today Magazine*, Vol. 8, March 1974, pages 35-40, with permission of the authors and *Psychology Today*. Copyright © 1974 Ziff-Davis Publishing Co.
**Dr. Baltes is Professor of Psychology and Director of the Division of Individual and Family Studies in the College of Human Development at Pennsylvania State University. Dr. Schaie is Associate Director for Research and Professor of Psychology at the University of Southern California Gerontology Center.

gitudinal studies suggested that intelligence during maturity and old age did not decline as soon as people had originally assumed.

As better intelligence tests became available, researchers began to realize that different intellectual measures might show different rates of decline. On measures of vocabulary and other skills reflecting educational experience, individuals seemed to maintain their adult level of functioning into the sixth, and even the seventh decade.

Resolving the Discrepancy. In 1956, one of us (Schaie) launched a major project aimed at resolving this disturbing discrepancy between the two kinds of study. Five hundred subjects, ranging in age from 21 to 70, received two intelligence tests, Thurstone and Thurstone's Primary Mental Abilities, and Schaie's Test of Behavioral Rigidity. Seven years later, we retested 301 of the subjects with the same tests.

The tests we used yielded 13 separate measures of cognitive functioning. Using factor-analysis methods, we found that the scores reflected four general, fairly independent dimensions of intelligence: 1) *Crystallized intelligence* encompasses the sorts of skills one acquires through education and acculturation, such as verbal comprehension, numerical skills, and inductive reasoning. To a large degree, it reflects the extent to which one has accumulated the collective intelligence of one's own culture. It is the dimension tapped by most traditional IQ tests [see "Are I.Q. Tests Intelligent? by Raymond Cattell, PT, March 1968]. 2) *Cognitive flexibility* measures the ability to shift from one way of thinking to another, within the context of familiar intellectual operations, as when one must provide either an antonym or synonym to a word, depending on whether the word appears in capital or lower-cases letters. 3) *Visuo-motor flexibility* measures a similar, but independent skill, the one involved in shifting from familiar to unfamiliar patterns in tasks requiring coordination between visual and motor abilities, e.g., when one must copy words but interchange capitals with lower-case letters. 4) Finally, *visualization* measures the ability to organize and process visual materials, and involves tasks such as finding a simple figure contained in a complex one or identifying a picture that is incomplete. The Schaie study did not contain sufficient measures of fluid intelligence, which encompasses abilities thought to be relatively culture free. Other researchers, e.g., Cattell and Horn, have reported a dramatic decline with age on fluid intelligence, though on the basis of cross-sectional data only.

If we analyze the data cross-sectionally (comparing the different age groups at a given point in time), we see the conventional pattern of early, systematic decline. But when we look at the results longitudinally (comparing a given age group's performance in 1956 with its performance in 1963), we find a definite decline on only one of the four measures, visuo-motor flexibility.

There is no strong age-related change in cognitive flexibility. For the most important dimension, crystallized intelligence, and for visualization as well, we see a systematic *increase* in scores for the various age groups, right into old age. Even people over 70 improved from the first testing to the second.

Intellectual Generation Gap. In cross-sectional studies, people who differ in age also differ in generation, since they were born in different years. This means that any measured differences in intelligence could reflect either age or generation differences, or both. Our study, however, allowed us to compare people from different generations at the same ages, because we tested people at two different points in time. For instance, we could compare subjects who were 50 in 1956 with subjects who were 50 in 1963. Our statistical analysis revealed that the differences between scores were due mainly to generational differences, not to chronological age. In other words, the important factor was the year a subject was born, rather than his age at the time of testing. Apparently, the measured intelligence of the population is increasing. The earlier findings of general intellectual decline over the individual life span were largely an artifact of methodology. On at least some dimensions of intelligence, particularly the crystallized type, people of average health can expect to maintain or even increase their level of performance into old age.

At present we can only speculate about the reasons for generational differences in intelligence. We believe the answer lies in the substance, method and length of education received by different generations. When we consider the history of our educational institutions, and census data on the educational levels attained by members of specific generations, it seems fair to assume that the older people in our study were exposed to shorter periods of formal education. Furthermore, their education probably relied more heavily on principles of memorization, and less heavily on those of problem-solving.

However, there are other possibilities that must be reckoned with before we can offer a more definite interpretation. Members of different generations may differ in their sophistication in test-taking or their willingness to volunteer responses. They may differ in the extent to which they have been encouraged to achieve intellectually. And tests developed to measure the abilities of one generation may be invalid for another. In any case, the existence of differences between generations makes the search for "normal" aging phenomena a Sisyphean task.

Drop Before Death. Klaus and Ruth Riegel, psychologists at the University of Michigan, have recently suggested that when intellectual decline does occur, it comes shortly before death [see "Life, or Death and IQ," News Line, May 1973]. In 1956, the Riegels gave intelligence tests to 380 German men and women between the ages of 55 and 75. Five years later they retested 202 of them. Some of the remainder had died, and others refused to be retested. When the Riegels looked back at the 1956 test scores of the subjects who had died, they discovered that on the average, the deceased subjects had scored lower than those who survived. Put another way, the low scores in 1956 predicted impending death.

The Riegels followed up their study in 1966 by inquiring into the fate of the people retested in 1961. Again, some people had died in the interim, and those who had died had lower scores than those who lived. Furthermore, people who had died since 1961 had declined in score from the first test session in 1956 to the second in 1961. These results pointed to a sudden deterioration during the five or fewer years immediately prior to natural death, or what the Riegels called a "terminal drop." Interestingly, the people who had refused to be retested in 1961 were more likely than the others to die before 1966. Perhaps their refusal reflected some kind of awareness of their own decline.

The Riegels' results may offer an alternative explanation for the general decline found by cross-sectional studies: the older groups may contain a higher percentage of people in the terminal drop stage, and their lower scores would not be typical of other people. If the researcher could foresee the future and remove from his study those subjects nearing death, he might observe little or no change in the intelligence of the remaining group. In fact, the Riegels found that elderly subjects still alive in 1966 did as well, on the average, as persons at the presumed period of peak performance, 30 to 34 years, which of course, is consistent with our own data.

While it is tempting to speculate on the reasons for terminal drop, we feel that the present state of the art is such that interpretation must be tentative at best. Most researchers would probably tend to relate the drop in intellectual functioning to neurophysiological deterioration. However, this position overlooks the possibility that psychological variables contribute both to the drop and the biological death.

Aged-Biased IQ Tests. The nature of the tests used to assess intelligence may also contribute to the apparent decline that is sometimes observed. Sidney L. Pressey (who now lives as an octogenarian in a home for the elderly and continues to make occasional but insightful contributions to psychology) first pointed out that the concept of intelligence, as well as the instruments to measure it, are defined in terms of abilities most important during youth and early adulthood. This is not really surprising, since IQ tests came into existence for the purpose of predicting school performance. The format and content of these tests may simply be inappropriate for tapping the potential wisdom of the aged. For example, older people tend to do relatively poorly on tests employing technical language such as the terminology of physics or computer programming. Their performance is better if items are worded in terms of everyday experiences.

Another problem is the distinction between a person's competence and his actual performance. Handicaps that have nothing to do with intrinsic ability may affect the way a person does on a test. For instance, Baltes and Carol A. Furry recently demonstrated that the aged are especially susceptible to the effects of fatigue; pretest fatigue considerably lowered the scores of older subjects, but did not affect the performance of younger ones.

Dwindling reinforcements may also affect the performance of the aged. Elderly individuals, because of their uncertain and shortened life expectancy, may cease to be sensitive to the sorts of long-range rewards that seem to control intellectual behavior in young people (e.g., education, career goals, and development of a reputation). Ogden Lindsley has proposed that the aged may become more dependent on immediate and idiosyncratic rewards.

Even when rewards are potentially effective, they may be unavailable to old people. Most researchers agree that the environment of the elderly is intellectually and socially impoverished. Family settings and institutions for the aged fail to provide conditions conducive to intellectual growth. The educational system discourages participation by the elderly, focusing instead on the young.

Recent work on age stereotypes indicates that some young people hold a negative view of old age. These views may influence them to withdraw reinforcements for competence in the elderly, or even to punish such competence. Aging persons may in time come to accept the stereotypes, view themselves as deficient, and put aside intellectual performance as a personal goal. In the process, the intellectual deficit becomes a self-fulfilling prophecy.

Compensatory Education for the Aged   Although educators have made massive attempts to overcome discrimination in early childhood, working through Government-funded compensatory programs, analogous efforts for the aged have barely begun. But, increasing numbers of gerontologists have felt encouraged by the reanalysis of intellectual decline to examine, probably for the first time in any vigorous manner, the degree to which intellectual performance can be bolstered. The results are still very sketchy, but they are promising.

Some researchers, working from a bio-behavioral perspective, have looked at the effects of physical treatments. For instance, hyperbaric oxygen treatment — the breathing of concentrated oxygen for extended periods to increase oxygen supply to the brain — seems to improve memory for recent events, although the outcome of such research is not at all free of controversy. Treatment of hypertension and conditioning of alpha waves also seem to be promising and deserve careful study. Other researchers concentrate on studying the psychological aspects of the learning process; they experiment with the pacing of items, the mode of presentation (for instance, auditory versus visual), the amount of practice, the delivery of rewards, training in mnemonics, and so on.

The speed with which a person responds, which is important on many intellectual tests, is usually assumed to be a function of biological well-being. But in a series of pilot studies, Baltes, William Hoyer and Gisela V. Labouvie were able to improve the response speed of elderly subjects rather dramatically, using Green Stamps as a reward for faster performance in canceling letters, marking answer sheets and copying words. After as little as two hours of training, women 65 to 80 years of age increased their speed as much as 20 to 35 percent. The researchers compared the performance of these "trained" subjects with that of untrained controls on 11 different intelligence tests. Although the transfer of the speed training to test performance was not earthshaking, the overall pattern was encouraging.

In the interest of rectifying some of the social injustices that have resulted from the branding of the aged as deficient, social scientists must continue to explore, with vigor and optimism, the research avenues opened during the past few years. This research should be guided by a belief in the potential of gerontological intelligence, and a rejection of the rigid, biological view that assumes an inevitable decline. We should not be surprised to find that the socialization goals and mechanisms of a society are the most powerful influence on what happens to people, not only during childhood and adolescence but also during adulthood and old age.

Social roles and resources can be assigned without regard to age only when the deleterious aspects of aging are eliminated. Toward this end, in 1971, an American Psychological Association task force on aging made some specific recommendations for eliminating the unnecessary causes of declining intellectual functioning. They included more forceful implementation of adult education programs; funding of research and innovative programs in voluntary (rather than mandatory) retirement, second-career training, and leisure-time activity, and better utilization of skills that are unaffected by age.

When we consider the vast spectrum of negative conditions, attributes and expectations that most Western societies impose on older people, we must acclaim the impressive robustness of our older population in the face of adversity. At the same time, we hope that society, aided by geropsychology, soon finds ways to make life for the elderly more enjoyable and effective. Acknowledging that intellectual decline is largely a myth is, we hope, a step in the right direction.

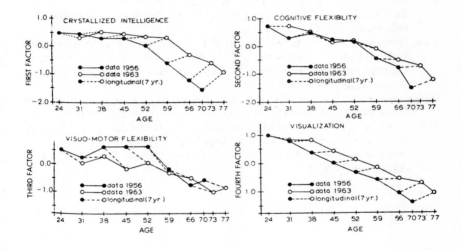

AGE & DIMENSIONS OF INTELLIGENCE. The solid lines slope downward, indicating that in both 1956 and 1963, older people scored lower than younger ones on various dimensions of intelligence. However, the dotted lines, which show how a given age group's performance changed from the first test occasion to the second, reveal that in the older groups crystallized intelligence and visualization go up and down.

128   *Basic Processes of Aging*

REFERENCES

Baltes, P. B. and G. V. Labouvie, "Adult Development of intellectual Performance: Description, Explanation and Modification" in *The Psychology of Adult Development and Aging,* Carl Eisdorfer and M. P. Lawton, eds. American Psychological Association, 1973.

Baltes, P. B. and K. W. Schaie, eds. *Life-Span Developmental Psychology: Personality and Socialization,* Academic, in press.

Horn, John L. "Organization of Data on Life-Span Development of Human Abilities" in *Life-Span Developmental Psychology: Research and Theory,* L. R. Goulet and P. B. Baltes, eds. Academic, 1970.

Jarvik, L. F. and D. Cohen, "A Biobehavioral Approach to Intellectual Changes With Aging" in *The Psychology of Adult Development and Aging,* Carl Eisdorfer and M. P. Lawton, eds. American Psychological Association, 1973.

Labouvie-Vief, G., W. J. Hoyer, P. B. Baltes and M. M. Baltes, "Operant Analysis of Intellectual Behavior in Old Age" in *Human Development,* 1974, in press.

Nesselroade, J. R., K. W. Schaie, and P. B. Baltes, "Ontogenetic and Generational Components of Structural and Quantitative Change in Adult Behavior" in *Journal of Gerontology,* Vol. 27, No. 2, pp. 222-228, April 1972.

Riegel, K. F. and R. M. Riegel, "Development, Drop and Death" in *Developmental Psychology,* Vol. 6, No. 2, pp. 306-319, March 1972.

Schaie, K. W., "A Reinterpretation of Age-Related Changes in Cognitive Structure and Functioning" in *Life-Span Developmental Psychology: Research and Theory,* L. R. Goulet and P. B. Baltes, eds. Academic, 1970.

11. Old Age Seen Negatively By Old as well as Young*

Old age is viewed negatively by old people, as well as by other members of society, Dr. Kahana reported.

The 124 subjects in his study included 33 children (ages 9-11), 17 adolescents (ages 15-17), 29 young adults (ages 20-25), 14 "establishment generation" adults (ages 30-40), and 31 elderly persons (ages 60-85). All were lower to upper middle-class in socioeconomic status.

One measure of the differences in perception of these subjects was a questionnaire in which they were asked to rate both sexes of the various age groups along the dimensions of Hopefulness, Activity, Independence, Involvement, Hardiness, Stability, and Wisdom.

The combined ratings of all age groups reveal a pattern that sets the tone for an understanding of intergenerational attitudes, Dr. Kahana said. Young adulthood is almost unanimously regarded as the most desirable age, followed by middle-age and adolescence in close succession. Old age is seen as the most undesirable.

"It is clear that the elderly share society's worship of youth," the speaker said. Young people are viewed as hardy, active, independent, and involved. The one unfavorable attribute applied to teenagers was lack of stability. The elderly, not surprisingly, are valued the least. They are seen as relatively hopeless, passive, uninvolved, and fragile. On the other hand, they are also depicted as wise and stable, though less so than middle-aged adults. Young people make little distinction between old men and old women in these evaluations, and young adults tend to have more negative view of the aged than adolescents do.

Some exceptions to the above generalities were noted:

• *Hopefulness.* The 25-year-old male is considered the most hopeful, but some votes were cast for the adolescent female by young men and middle-aged women. The elderly are considered most hopeless by all subjects except the adolescent males, who reserve that rating for adolescent females. And elderly subjects dissented from the others by rating the 40s as the most hopeful age group.

• *Independence.* Young women and middle-aged men were rated most independent, elderly females most dependent.

*Reprinted from *Geriatric Focus,* Vol. 9, No. 10, 1970, pages 1, 11-13 with permission of *Geriatric Focus.* This selection was abstracted by *Geriatric Focus* from a report by Dr. Kahana at the 1970 American Psychological Association meeting. Dr. Kahana is Associate Professor of Psychology at Oakland University in Michigan. At the time the paper was presented Dr. Kahana was at Washington University in St. Louis.

● *Involvement.* Subjects of various ages tend to rate themselves as most involved, old women as least involved. However, the elderly themselves regard older men as least involved.

● *Hardiness.* While adolescent males were generally rated as most hardy, they themselves designated young women as the hardiest. And middle-aged women cast their vote for middle-aged men.

● *Stability.* Middle-aged men and women were seen by all as the most stable, adolescent boys and girls the least steady. While the aged were generally depicted as quite stable, older males rated their age group as the least firmly rooted. "This finding has important implications," said Dr. Kahana. "It shows that poor self-evaluations may be independent of societal stereotypes."

● *Wisdom.* Adolescents were rated most foolish, and the middle-aged most wise. Young and middle-aged females, however, tend to regard old people as the wisest age group.

Significant data on self-perception, perception of one's age group, and perception of the opposite sex were also obtained. A number of fairly consistent trends were observed:

1. Subjects of both sexes and all ages tend to rank themselves above their age group in most of the dimensions studied.

2. Men of all ages regard themselves (and males in general) more favorably than they regard females. The sole exception is the old-age group, where males rated elderly women as generally more active, involved, hardy, and stable than elderly men. Even in this group, however, the men rated themselves higher than their age peers, female as well as male.

3. Women generally share this cultural stereotype, consistently rating themselves lower than men. (Except for females in their 30s, who tend to rate themselves superior to men.) "The picture is one of women of all ages saying: 'Men are equal to or better than women, although I think I am an exception among generally inferior womankind!' "

The data on devaluation of women is so pervasive that it might serve to document a diatribe for the women's lib movement, Dr. Kahana observed.

In contrast to other findings, he said, it is interesting to note that older adults — particularly older women — view themselves in rather favorable terms. People tend to report a more positive self-image with age, according to one observer. However, denial of faults also increases with age, suggesting that the reported improvement in image "may be a function of denial, rather than an actual increase in self-esteem."

Another measure of intergenerational perceptions employed by Dr. Kahana was an open-ended characterization of various age-sex groups. Subjects were asked to spontaneously think up three adjectives describing a "typical" 15-year-old, 24-year-old, etc. The aim was to elicit from these descriptions multidimensional definitions of youth and old age, as each respondent viewed it.

This was the picture of old age that emerged:

1. The 9-to 11-year-olds portray the aged as "scary," "mean," and "crabby." Together with age 1, old age was overwhelmingly regarded as the worst age to be. The reasons given were often phobic: for example, the infant can't move around much, the old person is close to death.

"These findings support hypotheses that negative views of the aged by children emerge initially as response to the fear of death associated with old age, rather than to the characteristics of the aged per se," Dr. Kahana observed.

2. The adolescents' stereotypes of old age are condescending and very negative. Significantly, they attribute a great deal of insecurity to all adults, and their hostility to the establishment is revealed in their overwhelmingly negative and even sarcastic descriptions of the 40-year-olds. "The only age group seen in positive, even utopian, terms is the young adult generation."

3. The elderly also view old age in negative terms, though less negatively than it is seen by younger groups. They regard it as a lonely time. Issues of engagement with the outside world continue to figure in some responses, while others reflect concern with quiet and relaxation.

"It is difficult to resist the temptation to see the different ages as grappling with various developmental tasks: the adolescent concerned with identity and self, the young adult engaged in society, and the aged concerned with maintaining a positive self-image in the face of a thankless and devalued position," Dr. Kahana said.

12. Personality and Patterns of Aging*

Robert J. Havighurst**

Happiness and satisfaction in the latter part of life are within reach of the great majority of people. The external conditions of life are better for people over 65 than they have been at any time in this century. Social Security benefits and company pensions are at record high levels. Medicare has underwritten much of the major medical expense. Almost no one is forced to work after the age of 65 if he prefers not to. Most of the states have programs, supported under the Older Americans Act, to improve the social adjustment of older people. In other words, society has done just about as much as anyone could ask it to do on behalf of older people. At least this is the conclusion one would draw from a superficial look at social statistics.

Yet we know that many people are unhappy and dissatisfied in their later years. Some of them suffer from poor health, but this is only a minority. The average person at age 65 will live 4 more years. According to research, the person who is in good health suffers very little impairment in his ability to learn, to initiate actions, to be effective in the ordinary relations of life until he is 85 years old or more.

Since a great many people after 65 have good enough health and enough income to support a life of happiness and satisfaction, we must turn to the psychologist to ask why some of these people are unhappy.

Theories of Successful Aging.—There are at present two contrasting theories of successful aging. Both are unsatisfactory because they obviously do not explain all the phenomena of successful aging. Yet both have some facts to support them. The first, one that might be called the *activity theory*, implies that, except for the inevitable changes in biology and in health, older people are the same as middle-aged with essentially the same psychological and social needs. In this view, the decreased social interaction that characterizes old age results from the withdrawal by society from the aging person; and the decrease in interaction proceeds against the desires of most aging men and

*Reprinted from *The Gerontologist,* Vol. 8, Part II, 1968, pages 20-23 with permission of the author and the Gerontological Society.
**Dr. Havighurst is Professor of Education and Human Development at the University of Chicago.

women. The older person who ages optimally is the person who stays active and who manages to resist the shrinkage of his social world. He maintains the activities of middle age as long as possible, and then finds substitutes for work when he is forced to retire and substitutes for friends and loved ones whom he loses by death.

In the *disengagement theory* (Cumming & Henry, 1961), on the other hand, the decreased social interaction is interpreted as a process characterized by mutuality; one in which both society and the aging person withdraw, with the aging individual acceptant, perhaps even desirous, of the decreased interaction. It is suggested that the individual's withdrawal has intrinsic or developmental qualities as well as responsive ones; that social withdrawal is accompanied by, or preceded by, increased preoccupation with the self and decreased emotional investment in persons and objects in the environment; and that, in this sense, disengagement is a natural rather than an imposed process. In this view, the older person who has a sense of psychological well-being will usually be the person who has reached a new equilibrium characterized by a greater psychological distance, altered types of relationships, and decreased social interaction with persons around him.

In order to test these two theories empirically, the data of the Kansas City Study of Adult Life were used, consisting of repeated interviews with 159 men and women aged 50-90, taken over the period from 1956 through 1962. The sample at the end of the study consisted of 55% of the people who were originally in the study. Of the attrition in the sample, 27% had been due to deaths; 12% to geographical moves; and the rest to refusals to be interviewed at some time during the series of interviews, usually because of reported poor health. There is evidence also that persons who were relatively socially isolated constituted a disproportionate number of the dropouts. The original sample excluded people living in institutions and those who were so ill that they could not be interviewed. The original sample also excluded people at the very bottom of the socioeconomic scale and a few people who would have been diagnosed as neurotic by a psychiatrist, as well as people who were chronically ill if the illness was one that confined a person to bed. Some of the sample became quite ill, physically or mentally, during the period of the study, but they were continued in the study if they could be interviewed.

The results of this study indicated that neither the activity theory nor the disengagement theory was adequate to account for the observed facts. While there was a decrease of engagement in the common social roles related to increasing age, some of the people who remained active and engaged showed a high degree of satisfaction. On the whole, those who were most active at the older ages were happier, but there were many exceptions to this rule.

Need for a Personality Dimension.—Since it is an empirical fact that some people are satisfied with disengagement while others are satisfied with a high degree of social engagement, it is clear that something more is needed to give us a useful theory of successful aging (Havighurst, Neugarten, & Tobin, 1964; Neugarten, 1965).

A substantial beginning on such a theory was made by Else Frenkel-Brunswik and her colleagues Reichard, Livson, and Petersen (1962) in their study of 87 elderly working men in the San Francisco area, 42 of them retired and 45 not retired. After interviewing these men intensively and rating them on 115 personality variables, the researchers rated them on "adjustment to aging" using a 5-point rating scale. Sixty men were rated either high (4 or 5) or low (1 or 2). Their personality ratings were subjected to a "cluster analysis" to identify men highly similar to one another. The high group produced three clusters and the low group produced two clusters, leaving 23 of the 60 not in any cluster. The five clusters or "types" of men were given the following names:

High on Adjustment	N	Low on Adjustment	N
Mature	14	Angry	16
Rocking-chair	6	Self-haters	4
Armored	7		

Among those judged successful in aging, the "mature" group took a constructive rather than an impulsive or a defensive approach to life. The "rocking-chair" group tended to take life easy and to depend on others. The "armored" men were active in defending themselves from becoming dependent. They avoided retirement if possible, and one of them who was ill complained of his enforced idleness, something the "rocking chair" type would have been glad to accept. Even the oldest of this group, an 83-year old, still worked a half-day every day.

Among those judged unsuccessful in aging, the "angry" men were generally hostile toward the world and blamed others when anything went wrong. They were poorly adjusted to work and several had been downwardly mobile socially. They tended to resent their wives. This group was especially fearful of death.

The "self-haters" differed primarily from the "angry" men by openly rejecting themselves and blaming themselves for their failures. They were depressed. Death for them was a longed-for release from an intolerable existence.

These types of men were making quite different behavioral adjustments to aging. Thus the "armored" and the "rocking-chair" were judged to be equally successful in adjustment to aging, but their adjustments were diametrically opposed. One group was active while the other was disengaged.

The Kansas City Study of Adult Life carried on this search for a personality dimension by studying women as well as men, over a social class range from upper-middle class through upper-working class. The 159 persons were rated on 45 personality variables reflecting both the cognitive and affective aspects of personality. Types of personality were extracted from the data by means of factor analysis. There were four major types, which we have called the integrated, armored-defended, passive-dependent, and unintegrated personalities.

Patterns of behavior were defined on the basis of a rating of *activity* in 11 common social roles: worker, parent, grandparent, kin-group member, spouse, homemaker, citizen, friend, neighbor, club and association member, church member. Ratings were made by judges on each of the eleven roles, based on a reading of the seven interviews with each person. The sum of the role-activity scores was used to divide the respondents into activity levels — high, medium, and low.

A third component of the patterns of aging was a measure of *life-satisfaction* or psychological well-being, which was a composite rating based on five scales recording the extent to which a person (a) finds gratification in the activities of his everyday life; (b) regards his life as meaningful and accepts both the good and the bad in it; (c) feels that he has succeeded in achieving his major goals; (d) has a positive image of himself; and (e) maintains happy and optimistic moods and attitudes.

The analysis based on these three dimensions (personality, role activity, and life satisfaction) was applied to the 59 men and women in the study who were 70 to 79. This is the group in which the transition from middle age to old age has presumably been accomplished. Fifty of these people were clearly one or another of eight patterns of aging, which are presented in Table 1.

Group A, called the *re-organizers*, are competent people engaged in a wide variety of activity. They are the optimal agers in terms of the American ideal of "keeping active, staying young." They reorganize their lives to substitute new activities for lost ones.

Group B are called the *focused*. They are well-integrated personalities with medium levels of activity. They tend to be selective about their activities, devoting their time and energy to gaining satisfaction in one or two role areas.

Group C we call the *successful disengaged*. They have low activity levels with high life satsifaction. They have voluntarily moved away from role commitments as they have grown older. They have high feelings of self-regard, with a contented "rocking-chair" position in life.

Group D exhibits the *holding-on* pattern. They hold as long as possible to the activities of middle age. As long as they are successful in this, they have high life satisfaction.

Group E are *constricted*. They have reduced their role activity presumably as a defense against aging. They constrict their social interactions and maintain a medium to high level of satisfaction. They differ from the *focused* group in having less integrated personalities.

Group F are *succorance-seeking*. They are successful in getting emotional support from others and thus maintain a medium level of role-activity and of life satisfaction.

Group G are *apathetic*. They have low role-activity combined with medium or low life satisfaction. Presumably, they are people who have never given much to life and never expected much.

Group H are *disorganized*. They have deteriorated thought processes and poor control over their emotions. They barely maintain themselves in the community and have low or, at the most, medium life satisfaction.

TABLE 1
Personality Patterns in Aging

Personality Type	Role Activity	Life Satis.	N
A. Integrated (re-organizers)	High	High	9
B. Integrated (focused)	Medium	High	5
C. Integrated (disengaged)	Low	High	3
D. Armored-defended (holding on)	High or medium	High	11
E. Armored-defended (constricted)	Low or medium	High or medium	4
F. Passive-dependent (succorance-seeking)	High or medium	High or medium	6
G. Passive-dependent (apathetic)	Low	Medium or low	5
H. Unintegrated (disorganized)	Low	Medium or low	7

These eight patterns of aging probably are established and predictable by middle age, although we do not have longitudinal studies to prove this proposition. It seems reasonable to suppose that a person's underlying personality needs become consonant with his overt behavior patterns in a social environment that permits wide variation.

In some ways the Kansas City Study and other studies of behavior and life satisfaction support the activity theory of optimal aging; as level of activity decreases, so also do the individual's feelings of contentment regarding his present activity. The usual relationships are high activity with positive affect; and low activity with negative affect. This relationship does not decrease after age 70.

At the same time, the data in some ways support the disengagement theory of optimal aging: there are persons who are relatively high in role activity who would prefer to become more disengaged from their obligations; there are also persons who enjoy relatively inactive lives.

Neither the activity theory nor the disengagement theory of optimal aging is itself sufficient to account for what we regard as the more inclusive description of these findings: that as men and women move beyond age 70 in a modern, industralized community they regret the drop in role activity that occurs in their lives; at the same time, most older persons accept this drop as an inevitable accompaniment of growing old; and they succeed in maintaining a sense of self-worth and a sense of satisfaction with past and present life as a whole.

The relationships between levels of activity and life satisfaction are influenced also by personality type, particularly by the extent to which the individual remains able to integrate emotional and rational elements of the personality. Of the three dimensions on which we have date — activity, satisfaction, and personality — personality seems to be the pivotal dimension in describing patterns of aging and in predicting relationships between level of activity and life satisfaction. It is for this reason, also, that neither the activity nor the disengagement theory is satisfactory, since neither deals, except peripherally, with the issue of personality differences.

This paper is a result of cooperation among the following three people: Bernice L. Neugarten, Sheldon S. Tobin, and Robert J. Havighurst. A description of the central research has been published by Dr. Neugarten under the same title in *Gawein J. of Psychol. Univ. Nijmegen 13*: 249-256, 1965.

REFERENCES

Cumming, E., and W. E. Henry: *Growing old*. Basic Books, New York: 1961.

Havighurst, R. J., B. L.: Neugarten, and S. S. Tobin: Disengagement, personality and life satisfaction in later years. In *Age with a future*. Munksgaard, Copenhagen: 1964.

Reichard, S., F. Livson, and P. G. Peterson: *Aging and personality*. Wiley, New York, 1962.

13. A Social-Psychological Perspective on Aging*

Robert J. Havighurst**

One of the principal unanswered questions about the human life cycle is — how do people structure their lives after about age 65? Under what conditions do they achieve satisfaction?

This is the central problem of the social psychology of aging. It is a problem worth studying both for its theoretical and its practical value.

As I read these two paragraphs, I ask myself — How would I have described the problem of adjustment in old age 22 years ago when I first began to work in this field? I think the main difference lies in our present emphasis on the *initiative* of the person who is growing older. I would not then have used such an active expression as "structure their lives."

The widespread but superficial view of aging in the 1940's saw it as a period of declines, losses, stresses, with the society outside the family doing very little to help older people make a satisfactory adjustment. Professor Burgess and I were members of the Social Science Research Council's Committee on Adjustment to Retirement, and we helped to make a survey of research on Social Adjustment in Old Age. With Ruth Cavan and Herbert Goldhamer and later with Ethel Shanas, we studied the lives of several occupational groups at and after the age of their retirement. We had a series of first-class doctoral students who studied retired teachers, YMCA secretaries, Methodist ministers, old age assistance recipients. For these studies we elaborated an interview schedule entitled "Your Activities and Attitudes." The Attitudes Inventory was a self-report measure of successful adjustment. Later we developed a rating scale for measuring personal-social adjustment, based on the Activities and Attitudes Inventory or on an interview.

We then studied the meanings of work and retirement to several occupational groups, including men and women generally in the age range from 60 to 70. My associates in these studies were Eugene Friedmann, William Harlan, Janet Bower, Ralph Ireland, and Dolores

*Reprinted from *The Gerontologist,* Vol. 8, No. 2, 1968, pages 67-71 with permission of the author and the Gerontological Society.
**Dr. Havighurst is Professor of Education and Human Development at the University of Chicago.

Grutens. We studied medical doctors, steel workers, coal miners, department store employees, and photo engravers

Our next step was to study a sample of older people in a small city by means of interviews. Dr. Ruth Albrecht made this study, which was published in the book, *Older People*. She took the very important step of defining a set of social roles which cover the ordinary social interaction of people and of working out a set of rating scales so that we could measure with a degree of accuracy the extent and intensity of social interaction. The morale and attitude toward life of these people was generally favorable, and we were coming to see old age more and more as a period with substantial rewards and satisfactions.

At this point we were convinced that we must study the *process* of growing old rather than the end product, and we moved to Kansas City for what was to be ten years of field work in two separate studies.

There were four characteristics of our Kansas City studies that we had learned were important in the social psychology of aging.

1. To study an adequate-sized sample of each of the major socioeconomic groups.
2. To study a group extending from middle age to old age.
3. To study the social interaction of people based on some kind of role analysis.
4. To study the personality structure of the members of our sample.

In the first of our two Kansas City studies the social role analysis was carried through in a fairly thorough manner, which was to serve as a basis for later social role studies. This was published in the monograph entitled *The Social Competence of Middle-Aged People*.

Upon this point in our Chicago studies I had generally taken the role of the psychologist while my colleagues were generally sociologists. However, with the advent of the Kansas City studies, we had several able psychologists on our research team, and I began to operate more as a sociologist.

The second Kansas City Study, generally known as the Kansas City Study of Adult Life, started in 1956 and completed field work in 1961. This was a more sophisticated work, both in sociological and psychological terms, than any of our earlier work. The first major publication was the book *Growing Old* by Elaine Cumming and William E. Henry. Reporting on a sample of people from 50 to 80, they showed systematically how persons change in their social interaction over time and also they began to explore the inner life or personality changes. They formulated the disengagement theory of successful aging, which was to become a stimulus for much discussion, writing, and further research. They proposed that social disengagement and "inner" or intrinsic disengagement were inevitable processes, and that the aged individual would be generally high in morale as he demonstrated in his own life these "natural" changes.

The second book had as its title *Personality in Middle and Later Life* and was organized by my colleague, Bernice Neugarten, who had taken the lead in making the personality studies in the Kansas City projects. This book presented various ways of studying personality change in adults, elaborating upon the problem of ego-development, and the relations between personality and adjustment, and it gave a factor-analytic treatment of the personality data which served as a basis for the study of personality types in middle-aged and older people. Among those working with Dr. Neugarten on this book were : William J. Crotty, Walter Gruen, David L. Gutmann, Robert F. Peck, Jacqueline Rosen and Sheldon S. Tobin.

The next step was taken in 1960, when the field work on the Kansas City study was nearing completion. Dr. Neugarten and I formed a clinical research group of graduate students to study intensively the seven rounds of Kansas City interviews. We needed better measures of social interactions and of personal adjustment (morale) than we had used in the past. At this time we developed the *Life Sastifaction Rating* which we have since used as a measure of personal-social adjustment or morale and we developed several measures of role performance, including role activity, satisfaction with role activity, ego-involvement in role activity, and change in role activity.

Our study of the relations of life satisfaction to social interaction in the Kansas City sample led us to a major modification of the disengagement theory. This was reported by us at the Copenhagen meeting of the International Gerontological Congress in 1963 and is about to appear in book form with the title *Patterns of Aging*. Dr. Neugarten, Dr. Tobin, and I are saying that both the activity theory and the disengagement theory of successful aging are insufficient to explain the patterns of aging to be seen in the Kansas City sample. There is no single manner in which older people combine social interaction and life satisfaction. Old people, like young people, are different. If anything, older people are more complex than younger people, because they have had such a wide variety of life-histories.

Some of the complexity of life for older people is pointed out by Williams and Wirths in their book *Lives Through the Years,* which is based on the Kansas City sample and pays special attention to the *social systems* of friends, family members, and acquaintances which center around each person.

THE CENTRAL POSITION OF PERSONALITY

This 20-year series of studies has brought us to the conclusion that personality organization and coping style is the major factor in the life adjustment of the individual as he grows older. It is the manner in which the individual deals with the various contingencies in his life, some of them social, some biological, which is the important fact. It is what one makes of the world that is the important thing.

The key concept is the concept of *adaptation*. The individual continually adapts himself to the conditions of his life. Adaptation is an active process, ruled by the ego. There are remarkably few people who refuse to try to adapt to changes in their circumstances. A very few give up the effort and commit suicide. Most people attempt to cope with whatever situation they face. For instance, a 65-year-old widow who had recently lost her strong and dominant husband spent a half hour telling an interviewer that she could not go on living without "Daddy." She wept almost continuously during the interview, and never ceased talking about her wonderful husband and how she could not get along without him. But six months later she had adapted reasonably well to this loss and was finding sources of satisfaction. Again, an elderly brother-sister pair had lived together for years in a small house heated by a coal-burning stove. Thy were becoming too feeble to look after their house in the cold winter months, and then the brother broke his hip. When this was mended enough to permit him to return home, the county health authorities decided that the couple must go to the county infirmary where they could get competent care. They both insisted that they would rather die than leave their home; but they were gently moved to the infirmary. After three months they had adapted reasonably well to the new life, where they were separated in different wings of the building, and could see each other only during daytime hours.

The Process of Adaptation. — In all segments of the life-span, growing older means an adaptation to: a) Changes in the structure and functions of the human body, b) Changes in the social environment.

The adaptation process is ruled, more or less actively and autonomously, by the ego or personality. What we call personal adjustment, measured in various ways and called by such names as *Life Satisfaction*, is a product of the adaptation process.

At a given place in the life cycle, adaptation is focused on certain roles and activities. These adaptation areas shift from one age level to another.

For example, during early adulthood the adaptive emphasis is on marriage and procreation and career-building, with the roles of spouse, parent, and worker the most important ones.

Then during middle age, the emphasis is on career performance, family life, and civic activity, with greatest importance given to the roles of worker, parent, and the complex of civic and associational activities.

Adaptation in the Sixties. — Up to the age of 60 or 65 the great majority of people can count on fairly good health, so that the state of their physicial organism does not generally count very much either in favor or against their adaptation. Still, those who are blessed with abundant vigor generally make a better adaptation than the average, and those who are physically weak generally have difficulty with their adaptation.

By the time a person reaches the decade from 60 to 70, he or she generally has to adapt to some marked changes in physical vigor and in the social environment. With respect to physical vigor, he cannot do as much heavy physical work as he has done formerly. This is a major problem especially for industrial workers, who often find it necessary to drop the worker's role or to change to a lesser job for reasons of health before they are ready to retire. Nobody escapes from the necessity to adapt his way of living to decreasing physical vigor and acuity if he lives to be 70.

The social environment changes in several ways so as to require adaptive effort by the aging individual. The majority of women lose their husbands before they are 70, and must adapt to widowhood. The great majority of employed men and women lose their roles as workers during this decade. People who have been active in social clubs and professional and civic organizations often find that they are relegated to positions of less importance than they have enjoyed during their middle years.

That part of the social environment which consists of the expectations that other people have of the individual as he moves through his 60's changes slowly but surely. He is expected to be less energetic, less autonomous, less creative than he was a decade earlier. At the same time he may have to adjust to a reduced income. The supportive environment of friends and colleagues thins out.

For the first time, for most persons, the adaptation process takes place against a set of negative changes in the body and the social environment. Some people have a kind of personality that accepts these negative changes in a passive-dependent manner. Others have a personality that seeks to replace lost roles by greater activity in other roles, especially those of grandparent, neighbor, friend, and church member.

Also, with time freed from earlier role-obligations, some people develop a set of free-time activities which give interest and enjoyment.

The end result of the adaptation process in the 60's is a reorganization of role-structure which is accomplished by the ego in the face of the losses and gains of the decade of life.

Adaptation in the Seventies. — Speaking in a general way about older people, one can say that the decade from 70 to 80 is one of *maintenance* of the reorganized role structure that resulted from the adaptations of the 60's. However, there is further role loss, such as widowhood for men as well as for women, and the loss of friends, with a general reduction in role activity caused by decreasing physical vigor. The *task* of the seventies for most people is maintenance of a structure of satisfactory activity which was developed by the reorganization process of the sixties.

Successful Aging. — Successful aging may be defined in various ways. It may be defined from the point of view of the friends and relatives and neighbors of an aging person. Does he or she do the things that we expect a person to do while growing older? It may be defined on the basis of a set of assumptions about what is "natural" as people grow older. One set of assumptions may lead to a definition of successful aging as the maintenance of the activities of middle age with little or no reduction. Another set of assumptions may lead to a definition of successful aging as progressive disengagement from much of the social interaction of middle age.

The writer will assume that successful aging consists of successful adaptation.

When there is a close "fit" between the personality, the social environment, and the physical organism, the adaptation will be relatively easy and aging will be successful. In general, the goodness of fit is maximized when:

1. The personality is strong and flexible.
2. The social environment is supportive.
3. The body is vigorous.

STUDYING THE ADAPTATION PROCESS

To understand the adaptation process in the latter part of the life cycle and to be able to predict the degree of life satisfaction of a particular individual we need to describe systematically for this person his:

1. Personality,
2. Social interaction,
3. Norms and expectations of sub-culture in
   which the person lives,
4. Economic security,
5. Health and vigor,
6. Societal provisions to assist adaptation.

The study of norms and expectations of the various sub-cultures and of the societal provisions to assist adaptation can best be made in a cross-cultural setting which amplifies the sub-cultural differences. For this reason we have taken part in a cross-national study that allows us to compare two occupational groups of retired men in six countries. In this research the social setting emerges clearly as a significant dimension of the adaptation process. For example, we have noted that older men living in Vienna are rated high on the extent of their individual expressive activities (attendance at theater and concert hall, summer excursions to the mountains, gardening, etc.) but relatively low on certain of the social interaction variables (especially participation in formal associations). This may be due to the liberal provision Vienna makes for expressive free-time activity. Again, we noted that retired Dutch teachers are much more active in church work than teachers from any of the other countries, but are rated relatively low on friendship activities. This may be due to the prominent place of the church in the social and political as well as religious life of Holland.

Another example of the influence of societal provisions was noted in the case of retired industrial workers of Milan. The members of our sample had all worked in a particular large industrial plant which provided housing for its workers and a social center for them. The retired workers continued to live in the apartment blocks maintained by the industry and they used the social center as a kind of club-house. Their ratings on friendship activities were higher than those of workers in any of the other national groups. This rating, as well as that on the acquaintance-colleague role, was higher than the ratings of retired teachers in these roles in Milan. Here the societal provision affected the forms of their adaptation to aging, through making it easy for them to interact practically every day for several hours a day with friends and former work-colleagues. In contrast, the retired teachers lived widely dispersed and had little easy opportunity to associate with old friends and colleagues. Their social interaction was more intensive with their families, and less with friends and colleagues than that of the industrial workers.

The cross-national study thus far has been only a pilot one, based upon only small samples, and therefore not sufficient for valid generalizations. Nevertheless, the findings point to the conclusion that, while particular patterns of role activity differ from society to society, the relationships between social interaction and life satisfaction are about the same as found in Kansas City. In other words, in various Western societies most people show greater life satisfaction if their general level of social activity remains medium or high, even though that activity takes place in a wide variety of behavior settings.

THE SIGNIFICANCE OF LIFE HISTORY

Another line of inquiry, independent of our Kansas City studies and primarily concerned with a somewhat different set of problems, has been under investigation by Tobin, Lieberman, and their students. They have been concerned with the function of memory, the place of reminiscence, and ways in which aged people reconstruct their life-histories.

The older person is continually integrating and reinterpreting his past, attempting to make of it a meaningful whole. Older persons always *adapt to the present in terms of a past history* — a past history which is, in a sense, an active component in present adaptation.

The individual is not only coping with a present biological state and a present social state but also with his past; and in a very active way, making sense of the present in terms of the past, and the past in terms of the present.

My colleague, Bernice Neugarten, has been especially concerned with the life history element in the adaptation process. From her we have learned to see adaptation in later maturity as a process in which the ego, or the personality, mediates between a set of biological processes, a set of social processes, and a past represented in the individual's memory.

PATTERNS OF AGING

The adaptation process can be studied empirically in groups of people when the several dimensions mentioned above are systemically measured and described. The actual forms of adaptation that result can be called *patterns of aging*. A pattern of aging is a coherent complex of behavior, including social interaction and use of free time, achieved by an individual through the interaction of his personality with his physical organism and with his social setting. There is a limited number of patterns which can be discovered empirically. Observers agree on assigning persons to these patterns, with a small number of exceptional persons who exhibit rare patterns that will only be observed repeatedly in relatively large samples.

The social setting and the physical organism give the ego or personality a set of possibilities, from which ego works out a pattern which is comfortable to him and is approved or at least tolerated by the society. The actual adaptation which the ego makes depends on his past experience, or his *life history*. The life history gives the ego a supply of experience and habits with which he makes up his own adaptation.

Next Steps

We have noted that there does not exist any study of the process of adaptation to aging which takes account of all of the dimensions of this process. Some useful studies have been made, but they are only partial. Generally the studies have been limited to people in reasonably good health and in a limited social class range, and in one country.

The most useful extensions of our present knowledge would probably come from extending the range of the health and vigor variable and extending the range of the social setting variable, combined with the best of our present personality and social interaction study techniques.

Through extension of cross-cultural studies as well as continued attention to comparative social-class studies we may be able to take into account the differing *group values* which are a part of the social setting. The system of values which is present in a sub-culture and which the individual has internalized, acts to mediate between the personality and the tasks presented to the individual by his society.

Finally, we do not yet understand the *individual psychological processes* by which individuals deal with the tasks of later maturity. We do have some understanding of the processes underlying the transition from adolescence to maturity, through close studies of individuals. We need analogous studies of the transition from middle age to later maturity. For this purpose it would be wise to make longitudinal studies, following persons for 10 to 15 years in the period from 50 to 70.

REFERENCES

Cumming, E., and W.E. Henry: *Growing old.* Basic Books, New York, 1961.

Friedmann, E., and R. J. Havighurst: *The meaning of work and retirement.* Univ. Chicago Press, Chicago, 1954.

Havighurst, R. J., R. Cavan, E. W. Burgess, and H. Goldhamer: *Personal adjustment in old age.* Science Research Associates, Chicago, 1949.

Havighurst, R. J., and R. Albrecht: *Older people.* Longmans, Green, New York, 1953.

Havighurst, R. J.: The social competence of middle-aged people. *Genet. Psychol. Monogr., 56:*297-375, 1957.

Havighurst, R. J., B. L. Neugarten, and S. S. Tobin: Disengagement, personality, and life satisfaction, *Age with a future,* Munsgaard, Copenhagen, 1964.

Neugarten, B. L., R. J. Havighurst, and S. S. Tobin: The measurement of life satisfaction. *J. Geront., 16:*134-143, 1961.

Neugarten, B. L.: *Personality in middle and late life.* Atherton Press, New York, 1964.

Neugarten, B.L.: Personality and patterns of aging. *Gawein, 13:*249-256, 1965.

Neugarten, B. L.: *Personality development in adulthood.* Paper presented at Amer. Psychol. Ass. meeting, Sept., 1966.

Williams, R. H., and C. Wirths: *Lives through the years.* Atherton Press, New York, 1965.

C.   SOCIAL ASPECTS

Because the sociology of aging embraces many facets, complete coverage of this topic could by no means be crowded into the limited space in this section. Nevertheless, these few readings do provide a sampling of both the concerns of social scientists today regarding the aged and their problems, and a view of some sociological approaches to these problems or concerns.

Margaret Blenkner describes the *normal* dependencies which many people experience *throughout* their lives. Among some aged groups these dependencies become more pronounced due to deprivations of a physiological, social, and economic nature. Such dependencies are bound to influence the adjustment of the aged person as well as how others interact with him. In discussing various solutions to dependency in old age, she argues that the general public is unlikely to support the development of adequate services for the aged, nor are the aged themselves likely to be comfortable about accepting such services until there has been a fundamental change in society's attitudes toward dependency in old age.

The next reading follows logically from the first in this section. In this paper Grant Youmans discusses one of the major theories about aging, the disengagement theory. This is the gradual withdrawing of the elderly person from his social contacts and the coincident withdrawal by society from that person. This characterization of the decreased interchange between the elderly person and his environment has been called disengagement. While many feel that the theory is oversimplified and perhaps incomplete, unquestionably some of the ideas stemming from disengagement theory have enabled a major improvement in our understandings about the elderly.

In a paper about social relationships among the aged in a public housing project, Barbara Pittard Payne and her colleagues emphasize the strong desire for independence in living arrangements among people of all ages. Public housing projects appear to be satisfactory to some inhabitants as long as they provide opportunities for interactions and interrelationships with peers and providing they are located within easy access to stores, parks, restaurants, and other urban advantages.

In the next reading, Jacquelyne Johnson Jackson documents the difficulties of the aged minorities, and especially of elderly blacks. Data are becoming available which allow such clear descriptions that the double jeopardy of being old and being black can be clearly demonstrated. In this review of the social gerontological literature on the black aged, Jackson has documented both the advances and understandings in this area, and has described the many problems of the black aged.

In a previously unpublished paper by J. T. Willis, political aspects and considerations relative to the elderly are discussed. While at various times the elderly have attempted to develop a voting block to influence legislation, their most successful efforts have had only minimal effects. In the 1930s the elderly were one of a number of deprived minorities which loosely grouped together in support of Roosevelt's New Deal politics. Experts on population growth do *not* project major increases in numbers of voting elderly to the point where a voting block of the aged is likely even in the distant future. It seems more likely that political influence will be exercised by the aged in more subtle ways. There is no danger that the aged will take over the world politically! There is more evidence that the political behavior of elderly voters will reflect their political attitudes and beliefs when younger.

Religion and philosophy play an increasing role in the lives of many persons as they grow older. The reading by David Moberg reviews the role of religion in the lives of the elderly. He distinguishes between the rituals of religious behavior and an individual's personal belief system. For those elderly who have been predisposed toward secular religious beliefs throughout their lives, these beliefs will play an increasingly important role in their lives as they grow older. However, for the person who did not participate in his earlier years, the philosophy and beliefs of organized religion provide him little comfort and support as he grows older.

In the last reading in this section, Ray Wingrove and Jon Alston review church attendance among different age groups. They find females consistently attending church more frequently than males. The relationship of religiosity to other social aspects of an individual's life is strongly suggested by the data. While documenting the importance of organized religions in the lives of people at all ages, the complexity of causative factors in this area prevents a simple explanation.

14. The Normal Dependencies of Aging*

MARGARET BLENKNER**

This paper is addressed to dependency as a state of being, not a state of mind; a state of being in which to be old — as to be young — is to be dependent. Such dependency is not pathological, it is not wrong; it is, in fact, a right of the old recognized by most if not all societies. It cannot be cured and the only way to forestall it is to die young. In short, it is the normal dependency or dependencies of old age that are the focus of what follows. These normal dependencies may be reduced to four basic categories:

1. *Economic dependency* stems from having crossed over from the productive to the consumer status in the economy. The older person typically finds himself dependent on income transfers from the currently working generation, provided primarily through taxes but also in contributions from children and other younger relatives (Kreps, 1965).

2. *Physical dependency* arises from the simple fact that in the process of aging, muscle strength inevitably diminishes, sensory acuity decreases, reflexes are slower, coordination is poorer, and the general level of energy is lower. The ordinary chores of living — personal self-care and grooming, keeping up one's living quarters, preparing or securing food, transporting oneself from place to place, shopping, participating in social functions, etc. — become increasingly difficult.

3. *Mental dependency* arises from a decline in the power of mentation paralleling the decline in physical power, but occurring more slowly or not reaching such magnitude as to be seen as a source of dependency until quite advanced old age. At that time, when deterioration or change in the central nervous system produces marked deficits in memory, orientation, comprehension and judgment, the old person, quite literally, no longer can use his head to solve his problems and direct his affairs; he must rely on the cognitive functions of others (Donahue, 1965).

4. *Social dependency* develops out of a complex of factors and losses. As the individual ages, he loses *persons* who are important objects and

*Reprinted from *Occasional Papers in Gerontology,* No. 6, August 1969, pages 27-37 with permission of the Institute of Gerontology at the University of Michigan and Wayne State University.
**Dr. Blenkner, now deceased, has served as Director of the Chronic Disease Module Project at the College of Human Medicine, Michigan State University, as Professor of Social Work and Director of Regional Institute for Social Welfare Research, at the University of Georgia, and as Director of Research at Benjamin Rose Institute in Cleveland, Ohio.

sources of affection, stimulation, and assistance. He loses *roles* that are the basis of status and power, and avenues to social participation. He loses *contemporaneity* as his knowledge, values, and expectations become obsolete in a fast changing society. He becomes without volition a progressively isolated and disengaged nonparticipant in the surrounding social world, increasingly dependent on bureaucratized substitutes for missing kith, kin, and agents of former days, increasingly dependent on recognition by others of his *rights* rather than his *power*. He becomes dependent on the social conscience of the generation in positions of authority, those who currently have all that he has lost in the way of vitality and performance. In other words, in old age, without the powers of his prime — economic, physical, mental, and social — one is dependent on the ethical responses of his fellow man (Rosow, 1962).

That these dependencies of the aged are intermixed and interacting hardly needs mention. The fact that they occur simultaneously, though at differing rates of development and force of impact at any given time, reduces considerably the possibility of defensive counteraction of substitutive maneuvers.

I have not included emotional dependency here because emotional dependency, in the sense of depending on others for love and emotional response, is part of the human condition. Man is a social animal. It is in his genes, whatever his stage of development or generational status. If disengagement theory and certain libidinal theories are to be believed, the need for intense emotional involvement with others may be less for the old than for the young and middle-aged.

There are three sources of help or types of solution for the normal dependencies of aging:

1. *Self-Solution,* whereby the older person himself seeks to modify his behavior or circumstances. For example, he balances his budget by restricting his consumption; he conserves his energy by restricting his activities: he bolsters his failing memory by writing notes to himself; he counters his social losses by social disengagement. This is the first line of defense. Such maneuvers are sensible and valid ways of coping, up to a point; beyond it they become increasingly pathological and dangerous until in an extreme form they may jeopardize the sanity and survival of the individual (Clark, 1967). Extreme and pathological forms of self-solution often are seen in the so-called "protective case" (Blenkner. Wasser and Bloom, 1967).

2. *The Kinship Solution,* the most common type among those of advanced years, requires the existence and proximity of children or

other relatives. For the aged who are fortunate enough to have concerned and capable kin, most of their dependent needs can be and usually are met by the care-giving services of such kin.

Typically, the old person remains in his own abode as long as he is capable of personal self-care. However, children or other relatives increasingly take on or assist with the heavier tasks of housekeeping and home maintenance, provide transportation and escort, manage his financial affairs, supervise his health care, nurse him in time of illness, and in general watch over him, substituting their strength, mobility, and judgment for his declining abilities. As he becomes more frail he is likely to move into the home of a relative where more personal care and protective supervision can be given. Only a small minority are institutionalized, and then only when the demand for intensive and skilled care rises beyond the capacity of family members (Stehouwer, 1968).

These too are sensible and valid solutions up to a point; but if carried too far they become destructive to both the old and their kin. An excessive burden of care can so overwhelm a family as to actually endanger its members' physical, emotional and social stability, or else result in a complete and irreversible rejection of the old person with all the accompanying guilt and suffering.

3. *The Societal Solution* consists of arrangements or programs through which society assists its members to cope with needs and problems beyond the resources of the individual or his primary group. It assigns consumer rights to goods and services by nonmarket criteria. Social insurance, public housing, and rent supplementation are good examples of such solutions.

Under the impact of modern living conditions (urbanization, increasing technology, mobility of population, disappearance of the three-generation household, extension of the retirement years), there is a tremendous need to develop and expand imaginative and inventive societal solutions to the normal dependencies of aging. Commenting on the "pressing requirements of a fast-growing aged population," Robert Morris in 1965 asserted that "no organization, no agency, no community is yet ready to organize itself on a mass basis that will be sufficient to ensure all the necessary services for all the elderly whenever they may require such services." That statement is as true now as it was then.

With the sole exception of Medicare, in the past decade we have made little or no progress in the United States toward realistic societal solutions *on a mass basis* to problems arising from the normal, to-be-expected dependencies of aging. Professional social work, which should be in the vanguard in developing such solutions, still acts as though counseling and custodialism were major answers to the problems of growing old in America. Attempts to encourage new programs specifically geared to the aged are met with the Social Work Establishment's territorial cry "duplication of service!" This is supposed to scare off encroachers on established ways of cutting the welfare pie. Anyone who is not completely naive knows it never is raised in defense of clients, only budgets. No client ever complained of duplication of service. Most would welcome the opportunity to do some comparative shopping.

The remainder of this paper is devoted to a rundown of some of the things we now have in the way of societal solutions to the economic, physical, mental, and social dependencies of normal aging, and to a brief commentary on how well and in what manner our existing systems of income maintenance, social services, and health care function in respect to these dependencies. Admittedly this is a presumptuous undertaking, one not calculated to win friends and influence people. But it may be useful in demonstrating how far we still have to go to meet the needs of the aged.

Despite the woeful inadequacies of our present income maintenance system, we are further along the road to solution in the economic sphere than any other. We know the answer; the question is, do we have the generosity? The obvious answer to economic dependency among persons no longer in the labor market is either to supply them with money, or to pay their bills. This in effect is what we have done in the United States for the older person; but we have done it penuriously and, for too many, we have done it demeaningly.

Building on our present social insurance system, we could take care of this particular dependency by instituting universal coverage of all retired or disabled persons 60 years and over, and making the minimum benefit sufficient to secure a modest but adequate standard of living. We could remove the questionable co-insurance and deductible provisions from Medicare, add some provisions for "preventicare," and thus insure that all — not just part — of the elderly's medical bills will be paid. We could, once and for all insofar as the aged are concerned, get rid of the means test approach to economic dependency. We could and probably shall do all these things before too long, regardless of which party dominates the political scene in the next decade.

Presently, neither old age insurance nor old age assistance is meeting the economic need of our older citizens. If they were, the old would not comprise one-fourth to one-third of the poor we talk so much about today. The war on poverty, in the aged sector, can be won easily as soon as we grant that the main cause of poverty is lack of money, and set about providing it.

Many schemes for meeting economic need are in the air these days. We hear talk of the guaranteed income, the negative income tax, the universal demogrant, etc. There is no group for whom it is more politically feasible to move toward these modern concepts of income maintenance than the aged. In fact, we already have moved toward the universal demogrant in extending Social Security coverage to persons without a history of eligible employment. To end most of the poverty among our older citizens we need only extend coverage to all retired persons over a given age, and increase substantially the minimum benefit (doubling, or better tripling, the present amount and instituting some cost-of-living device to protect against further inflation).[1] For those who worry about the prosperous oldster who might get money he doesn't need, changes in our income tax laws regarding exemptions could tax it right back, if we wish.

Generously meeting the economic dependency of the aged will do much to solve or forestall the rise of problems in other areas. In fact, *satisfactory solutions to dependency needs in other areas hinge on first satisfactorily and adequately solving the problem of economic dependency*. Failure thus far to solve this problem is a major source of failure and confusion in our efforts in other dependency areas, as will be seen later.

Problems of physical dependency may be met by various congregate and protective living arrangements of an institutional or semi-institutional character, or by services delivered to the old in their own homes or those of relatives or friends. In the United States, despite lip-service to the slogan "keep the old in their own homes," most money and manpower directed specifically toward services and facilities for the aged segment of the population are designed to remove the old from their own homes.

With public funds and through public policy, we have subsidized the development and expansion of the proprietary nursing home into a major industry (Blenkner, 1968). Private philanthropic money for the aged is nearly all concentrated in congregate care facilities of one sort or another, as is professional personnel employed by the voluntary agencies to serve the aged. The one program that could put action into

---

[1] To assure the old a continuing share in the economic growth of the nation will require that in the future some part of the cost be met from general revenue, in addition to employee-employer contributions.

the slogan of keeping the old in their homes — an extensive system of home help services (visiting housekeepers or home aides, home handymen and maintenance aides, transport and escort aides, etc.) is grossly underdeveloped in the United States in contrast to other advanced industrialized societies (Townsend, 1968). Even worse, under the impact of Medicare legislation, such service as has been developed is now being distorted and sidetracked into a restricted type of health care. It is available only on prescription and limited to part-time, intermittent, personal care services, instead of being developed in its own right as a *major societal solution* to the normal physical, mental and social losses incurred in old age (Harris, 1968).

Home aides can readily be recruited and trained to perform responsibly any task around the home or neighborhood that the older person would ordinarily do for himself if he were able, or that a family member (if available) might do for him. Aides in our projects[2] have done housecleaning, meal planning and grocery shopping, laundering and mending; they have given assistance in bathing, grooming and dressing; they have overseen and assisted in the taking of prescribed medications, and in physical and occupational therapy exercises; they have read to, talked with, written letters for, chauffered, and escorted old people living at home or in the homes of relatives and friends. For many, this service has proved a means of social stimulation and reorientation to the outside world, as well as a way of improving physical care and environment. It has enabled several participants in the projects to live out their lives and die in familiar surroundings — a rare privilege in this day, when death is something we hide from sight, putting out our old to die antiseptically among strangers.

A program that should be available as a *social utility on user initiative*, to any older citizen who wishes to use it, generally is available only in package deals and tie-in sales with professional services (Kahn, 1965). The old person should not have to be sick or disturbed and under treatment by a physician, nurse, or social worker to receive home aide services. Age itself should constitute an entitlement. Fees should be charged that reflect the amount of service received, but it is no more practical to charge individuals the full cost of such service than it is to expect younger individuals to pay the full cost of their education. Heavy but by no means complete subsidization is necessary; devices

[2] Conducted by the Bejamin Rose Institute, Cleveland, Ohio and supported in part by Welfare Administration Grant No. 175 and Public Health Service Grant No. CD-00213, Department of Health, Education and Welfare, Washington, D.C., and the Macgregor Home, Cleveland, Ohio.

analogous to tuition scholarships for the educationally indigent should be invented for persons unable to pay even nominal costs. However, the number of such persons will be considerably reduced if and when our income maintenance system catches up with present day realities.

The crying need in the field of home help services is for creative thinking and the planning of ways and means *to finance and structure such services to reach the mass of older people* and their families. While Ellen Winston, at a meeting of the National Council on Homemaker Services (1968), called for 200,000 homemakers, the Council boasts that the number has more than doubled in the last few years — there are now almost 12,000! These figures include *all* home aides, only a minority of whom are serving the old. Sweden, with a population less than 1/20th that of the United States, had more than 12,000 home helpers in 1961 (Eltz, 1963). To catch up with let alone surpass the volume of service established years ago in Sweden and Britain, we would require *at least* 200,000 homemakers and home aides for the elderly alone. (Winston's projections are very modest.)

Meanwhile, in the face of this need and potential demand, the professionals who administer such programs as we have bury their heads in the sand of standards and jurisdictional disputes — a ridiculous posture, but also a tried and true bureaucratic way of putting the brakes on any expansion that threatens the status quo. Solutions to *social* dependency have become confused with solutions to *mental* dependency. This is evident on the social welfare scene in the newly developing programs of protective service. Although directed toward the aged person whose behavior is such as to render his *mental* competence suspect, a review of services usually included under the "protective service" rubric reveals that many of them may be needed by any old person at one time or another, especially if he is without accessible relatives, friends, or personal agents to help him manage.

The social characteristic of being "without anyone reliable, ready, willing, and able to act on his behalf" is sufficient to identify a public assistance recipient as "one who needs protective services."[3] There is danger in such confusion of social and mental characteristics. Although done with the best intentions, i.e. to make scarce services available to the largest number of older persons, it tends to cast an aura of marginal mentality and civil status over all older persons seeking social services. It reinforces an already existing tendency to deny self-determination to persons in the client/patient role, to assume that the professional always knows best (Blenkner, 1967).

No one has yet demonstrated that the average client cannot do just as good a job as the average caseworker in deciding what his major problem is, and what service would be most effective in solving or ameliorating it. With old people who in the past have managed their lives and filled their social roles adequately, this is a particularly tenable hypothesis. Some of our touted procedures of study and diagnosis that characterize practice in the "best" agencies look a bit ridiculous from the client's side of the desk.

I'll never forget an old man who applied for admission to an apartment house for older people, operated by a social agency for which I was then directing a study of a model program of services to the aging (Blenkner, Jahn, and Wasser, 1964). We gave him the works in the way of study and diagnosis. The caseworker interviewed him, a public health nurse visited him, a physician examined him, he made a trial visit to the apartment house, he met and talked with house staff and residents, we held innumerable staff conferences about him. I can't recall whether we had a psychiatric consultation, but we probably did. Altogether it was a glorious interdisciplinary experience in psychobiosocial diagnosis for all — except the old man. After several weeks we concluded our deliberations and decided that he was a proper candidate for residence in the house. He was called in and the service director, exuding the warmth of the professional offering a tangible reward for good client performance, informed him of our decision. Puzzled by his somewhat flat response, she asked "Aren't you pleased?"

The old man sighed: "I guess so." Then, with rising inflection: "But that was a hell of a lot to go through just to rent a room!"

---

[3] One who needs protective services is identified as: An applicant or recipient of public assistance (current, former, or potential) who has one or more of the following characteristics:

(1) Has physical or mental limitations that render him unable to act on his own behalf, to manage money, and/or to carry on activities of daily living;
(2) Behaves in a way that is harmful to self or others;
(3) Is mentally incompetent to the degree that legal measure are, or foreseeably will be, necessary and are to be invoked for his own or others' protection, e.g., legal representative, guardianship, and commitment;
(4) Living in unsafe or hazardous conditions;
(5) Neglected or exploited;
(6) Without anyone reliable, ready, and willing or able to act on his behalf, e.g., a family member, relative, friend.

Source: *State Letter No. 925. Four Model Demonstration Projects — Services to Older Adults in the Public Welfare Program.* Bureau of Family Services, Welfare Administration, September 1, 1966.

My enthusiasm for professional procedures has been somewhat tempered ever since.

Solutions to social dependency may also be confused with *economic* solutions, as witness the development of programs to put old people to work in hospitals, clinics, schools, social or recreational agencies, and beautification efforts. Are these programs promulgated because they provide meaningful roles to the old whose life has lost meaning, or because they provide needed cash income to those who work in the programs, or because they promise a source of cheap labor to a segment of our economy where unionization and minimum wage legislation are rapidly raising labor costs? Does the activation of such programs meet a basic social need for a considerable number of the aged, or does it serve primarily to distract us from the larger issue of inadequate Social Security benefits? How many of the old would choose to work, if they had adequate retirement incomes?

These are many questions, but I think we must ask theem as long as retirement is synonymous with poverty for large numbers of older Americans.

These are nasty questions, but I think we must ask them as long as retirement is synonymous with poverty for large numbers of older Americans.

Confusions and contradictions such as these reflect the difficulty we in the social and behavioral sciences, and the applied fields of social welfare and mental health, have encountered in coming to grips with normal old-age dependency as a development that must be planned and provided for, and is unlikely to be cured, treated, rehabilitated, or exorcised away.

REFERENCES

Blenkner, M. "Prevention or Protection: Aspects of Social Welfare Services for the Mentally Impaired Aged." Paper prepared for First Workshop on Comprehensive Services for the Geriatric Mental Patient, Washington, D.C., November 30-December 1, 1967. (To be published in *Proceedings.*)

Blenkner, M. "The Place of the Nursing Home Among Community Resources." *Journal of Geriatric Psychiatry,* 1 (Spring, 1968), 135-150.

Blenkner, M., Jahn, J., and Wasser, E. *Serving the Aging: An Experiment in Social Work and Public Health Nursing.* New York: Community Service Society, 1964. Mimeo.

Blenkner, M., Wasser, E., and Bloom, M. *Protective Services for Older*

People: Progress Report, 1966-67. Cleveland: Benjamin Rose Institute, 1967. Mimeo.

Clark, M. "Is Dependency in Old Age Culture Bound?" Paper read at Annual Meeting of the Gerontological Society, November 10, 1967.

Donahue, W. "Psychological Changes with Advancing Age." In: *Planning Welfare Services for Older People.* Papers presented at the Training Institute for Public Welfare Specialists in Aging, Cleveland, June 13-24, 1965. Washington, D.C.: Government Printing Office, 1965.

Eltz, S. *Housing for the Aged and the Disabled in Sweden.* (Sweden Today Series.) Stockholm: Swedish Institute, 1963.

Harris, I. (ed.) *Final Report: Homemaker – Public Health Nurse Demonstration Project Serving Incapacitated Adults.* San Diego: Homemaker Service of San Diego, Inc., 1968.

Kahn, A. "Social Services in Relation to Income Security: Introductory Notes." *Social Service Review,* 39 (December, 1965), 381-389.

Kreps, J. "The Economics of Intergenerational Relationships." In: E. Shanas and G. Streib, (eds.) *Social Structure and the Family: Generational Relations.* New York: Prentice-Hall, 1965.

Morris, R. "Principles and Processes of Community Planning, Coordination, and Development." In: *Planning Welfare Services for Older People.* Papers presented at the Training Institute for Public Welfare Specialists in Aging. Cleveland, June 13-24, 1965. Washington, D.C.: Government Printing Office, 1965.

Rosow, I. "Old Age: One Moral Dilemma of an Affluent Society." *The Gerontologist,* 2 (December, 1962), 182-191.

Stehouwer, J. "The Household and Family Relation of Old People." In: E. Shanas, *et al., Old People in Three Industrial Societies.* New York: Atherton Press, 1968.

Townsend, P. "Welfare Service and the Family." In: E. Shanas, *et al., Old People in Three Industrial Societies.* New York: Atherton Press, 1968.

Winston, F. "The ABC's of Homemaker-Home Health Aide Service." Paper presented at the National Council for Homemaker Services Forum, April 24, 1968.

15. Some Perspectives on Disengagement Theory*

E. GRANT YOUMANN**

Research efforts in a relatively new field such as social gerontology have proceeded for the most part with little attention to explicit theory. Social gerontologists have been concerned primarily with the practical issues and problems confronting older persons. Philibert (1965) and Kastenbaum (1965) criticize social gerontology for being a mixture of findings made by older and established disciplines, each of which has its own methods and theories, and each of which deals with some aspects of human aging. These critics maintain that a collection of findings does not offer adequate understanding of the aging process and that a comprehensive theoretical framework is needed to facilitate the collection of integrated knowledge about human aging.

Cumming and Henry (1961) proposed a general theoretical explanation of the social psychological aspects of human aging that was labeled disengagement theory. The older person was conceived as being at the center of a network of social interactions and, as he aged, his social life constricted and he experienced a curtailment of involvement in social systems — an inevitable and a universal process beneficial to both the individual and society. Parsons predicted that the theory would serve as an important focus of discussion in social gerontology for some time (Cumming & Henry, 1961). Apparently this prediction was correct. Disengagement theory not only has instigated many lively discussions among social gerontologists, but has stimulated considerable research and provoked substantial controversy.

Published materials by social gerontologists suggest a negative view of disengagement theory and a need for modification. Brehm (1968), Kutner (1962), and Maddox (1964) question the alleged universality and inevitability of the theory and maintain that the process of disengagement is applicable to only a portion of older people. Rose and Peterson (1965) suggest that alleged disengagement in later life may be

*Reprinted from *The Gerontologist,* Vol. 9, No. 4, 1969, pages 254-258, with permission of the author and the Gerontological Society.
**Dr. Youmans is Adjunct Professor of Sociology at the University of Kentucky in Lexington. At the time the paper was written Dr. Youmans was also with the U. S. Department of Agriculture.

a continuation of life-long patterns of low social participation. Havighurst (1961) and Kleemeier (1964) suggest that disengagement is not necessarily beneficial to older people, since it is the engaged person who is usually happiest. Neugarten (1964) maintains that psychological disengagement precede social disengagement and that this phenomenon occurs by the mid-forties. Williams and Wirths (1965) suggest that some older persons must cope with disengagement and that it can occur in different aspects of a person's behavior and at different rates in these various aspects. In rating 295 older persons aged 54 to 93 years on an index of disengagement, Carp (1968) maintains that the component parts of disengagement from family and friends has different meanings for different people, and that the loosening of the bonds of parenthood do not necessarily mean a loosening of other social ties.

In a study of emeritus professors, Roman and Taietz (1967) suggest that disengagement theory needs to be modified by incorporating the intervening variable of opportunity structure. Tallmer and Kutner (1969) offer evidence that it is not age which produces disengagement but the impact of physical and social stress that may be expected to increase with age.

A liberal sampling of empirical studies offers little support to disengagement theory. Available evidence suggests that while many older persons lose their major adult roles, such as those of occupation for men and child-rearing for women, these losses do not necessarily mean disengagement from other social relationships. Kapnick, Goodman, and Cornwell (1968), in a study of delegates to the New York and Rhode Island constitutional conventions, found no support to the proposition that older men would be underrepresented, be less active, and be more conservative than the younger men. These authors found support for the proposition that the older delegates occupied their full quota of leadership roles. Streib (1965) summarized studies relevant to the aged as a minority group and concluded that the aged are not systematically deprived of power and privileges, are not excluded from public facilities, and are not precluded from jobs they are qualified to perform.

Glenn and Grimes (1968), from a study of national surveys of political behavior, concluded that political interest and participation increased with advances in age. Prasid (1964) in a study of 900 retired industrial workers in five industrial centers concluded that the disengagement theory postulate — that most men are ready to disengage — finds no support among industrial workers in the modern era. In a study of a representative sample of men and women aged 45 to 60 living in a rural county in Kentucky, Youmans (1968) found no evidence of anticipatory social disengagement from present hobbies or community activities. Shanas (1968), in a study of 2,500 non-institutionalized persons aged 65 and over, concluded that while old people do tend to become increasingly preoccupied, there seems to be no evidence for a decrease in response to normative controls, as suggested by disengagement theory.

Two studies of family relationships give negative support to disengagement theory (Youmans, 1967a, 1967b). These studies involved representative samples of men and women aged 60 and over living in a rural county and in a metropolitan center. In comparing the women aged 60 to 64 with those aged 75 and over, no statistically significant differences were found in the frequency of visits with siblings who lived apart, in the proportions who said their children came to them for advice, in the proportions who said they helped their children in some way, in the proportions who said relatives came to them for advice, or in the proportions who said they helped their brothers or sisters in some way. While the men experienced substantial disengagement from paid employment, they evidenced no disengagement from family life or leisure-time activities. Palmore (1968), in a longitudinal study of 127 Ss with a mean age of 78 years, found no significant over-all decrease in activities among the men and only a slight decrease among the women.

A recent publication by Shanas, Townsend, Wedderbum, Friis, Milhoj, and Stehouwer (1968) provides substantial negative evidence concerning disengagement in later life. Using national samples of persons aged 65 and over in Denmark, Britain, and the United States, these authors explored older persons' physical capacities, social roles, incomes, and attitudes. These authors concluded that older persons are more strongly integrated into industrial society than is often assumed. Their data suggest that *independent* of growing infirmity, social disengagement is not a widespread phenomenon and subjective disengagement is very meager.

A study initiated by the National Institute of Mental Health has special significance to disengagement theory. In 1955-1957, a research team of physiologists, medical clinicians, psychiatrists, psychologists, and sociologists examined a broad range of biological and behavioral characteristics of 47 healthy older men with a mean age of 71 years (Birren, Butler, Greenhouse, Sokoloff, & Yarrow, 1963). In 1961, a follow-up of this group of healthy aged Ss provided an opportunity to replicate some of the analyses used in the earlier study and to obtain a limited "longitudinal" view of human aging (Yarrow, Blank, & Murphy, 1968; Yarrow, Blank, Quinn, Youmans, & Stein, 1963). In the 5-year follow-up, assessment was made of the social environment, daily behavior, interests, satisfactions, and attitudes of the 38 surviving men. The data on the group of men at the beginning and end of the 5-year interval in old age do not support the contention of disengagement theory that the aged person withdraws from his social environment or that the social environment fails to support the aging person. The men in this longitudinal study maintained a reasonably steady and consistent course in their activities, relationships, and general feelings toward life. It is noteworthy that almost half of the men reported more social activities outside of their families at the time of the follow-up than at the time of the original interview 5 years earlier. A 10-year follow-up study of the survivors of this cohort of healthy older men is now in progress. Preliminary analysis suggests that highly stable patterns have been maintained with respect to the organization and complexity of the men's daily living and with respect to relationships and integration with other persons. Changes have occurred over the 10-year period of time, but these changes are not ones of general disengagement.

The foregoing data suggest serious limitations about the adequacy of disengagement theory to serve as a guide for researchers and practitioners in social geronotology. It is suggested that some theoretical progress may be achieved by considering the "life course" frame of reference. Despite the fact that few researchers appear interested in the entire life-span, the data are overwhelming in their abundance and diversity and continue to accumulate from biological, demographic, anthropological, sociological, historical, and political studies (Cain, 1964). It is not the intent here to sift and sort these data into a coherent theoretical scheme but to examine a few salient aspects of life course phenomena.

Essentially, the notion of the life course suggests that every person, if he survives, moves through various stages of development — infancy, childhood, young adulthood, maturity, and old age. For many persons, retirement also may be designated a stage in life (Simpson, 1968). Disengagement theory recognizes an underlying model of human development and maintains it is one of inevitable and universal disengagement. The life course idea suggests that there is much more to human aging than only engagement or disengagement. Every society is concerned with the universal phenomenon of movement through the life course. To function effectively, a given society must provide the means by which a person can move in an orderly fashion from one status position to another, and a society also must provide the motivations for individuals to fulfill the roles associated with each status position. Every phase of the life course is marked by important changes and these are related to those that occurred earlier. The older-age period of life brings changes in physical and psychological capacities and changes in social circumstances and opportunities which impose the need for substitutions and reorganization of behavior.

A full understanding of human aging requires that the cultural expectations and abilities associated with older age be compared with those of earlier stages of life. It is generally recognized that we have a youth-centered society in the United States, and this is evidenced in the many organizational structures which give support to the achievement activities of young people. There seems to be a fairly good fit between social expectations and the abilities of young people to perform. During later middle age, however, an interesting paradox occurs. At a time in life when the individual experiences slight decrements in abilities and energies, the expectations of society continue to press for achievement. There is a disparity between social expectations and the abilities of individuals to meet these expectations. In older age, the abilities and energies continue their gradual decline. However, this stage of the life course reveals a sharp contrast to previous stages. In old age, social expectations and social supports decline sharply below the level of abililties of older people. There is an inadequate fit between the potentials of old persons and the structure of society. There is a lack of organized group life to sustain the social functioning of older people, and the aged person in the United States, typically, is confronted with the prospect of a "roleless role."

Examination of stages in the life course permits insight into coping behavior and adjustment patterns manifest in different stages. Each stage may have its dominant values and sentiments (Peck, 1956). The life course approach suggests that the biological model of organic decline may not be appropriate for the social aspects of human aging. The life course idea suggests that many difficulties attributed to old age may be merely bad habits acquired at an earlier age. The life course concept offers a model for studying a wide range of phenomena associated with aging, such as family roles, occupational and avocational careers, consumer patterns, political and religious activities, and deviant behavior.

In viewing the life course as a sequence of development stages, recognition is given to the importance of social change in understanding human aging. Rose and Peterson (1965) point out that the disengagement theory offers a poor interpretation of socio-cultural change and that certain social trends in American society tend to counteract conditions which might influence some older persons to disengage.

Among these changes and trends which tend to foster continued engagement in older age are *(a)* advances in medical science and health practices which have permitted increasing proportions of older persons to maintain physical vigor, *(b)* earlier retirement for men and the freeing of women from close responsibility of child-care at an early age, *(c)* the rising economic security and educational level of old persons, *(d)* the rapidly increasing number of organized activities and programs for the aged, and *(e)* a redefinition of leisure-time activities so that retired males may participate in a variety of activities formerly defined as feminine. While these trends may provide conditions favorable for the engagement of older persons, the ability of the individual to become a participating member in a meaningful way depends, in large measure, on the roles he has performed in the earlier stages of his life course. Simpson, Back, and McKinney (1966) provide evidence that social participation among retired workers is correlated with participation in earlier stages of the life cycle.

In contrast to disengagement theory, the life course concept acknowledges the importance of generational phenomena in understanding human aging. The pervading presence of young people with their distinctive styles of life certainly are a significant factor in explaining the social psychology of aging. Each younger generation in Western society differs to some degree from the older generation by virtue of exposure to different historical experiences. Reinforced by peer group association and by the changing content of formal education and popular culture, these experiences influence the young to develop responses to life different from those who are older than they. New generations provide the opportunity for social change to occur.

One example of generational analysis may be cited to indicate the relevance to social gerontology. Cain (1967, 1968) examined the hypothesis that persons already past 65 in America have needs and aspirations in sharp contrast to those of persons just beginning to enter the old-age category. Those born in the decade preceding 1900 were directed down one path of life, while those born in the decade after 1900 followed a different path. The latter group is a "favored" generation. Its members have fewer children, have more double paychecks in the family, and have been riding the crest of probably the longest period of uninterrupted prosperity in the nation's history.

The generational analysis cited suggests important questions concerning the formation of public policies for older people in the United States. If public policies are based solely on studies of persons already in the old age category, the programs and facilities may not be appropriate for coming generations of old people. The present generation of aged persons grew up in a period when work and personal responsibility for financial security were fundamental and feasible values (Taves, 1964). The new generations of elderly persons will have seen personal efforts frustrated and made ineffective by social forces beyond individual control. They tend to accept the principle of public responsibility for individual welfare. The new generations of older people will demand more and also offer more. They will be better educated, more urbane and sophisticated, more mobile and secular, and they will more often live to a very old age. It is probably a safe prediction to say that the newer generations of elderly will find their greatest satisfaction from a responsible role in the mainstream of life commensurate with their skills, physical stamina, and earlier social status. It is reasonable to expect that older people will want to share in what Benson (1969) calls the "irrepressible world revolt" for autonomy and for the right to take part in decisions that affect their lives.

SUMMARY

The foregoing perspectives on disengagement theory — the need for modification, the lack of empirical supports and inadequate recognition of social change — suggest a lack of confidence in its usefulness as a general theoretical explanation of the social pychological aspects of human aging. It is recognized that some older persons disengage from social relationships, and the factors and conditions producing this behavior need to be studied. It is suggested that a development concept such as the life course offers a more comprehensive and promising framework for research and application in social gerontology.

Acknowledgment for helpful suggestions is made to A. Lee Coleman and James H. Copp.

REFERENCES

Benson, L. The irrepressible world revolt. *New Republic*, 1969, 160, No. 3, 17-22.
Birren, J. E., Butler, R. N., Greenhouse, S. W., & Yarrow, M. R. (Eds.), *Human aging: A biological and behavioral study*. Washington: Public Health Service Publication No. 986, 1963.

Brehm, H. P. Sociology and aging: Orientation and research. *Gerontologist,* 1968, 8, 24-31.
Cain, L. D., Jr. Life course and social structure. In R. E. Faris (Ed.), *Handbook of modern sociology.* Chicago: Rand McNally, 1964.
Cain, L. D., Jr. Age status and generational phenomena: The new old people in contemporary America.. *Gerontologist,* 1967, 17, Pt. I, 83-92.
Cain, L. D., Jr. Aging and the character of our times. *Gerontologist,* 1968, 8, 250-258.
Carp, F. M. Some components of disengagement. *Journal of Gerontology,* 1968, 23, 382-386.
Cumming, E., & Henry, W. E. *Growing old.* New York: Basic Books, 1961.
Glenn, N. D. & Grimes, M. Aging, voting, and political interest. *American Sociological Review,* 1968, 33, 563-575.
Havighurst, R. J. Successful aging. *Gerontologist,* 1961, 1, 8-13.
Kapnick, P. L., Goodman, J. S., & Cornwell, E. E., Jr. Political behavior in the aged: Some new data. *Journal of Gerontology,* 1968, 23, 305-310.
Kastenbaum, R. Theories of human aging: The search for a conceptual framework. *Journal of Social Issues,* 1965, 21, 13-36.
Kleemeier, R. W. Leisure and disengagement in retirement. *Gerontologist,* 1964, 4, 180-184.
Kutner, B. The social nature of aging. *Gerontologist,* 1962, 2, 5-8.
Maddox, G. L., Jr. Disengagement theory: A critical evaluation. *Gerontologist,* 1964, 4, Pt. I, 80-82.
Neugarten, B. L. *Personality in middle and late life: Empirical studies.* New York: Atherton, 1964.
Palmore, E. B. The effect of aging on activities and attitudes. *Gerontologist,* 1968, 8, 259-263.
Peck, R. Psychological developments in the second half of life. In J. E. Anderson (Ed.), *Psychological aspects of aging.* Washington: American Psychological Association, 1956.
Philibert, M. A. J. The emergence of social gerontology. *Journal of Social Issues,* 1965, 21, 4-12.
Prasid, S. B. The retirement postulate of the disengagement theory. *Gerontologist,* 1964, 4, 20-23.
Roman, P., & Taietz, P. Organizational structure and disengagement: The emeritus professor. *Gerontologist,* 1967, 7, Pt. I, 147-152.
Rose, A. M., & Peterson, W. A. *Older people and their social world.* Philadelphia: F. A. Davis, 1965.

Shanas, E. A note on restriction of life space: Attitudes of age cohorts. *Journal of Health & Social Behavior,* 1968, 9, 86-89.

Shanas, E. Townsend, P., Wedderbum, D., Friis, H.; Milhoj, & Stehouwer, J. *Old people in three industrial societies.* New York: Atherton Press, 1968.

Simpson, I. H. Problems of the aging in work and retirement. In R. R. Boyd (Ed.), *Older Americans: Social participants.* Spartanburg, S. C.: Converse College, 1968.

Simpson, I. H., Back, K. W., & McKinney, J. C. Attributes of work, involvement in society, and self-evaluation in retirement. In I. H. Simpson & J.C. McKinney (Eds.) *Social aspects of aging.* Durham, N. C.: Duke University Press, 1966.

Streib, G. F. Are the aged a minority group? In A. W. Goulder & S. M. Miller (Eds.), *Applied sociology.* New York: Free Press, 1965.

Taves, M. J. A resume; New perspectives in aging. In D. E. Alleger (Ed.), *Social change and aging in the twentieth century.* Gainesville; University of Florida, 1964.

Tallmer, M., & Kutner, B. Disengagement and the stress of aging. *Journal of Gerontology,* 1969, 24, 70-75.

Williams, R. H., & Wirths, C. G. *Lives through the years.* New York: Atherton, 1965.

Yarrow, M. R., Blank, P., & Murphy, H. S. A longitudinal study in human aging. Unpublished manuscript, National Institute of Mental Health, Bethesda, Md., 1963.

Yarrow, M. R., Blank, P., Quinn, O. W., Youmans, E. G., & Stein, J. Social psychological characteristics of old age. In J. E. Birren, R. N. Butler, S. W. Greenhouse, L. Sokoloff, & M. R. Yarrow (Eds.), *Human aging: A biological and behavioral study.* Washington, D.C.: Public Health Service, Publication No. 986. 1963.

Youmans, E. G. Family disengagement among older urban and rural women. *Journal of Gerontology,* 1967, 22, 209-211. (a)

Youmans, E. G. Disengagement among older rural and urban men. In E. G. Youmans (Ed.), *Older rural Americans.* Lexington: University of Kentucky Press, 1967. (b)

Youmans, E. G. Orientations to old age. *Gerontologist,* 1968, 8, 153-158.

16. Family and Other Relationships of Residents of A Public Housing Project for Older People*

BARBARA PITTA PAYNE, RAYMOND PAYNE, AND C. RAY WINGROVE**

INTRODUCTION

This paper reports on one portion of a survey of health and related matters among older people in public housing apartments in Atlanta, Georgia.

This phase of the survey documented (1) the relationship and interaction patterns between subjects and their families, and (2) subjects' attitudes and feelings about those relationships.

Interviews were held with 51 persons. All were Negroes 62 years old or older, residing in Anton Graves Center, 126 Hillard Street, S.E., a segment of Grady Homes Housing Project.

The subjects were selected at random to represent the 227 persons then living in the Center. Eight of the subjects were male, 43 female. Five persons (three females and two males) were married and living with their spouses. Eight were divorced or separated.

Each subject was interviewed personally in his apartment by sociology students from Georgia State University; data were analyzed at the University of Georgia.

FAMILY RELATIONSHIPS

None of the subjects was dependent upon children or other relatives for major support. (All but one reported have one or more living relatives.)

*Original paper written for this book.
**Dr. Barbara Payne is Professor of Sociology at Georgia State University. Dr. Raymond Payne, now deceased, was Professor of Sociology at the University of Georgia. Dr. C. Ray Wingrove formerly at the University of Georgia, is presently Professor of Sociology at the University of Richmond and is an editor of this book.

Several reported receiving some help from relatives. Seven said family members visited them, three had errands run for them, one had relatives visit for meals, and two had received clothes. One had a relative who "took her places."

Altogether, 15 percent had received some kind of help from relatives. About half of the subjects were without "active relationships" with family members.

Frequency of contacts with relatives varied greatly.

27 per cent were not in contact with relatives, or had seen relatives no more than once in the preceding five years.

16 percent were seeing relatives several times a year.

41 percent were seeing relatives weekly or several times each month.

12 percent were seeing relatives daily.

Most (72 percent) had never lived with family members (spouses excepted), and 70 percent *did not now want to do so*. They preferred "living independently" as they were doing.

Subjects were asked what they would like to have changed about their families, or what they wanted that they were not getting. Most (62 percent) said they wanted no change, and another 24 percent could think of nothing. Thus, over four-fifths were satisfied (or, at least, uncomplaining) about the treatment they were receiving from family members. However, some may simply have been convinced that nothing could be done, so were uncomplaining.

Several were doing things for family members. A few (4 persons) were contributing financially. Five others were doing baby sitting, helping sick relatives, or rendering other service.

Residents considered religion and church activities to be quite important. These provided friends and social contacts outside the apartment. More time was spent this way than in all others combined. Over a third of the subjects made no reference to religion. Of the others, 14 were Baptists, three Methodists, two spiritualists, two Holiness, one was a member of the Church of God, and two were Jehovah's witnesses. Seven belonged to no particular denomination but "visited different churches."

Over a third of the cases admitted to loneliness. They said they didn't have "much" company; some were "very lonely."

The other almost two-thirds spent some time with friends or relatives. Most (18) spent time with friends *within* the apartments, and six spent most of their visiting time with friends *outside* the apartments.

The other not-so-lonely persons spent most of their visiting time with relatives.

In the informal portions of the interviews, the subjects almost all admitted to some loneliness, but were eager to express satisfaction with the Center. They liked its location — downtown, close to city hospital, clinics, stores, and overlooking the city. They liked watching the city, both day and night. Also, there had developed a high degree of pride in the Center. It is well managed and maintained, and has come to carry some prestige as a place of residence in the inner city.

DISCUSSIONS AND CONCLUSIONS

These older people, residents of a public housing center operated especially for this age group, were found to be generally satisfied insofar as their family relationships were concerned. That is, adjustments had been made and most were accepting their lots. Few if any wished to trade their present living arrangements for closer association with families. Loneliness was present and reported, but our research failed to investigate the extent to which our subjects had *chosen* to separate themselves from their family, or were refusing to respond (for whatever reasons) to overtures from family members. Nor can we know from these results how representative these cases are of older people in public housing. However, our findings indicate that such housing arrangements can provide opportunities for friendly association while allowing the person to live "independently" of family, apparently an important consideration within the value system of older people. At this stage in life — when people, through their own aging process, are typically losing friends and relatives, a Center such as this is capable of providing satisfying experiences in a peer group. Residents can enjoy "outside" company while at the same time engaging in dependable relationships within the complex. It would seem especially important for the morale and satisfaction of residents to have their apartment complex located in the inner city, to have an organized program of intra-project activities. Under these conditions the relative absence of family relationships will not be critical in the lives of oldsters.

17. The Blacklands of Gerontology*

JACQUELYNE JOHNSON JACKSON**

Previous visits to *The Blacklands of Gerontology* (Jackson 1967; 1971a) have focused largely upon a presentation and critique of selected literature pertinent to aging and aged blacks, emphasizing especially the paucity *and* inconclusive findings of much of the available data, emergent issues arising therefrom (such as those of relationships between and among race, aging, religion, family and kinship, and health, as well as methodological ones principally concerned with inadequate conceptualizations and collection and interpretation of the data), the usually low socioeconomic statuses of black aged, and critical research and social policy needs.

THE STATE OF THE LITERATURE

In general, *The Blacklands of Gerontology* are more fertile than they were two decades ago as there has been a continuing and slowly proliferating availability of more heterogeneous literature on black aged. More black subjects are being included in study populations containing white subjects, with a tendency (still conspicuously absent in some cases) of increasing sampling sizes to permit more sophisticated data analyses by race, as well as the very important trend of restricting samples to black subjects alone. This allows isolation of similarities and differences among processes of black aging, clearly recognizing (as many still do not) that blacks are highly variable.

A greater emphasis and concern is being given to minority aged (including blacks) by The Gerontological Society, as exemplified by its sponsorship of roundtable discussions on minorities at recent annual meetings and the special series of articles on elderly minorities in *The Gerontologist*, 11:26-98, 1971. The National Council on Aging has also pursued field work among minority elderly funded largely by the office of Economic Opportunity, and focused on them at its Annual Conference, March, 1971. The Institute of Gerontology at The Uni-

*Reprinted from *The International Journal of Aging and Human Development,* Vol. 2, 1971, pages 156-171 with permission of the author and the Baywood Publishing Company. Copyright © Baywood Publishing Co., Inc., 1971.
**Dr. Jackson is Associate Professor of Medical Sociology at the Duke University Medical Center.

versity of Michigan-Wayne State University shows increased inclusion of minority group students in training programs and recently held a Symposium on "Triple Jeopardy: The Plight of Age Minorities in America," April, 1971. The Gerontological Center at the University of Southern California has been making training contributions, sought involvement in various community programs, and developed a Workshop of Ethnicity, Mental Health, and Aging. The significant contributions of the U. S. Senate Special Committee on Aging under the direction of William Oriol include its temporary contract with Dr. Inabel Lindsay to provide a systematic review of available knowledge of black aged.

A small but growing band of black gerontologists and other blacks interested in the aged has emerged.* There has been continuing interest and activities underfoot by the National Urban League to conduct research on and promote concern for the black aged. There is a strong possibility that the Administration on Aging, U. S. Department of Health, Education, and Welfare, will fund, for the first time, a gerontological training program at a black institution (probably at Fisk University where adequate personnel are already available and/or Tennessee State University, both in Nashville) which should contribute significantly towards a reduction of the shortage of trained black researchers and service-providers.

A *Research Conference on Minority Group Aged in the South* is planned, to be funded by the National Institute of Child Health and Development, to permit a systematic assessment of the current status of research on the black aged, tentatively scheduled for early October, Nashville, Tennessee. Perhaps the most important development is the formation of the *National Caucus on the Black Aged* in November, 1970, under the leadership of Hobart C. Jackson (Chief Administrator, the Stephen

* I am often among those asked to identify black gerontologists and/or those behavorial scientists interested in aging. A partial listing would include Dr. Stanley H. Smith (Fisk University); Dr. James E. Blackwell (University of Massachusetts at Boston); Dr. Maurice Jackson (University of Southern California); Dr. Robert Staples (University of California, Irvine); Miss Gloria Walker and Mrs. Marguerite Howie (South Carolina State College); Dr. Wilbur Watson (Rutgers University and the Stephen Smith Geriatric Center, Philadelphia); Dr. Hubert Ross (Atlanta University); Dr. Jesse Gloster (Texas Southern University); Dr. Barbara Solomon (University of Southern California); Dr. James E. Conyers (Indiana State University, Terre Haute); Dr. Ralph H. Hines (Meharry Medical College); Dr. Adelbert H. Jenkins (New York University); Dr. Charles U. Smith (Florida A. and M. University); Dr. Floyd Wylie (Wayne State University); Dr. Robert Hill (National Urban League; Washington, D.C.); Dr. Inabel Lindsay (Washington, D.C.); Mr. Abraham Davis, Jr. (HEW, Washington, D.C.); Dr. Percil Stanford; and Mrs. Mercedee Thompson (St. Louis).

Smith Geriatric Center, Philadelphia) and Robert J. Kastenbaum (Director, Center for the Study of Death, Dying and Lethal Behavior, Wayne State University).

It is significant that those responsible for planning the forthcoming 1971 White House Conference on Aging failed to provide for policy formulations focusing specifically upon the acute problems and needs of minority group aged, especially those who are in "quadruple jeopardy" by being black and female and old and poor. This glaring omission particularly as it relates to critical needs in the areas of housing, income, health and retirement roles and activities, should be corrected. A step in this direction may well be a possible *National Conference on Black Aged,* tentatively scheduled for Washington, D.C., November, 1971. The organization of an effective and permanent "Committee of One Hundred Elderly Black Statesmen," composed largely of those sixty-five or more years of age who have had active professional and civic careers, could do much to spark the needed attention upon the deplorable plight of many black elderly. It would certainly provide a "Black House" of cogent policies for legislative and other remedies.

Despite the fertility of *The Blacklands of Gerontology,* certain critical research, training, and service needs remain extant. These have been identified, particular by Bourg (1971), Havighurst (1971), H. Jackson (1971), J. Jackson (1967; 1970; 1971a; 1971b; 1971c), Jenkins (1971), Kalish (1971), Kastenbaum (1971), and Kent (1971a; 1971b; 1971c), as well as the issue of the implications of recent black militancy on the psychological well-being of aged blacks dividing Elam (1970) and Solomon (1970). These attest to the need for carefully executed, intensive, interdisciplinary studies employing national, random samples of aging and aged blacks. Also needed are an enlarged cadre of gerontologists (especially black) focusing upon black aged, substantial training and research funds for this research, crucial improvements in the services available to black aged, and their satisfactory utilization of such services. Almost all of the behavioral scientists cited recognize the critical and varying impacts of racial discrimination upon aging.

This literature review, with some notable exceptions, is restricted to what has become available within the last several years, as well as certain projections about what is likely to be available within the next year. The search is not exhaustive, and additional information on existing and projected literature and demonstration and service projects would be particularly welcomed. The four areas to be investigated in this review are aging and: (a) health, life expectancy, and race; (b) psychology and race; (c) social patterns, policies, and resources; and (d) additional related information.

HEALTH, LIFE EXPECTANCY, AND RACE

The bulk of the literature under consideration relates directly or indirectly to: (1) physical and mental health; (2) factors affecting the delivery and utilization of health-care services; (3) racial differentials in body age, life expectancy, and mortality; and (4) aged sexual behavior.

Physical and mental health. All available data tend to suggest that black males seventy-five or more years of age tend to be in better health than their female or white counterparts. This fact may be attributed to the much earlier deaths of black males who were physiologically, psychologically, and socioculturally less advantaged. Aging blacks are afflicted by various health disabilities associated with increasing age. However there is still need for a careful study of their physical and mental health in later years.

The National Center for Health Statistics has published some limited but useful data on health patterns of blacks. Included in the most recent National Health Surveys, beginning around 1959, are statistics from medical examinations performed upon a probability sample of noninstitutionalized persons, eighteen to seventy-nine years of age, and later with the Health Interview Surveys. Plans are underfoot to examine the available data systematically. Table 1 provides some selected data on health characteristics of black and white males and females in varying age groupings. These data from the National Health Examination Survey tend to support the expected racial variations in health conditions. They also reveal certain interesting lineal and curvilineal variations by age, sex, and race.

Perhaps one of the most impressive statistics is the finding that a far larger proportion of blacks of both sexes needed dental care than was true of whites — impressive if it points towad the establishment of "Denticare" for the aged. However, the average simplified oral hygiene index is better for black males, seventy-five to seventy-nine years of age than for white males of corresponding ages. Also *fewer* edentulous persons, sixty-five to seventy-four years of age, were found among the blacks than the whites.

Rheumatoid arthritis was more prevalent among females than among the males of both races. With the exception of black males,

osteoarthritis tended to increase with age. For the black males, osteoarthritis was curvilineally related to age.

TABLE 1
Selected statistics from the National Health Survey,
1960-1962, by race, sex, and age*

Health characteristic	Black males	Black females	White males	White females
Average simplified oral hygiene index				
Total, 18-79 years	2.4−	2.0−	1.7−	1.3−
55-64 years	2.8−	2.7−	1.9−	1.4−
65-74 years	3.3−	2.5−	2.3−	1.6−
75-79 years	2.7−	2.1−	4.6−	1.5−
Mean no. of decayed, missing, and filled teeth, including edentulous				
persons, Total, 18-79 years	12.9	15.7	20.6	21.9
55-64 years	18.4	25.4	21.2	26.2
65-74 years	23.7	26.9	25.2	27.9
Prevalence rates of edentulous persons				
Total, 18-79 years	7.8	17.7	14.3	20.6
55-64 years	19.5	37.0	29.1	39.1
65-74 years	36.3	45.8	60.7	52.8
Average periodontal index, Total, 18-79 years	1.8−	1.4−	1.3−	0.8−
Percent of dentulous adults needing				
early dental care, Total, 18-79 years	65.9	57.5	42.9	32.7
55-64 years	78.5	79.2	46.4	31.3
Mean serum cholesterol levels,*				
55-64 years	230	243	234	265
65-74 years	224	266	230	267
Prevalence of rheumatoid arthritis, Rate/100 Adults, Total, 18-79 years	1.5	4.7	1.7	4.6
Prevalence rates (Per 100 adults) for all degrees, Osteoarthritis,				
Total 18-79 years	39.4	34.5	37.8	37.8
55-64 years	66.3	66.4	63.4	75.9
65-74 years	55.6	75.9	77.5	85.7
75-79 years	78.6	78.0	81.1	90.6
Prevalence of definite heart disease				
% Total, 18-79 years	23.8	24.8	11.5	12.5
% 55-64 years	41.6	52.2	22.5	23.7
% 65-74 years	56.9	70.1	31.3	43.5
% 75-79 years	32.3	69.5	39.3	44.8

TABLE 1
Selected statistics from the National Health Survey
1960-1962, by race sex, and age — cont'd

Health Characteristic	Black males	Black females	White males	White females
Prevalence rates (per 100 adults) of definite coronary heart disease,				
Total, 18-79 years	3.2	2.0	3.8	2.1
55-64 years	5.7	5.5	10.3	4.7
65-74 years	3.4	5.1	12.2	8.2
Prevalence rates of definite hypertensive heart disease,				
% Total, 18-79 years	19.1	22.2	6.5	9.8
% 55-64 years	33.1	46.4	11.7	19.5
% 65-74 years	50.2	66.4	16.3	37.5
% 75-79 years	32.3	69.5	24.0	37.1
Percent reactive to the KRP syphilis test				
Total, 18-79 years	22.9	16.3	2.3	2.1
55-64 years	31.0	35.2	3.5	4.1
65-74 years	32.6	13.1	4.0	2.4
Mean systolic blood pressures in mm, Hg				
Total, 18-79 years	136.2	136.3	130.6	129.4
55-64 years	148.3	155.7	139.7	145.8
65-74 years	158.3	175.2	147.1	159.2
75-79 years	156.5	162.8	154.1	156.5
Mean diastolic blood pressures in mm, Hg.				
Total, 18-79 years	83.3	83.2	78.3	77.5
55-64 years	89.3	91.9	82.6	84.2
65-74 years	86.9	89.7	80.5	83.3
75-79 years	84.9	82.9	78.9	79.1
Mean blood hematocrit, ml.%				
Total, 18-79 years	45.8+.	40.8+.	46.5+.	42.5+.
55-64 years	44.2+.	42.1+.	46.3+.	42.1+.
65-74 years	44.1+.	41.9+.	45.9+.	43.3+.
Mean glucose levels in mg. %				
Total, 18-79 years	118.5	126.1	115.4	126.5
55-64 years	131.7	141.9	130.2	145.5
65-74 years	150.8	166.2	139.0	159.5
75-79 years	201.1	187.2	151.6	177.5

Distance Vision, 20/20 or better Uncorrected Acuity, Rate/100				
adults, Total, 18-79 years	60.0	52.9	57.3	50.4
55-64 years	23.0	12.9	25.1	17.8
65-74 years	15.3	10.2	8.8	2.4
Near Vison, 14/14 or better Uncorrected Acuity, Rate/100				
adults, Total, 18-79 years	47.8	45.6	47.3	26.7
Hearing Level (−5dB or less at 1000 cycles/second) Rate/100				
population, Total, 18-79 years	62.3	63.2	56.1	60.8
55-64 years	38.8	47.7	44.8	36.1
65-74 years	27.7	32.6	25.1	24.2
75-79 years	30.1	10.2	10.2	8.9
Prevalence of Self-reported Nervous Breakdowns				
% Total, 18-64 years	2.8	10.4	3.2	6.0
% 18-79 years	4.2	24.4	5.6	11.6
% 65-74 years	8.2	23.5	5.2	9.7

− = the higher the score the less desirable; + = the lower, the less desirable.
* All data projected for the United States population, 18-79 years of age, with the specific exception of that for mean serum cholesterol levels, which applies only to the sampled whites and the Southern blacks in the Health Examination Survey.
Source: U. S. Public Health Service, National Center for Health Statistics. "Vital and Health Statistics," Data from the National Health Survey," Series 11, #3, 5, 6, 7, 9, 10, 12, 13, 15, 16, 17, 18, 22, 23, 24, 25, 26, 27, 34, 36, and 37."

Definite heart disease was more prevalent among blacks than whites and females than males, with the exception of those seventy-five to seventy-nine years of age. Coronary heart disease was more prevalent among whites, while hypertensive heart disease was more typical of blacks. Curvilineal rates by age characterized coronary and hypertensive heart patterns among the blacks and the latter among white females. Mean serum cholesterol levels were higher for females than for males, whites than for blacks.

The proportion of subjects reactive to the KRP test for syphilis tended to increase with age among all but white females. Mean blood pressure rates were curvilineal with age among blacks and white females. The systolic was lineal and the diastolic, curvilineal among white males. Both black and white males at all age levels had higher mean blood hemocrit levels than was the case for the females, with the latter displaying increases in the later age stages as opposed to decreases among the remaining groups.

Diabetic conditions were more typical among blacks. Mean glucose levels were higher than among the whites for those seventy-five to seventy-nine years of age, with definite lineal increases by age among each group. Black male rates were lower than those of black females until age seventy-five; then the pattern reversed.

In general, a higher proportion of blacks in the late stages maintained better visual acuity and hearing levels than did whites. The hearing levels of black males, especially those of seventy-five to seventy-nine years of age, tended to be much better than those of their white counterparts. Racial differentiations among the females were not as clear.

Self-reported nervous breakdown data revealed higher proportions among black females than any of the others at all age levels. Special attention should be given to eliciting causal factors contributing to almost 25 percent of black females, fifty-five or more years of age, reporting a nervous breakdown. Some might argue that such self-reported data is unreliable, but it is important to investigate the *meaning* of a situation assigned by the actors involved as well as the so-called objective investigators.

Other data on such variables as chronic conditions, hospitalization, medical visits, and mortality are also available and under systematic investigation. Walker (1970) utilized secondary data in her investigation of relationships between reported chronic ailments and socioeconomic status of the inner-city aged of Nashville, Tennessee. Most of the black and white subjects reported few ailments, but those most often reported revealed certain sex and social class differences. Modal ailments were heart and circulatory disorders among the males, arthritic and other bone disorders among black females, and both skin and arthritic and other bone disorders among white females.

Hypotheses suggested for future investigations are worth noting: (a) the "lower the SES level, the greater the likelihood of a subject feeling ill; (b) there is no significant variation by race for most chronic ailments; (c) where there is such a difference, black females are far more likely to report (or to have) ailments at least partially induced by stress and strain; and therefore (d) both blacks and females are more likely to be affected adversely by the external environment than are white males." (Walker, pp. 50-51.)

The higher rates of perceived nervous breakdowns among black females have already been noted, as well as their greater institutionalized rates in state mental institutions in the late age stages. Mental health in old age may be affected in a number of ways. One of the most important issues now being raised in the literature in this respect is the aforementioned one of the impacts of increased black militancy upon the self-images of older blacks. Moore's (1971) failure to realize what is probably the compatibility of Elam (1970) and Solomon's (1970) positions may be due to a tendency to overgeneralize about blacks. Both positions make sense; they must be applied to the subpopulations rather than the total population. A continuing issue about the mental health of the aged is that of their ability to cope with the addition of age discrimination after having already been subjected to racial discrimination throughout their lives. Careful study is also needed here, for data are highly inconclusive (cf. Jackson, 1967 and Moore, 1971).

Factors affecting the delivery and utilization of health-care services. The work of Fabrega, et al. (1969) and Gordon and Rehr (1969) point to some of the problems affecting adequate delivery and utilization of such services. What is most important are their stresses upon the attitudes of care-givers in making distinctions and certain apparent ethnic differences in reaching out for assistance when in need. Probably the most important implication is that black aged, in particular, need increasing awareness of the medical system so as to adapt better to it and make it adapt better to them.

Racial differences in body age, life expectancy, and mortality. The most exciting for me is Morgan's (1968) finding that differential physical aging among black and white males tends to justify assumptions that black males are indeed old earlier than white males:

> Negro males of 30 calendar years on have an older body age than their white counterparts. The biggest jump in body age is between 21 and 30, after which Negroes hold a 5-yr. body-age differential until 60 (then increasing further) (p. 598).

Such a finding provides further support for differential minimum age-eligibility requirements for recipients of *Old-Age Assistance, Survivors, Disability, and Health Insurance* (OASDHI) so as to reflect racial differentials in life expectancies (Jackson, 1970; 1971c) and, now, body ages.

Additional support is garnered in Demeny and Gingrich's (1967) careful critique of American black-white mortality differentials:

Unless it is assumed that age patterns of death for United States Negroes were extremely deviant from those found in populations with reliable census and vital statistics, one must conclude that the official figures grossly underestimate early childhood mortality for Negroes, at least for the period, 1910-1940. It follows that, during those decades, *Negro-white mortality differentials in terms of expectation of life at birth were also substantially higher than is suggested by the official estimates* (p. 820, *italics added*).

Finally, Hill (1971) has pointed out that recently the life expectancy for black males has *decreased*. That may be affected by the increases noted in infant mortality among blacks in certain metropolitan areas over the past decade.

Aged sexual behavior. In their mortality and survival comparisons of black eunuchs and intact persons in a mentally retarded population in Kansas, Hamilton and Mestler (1969) suggested that the eunuchs tended to survive longer, but the significant difference found among the comparable whites did not appear among the blacks:

> The difference between eunuchs and intact men with regard to duration of life was significantly more in whites than in non-whites (13.5 vs. 3 years). The detrimental effects of testicular fuction upon viability, and the benefit from orchiectomy, may prove to be more in white than in non-white males (p. 410).

As in other studies, the small sampling size of the blacks tended to prohibit more elaborate data analyses.

Pfeiffer, Verwoerdt, and Wang (1968; 1969) included blacks in their analyses of aged sexual behavior, most often without racial separation of the data. They held that the "Negro and white Ss did not differ significantly from one another in respect to age-related patterns of sexual interest and activity" (p. 197). If so, their findings are supportive of other accumulating data which refute the notion of "black sexual bestiality." They did indicate the need to study subjects under sixty years of age, and especially women, so as to amass more information on sexual behavior and aging. It would be very interesting to determine whether earlier decreases in sexual behavior tended to occur among black females then white females when they are subjected to more years without a spouse.

Psychology and Race

Most psychological literature on the aged has avoided the utilization of black subjects. Where they have been utilized, the problems under investigation have been perceived as unaffected by race. Recent literature has shifted some attention to the dynamics of race and age, with the most significant being that of Kastenbaum (1971), Jenkins (1971), and Brunswick (1969-1970).

Kastenbaum's (1971) investigation of differential attitudes toward future optimism and subjective life expectancies among young black and old whites is most intriguing. Noting the foreshortened time perspective typical of deprived, depressed, aged, or dying subjects, he has applied this model to *hard-core unemployed* black males recruited for participation in a job opportunity program (Teahan and Kastenbaum, 1970). Comparisons of those who remained in and who left the program at one and six month intervals led him to the formulation of an hypothesis under further investigation: "there is at least a partial functional equivalence between the phenomenologic world of young-and-black and the old-and-white." Incidentally, this study also appears promising in the accumulation of more data attesting to the earlier *oldness* occurring among black, than among white males.

Jenkins (1971) has employed an Eriksonian model in providing therapeutic treatment to a young black male experiencing life-adjustment difficulties, and has suggested that racial factors prohibiting adequate achievement of ego integrity in the earlier years are dysfunctionally related to mature adaptation to old age. Thus, he emphasizes the necessity to reform society so as to promote healthier aging among blacks.

Brunswick's (1969-70) analysis of black and white intergenerational differences in outlook on life, interracial tolerance and hostility, and attitudes toward advocacy of violence note especially differential attitudes among younger and older subjects. She has stressed her belief that "education is at least as important a divider, or determiner of generations, as age" (p. 369), and her article is fraught with implications for further investigations of possible generation gaps by age and other variables among blacks and whites. I suspect that self-concept may well be an important divider among blacks.

Byrne's, et al. (1969) findings about the relative universality of responding positively to strangers expressing attitudes similar to one's own and negatively to those bearing dissimilar attitudes portends significant implications for relationships in direct services to the elderly especially, and could, perhaps, be tied in with the Thune (1969) studies of racial attitudes among white and black subjects in a Nashville Senior Citizens Center.

SOCIAL PATTERNS, POLICIES, AND RESOURCES

The bulk of the recent literature falls within the areas of social patterns, policies, and resources. Demographic aspects are also of interest, given the projected data from the U. S. Bureau of the Census (and a possibility that a special report on black aged in the fifty largest cities may be forthcoming from that agency).

In 1970, the reported 1,565,897 blacks, sixty-five or more years of age, represented an increase of about one-third percent over those reported in 1960. As expected, most (56.7%) were females, and most (60.8%) resided in the South. North Dakota had the fewest (twelve males and ten females), while New York had the largest number of females (67,509), and Texas, the largest number of males (50,965). Table 2 contains data on the proportion of blacks sixty-five or more years of age within each state. As shown, West Virginia had both the largest proportion of males and females, while Hawaii and North Dakota had the least.

Hill (1971) has detailed available recent demographic characteristics of the black aged, noting especially their patterns of residence, marital status and household compositions, income, education, employment, and health. Of special significance is the fact that he plans to provide a succinct demographic analysis when sufficient data are available. Herman Brotman (Administration on Aging) is also in the process of continuing his highly competent compilation of statistical data on the aged, including black aged, and will be providing information particularly about changes within the last decade. Finally, Inabel Lindsay (Member, Task Force on Problems of the Aging, appointed by President Richard M. Nixon, 10 October 1969) was in the process of summarizing available information on black aged in her role as a temporary consultant to the U. S. Senate Special Committee on Aging (a role which occurred as one of the responses to the *National Caucus on the*

TABLE 2
Percentages of persons 65 or more years of age
within the total black population, by sex and state, 1970

State	Males	Females	State	Males	Females
West Virginia	14.2	13.7	Michigan	5.4	5.9
Arkansas	11.8	12.5	Maryland	5.3	6.0
Oklahoma	9.6	10.8	Illinois	5.2	5.9
Mississippi	9.3	10.1	Oregon	5.2	5.2
Kentucky	9.3	11.1	Wyoming	4.9	6.5
Alabama	8.6	10.3	District of Columbia	4.8	6.2
Tennessee	8.5	9.6	Massachusetts	4.7	6.0
Kansas	7.9	9.6	New Jersey	4.7	5.8
Missouri	7.8	8.7	Rhode Island	4.7	6.7
Louisiana	7.5	8.8	New Mexico	4.7	4.9
Texas	7.5	8.5	New York	4.5	5.8
Pennsylvania	7.1	7.9	California	4.3	5.5
Virginia	6.7	8.2	Idaho	4.2	3.9
Iowa	6.7	7.6	Montana	4.1	5.5
Arizona	6.6	6.6	Maine	4.0	5.9
Ohio	6.4	7.0	Colorado	3.8	5.9
North Carolina	6.3	7.8	Washington	3.7	4.4
Georgia	6.2	8.5	Utah	3.6	6.9
Florida	6.0	6.9	Connecticut	3.5	4.5
Indiana	6.0	6.8	Wisconsin	3.2	3.4
South Carolina	5.7	7.7	South Dakota	3.1	4.0
Delaware	5.7	6.5	Nevada	3.0	3.2
Nebraska	5.6	6.5	New Hampshire	2.5	3.2
Vermont	5.6	6.9	Alaska	1.1	1.4
Minnesota	5.4	6.3	North Dakota	0.8	1.0
			Hawaii	0.8	1.2

Source of raw data: U. S. Bureau of the Census. Advance Report, United States, General Population Characteristics, PC(V2)-1, U. S. Department of Commerce, Washington, D. C., February, 1971.

Black Aged). All of these compilations will attest to the continued gener-ally low socioeconomic statuses of black aged, and, perhaps, to a slightly rising rate of institutionalization among them.

Utilization of Census and the National Center for Health Statistics data clearly point to the need, as Kent has implied (1971a), for substan-tially enlarged sample sizes involving blacks, so as to permit far more sophisticated data analyses. Also, given the nature of the times and the need to "check out" the rapidity of change, national data collected at least five-year intervals (instead of decennially) and reported sepa-rately (i.e., not as "non-white") for blacks would be of great value. The racial separation apparent in the last few years is a welcome step in the right direction.

Familial, kinship, and retirement roles. Major research developments include the likelihood of publication of data from the Philadelphia Aged Services Project under the direction of Donald P. Kent, and from J. Jackson's "Roles and resources of older, urban blacks" (should I cease writing reviews!) within the next year. Such publications will tend to document specific kinship patterns, as well as other data, among urban blacks in Philadelphia, Pennsylvania, and Durham, North Carolina, respectively. As far as I know no similar studies involving rural aged blacks are underway (in fact, I have not yet located a recent research study on them). These sets of expected publications will probably emphasize strengths and weaknesses of specific subgroups of aged blacks, and the Philadelphia series will provide racial comparisons, and emphasize the feasibility of a network of "caretakers" often found and trained among deprived populations. I wish to again stress my belief that the Philadelphia study can provide an excellent model of "how-to-do-research," for its concerns have not been merely with collecting data, but with providing assistance to the subjects!

My data on kinship patterns and processes among predominantly low-income urban black aged reveal primarily their effective kinship newtorks or substitutes. They also provide specific information on relationships with parents, children, siblings, grandchildren, cousins, and best friends. The preliminary report on grandparent-grandchild interaction (Jackson, 1971c) shows that the grandparental subjects preferred grandchildren living near them (but not with them) and younger (rather than older) grandchildren. Relationships among their affectional closeness, value consensus, and identification with their grandchildren were unclear, but preferences did appear to be related to particular grandchild types. The data also suggested the implausibility of a general postulation of a "generation gap," because age proved to be a highly insufficient variable, particularly among the males. The findings also debunked the usual myths about disintegrating black families, while sustaining the picture of the important roles many of them actually serve as "Individual Departments of Welfare" when the society fails to provide adequate education, employment, income, and housing for themselves, their children, and their children's children.

"Sex and social class variations in black older parent-adult child relationships" (Jackson, 1971b) did reveal certain significant differences found among a pilot sample of largely middle-class aged blacks in

Durham. While most of the parental subjects received some instrumental assistance from children, middle-class parents were more likely
than lower-class parents to receive this assistance, and, as expected,
daughters tended to be more likely than sons to provide it. The study
also suggests the need for greater analysis of parental-child sex preferences in black families.

A most impressive research study in process, particularly by virtue of
its utilization of a national sample (3,340 whites and 487 blacks) is that
undertaken by Rubenstein (1971). His comparisons of the social participation — largely familial and kinship, among aged whites and
blacks has led him to conclude that there are no racial differences in the
proportion of those living alone and isolated and in their emotional
state of well-being or morale. He does expect to report finally that the
blacks fare more poorly as measured by education, occupation, income, and employment, which is, of course, in agreement with existing
findings. Lambing's (1969) study of retired blacks in an urban setting
in Florida contributes, as well, to a growing body of highly localized
data on aged blacks.

Fillenbaum's (1971) report of relationships between job and retirement attitudes found among nonacademic employees in a North
Carolina university and medical center indicated that those relationships were quite minimal. She concluded that "only where work holds
the central organizing position in a person's life (which here it does not)
should job attitudes influence retirement attitudes" (p. 247). What is of
greater significance for present purposes is the finding that the white
and black subjects could not be racially distinguished by their attitudes
toward retirement. However, she did find a racially significant difference in that the negative association between achievement (i.e., "possible acquisition of further knowledge and skills") and retirement typical
of the whites was not typical of the blacks. I could not determine
whether this was a spurious finding since she provided no *specific*
occupational data on the subjects by race. However, almost all, if not all,
of the lower echelon "housekeeping" personnel in the populations
under study were black, and almost none of the remaining
nonacademic employees were in the upper echelon slots at the time
that the data were collected. In other words, further investigation of
the finding is warranted.

Housing and social resources. A preliminary report from an analysis of
impacts of housing relocation among older blacks (Jackson, 1970)
revealed many similarities among applicants to an age-segregated pub-

lic housing complex, as measured by the Carp Housing Schedule (Carp, 1965). The most significant finding is that of the differences separating the successful and nonsuccessful applicants. Briefly, those who were male, younger, and married were more successful, portending grave implications for black aged, for, in some sense, those who were the least deprived were those most likely to gain acceptance by the white admission agents. It would be unfortunate if the usual pattern of rejecting those blacks most in need of educational, employment, and other opportunities comes to characterize the aged as well.

Bourg (1971) has issued a preliminary report on his ongoing investigation of "Life styles and mobility patterns of older persons in Nashville-Davidson County" (Tennessee). This study is primarily concerned with a description of various settings surrounding the elderly and with developmental processes involved in their psychological and sociocultural aging. Findings from his sample of 297 black aged (no other group is under investigation) emphasize their conspicuous diversity "in the functions provided by their social relationships" and their mobility differences. The second phase utilizes a panel of subjects to obtain more detailed information on "the relationship between mobility patterns with small boundaries and dependence on the immediate environment." His study is of special value in that the restriction to blacks only helped to focus upon their differences. He calls attention to the need to explore "the differences amid the similarities" and "the similar components which emerge among the differences."

Lopata's (1970) study of "Social relations of widows in black and white urban communities" could well benefit from utilizing at least a twofold comparative model: (a) racial comparisons with whites, as she has done; and (b) comparisons holding race constant. Her characterization of the black widows tends to fall within the traditional pathological mold, and one cannot determine readily if the widows themselves were fairly interpreted or if the interpreter unduly influenced her data. Her conceptualization of black widows are being untrained in "skills which facilitate the conversion of strangers into friends" and "often unable to enter any social relation with a great deal of intimacy" (pp. 29-30) represented her value judgement and, perhaps, attests anew to the critical importance of black people performing their own research in such cases. We are given no indication of the variety of black widows located in the Chicago Metropolitan Area.

H. Jackson (1971) has aptly summarized priorities requiring attention to promote the welfare of the aged. The greatest need is for an adequate income, with a minimal floor of $6,000 for an individual and

$9,000 per married couple for those sixty-five or more years of age. When necessary, annual adjustments should be made to maintain the equivalent of this income. Other needs given high priority included employment, health, and a nationwide network of community services. In his role as a private citizen and as National Chairman, the National Caucus on the Black Aged, he is committed to strive to achieve these goals.

Related Literature

In addition to suggested references covering the topics discussed above, the bibliography contains a section on "additional related literature" pertinent to those areas. They are primarily concerned with the "generation gap," political involvement of the aged, and the provision of social services, such as in health and transportation.

Summary

This third review of social gerontological literature on black aged has focused largely upon recent developments in available data on health and longevity (including body age), psychology and race, and social patterns, policies and resources, as well as related organizational developments. An increasing number of investigators of and investigations on black aged have appeared within the last few years, but none have yet embarked upon a clearly mandated highly sophisticated, interdisciplinary study involving a *large*, random sample of aging and aged blacks throughout the nation. Also, few of these investigators have been black, but the possibility of the development of a social gerontological training program in research at Fisk University may reduce this problem somewhat, as has, indeed, the significant contributions already made by such institutions as Duke University, The University of Michigan, Wayne State University, and the University of Southern California.

There has been far less interest recently in cataloguing the objective social conditions, and far more interest in studying the processes of aging and the specific environmental conditions of black aged. Greater attention has been given to investigations of the influence of race upon aging (e.g., Kastenbaum, 1971: Jenkins, 1971) and upon differences among black aged (e.g., Bourg, 1971; Jackson, 1970; 1971b). More progress has also been made in identifying commonalities among black and white aging and aged persons (e.g., in Kent's Philadelphia Aged Services Project; Fillenbaum, 1971; Pfeiffer, et al., 1969). Two of the most critical research needs are mental illness among the black aged, and trends in the use or non-use of nursing homes by the black aged.

The formation of the National Caucus on the Black Aged in November, 1970, was very significant. It may well serve as a viable catalyst in producing desired research, training, and services for black and other aged Americans.

While it is no longer true that almost nothing is known about black aged, it is still true that we've got a long way to go! It would be helpful if some of the research, training, and service needs already identified here and elsewhere were executed with greater speed. Finally, it would be extremely helpful if Nathan Shock were to extend his bibliographic captions to include a section on "Minority Group Aged."

SELECTED BIBLIOGRAPHY

I. HEALTH, LIFE EXPECTANCY AND RACE

Conley, Ronald W.: "Labor force loss due to disability." Public Health Reports, 84:291-298, 1969.

Demeny, Paul, and Paul Gingrich: " A reconsideration of Negro-white mortality differentials in the United States." *Demography,* 4:820-837, 1967.

Elam, Lloyd C.: "Critical factors for mental health in aging black populations." Paper delivered at the Workshop of Ethnicity, Mental Health, and Aging, Los Angeles, 1970.

Fabrega, Horacio, Jr., Richard J. Moore, and John R. Strawn: "Low income medical problem patients: some medical and behavioral features." *Journal of Health and Social Behavior,* 10:334-343, 1969.

Gordon, Barbara, and Helen Rehr: "Selectivity biases in delivery of hospital social services." *Social Service Review,* 43: 35-41, 1969.

Hamilton, James B., and Gordon F. Mestler: "Mortality and survival; comparison of eunuchs with intact men and women in a mentally retarded population." *Journal of Gerontology,* 24:395-411, 1969.

Metropolitan Life Insurance Company: "Trends in mortality of non-whites." *Statistical Bulletin,* 51:5-8. 1970.

Morgan, Robert F.: "The adult growth examination: preliminary comparisons of physical aging in adults by sex and race." Perceptual and motor skills, 27: 595-599, 1968.

Pfeiffer, Eric, Adriann Verwoerdt, and Hsioh-Shan Wang. "The natural history of sexual behavior in a biologically advantaged group of aged individuals." *Journal of Gerontology,* 21: 193-198, 1969.

Pfeiffer, Eric, Adriann Verwoerdt, and Hsioh-Shan Wang: "Sexual behavior in aged men and women." Archives of General Psychiatry, 19:753-758, 1968.

Solomon, Barbara: "Ethnicity, mental health and the older black aged." Gerontological Center, University of Southern California, Los Angeles, 1970.

U.S. Department of Health, Education, and Welfare, Public Health Service, National Center for Health Statistics: "Vital and health statistics, Data from the National Health Survey" U.S. Government Printing Office, Washington, D.C.

—: "Binocular visual acuity of adults, United States, 1960-1962," Series 11, Number 3; 1964.

—: "Binocular visual acuity of adults by region and selected demographic characteristics, United States, 1960-1962," Series 11, Number 25; 1967.

—: "Blood glucose levels in adults, United States, 1960-1962," Series 11, Number 18, 1966.

—: "Blood pressure as it relates to physique, blood glucose, and serum cholesterol, United States 1960-1962," Series 11, Number 34, 1969.

—: "Blood pressure of adults by race and area, United States, 1960-1962," Series 11, Number 5, 1964.

—: "Chronic conditions and limitations of activity and mobility, United States, July, 1965-June, 1967," Series 10, Number 61, 1971.

—: "Coronary heart disease in adults, United States, 1960-1962," Series 11, Number 10, 1965.

—: "Decayed, missing, and filled teeth in adults, United States, 1960-1962," Series 11, Number 23, 1967.

—: "Differentials in health characteristics by color, United States, July, 1965-June, 1967," Series 10, Number 56, 1969.

—: "Family use of health services, United States, July, 1963-June, 1964," Series 10, Number 55, 1969.

—: "Findings on the serologic test for syphilis in adults, United States, 1960-1962," Series 11, Number 9, 1965.

—: "Hearing levels on adults by race, region, and area of residence, United States, 1960-1962," Series 11, Number 26, 1967.

—: "Heart disease in adults, United States, 1960-1962," Series 11, Number 6, 1964.

—: "Hypertension and hypertensive heart disease in adults, United States, 1960-1962," Series 11, Number 13, 1966.

—: "Mean blood hematocrit of adults, United States, 1960-1962," Series 11, Number 24, 1967.

—: "Need for dental care among adults, United States, 1960-1962," Series 11, Number 36, 1970.

—: "Oral hygiene in adults, United States, 1960-1962," Series 11, Number 16, 1966.

—: "Periodontal disease in adults, United States, 1960-1962," Series 11, Number 12, 1965.

—: "Persons hospitalized by number of hospital episodes and days in a year, United States, July, 1965-June, 1966," Series 10, Number 50, 1969.

—: "Persons injured and disability days due to injury, United States, July, 1965-June, 1967," Series 10, Number 58, 1970.

—: "Prevalence of osteoarthritis in adults by age, sex, race, and geographic area, United States, 1960-1962," Series 11, Number 15, 1966.

—: "Prevalence of selected impairments, United States, July, 1963-June, 1965," Series 10, Number 48, 1968.

—: "Rheumatoid arthritis in adults, United States, 1960-1962," Series 11, November 17, 1966.

—: "Selected dental findings in adults by age, race, and sex, United States, 1960-1962," Series 11, Number 7, 1965.

—: "Serum Cholesterol levels of adults, United States, 1960-1962," Series 11, Number 22, 1967.

—: "Selected symptoms of psychological distress, United States," Series 11, Number 37, 1970.

—: "Total loss of teeth in adults, United States, 1960-1962," Series 11, Number 27, 1967.

—: "Volume of physican visits, United States, July, 1966-June, 1967," Series 10, Number 49, 1968.

Walker, Gloria V.: "The relationship between socioeconomic status and chronic ailments of the aged in Nashville, Tennessee." Unpublished master's thesis, Fisk University, Nashville, Tennessee, 1970.

II. PSYCHOLOGY AND RACE

Brunswick, Ann F.: "What generation gap? A comparison of some generation differences among blacks and whites." *Social Problems,* 17:358-370, 1969-1970

Byrne, Donn, William Griffitt, William Hudgins, and Keith Reeves: "Attitude similarity-dissimilarity and attraction: generality beyond the college sophomore." *The Journal of Social Psychology,* 79:155-161, 1969.

Jenkins, Adelbert H.: "Growth crisis in a young black man: its relationship to family and aging." Paper presented at the annual meeting of the Eastern Psychological Association, New York City, 1971.

Kalish, Richard A.: "A gerontological look at ethnicity, human capacities, and individual adjustment." *The Gerontologist,* 11:78-87, 1971.

Kastenbaum, Robert J.: "Time without a future: on the functional equivalence between young-and-black and aged-and-white." Paper presented at the annual meeting of the Eastern Psychological Association, New York City, 1971.

Teahan, John, and Robert Kastenbaum: "Subjective Life Expectancy and Future Time Perspective as Predictors of Job Success in the 'Hard-Core Unemployed.'" Omega, 1, No. 3, 189-200, 1970.

Thune, Jeanne M.: "Group portrait in black and white." Senior Citizens, Inc., Nashville, Tenneessee, 1969.

III. SOCIAL PATTERNS, POLICIES AND RESOURCES

Bourg, Carroll: "The changing environment of older persons." Paper presented at the 35th annual meeting of the Association of Social and Behavioral Scientists, Montgomery, Alabama, 1971.

Cohen, Elias S.: "Welfare policies for the aged poor: a contradiction." Paper delivered at the Symposium on Triple Jeopardy: The Plight of Aged Minorities in America. The Institute of Gerontology, The University of Michigan-Wayne State University, Detroit, April, 1971.

Fillenbaum, Gerda G.: "On the relation between attitude to work and attitude to retirement," *Journal of Gerontology.* 26: 244-248, 1971.

Havighurst, Robert J.: "Report of a Conference on Flexible Careers." *The Gerontologist,* 11: 21-25, 1971.

Hays, David S., and Morris Wisotsky; "The aged offender: a review of the literature and two current studies from the New York State Division of Parole." *Journal of the American Geriatric Society,* 17: 1064-1073, 1969.

Hill, Robert: "A profile of the black aged." Paper delivered at the Symposium on Triple Jeopardy: The Plight of Aged Minorities in America. The Institute of Gerontology, The University of Michigan-Wayne State University, Detroit, April 1971.

Jackson, Hobart C.: "National goals and priorities in the social welfare of the aging." *The Gerontologist.* 11:88-94, 1971.

Jackson, Jacquelyne J.: "Social gerontology and the Negro: a review." *The Gerontologist,* 7:168-178, 1967.

Jackson, Jacquelyne J.: "Social impacts of housing relocation upon urban, low income, black aged." Paper delivered at the annual meeting of the Gerontological Society, Toronto, Canada, 1970.

Jackson, Jacquelyne J.: "Negro aged: toward needed research in social gerontology." *The Gerontologist,* 11:52-57, 1971a.

Jackson, Jacquelyne J.: "Sex and social class variations in black older parent-adult child relationships." *Aging and Human Development,* in press, 1971b.

Jackson, Jacquelyne J.: "Aged blacks: A potpourrie in the direction of reduction of inequities." Phylon, in press, 1971c.

Jackson, Jacquelyne J.: "Compensatory care for aged minorities," Paper delivered at the Symposium on Triple Jeopardy: The Plight of Aged Minorities in America. The Institute of Gerontology, the University of Michigan-Wayne State University, April, 1971d.

Kent, Donald P.: "The delivery of welfare services: reordering the system," Paper deliverd at the Symposium on Triple Jeopardy: The Plight of Aged Minorities in America. The Institute of Gerontology, the University of Michigan-Wayne State University, April, 1971b.

Kent, Donald P.: "The elderly in minority groups: variant patterns of aging." *The Gerontologist,* 11:26-29, 1971a.

Kent, Donald P.: "The Negro aged." The Gerontologist, 11:48-51, 1971c.

Lambing, Mary L.: "A study of retired older Negroes in an urban setting." Unpublished Ph.D. dissertation, University of Florida, Gainesville, 1969.

Lopata, Helena Z: "Social and family relations of black and white widows in urban communities." Administration on Aging Publication #25, U.S. Department of Health, Education and Welfare; 1970.

Moore, Joan W.: "Situational factors affecting minority aging." *The Gerontologist,* 11:88-93, 1971.

Rubenstein, Daniel I.: "An examination of social participation found among a national sample of black and white elderly." *Aging and Human Development,* 2, 1971.

The Gerontologist, 11:26-98, 1971.

IV. ADDITIONAL RELATED REFERENCES

(African aged)

Arth, Malcolm J.: "An interdisciplinary view of the aged in Ibo culture." *Journal of Geriatric Psychiatry,* 2:33-39, 1968.

Arth, Malcolm J.: "Ideals and behavior: a comment on Ibo respect patterns." *The Gerontologist,* 8:242-244, 1968.

Shelton, Austin J.: "Ibo child-raising eldership and dependence: further notes for gerontologists and others." *The Gerontologist,* 8:236-241, 1968.

(Other references)
Adams, Bert N.: "Isolation, function, and beyond: American kinship in the 1960's." *Journal of Marriage and the Family,* 32:575-597, 1970.
Brody, Stanley J., Harvey Finkle, and Carl Hirsch: "Benefit Alert, a public advocacy program for the aged." Paper presented at the 8th International Congress of Gerontology, Washington, D.C., 1969.
Cantor, Marjorie H.: "Elderly ridership and reduced transit fares: the New York City experience." Administration on Aging Publication, #23, U.S. Department of Health, Education, and Welfare.
Cantor, Marjorie, Karen Rosenthal, and Mary Mayer: "The elderly in the rental market of New York City." Administration on Aging Publication, #26, U.S. Department of Health, Education, and Welfare.
Carey, Jean Wallace: "Senior advisory service for public housing tenants." Paper delivered at the annual meeting of the Gerontological Society, Toronto, Canada, 1970.
Carp, Frances M.: A future for the aged, Victoria Plaza. The University of Texas Press, Austin, 1966.
Carp, Frances M.: "Public transit and retired people." Administration on Aging Publication, #32, U.S. Department of Health, Education, and Welfare.
Hoffman, Adeline (ed.): "The daily needs and interests of older people." Charles C. Thomas, Publisher, Springfield, Illinois, 1970.
McGuire, Marie C.: "The status of housing for the elderly." *The Gerontologist,* 9:10-14, 1969.
Shapiro, Sam, Eve Weinblatt, Charles W. Frank, and Robert V. Sager: "Social factors in the prognosis of men following first myocardial infarction." Milbank Memorial Fund Quarterly, 47:56-63, 1969.
Suchman, Edward A., and A. Allen Rothman: "The utilization of dental services." Milbank Memorial Fund Quarterly, 47:56-63, 1969.
Trela, James E.: "Age graded secondary association memberships and political involvement in old age." Paper presented at the annual meeting of the Gerontological Society, Toronto, Canada, 1970.
Troll, Lillian E.; "Issues in the Study of Generations." *Aging and Human Development,* 1:199-218, 1970.

U. S. Bureau of the Census. "Advance report. General Population Characteristics." PC(V2)-1, U. S. Department of Commerce, Washington, D.C., February, 1971.

U. S. Senate Developments in Aging, 1970, A Report of the Special Committee on Aging, Report No. 92-46, U. S. Government Printing Office, Washington, D.C., 1971.

(References not examined)

Dominick, Joan: "Mental patients in nursing homes: four ethnic influences." *Journal of American Geriatric Society,* 17:63+, 1969.

Gregory, R.J.: "A survey of residents in five nursing and rest homes in Cumberland Country, North Carolina." *Journal of American Geriatric Society,* 18:501-506, 1970.

18. Aging, Politics, and Political Attitudes*

J. T. WILLIS**

"Intelligence, and reflection, and judgment, reside in old men and if there had been none of them, no state could exist at all."

CICERO
DE SENECTUTE, XVII

At the other extreme is the brashness of Ralph D. Abernathy (1), president of the Southern Christian Leadership Conference as expressed in a speech and quoted in the *Athens Banner Herald* on Sunday, May 24, 1970: "What we need is some young 'soul power' to drive them out of office, for we are tired of old folks running the country." Earlier in the speech, Abernathy had urged the rally in Atlanta to defeat several office holders whom he described as "wrinkled old souls in positions of trust."

Somewhere between these two extremes we find the attitudes of most of our politicians. They have been responsive to an extent to the needs of senior citizens either because of pressure or compassion.

WHO ARE THE OLD FOLKS?

Without formal definition, and without intent, Botwinick (2) says that law makers have defined old age as being 65 or older. This is the age at which most people become eligible for retirement with social security benefits.

A more appropriate name for those 65 and older and one that is seen in print often is "senior citizen." According to the 1970 census, senior citizens numbered about 20.9 million people or about 15 per cent of the total U.S. population of voting age. Their number increases by 300,000 each year.

In 1870, those 65 and over constituted approximately 3 per cent of the total population, numbering 1,153,649; in 1930, this group com-

*Original paper written for this book.
**Dr. Willis is presently Director of the South Carolina Opportunity School in West Columbia.

197

posed 5.4 per cent or 6,633,805. The total population by 1930 had increased threefold since 1870, but the number of those 65 and over was nearly six times as large as before. By 1970, the total population had increased six fold and the number of those 65 and over was about 19 times as many.

Most senior citizens are women. Most men are husbands and most women are widows. Half never got to high school. Seventeen per cent are illiterate or functionally illiterate.

Senior citizens have an aggregate income of $45,000,000,000,000 yearly. Almost half of their income is from retirement and welfare programs. About one third of their income is derived from employment and about one fifth from investments and contributions.

In the late 1800s, the vast majority of the United States population lived in the rural areas and were engaged in agriculture. The farm homes were large enough that children could continue to live in the home of parents even after marriage. This lessened the number of problems experienced with senior citizens relative to their personal care. By 1930, over 50 per cent of people 65 and older lived in urban centers and were engaged in or retired from an industrial or non-agricultural occupation. In the transition from a land economy to a money industrial economy, the contribution which old people could make lost much of its former value. Industry could no longer use them and retirement and pension plans were almost non-existent. No longer did they live in a farm dwelling adequate for sheltering married children and grandchildren. They lived in smaller units, many times alone because of the death of the mate, and with fewer children to provide for them. The Great Depression, which forced many people out of work, made the conditions worse.

IS THE PRESENT WELFARE OF SENIOR CITIZENS A RESULT OF POLITICS?

Only in recent years have senior citizens become involved in politics to any degree of effectiveness. Because of longer life expectancy now, many more older people are living longer and statistics show that they vote until about age 80. They have a reputation of moving from the inner city to the suburbs and then back to the inner city. This causes some problems for the politicians. In many instances they have held the balance of power among interest groups and could have used this power effectively had they been organized.

Cottrell (6) has indicated that the rural areas of our country have been over-represented in state legislatures because of the sparseness of population in those areas. Since most senior citizens live in urban areas, they have not been adequately represented in state and federal government.

In the late 1800s, people 65 and older were only 3 per cent of the total population and they were not organized for political action. In 1970, they composed about 10 per cent of the total population and about 15 per cent of the voting population. This trend in population can be effective politically. Coiro (5) has written that seniors over 55 cast about 33⅓ per cent of all ballots in any election.

In the years between 1920 and 1930, there were many elderly people who migrated to the West coast and primarily to California. The population of California as a whole increased by 65 per cent but the aged population increased over 80 per cent. The population of people 65 and older over the nation during this period increased by only 14 per cent.

The migration of large numbers of senior citizens to California and to such areas as Los Angeles, Long Beach, San Diego, and Pasadena laid the ground work for political action at a time when the senior citizens were suffering. The Great Depression had hit hard and their savings and retirement incomes were wiped out. Holtzman (8) said that the state itself provided a political atmosphere conducive to the rise of old age reform movements which benefitted senior citizens all over the United States. He said that old-age pension organizations, supported by an articulate, group conscious segment among the aged population, have since 1933 constituted a new force on the American political scene.

Dr. Francis E. Townsend was a leader of one such group known as the Townsend Movement. Seated by a window in his home one morning, so the story goes, Dr. Townsend was startled to see three old women rummaging in garbage cans for edibles. Horrified at this sight and the thought that he too was out of work and might face such a degradation, Townsend began to think seriously of ways to assure a better future for himself and old people in general. He conceived of a plan whereby every person over sixty would receive $200 a month on the condition that that person would spend all of the $200 during the next month. During this period of time, it was considered that one person could produce about $2,500 worth of goods in a year. Townsend's plan provided for one person, under sixty and at work, to provide enough goods for one retired person. The retired person would spend all of his retirement income ($2,400 yearly) to purchase goods. Thus there would be at least as many people provided with work as there were retired people. Townsend and his followers used such slogans as "$200 a Month at Sixty," "Revolving Pensions and Prosperity," and "Honor Thy Father and Mother."

In addition to espousing the Townsend Movement, Townsend and his supporters organized clubs all over the United States to help promote the movement. Within two years, there were 7,000 clubs with 1,500,000 aged people as members and another 25,000,000 of all ages supporting the movement.

While the movement became very popular and attracted many followers, it was never accepted by the Congress of the United States. Some lasting good may have resulted from it for Holtzman (7) credits the Townsend Movement for the enactment of the Social Security Act of 1935. He wrote:

> The old-age provisions of the Social Security Act, that keystone of the welfare state, memorialize the impact of the Townsend Movement upon national public policy. Agitation for the Townsend plan greatly accelerated the time schedule for the appearance of a national old-age security program. In crystalizing an overwhelming public clamor for action, the Townsend Movement afforded that program tremendous popular support, the political overtones of which neither the President nor the Congress could ignore.

Other writers such as Cottrell (6) attribute the enactment of the Social Security Act to the Great Depression of the 1930's.

As the aged population increased in numbers and their conditions were more widespread and their needs better known, other groups were formed to do something to service those needs. Often the groups were organized to provide service in a local community. As other groups formed, sometimes two groups would merge into a third group. Often their service was so effective that a pressure group would be formed by them. If the service proved to be worthwhile but its means were inadequate for expansion, this group may have been the starting point of a new government agency either on a state or national level.

Some other movements started for the welfare of the aged population were the Utopian Society, the Technocrats, Upton Sinclair's End Poverty in California (EPIC), the Ham and Egg movement and George McLain's California Institute of Social Welfare.

The Utopian Society was organized in 1934 to secure financial aid for the elderly. It boasted a membership of 500,000 and held as many as 250 meetings in one night in Los Angeles. Fifty thousand elderly people are reported to have attended one meeting.

The Technocrats was an organization begun in New York and later moved into Southern California in the early 1930s. This organization provided impetus for old age politics.

Koller (10) wrote that such movements and concerns over aging citizens stirred federal, state, and local governments into enacting a variety of programs designed to prevent and relieve the problems of the aging.

Some of the programs developed by government at various levels have resulted in the following action as listed by Kent (9).

> By the $15 billion it spent, or administered, for the economic welfare of persons 65 and over.
>
> By the pleasure a 57 year old widow in Cleveland gets from her new apartment built in 1961 partly with Federal funds under the new 'Housing for the Elderly' program.
>
> By the scientific research sponsored or constructed by the Public Health Service to wipe out cancer, heart disease, and diabetes.
>
> By the special job-finding help of the Federal-State Employment Security System that returned many older people to employment.
>
> By the hospital care the Veterans Administration gave to many thousands of World War I veterans who couldn't afford it elsewhere.
>
> By the new interest in the plight of older people created by the White House Conference on Aging.
>
> By the many who received assistance in setting up small businesses to help supplement their retirement income.
>
> But, no matter how you measure the Government's help — with cold statistics, in warm, human terms, or as a new dimension of dignity — the end result is an amazing phenomenon of recent years.

Kent concluded that what has been done is good but there is much yet to be done.

The following is a brief list of agencies and divisions of the Federal Government which share in the administration of the affairs of the aged. Some of them have direct responsibility and others only indirect responsibility for the programs previously mentioned. The agencies are: Department of Health, Education, and Welfare; Department of the Treasury; Department of the Interior; Department of Agriculture; Department of Commerce; Department of Labor; Office of Defense

Mobilization; Housing and Finance Agency; the National Science Foundation; Small Business Administration; Civil Service Commission; and the Veterans Administration.

President Roosevelt brought several of the above named agencies concerned with welfare, health, and education of the senior citizens under the care of a single organization, the Federal Security Agency. President Eisenhower's administration converted this agency into the Department of Health, Education, and Welfare with cabinet status. Even this left the affairs of the aging under a scattered number of agencies. To alleviate some of the overlapping of services and to reduce some bureaucracy, the Federal Council on Aging was established in 1956. The membership of the Council consisted of representatives from all of the agencies listed above. Even though the Council is purely advisory, the various committees functioning as a part of the council can be very effective in influencing government.

Just prior to the organization of the Federal Council on Aging, the Governors' Conference called upon the Council of State Government in 1954 to study the problems of the aged and report its findings to the 1955 annual meeting of that Conference. As a result of the study, a 176 page report was written and published entitled "The State and Their Older Citizens." Included in the report was a "Bill of Objectives for Older People" and a "Program of Action in the Field of Aging." This report, along with work at the national level, induced President Eisenhower to create the Federal Council on Aging.

Carlie (4) wrote a brief report of the findings of four investigators relative to the effectiveness of senior citizens in politics. A summary of their findings follows.

Cottrell found that senior citizens have a great potential of voting power but they are scattered over a great many different interest groups, most of which do not make the welfare of the aged their primary goal. This potential has never been realized.

Tibbits found that there was a growing recognition of the aged and of their children as a political force that has led to increased commitments on the part of political parties and office seekers. However, the broad scale political action came on behalf of, rather than by, older people.

Rose found that the most effective lobbyists for legislation for the aging were those organizations with general welfare interests that were not age-based.

Holtzman found that the movement for old age security up to the time of the depression was almost completely divorced from economic or political expression.

While politicians probably lost no votes over enactment of legislation that benefitted senior citizens, it was not because of political power that senior citizens were the benefactors of the legislation.

CAN SENIOR CITIZENS INFLUENCE POLITICS?

The essence of senior power is in the growing numbers of seniors speaking out and taking stands on local and national issues, as well as working within their communities for better living conditions.

Newsweek (11) carried an unsigned article stating that senior citizens, bolstered by their success in winning medicare in 1966 and worried by the erosion of their fixed incomes by inflation, have recently begun to organize across the country, creating the latest pressure group to appear on the American political scene — Senior Power. The magazine quotes William Hutton, executive director of the 25,000 member National Council of Senior Citizens as saying that all these people needed was some organization. Political action makes old people feel important again. It gives them a psychological uplift.

Butler (3) wrote that our elderly have at last reached the point where they can no longer be ignored and there are already signs that their problems might easily become the next big cause now that issues like civil rights, the war, and ecology seem to be fading into the background. While it isn't likely that anyone's grandparents are going to start riots, plant bombs or seize social security offices in the name of "Senior Power," the more active ones aren't waiting for any young crusaders to fight their battles for them.

There is some real activity on the part of senior citizens according to Butler. He said, "At the local level, retirees are beginning to use some of the same techniques as other deprived minorities. Three years ago, for example, 2,000 elderly people had a rally at Boston's Faneuil Hall to protest a 25 cent bus and subway fare. Before the meeting was over, nearly 40 politicians were lined up waiting to speak. Not long afterward, senior citizens' fares were reduced to ten cents.

In 1972, a year for national elections, both major political parties took great pains to court the favor of elderly voters according to a report in *U. S. News and World Report* (13). According to the report, the Republicans and Democrats had knowledge that people 65 and over comprise what may be the most powerful single group headed for the polls. Sixty-six percent of that age group voted in 1968 compared to 61 per cent of all people of voting age.

Small delegations of oldsters even announced plans to demonstrate at both national political conventions along with black militants, women's libbers, and anti-war groups according to Butler (3). Usually, elderly people are patriotic and even though a great majority are reluctant to challenge a system that they feel they must depend on for their very lives, a system that they helped to build, more and more of them are beginning to wonder if they really have much to lose by challenging it.

Political parties will continue to give serious consideration to the senior citizens. Tibbitts (12) wrote that young people, becoming eligible to vote tend to identify themselves as independent voters, but as they become older they move toward a specific party, usually conservative. By the time they reach age 70, they have become very strong party identifiers. Older people go to the polls and vote. According to Tibbitts, the proportion voting in national elections rises from about 52 per cent at age 21 to a maximum of 80 per cent from about age 50 to 65 and then dropping to approximately 65 per cent about age 80. These statistics are important to political parties.

Party platforms are built as a means to election of their candidates and they differ very little between parties. The behind the scene commitments are a different matter though. These commitments show increasing concern for the problems of the aged. While there is a tendency toward continued identification with the original choice of party, older persons tend to switch to the Republican Party. From age 21 through age 44, fifty per cent of the voters identify with the Democratic party. The proportion drops to around 45 per cent among those in middle age to slightly below that in later maturity and old age. Forty per cent of those 65 and older belong to the Republican party.

SUMMARY

A characteristic of senior citizens, and one that adds to their happiness, is independence. However, this may not always be favorable to their welfare and may be one reason for their ineffectiveness politically. Much good can be accomplished and the plight of older people improved through cooperation with other groups. Coiro (5) quoted William E. Adams, state senator from New York, as saying that social action programs and activities are an excellent way to bridge the so-called "generation-gap." He's observed an interesting parallel between the needs, goals, and aspirations of seniors and youths. They all desire to have identity, to be active in the community, and to be part of the forces shaping the policies of today and tomorrow.

The needs of our senior citizens are felt in every community of our country. Machinery exists today to translate these needs into political action designed to meet these needs. Efforts have been fragmentary because of the lack of organization among senior citizen organizations. Carlie (4) wrote that the responsibility for the enactment of legislation pertaining to the aged stemmed from organizations which were not age-based and not from old age political interest groups directly. Kent (9) said that co-ordinated approaches must be made, and perhaps most important, efforts should be continued to develop widespread public awareness and sympathy. Unless they do, Dr. Irving Latimer, formerly with the National Better Business Bureau, was quoted by Coiro (5) as saying, "Older people will remain potential victims of their own lack of appeal unless they insist on their rightful role as consumers by registering their demands with dollars and votes."

REFERENCES

(1) Abernathy, Ralph D. " 'Old Souls Must Fall, Rally Told," *Athens Banner Herald.* Sunday, May 24, 1970. p. 1.
(2) Botwinick, Jack. *Aging and Behavior*. Springer Publishing Company, Inc.: New York. 1973. p. 1.
(3) Butler, Patrick. "Senior Power," *America*. December 2, 1972. pp. 472-473.
(4) Carlie, Michael Kaye. "The Politics of Age: Interest Group or Social Movement," *The Gerontologist*. Vol. 9, No. 4. Winter, 1969. pp. 259-264.
(5) Coiro, Cynthia. "Senior Power Breaks the Barrier," *Harvest Years*. October, 1970. pp. 6-12.
(6) Cottrell, F. "Governmental Functions and the Politics of Age," *Handbook of Social Gerontology*. The University of Chicago Press: Chicago. 1960. pp. 624-664.
(7) Holtzman, Abraham. *The Townsend Movement*. Bookman Associates, Inc.: New York. 1963. pp. 17-33.
(8) Holtzman, p. 207.
(9) Kent, Donald P. "Aging and Government Policy: Outlook for Progress in the 1960's," *Aging and the Economy*. The University of Michigan Press: Ann Arbor. 1963. pp. 195-208.
(10) Koller, Marvin R. *Social Gerontology*. Random House: New York. 1968. pp. 133-137.
(11) Unsigned article in *Newsweek*, October 12, 1970. 76: 101.

(12) Tibbitts, Clark, "Politics of Aging: Pressure for Change," *The Politics of Age*. The University of Michigan Press: Ann Arbor. 1962. pp. 16-25.
(13) Unsigned article in *U. S. News and World Report*, November 6, 1972. 73: 35-7.

19. Religiosity in Old Age*

DAVID O. MOBERG**

Geriatricians and gerontologists hold divergent opinions about the importance of religion in the later years of life. The differences reflect a combination of facts and personal biases. Religious persons tend to praise the influence of religious faith and practice and to believe that people become more religious as they approach death, while secularists are prone to believe religiosity declines and to condemn the "ill effects" of both personal and organized religion.

There is no question about the relative importance of the church among voluntary association memberships of the aged. Study after study in various parts of the nation and in different types of communities have found that the aged (like most younger people) are more apt to be church members than members of any other one type of voluntary organization and, indeed, than of all other associations together. Disagreements arise, however, on several topics: What are the trends of personal religion over the life cycle? (Are the aged more likely to be church members than middle-aged and young adults? What is their comparative rate of participation in the church?) What are the effects of church participation? (Does it promote personal adjustment or does it reflect a search for security by maladjusted persons?) What are the characteristics of religious faith among the elderly? (Do they revert to the religion of their childhood? Are they progressively emancipated from traditional religion?)

Contradictory answers to questions of these kinds are based not only upon the personal opinions of experts but also upon empirical data from research surveys of behavioral scientists. The confusion that results leads to both traditionalistic attempts to perpetuate past practices and radical proposals that religion be drastically changed or else ignored entirely in geriatric programs.

The confusion of gerontologists about the role of religion is readily transferred to geriatricians, for scientific generalizations eventually influence practical action.

After considerable study and research, I have concluded that the confusion and contradictions about religion in old age are a product of more than a simple lack of research on the subject. The concept of

*Reprinted from *The Gerontologist*, Vol. 5, 1965, pages 78-87, and 111-112, with permission of the author and The Gerontological Society.
**Dr. Moberg is Chairman of the Department of Sociology and Anthropology at Marquette University in Milwaukee.

207

"religion" is very broad, and it is defined in the research operations of social scientists in a variety of ways. The "religiosity" of scientist A is so greatly different from the "religiosity" studied by scientist B that they are not dealing with the same subject even though the same words may be used in their reports. Examination of the "operational definitions" (questions asked and other techniques used to describe and classify people's religious behavior) of relevant research projects reveals several types of "religiosity."

The best analysis of this conceptual problem is the five-fold classification of "dimensions of religiosity" developed by Professor Glock of the Survey Research Center at the University of California (Berkeley). I shall briefly describe each of his five modes or types of religious expression and then summarize some findings on each dimension from studies about religion in old age.

DIMENSIONS OF RELIGIOSITY

Glock's (1962) analysis of the "core dimensions of religiosity" within which "all of the many and diverse manifestations of religiosity prescribed by the different religions of the world can be ordered" provides the most satisfactory extant frame of reference for studying and assessing religion scientifically.

1. The *experiential* dimension reflects the expectation that religious persons "will achieve direct knowledge of ultimate reality or will experience religious emotion," although the emotions deemed proper or experienced may vary widely from one religion or one person to another. Subjective religious experience or feeling is difficult to study but may be expressed chiefly in terms of "concern or need to have a transcendentally based ideology," cognition or awareness of the divine, trust or faith, and fear.

2. The *ideological* dimension concerns beliefs that the followers of a religion are expected to hold (official doctrine), the beliefs they actually hold, the importance or saliency of beliefs, and their functions for individuals.

3. The *ritualistic* dimension has to do with the religious practices of adherents to a religion. It includes public and private worship, prayer, fasting, feasting, tithing, participation in sacraments, and the like.

4. The *intellectual* dimension deals with personal information and knowledge about the basic tenets and sacred writings of one's faith. Again official expectations and the actual achievements of constituents tend to diverge considerably and need to be clearly distinguished from

each other. Misconceptions, intellectual sophistication, and attitudes toward both secular and religious knowledge are important aspects.

5. The *consequential* dimension "includes all of the secular effects of religious belief, practice, experience, and knowledge on the individual." It includes all specifications of what people ought to do and to believe as a result of their religion. In Christianity it emphasizes the theological concept of "works" and especially Christian perspectives on man's relationships to other men, in contrast to his relationships to God. Rewards and punishments, expectations and obligations, commandments and promises are all aspects of this measure of religiosity.

Obviously, there are distinctions both in kind and in degree within each of the five dimensions. Just as religiosity itself is not a unilateral concept, each of its major dimensions may also be complex and multidimensional. The areas of religious commitment are all inextricably bound up with each other in real life; none can be studied effectively without recognition of and consideration for the others.

The attempt to clarify the present status of knowledge about religion in old age through use of Glock's dimensions is not simple, as we shall see in the following summary. A wide variety of techniques has been used. Measuring instruments and operational definitions of concepts have not been the same; therefore the actual phenomena studied are not identical even when presented under the same terms. The studies have had divergent objectives and in many additional ways have not been directly comparable. Can order be introduced into such a conglomeration of findings and interpretations?

RELIGIOUS FEELINGS

On the basis of her 25 years of medical practice, Dr. Nila Kirkpatrick Covalt (1960), Director of the Kirkpatrick Memorial Institute of Physical Medicine and Rehabilitation in Winter Park, Florida, stated that she found no evidence to support the common assumption that people turn to religion as they grow older. Patients do not talk with their physicians about religion. The religious attitudes of most old people are those they grew up with. Patients' thoughts, visions, and dreams when regaining consciousness are often given a spiritual significance, Dr. Covalt stated, but

> I recall no person who called out to God or audibly prayed when he knew he was dying. Usually these persons are exerting every bit of energy in a struggle to keep alive.

At least the overt manifestations of their feelings do not indicate a high degree of experiential religiosity.

Contrary evidence is also available, however. The panel of persons in the Terman Gifted Group apparently had greater interest in religion in 1960 (at their median age of 56) than they had in 1940 and 1950 (Marshall & Oden, 1962). Over half (54.1%) of 210 people past age 65 in a Chicago working-class area said religion had become more helpful over the preceding decade; 30.1% said that it had not become more helpful, and 6.2% said that there had been no change (9.6% gave no answer) (O'Reilly & Pembroke, n.d.).

Jeffers and Nichols (1961) found in their study of 251 persons in North Carolina past age 60 that religion means more to most Ss as the years go by and the end of life approaches and that this is especially true of disabled persons for whom the end is more imminent. Similarly, 57% of 140 retired Negroes in South Carolina reported that religion and the church held more meaning since retirement than they did before; 42% reported that they held the same meaning, and only two persons said they held less meaning (Lloyd, 1955).

A large study of 1700 elderly Minnesotans found that only from 7 to 19% of the subcategories of men and from 2 to 5% of the women reported that religion does not mean much to them. In contrast, 52 to 55% of the women reported that religion does not mean much to them. In contrast, 52 to 55% of the men and 66 to 71% of the women reported religion was the most important thing in their lives (Taves & Hansen, 1963). Among the 143 older people in a rural New York community, the church and clergy were much more important than formerly to 34 persons, somewhat more important to 28, about the same to 56, somewhat less important to 10, and much less important to only 7. Corresponding answers about the meaning of God and religion ranged from 46 who said they held much more meaning than formerly, through 25, 59, and 3 in the respective intermediate categories, to only 1 who said they held much less meaning (9 gave no response). Yet only 13 mentioned religion as one of the things that provided them the greatest satisfaction (Warren, 1952).

Wolff's (1961) summary of psychological aspects of aging includes the statement that geriatric patients have ambivalent feelings toward life and death and may turn toward religion, which "gives them emotional support and tends to relieve them from the fear that everything soon will come to an end."

The contrasting results of studies which refer to religious feelings of the aged may result from a basic difficulty in scientific research on religious feelings. American societal expectations hold that religion is helpful in any time of trouble. Anyone who expresses a perspective contrary to the position that religion helps the aged may feel that he is in danger of being socially rejected for his seemingly heretical views. With the fear of such reprisals, biased responses to questions about religious feelings may distort the results of questionnaire as well as interview studies. A type of self-fulfilling prophecy mechanism also may be at work: the expectation that religion will help may lead the person to receive genuine help through religious channels or at least to feel as if he had.

While the bulk of the evidence available to date indicates that religious feelings increase for more people than those for whom they decrease, we must retain an open mind on this subject while awaiting additional research.

Religious Beliefs

There is some evidence from public opinion survey data that belief in life after death may increase with age; at least a higher proportion of old people than of younger generations believe that there is a life after death. Older people also are more certain that there is a God and apparently are more inclined to hold to traditional and conservative beliefs of their religion. (Gray & Moberg, 1962).

A study of 496 persons in New York City, 325 of whom were Jewish, found that the proportion who believed in a life after death (heaven) increased from 30.1 to 40.5% from ages 30-35 to ages 60-65. Nonbelief for the same age categories diminished from 36.1 to 25.1, with the remainder uncertain (Barron, 1961). The nationwide *Catholic Digest* (Anon., 1952) survey revealed that 81% of the respondents aged 65 and over compared to 79% of all and 76% of those aged 45-54 thought of God as a loving Father. Belief in God was held the most certainly by persons aged 65 and over, and a somewhat higher proportion of the aged (56%) than of the total sample (51%) believed one should prepare for life after death rather than be concerned with living comfortably. This lends some support to the opinion of Starbuck (1911), the pioneer in the psychology of religion, that religious faith and belief in God grow in importance as the years advance. His research data were skimpy and his highest age category was "40 or over," but his conclusion has been adopted so widely that Maves (1960) has called it a "part of the folklore of the psychology of religion."

Surveys have revealed that older people as a whole tend to have more conservative religious perspectives than younger adults. Indirect evidence of this also comes from St. Cloud, Florida, where more than half the population in the mid-1950's was aged 60 and over. Its churches were generally more fundamentalistic than was usual in peninsular Florida, and over one-third were evangelical and sectarian (Aldridge, 1956).

Whether the differences in religious beliefs between the generations are a result of the aging process or of divergent experiences during the formative years of childhood and youth, which are linked with different social and historical circumstances, is unknown. Longitudinal research might reveal considerably different conclusions from the cross-sectional studies which provide the foundation for current generalizations about age variations in the ideological dimension of religion.

Religious Practices

The ritualistic dimension has received considerable attention from social scientists, perhaps because the observation of most religious practices is relatively simple. The findings are not wholly consistent, however.

All American studies which have come to my attention indicate that more of the formal social participation of the elderly, as well as of other age groups, is in the church than in all other voluntary community organizations together. This holds true whether measured by membership, attendance, or other indicators. For example, 87% of 1,236 persons aged 60 and older in two Kentucky communities participated in the church, 35% in Sunday school, and 8% in other church activities. The next highest participation was 6% in "service and welfare organizations." As also is consistently true, women participated in the church to a somewhat greater extent than men, 94% compared with 85% of the men in a Lexington sample and 93 and 73%, respectively, in a Casey County sample (Youmans, 1963).

The highest Chapin social participation scores for religious participation among the heads of household in four rural New York communities studied in 1947-1948 were found among men aged 75-79, followed closely by those aged 45-54. Among homemakers in the same study, the highest scores were found among those aged 70-74 and 75-79, with women aged 60-64 in third place and 45-54 fourth. Female participation in religious organizations exceeded that of the males at every age, but male participation exceeded that of the females in nonreligious organizations (Taietz & Larson, 1956). (Chapin scores are based upon a combination of membership, attendance, financial contributions, committee positions, and offices held.)

The peak of intensity of social participation, based on Chapin's scale among 1,397 persons aged 10 and over in two North Carolina localities, came at age 55 to 59 with a sharp drop thereafter. Four-fifths of this participation was in religious activities, and six-tenths of the persons participated only in churches and their auxiliary organizations (Mayo, 1951).

Some studies have revealed increases in religious practices in old age. Public opinion poll data indicate consistently higher figures for church attendance, Bible reading, and prayer among persons aged 50 and over than among younger groups (Toch, 1953). Age among 597 institutionalized women aged 65 or older living in Protestant homes for the aged was positively correlated with increased religious activities as well as with increased dependence upon religion (Pan, 1954). Contrasting evidence from other samples of older people suggests that the relative youthfulness of the "over 50" group compared to samples with a higher minimum age and the unusual environmental circumstance of residents in Protestant church homes, which facilitate participation in organized religious activities, may account for the variation between these two studies and others reported below.

A survey of 100 first admissions of persons aged 60 and over to a county hospital found evidence which was interpreted tentatively as contrary to the common assumption that people become more interested in religion as they grow older. Several were found to attend church less frequently than at age 50, and few attended more often than before (Fiske, 1961). (The report sensibly qualifies the finding by suggesting that a change in behavior does not necessarily imply less concern with spiritual matters. It refers to a University of Chicago study which found that the decrease in church attendance among aging persons is accompanied by increased listening to religious programs on radio and television.)

In the "Back of the Yards" Chicago study (O'Reilly & Pembroke, n.d.) approximately equal proportions of men attended church more (34%) and less (32%) than they did before the age of 65, but among women the respective figures of 27 and 46% indicate a decrease in attendance. Increasing age among Catholics in Fort Wayne, Indiana, was associated with decreasing church attendance, chiefly because of poor health (Theisen, 1962). Fichter's (1954) study of 8,363 active white Catholic parishioners found that the percentage who received monthly Communion diminished fairly consistently in each 10-year category from age 10 to 60-and-over. However, a higher percentage of the eldest category (86.6) made their Easter duties (confession and

Holy Communion) than any other age except the youngest (ages 10-19, 92.1%), and only the youngest exceeded the elderly in the percentage attending Mass every Sunday (92.8 versus 90.9%). Physical disabilities may account for differences. Although variations over the total life span cannot be accounted for solely on the basis of age, both the young and the old were significantly more religious as measured by these practices than persons aged 30-39, who had the lowest record for both sexes (63.4% made their Easter duties, 69.3% attended Mass every Sunday, and 31.6% received monthly Communion).

Only 4% of a representative stratified sample of people aged 65 and over studied in 1948-1949 in a small midwestern city rejected religion and the church, but an additional 18% had no church affiliation and no attendance, and 15% had only a passive interest. The other 63% participated in religious activities frequently and actively. Most people evidently continued to carry on the religious habits of their middle years, but they also customarily dropped gradually out of church leadership positions after the age of 60 (Havighurst & Albrecht, 1953). In a metropolitan Kansas City study (Cumming & Henry, 1961) the proportion of persons aged 50 and over who seldom attended church was lowest at age 60-64 in both sexes and reached its highest figure among those aged 75 and over (64.3% of the men and 75.0% of the women).

Senior citizens surveys of a cross-section of the population aged 65 and over in Long Beach, California (McCann, 1955), and Grand Rapids, Michigan (Hunter & Maurice, 1953) indicated a definite tendency of the aged to attend church less often than they did ten years earlier, and increasing non-attendance accompanied increasing age. Problems of physical mobility and finances were among the most significant factors related to declining attendance. Listening to religious services on radio or television and "lost interest" followed health or physical condition in importance among the reasons respondents gave for attending church less often than they had a decade earlier; where the former is a major reason for decreased attendance (17.1% of the Long Beach and 33.9% of the Grand Rapids sample), non-attendance can hardly be accepted as an indicator of a loss of religiosity.

Fifty-five per cent of 131 aged members of two urban Baptist churches in Minnesota attended church every Sunday. The percentages ranged from 71.4 among the 14 persons aged 80-84 to 20 among the 5 aged 85-89. Nearly half (45.6%) of the persons aged 75 and over attended church every Sunday, compared with 64.5% of those aged 65-69 and 60.5% of those aged 70-74. The evidence pertinent to attendance at other church activities clearly supported the hypothesis that participation declines in old age. This decline was even more pronounced in regard to holding lay leadership positions, which reached its peak in both churches at the age of 25-44. Only 4.6% said that they were more active in the church now than they were in their fitties, but 72.5% said that they were less active than in their fifties (Moberg, 1965).

The survey (Barron, 1961) of 496 residents of New York City (325 of whom were Jewish, 98 Roman Catholic, 65 Protestant, and 8 of other or no faiths) found only insignificant differences between the age categories 30-35, 40-45, 50-55, and 60-65 in the proportion that attended church or synagogue "often" in contrast to "sometimes" and "hardly ever" or "never."

The strongest criticism of the "contemporary folklore that 'older' people are more religious than others . . . , and that there is a turning to religion in old age" comes from Orbach's (1961) interpretations and research. In support of his position, Orbach appealed to sociological interpretations of the functions of religion in our "youth-centered society," evidence of the significance of religious beliefs, feelings, and conversion among the young rather than the aged, and empirical findings from studies like those mentioned above which indicate that participation in religious activities decreases in old age.

Since other studies are weak on the levels of both sampling and the analysis of relevant sociological variables other than sex, Orbach made a careful analysis of five probability samples of 6,911 adults aged 21 and over who resided in the mid-1950's in the Detroit Metropolitan Area. Church attendance on a five-point scale from once a week to never was related to age in five-year intervals with sex controlled. Age *per se* was found to be unrelated to changes in church attendance; there was no indication of an increase in attendance in the later years, although the data suggest that there is a polarizing effect in which intermediary categories of "casual" and "cursory" churchgoers tend to shift into a dichotomous distribution of regular church attenders and non-attenders.

When the data were grouped into four age categories (21-39, 40-59, 60-74, 75 and over), the most striking finding was the constancy of attendance in all age groupings, with the one exception of significantly increased non-attendance among the oldest group, which can be attributed at least partly to the effect of age on physical health. Mul-tivariate analysis of church attendance in relationship to age with religious preference, sex, and race as control variables found only Protestant Negro males and Jewish males and females to show increased attendance with age. The small number of cases of Negro males in the oldest age category and the historical decline of Jewish orthodoxy, which is directly reflected in the age groupings, may account for these exceptions to the general pattern of declining attendance as age increases. When other sociological variables were controlled, the relationships between age and attendance were mixed and inconsistent and lent no support to the hypothesis that religiosity increases with age.

The bulk of reliable evidence thus indicates that church attendance of people generally remains fairly constant but tends to decline in the later years compared with younger ages. It is hazardous, however, to assume that church attendance is anything more than a crude indicator of religiosity; it is only one subdimension of religious practices, which themselves comprise but one of Glock's five major dimensions of religious commitment.

Orbach (1961) states that "participation in religious bodies through attendance and involvement in ceremonial worship is perhaps the most crucial and sensitive indicator of overt religiosity." This may apply satisfactorily to the most sacramentally oriented religions — those which believe that the religious institution is the channel of God's grace and that salvation is bestowed upon the individual only through institutionalized participation in church rituals. It probably does not apply to non-sacramental Protestants and to Jews. Orbach (1961) also wisely reminds us that "objective criteria such as attendance cannot replace study of the area of religious beliefs and attitudinal changes or approximate the subjective aspect of inner religious feelings." Attendance is easier to study, but it should be used as a measure of religiosity only provisionally and with a clear recognition of attendant dangers.

Although church attendance tends at most to remain constant with increasing age in cross-sectional studies of the population and more often to decline, regular listening to church services and other religious broadcasts on the radio and reading from the Bible at least weekly have been found to increase among the elderly with advancing age (Cavan, Burgess, Havighurst, & Goldhamer, 1949). Evidently religious practices outside the home diminish while those within the home increase. Physical condition may be the chief intervening variable responsible for such trends. Comparative studies reveal that participation in other social organizations declines at a much more rapid rate than participation in the church.

RELIGIOUS KNOWLEDGE

Relatively little research has been done on age differences in the intellectual dimension of religiosity among older adults. I have been unable to locate any published research which bears directly upon this topic.

EFFECTS OF RELIGION

Although many of the other dimensions of religiosity have been only crudely defined, they have been used as independent variables in research designed to discover the effects of religion upon other aspects of personal and social life. Examples of some of these explorations of the consequential dimension of religion will be presented here.

A number of studies have demonstrated that church members hold a larger number of memberships in voluntary community associations and other organizations than those who are not members and that lay leaders in the church are more active in non-church organizations than are other church members (Moberg, 1962), but relatively little attention has been given to age variations in this pattern.

A national survey of adults (Lazerwitz, 1962) in the spring of 1957 related the age of persons with Protestant and Catholic religious preference to the number of voluntary association memberships they held. It was found that the lowest membership levels prevailed among Protestants in the youngest (21-24) and oldest (60-64 and 65 and over) categories and the highest membership rates at ages 30-59. Among Catholics the highest percentage of persons with no organizational memberships was at ages 65 and over and 45-49, with the greatest number of memberships at ages 35-44. Most of the Protestants and Catholics who seldom or never attended church also lacked membership in voluntary associations, while most of those who attended faithfully had one or more such memberships.

Other studies support the conclusion that there is a positive correlation between church participation and other formal social participation at all ages. It is not unreasonable to think that associating with people in church-related activities and organizations contributes to knowledge of other voluntary organizations; friendships in the church with persons who are members of other groups may lead to social participation in them. The lower organizational membership levels of Catholics hence could result from their lesser stress upon "fellowship" in the church as compared to Protestants, as well as from their somewhat lower position in the social class structure of American society.

Barron's (1961) New York City study included a question about the respondent's self-image, "Would you say you are a religious person, or doesn't religion mean very much to you?" Of all the respondents,

44.7% responded affirmatively and 25.2% expressed an irreligious self-image. Among the 116 persons aged 60-65, however, the respective percentages were 55.1 and 19.9 (25.0% were undecided compared with 30.1% in the total sample).

> The most significant aspect of the chronological age distribution in answer to this question was the steadily increasing proportions of the religious self-image and the steadily declining proportions of indecision regarding the self-image in the ascension of chronological age.

The relationship of religion to personality problems has been observed and commented upon by a number of behavioral scientists. Religion was the preferred topic of discussion in group therapy sessions with geriatric patients at a state hospital. Religious beliefs and faith in God helped disorganized members to overcome their grief when unhappy, lonesome, and despondent. They were eager to discuss a better life after death; other members sensed the support religion gave them because they themselves also received greater "Ego strength" from religion. Delusions and hallucinations involving religious symptoms were, however, not accepted by other members of the group as true and correct; when they occurred the possibility of a mistake or incorrect interpretation was discussed (Wolff, 1959a).

Elderly patients who have ambivalent feelings toward life and death often want to die, since they believe they have nothing for which to live. Yet as they sense death is approaching, they may become disturbed and insecure, want others near at all times, and fear the dark. They may attend church more often than previously, confess, and ask that their sins be forgiven. They thus turn toward religion, which gives them emotional support and relief from the fear that everything soon will end (Wolff, 1959b).

Fear of death was one topic probed in a study of 260 community volunteers aged 60 and over in North Carolina. Such fear was found to be significantly related (at the 1% level of confidence) to less belief in life after death and less frequent Bible reading (Jeffers, Nichols, & Eisdorfer, 1961). Swenson's (1961) psychological study of 210 Minnesota residents aged 60 and over similarly found a significant relationship between death attitudes and religiosity as measured by both religious activity and the MMPI religiosity scale, a measure of devotion to religion. "Persons with more fundamental religious convictions and habits look forward to death more than do those with less fundamental convictions and less activity. Fearful attitudes toward death tend to be found in those persons with little religious activity. . . . it seems logical to infer that the eschatologically oriented person contemplates death in a positive manner."

These findings support the conclusion that a sense of serenity and decreased fear of death tend to accompany conservative religious beliefs. This does not necessarily prove, however, that religious faith removes the fear of death. It is conceivable that attitudes toward death of the religiously faithful differ from those of nonreligious people because of differences in their social integration (Treanton, 1961); the religious have a reference group that gives them support and security and the nonreligious are more likely to lack such social support. Swenson's finding that fear of death is related to solitude supports this hypothesis; social isolation may be an intervening variable explaining the observed relationships.

The traditional cultural definition of death complicates research on this subject among people of Christian convictions. The faithful believer is expected to rest upon the promise of his salvation that he has no fear of death; he is expected to see death as a portal to immortality. His affirmation that he does not fear the advent of death could be an expression of a neurotic personality which disguises death and pretends that it is not a basic condition of all life (Fulton, 1961). Feifel (1956) has hypothesized that "certain older persons perceive death as the beginning of a new existence for the purpose of controlling strong anxieties concerning death." While this hypothesis may be perceived by some religious people as an impudent attack upon the genuineness of religious faith, it may also be viewed as a compliment to it. If the hypothesis is verified, one of the social-psychological functions commonly attributed to religion by even the most faithful when they seek comfort in biblical teachings about the resurrection will have received scientific support.

Happiness was significantly related to frequency of church attendance among both Catholics and non-Catholics in the Chicago "Back of the Yards" study. The "very happy" attended church the most frequently, the "moderately happy" the next most frequently, and the "less happy" persons attended the least of all. Lonely Catholics tended to be less active in the practice of their religion, but the relationship was not statistically significant (O'Reilly & Pembroke, n.d.).

Feelings of satisfaction and security were provided older persons by religion and church participation in a small midwestern community studied by McCrary (1956). Yet in her general medical practice in Muncie, Indiana, Dr. Covalt (1958) observed little or no relationship between religion and good adjustment to illness. The patient who brought a Bible to the hospital with him thereby gave the physicians a sign of anticipated trouble, for the stable, secure person did not bring a Bible. These insecure individuals often were members of fringe-type religious sects. They were uncooperative, did not carry out instructions, fought the nurses, complained about even the most minor matters, and unpleasantly hindered their own recovery.

Contradictory evidence thus emerges on the matter of whether religion performs such functions as promoting happiness, increasing personal security, combatting loneliness, and removing the fear of death. Several of these concepts are reflected in studies of personal adjustment or morale in old age. To discuss the techniques and findings of these in any detail is impossible in the short space available here, but a brief summary of some of the major studies will help to illuminate this aspect of the consequential dimension of religion. More thorough surveys are found in Gray and Moberg (1962) and Maves (1960).

These studies generally have found that there is a direct relationship between good personal adjustment and such indicators of religiosity as church membership, church attendance, Bible reading, regular listening to radio church services, belief in an after life, and religious faith. Yet a carefully planned experimental design to explore this relationship further, with the use of the Burgess-Cavan-Havighurst Attitudes Inventory as the measure of personal adjustment, revealed that controlling other factors which also are linked with good adjustment removed the correlation between adjustment and church membership (Moberg, 1953a). The relationship observed in cruder studies must be a result of linking with church membership certain other factors which contribute to adjustment rather than a result of church membership in and of itself.

Further analysis (Moberg, 1956) through additional experimental designs demonstrated that religious activities (church attendance in the past and present, lay leadership in the church, grace at meals, reading from the Bible and other religious books, family prayers, etc.) were significantly correlated with high adjustment scores. It was concluded that either those who are well-adjusted engage in many religious activities or else engaging in many religious activities contributes to good adjustment in old age.

Similarly, an experiment designed (Moberg, 1953b) to analyze the relationships between adjustment and leadership in the church, as indicated by office-holding and committee work in the past and present, revealed that personal adjustment was positively related to lay leadership. An investigation (Moberg, 1958) of Christian beliefs about sin, prayer, the future, the Bible, and Jesus in relationship to personal adjustment also revealed a positive relationship between holding conventional Christian beliefs and good adjustment in old age when other factors were controlled. The evidence from these experimental designs, based upon institutionalized persons in homes for the aged, a county home, and a soldiers' home, supports the conclusion that religious beliefs and activities, in contrast to church affiliation *per se*, contribute to good personal adjustment in old age.

This conclusion is supported by additional studies of elderly people. The most significant of these (Moberg & Taves, 1965) involves over 5,000 persons aged 60 years and over interviewed in five surveys in four midwestern states. It was found that the adjustment scores of church "leaders" (church officers and committeemen), other church members, and non-church members were significantly different, with the leaders consistently highest and non-members lowest. Cross-tabulations of the data for 1,340 urban respondents in one of the states demonstrated that these differences remained

> statistically significant at the .001 level when analyzed within categories of sex, age, education, marital status, home ownership and type of residence, participation in civic, social, and professional organizations, organizational activity levels compared to those during the respondents' fifties, self-rating of health, and self-identification of age. Only in the area of employment were the variations non-significant, but even these were in the anticipated direction,

so the hypothesis that church participation is related to good personal adjustment in old age was overwhelmingly supported by the evidence.

A study (Oles, 1949) of Orthodox Jews aged 65 and over also found that adjustment was related to religious adherence. No non-religious persons were in the well-adjusted category; all were intensely or fairly religious. Three-fourths of the fairly adjusted group were intensely or fairly religious, but only 35% of the poorly and very poorly adjusted group were.

Religious beliefs and activities seem, on the basis of these and other studies, to be positively related to good personal-social adjustment in old age. Contrary evidence, but on a somewhat different basis, comes from Barron's (1961) New York City study. Only 39% mentioned that religion and the church gave them the most satisfaction and comfort in their lives today. This was exceeded by being home with the family, keeping house, "doing things I like to do by myself at home," having relatives visit, and spending time with close friends. Worry about getting older was significantly less among these who found religion comforting only for the age group 40-45; the comparative figures for all ages indicate that 37% of those who derive comfort from religion worry about aging compared with 40.6% of those who do not find religion comforting. Both of these measures of religiosity are very limited, but this finding suggests the need for further research before making sweeping generalizations about the impact of religion upon personal adjustment.

Another consequential aspect of religion is the large number of retirement homes and communities, nursing care facilities, social clubs, literary projects, counseling centers, volunteer services programs, educational activities, and other programs by and for the aged which are under church sponsorship (Culver, 1961). While these, like all human behavior, are based upon a wide range of economic, social, political, psychological, and humanitarian interests, the very fact that religiously based institutions are their sponsors demonstrates this to be a consequence of organized religion. Religious beliefs, feelings, knowledge, and practices undoubtedly are an underlying factor in much of the humanitarian work that is done through other institutional structures as well. The educational and inspirational work of the church often is directly oriented toward such goals; to whatever extent it is effective, it serves as an enlightening and motivating influence in society, and more often produces change through its constituents than through formal institutional action. This aspect of the consequental dimension of religious commitment is obviously very difficult to study empirically because it is so intricately woven into the total fabric of society.

INTERRELATIONS OF THE DIMENSIONS

Some studies have shown both the interconnectedness and the relative independence of various dimensions of religious commitment. The biserial correlation coefficient between the religious activity and religious attitude scores in the Chicago Activities and Attitudes Inventories by Burgess, Cavan, and Havighurst, for example, was significant at the .001 level of confidence in a North Carolina study (Jeffers & Nichols, 1961). The correlation co-efficient between attitudes toward religion and frequency of attendance at religious services in the original Chicago study was .55 among 1,024 males and .37 among 1,894 females (Cavan et al., 1949). In a study (Moberg, 1951) of 219 institutionalized aged persons, the product-moment correlation of a religious activities score and a religious belief score was .660 with a standard error of .038.

Such relationships are the kind one would expect; if a person has religious faith, he is more apt to participate in the personal and social activities which simultaneously nourish that faith and are consequences of it. Belief in life after death thus is significantly associated with more frequent church attendance, more frequent Bible reading, a greater number of other religious activities, a feeling that religion is the most important thing in life, less fear of death, and stronger religious attitudes than are found among those who lack such a belief (Jeffers et al., 1961).

Nevertheless, it is a fallacy to assume that *all* dimensions of religiosity are highly intercorrelated. Hospitalized old people, we know, are somewhat more likely than the elderly in the community to identify with a religious group, but they also are considerably less likely to attend religious services than nonhospitalized old people (Fiske, 1960). To judge the totality of the religiosity of a person on the basis of one of the five major dimensions of religious commitment or, as is a common practice, of but one subdimension thereof, can lead to serious errors. Religious preference, church attendance, religious self-identification, and other simple indicators of religiosity must be used with great caution of interpretation. Religious commitment is a complex phenomenon with many ramifications. Until research has demonstrated the ways in which and the extent to which the experiential, ideological, ritualistic, intellectual, and consequential dimensions of religious commitment are inter-correlated, it is wise to refrain from jumping to conclusions about any of them on the basis of evidence only from another.

SUMMARY AND CONCLUSIONS

Research to date seems to indicate fairly conclusively that ritualistic behavior outside the home tends to diminish with increasing age, while religious attitudes and feelings apparently increase among people who have an acknowledged religion. To use Kuhlen's (1962) words in his summary of research findings on adult religion,

> . . . in all studies examined, with the exception of those relating to church attendance, trends indicate an increased interest in and concern about religion as age increases, even into extreme old age.

In other words, religion as a set of external extradomiciliary rituals apparently decreases in old age, while the internal personal responses linked with man's relationships to God apparently increase among religious people. Thus both disengagement from and re-engagement with religion are typical in old age!

We have seen that some religious practices decline in the later years, but religious feelings and beliefs apparently increase. These contrasting tendencies account for most of the apparently contradictory statements about the place of religion in old age. The use of non-comparable "indicators" or "measures" of religiosity has led to confusion. More research is needed on the major dimensions of religiosity; it will have implications for the specialist in geriatrics as well as for churchmen and gerontologists.

This distinction is related to the age-old contrast between faith and "works." Most of the objective practices ("works") of religion become increasingly difficult to perform in old age as the body and mind gradually show the effects of the aging process. Yet in his "spirit" the religious person may remain devout; his religius beliefs and feelings can become more intense even though his institutionally-oriented religious practices diminish.

Recognition of these distinct dimensions of religiosity thus helps to resolve differences of opinion about the role of religion among the elderly. Research can clarify the subject further; it also can lead to more realistic and wholesome relationships between clergymen and psychologists, social workers, and medical personnel and to keener awareness of the religious implications of geriatric practice.

REFERENCES

Aldridge, G. J.: The role of older people in a Florida retirement community, *Geriatrics, 11*:223-226, 1956.

Anon.: Do Americans believe in God? *Cath. Digest, 17*:1-5, Nov. 1952.

Barron, M. L.: *The aging American: an introduction to social gerontology and geriatrics.* Thomas Y. Crowell, New York, 1961, pp. 164-183.

Cavan, R. S., E. W. Burgess, R. J. Havighurst, and H. Goldhamer: *Personal adjustment in old age.* Sci. Res. Assoc., Chicago, 1949. pp. 58, 198.

Covalt, N. K.: The meaning of religion to older people — the medical perspective. *In*: D. L. Scudder (Editor, *Organized religion and the older person.* Univ. Florida Press, Gainesville, 1958, pp. 78-90.

Covolt, N. K.: The meaning of religion to older people. *Geriatrics,* 15:658-664, 1960.

Culver, E. T.: *New church programs with the aging.* Association Press, New York, 1961.

Cumming, E., and W. E. Henry: *Growing old: the process of disengagement.* Basic Books, New York, 1961, pp. 91-94.

Fiefel, H.: Older persons look at death. *Geriatrics 11:* 127-130, 1956.

Fichter, J. H.: *Social relations in the urban parish.* Univ. Chicago Press, Chicago, 1954, pp. 83-93.

Fiske, M.: *Some social dimensions of psychiatric disorders in old age.* Langley Porter Neuropsychiat. Inst., San Francisco, 1960, p. 13 (mimeo.).

Fiske, M.: Geriatric mental illness: methodologic and social aspects. *Geriatrics, 16:* 306-310, 1961.

Fulton, R. L.: Symposium: death attitudes. Comments. *J. Geront., 16:* 63-65, 1961.

Glock, C. Y.: On the study of religious commitment. *Relig. Educ., 57:* S-98-S-110, 1962.

Gray, R. M., and D. O. Moberg: *The church and the older person.* Wm. B. Eerdmans, Grand Rapids, 1962, pp. 41-43, 153.

Havighurst, R. J., and R. Albrecht: *Older people.* Longmans, Green, New York, 1953, pp. 201-203.

Hunter, W. W., and H. Maurice: *Older people tell their story.* Univ. Mich., Ann Arbor, 1953. pp. 62-63.

Jeffers, F. C., C. R. Nichols: The relationship of activities and attitudes to physical well-being in older people. *J. Geront., 16:* 67-70, 1961.

Jeffers, F. C., C. R. Nichols, and C. Eisdorfer: Attitudes of older persons toward death: a preliminary study. *J. Geront.,* 16:53-56, 1961.

Kuhlen, R. G.: Trends in religious behavior during the adult years. *In:* L. C. Little (Editor), *Wider horizons in christian adult education.* Univ. Pittsburgh Press, Pittsburgh, 1962, p. 23.

Lazerwitz, B.: Membership in voluntary associations and frequency of church attendance. *J. Scient. Study Religion, 2:* 74-84, 1962.

Lloyd, R. G.: Social and personal adjustment of retired persons *Social. soc. Res., 39:* 312-316, 1955.

Marshall, H., and M. H. Oden: The status of the mature gifted individual as a basis for evaluation of the aging process. *Gerontologist, 2:* 201-206, 1962.

Maves, P. B.: Aging, religion, and the church. *In:* C. Tibbitts (Editor), *Handbook of social gerontology.* Univ. Chicago Press, Chicago, 1960, pp. 698-719.

Mayo, S. C.: Social participation among the older population in rural areas of Wake County, North Carolina, *Soc. Forces, 30:* 53-59, 1951.

McCann, C. W.: *Long Beach senior citizens' survey.* Community Welfare Counc., Long Beach, 1955, pp. 50-52.

McCrary, J. S.: *The role, status, and participation of the aged in a small community.* Ph.D. thesis, Washington Univ., St. Louis, 1956.

Moberg, D. O.: *Religion and personal adjustment in old age.* Ph.D. thesis, Univ. Minnesota, Minneapolis, 1951, p. 105.

Moberg, D. O.: Church membership and personal adjustment in old age. *J. Geront., 8:* 207-211, 1953 (a).

Moberg, D. O.: Leadership in the church and personal adjustment in old age. *Social. soc. Res., 37:* 312-316, 1953 (b).

Moberg, D. O.: Religious activities and personal adjustment in old age. *J. soc. Psychol., 43:* 261-267, 1956.

Moberg, D. O.: Christian beliefs and personal adjustment in old age. *J. Amer. Sci. Affil., 10:* 8-12, 1958.

Moberg, D. O.: *The Church as a social institution.* Prentice-Hall, Englewood Cliffs, N. J., 1962, pp. 393-395, 414-418.

Moberg, D. O.: The integration of older members in the church congregation. In: A. M. Rose and W. A. Peterson (Editors). *Older people and their social world.* F. A. Davis, Philadelphia, 1965.

Moberg, D. O., and M. J. Taves: Church participation and adjustment in old age. In: A. M. Rose and W. A. Peterson (Editors), *Older people and their social world.* F. A. Davis, Philadelphia, 1965.

Oles, E. S.: *Religion and old age, a study of the possible influence of religious adherence on adjustment.* Thesis, Bucknell Univ., Lewisburg, Pa., 1949, Reviewed in *J. Geront., 5:* 187, 1950.

Orbach, H. L.: Aging and religion: church attendance in the Detroit metropolitan area. *Geriatrics, 16:* 530-540, 1961.

O'Reilly, C. T., and M. M. Pembroke: *Older people in a Chicago community.* Loyola University, Chicago, n.d. (survey made in 1956).

Pan, J. S.: Institutional and personal adjustment in old age. *J. gen. Psychol., 85:* 155-158, 1954.

Starbuck, E. D.: The psychology of religion (3rd ed.). Walter Scott, New York, 1911, p. 320.

Swenson, W. M.: Attitudes toward death in an aged population. *J. Geront., 16:* 49-52, 1961.

Taietz, R., and O. F. Larson: Social participation and old age. *Rur. Sociol., 21:* 229-238, 1956.

Taves, M. J., and G. D. Hansen: Seventeen hundred elderly citizens. *In:* A. M. Rose (Editor), *Aging in Minnesota.* Univ. Minnesota Press, Minneapolis, 1963, p. 172.

Theisen, S. P.: *A social survey of aged Catholics in the deanery of Fort Wayne, Indiana.* Ph.D. thesis, Univ. Notre Dame, Ind. 1962.

Toch, H.: Attitudes of the "fifty plus" age group: preliminary considerations toward a longitudinal study. *Publ. Opin. Quart., 17:* 391-394, 1953.

Treanton, J. R.: Symposium: death attitudes. Comments. *J. Geront., 16:* 63, 1961.

Warren, R. L.: Old age in a rural township. *In: Old age is no barrier. N. Y. State Jt. Legis. Com. on Problems Aging, Albany, 1962. pp. 155-166.*

Wolff, K.: Group psychotherapy with geriatric patients in a state hospital setting: results of a three year study. *Group Psychotherapy. 12:* 218-222, 1959 (a).

Wolff, K.: *The biological, sociological and psychological aspects of aging.* Charles C. Thomas, Springfield, Ill., 1959, p. 75 (b).

Wolff, K.: A Co-ordinated approach to the geriatric problem. *J. Amer. ger. Soc., 9:* 573-580, 1961.

Youmans, E. G.: Aging patterns in a rural and an urban area of Kentucky. *Univ. Ky. agric. Exp. Sta. Bull. 681,* 1963, p. 45.

20. Cohort Analysis of Church Attendance, 1939-1969*

C. Ray Wingrove and Jon P. Alston**

A recurrent topic in the fields of both gerontology and sociology of religion is the relationship between church attendance and age.

Howard M. Bahr (1970) presents comprehensive descriptions of four models which have been used to categorize the findings of research on the relationship between aging and church attendance.[1] He calls these four models *traditional, stability, family-cycle,* and *disengagement.* The traditional model views church attendance as reaching a low between the ages of 30 and 35, then increasing steadily until old age. The stability model sees church attendance as unrelated to age and as being fairly constant throughout one's lifetime. The family-cycle model suggests a relationship between age and church attendance dependent upon age linked marriage and child rearing stages. According to this model, the peak in church attendance appears among young parents assumed to be concerned about their children's religious education. Finally, the disengagement model implies a gradual decline in church attendance from middle to old age. As the person ages, he gradually reduces his church-related activity.

The research of Fichter (1952, 1954), Cauter and Downham (1954), O'Reilly (1957), Smith (1966), Glock, *et al* (1967), as well as the writing of Argyle (1959:69) support the traditional model. That of Lazerwitz (1961), Orbach (1961), Catholic Digest (1953), 1966) and to some extent Screib (1965-a) advocate the stability model. Albrecht (1958) seems to be the chief exponent of the family life-cycle model, although Lazerwitz (1961) did find increased regularity of church attendance among Protestants with children 5 years old and older. The disengagement model finds support from the works of Mayo (1951), Hunter and Maurice (1953), McCann (1955), Catholic Charities of St. Louis (1955), and Barron (1958, 1961).

*Reprinted from *Social Forces,* Vol. 53, Number 2, December 1974, pages 324-331 with permission of the authors and *Social Forces.*
**Dr. Wingrove is Professor of Sociology at the University of Richmond and is an editor of this book. Dr. Alston is Associate Professor in the Department of Sociology at Texas A & M University.

A major source of confusion seems to arise from the two major methodological strategies utilized by the researchers noted above. We suspect that the existence of four empirically tested, yet contradictory models is due to the use of methodologies inappropriate for the problem. With the exception of a few restricted longitudinal studies (Streib, 1965-a), most of the research in this area can be classified as either cross-sectional or retrospective in nature. Cross-sectional analyses assume that the activity pattern of those in younger age categories accurately portrays that of older people when they were younger. Such an approach ignores changes in behavior due to inter-generational differences as well as the possible existence of social change taking place during the lifetimes of respondents. In short, the cross-sectional approach presents a static view of behavior which often results in erroneous conclusions (*Geriatric Focus,* 1973).

The retrospective approach attempts to approximate life cycle patterns in church attendance with the assumption that the memories of respondents serve them well enough to remember accurately church attendance patterns of earlier ages. Not only might memories be fuzzy, but there might also be a tendency for people to idealize their past religious behavior. Such biases would tend to produce support for the disengagement model as indeed the retrospective studies do. This becomes apparent from Bahr's (1970) summary presentation of the patterns of aging and church attendance found in the selected studies which he uses. At a later point in his article, Bahr (1970) also points out discrepancies in his own study resulting from the use of retrospective versus cross-sectional data.

Perhaps the ideal method which would avoid the obvious weaknesses of both the cross-sectional and retrospective approaches would be a panel study of a representative national sample. Such a study would adequately demonstrate how people change as they grow older. Of course, time, money, and human impatience greatly discourages serious consideration of such a project (Glenn and Zody, 1970). Many scholars in the field (cf., Orbach, 1961: Riley, and Foner. 1968: Hammond, 1969; and Glenn and Zody, 1970) recognize the inherent weaknesses of the cross-sectional and retrospective approaches and the improbability of a national panel study. They have suggested cohort analysis as perhaps the most applicable methodological alternative.[2] One of the major problems hindering cohort analysis, of course, has been the non-availability of comparable secondary data which cover enough time to allow the kind of analysis in which the researcher is interested. Until recently, such data were unavailable, and thus, a cohort analysis of life-long church attendance as related to age was impossible.

This study presents a cohort analysis of church attendance which spans a thirty-year interval (1939-1969) and offers for the first time data on church attendance of a longitudinal nature which can be compared to the findings of the growing body of literature based on cross-sectional and retrospective methodologies.

METHODOLOGY

The data on church attendance used in the present study derive from six national surveys of the American population conducted by the American Institute of Public Opinion (the Gallup Poll) during the years 1939, 1950, 1955, 1960, 1965, and 1969.

The earlier polls used quota samples, while those taking place after 1955 are based on more representative sampling procedures using probability samples (Glenn, 1970). By 1960, the Gallup organization had completed its transition from the use of quota to probability samples (Glenn and Zody, 1970). Therefore we standardized the church attendance figures for the 1950 and 1955 polls using the educational distribution of corresponding age groups from the 1960 survey (See Glenn and Zody, 1970, for a discussion of this technique).

Church attendance is measured by responses to the question, "Did you, yourself, happen to attend church or synagogue in the last seven days?"[3] Those respondents who answered neither "yes" or "no" to these questions were omitted from our analysis.

The samples consist of the total white populations, including non-Christians, since the present focus is upon the church attendance patterns of the American population as a whole rather than of a specific religious group. Although the Jewish population has a different church attendance pattern than do the Christians (Alston, 1971), the use of the total white population maintains the representativeness of the samples. However, the non-Christian sample was very small in all surveys so that the data essentially refers to Protestants and Catholics.

Nearly all (98.5-100%) respondents in the surveys used were willing to answer whether or not they had attended church services. The total sample sizes varied from roughly 1,000 respondents (1955, 1965, and 1969), 2,000 respondents (1950), to 3,000 respondents (1939 and 1960). Since the time between dates for which our data are presented is unequal as well as relatively short, it was impossible to arrange the data in a matrix which would permit comparison within and among cohorts.[4] Therefore, our data are presented in tables in which each cohort can be traced through time by reading across a row, in which partial cross-sectional analysis for any year can be viewed by reading down the column under the year. We decided that the age span for cohorts should be ten years as this was the shortest span which would still allow adequate sample size for analysis.

The youngest of five cohorts used here is composed of those white respondents born between 1925 and 1934 and who were, therefore, 16-25 years old when interviewed in 1950. Since this cohort is so young, it figures into our analysis only minimally. Our oldest cohort consists of individuals born during 1885-1894, and who were 45-54 years old in 1939.

In order to facilitate the observation of trend lines, we present profiles of each cohort based on data from Table 1. Profiles were drawn by plotting the church attendance for each cohort by the median age of each cohort during the year in which the survey was conducted (See Figure 1). Thus, life-long church attendance patterns for each cohort are presented based upon the median age of each cohort at the time of survey.

FINDINGS

One of the first patterns to become apparent from figure 1 is that while church attendance seems to vary by age, each cohort is characterized by its own peculiar profile. Cohort #1, although restricted in age-span, exhibits a peak during the mid-twenties, a pattern atypical of the remaining cohorts. These were individuals maturing during the post World War II religious "boom."

Although interpretation is hazardous because of the small age range forming cohort #1, we suspect that this "generation" was, when young, influenced by the increased interest among Americans in religious activity — though the extent and character of this religiosity is beyond the present analysis (Herberg, 1955; Lipset, 1959; Fichter, 1960).

It is interesting that while the first cohort achieved its attendance peak relatively early in life, the extent of attendance is not much higher than the other cohorts. That is, this cohort's interest in religion (as measured by church attendance) seem relatively transitory and not especially greater in degree than other cohorts. It may very well be true (Lipset, 1959) that the post-war renewal in religious interests primarily reflected secular rather than religious characteristics. However, we also note that with one exception (Cohort #4, which nears its peak in 1955) the attendance-peak for all cohorts was reached during the

TABLE 1.
*Percentage of White Respondents
Who Said They Attended Church in Six 10-year
Cohorts By Sex – 1939, 1950, 1955, 1960, 1965, 1968*[a]
(N's are in parentheses)

	1939[b]	1950	1955	1960	1965	1969
Cohort No. 1						
(1925-1934)-ages		16-25	21-30	26-35	31-40	35-44
Total		34(105)	49(287)	46(507)	47(609)	43(256)
Males		28(39)	44(121)	43(216)	42(284)	34(118)
Females		34(66)	53(166)	48(291)	52(325)	51(138)
Cohort No. 2						
(1915-1924)-ages	15-24	26-35	31-40	36-45	41-50	45-54
Total	40(445)	38(284)	45(329)	52(627)	50(638)	48(280)
Males	38(277)	32(138)	35(138)	42(309)	50(315)	44(138)
Females	44(168)	43(146)	51(191)	61(318)	50(323)	51(142)
Cohort No. 3						
(1905-1914)-ages	25-34	36-45	41-50	46-55	51-60	55-64
Total	38(729)	43(272)	54(300)	44(448)	45(553)	38(246)
Males	35(499)	36(126)	52(150)	43(237)	40(266)	30(118)
Females	44(230)	51(146)	56(150)	44(211)	50(287)	45(128)
Cohort No. 4						
(1895-1904)-ages	35-44	46-55	51-60	56-65	61-70	65-74
Total	35(679)	46(192)	49(201)	47(307)	52(360)	46(128)
Males	31(460)	39(95)	39(98)	39(158)	46(192)	48(75)
Females	44(219)	52(97)	56(103)	55(149)	59(168)	43(53)
Cohort No. 5						
(1885-1894)-ages	45-54	56-65	61-70	66-75	71-80	75-84
Total	42(556)	48(150)	40(167)	39(254)	40(200)	35(51)
Males	38(367)	39(78)	34(96)	39(109)	31(115)	30(27)
Females	50(189)	56(70)	48(71)	40(145)	51(85)	42(24)

[a] Percentages for 1950 and 1955 are standardized to the educational distribution in the cohort as shown by the 1960 data. (See Glenn and Zody: 1970).

[b] Data for 1939 are presented as a matter of interest but not as part of the analysis due to the incomparability of sampling procedures and insufficient information to permit standardization.

FIGURE 1.
Percentage Church Attendance By Age For Cohorts 1-5

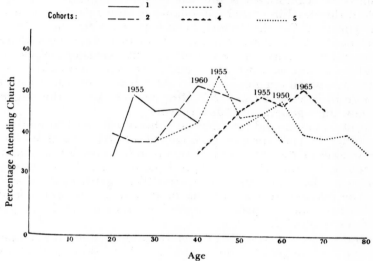

decade, 1950-1960. Thus, different age groups took part in the increased attendance rates during the 1950's. After 1965, all cohort profiles decline irrespective of specific age of respondents at the time.

Cohorts #2 and #3 reach their peaks in attendance before age 50 while Cohorts #4 and #5 reach theirs after age 55. Also, some cohorts are typically high in church attendance while others are, on the average, low (See figure 1). Moreover, it is interesting to note that the age at which the four overlapping cohorts are closest in church attendance is the 45-55 age category, when the inter-cohort attendance range is from 42% for cohort #5 to 48% for cohort #2. This suggests that, while each cohort is slightly different from the rest, external social pressures must exist to achieve such homogeneity at age 45-55.

Figure 2 presents attendance data by sex as well as individual cohort. As expected (Argyle, 1951), females are generally higher than males in terms of church attendance. However, it is more important to point out that the sexes tend to follow the same trend. The exceptions to this pattern are found in cohorts #2 and #4. In cohort #2, attendance for the sexes is equal during ages 40-50. This convergence is due to an increase in male attendance and a decrease in female attendance. For cohort #4, male-female attendance differences are almost erased after age sixty-five. Cohort #4 is singular in another manner. Its male-female differential in church attendance is both relatively large *and* highly constant. For this cohort, born between 1895 and 1904, the double standard (in terms of church attendance) is represented at its highest and most consistent level until the extreme ages are reached.

There is no age at which males and females are most alike for all cohorts. Males and females in cohorts #2 and #3 converge before age 50; those in cohorts #4 and #5, after age 65! Again, this suggests consistent inter-generational differences.

Two observations indicate that all cohorts may be responding to forces other than just chronological age. *All* cohorts, regardless of their respective ages at the time, are at or very near their peaks in attendance between 1950 and 1960 (exception cohort #4). Also, they *all* experience a decline in attendance after 1965 regardless of age at that date. The religious revival in terms of attendance apparently ended after 1965 and was felt throughout all of the white population, regardless of age (Alston, 1971).

Secondly, there is typically greater variation in church attendance from one age category to another within cohorts (longitudinal) than there is from one age category to another in any single year (cross-sectional). (See Table 2) These observations suggest that all cohorts respond in some degree to the social pressures of the times. When the fashion ends, all ages are equally as likely to change behavior.

Thus, we have suggested three factors other than age itself which seem to influence church attendance: first, the cohort (when born) to which one belongs, since each cohort manifests a distinct and separate profile; secondly, sex, which all studies prior to this have also shown; and thirdly, the social pressures of the time which is operationalized here as the decade in which the poll was taken.

To ignore any of these factors increases the likelihood of incomplete interpretation. For example, females are generally higher in attendance than are males, except for certain cohorts at the upper age levels. However, males in some cohorts have equal or higher attendance rates than females at the same age in another cohort. For example, the males 41-50 years old in cohort #3 were slightly higher in attendance than females 41-50 years old in cohort #2. Although sex is a very important variable associated with church attendance, one cannot minimize the impact of cohort membership and the prevailing trends of a specific time period.

FIGURE 2. *Church Attendance By Age And Sex For Cohorts 1-5*

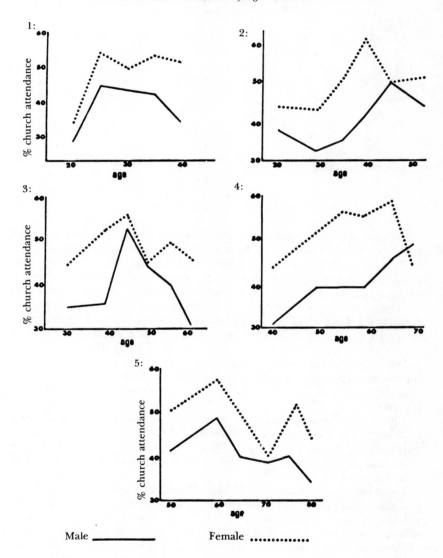

Male _____   Female ••••••••••••

TABLE 2 [a]

Range in Church Attendance Percentages,
By Cohort and Year

Cohort	Range Percentage Low-High	Range	Year	Range Percentage Low-High	Range
# 1	34-49	15	1950	34-48	14
2	38-52	14	1955	40-54	14
3	37-54	17	1960	39-52	13
4	35-52	17	1965	40-53	13
5	35-48	13	1969	35-48	13

$\bar{x} = 15.20$ $\bar{x} = 13.40$

[a]*Source:* Table 1

Summary and Conclusions:

In contradiction to the stability model, our data suggest that church attendance varies somewhat by age; however, our cohort analysis reveals no consistent pattern in this relationship. One observes little evidence in support of any of the four models which typically categorize data in this area.[5] The traditional model is supported by the profile of cohort #4 (born 1895-1904) but contradicted by those of cohorts #2 (born 1915-1924) and #3 (born 1905-1944). The minimum range in church attendance is found in cohort #5 (born 1885-1894) which varies from 35% for those aged 75-85 to 48% for those aged 60-70. The younger cohorts manifest an even greater range which is hardly an argument for the stability model which supports the view that the rate of church attendance is fairly constant throughout one's lifetime.

The disengagement model receives some support from the patterns of cohorts #2 (born 1915-1924) and #3 (born 1905-1914) but is clearly contradicted by cohort #4 (born 1894-1904) which continues to exhibit increased church attendance from those aged 35-45 (35%) to a high of 52% for ages 61-70.

Likewise, the continuation of high church attendance into later age categories for cohorts #4 and #5, especially for #4, casts doubt on the validity of the family cycle model. Church attendance is strongly associated with sex, as females consistently have much higher rates of attendance than do males. Nevertheless, both sexes from the same cohort exhibit similar profiles, with the males being consistently lower.

Church attendance also appears related to the mood of the times. Most of our cohorts experienced their peaks in attendance during the ten year interval from 1950-1960 which some refer to as the period of religious revival in the U. S. Furthermore, *all* cohorts do show a decline in attendance after 1965, regardless of their ages at the time. Other research, for example, that of Irving Webber (1954) and some cited by Barron (1961) also suggests the influence of social climate on church attendance.[6] Consequently, it seems that church attendance varies greatly in frequency and in time of peak occurrence from one cohort to another.

Additional use of cohort analysis would profit from an increased availability of data. As other surveys are made available to scholars by existing data banks (Hyman, 1972), more controls could be introduced by collapsing a number of surveys into larger samples. This would allow for the use of such controls as region, city size, and occupation, all of which influence the levels of church attendance (Alston, 1972). In addition, larger samples would allow for the analysis of the influence of denominational membership, which is impossible at the present time (Glenn, 1973).

Our data suggest that church attendance patterns should not be investigated in a social vacuum. Additional data might reveal long term cycles responding to social pressures which characterize the social milieu. Further research should show more clearly what these social pressures are. Thus, we conclude that even though church attendance varies by age, no single model fits every cohort, and many other factors must be taken into consideration. The present study suggests that in addition to sex, specific cohort membership and the general societal environment be taken into account as causative factors. These, plus other factors such as income, education, occupation, denomination, familial status, and individual group levels of religiosity prevent any definite statement on the association between age and church attendance at the present time.

FOOTNOTES

1. For a more complete summary and discussion of studies in this area, see Moberg (1965) and Orbach (1961).

2. A number of advantages in the use of separate surveys for cohort analyses (Hyman, 1972; Glenn 1970 and 1973), although both panel and cohort studies allow for the study of change during a period of time. Studies using the panel design necessarily involve a large amount of time, and also entail a high cost. A thirty-year panel study would be difficult to maintain, even ignoring such problems as the attrition of subjects. In addition, repeated interviews, as are done in panel studies, may influence the response patterns (Babbie, 1973). Unlike the use of the retrospective method, cohort analysis uses responses based on contemporary attitudes and behavior does not rely upon the memory of the respondents.

3. Michael Argyle (1959) argues that asking respondents if they went to church last Sunday leaves much less room for distortion than asking how often they attend.
4. Since data did not permit the use of age intervals equal to the time intervals between surveys, there is an overlap in ages of the same cohort from one survey date to the next. For example, those 16-25 in 1950 were 21-30 by 1955. It is only when age intervals equal the time interval between surveys that no overlap occurs, and that the data can be arranged in a matrix that facilitates comparisons within and among cohorts (Glenn and Zody, 1970, and Hyman, 1972).
5. As Glenn and Zody point out (1970) tests of significance are not really applicable to corrected percentages such as we have used in our analysis. They do say it is permissible if one allows a greater difference for statistical significance than he would with raw percentages. Casual observation of our data indicates that more stringent tests of significance would seldom yield significant differences in percentages, so the authors decided against any such analysis. However, with perhaps the exception of the stability model, one need not apply statistical tests to see that our data provide no support for the models discussed in this paper.
6. For discussions of factors related to participation by the aged see Bultena (1949), Lenski (1953), Taietz and Larson (1956), and Cowhig and Schnore (1962).

REFERENCES

Albrecht, R. E. 1958. The Meaning of Religion to Older People — The Social Aspect. In *Organized Religion and The Older Person,* edited by D. L. Scudder. Gainesville, Florida: University of Florida Press.

Alston, J. P. 1971. Social Variables Associated with Church Attendance, 1965 and 1969. *Journal for the Scientific Study of Religion,* 10:233-236.

Alston, J. P., 1972. Church Attendance and size of community. *Journal for the Scientific Study of Religious* 11:182-184.

Argyle, M. 1959. *Religious Behaviour.* Glencoe, Illinois: The Free Press.

Babbie, E. R. 1973. *Survey Research Methods.* Belmont, California: Wadsworth Publishing Company, Inc.

Bahr, H. M. 1970. Aging and Religious Disaffiliation. *Social Forces* 49:60-71.

Barron, M. L. 1958. Role of Religion and Religious Institutions in Creating the Milieu of Older People. In *Organized Religion and the Older Person,* edited by D. L. Scudder. Gainesville, Florida: University of Florida Press.

____1961. *The Aging American: An Introduction to Social Gerontology and Geriatrics.* New York: Crowell.

Bultena, L. 1949. Church Membership and Church Attendance in Madison, Wisconsin. *American Sociological Review* 14:384-389.

Cauter, T., and S. Downham. 1954. *The Communication of Ideas.* London: Chatto & Winders.

Catholic Charities of St. Louis. 1955. "Older People in the Family, the

Parish and the Neighborhood." St. Louis: Catholic Churches of St. Louis.

Catholic Digest. 1953. "How Important Religion Is to Americans." 17:7-12.

———. 1966. "Do Americans Go to Church?" 30:24-32.

Cowhig, J. D., and L. F. Schnore. 1962. "Religious Affiliation and Attendance in Metropolitan Centers." *American Catholic Sociological Review* 23:113-27.

Fichter, J. H. 1952. "The Profile of Catholic Religious Life." *American Journal of Sociology* 58 (July): 145-50.

———. 1954. *Social Relations in the Urban Parish.* Chicago: University of Chicago Press.

———. 1960. "The Americanization of Catholicism." In Thomas T. McAvoy (ed.), *Roman Catholicism and the American Way of Life.* Notre Dame: University of Notre Dame Press.

Geriatric Focus. 1973. Institutionalized Aged: The 4 Percent Fallacy 12:No. 3:1.

Glenn, N. D. 1970. Problems of Comparability in Trend Studies with Opinion Poll Data. *Public Opinion Quarterly* 34:82-91.

———. 1973. The Social Scientific Data Archives: The Problem of Underutilization. *The American Sociologist* 8:42-45.

———, and R. E. Zody. 1970. Cohort Analysis with National Survey Data. *The Gerontologist* 10, Part I: 233-240.

Glock, C. U., et al. 1967. *To Comfort and Challenge.* Berkeley: University of California Press.

Hammond, P. E. 1969. Aging and the Ministry. In *Aging and Society,* Vol. II, *Aging and the Professions,* edited by Matilda W. Riley *et al.* New York: Russell Sage Foundation.

Herberg, W. 1955. *Protestant – Catholic – Jew.* New York: Doubleday.

Hunter, W. W., and H. Maurice. 1953. *Older People Tell Their Story.* Ann Arbor: Institute for Human Adjustment, Division of Gerontology, University of Michigan.

Hyman, H. 1972. *Secondary Analysis of Sample Surveys: Principles, Procedures, and Potentialities.* New York: John Wiley & Sons, Inc.

Lazerwitz, B. 1961. Some Factors Associated with Variation in Church Attendance. *Social Forces* 39: 301-309.

Lenski, G. H. 1953. Some Correlates of Religious Interest. *American Sociological Review* 18: 533-544.

Lipset, S. M. 1959. Religion in America: What Religious Revival? *Columbia University Forum* 2: 17-21.

Mayo, S. C. 1951. Social Participation Among the Older Population in

Revival Areas of Wake County, North Carolina. *Social Forces* 30: 53-59.

McCann, C. W. 1955. *Long Beach Senior Citizens' Survey.* Long Beach, California: Community Welfare Council.

Moberg, D. O. 1965. Religiosity in Old Age. *The Gerontologist* 5: 78-87.

Orbach, H. L. 1961. Aging and Religion: A Study of Church Attendance in the Detroit Metropolitan Area. *Geriatrics* 16: 530-540.

O'Reilly, C. T. 1957. Religious Practice and Personal Adjustment of Older People. *Sociology and Social Research,* 42: 119-121.

Riley, M. W., and A. Foner. 1968. *Aging and Society. Vol. I An Inventory of Research Findings.* New York: Russell Sage Foundation.

Smith, J. 1966. The Narrowing Social World of the Aged. In *Social Aspects of Aging,* edited by Ida H. Simpson and John McKinney, Durham, N. C.: Duke University Press.

Streib, G. 1965a. Longitudinal Study of Retirement, Final Report to the Social Security Administration, Washington, D.C.: Govt. Printing Office.

Taietz, P., and O. F. Larson. 1956. Social Participation and Old Age. *Rural Sociology* 21: 229-238.

Webber, Irving L. 1954. The Organized Social Life of the Retired in Two Florida Communities. *American Journal of Sociology* 59: 340-346.

III
CONCERNS
FREQUENTLY
CONFRONTING THE
AGED

SEX, RETIREMENT, DEATH AND DYING

Concerns of the aged are not too different from those of the rest of the population. Old people are interested in meeting basic human needs such as having adequate housing and food, finding meaningful endeavors to fill up their time, and in loving and being loved. Nevertheless, some concerns appear to grow more salient or more frequent as people grow older. We have been selective and deal with only a few major concerns in this section as the title indicates.

Sex is included not so much because it is a special concern of the aged, but because it was thought for so long *not* to be a concern at all. Retirement perhaps is more nearly an exclusive concern of the elderly among the healthy population, and, thus, fits the image of an interest which becomes more salient with age. Death and dying while not a unique concern of the elderly are nevertheless a certainty which looms more prominently upon the horizon as one moves into his later years.

A.   SEX

The first article in this section by Isadore Rubin challenges the presumptive myth of the "sexless older years." Rubin demonstrates that sexual needs for many older people may be as great as for those at any other age. Admitting and facing these needs is but one step in the direction of helping the older person lead a more normal life, and they should not be ignored by practitioners, family and friends.

The next paper by Wingrove illustrates the persisting interest that the older person has in normal sexual experiences. While some of the elderly may develop physiological limitations, earlier patterns of sexual adjustment will persist into old age, as is true of so many other adjustment patterns. A major problem for the elderly in this area of the sexual adjustment is the diminished opportunity for normal sexual relationships. Among the very old, the small number of men as compared to women, and the somewhat limited privacy in their living arrangements often limit the opportunity for sexual experience.

A survey and synthesis of recent medical studies leads to the conclusion that there is no psychological reason why older people in reasonably good health should not have an active and satisfying sex life. In view of these findings, it is time that society relinquishes its image of the aged as sexually neuter objects with any variation being considered deviant. A healthy outlook in youth may be all many need to prevent the "sexless older years" from becoming a self-fulfilling prophecy.

21. The "Sexless Older Years"—A Socially Harmful Stereotype*

ISADORE RUBIN**

The stereotype of the "sexless older years," which has placed its stamp upon our entire culture and which, in many cases, acts as a "self-fulfilling prophecy," has done considerable damage to our aging population. Although no studies of sexual behavior and attitudes of the aging have been done on a sufficiently representative sample to provide us with norms, a growing body of research makes clear that there is no automatic cutoff to sexuality at any age and that sex interests, needs, and abilities continue to play an important role in the later years. This is true not only for the married, but also for the single and widowed. Unless our entire culture recognizes the normality of sex expression in the older years, it will be impossible for older persons to express their sexuality freely and without guilt.

It has been suggested that our culture has programmed marriage only until the child-raising period has been completed.[1] If this is true of marital roles in general, it is especially true of sexual roles in the later years. Society has not given genuine recognition to the validity of sexual activity after the child-bearing years, creating a dangerous stereotype about the "sexless older years" and defining as deviant behavior sex interest and activity which may continue vigorously into these older years.

A SELF-FULFILLING PROPHECY

This stereotype has until recently placed its unchallenged stamp upon our culture. In the late 1950s, undergraduates at Brandeis University were asked to take a test to assess their attitudes toward old people.[2] Those taking the test were requested to complete this sen-

*Reprinted from *The Annals of the American Academy of Political and Social Sciences,* Vol. 376, March 1968, pages 86-95, by permission. Copyright © by The American Academy of Political and Social Science.
**Dr. Rubin, now deceased, was for many years the editor of the magazine, *Sexology.* He was a Fellow of the Society for the Scientific Study of Sex.

tence: "Sex for most old people. . . ." Their answers were quite reveal-
ing. Almost all of these young men and women, ranging in age from
seventeen to twenty-three, considered sex for most old people to be
"negligible," "unimportant," or "past." Since sex behavior is not only a
function of one's individual attitudes and interactions with a partner,
but also a reflection of cultural expectations, the widespread belief
about the older person being sexless becomes for many a "self-fulfilling
prophecy." Our society stands indicted, says psychiatrist Karl M. Bowman, of grave neglect of the emotional needs of aging persons:

> Men and women often refrain from continuing their sexual rela-
> tions or from seeking remarriage after loss of a spouse, because
> even they themselves have come to regard sex as a little ridicu-
> lous, so much have our social attitudes equated sex with youth.
> They feel uncertain about their capacities and very self-conscious
> about their power to please. They shrink from having their pride
> hurt. They feel lonely, isolated, deprived, unwanted, insecure.
> Thoughts of euthanasia and suicide bother them. To prevent
> these feelings, they need to have as active a sex life as possible and
> to enjoy it without fear.[3]

Most of our attitudes toward sex today still constitute — despite the
great changes that have taken place in the openness with which sex is
treated publicly — what a famous British jurist has called "a legacy of
the ascetic ideal, persisting in the modern world after the ideal itself has
deceased."[4] Obviously, the ascetic attitude — essentially a philosophy
of sex-denial — would have far-reaching effects upon our attitude
toward the sexual activity of those persons in our society who have
passed the reproductive years. Even so scientific a writer as Robert S.
de Ropp, in his usually excellent *Man against Aging,* betrays the unfortunate effects of our ascetic tradition when he says:

> For sexual activity, enjoyable as it may seem in itself, still has as its
> natural aim the propagation of the species, and this activity be-
> longs to the second not the third act of life's drama.[5]

In addition to our tradition of asceticism, there are many other
factors which undoubtedly operate to keep alive a strong resistance to
the acceptance of sexuality in older people. These include our general
tradition of equating sex, love, and romance solely with youth; the
psychological difficulty which children have of accepting the fact of
parental intercourse; the tendency to think of aging as a disease rather
than a normal process; the focusing of studies upon hospitalized or
institutionalized older people rather than upon a more typical sample

of persons less beset by health, emotional, or economic problems; and the unfortunate fact that — by and large — physicians have shared the ignorance and prejudices equally with the rest of society.[6]

It is significant, however, that centuries of derogation and taboo have not been successful in masking completely the basic reality that sex interest and activity do not disappear in the older years. Elaine Cumming and William E. Henry point out that our jokes at the expense of older people have revealed considerable ambivalence in the view that all old people are asexual.[7] The contradictory attitude which people possess about sexuality in the later years is also well illustrated by the history of the famous poem "John Anderson, My Jo," written by Robert Burns almost two centuries ago. In the version known today, the poem is a sentimental tribute to an old couple's calm and resigned old age. The original folk version — too bawdy to find its way into textbooks — was an old wife's grievance about her husband's waning sex interest and ability which makes very clear that she has no intention of tottering down life's hill in a passionless and sexless old age.[8] It is also interesting to note that sexuality in older women was an important part of one of Aristophanes' comedies. In his play *Ecclesiazusae* ("Women in Parliament"), Aristophanes described how the women seized power and established a social utopia.[9] One of their first acts was to place sexual relations on a new basis in order to assure all of them ample satisfaction at all times. They decreed that, if any young man was attracted to a girl, he could not possess her until he had satisfied an old woman first. The old women were authorized to seize any youth who refused and to insist upon their rights also.

The Harmful Influence of the Myth

A British expert in the study of aging has suggested that the myth of sexlessness in the older years does have some social utility for some older women in our society who may no longer have access to a sexual partner.[10] However, the widespread denial of sexuality in older persons has a harmful influence which goes far beyond its effect upon an individual's sexual life.[11] It makes difficult, and sometimes impossible, correct diagnoses of medical and psychological problems, complicates and distorts interpersonal relations in marriage, disrupts relationships between children and parents thinking of remarriage, perverts the administration of justice to older persons accused of sex offenses, and weakens the whole self-image of the older man or woman.

A corollary of the failure to accept sexuality as a normal aspect of aging has been the tendency to exaggerate the prevalence of psychological deviation in the sexual behavior of older men and to see in most old men potential molesters of young children. Seen through the lenses of prejudice, innocent displays of affection have often loomed ominously as overtures to lascivious fondling or molestation. It is common, too, to think of the exhibitionist as being, typically, a deviation of old age.

Actually, the facts indicate the falsity of both of these stereotypes. As research by Johann W. Mohr and his associates at the Forensic Clinic of the Toronto Psychiatric Hospital showed, "contrary to common assumption the old age group is the relatively smallest one" involved in child-molesting.[12] The major age groups from whose ranks child-molesters come are adolescence, the middle to late thirties, and the late fifties. The peak of acting out of exhibitionism occurs in the mid-twenties; and, in its true form, exhibitionism is rarely seen after the age of forty.

In relatively simple and static societies, everyone knows pretty much where he stands at each stage of life, particularly the older members of the group. "But in complex and fluid social systems," notes Leo W. Simmons, "with rapid change and recurrent confusion over status and role, no one's position is so well fixed — least of all that of the aging."[13] For many aging persons, there is a crisis of identity in the very sensing of themselves as old, particularly in a culture which places so great a premium upon youth. David P. Ausubel notes that, just as in adolescence, the transition to aging is a period where the individual is in the marginal position of having lost an established and accustomed status without having acquired a new one and hence is a period productive of considerable stress.[14] Under such conditions of role confusion, aging persons tend to adopt the stereotype which society has molded for them, in sex behavior as in other forms of behavior. But they do so only at a very high psychic cost.

For many older people, continued sexual relations are important not so much for the pleasurable release from sexual tension as for the highly important source of psychological reinforcement which they may provide. Lawrence K. Frank has said:

> Sex relations can provide a much needed and highly effective resource in the later years of life when so often men face the loss of their customary prestige and self-confidence and begin to feel old, sometimes long before they have begun to age significantly. The premature cessation of sexual functioning may accelerate physiological and psychological aging since disuse of any function usually leads to concomitant changes in other capacities. After

menopause, women may find that continuation of sexual relations provides a much needed psychological reinforcement, a
feeling of being needed and of being capable of receiving love
and affection and renewing the intimacy they earlier found desirable and reassuring.[15]

THE GROWING BODY OF RESEARCH DATA

Gathering data about the sexual behavior and attitudes of the aging
has not been an easy task. To the generalized taboos about sex research
have been added the special resistance and taboos that center around
sexuality in older persons. For example, when the New England Age
Center decided to administer an inventory to its members, they included only nine questions about sex among the 103 items.[16] The nine
questions were made deliberately vague, were confined largely to past
sexual activities, and were given only to married members. Leaders of
the Center felt that if they had asked more direct questions or put them
to their unmarried members, these people would not have returned to
the Center. In California, a study of the attitudes of a sample of persons
over sixty years old in San Francisco during the early 1960s included
just one general open-ended question about sexual attitudes, apparently because of the resistance which many of the researchers had
about questioning subjects in the area of sex.[17] Psychiatrists reporting
on this research befor the Gerontological Society noted that the people
involved in research in gerontology are being hamstrung by their own
attitudes toward sex with regard to the elderly in much the same way in
which the rest of society is hamstrung with regard to their attitudes
toward the elderly in such matters as jobs, roles, and those things which
go into determining where a person fits into the social structure.

Fortunately, although no sample has yet been studied that was sufficiently broad or typical to present us with a body of norms, a sufficient
amount of data now exists which leaves no doubt of the reality of sex
interests and needs in the latter years. While it is true that there are
many men and women who look forward to the ending of sexual
relations, particularly those to whom sex has always been a distasteful
chore or those who "unconsciously welcome the excuse of advancing
years to abandon a function that has frightened them since
childhood,"[18] sexual activity, interest, and desire are not the exception
for couples in their later years. Though the capacity for sexual response does slow down gradually, along with all the other physical
capacities, it is usually not until actual senility that there is a marked loss
of sexual capacity.

With the research conducted by William H. Masters and Virginia E. Johnson, who observed the anatomy and physiology of sexual response in the laboratory, confirmation has now been obtained that sexual capacity can continue into advanced old age.[19] Among the subjects whose orgasmic cycles were studied by these two investigators were 61 menopausal and post menopausal women (ranging from forty to seventy-eight) and 39 older men (ranging from fifty-one to eighty-nine). Among the women, Masters and Johnson found that the intensity of physiologic reaction and the rapidity of response to sexual stimulation were both reduced with advancing years. But they emphasized that they found "significant sexual capacity and effective sexual performance" in these older women, concluding:

> The aging human female is fully capable of sexual performance at orgasmic response levels, particularly if she is exposed to regularity of effective sexual stimulation. . . . There seem to be no physiologic reasons why the frequency of sexual expression found satisfactory for the younger woman should not be carried over into the postmenopausal years. . . . In short, there is no time limit drawn by the advancing years to female sexuality.

When it comes to males, Masters and Johnson found that there was no question but that sexual responsiveness weakens as the male ages, particularly after the age of sixty. They added, however:

> There is every reason to believe that maintained regularity of sexual expression coupled with adequate physical well-being and healthy mental orientation to the aging process will combine to provide a sexually stimulative climate within a marriage. This climate will, in turn, improve sexual tension and provide a capacity for sexual performance that frequently may extend to and beyond the eighty-year age level.

These general findings have been supported by various types of studies which have been made over the course of the years. These studies include the investigation by Raymond Pearl in 1925 into the frequency of marital intercourse of men who had undergone prostatic surgery, all over the age of fifty-five;[20] Robert L. Dickinson and Lura E. Beam's studies of marriages and of single women, including a number of older single women and widows;[21] the Kinsey studies of the male and the female;[22] older men studied at outpatient clinics by urologists at the University of California School of Medicine at San Francisco;[23] extended study by Duke University psychiatrists of Negroes and whites living in the Piedmont area of North Carolina;[24] Joseph T. Freeman's study of older men in Philadelphia;[25] a study of patients attached to a geriatric clinic in New York;[26] a survey of veterans applying for pensions;[27] a questionnaire survey by *Sexology* magazine of men over sixty-five who were listed in *Who's Who in America;*[28] and a study of sex attitudes in the elderly at the Langley Porter Neuropsychiatric Institute in San Francisco.[29]

NO AUTOMATIC CUTOFF DATE

All of these studies indicate the continuation of sex needs, interest, and abilities into the later years despite the gradual weakening that may take place. The Kinsey group, quite contrary to general conceptions of the aging process in sex, found that the rate at which males slow up sexually in the last decades of life does not exceed the rate at which they have been slowing up and dropping out of sexual activity in the previous age groups.[30] For most males, they found no point at which old age suddenly enters the picture. As far as females were concerned, the Kinsey investigators — like Masters and Johnson later — found little evidence of any aging in their capacities for sexual response.[31] "Over the years," they reported, "most females become less inhibited and develop an interest in sexual relations which they then maintain until they are in their fifties or even sixties." In contrast to the average wife, the responses of the husband dropped with age. Thus, many of the younger females reported that they did not desire intercourse as often as their husbands. In the later years of marriage, however, many of the wives expressed the desire for coitus more often than their husbands were then desiring it.

The Duke University survey — reported by Gustave Newman and Claude R. Nichols — found that only those persons who were seventy-five or older showed a significantly lower level of sexual activity.[32] This study found that Negro subjects were sexually more active than white subjects; men were more active than women; and persons lower in social and economic scale were more active than those in the upper-income group. A possible explanation of the greater activity reported by males lies in the fact that men and women of the same age were reporting on different age groups. The wives, on the average, would be reporting on sex activity with a husband who was perhaps four years older.

Despite the fact that masturbation has been usually considered an activity that ends with maturity, for many older persons, this practice apparently continues to serve as a satisfactory form of release from sexual tensions when a partner, is for one reason or another, not available.[33]

Several of the studies suggest a correlation between early sex activity and a continuation into the late years. The Kinsey group found that, at age fifty, all of the males who had been sexually active in early adolescence were still sexually active, with a frequency about 20 percent higher than the frequency of the later-maturing males.[34] They report:

> Nearly forty years maximum activity have not yet worn them out physically, physiologically, or psychologically. On the other hand, some of the males (not many) who were late adolescent and who have had five years less of sexual activity, are beginning to drop completely out of the picture; and the rates of this group are definitely lower in these older age periods.

They conclude:

> The ready assumption which is made in some of the medical literature that impotence is the product of sexual excess, is not justified by such data as are now available.

Freeman[35] found that the sex urge of persons in advanced years correlated strongly with their comparative sex urge when young, and a similar finding was reported by the Duke University survey.[36]

Masters and Johnson report the same finding, with additional emphasis upon regularity of sexual expression as the essential factor in maintaining sexual capacity and effective performance for both males and females: [37]

> When the male is stimulated to high sexual output during his formative years and a similar tenor of activity is established for the 31-40 year range, his middle-aged and involutional years usually are marked by constantly recurring physiologic evidence of maintained sexuality. Certainly it is true for the male geriatric sample that those men currently interested in relatively high levels of sexual expression report similar activity levels from their formative years. It does not appear to matter what manner of sexual expression has been employed, as long as high levels of activity were maintained.

FACTORS RESPONSIBLE FOR DECLINING SEX ACTIVITY

On the basis of present data, it is not possible to sort out the emotional element from the purely physiologic factors in the decline in sexual activity of the older male. Some animal experiments have shown that changes in the external environment can result in changes in sexual drive. When aging rats had the opportunity for sex activity with a number of partners, for example, the number of copulations increased considerably.[38] However, as soon as male rats reached a certain age, they failed to respond to females.[39]

Many men also find that, with a new partner, a new stimulus is given to their virility.[40] However, often these men return to their old level within comparatively short periods of time.[41] Present data lead us to conclude, with the Kinsey investigators:

> The decline in sexual activity of the older male is partly, and perhaps primarily, the result of a general decline in physiologic capacity. It is undoubtedly affected also by psychologic fatigue, a loss of interest in repetition of the same sort of experience, an exhaustion of the possibilities for exploring new techniques, new types of contacts, new situations.[42]

Masters and Johnson, on the basis of their clinical work with older males, describe six general groups of factors which they believe to be responsible for much of the loss of sexual responsiveness in the later years: (1) monotony of a repetitive sexual relationship (usually translated into boredom with the partner); (2) preoccupation with career or economic pursuits; (3) mental or physical fatigue; (4) overindulgence in food or drink; (5) physical and mental infirmities of either the individual or his spouse; and (6) fear of performance associated with or resulting from any of the former categories.

The most constant factor in the loss of an aging male's interest is the problem of monotony, described by the Kinsey group as "psychologic fatigue." According to Masters and Johnson, many factors may produce this: failure of the sexual relationship to develop beyond a certain stage; overfamiliarity; lack of sexual interest on the female's part; aging and loss of personal attractiveness of the female.

A major deterrent for many men is preoccupation with the outside world and their careers. Overindulgence in food and drink, particularly the latter, takes a high toll. According to Masters and Johnson, secondary impotence developing in the late forties or early fifties has a higher incidence of direct association with excessive alcohol consumption than with any other single factor.

As each partner ages, the onset of physical or mental infirmities is an ever-increasing factor in reducing sexual capacities. The harmful effect of this is sometimes multiplied by the negative or discouraging attitude of the physician. Once a failure in performance has occurred because of any of the factors, the fear of failure becomes an additional factor in bringing about withdrawal from sexual activity. "Once impotent under any circumstances," remark Masters and Johnson, "many males withdraw voluntarily from any coital activity rather than face the ego-shattering experience of repeated episodes of sexual inadequacy."

The very scanty data concerning the sexual attitudes of older persons suggest a more positive attitude toward sex among men than among women, with women being more "culture-bound" and still showing strong evidences of the effects of the Victorian age in which they acquired their attitudes toward sex.[43] A study of dreams of residents of a home for the aged and infirm, on the other hand, indicates a contrasting difference in emotional tone of the sexual content of the dreams of men and women: "Whereas in men sexual dreams revealed anxiety, failure, and lack of mastery, in women they usually depicted passive, pleasurable gratification of dependent needs."[44]

THE UNMARRIED HAVE SEX NEEDS TOO

It is not only the married who have sexual needs. Aging widows, widowers, and single persons, who make up an increasingly large segment of our population, face even greater problems in respect to sex than do the married. In the survey by Newman and Nichols, only seven of the 101 single, divorced, or widowed subjects reported any sexual activity with partners.[45] Apparently, the strength of the sexual drive of most elderly persons is usually not great enough to cause them to seek a sexual partner outside of marriage in the face of social disapproval and the difficulties of such an endeavor. Interestingly, however, thousands of older couples were reportedly living "in sin — or what they think is sin" because marriage would mean loss of social security payments.[46]

Dickinson and Beam reported that in their study of widows ranging from sixty to eighty years of age there was evidence of masturbation.[47] They reported that when these women underwent pelvic examinations they showed such marked sexual reactions that they found that "it is desirable to relieve the patient's embarrassment by hurting her, lest she have orgasm." Since many older women are quite troubled by their practice of masturbation, marriage counselors have stressed the importance of helping older persons to accept this practice as a valid outlet when they feel the need for it.[48]

The Great Need for Information

Persons who have worked with "senior citizens" and "golden age" clubs have reported the great need for knowledge, the confusion, and the eager hunger for information about sex shown by persons in these clubs.[49] The many perplexing problems that they raise indicate the extent to which such information is needed to help people solve broader questions of remarriage and interpersonal relationships during their later years. The growing incidence of disease states in these years — each of which may require a difficult readjustment in sexual and other relationships — makes it essential that older people be provided with this information openly and consistently.[50]

It should be clear, however, that unless our entire culture recognizes the normality of sex expression in the older years, it will be impossible for older persons to express their sexuality freely and without guilt. Physicians are particularly crucial in this respect; unless they are convinced of the psychological importance of sexual functioning in the later years, they can do irreparable harm to their patients' sexuality.[54] Fortunately, at long last, medical schools and medical publications have begun to take steps to correct the glaring lacks in the education of medical students, which have in the past resulted in the creation of a body of medical practitioners who, by and large, shared the general prejudices of our society concerning sexuality in older persons.

REFERENCES

1. E. Cumming and W. E. Henry, *Growing Old.* New York: Basic Books, 1961, p. 155.
2. P. Golde and N. Kogan, "A Sentence Completion Procedure for Assessing Attitudes Toward Old Poeple," *Journal of Gerontology*, Vol. 14, July 1959, pp. 355-363.
3. K. M. Bowman, "The Sex Life of the Aging Individual," in M. F. DeMartino (ed.), *Sexual Behavior and Personality Characteristics.* New York: Citadel, 1963, pp. 372-375.
4. G. Williams, *The Sancity of Life and the Criminal Law.* New York: Alfred A. Knopf, 1957, p. 51.
5. R. S. de Ropp, *Man against Aging.* New York: Grove Press, 1962, p. 252.
6. H. I. Lief, "Sex Education of Medical Students and Doctors," *Profile Medicine and Surgery*, Vol. 73, February 1965, pp. 52-58.

7. Cumming and Henry, *op. cit.*, footnote, p. 21.
8. R. Burns, *The Merry Masses of Caldeonia*, J. Barke and S. G. Smith (eds.). New York: Putnam, 1964, pp. 147-148.
9. H. Einbinder, *The Myth of the Britianica.* New York: Grove Press, 1964, p. 94.
10. A. Comfort, "Review of *Sexual Life after Sixty*," by Isadore Rubin, *British Medical Journal*, II, March 25, 1967, p. 750.
11. Isadore Rubin, *Sexual Life after Sixty.* New York: Basic Books, 1965, Chap. 1.
12. J. W. Mohr, R. E. Turner, and M. B. Jerry, *Pedophilia and Exhibitionism.* Toronto: University of Toronto Press, 1964.
13. L. W. Simmons, "Social Participation of the Aged in Different Cultures," in M. B. Sussman (ed.), *Sourcebook in Marriage and the Family,* 2nd ed. Boston: Houghton Mifflin, 1963.
14. D. P. Ausubel, *Theory and Problems of Adolescent Development.* New York: Grune and Stratton, 1954, pp. 53 ff.
15. L. K. Frank, *The Conduct of Sex.* New York: Morrow, 1961, pp. 177-178.
16. E. B. Armstrong, "The Possibility of Sexual Happiness in Old Age," in H. G. Beigel (ed.), *Advances in Sex Research. New York: Hoeber-Harper, 1963, pp. 131-137.*
17. E. H. Feigenbaum, M. J. Lowenthal and M. L. Trier, "Sexual Attitudes in the Elderly." Unpublished paper given before the Gerontological Society, New York, November 1966.
18. *W. R. Stokes, Married Love in Today's World.* New York: Citadel, 1962, p. 100.
19. W. H. Masters and V. E. Johnson, *Human Sexual Response.* Boston: Little, Brown, 1966, sec. on "Geriatric Sexual Response," pp. 223-270.
20. R. Pearl, *The Biology of Population Growth.* New York: Alfred A. Knopf, 1925, pp. 178-207.
21. R. L. Dickinson and L. E. Beam, *A Thousand Marriages.* Baltimore: Williams & Wilkins, 1931, pp. 278-279, 446; and R. L. Dickinson and L. E. Beam, *The Single Woman.* Baltimore: Williams & Wilkins, 1934, p. 445.
22. A. C. Kinsey, W. B. Pomeroy, and C. E. Martin, *Sexual Behavior in the Human Male.* Philadelphia: W. B. Saunders, 1948; and A. C. Kinsey, W. B. Pomeroy, C. E. Martin, and P. H. Gebhard, *Sexual Behavior in the Human Female.* Philadelphia: W. B. Saunders, 1953.
23. A. L. Finkle et al., "Sexual Function in Aging Males: Frequency of Coitus among Clinic Patients," *Journal of the American Association,* Vol 170, July 18, 1959, pp. 1392-1393.

24. G. Newman and C. R. Nichols, "Sexual Activities and Attitudes in Older Persons," *Journal of the American Medical Association,* Vol. 173, May 7, 1960, pp. 33-35.
25. J. T. Freeman, "Sexual Capacities in the Aging Male," *Geriatrics,* Vol. 16, January 1961, pp. 37-43.
26. L. Friedfeld, "Geriatrics, Medicine, and Rehabilitation," *Journal of the American Medical Association,* Vol. 175, February 18, 1961, pp. 595-598; and L. Friedfeld et al., "A Geriatric Clinic in a General Hospital," *Journal of American Geriatrics Society,* Vol. 7, Octoer 1959, pp. 769-781.
27. L. M. Bowers, R. R. Cross, Jr., and F. A. Lloyd, "Sexual Function and Urologic Disease in the Elderly Male," *Journal of the American Geriatrics Society,* Vol. 11, July 1963, pp. 647-652.
28. I. Rubin, "Sex over Sixty-five," in H. G. Beigel (ed.), *Advances in Sex Research.* New York: Hoeber-Harper, 1963.
29. Feigenbaum et al., *op. cit.*
30. Kinsey et al., *Sexual Behavior in the Human Male,* pp. 235-237.
31. Kinsey et al., *Sexual Behavior in the Human Female,* pp. 353-354.
32. Newman and Nichols, *op. cit.*
33. Rubin, "Sex over Sixty-five"; and Dickinson and Beam, *A Thousand Marriages.*
34. Kinsey et al., *Sexual Behavior in the Human Male,* pp. 319-325.
35. Freeman, *op. cit.*
36. Newman and Nichols, *op. cit.*
37. Masters and Johnson, *op. cit.*
38. J. Botwinick, "Drives, Expectancies, and Emotions," in J. E. Birren (ed.), *Handbook of Aging and the Individual.* Chicago: University of Chicago Press, 1959, pp. 739-768.
39. L. F. Jakubczak, Report to the American Psychological Association, August 31, 1962.
40. J. Bernard, *Remarriage.* New York: Dryden, 1956, p. 188.
41. Kinsey et al., *Sexual Behavior in the Human Male,* pp. 227-229; and A. W. Spence, "Sexual Adjustment at the Climacteric," *Practitioner,* Vol. 172, April 1954, pp. 427-430.
42. Kinsey et al., *Sexual Behavior in the Human Male,* pp. 226-235.
43. Feigenbaum et al., *op. cit.*
44. M. Barad, K. Z. Altshuler, and A. I. Goldfarb, "A Survey of Dreams in Aged Persons," *Archives of General Psychiatry,* Vol. 4, April 1961, pp. 419-424.
45. Newman and Nichols, *op. cit.*
46. *New York Times,* January 12, 1965.
47. Dickinson and Beam, *A Thousand Marriages.*

48. L. Dearborn, "Autoerotism," in A. Ellis and A. Abarbanel (eds.), *The Encyclopedia of Sexual Behavior.* New York: Hathorn, 1961, pp. 204-215; and L. Hutton, *The Single Woman.* London: Barrie & Rockcliff, 1960, p. 58.
49. Feigenbaum et al., *op. cit.*
50. Rubin, *Sexual Life after Sixty,* Chaps. xi-xiii.
51. J. S. Golden, "Management of Sexual Problems by the Physician," *Obstetrics and Gynecology,* Vol. 23, March 1964, pp. 471-474; and A. L. Finkle and D. V. Prian, "Sexual Potency in Elderly Men before and after Prostatectomy," *Journal of the American Medical Association,* Vol. 196, April 11, 1966, pp. 139-143.

22. Sex and the Aged*

C. Ray Wingrove**

"Don't give up sex!" This is the advice a 79-year-old widow gives her contemporaries in a recent article appearing in the *Richmond News Leader* (3). The newspaper account is based upon a videotaped interview which carried this remarkable lady into classes on aging and retirement readiness being taught at the University of Washington in Seattle. Calling herself Ms. Something — the Ms. to be modern, and the Something to avoid recognition by friends and relatives — she relates before camera the full saga of her sexual experiences during the past 23 years of widowhood. Since becoming a widow at 56, her varied experiences include 35 "adventures" with men ranging in age from 15 to 82. Her most recent suitor wants an affair, but she is a little concerned about the gossip of neighbors.

If true, Ms. Something's account certainly punches holes in the image of *all* old people as sexually inactive beings. Clearly some of them are not only still sexually active, but are enjoying it immensely. Of course, as any researcher will tell you, individual reports should never be used as evidence of normative patterns of behavior but limited instead to purposes of illustration and sources of hypotheses. However, empirical evidence is accumlating which suggests that Ms. Something is not just an isolated case of sexual aberation, but perhaps rather a highly "successful" representative of a large segment of the aged population. Witness findings from the research of Kinsey, Masters and Johnson, Alexander Leaf, the Duke University Longitudinal Studies and others over the past two and one half decades (4, 5, 8, 11, 12, 13, 15, 16). More and better knowledge about the sex life of older citizens is becoming available not just to professionals, academicians and those who read the learned journals but to the general public as well. Many old people themselves are beginning to learn about the sexual behavior of their peers for the first time and are being given a yardstick against which to measure how they stack up.

Even though everyone seems to be looking at, talking about, and participating in sex more openly today, and in spite of the mild burgeoning of new knowledge about the sexual behavior of the aged, ignorance is great and many long held myths about the aged and sex

*Original paper written for this book.
**Dr. C. Ray Wingrove is Professor of Sociology at the University of Richmond and is one of the editors of this book.

still prevail. What are they, why do they exist, and just how much if any validity do these myths hold?

PREVAILING MYTHS

I was interested in noting the reactions of friends and colleagues as I had them read the newspaper account of Ms. Something. Reactions ranged from disbelief, shock and indignation to mild hilarity and a complacent "so what" attitude — reactions which probably reflect the variety of commonly held stereotypes of the aged person as a sex object in our society. Any list of these stereotypes must include the ideas that sexual desire and activity cease with the onset of old age, that sexual desire and activity *should* cease with the onset of old age, that the old who claim to be interested or active in sex are either perverse, liars or perhaps both, that the old are too fragile for sex and might be injured by engaging in such activities, and that they are physically unattractive and therefore, sexually undersirable (1, 16).

Why have such stereotypes persisted for so long? Eric Pfeiffer thinks it is because of the generalized taboo in our society against sex in old age (16). This taboo has hindered research and hence the accumulation of knowledge in this area. Cooperation from subjects has been difficult to obtain. It has been even more difficult to obtain cooperation from the families of willing subjects. Most physicians lack the training and most behavioral scientists the courage and motivation to undertake research in what they hold to be too sensitive or too upsetting a topic. Too often they have not been able to overcome their own hesitancy or embarassment. The nature of this taboo has its roots in several facets of our culture. Ideally, sex is for procreation rather than recreation. Sex for those of child bearing age may involve the likelihood of pregnancy and hence the albeit sometimes reluctant approval of society. However, old people cannot hide behind this facade. Others see the taboo against sex in old age as an extension of the Oedipal Complex. The discomfort felt by children imagining the sexual activity of their parents is widespread. To the extent that old people represent the parent generation, their sexual behavior may create anxiety among those who are younger. Another hypothesis is that relegating the old to a sexually barren wasteland eliminates a sizeable force from the competitive arena of the young.

CURRENT RESEARCH

Regardless of its origin, cracks are beginning to appear in this taboo against sex for the old — at least enough so that research in the area is gaining some momentum — and stereotypes are beginning to come under attack. Predictably enough, stereotypes about the sex life of the aged (like all stereotypes) are being found deficient in explaining individual variations. Two general conclusions emerge from the findings of diverse studies, viz., that sexual interest and activity are far from rare among those over 60, and that although great variability exists in sexual behavior among members of either sex, there are significant differences between males and females on both sexual behavior and sexual interests (16).

Kinsey's findings suggested a gradual decline but by no means a disappearance of sexual activity and interest among the aged in his sample. Masters and Johnson provide even more support for this idea. However, both the pioneering work of Kinsey and the more imaginative and innovative study of Masters and Johnson suffer not only from the normal limitations of the cross-sectional design but from the inadequacies of small and non-representative samples as well. Fortunately, we now have a more substantial source of data. The longitudinal study of subjects participating in the research of Duke University's Center for the Study of Aging and Human Development not only provides more convincing data in support of earlier speculations, but indicates that the frequency and range of sexual behavior among the aged is probably greater than the earlier studies of Kinsey suggest or the scope of the Masters and Johnson studies would allow (4, 5, 16).

The Duke interdisciplinary and longitudinal study of old people began in 1954 and continues today. The original sample included 254 subjects 60-94 years old, roughly equal numbers of males and females, blacks as well as whites, and 31 intact couples. The latter characteristic of their sample provided an excellent opportunity for cross-validation of information from marital partners, and therefore, a way to combat a long standing criticism stemming from the questionable truthfulness of subjects. Subjects were seen repeatedly at 3-4 year intervals (4, 5, 16).

Synthesizing findings largely from the Duke studies and to some extent from Kinsey, Masters and Johnson, Newman and Nichols, and even more specialized studies like that on penile erections of aged males during REM sleep (1, 2, 4, 5, 7, 8, 11, 16), we find evidence for the following statements about *sexual behavior among aged males:*

1. Sexual activity declines with advancing age but varies greatly from 40-60 per cent of those 60-70 claiming they still engage in sexual intercourse to only 10-20 per cent of those 80 or above.

2. Sexual interest also tends to wane with advancing age but much less so than activity. Interest varies considerably and even

increases for a small percentage of the very old (over 80). This may be a function of the fact that those who reach extreme old age are a biologically advantaged group.

3. Those who continue to be sexually active engage in intercourse anywhere from 3 times per week to once every other month.

4. Most studies do not record marked differences between married and unmarried males in reported sexual interest and activity.

5. Although variation is great, many males maintain the capacity for erection into extreme old age.

6. Older males who continue to be sexually active are likely to find they are slower to be aroused, slower to develop erection, slower to effect intromission, and slower to achieve ejaculation.

7. Sex drive remains fairly constant throughout life, i.e., barring chronic physical incapacity, the male who enjoyed a high level of sexual activity throughout his middle years, can expect to be able to continue sexual activity into the 70's and 80's.

There are fewer reports on females; however, the following statements appear to summarize some of what we know about *sexual behavior among old women:*

1. Biologically, females suffer less sexual impairment with age than do males. The capacity to reach orgasm does not seem to diminish among those who have regular sexual stimulation throughout the middle years.

2. Although more old women than old men are probably still capable of sexual activity, far fewer are interested. However, there is no noticeable change in interest with age as among males.

3. Far fewer old women claim to be sexually active, but again those who are tend to remain active into very old age. Only 20% of the Duke sample reported regular intercourse at the beginning of the study, but this proportion did not decline over a 10 year period. The lack of available sex partners accounts for much of the discrepancy between male and female activity and interest.

4. Unlike males, married women differ substantially from the single in experiencing greater sexual interest and activity.

An observation which becomes apparent as one surveys the literature is that there is a great gap between the potential sexual activity of the aged and their actual performance. Again although similarities exist, there are explanations for this which differ by sex (1, 15). *Reasons why males do not live up to their sexual potential in old age include the following:*

1. Fear of failure. Many older males fear failure in sexual endeavors, and hence do not risk it by attempting them.
2. Persistence of the Victorian idea that old men lack sexual identity. The aged are victims of cultural beliefs as are the rest of the population. Stereotypes of appropriate or expected age related behavior often becomes a self fulfilling prophecy.
3. Physical limitations. Impotence among males may result from artereosclerotic, endocrine, cardiorespiratory, genitourinary, hematological, neurological, or infectious disorders. Diabetes Milletus, perineal prostatectomy and sometimes suprapubic and uretheal prostatectomy may also cause impotence.
4. Boredom with one's partner.
5. Overindulgence in food or drink.
6. Drugs and medication.
7. Preoccupation with financial problems, unemployment, etc.

Reasons why females do not live up to their sexual potential in old age include:

1. Scarcity of sex partners. Most old women are widows, and there are more old women than old men.
2. Menopause may have a negative psychological effect. Although this has been disputed as a biological factor in diminished sexual capacity, it continues to act as such because many women believe it does.
3. Many aged husbands are impotent.
4. More women than men profess disinterest in sex at all ages. The old sometimes use their age as a handy excuse.
5. Steroid starvation which causes pain during coitus. Masters and Johnson consider this a primary cause of reduced sexual activity in old females and recommend hormone treatment to ameliorate the situation. They argue that hormone treatment results in greater sexual activity not because of any relation to sexual stimulation as some claim, but because it reduces the pain of sexual intercourse.
6. The Victorian concept that females should really have no interest in sex. Females as well as males are victims of their cultural beliefs which become self-fulfilling prophecies.

7. Physical changes. Here again the loss of sexual interest may be psychological in nature rather than biological as witnessed by the reaction of many women following a hysterectomy.

8. Miscellaneous factors including boredom with partner, drugs, medication, anxiety, etc.

Finally, of course, all old people — both male and female — live in a society which struggles to place and to keep them in a neuter mold, and which punishes them if they dare to project another image. The sexual overtures of old people are ridiculed. "Don't be an old fool," is a frequent put down in such a context. Our institutions provide little privacy and most still prohibit coed living arrangements. Even the life styles of most American families discourages sexual activity of older relatives who might be sharing the home. This simplifies life for staff, personnel, and family; life would probably be simpler for all in a sexless world, but most would consider it a high price to pay. Why make the old pay a price for convenience and simplicity which the rest of society escapes? They least of all can afford the sacrifice. Punishment of the old sexual offender is swift and harsh and reflects society's general abhorrence of sex among the aged. This has led some to view the geriatric sex offender as one of the most maligned individuals in our society (6).

CONCLUSIONS

Our new found knowledge about sex in old age should be useful to at least three categories of people in society, viz., to the old themselves, to the general public, and to practitioners. Sex does not have to be the source of just one more restriction for the aged. The knowledge that many people continue to enjoy active sex lives into their later years may reduce the anxiety which contributes to impotence in many males. The knowledge that one isn't alone in having sexual fantasies after 65 may allow more old people to feel normal, unashamed, and guilt free about their own thoughts. The knowledge which corrects erroneous ideas about the harmful physical effects of sexual intercourse in old age may permit more to enjoy sex without fear of sudden death from stroke or heart attack. The knowledge of available hormone treatments may allow more old women to seek once more a fulfilling sex life without fear of pain. The knowledge that one's husband may avoid sex out of fear of failure may make women feel less rejected and give them the understanding their spouses deserve. And finally, such knowledge may encourage more old people to stand up and demand their rights to as full a life as possible for as long as possible.

For the general public, the discovery of sex in old age may help dispel the unfounded myths of the sexless older years and lead to a modification of prejudicial attitudes and discriminatory behavior. For the practitioner, this discovery may serve as another avenue of aid to his elderly clients.* He may convey the idea that sex among the aged is normal and widespread and hence help alleviate anxieties and banish non-acceptance. As a matter of fact, there is some evidence that sex may even be therapeutic for some aged persons. Butler and Lewis state,

> There is some evidence, for example, that sex activity helps arthritis, probably because of adrenal gland production of cortisone. The sexual act itself a form of physical activity, helping people stay in good physical condition. It helps to reduce tensions, which are both physical and psychological (2, p. 102).

One word of caution should be heeded in this area, however. Dr. Marcel Heiman likens the accumulating knowledge about sex in old age to the discovery of the female orgasm. Once found, its presence was equated to the ultimate bliss, and its absence, the worst of fates. Dr. Heiman warns against imposing geriatric sex upon everyone. He states,

> In our zeal we frequently overlook the fact that some old people may already have found a solution of their own. May we not ask ourselves — and them — if they want sex and/or need it? (9, p.1)

Practitioners and scientists alike must be careful lest they inadvertently equate happiness in old age to sexual happiness.

In sex, as in many other areas, the generation gap may not be so great after all. The old may be quietly joining the sexual revolution in America. To the extent that it brings happiness, a sense of meaning to lives, and an opportunity to remain a part of the human race, their joining should be welcomed.

REFERENCES

1. Atchley, Robert C., *The Social Forces in Later Life*. Belmont, California: Wadsworth Publishing Company, 1972.

* For a discussion of solutions to loneliness in old age, see Dr. Mary Carlderone's chapter on sex in *Sex in Education for the Aging,* edited by Stanly M. Grabowski and W. Dean Mason.

2. Butler, Robert N. and Myrna I. Lewis, *Aging and Mental Health: Positive Psychosocial Approaches.* St. Louis: The C. V. Mosby Company, 1973.
3. Fjermedal, Grant, "79-Year-Old Widow Enumerates Her Lovers Chattily." *Richmond News Leader* (Richmond, Virginia), Thursday, September 19, 1974.
4. *Geriatric Focus.* "Sexual Attitudes and Behavior in the Elderly," Vol. 12. No. 5, 1973.
5. _____. "Normal and Abnormal Sex Behavior in Aging," Vol. 7, No. 13, 1968.
6. _____. "The Geriatric Sex Offender: Most Maligned Individual," Vol. 7, No. 2, 1968.
7._____. "REM Sleep and the Libido in Elderly Males," Vol. 7, No. 1, 1968.
8._____. "Survey of the Literature Reveals Geriatric Sex is Here to Stay — Despite Cultural Disapproval," Vol. 7, No. 1, 1968.
9. _____. "Suggests 'Happy Balance' Between Sex, Sublimation," Vol. 7, No. 1, 1968.
10. Grabowski, Stanly M. and Mason, Dean W. (Editors). *Education for the Aging.* Washington, D. C.: Capitol Publications, 1974.
11. Kinsey, A. D., et al. *Sexual Behavior in the Human Male.* Philadelphia: Saunders, 1948.
12. _____. *Sexual Behavior in the Human Female.* Philadelphia: Saunders, 1953.
13. Leaf, Alexander, "Every Day is a Gift When You Are Over 100," *National Geographic.* January, 1973.
14. Lobsenz, Norman M., "Sex and the Senior Citizen." *New York Times Magazine.* January, 1974. A condensed version also appears in *Readers Digest,* April, 1974.
15. Masters, W. H., and Johnson, V. E., *Human Sexual Response.* Boston: Little, Brown and Company, 1966.
16. Pfeiffer, Eric, "Sexual Behavior in Old Age." Chap. 8 in *Behavior and Adaptation in Late Life,* edited by Ewald W. Busse and Eric Pfeiffer. Boston: Little, Brown and Company, 1969.
17. *Time.* "Romance and the Aged," June 4, 1973.

B. RETIREMENT

The readings which are grouped together here deal with the increasingly significant stage of life known as retirement. The paper by Frances Carp views aging within a developmental context, i.e., as part of a process which begins at birth and continues until death. Carp points out the lack of research on the later phases of adult development and discusses the consequences of the "unknown quality" which surrounds growing old. A look at some possible trends in retirement patterns of the future is especially provocative.

The next two articles get away from the abstract, theoretical aspects of retirement and deal more with the specifics of reality. Erdman Palmore reviews and summarizes the pros and cons of compulsory vs. flexible retirement policies, and concludes with several of his own proposals for increasing flexible retirement and, thereby, reducing human obsolescence. Gerda Fillenbaum deals with the emerging field of preretirement planning and the pervasive unmet needs in this area. Her research suggests topics to cover in planning, ways to motivate participation in planning, the age at which planning should begin, and other specifics of interest to the practitioner.

The retirement problem is complicated by economics. With inflation and the ever increasing cost of living, it is impossible for the average person to provide for his post-retirement years. He must either work for pay beyond retirement or belong to a retirement program which compensates automatically for the decreasing value of the dollar. The many problems related to retirement are suggested in these three papers. Solutions are much harder to come by!

23. Background and Statement of Purpose*

FRANCES M. CARP**

The Life Span Development Context

Development is perceived as coterminous with life. It is continuous, sequential, and consequential — a concatenation of process of growth, maturation, retrogression, and deterioration. It expresses the interaction of biological, psychological, and cultural forces, and is expressed in physiological, behavioral, and social terms.

Genetic factors set limits upon development, but these bounds are rarely, if ever, reached. Other factors interfere with development or fail to support it. The determinants of developmental processes must be defined and measured, and their consequences specified and evaluated.

There is reluctance, or at least inertia, to perceive development as lifelong and continuous.

But changes do occur throughout life, more rapidly during certain periods, more slowly during others. Changes at any point in the life history are dependent on those which occurred earlier, and they in turn affect those yet to come. Normal development involves coordinated increments and decrements. During early life, increments seem to predominate. During late life, decrements are observed more commonly. It remains to be determined whether all changes past any given age are decremental or deteriorative.

Little attention has been given to the conceptualization and systematic investigation of the developmental stages of adult life — the periods of relative stability and the critical periods or turning points between them.

*Reprinted from Chapter I of *The Retirement Process,* USPH Monograph No. 1778, NICHD Conference Report at Gaithersburg, Dec. 1966, edited by Dr. Carp with permission of the author.
**At the time this chapter was written, Dr. Carp was a Health Scientist at the National Institutes of Health. Presently she is a Project Director at the Wright Institute in Berkeley, California.

269

Adolescence, a critical period of dramatic shifts in the environment and striking changes in the individual, is understandably intriguing to investigators. It involves the resolution of a complex and often conflictive interplay of biological, psychological, and social changes. The word "adolescence" evokes a fairly clear, comprehensive, and common image of the life stage leading from childhood to maturity.

AN ANONYMOUS PERIOD OF TRANSITION

A later transitional period has received scant attention from investigators, though it must be as complex as adolescence and potentially as fascinating. This is the transition which follows the relatively stable phases of life which are initiated by adolescence. So totally has this transition in later adult life been ignored — or avoided — that it remains unnamed. The next transitional term in our developmental vocabulary after "adolescence" is "senescence," which refers to the transition into old age. Obviously other phases of life intervene between adolescence and senescence — at least early adulthood, middle maturity, and later maturity.

There are not even adequate descriptions of the transition from young adult status to the next relatively stable period in the life history. The person experiences decline in sensory-motor functions, perhaps diminution of stamina and endurance, probably some accumulation of ailments. Until recently, it was thought that his intellectual competence must be diminishing, though recent studies cast doubt on this. (3) (4) (5) Significant changes in intelligence may not occur until very old age, except in persons who sustain brain damage or those nearing death. (6) Menopause and reduction in sexual performance are relevant, though probably they are even less synonymous with the anonymous development period than is puberty with adolescence. Neugarten's findings indicate that the menopause is not necessarily traumatic. (7) Important alterations occur in social press and social roles, (8) (9) and in ego processes. (10) Changes during the later transition often reverse those of adolescence, though many issues are the same: dependence versus independence, usefulness versus uselessness, and self-esteem versus self-devaluation.

For the adolescent it is fairly clear how these and other developmental issues should be resolved, because the goal is ability to function as an adult. Independence, productiveness, activity, and social involvement obviously are good outcomes in our culture at the present time. However, society has not decided whether, as a person moves past young adult status, he should become more or less independent, sociable, or active. As Rosow puts it, society has defined no role models for developmental stages beyond early maturity. (*11*)

Everyone knows, in general terms at least, the major developmental tasks for infancy, childhood, adolescence, and young adulthood, and there is common recognition of behaviors which are appropriate and inappropriate to each. For subsequent periods of life, no culture norms are available to serve as models and goals. Generally, changes in later life are assumed to be losses, perhaps because, in the absence of age appropriate models, variables are selected which are relevant to earlier life stages (and for which measuring instruments are available), and performance is measured against standards of earlier years. This interpretation tendency is reinforced by clearly documented decrements in sensory-perceptual-motor performance. (*12*)

Change must, of necessity, be measured and interpreted in reference to some standard. Until the stages of later maturity are described and accepted as legitimate parts of life span development, the changes which occur during the period of transition into later maturity cannot be assessed adequately. To take a ridiculous example, we say that the older person shows decrement because the speed of his response is slowed, but it would never occur to anyone to interpret as "loss" the inability of the teenager to creep or crawl as well as he once did, or the inefficiency of a 5-year-old with a nursing bottle. Early stages of development are known to require relinquishing some behavior patterns as well as acquiring others. This principle is rarely applied to adult behavior.

For early periods it is also commonly agreed that development is best assisted by defining goals so that they are clear to the developer, and by managing rewards so that the "best carrot" is ahead and the satisfactions relevant to earlier stages are less. The "stick" is recommended for limited use because its application may "fix" undesired behavior or lead to unpredictable consequences. (*13*) (Punishment may have favorable effects if it clarifies the situation for the learner.)

An overweight adolescent comes home crying from a dance at which she was a wallflower. We say her mother acts against the girl's developmental best interest if she offers her the consolation of cake and ice cream. Rather, she should help the girl implement a constructive course of action — diet, beauty parlor, dancing lessons — which will enable her to experience success in heterosexual activities appropriate to her age. The girl's development depends upon establishing satisfactions relevant to the tasks of adolescence.

A man aged 65 is retired by company policy, or one over 40 loses his job and remains unemployed. The "sticks" are apparent, but where is the"carrot"? What are the cognitive and motivational factors that guide his development? The satisfactions of early maturity — from income growth, career development, community service, child-rearing, youth, and possibly good looks — are reduced, it is true; but do relatively greater satisfactons lie ahead? Or is the person faced with negative alternatives only? The future may seem sterile or even threatening and he is barred from the past.

The stress from a double-avoidance situation is more intense if the person perceives the situation as one attributable to himself, and it must be difficult to avoid recognition that it is *his* age, *his* health, *his* job, *his* fading youth, and *his* failure to capitalize on opportunities when he had them that now affect his state. Would biological and behavioral aging be decelerated if society established gratifications in later maturity which would outweigh the now unavailable ones of earlier maturity, and so guide development with less stress?

Alternatively, some atypical behavior of older people may result neither from intrinsic processes of aging nor from unresolved conflict but, quite the opposite, from reduction in stress to the point of inadequate stimulation. During most of the life history, development is seen to depend upon goal-directed striving, and mental health upon cycles of problem-solving behavior and consequent stress reduction. Older adults who are inactive, unsociable, and unhappy may be reacting as would persons of any age to a similarly sterile and unchallenging situation.

Persons entering later maturity cannot have a clear picture of how they should behave until society has decided what the later periods of human life ought to be. The learning task is cognitively obscure and motivational elements are largely negative. Appropriate motivations cannot be offered until we know what later maturity is all about, nor can they be established until we identify the intrinsic motives of persons in later maturity. Rewards should lead the individual toward the desired behavior. To do this, rewards must be relevant not only to the prescribed performance, but also to the needs and drives of the actor. We would not get far with toilet training a toddler if we used a baby blue Cadillac as reward, though the behavior of a college student might be managed well with that inducement. The dictum of learner-relevant rewards probably holds at all ages. Yet we know little about the needs and drives of older adults.

In summary, the period of transition from young adult life to a later stage of adult life is poorly understood and, unless special efforts are made, it seems likely to remain so. Such efforts should be made, because this transition from young adult life will determine the nature of the succeeding, relatively stable period. As at adolescence, in the transition to later life the organism undergoes change at all levels — biological, psychological, and social. The determinants and consequences of this change must be understood in order that developmental processes can realize the potentials of this period of life and prepare the individual for succeeding stages.

The Problem

In need of investigation, then, are: transitions related to completion of personal and societal expectations regarding participation in the labor force, child-rearing, or spousehood or: developmental processes involved in preparation for, realization of, and reestablishment of life following retirement from the major life work of early adult years.

Different Meanings of Retirement

Retirement has many meanings to those undergoing it: the end of individual worth and social contact, a haven of rest, relief from an unpleasant, overtaxing, or health-draining job, or completion of commitment to society and initiation of self-realization. It may be a ceremony between one career and another; it may represent the opportunity to start one's "real" lifework or to draw two paychecks. Second and even third careers are becoming more common among men and among women whose first career is motherhood.

Investigators use different definitions of retirement in their studies. Some equate retirement with withdrawal from the labor force, usually within certain age brackets, and perhaps for certain reasons, others, with termination of career job, regardless of what the person does subsequently. In some studies, retirees are all those past normal retirement age, usually 65. In others, they are persons who say that they have quit working or no longer work full time. Included may be persons who consider themselves unemployed and who continue to seek work, and those who do not admit to earnings which jeopardize social security or old-age assistance benefits.

Some investigators suggest that, to understand the potentials of retirement, studies should focus on leisure rather than on retirement. Leisure should be distinguished from unemployment and illness and is characterized by voluntary acceptance of the status, personal satisfaction in it, and perhaps noninstrumentality of activities. Defining retirement in terms of leisure would be particularly useful, because retirement is only one manifestation of the expansion of leisure throughout our society and, insofar as possible, research on retirement should speak to the larger issue.

Leisure is sometimes defined as the antithesis of work in terms of economic function: work produces, leisure does not. This definition seems nicely objective; retired persons, by definition, do not contribute to the gross national product. It is, however, an oversimplification. Some time during retirement is spent at nonleisure activities. These include housework, yardwork, cooking, grooming, health care, and, for some people, illness and job hunting. Old persons with low morale are unable to account for a significant proportion of their days. (25) This "lost time" surely is not leisure. Other categories of use of time and energy. must be added to those of work and leisure.

During working years,"recreation" is stressed as a function of leisure, usually with the implication of renewal to return to the job. This approach has little relevance to the definition of retirement leisure unless recreation is more broadly defined.

Freedom or autonomy may be the essential element of leisure as contrasted to work. The freedom-versus-compulsion polarity would avoid some of the difficulties encountered with other bases for distinguishing leisure from work. It seems to apply particularly well to retirement leisure. Most investigators find independence to be a strong need among older adults. There is general agreement that, with age, individual differences widen and each person becomes "more and more like himself." Some older persons express pleasure in being able, at last, to say what they think and do what they like when they want to; that freedom may be one of the few rewards of age, and an essential ingredient in retirement leisure.

At present there is no clear and single meaning for retirement. The word evokes many different connotations and is used in many different ways. This accumulation of discrepant connotations is a source of confusion. The word must be defined specifically for any research use. There are various patterns of retirement. For example:

1. Retirement at the normal retirement age under a formal retirement system;
2. Early retirement under a formal system;
3. Late retirement under a formal system;
4. Retirement from a firm without formal retirement;
5. Retirement from self-employment and
6. Increasing difficulty in obtaining employment until it ceases.
7. In addition, women who have never been in the labor force constitute a sizable proportion of the "retired" group.

To complicate matters further, individuals from any group except No. 6 may take up other employment, either full- or part-time. Are they, then, retired?

Probably the most typical pattern today is retirement from a steady job in a firm which has no pension plan. (At present a minority of workers retire under the provision of retirement systems, but the proportion is growing. There is evidence that many workers would retire sooner if they could look forward to adequate retirement income.) Among this group, at present, the commonest reason given for retirement is ill health. However, the rate of retirement of older workers rises disproportionately when there is any rise in unemployment, which suggests that economic pressure is important in putting the older worker at a disadvantage. "Health" may be used euphemistically in explanation. "Voluntary" retirement may encompass a wide spectrum of explanation for leaving the labor force.
Another way to divide retirement patterns is:
1. Refusal;
2. Retirement to a planned life (which may or may not turn out as expected); and
3. Retirement without previous planning (which probably is the most common pattern).

At present there are many paths to retirement, and retirees are a heterogeneous group. They include the disabled, the unwell, the vigorous; the unwilling, the voluntarily retired; those who add earnings to retirement benefits, those who are unable to work or to qualify for disability payments; men who have been "unemployed" for years; and many others.

"Retirement" as a Working Title

To recapitulate: the long-range goal is to extend understanding of development (including retrogression) beyond achievement of maturity. A transition period in later maturity probably is of great consequence and should receive immediate attention. One issue during this transformation period is completion of work role. This issue has been selected as an entry point for investigation of the transition period. As the nature of the period in development comes to be understood, a name comparable to "adolescence" and "senescence" should become available. It will supplant the working title, and its adoption will broaden the research domain to its natural dimensions. Initial efforts will be concentrated upon the determinants and consequences of severance from the major work of young adult life. Attention will center upon retirement as a process rather than as an event or as a status.

EMERGENCE OF A NEW PHASE IN HUMAN DEVELOPMENT

One reason for the dearth of information regarding postwork phases of the life history is that only recently have there been significant numbers of persons in them. As the efficiency and productivity of the economy increase, the age for retirement goes down. Simultaneously, advances in medical science and care keep more persons alive into mature years, probably improve competence and well-being during them and, to a lesser extent, increase longevity. Further increases seem imminent.

Tibbitts (26) has pointed out that the highly developed, high energy economies of this and several other countries have produced a new social class. In developmental terms, these economic and medical trends have created a new phase in the normal life span, a retirement-leisure period which almost everyone will experience.

Until fairly recently the life history went through gestation, birth, infancy, childhood, adolescence, adulthood, senescence, and death. In general, people played in infancy, were educated or trained in childhood and adolescence, worked in adult years, quit about the time it was no longer possible to work, and died soon thereafter. In some parts of the world this is still true. However, in this country and some others, an increasing number of years lies between end of work and end of life. These years provide opportunity for attainment to "higher developmental levels" of human nature (10) (27) with consequent benefits to individuals and to society. However, extending years of obsolescent existence constitute a drag on society, disrupt development of younger generations, and are less than a blessing to those who have them.

This emerging phase can be frustrating and degrading or it can be a fulfilling and creative segment of life. People in it have, to perhaps a greater extent than at earlier stages of life, wisdom, understanding, compassion, and perspective — traits badly needed in our time, with its dangerous gap between technology and the solution of personal and group conflicts. Understanding of forces underlying this evolving life phase and consideration of factors which influence it are of crucial importance in determining whether it will elevate or degrade human life. Because of the number of persons anticipated in the new developmental period, such study should not be delayed.

PERSONS IN THE NEW RETIREMENT-LEISURE PERIOD

The rise in number of retired persons is rapid, both absolutely and in proportion to other age groups. In 1900 there were 3 million people aged 65 and over in the United States; it is estimated that there were 18.2 million in 1965. The proportion of the population 65 and over rose from 4 percent in 1900 to 5 percent in 1930 and to nearly 9 percent in 1960. Individuals tend to live longer. See table 1 for life expectancy figures of 50-year-olds from 1900 to 1965.

TABLE 1.
Expectation of life in the United States, at age 50

	White male	White female	Nonwhite male	Nonwhite female
1900-1902	20.76	21.89	17.34	18.67
1909-1911	20.39	21.74	16.21	17.65
1919-1921	22.22	23.12	20.47	19.76
1929-1931	21.51	23.41	17.92	18.60
1939-1941	21.96	24.72	19.06	20.95
1949-1951	22.83	26.76	20.25	22.67
1965	23.20	28.50	21.00	25.00

Source: Statistical Bulletin of the Metropolitan Life Insurance Co. Compiled from various publications of the National Vital Statistics Division, National Center for Health Statistics, and the Bureau of the Census.

Probably these trends will continue and perhaps they will accelerate as medical science attacks the killers of the later years of life and masters biological aging. Also, both length of life and competence during the later years should be affected favorably by recent provisions for health care through private insurance protection and public care programs, and by projected advances in environmental design of residential units, communities, and transportation facilities.

While longevity increases, and more people live to be old and to be well in old age, the number of years they are needed or tolerated in the labor market decreases. Our economy is no longer one in which a person normally is economically productive until life's end or very near it.

If production trends are maintained — and probably they will accelerate — persons in younger age groups will of necessity experience this transition from economic activity to economic inactivity, either because of a continual lowering of retirement age or through some new pattern of distributing work, education, and leisure through the adult years. Older workers are the "trial piece" on which society will learn about the new leisure, but retirement can no longer be equated with old age.

THE MEANINGS OF WORK AND LEISURE

For the first time in history, significant numbers of people have completed their work well before the end of their life span. Ironically, that same society which added years to life with improved health and economic security, also ingrained into members of today's older generation strong habits of work and respect — almost reverence — for labor. Older people tend to equate industry with virtue and they have had little acquaintance with leisure.

In the long view of history, work has been a major trial and tribulation to mankind. Adam's punishment for "the fall" was the necessity henceforth to toil for a living: "In the sweat of your face you shall eat bread . . ." (*30*) During the golden days of Greek civilization, leisure was the perquisite of a small favored upper class. Medieval man perceived no strong polarity between work and play. Only in 19th century Western culture did work become a good in itself.

Even today this compulsion is not universal. Serious misunderstandings exist within this country because persons in some subcultures use work as means only, whereas for members of the dominant society work is as much end as means. Stereotyping certain ethnic groups as shiftless and immature is a result in part of the tendency of members of these groups to work when they feel that they need the money and not to work when they feel that they have sufficient funds to cover their needs — which may be quite different from ours also. We do not recognize the recency or provincialism of the majority ethic. It is so deeply woven into our moral fabric that we cannot see it. For older adults in America, work is not only a way to live, it is also the way of life.

Those in their sixties and seventies are therefore on the frontiers of an ideological revolution. How does a whole society replace work as the major source of meaningful life? (*31*) Incomes normally decline abruptly upon retirement, and it is not yet known how much of the reported effects of retirement are contingent upon this fiscal concomitant. This is a serious question whether money is the only or even the major derivative of work to the worker. It is by no means certain that older persons in our culture today — even those with adequate income — can be happy without work.

Because increasing years of leisure toward the end of life seem to be in store, it is important to study possibilities for change from the motivational centrality of work. At stake is not only the happiness of individuals as they retire, but also the well-being of society, which will be penalized by their resentment and despair or enriched by their fulfillment and contribution.

At present the factors which largely define success in life and therefore provide satisfaction and fulfillment are money, activity, and youth. All are intimately bound up with work. Retirement reduces income, creates conditions conducive to inactivity, and confronts the person with loss of youth. For many persons, retirement offers nothing to make up for the loss of these supports to self-esteem. Poverty is not a virtue. Contemplation and introspection usually are equated with "vegetation," and volunteer work with "being a sucker" or "basket weaving." Madison Avenue sells few products by associating them with old age. The Oldsmobile Co. now advertises its "Youngmobiles."

SOCIAL CHANGES WHICH MAY AFFECT THE MEANINGS OF WORK AND LEISURE

Experience With Leisure. Changes are underway. Colleges, high schools, and even elementary schools are beginning to train and educate for leisure. Workers experience increasing contact with leisure, and it may turn respectable through familiarity. Workdays and workweeks are shorter than they were when today's retired persons were young. Paid vacations are longer and extend to more of the labor force. Innovations such as the 13-week vacation for members of the steel union are being tried.

Motivational Relocations. More persons are enrolled in retirement benefit plans. Economic security in retirement would reduce preoccupation with money. A relocation of values may also be underway throughout society, a shift from money as the primary measure of personal worth. Today's retired person tends to feel that, unless an activity is performed for pay, it is only "busy work" not truly valued by society. *(32)* The group studied was poor (one-third of the persons aged 65 and over have incomes below the poverty line), and the experience of this generation with the depression has sensitized them to economic want. In a few years the depression will be an historical event rather than a personal experience, and the effects of impoverishment during early years will be seen only in minority and other subgroups of the population.

However, it is by no means clear that the affluent old do not want payment. Desire for pay sometimes seems as much a request for reassurance regarding the worth of the activity and the person as it is a demand for purchasing power.

Nonmonetary motivations are operant. Some members of both the prework and the postwork generations are concerned with social problems and their solution, and relegate financial remuneration to secondary importance. Participation in such programs as the Peace Corps and VISTA is an example. Even among poor old people today there is frequent expression of the need to make a meaningful contribution to the welfare of others. (25)

Volunteering is not made easy for older persons. The Peace Corps has been criticized for the small number of older volunteers, for confining recruitment efforts to campuses, and because it has used selection, training, and assignment standards for older persons which were developed for college students. The physical obstacle course may be irrelevant to selection of schoolteachers or agricultural advisors. The 22-year-old "A.B. generalist" tends to be upset if he does not get the assignment he requested. How much more disconcerting it must be for the retired physician to find himself planning irrigation systems in an area without medical care, or for the retired farmer to work as a medical technician in a country in desperate need of updating its agriculture. The few volunteers past retirement age receive publicity, but the Peace Corps, like most social welfare programs, does not shape its policy for this group.

In 1960-61 (before Headstart) a group of retired schoolteachers in a housing project for the elderly in San Antonio, Tex., wanted to start a preschool program. Most children in the neighborhood entered first grade knowing no English, and the ex-teachers were aware of the handicap this imposes. All volunteers were in good health and seemed competent. They wanted no pay. However, no person or organization in the community would help them find space or contact parents.

Many could provide similar anecdotes. Few volunteer programs are geared to the needs of retired persons or attempt to utilize their special capabilities to contribute to the welfare of others. This human resource may become highly valued if, as seems possible, definitions of human worth begin to emphasize terms other than money. The "hippies" may be expressing, in fringe form, a tendency endemic to our time which is expressed in less extreme form in proposal of a senior service corps.

An improved financial status through social security and other retirement-benefit programs could provide a foundation for the development of noneconomic bases of worth. If the time and energy of retired persons were not preempted by efforts to subsist on inadequate incomes, if their possibilities for activity were not so severely restricted by lack of money, and if society valued their participation, who knows what the response of older people might be to humanity's needs? Perhaps new tasks and new rewards are evolving for the experienced person who has time for society's problems because he no longer must compete in the labor force.

Alternatively, retirement may come to be defined as the phase of life after the individual's obligation to society has been met and he is free to pursue his own ends, to live his own life, at last, as he likes. The person who retires according to the second pattern may be, incidentally to his purpose, of unique value to the society in which he lives, as model, commentator, and appreciator. If retirement acquires a positive valence because it is an acceptable segment of life, and if people learn how to use its leisure, retired individuals and all of society will benefit from the emergence of the new life stage.

Toward this end, the needs satisfied by work, and the possibility of altering, relocating, or supplanting these motivations, should be investigated. History assures us that the present value dominance of work is not unalterable. Attitudes toward retirement are becoming more favorable. Knowledge of the reasons for this shift will be helpful in assisting it and in assuring that retirement becomes not a discouraged acceptance of the inevitable, but a redefinition of life with meaning.

Material success, occupational advancement, and social status — the dominant motives of today's adults — may be diminished in tomorrow's. We do not know what the adult goals and motives of young people and children will be. Retirement may have quite different meanings in 10 or 20 years.

Look to the Future

Whether society continues to take its surplus production in end-of-life leisure or chooses some other distribution, adults in the "leisure years" of the future will not be like those in them today. Younger persons, and probably people in better health and with improved economic resources, will be involved.

Never again will a retired population in this country include such large numbers of immigrants and of second-generation Americans or so many people with so little education. No other generation, we hope, will undergo two world wars and a "great depression" during their earning years, and a "great inflation" while they try to live on their savings. Attitudes toward work and leisure will be different from the "Pepsi generation," the "beatniks," and the "hippies."

Society may legitimatize activities other than work and may even revert to idealization of leisure. Society's view may so change that activity and involvement, whether at work or leisure, will not be requisite to personal worth.

Labor Force and Human Development Needs

Projections of present rates of population and productivity growth imply that by 1985 only about one-half the labor force will be needed to maintain the gross national product (GNP).*(33)* If society is content with the level of production, there are alternative courses of action to balance the labor force: delay entry, withdraw about half the work force for retraining or reeducation at all times, reduce the workweek to 22 hours or the work year to less than 7 months, distribute leisure throughout the adult life span, reduce retirement age to 38, or, what is more likely, some combination of these.

Any solution will have far-reaching effects on persons of all ages. Reduction in retirement age, which is likely to continue if there is no major policy shift, will have tremendous impact on "older" adults. Drastic policy change seems unlikely, because the forces which have led to earlier retirement are numerous and persistent, and maintenance of economic equilibrium largely through lowering retirement age has become a habit. This may be the best solution. However, it seems to occur by default rather than by explicit decision based on consideration of the socioeconomic and personal consequences of the various possibilities. Personal and social consequences of each alternative and combination of alternatives should be projected, and policy decisions should be made in light of these as well as economic considerations.

Economists are concerned with the need for a conceptual framework for analyzing lifetime allocations of work, income, and leisure in relation to productivity. They point out that, as output per man-hour increases, a man's lifetime output of goods and services grows. Should he have more and more income or greater leisure or some of each? In what proportions? How apportioned through the life span? Biological, behavioral, and social scientists should become concerned with the differential impact on human development of the various alternatives — increased age at entry to the labor force, lower retirement age, decreased workweek, retraining, intermittent leisure, or increased goods and services. Investigators should also entertain the possibility of increasing the flexibility of work-nonwork schedules, both between individuals and within the career duration of one individual.

Balancing Production by Earlier Retirement

To point up the possibilities by exaggerating them, assume that excess production is balanced totally by adjusting retirement age and imagine what would be going on in 1985.

The Retired and the Retiring. If retirement age approximates 38 in that reference year, the "cool kids" will be leaving the work force and joining the "beat generation," which will be in retirement. The oldest offspring of the newly retired will be college undergraduates; families may not yet be complete. End of worklife may normally precede, rather than follow, completion of child-rearing or even childbearing. A typical retirement dream sponsored by airlines today is travel for two. Depending upon family size and spacing of children, the first postretirement period may, instead, involve two-parent concentration on children and produce a new phase in family organization. New retirees' parents will be approximately the age at which retirement takes place today; they are the people who, by today's standards, expect to retire about 1985.

The economic position of retired persons in 1985 depends upon the extent to which young and middle-aged adults must assume financial responsibility for the children and parents, both in 1985 and in 1967. College education, newly becoming a "must" for the majority and increasing in duration for many, now occurs in peak earning years of parents. In the future, reduction of income at retirement may precede college attendance of offspring.

Two-generation retirement occurs now. Some retired persons' most serious problem is financial, social, or emotional support of aged parents. What multigenerational patterns of retirement will appear? What economic and interpersonal patterns will evolve? Only recently has it been recognized that the "retired" do not comprise a homogeneous group and that retirement must contain several life stages. In less than 20 years it may encompass several more.

Probably the population, the proportion of it in older age brackets, and the preponderance of women among older persons, will continue to grow. Age-segregated retirement facilities will increasingly resemble old ladies' homes, and widows will comprise an even larger majority of older persons.

Industrialization, Automation, and Education. How will industrialization and mechanization affect the distribution of jobs by 1985, and how will the job distribution, in turn, affect retirement? Industrialization lowers retirement age. Nevertheless, it creates working conditions more congenial to older workers: less physical energy and strength are required, the variety of jobs provides some work more congenial in content, and geographical shifts are toward more temperate climates. Negative factors remain, such as the educational disadvantage of older persons and their avoidance of skill retraining and professional recycling programs. Obsolescence has been a problem in industry. It will become an increasing hazard in administrative, professional, and scientific positions. On the other hand, will industry and the professions suffer from the loss of persons at age 38?

Educational requirements probably will continue to proliferate. At present, unemployment and labor force withdrawal by older men are closely correlated with their educational and skill levels. The uneducated and unskilled are first denied jobs when there is a labor surplus, and they are most likely to reach retirement early and as the surrender phase of continued unemployment. At the other end of the scale, unless some educational revolution makes it possible to prepare scientists and professional people much more efficiently, they will hardly be ready to work before they reach "retirement age." Today, retirement is later for the self-employed, the better educated, and those in higher job levels. Perhaps these differentials will continue and accentuate, so that, by 1985, some persons will stop work well ahead of the average retirement age, while others will work far beyond it. This may occur as part of a general move to shape work to accommodate the characteristics of individual workers rather than, as now, the reverse. *(34)*

Distribution of GNP. Income is a basic determinant of retirement behavior. At present a sharp reduction in income is concurrent with retirement, and that drop carries many people to the poverty level. Most retired persons are on fixed incomes. As technological advances increase production and therefore worker income, the relative position of these retired persons declines. Will future retirees share in the benefits of economic growth or be penalized by cost-of-living rises? What will the effects on retirement behavior be if a universal guaranteed minimum income is provided by 1985? What will happen to man's motivations to remain active when he is given security without striving? Will younger personalities grow and strengthen in the absence of economic demands and stress? What will be the effects of sharply reduced income at age 38 as a normal occurrence?

Medical Science and Medical Care. Retirement at 38 in 1985 would occur approximately halfway through the life span and would initiate a long postwork period of competence and good health for most people. By 1985, biochemists may have identified the basic processes of physiological aging and ways to retard or arrest them.*(35)* Perhaps by then it will be possible to instruct the aging human eye to generate a new lens, as the Drs. Coulombre observe occurring now in the eye of the chick embryo.*(36)* What a difference this would make in the experience and behavior of the many older people who have cataracts and others lens defects! Replacement or regeneration of parts of the human body may, by then, be relatively routine.

Medical science promises new breakthroughs which may have an even more dramatic impact on living for the older adult by minimizing the effects of cumulative injury and disease, and by preventing or curing the major killers and cripplers of later life. In addition, advances in medical care should maintain competence and well-being during more of adult life. Through medical science and care, longevity should be increased and good health should characterize more of the older population. Lowenthal's data suggest that physical well-being will be reflected in low psychiatric rates for the older members of society.(*20*)

According to the Surgeon General: "The implications of some developments in biochemical science are so sweeping that we are barely beginning to grasp them conceptually and have not yet begun to handle them practically." and, "If bodies and minds can be shaped in the womb; if personality and physical capability can be manipulated throughout life; and if life can be extended well beyond our present span — then we are approaching a peak where the prospect is dazzling but the precipices are very steep."(*37*)

There may be interesting problems regarding utilization of medical services. This is suggested by the lack of increase in medical care use immediately following passage of the medicare bill. Provision of services will not improve health unless they are used. This may be only a short run problem due to novelty of the program, and utilization rates may soon rise. It may be a problem temporary in terms of generations. Today's older persons tend to view "giving in to illness" as indicative of poor moral fiber. Such a view may not be held in old age by today's younger adults, for most of whom medical care has been routine throughout life. It is interesting to speculate on the reactions of today's children to the diseases of old age unless there are major medical science advances before they reach that period. Because of the rapid strides in preventive and ameliorative measures against childhood diseases, the first experience with serious illness will occur in middle age or later maturity, for many of them.

Environmental Design. Urbanization will probably continue, and cities and towns will be planned for their users, at least to a greater extent than is true today. Environmental design which minimizes wear and tear on human beings should have a differentially favorable effect on aging persons.

By 1985 there will be "new towns" in which residence modules are tailored to occupants' needs and are movable and exchangeable as these needs alter with time. Transportation may be an effortless (and smogless) matter of entering, at the door of one's residence module, a private "pod" which operates at the command of an IBM card into which the traveler punches his destination.

Shopping may be accomplished at home via color televiewer, and cooking and housework may require only knowing how to direct a computer. Emotional needs of housewives may inhibit the utilization of such technologic possibilities. On the basis of current marketing research, producers of ready-mix products purposely require more participation by the cook than is necessary. For example, cake mixes sell better when the housewife must add fresh eggs — though powdered egg could be included in the mix with no loss in flavor or texture. A current sales promotion program of one large company promises the housewife that their newest product also allows her to add the butter.

POLICY ALTERNATIVES

Alternatives to earlier retirement should be considered seriously in attempts to balance the labor force and the labor requirement. According to some philosophies, reduction of production through early retirement is incongruous for a nation which talks about improving the quality of life for its citizens and for those of other countries. According to this view, reduced labor force participation is better justified on the basis of the superior value of education and leisure over goods.

Full employment. Full employment may become the national goal. Military commitments have reduced unemployment to 4 percent. A similar rate might be achieved during peace by commitment to eliminate air and water pollution, or urban ugliness, or to meet the service needs of the elderly, or to provide a higher standard of living to a greater proportion of the population of this and other countries. Implementation of such programs would have dramatic impact on the number, characteristics, and behavior of persons in retirement. However, the complexity of relationships among population growth, gross national product, and age-specific labor force participation suggests that achieving full employment would not be easy, even if it became the nation's goal. Increased leisure is in store.

Distributed Leisure. To gain perspective, developmental scientists should view the present retirement pattern as one form of leisure allocation which may have greater or lesser human development advantage than other possible patterns. Various distributions of intermittent leisure and education during adult life should be considered as alternatives to early retirement. Economists can create models showing the approximate changes in lifetime production which would result from changes in total working time and in its distribution. Developmental scientists should explore the personal and social consequences of each variation.

REFERENCES

(*1*) Farnsworth, P. R. (Ed.): *Annual Review of Psychology*. Palo Alto, Calif., Annual Reviews, Inc., 1967, vol. 18, 606 pp.

(*2*) Farnsworth, P. R. (Ed.): *Annual Review of Psychology*. Palo Alto, Calif., Annual Reviews, Inc., 1965, vol. 16, 571 pp.

(*3*) Jarvik, L. F., Kallman, F. J., and Falek, A.: Intellectual changes in aged twins. *J. Geront. 17: 289-294, 1962*.

(*4*) Eisdorfer, C.: The WAIS performance of the aged: a retest evaluation. *J. Geront. 18: 169-172, 1963*.

(*5*) Pierce, R. C., and Berkman, P. L.: Change in intellectual functioning. In Lowenthal, M. F., Berkman, P. L., and Associates (Eds.): *Aging and Mental Disorder in San Francisco*. San Francisco, Jossey-Bass, 1967, pp. 176-189.

(*6*) Birren, J. E.: Increments and decrements in the intellectual status of the aged. Paper presented at a Regional Research Conference on Aging in Modern Society: Psychological and Medical Aspects, at the University of California San Francisco Medical Center, March 1967.

(*7*) Neugarten, B. L., Wood, V., Kraines, R. J. and Loomis, B.: Women's attitudes toward the menopause. *Vita Humana. 6: 140-151, 1963*.

(*8*) Parsons, T.: Old age as consummatory phase. *The Gerontologist. 3: 53-54, June 1969*.

(*9*) Reisman, D.: Some clinical and cultural aspects of the aging process. In Reisman, D. (Ed.): *Individualism Reconsidered*. Glencoe, Ill., The Free Press, 1954, pp. 484-491.

(*10*) Erikson, E. H. (Ed.): Identity and the life cycle. Entire issue of *Psychol. Issues. 1: 1-171, 1959*.

(*11*) Rosow, I.: Adjustment of the normal aged. In Williams, R. H. Tibbitts, C., and Donahue, W. (Eds.): *Processes of Aging*. New York, Atherton Press, 1963, vol. 2, pp. 195-223.

(*12*) Birren, J. E.: *The Psychology of Aging*, Englewood Cliffs, N.J., Prentice-Hall, 1964, 288 pp.

(*13*) Maier, N. R. F.: *Frustration*. New York, McGraw-Hill, 1949, 264 pp.

(*14*) Selye, H.: The general-adaptation-syndrome in its relationships to neurology, psychology, and psychopathology. In Weider, A. (Ed.): *Contributions Toward Medical Psychology*. New York, Ronald, 1953, vol. 1, pp. 234-274.

(*15*) Cumming, E., and Henry, W.E.: *Growing Old*. New York, Basic Books, 1961, 293 pp.

(*16*) Kleemeier, R. W. (Ed.): *Aging and Leisure*. New York, Oxford Press, 1961, 432 pp.

(*17*) Tibbitts, C.: Retirement problems in American society. *Amer. J. Sociol. 59: 301-308, Jan. 1954*.

(*18*) Shanas. E.: Health and adjustment in retirement. Paper presented at the 19th Annual University of Michigan Conference on Aging, July 1966.

288   *Concerns Confronting The Aged*

(*19*) Crippen, D. M.: Employment after retirement. *Modern Maturity. 6: 56-59, Apr.-May,* 1963.
(*20*) Lowenthal, M. F., Berkman, P. L., and Associates (Eds.) *Aging and Mental Disorder in San Francisco: A Social Psychiatric Study.* San Francisco, Jossey-Bass, 1967, 341 pp.
(*21*) Swartz, F. C.: *Foreword. Retirement: A Medical Philosophy and Approach.* Chicago, Committee on Aging, American Medical Association, 9 pp.
(*22*) Bortz, E. L.: *Creative Aging.* New York, MacMillian, 1963. 179 pp.
(*23*) McMahan, C. A., and Ford, T. R.: Surviving the first five years of retirement, *J. Geront. 10: 212-215, 1955.*
(*24*) Thompson, W. E., and Streib, G.: Situational determinants, health and economic deprivation in retirement. *J. Soc. Issues, 14: 2, 18-34, 1958.*
(*25*) Carp, F. M.: *A Future for the Aged: Victoria Plaza and Its Residents.* Austin, The University of Texas Press, 1966, 287 pp.
(*26*) Tibbitts, C.: Introduction. Social gerontology; origin, scope and trends.*Int. Soc. Sci. J. 15: 339-354, 1963.*
(*27*) Maslow, A. H.: *Motivation and Personality.* New York, Harper, 1954, 411 pp.
(*28*) Anderson, J. E.: Research problems in aging. In Anderson, J. E. (Ed.): *Psychological Aspects of Aging.* Washington, D.C., American Psychological Association, 1956, pp. 267-289.
(*29*) Donahue, W., Orbach, H. L., and Pollak, O.: Retirement: the emerging social pattern. In Tibbitts, C. (Ed.): *Handbook of Social Gerontology.* Chicago, The University of Chicago Press, 1960, pp. 330-397.
(*30*) Genesis 3:19.
(*31*) Kaplan, M.: The uses of leisure. In Tibbitts, C. (Ed.): *Handbook of Social Gerontology.* Chicago, The University of Chicago Press, 1960, pp. 407-435.
(*32*) Carp, F. M.: Differences among old workers, volunteers, and persons who are neither. *J. Geront.* (in press).
(*33*) Kreps, J. M., and Spengler, J. J.: The leisure component of economic growth. In *The Employment Impact of Technological Change,* Appendix, vol. 2, National Commission on Technology, Automation, and Economic Progress, Wash., D.C., Govt. Print. Off., 1966, pp. 353-397.
(*34*) Galbraith, J. K.: *The New Industrial State.* Boston, Houghton Mifflin Company, 1967, 427 pp.
(*35*) Strehler, B. L.: Cellular aging. *Annals N. Y. Acad. Sci. 138: 661-679, 1967.*
(*36*) Coulombre, A., and Coulombre, J.: Lens reconstruction from lens epithelial transplants. *Anat. Record. 157: 231, Feb. 1967* (abstract).
(*37*) Stewart, W. H.: The role of the Public Health Service in health affairs. Presented at American Hospital Association's Midyear Conference for presidential officers and executives of Allied Hospital Associations, Chicago, Ill., Feb. 3, 1966 at 11:00 a.m.

24. Compulsory Versus Flexible Retirement: Issues and Facts*

ERDMAN PALMORE**

Compulsory retirement is increasing so that about half of wage and salary workers who retire at age 65 do so because of compulsory retirement. Compulsory retirement is discrimination against an age category and prevents many older workers from continuing employment. Flexible retirement would better utilize the skills and experience of older persons and increase the income of the aged. It may also increase life satisfaction and longevity. The facts do not support most arguments for compulsory retirement.

The local, state, and national conferences involved in the 1971 White House Conference on Aging have increased concern with one of the most controversial issues in gerontology: that of compulsory retirement at a fixed age versus flexible retirement based on ability. Debate on this perennial issue also seems to increase as compulsory retirement policies affect more and more workers who are still able to work and as the national costs of maintaining incomes and health care for the retired steadily escalate.

Various arguments and theories supporting one side or the other have appeared in scattered reports and articles (Busse & Kreps, 1964; Havighurst, 1969; Hyden, 1966; Kreps, 1961; Koyl, 1970; Lambert, 1964; Mathiasen, 1953; Palmore, 1969a). This article attempts to summarize these arguments and present the relevant facts as a basis for future private and public policy.

We will first present the facts on the extent of compulsory retirement, then discuss the theories and facts supporting flexible retirement, and third, discuss those supporting compulsory retirement. Finally, we will present proposals for encouraging flexible retirement policies.

EXTENT OF COMPULSORY RETIREMENT

The practice of compulsory retirement apparently became widespread only in this century and grew along with the swift industrializa-

*Reprinted from *The Gerontologist*, Vol. 12, 1972, pages 343-348 with permission of the author and the Gerontological Society.
**Dr. Palmore is Professor of Medical Sociology at the Center for the Study of Aging and Human Development, Duke University Medical School.

tion and growth of large corporations in the early 1900s (Mathiasen). A series of national surveys conducted by the Social Security Administration and others show that compulsory retirement policies affect a large and growing proportion of older workers. A comparison of the reasons for retirement given in the 1951 and the 1963 Social Security surveys of the aged indicated that the proportions of male beneficiaries who retired because of compulsory retirement provisions doubled during those 12 years (11% in 1951 and 21% in 1963 for wage and salary workers retired within the preceding 5 years [Palmore, 1967]). In their 1969 Survey of Newly Entitled Beneficiaries, the Social Security Administration found that 52% of the nonworking beneficiaries, who had been wage or salary workers and who became entitled at age 65, had retired because of compulsory retirement (Reno, 1971) (those who retired before they reached 65, about 2/3 of the new beneficiaries, usually gave poor health or job discontinued as the main reason, rather than compulsory retirement). A national survey of retirement policies found that 73% of companies with pension plans (which includes most large companies) had compulsory retirement at a fixed age for some or all workers (Slavick & McConnell, 1963). The majority of these had compulsory retirement at age 65. The 1966 SSA survey of retirement systems in state and local governments found that 79% had compulsory or automatic retirements at a fixed age (Waldman, 1968). This is an increase from the less than one-half of the systems in 1944.

Thus, it apppears that compulsory retirement policies may affect about half of the male wage and salary workers retiring at age 65 and will affect more in the future if recent trends continue.

The Case for Flexible Retirement

1. Compulsory retirement is by definition discrimination against an age category, contrary to the principle of equal employment opportunity. Federal law now prohibits discrimination in employment based on race, sex, or age for persons under 65. It is ironic that the present law against age discrimination in employment is limited to persons under 65, because persons over 65 are the ones who are most likely to be discriminated against by such policies as compulsory retirement. It seems possible that restricting this law to persons under 65 could be considered unconstitutional in the sense that it does not provide equal protection of the law to all persons.

Supporters of compulsory retirement might argue that such discrimination is as legal and justifiable as child labor laws and policies which restrict the employment of children. However, there seems to be a valid difference in that child labor restrictions are designed primarily for the protection of children while compulsory retirement policies are usually justified on grounds other than those of protecting older persons.

2. Age, as the sole criterion for compulsory retirement, is not an accurate indicator of ability because of the wide variation in the abilities of aged persons. Twenty years ago the National Conference on Retirement of Older Workers concluded that

> Both science and experience indicate that the aging process and its effects show such wide variance among individuals as to destroy the logic of age as the sole factor in determining whether a person should retire or continue to work (Mathiasen. 1953).

Recently the Gerontological Society's Committee on Research and Development Goals in Social Gerontology echoed this conclusion by stating

> age limitations for employment are both socially and economically wasteful, since chronological age is rarely a reliable index of potential performance (Havighurst, 1969).

All the available evidence agrees that despite the declining abilities of some aged, most workers could continue to work effectively beyond age 65 (Riley & Foner, 1968).

3. Flexible retirement would better utilize the skills, experience, and productive potentials of older persons and thus increase our national output. If the millions of persons now forced to retire were allowed to be gainfully employed, the national output of goods and services could increase by billions of dollars. In a previous review (Palmore, 1969a) we concluded,

> Many gerontologists have pointed out that because of the aged's extensive experience and practice, many have developed high levels of skills, emotional stability, wise judgment, and altruism. They agree that these abilities can and should be channeled into constructive roles.

4. Flexible retirement policies would increase the income of the aged and reduce the transfer payments necessary for income maintenance. Since the average income of retired persons is about one-half that of aged persons who continue to work (Bixby, 1970), it follows that flexible retirement policies might double the average incomes of those who were forced to retire but are willing and able to work. Similarly, over twice as large a proportion of retired aged persons have incomes below the poverty level as do aged persons who continue to work. Thus the millions of aged persons with poverty incomes might be substan-

tially reduced by flexible retirement, which would increase their employment opportunities. This in turn would substantially reduce the amount of old age assistance and other welfare payments currently given to the aged with inadequate incomes. Similarly, Social Security payments could be reduced substantially because of the provision which reduces retirement benefits for earnings of over $1,680 per year. Considering the fact that over 20 billion dollars a year are paid by Social Security to retired workers and their dependents, it is easy to see that several billion dollars could be saved from income maintenance programs if only a minority of the aged could avoid forced retirement.

5. Flexible retirement, in providing more employment, would improve life satisfaction and longevity of the aged. Most evidence indicates that retirement does tend to decrease life satisfaction. A recent review concluded:

> Overall satisfaction with life is greater among older persons who are still working than among those who have retired. This pattern seems to arise in part (but only in part) because the kinds of people who remain in the labor force are very different from those who retire (tending to be healthier, better adjusted, more advantaged on the whole). Yet quite apart from such factors as health or socioeconomic status, the pattern of lower satisfaction among the retired persists. (Riley & Foner, 1968).

Streib (1956) found that even for persons with similar levels of health and socioeconomic status, morale still tends to be comparatively higher among the employed. Thompson (1960) found that decreases in satisfaction over a 2-yr. period were somewhat greater among older persons who retired than among those who continued to work; and decreases in satisfaction were substantially greater among reluctant retirees. The Duke Longitudinal Study (Palmore, 1968) found that reductions in economic activities including retirement were closely associated with reduction in life satisfaction. Dr. Thomas Green (1970), of Syracuse University's Educational Policy Research Center, has concluded,

> Surely there is nothing more damaging to the human spirit than the knowledge — or belief — that one's capacities are unused, unwanted . . .

There is less evidence supporting the idea that retirement has negative effects on health and longevity. Most of the association of poor health and greater mortality with retirement is probably due to the fact that people in poor health and with shortened life expectancies are the ones who tend to retire (Martin, Doran, 1966; Riley, 1968). However, we found that work satisfaction was one of the strongest predictors of longevity in our longitudinal study of normal aged (Palmore, 1969b). It may be that lack of work satisfaction, which can occur among the employed as well as among the retired, is the factor which reduces longevity.

6. Flexible retirement reduces the resentment and animosity caused by compulsory retirement. Apparently, many workers bitterly resent being thrown on the trash dump while they are still capable of working. Flexible retirement policies, by allowing such workers to continue to work, eliminates this problem.

The Case for Compulsory Retirement

1. Compulsory retirement is simple and easy to administer. Flexible retirement would require complicated tests which would be difficult to administer fairly and difficult to explain and justify to the worker. This may be the main reason for the popularity of compulsory retirement among administrators. Proponents of flexible retirement agree that it would be somewhat more difficult to administer, but many with experience in the administration of flexible retirement plans assert that the complications have been exaggerated and that adequate tests of retirement based on ability are "not the monsters they were made out to be" (Mathiasen, 1953). Various groups have been working on improving techniques for measuring functional ability as a basis for retirement practices (Koyl, 1970).

In fact, most organizations have implicit or explicit standards, more or less based on ability and merit, which they use to decide who should be hired, fired, transferred, or promoted among workers under 65. Flexible retirement policies can use these same standards, or somewhat more exacting standards, to decide who should be retrained and who retired among workers over 65.

2. Compulsory retirement prevents caprice and discrimination against individual workers. Proponents of flexible retirement also grant this point, but point out that prevention of individual discrimination is bought at the price of wholesale discrimination against an entire age category. They argue that the net number of workers willing and able to work who are forced to retire would be much less under policies of flexible retirement.

3. Compulsory retirement provides predictability. Both employer and employee know well in advance that the employee must retire on a fixed date. Thus, both can plan ahead better. On the other hand, some predictability can be built into flexible retirement by requiring workers

and management to give a certain amount of advance notice to the other party of any intended retirement.

4. Compulsory retirement forces management to provide retirement benefits at a determined age. Most compulsory retirement plans are accompanied by retirement pension systems (Slavick & McConnell, 1963). On the other hand pension systems are often combined with flexible retirement policies with no great difficulty (Mathiasen, 1953).

5. Compulsory retirement reduces unemployment by reducing the number of workers competing for limited jobs. This is especially important in declining or automating industries or plants with an over supply of workers. On the other hand, it could be pointed out that compulsory retirement tends to increase unemployment among older workers by forcing them to leave one job at which they are experienced and seek another job in a new area in which they may be disadvantaged. Using compulsory retirement to reduce unemployment is analogous to firing all women or all blacks in order to reduce the number of workers competing for jobs. A better solution to the unemployment problem is for the government to stimulate the economy or to create additional jobs by being the "employer of the last resort." In a previous analysis we concluded,

> The idea that society can provide only a limited number of jobs and that therefore it cannot provide enough jobs for aged workers is no longer accepted by most modern economists. Society could create a useful role for every adult if it were willing to devote the necessary attention and resources to this end. Certainly there would be major economic and political problems involved. But there is an unlimited amount of goods and services needed and desired in our American society (Palmore, 1969a).

If a smaller work force is really desired, this could be accomplished by shorter work weeks, longer vacations, delayed entry into the labor market by more education, etc. (Kreps, 1969).

6. Compulsory retirement prevents seniority and tenure provisions from blocking the hiring and promotion of younger workers. This is certainly true when seniority and tenure provisions are used to retain workers who have become less efficient and productive. A solution to this problem under flexible retirement would be to eliminate seniority and tenure provisions at a fixed age and require the older workers to compete periodically for their jobs on the basis of ability rather than seniority.

7. Compulsory retirement forces retirement in only a few cases because most workers 65 and over want to retire or are incapable of

work. This claim is probably not true as shown by the surveys cited earlier.

It is true that 69% of men over 65 not at work say they are not well enough to work and another 16% say they are not interested in work, but many of these responses may be rationalizations for inability to find suitable employment (Palmore 1967; Sheppard, 1969). The only way to accurately determine how many older workers are forced to retire, but are willing and able to work, is to eliminate compulsory retirement and count how many take advantage of the opportunity to continue working.

8. Compulsory retirement saves face for the older worker no longer capable of performing adequately. The older worker does not have to be told and does not have to admit that he is no longer capable of working but can blame his retirement on the compulsory retirement policy. Such a face-saving device undoubtedly has important value for many workers, but the number of such workers should be balanced against the perhaps equal number of capable workers forced to retire by compulsory retirement and the resulting frustration, loss of status, reduction of income and of national productivity.

9. Most workers 65 years old have impaired health or only a few years of health left. The facts do not support this argument. Life expectancy for a 65-year-old person is now about 15 years, and the majority of aged do not appear to have disabling impairments. Only 37% of persons 65 and over report any limitation in their major acitivity (National Center for Health Statistics, 1971).

Seventy percent of the Social Security male beneficiaries retiring at age 65 because of compulsory retirement report no work limitation (Reno, 1971). Furthermore, despite compulsory retirement and other discrimination against the aged, about one-third of men over 65 continue to do some work (Bogan, 1969). Thus, it appears probable that the majority of workers age 65 can expect a substantial number of years in which they will be capable of productive employment.

10. Most older workers are inferior and cannot perform most jobs as well as younger workers. This appears to be another of the stereotypes about the aged which has little or no basis in fact. A recent review of the evidence concluded,

> Studies under actual working conditions show older workers performing as well as younger workers, if not better, on most, but not all, measures. Thus, those men and women who remain in the labor force during their latter years are not making generally inferior contributions, despite their frequently poor performance under laboratory conditions (Riley & Foner, 1968).

11. Compulsory retirement does little harm because most workers who are forced to retire could get other jobs if they wanted to. Again the evidence is contrary to this theory. When workers 65 and over lose their jobs, they have much more difficulty in getting another one than younger men. The proportions of older workers in the long-term unemployed categories are about twice as high compared to workers age 20-35 (Riley & Foner, 1968). Educational differences do not explain these differences in long-term unemployment (Sheppard, 1969). More than one-half of all private employees in states without age-discrimination legislation in 1965 admitted age limits in hiring practices and many more probably informally discriminate against older workers (Wirtz, 1965).

12. Most workers forced to retire have adequate retirement income. Again the facts appear to be to the contrary. We do not know exactly what percentage of those forced to retire are in poverty, but 30% of all retired couples and 64% of the retired nonmarried persons have incomes below the official poverty level (Bixby, 1970). And it is precisely those forced to retire early who have incomes substantially lower than those who retire early voluntarily (Reno, 1971).

PROPOSALS FOR INCREASING FLEXIBLE RETIREMENT

As may be obvious from the preceding review, I favor flexible retirement policies primarily because I conclude compulsory retirement is unfair to the capable older worker, psychologically and socially damaging, and economically wasteful. The remaining question then is how to bring about more flexible retirement policies.

The most extreme proposal would be to outlaw all compulsory retirement by removing the age limitation in the present law against age discrimination in employment. The main objections to such a proposal is that at present it would be politically difficult if not impossible to pass such a law and that even if it could be passed it would be extremely difficult to enforce effectively. A counter-argument would be that the difficulty of enforcement should not prevent passage of a just law. We have many excellent laws which are difficult to enforce, such as laws against murder, robbery, and racial discrimination. Another serious objection is that while compulsory retirement may usually be unjust, in some situations it may be less unjust than a system with no retirement criteria or with completely arbitrary decisions as to who must retire.

A more moderate proposal would be to provide tax incentive for flexible retirement policies. A reduction in the amount of Social Security tax paid by the employer with flexible retirement policies could be economically justified by the savings in Social Security benefits that would result from continued employment of workers not forced to retire.

The most modest proposal would be to encourage some kind of compromise between complete compulsory retirement and flexible retirement based on ability alone. Brown (1950) of Princeton University proposed such a compromise plan over 20 years ago. Under this plan a definite age would be set at which all employees recognize that the promise of continued employment ends. At this time all seniority rights and further accumulation of pension credit ends. Then retired employees can be recalled to work as temporary employees, subject to the needs of management.

> In this way, selected individuals can be recalled for specific needs on the basis of changing demands for personnel and the physical, mental, and personality adjustment of the particular worker to advancing age.

Such plans are in fact already operating smoothly in many businesses and institutions.

In conclusion, I hope that this article may clarify the issues and facts involved and may become a basis for reducing the millions of cases of compulsory retirement and the resulting social and economic waste of our older citizens' talents and skills.

REFERENCES

Bixby, L. Income of people aged 65 and older. *Social Security Bulletin,* 1970, 33, 4, 3-34.

Bogan, R. Work experience of the population. *Monthly Labor Review,* 1969, 92, 44-50.

Brown, J. The role of industry in relation to the older worker. In *The aged and society.* New York: Industrial Relations Research Assn., 1950.

Busse, E., & Kreps, J. Criteria for retirement: a reexamination. *Gerontologist,* 1964, 4, Pt. 1, 117-119.

Gould, D. Let's ban retirement. *New Statesman,* 1968, 75, 411.

Green, T. Panel examines new technology. *New York Times,* Jan. 30, 1970.

Havighurst, R. J. (Ed.). Research and development goals in social gerontology. *Gerontologist,* 1969, 9, Part II.

Hyden, S. *Flexible retirement age.* Paris: Organization for Economic Cooperation & Development, 1966.

Koyl, L. A technique for measuring functional criteria in placement and retirement practices. In H. Sheppard (Ed.), *Towards an industrial gerontology*. Cambridge, Mass: Schenkman, 1970.

Kreps, J. Case study of variables in retirement policy. *Monthly Labor Review*, 1961, 84, 587-91.

Kreps, J. Economics of retirement. In E. Busse & E. Pfeiffer (Eds.), *Behavior and adaptation in late life*. Boston: Little, Brown, & Co., 1969.

Lambert, E. Reflections on a policy for retirement, *International Labor Review*, 1964, 90, 365-75.

Martin, J., & Doran, A. Evidence concerning the relationship between health and retirement. *Sociological Review*, 1966, 14, 329-343.

Mathiasen, G. (Ed.), *Criteria for retirement*. New York: G. P. Putnam's Sons, 1953.

National Center for Health Statistics. Current estimates from the Health Interview Survey — 1969. *Vital & Health Statistics*, Ser. 10. No. 63, 1971.

Palmore, E. Retirement patterns. In L. Epstein & J. Murray, *The aged population of the United States*. Washington: Government Printing Office, 1967.

Palmore, E. The effects of aging on activities and attitudes. *Gerontologist*, 1968, 8, 259-263.

Palmore, E. Sociological aspects of aging. In E. Busse & E. Pfeiffer (Eds.), *Behavior and adaptation in late life*. Durham: Duke Univeristy Press. 1969, (a).

Palmore, E. Predicting longevity. *Gerontologist*, 1969, 9, 247-250. (b).

Reno, V. Why men stop working at or before age 65: Findings from the Survey of New Beneficiaries. *Social Security Bulletin*, 1971, 34, 6, 3-17.

M. Riley & A. Foner, *Aging and Society*, Vol. II. New York: Russell Sage Foundation, 1968.

Sheppard, H. Aging and manpower development. In M. Riley & A. Foner, *Aging and Society*, Vol. II. New York: Russell Sage Foundation, 1969.

Slavick, F., & McConnell, J. Flexible versus compulsory retirement policies. *Monthly Labor Review*, 1963, 86, 279-81.

Streib, G. Morale of the retired. *Social Problems*, 1956, 3, 270-276.

Thompson, W., Streib, G., & Kosa, J. The effect of retirement on personal adjustment. *Journal of Gerontology*, 1960, 15, 165-169.

Waldman, S. *Retirement systems for employees of state and local governments*, 1968. Washington: Government Printing Office, 1968.

Wirtz, W. *The older American worker*. Washington: Government Printing Office, 1965.

25. Retirement Planning Programs At What Age, and for Whom?*

Gerda G. Fillenbaum**

Responses of a randomly selected group of employees who were questioned about their attitudes concerning a proposed retirement planning program indicated that while there was almost universal agreement that such a program was desirable and age 45 an appropriate one at which to start, attendance would differ markedly with occupational status. Regardless of age, upper occupational status persons showed no interest, older (i.e., over age 44) middle-occupational status persons are more interested than are younger, but lower occupational status employees of all ages said they would attend such a program. The latter being the case, it was suggested that a retirement planning program which was also concerned with improving the present situation might be more beneficial than one which concentrated on post-retirement life.

Inquiries into the effectiveness of retirement planning programs (Greene, Pyron, Manion, & Winklevoss, 1969; Hunter, 1962, 1968), have shown them to have some beneficial effect where retirement preparation (Hunter, 1962), satisfaction with retirement, (Hunter, 1968) and adjustment to retirement (Greene et al., 1969) are concerned. However, where these programs are voluntary only some who are eligible attend, and of the latter not all recall doing so when asked about this later. Thus, Greene et al. (1969) reported that only 57% of their sample of preretirees aged 60 and over attended the available voluntary program (but some preretirees were ineligible since certain retirement planning programs were only offered to those aged 62 and over), and while 72% of the retirees from these firms had attended such courses, less than half could recall doing so.

In addition, little attention seems to have been paid to determining the most appropriate age at which to introduce such programs, al-

*Reprinted from *The Gerontologist*, Vol. 11, 1961, pages 33-36, with permission of the author and the Gerontological Society.
**Dr. Fillenbaum is a member of the staff of the Center for the Study of Aging and Human Development at Duke University Medical Center.

though this should influence program content. The present manner of deciding the appropriate age at which to offer a retirement planning program appears to be somewhat haphazard and based more upon a general expectation of what is a plausible appropriate age than on empirical information. Thus Wermel & Beideman (1961) suggest starting 15 to 18 years before the expected age of retirement (i.e., around age 50) in order to permit time for financial planning. Only rarely (Davidson & Kunze, 1965; Heron, 1962) do we read that some particular starting age has been selected because employees' needs point to that age.

Before setting up a retirement planning program for the non-academic employees in a large university and medical center complex we decided that it would be helpful to know whether such a program was desired, by whom, and how old these persons were. Naturally, our findings apply only to our special case, and only at the present time, but since little information of this nature appears to be readily available, our data may be useful to others who are also considering offering retirement planning programs.

MATERIALS AND METHODS

Subjects The non-academic population consists of nearly 6,000 persons of both sexes, different races, ranging in age from 17 to 74 years, and in length of time employed from the newly hired to those with over 30 years of service. The occupational structure is such that well over 1,000 persons fall into each of the main groupings of professionals, technicians, office and clerical, and service workers. Age and level of education (and consequently occupational status) are inversely related in this group. Younger persons have had more education and are more likely to hold upper occupational status positions and to be white.

A random selection of 100 persons from each of the decades 25-34; 35-44; 45-54; 55-64 was planned, but due to programming errors, 450 persons were selected instead of 400. Selection, however, was still random within each decade. The mandatory retirement age is 65. Comparison of the randomly selected group with the total population indicated that the randomly selected group was representative on all relevant variables (sex, race, length of time employed, occupational status).

Questionnaires on which anonymity was ensured were mailed to all those selected. Of these, 19 never reached their destination, and replies were obtained from 56% (243) of the remainder. The nonrespondents did not differ significantly from the respondents on race, occupational status, or length of time employed. A significantly larger proportion of those aged 45-54, however, and of women, returned the questionnaire. The youngest age group returned the fewest questionnaires.

Information was requested on a wide variety of topics. Answers to two of these topics: the acceptability of a retirement planning program, and retirement plans, are immediately relevant here.

ACCEPTABILITY OF A RETIREMENT PLANNING PROGRAM

Three questions were asked:

1. Do you think that a program which would tell people about some of the problems of aging and retirement, and which would suggest ways of dealing with these problems, would be useful? Yes   No

2. If such a program were available here, what might be the likelihood of your making use of it? (1) would certainly go, (2) might go, (3) would not go, (4) would go if I were older than I am, or (5) would have gone when I was younger, too late now.

3. Would you be more likely to go if you were allowed time off from work? Yes   No

Nearly everybody (227/235) believes that a retirement planning program would be useful; 44% would certainly go, 32% might go, 24% would not go (of the latter 41/58 are under 45). The proportion of those who "would certainly go" increases with each decade (25-34, 23%; 35-44, 42%; 45-54, 49%; over 54, 55%), and the proportion who "might go" jumps suddenly with the 45-54 age group (25-34, 26%; 35-44, 26%; 45-54, 37%; over 54, 35%). As a group those aged 45 and over express the most interest.

Interest in a retirement program increases as occupational status decreases (upper, 17% interested; middle, 50%; lower, 65%), and, probably concomitantly, as educational level decreases. Interest is a function of both age and occupational status. When, for each occupational status, those aged 45 and over are compared with younger persons, upper occupational status persons of all ages express a similar lack of interest in a retirement planning program (only 26% of the older and 12% of the younger are interested), the older middle occupational status persons are somewhat more interested than the younger (56% of the older and 42% of the younger), and both older and younger lower occupational status persons are interested (61% and 78%, respectively).

Finally, time off from work might induce some additional persons to make use of a retirement planning program. An additional 20% in all age groups except the oldest say that they would be more likely to go if allowed time off from work.

PLANNING FOR RETIREMENT

Employees were asked whether people *should* make plans for retirement, and if so, when; whether *they* had thought about retirement and made plans and when they had done this.

Nearly all (225/232, 97%) believe that people *should* make plans, but only 66% report thinking of retirement and only 28% have made any plans. Not surprisingly, the older the age group, the larger the proportion who report having thought about retirement. No differences are found as a function of sex, race, or occupational status, but the greater the length of time employed and the *lower* the level of education (matters which are closely related in this population), the more likely the respondent is to report having thought about retirement. While thinking about retirement is inversely related to level of education, planning for retirement is positively related to it (percentages in each educational grouping are: (grades 0-8, 11%; grades 9-12, 17%; up to and including 4 years of college, 38%; more than 4 years of college, 43%) and is also, consequently, related to occupational status. The higher the occupational status the greater the likelihood that retirement plans have been made. Strangely, planning for retirement is not related to age, neither is it related to sex or race. It is as though the worse one's position the more one worries about retirement, but the less one actually does anything about it, probably because one cannot.

Plans *should* be made "a good deal before retirement," "when the work career is started," "when a person is becoming established," etc. The specific time range covers anything from 1 to 47 years before retirement, with 20 and 30 years before retirement being the most frequently recommended times. Needless to say, this is not when people report that they actually made plans; plans tend to be made much closer to retirement.

DISCUSSION

Our data seem to indicate that, for the age group examined, the desirable time to introduce a retirement planning program is around the age of 45. It is clear that interest in retirement becomes more evident at this age, as indicated by the greater proportion of persons who say that they would be interested in attending, by the larger number of questionnaires returned by those aged 45-54, and by the general belief that planning should start some 20 years before retirement. This is slightly earlier than either the 15 to 18 years before retirement recommended by Wermel & Beideman (1961) for a model retirement preparation program, or than the starting age suggested by the company-directed employee opinion polls which they report. It may reflect the trend towards a greater acceptance of retirement (Ash, 1966).

Further evidence in support of introducing a retirement planning program at this age comes from a knowledge of the changes in the family life and personal interests of these individuals. Among those aged 45-54 in this sample the nuclear family (husband, wife and unmarried children) is still the most common unit, but there is an increase in the number of childless households, although only one person was living alone. However, in the next older decade, the childless nuclear family is preponderant, and many people are living completely alone. This is a foretaste of the early stages of retirement. While the 45-54-year-old people are still active in associations, they report that their involvement is less than it was 10 years previously. If these interests are to be maintained, and participation in pre-retirement education programs encourages involvement in activities since this leads to better adjustment in retirement (Greene et al., 1969; Hunter, 1968), intervention needs to start by this age.

Like Burgess, Corey, Pineo, & Thornbury (1958) we too find that lower occupational status persons need guidance in the plans they should (or could) make for retirement, for they worry but they do not plan. What we find especially heartening is that these same people express an interest and willingness to make retirement plans. Clearly, if a retirement planning program can only be offered to a limited group, then it should be offered to lower occupational status persons. After all, upper occupational status persons do make plans for retirement and, as shown by Stokes and Maddox (1967), maintain their satisfaction with retirement.

The present subjects were not asked which topics they wished to see included in a retirement planning program. Thirty years or so before the event few would have been willing to make suggestions, but from present indications of which persons are most interested in a program of this type, and from reports of factors related to adjustment after retirement, certain recommendations can be made.

The aim of retirement planning programs is to improve adjustment to retirement and reduce problems which may be caused or exacerbated by retirement. Present evidence indicates that those whose income, level of activity, and job satisfaction are greater, whose health is better, and whose attitude to retirement is more favorable, tend to adjust better to retirement (Greene et al., 1969; Simpson, Back, & McKinney, 1966; Thompson, 1958; Thompson & Streib, 1958). Presumably, then, any retirement planning program should concentrate on such matters in order to improve adjustment to retirement, and possibly, since financial condition plays such an overwhelming role in this area and is related to nearly all other variables mentioned, greater emphasis should be placed on economic considerations than on other matters. The manner in which this is done may vary with closeness to retirement. For instance, where retirement is imminent, financial position can be made clear and methods of coping with the available income can be outlined, but little can be done to noticeably increase either present or future income.

Instruction which begins 10 or 15 years before retirement can introduce the concept of financial planning for old age, but may be too late to markedly improve the worker's pre-retirement economic position. However, at an earlier stage, say 30 years before retirement, attempts can be made to improve both pre- and post-retirement economic position by pointing out the virtues of, say, further education and retraining and of financial planning. While matters such as retraining may not generally be perceived as a form of retirement planning, they may be expected to have an effect on adjustment to retirement which is similar to that sought by more conventional approaches to retirement planning.

Retirement should not be viewed as an entirely separate stage of life, unconnected with what went before — it is not. Income in later years may be much affected by pre-retirement income and specific job; health in old age may be related to health care when younger. Improvements made to life at an earlier age may well have a greater effect, and for a longer period of time, than advice given shortly before retirement. We need to view retirement as part of the *continuum* of life, and if we offer programs to younger persons it is essential that retirement should be seen in this way. Matters on which they are given guidance should not be of use only 30 years hence, but should also have some value in the more immediate future. While they must be made aware of the problems to be faced in retirement, they can also be shown how improvements in their present status may also have a desirable effect after they retire.

REFERENCES

Ash, P. Pre-retirement counseling. *Gerontologist*, 1966, 6, 97-99, 127-128.

Burgess, E. W., Corey, L. G., Pineo, P. C., & Thornbury, R. T. Occupational differences in attitudes toward aging and retirement. *Journal of Gerontology*, 1958, 13, 203-206.

Davidson, W. R., & Kunze, K. R. Psychological, social and economic meanings of work in modern society: their effects on the worker facing retirement. *Gerontologist*, 1965, 5, 129-133, 159.

Greene, M. R., Pyron, H. C., Manion, U. V., & Winklevoss, H. Pre-retirement counseling, retirement adjustment, and the older employee. Graduate School of Management and Business, College of Business Administration, University of Oregon, Oct., 1969, Unpublished report.

Heron, A. Preparation for retirement. A new phase in occupational development. *Occupational Psychology*, 1962, 36, 1-9.

Hunter, W. W. Trends in pre-retirement education. Background paper and bibliography prepared for the Welfare planning council of the Los Angeles Region conference on Pre-retirement counseling: a community responsibility, Nov. 28-30, 1962.

Hunter, W. W. *Preparation for retirement*. Division of Gerontology, University of Michigan, Ann Arbor, 1968.

Simpson, I. H., Back, K. W., & McKinney, J. C. Attributes of work involvement in society and self-evaluation in retirement. In I. H. Simpson and J. C. McKinney (Eds.), *Social aspects of aging*. Duke University Press, Durham, N.C., 1966.

Stokes, R. G., & Maddox, G. L. Some social factors on retirement adaptation. *Journal of Gerontology*, 1967, 22, 329-333.

Thompson, W. E. Pre-retirement anticipation and adjustment in retirement. *Journal of Social Issues*, 1958, 14, 35-45.

Thompson, W. E. & Streib, G. F. Situational determinants: health and economic deprivation in retirement. *Journal of Social Issues*, 1958, 14, 18-34.

Wermel, M. T., & Beideman, G. M. *Retirement preparation programs: a study of company responsibility*. Pasadena: Industrial Relations Section, California Institute of Technology, 1961.

C. DEATH AND DYING

The next series of papers are concerned with attitudes toward death and dying and alternative ways of facing this inevitability. This section seems particularly timely as more and more researchers and writers continue to break down the barriers surrounding this taboo. It is becoming increasingly apparent that people of all ages — not just the old — demand and deserve the right to live *and* die with a sense of self-worth and dignity.

The first paper in this section presents excerpts from a symposium on death and attitudes toward death which considers the taboo surrounding death, the possibility of euthanasia, and how to deal with dying patients.

Following the symposium report, a brief synopsis is given of Elizabeth Kubler-Ross' five psychological stages preparatory to death. These are the stages or ways of coping with death which are covered so thoroughly in her brilliantly written book *Death and Dying*. The student interested in more depth might enjoy reading the book from which this description is taken.

The final article in this series by David Sudnow concerns the harsh and cruel realities of dying in our contemporary American society. Today's dying patient is too often subjected to a dehumanizing environment in his last days rather than being surrounded by the warmth and love of those who could make his last experience in life more bearable.

26. Symposium on Death and Attitudes Toward Death*

STACY B. DAY, MULFORD Q. SIBLEY, B. J. KENNEDY, ROBERT FULTON, RICHARD SIMMONS, JOHN BRANTNER, ROBERT A. GOOD, I. E. FORTUNY, ROBERT C. SLATER**

Is death a taboo subject?
What do you tell the patient?
Is euthanasia coming?

INTRODUCTION

"It has been said that ever since men began to think the subject of death has exercised their minds, yet it is true no less that it is only in these last few years that the conditions and circumstances of dying have become of increasing importance and concern. . . ."

With these words, Dr. Stacey B. Day introduced the first session of a Symposium on Death and Attitudes Toward Death. The symposium was presented as part of an ongoing curriculum development program of the Bell Museum of Pathology and the Department of Pathology of the University of Minnesota Medical School, Minneapolis. Dr. Day, conservator of the Bell Museum, and Dr. Robert A. Good, chairman of the department, enlisted the aid of faculty members and other persons from the community to provide a broad look at many aspects of dying and death.

The questions and answers included here are only those that the editors considered most pertinent to physicians treating patients of middle age and old age. Most of the questions were submitted by medical students and were presented to the panelists by Dr. Day. The questions are paraphrased in these excerpts and only key portions of individual answers are given.

*Reprinted with permission of the authors from *Geriatrics,* Vol. 27, Number 8, August 1972, pages 52-55, and 58-60. Copyright The New York Times Media Co., Inc.
**Dr. Day is Professor of Biological Sciences at the Cornell University Medical Center. The rest of the symposium participants are at the University of Minnesota. Dr. Sibley is Professor of Political Science. Dr. Kennedy is Professor of Medicine and Medical Oncology. Dr. Fulton is Professor of Sociology. Dr. Simmons is Associate Professor of Surgery and Microbiology. Dr. Brantner is Professor of Clinical Psychology. Dr. Good is Professor of Pathology. Dr. Fortuny is Associate Professor of Medicine. And, Dr. Slater is Director of the Mortuary Science Division.

Dr. Stacey B. Day: We have been asked whether attitudes toward discussions about death are changing, or whether death is still a taboo subject. Professor Sibley, why don't you start on that question?

Prof. Mulford Sibley: I think the attitude toward death is changing very sharply. Last year I attended a conference on death sponsored by the Department of Sociology at Hamline University (St. Paul) and it was packed. The interesting thing is that a high percentage of people who attended that conference were high school and college students. So I believe the ban on discussing death is breaking down very much in contemporary American society. It is not merely medical schools that are getting concerned.

Dr. Day: Dr. Kennedy, you see a great deal of death, especially in the cancer unit. How would you answer this?

Dr. B. J. Kennedy: The audience here demonstrates the fact that death is a very voguish subject. Physicians who deal with dying cancer patients have been identified with the subject for a long time; we have been teaching about death for a great number of years. With cancer patients, death and the disease have been interrelated. A patient frequently will ask, "Am I going to die?" My usual answer is that *absolutely, I will guarantee that all my patients will die.*

It's surprising that a number of patients are amazed that a physician would say they are going to die — maybe not today or tomorrow, but some day — and that the physician is willing to talk with patients who are interested in whether or not they are going to die. Death has been something that physicians did not discuss with their patients. As a result there was always a gap in communication between the doctor and the patient. In fact it still exists where physicians refrain from talking about potential death.

Patients want to talk about death. There is no problem in talking about death. I think what is happening is that the public is learning that you *can* talk about death.

Dr. Day: Professor Fulton, you aren't a physician, yet I know you have been working in this area for a long time. What are you going to say in answer to the question?

Prof. Robert Fulton: I think this audience tells us, and the one that Professor Sibley describes at Hamline tells us, that this is the first "death-free" generation in the history of the world, a generation that is being confronted with the question of longevity for what? You have two generations coming into conflict here — a generation that, in its own private life, has never really experienced death, and a generation of elderly people who constitute the largest and fastest growing population of elderly people this country has ever seen. This elderly group is, in terms of the Hippocratic Oath, a group that must be kept alive, that must be assisted and aided in every way possible.

The directive reads: "Primum non nocere" — first of all do no harm. So we are trapped at this particular time in our history with a generation that is very health oriented, very life oriented, and very welfare oriented — and a generation that is most eligible to die. Among the things we see moving and pushing us are the questions about life. Longevity for what? Organ transplants for what? Extension of life for what? Extraordinary measures for what?

According to all government statistics and reports, the elderly have very little to look forward to regardless of how good their health might be. The segregation, the abandonment, and the isolation of the elderly population raises fresh moral and ethical issues, issues that have always been here but not in such a fashion.

This is the point that I would make in commenting on Dr. Kennedy's remarks. Of course we have always had death. The point is not that death is voguish or that death is new or that we are coming to recognize it; it is just that the whole sociologic structure within which living and death occurs has changed. Health care professionals are just now becoming aware of the situation because the stresses and strains within the various institutions are becoming intolerable for many, not the least of whom is the dying patient.

Dr. Day: Dr. Simmons is our transplant surgeon. Dick, have a go!

Dr. Richard Simmons: Is the discussion of death taboo? I think death is almost like sex: If we had had a sex conference we couldn't have driven more people in here! Discussions of death are like sex — they are free and open to the public. You can watch sex in a movie theater but discussing it with your children is slightly embarrassing. In fact, however, it is more embarrassing to discuss death with your children than it is to discuss sex nowadays. Certainly it is with me and my family; there are lots of sssshhhhs around, particularly from the grandparents, when the problem of death comes up in the family.

The other private realm of death is in the patient; death in the patient under your care is a very private matter. I think a doctor tends not to bring the subject up very often with the patient, and when he does, he intellectualizes it, as we are doing here. For example, before transplantation I always tell the patient his chances of dying in just so many words: "You have a 10 percent chance of dying one year following the operation tomorrow morning." This point is important for a patient to know because he has a feeling that he is going to get this organ and by gosh he is going to run. He is not, and by at least pointing out to him that it is troublesome — that there are problems including death along the line — you give him and his family a more realistic attitude about the matter.

I must say I don't do that to my general surgical patients, where death is far less of a probability, because it is slightly embarrassing to raise the possibility of a failure. We, as physicians, do not like to contemplate failure.

Dr. Day: Dr. Brantner, would you like to add a postscript to this?

Dr. John Brantner: To answer the question about death — is it still a taboo subject? — I think the change in attitude is one of the most profound changes that has happened in our society in the last five years or so. People are beginning to question the assumptions, the hypotheses, on which we have based our lives. And I think people are beginning to see that by ignoring death, by denying death, by closing it out from our consideration, we have done things we didn't want to do about our lives.

We are beginning to see that death underlies many of our moral questions, many of our political questions, so many things. Do we eat meat? If we do perhaps we should examine this in the context that we are dining on death. Would we be willing to slaughter in order to eat meat? The question of vegetarianism or omnivorousness is one that involves death. And we cannot approach it intelligently and unemotionally if we exclude death from our consideration. This is perhaps a trivial example, but death pervades all the questions of war, the question of our traffic laws, the question of abortion and contraception. So many other things which are important to us now cannot be answered fully unless we have experienced, as a society, a confrontation with death, and we are beginning to realize this.

Dr. Day: I'm going to move on to another question and ask Professor Fulton to answer. The question is: Birth is no longer blindly accepted but increasingly is planned and timed. Does this development and growing acceptance of abortion indicate a readiness to consider euthanasia?

Prof. Fulton: Some of you are acquainted with the second World War gold stars that used to hang in the windows of many homes across this country. The impulse toward euthanasia is growing so fast and so strong that I wouldn't be a bit surprised if, within this decade, the decade that I have labeled "The Decade of Death," the young people of America will be putting up such stars in the windows of their homes across the country with the slogan, "We Gave." And it will be their parents or their grandparents who were "given."

We will have 25 million people over 65 at the end of the decade. They are the most eligible to die. Almost 8 million people are over 75, and 20,000 people are over a century old. We don't know what to do with them. We have no place for them. Society has changed so profoundly that most of them are economically obsolete. They are sociologically obsolete. In terms of the change of family structure of American society, they are obsolete as family members. They are separated and isolated from their families, psychologically if not physically, simply by virtue of the fact that this is a youth-oriented society — a two-generational society. Yet we have a four-generational population demographically. And we don't know what to do.

What has been suggested in England is a bill giving the right to a patient to request a doctor to kill him. The whole question of the right to die, to take one's own life when he so chooses, when he no longer, in his terms, is willing to accept the conditions of his life, is becoming more and more acceptable to the American public all the time. The right to take one's own life is popular among the young and growing in acceptability among us, because we look to the elderly to commit that act for us and solve many of the ethical and moral problems that at the time are beyond our capabilities.

Prof. Sibley: May I ask a question in that connection? Do you personally approve of euthanasia?

Prof. Fulton: No, I don't.

Prof. Sibley: I don't either.

Dr. Day: Dr. Brantner, what have you got to say about that?

Dr. Brantner: It is coming. Many of us in this room will be faced with the question of deciding for ourselves, legally and not feloniously, under what conditions life is acceptable to us. I hope we will never be faced, any of us in this room, with the question that has been posed under the context of euthanasia — under what conditions is life acceptable for others? We are thinking of voluntary, statutory euthanasia. It will come. Many of us will have to ask ourselves the very, very basic fundamental question: When is death an acceptable event in my life? And there is another question that we will then face. What are the appropriate conditions of death, if we decide we are eligible for death and death has become an acceptable outcome?

For those in the whole health care business, the "appropriateness of death" is a basic question. How should people die under those circumstances? It relates very directly, the right to die, not only to the question of asking my physician to cease medical treatment but asking him to kill me since I am unable to kill myself under many of the conditions that I would define. And reserving for myself the right to kill myself. I would also express my *personal* belief: I see this coming. I suppose I am willing to defend it as a right for others. I can conceive of no circumstances under which I would avail myself of this right.

Dr. Day: Dr. Simmons, let us say that you open me up in the operating room and find I have an inoperable cancer. I tell you that I wish to die. What are you going to say to me?

Dr. Simmons: In one sense we already have euthanasia. A patient can refuse further treatment, and some patients choose to do just that. If we point out to these patients what their chances are if they have such and such an operation, a number will say this is not acceptable. They will not accept further hemodialysis treatment, or immunosuppressive treatment for transplantation, or chemotherapy for cancer. The patient will withhold treatment and go elsewhere. Euthanasia, in that sense, has already arrived.

Dr. Day: I have a group of questions now, and I will present one each to a separate member of the panel. Dr. Kennedy, do you have any suggestions on how to develop a healthy realistic attitude toward death?

Dr. Kennedy: I think the average person must, in his own judgment, begin to decide what his purpose is in living, what his goals are, and then accept the realistic fact that some day he will die. In so doing, when he is faced with the reality of death, it will not be as traumatic to him as it will be to the person who has blinded himself to the fact that death is going to occur. Making a will is a good illustration that he accepts the fact that he is going to die.

Dr. Day: Dr. Brantner, how do you view your own death? Do you ever think about it?

Dr. Brantner: Following Dr. Kennedy's advice, I think about it daily. As a deliberate discipline. I would carry that advice further. I would recommend some practical means of carrying out a kind of confrontation with your own death. Not only with your own death, but also with your own disability — the planning for disaster and death. Regardless of how much we think of this, when it arrives it is going to be seen by us as a disaster. But we can prepare for disaster. We can consider, those of us who wear spectacles, what we will do in those days when we cannot read. We can anticipate our own paraplegia, our own strokes. We can make this blow less in that we will have thought about it. And I think this is one of the keys for death. Think daily on it. In the context of your prayers, your meditations, while brushing your teeth, at any regular time whatever, think daily on it. Accustom yourself to looking at your possessions and your relationships with others in this context. On parting from another, remind yourself — not in a morbid gloomy way, but in a way that may catch you up in a quarrel, or catch you up in hasty words — remind yourself that this could be your last parting from this person.

Dr. Day: I am going to give this question to Dr. Simmons. Am I pledged to maintain existence in all my patients? Must I initiate procedures which will keep ventilation and circulation going when I know that each day of existence depletes the material reserves of the family, uses up valuable economic resources, and offers no chance for the patient to enjoy again a normal life?

Dr. Simmons: With respect to other members of the panel, who I hope will remain my friends, it sounds as if death is a desirable thing; personally I think death is not very desirable. It may be socially desirable, and it may be ecologically important for society, but it is not a desirable thing for the person involved. Should one do everything possible to save the heart-beating, presumably brain-living cadaver? The answer is yes, even if you think otherwise, because you will be wrong on occasion. As long as you really think there is a possibility of continuing existence, recovery is possible.

I think the point that there is dignity in dying is overstated. I don't see that it is very dignified. And death is no more or less dignified for a patient on a respirator than it is for a person falling in the middle of the street in a car accident. I think the patient deserves an attempt to save his life. On the other hand, when failure to save his life has occurred, he also deserves to be made as comfortable as possible and to die as quickly as possible without euthanasia. Thus, some rational decisions must be made. Perhaps transplantation has helped make those decisions by deciding when brain death has occurred. You can decide when brain death has occurred and turn off the respirator even if the organs are not going to be used for somebody else. I don't think this is, in fact, a really difficult decision in medical practice.

Dr. Day: Dr. Simmons, does the patient fall into a conspiracy of silence, a mutual conspiracy of silence with his doctor, when facing death?

Dr. Simmons: Yes, I think most patients fall into a "conspiracy of silence." When they are acutely ill, you have to bring up the subject of death to them. The patients are in the hospital to prevent death. They really are, in a sense, denying the reality of death when they come to the hospital because they come to get well. As Dr. Kennedy said, he is happy when the patient asks, "Am I going to die?", because he knows how to deal with it and he knows the patient needs it dealt with. The patient, however, doesn't always ask, or it takes a long time for him to ask.

Dr. Day: Dr. Good, the same question.

Dr. Robert Good: There are a number of aspects we should bring out. First of all, I think physicians dealing with the issue of death, and Dr. Simmons indicated this in his discussion, really are afraid to deal with this question. They have a very tough time, and for a very special reason, for from the very earliest phase of their lives, many times these people are selected. Their mothers selected them and they were selected all the way through school and they get a sense that they are omnipotent. Facing death for a physician is facing failure in our modern outlook. I think this is one of the problems. As a pathologist I see this in a very special way. One of the hardest things is to get physicians to come to the postmortem room. They don't want to come. It is a recognition of their failure in dealing with disease. And this is very tough for doctors.

Dr. Day: Dr. Fortuny what do you say?

Dr. Ignatio Fortuny: One of the things I would like to stress is the conspiracy of silence, tying it in with what Dr. Good said. This results from the inadequacy of the individuals caring for the patient, namely, the doctors and nurses; they too fail. We don't like to see failure. Therefore, if we haven't got the courage to face the reality of this person's life and answer the question frankly, when the question is posed to us, "Are we going to live?", we fumble by using very objective and scientific terms to answer something we really don't know about. That's how the conspiracy begins, because then the doctor or the nurse gets caught in the game of trying to give an answer to something he or she doesn't know. The patient doesn't get any help at all, just the fumbling of words regarding his body. I think the conspiracy of silence, then, is a very real thing that never happens when whoever is responsible shares with the patient the reality of his state — whether it is immediate or distant death. Once the truth has been told to the person, and once the doctor has opened the gates, the basis for the conspiracy is removed. In facing the reality of your own dying, you can put it aside only when it has been looked at and defined honestly; then acceptance follows.

Dr. Day: Thank you very much. I am going to give Professor Slater a new question. Can we prepare for sudden acute death arising from accidents or some unforeseeable circumstances?

Prof. Robert Slater: I would like to approach it in two ways. There is a group which calls itself Equinox surrounding the Harvard campus and medical center that is doing some work in this regard with a health care team. Before a patient dies, the group has a funeral director who participates in group therapy sessions to answer questions this patient might have about his death. What happens? When does it happen? I think this is one way in which we might follow very carefully a study where they are looking at preparation for death. But I think our culture prepares us for the kind of death you are talking about — sudden death — in another way. Sudden death is practically contagious in our society and it is looked upon as unclean unless you die a hero's death. It is one thing to die from some wasting disease but it is another thing to be killed going down the highway at 80 miles an hour. Our culture seems to approve of death in one instance and to look upon it with much suspicion in another instance. Preparation for death has been with us a long time in all writings, in mythology, for instance, yet we seem to do an awfully good job of flunking the exam in preparing for it.

Dr. Day: Dr. Good?

Dr. Good: I think there is only one way to prepare for sudden and unexpected death and that is through our cultural heritage. Our poets constantly think on death, they constantly help us face the possibilities of death. I really don't think that it is very active living or very exciting living to be avoiding death constantly in a way that some have suggested. Look at all you youngsters going out there and skiing. What happens with skiing is that you are constantly seeking to be close to death and still to avoid it! I think this is a part of living.

The real way of avoiding death on the highway is not to overcrowd the highway. Seat belts are really an inconsequential, although temporarily slightly effective, preventive measure. They are not the real business. It is those overcrowded highways and the *chance* of accidents. I think that we, in our scholarly pursuits, have to be prepared to deal with the potentiality, in our way of living, of sudden death. I would answer this question by saying that there is only one preparation, one way of preparing for the eventuality of unexpected death and that is to do as Dr. Brantner earlier said, "think on it whenever we get a chance." I have been practicing all week long. Thinking about death when I shave!

Prof. Slater: It seems to me that if we look at the intention for which a funeral is given in most cultures — and they tell us they haven't found a culture yet that has not had some sort of a ceremony or funeral rite — we emphasize that it gives approval to the feelings and the emotions people have at the time of a separation crisis, in this instance, death. All of our functions where we express strong emotions have had rites and ceremonies established around them. They help many people act through or say things that they cannot ordinarily express on their own without the help of a liturgy or a rite.

I think there is something further that is important in this culture. We talk a lot about death and the relationships that go with it. The real importance of a funeral has to be as much a testimony to the fact that a life has been lived as to the fact that a death has occurred. The death is an empirical fact. The life that has touched many people, whether they were important or unimportant, is very important to that family circle, however large it might be. The purpose of the funeral is to give people the ability to work through the strong feelings that are in our culture in this current time, and I think history will prove it has been the same throughout the ages.

27. Psychological Stages Preparatory to Death*

Since death is as intrinsic a human experience as life, after all the millennia mankind should have developed some expertise in helping dying people, Dr. Ross told the institute on "The Dying Patient and His Family." Not just helping them to die, but helping them to "live until they die," she explained.

Instead, our society has converted death into a terribly lonely, depersonalized affair. Terminal patients in our hospitals — particularly those in intensive care units — are treated as though no longer human. People avoid looking at them or listening to them.

Research papers suggest that most people in health care believe terminal cancer patients should not be told about their condition, Dr. Ross said. Yet she has found that terminally sick patients always know they are dying, whether they have been told or not. Visit their rooms, and within minutes they are talking about malignancy, metastasis, dying. "They will talk about it, if you are ready to talk. But if you resort to denial, the patient will use denial."

She cited the case of an irascible, difficult, 50-year-old patient who was dying of metastasis. His wife had made arrangements to transfer him to a Nursing Home; but nobody knew how to break the news to him.

On the way to the interview room, the following day, Dr. Ross asked him why he had accepted her invitation. He replied: "It was because you used the word 'communicate'. I have been trying for two years to communicate with my wife. And now I have such a short time left."

"How sick are you?" she asked.

He looked at her, and said: "Do you really want to know? I'm riddled with cancer!"

In this country we have difficulty talking about death. It is different in Europe, where most people die at home, asserted the speaker.

"They remain in a familiar environment, in their own bed, surrounded by their family. Most important, perhaps, the children are not sent away; they are permitted to share in some of the responsibilities

*Reprinted from the *Geriatric Focus,* Vol. 9, April 1970, pages 1, 9 and 10, with permission of *Geriatric Focus.* This selection was abstracted by *Geriatric Focus* from a report at a professional meeting by Dr. Kubler-Ross, and is further described in her book *On Death and Dying,* New York: MacMillan, 1969. Dr. Kubler-Ross is Medical Director of the Family Service and Mental Health Center of South Cook County in Chicago.

caring for the dying person, and in the preparatory grief. They see animals (and sometimes people) born, they see them die; they learn from early childhood that life has a natural beginning, and a natural end."

When the patient dies, they don't embalm the corpse or paint the face in a grotesque attempt to make it appear that he's just asleep. They do not attempt to deny reality, as we do. And that is what makes death so much more difficult for us. "Dying is not so terrible, if you have learned through experience that it is part of life."

The best teachers are dying patients, Dr. Ross observed. Thus far she has interviewed some 400 of them. Only three refused to talk about death, and they were "exceptionally tragic cases."

When patients are seriously ill, denial doesn't work. In bed all day, with little input from the outside, they become good observers. They see relatives come in with swollen eyes and cheeks; they see old friends who once were casual become stilted strangers. They perceive the tension, anxiety, and discomfort in the attitude of personnel. They know they are getting weaker, that they need more and more medication, that the pain doesn't go away. Adding these things up, they know they are close to death. "They will even convey to you the time of death — if you listen for it!"

All terminal patients go through five psychological stages in preparation for death, Dr. Ross said. She listed them as follows:

Stage 1, shock or denial. ("No, not me!") Somebody made a mistake, read the slides or x-rays wrong. They go into hibernation, refuse to talk about their condition or hear about it. Or they frantically shop around from doctor to doctor, from clinic to clinic, seeking a miracle.

Stage 2, anger, rage. ("Why me?") They are bitter about everything and irate with everyone, including God. They turn on their families, are nasty, mean, ungrateful, perpetually complaining. They snarl at doctors and nurses — and suffer for it. A California study showed that it took nurses twice as long to respond to the bell or light of a terminal patient as to the signal of other patients.

Stage 3, bargaining. ("Yes, me, but . . .") The angry, demanding patient suddenly becomes quiet and nice. He has called a truce, he says in effect: "Give me one more year, and I'll be good. I'll say my prayers, go to church; I'll do this or that . . ." He's trying to buy time.

Dr. Ross cited the case of a very disagreeable female patient who suddenly turned sweet and nice as the date of her son's marriage approached. Suffering severely from disease, she depended on round-the-clock injections to ease her pain. "Give me just one day without pain so I can attend my boy's wedding, and I'll be very good," she begged. "I won't ring the bell all the time."

At the appointed time, sporting a new hairdo and a becoming new dress and provided with sufficient medication to ease painlessly through the day, she took off for the wedding. She returned to the hospital late that evening exhausted and quite ill. As they helped her into bed, she said: "Don't forget, Dr. Ross, I have another son!"

Stage 4, depression, preparatory grief. ("Woe is me!") Some whine and complain, some cry all the time. More commonly, they just sit and grieve silently "not for what they have already lost, but for what they are in the process of losing." They are preparing themselves for the break in family ties, the final separation from humanity. It is a time to do what has to be done, and say what has to be said; it is a time to bid farewell to relatives, children, and friends.

Stage 5, acceptance. ("I am ready.") They have disposed of unfinished business, said their good-byes, cut all personal ties. They don't want to see any more relatives and friends. Usually all they want is to lie back quietly on the pillow, perhaps have one person with whom they are comfortable sit with them. This is not resignation, Dr. Ross declared, it is something much more positive and courageous. It is not a happy acceptance; but neither is it painful or sad surrender.

She told of an attractive, courageous, young black woman who came to the hospital with a terminal kidney condition. "There was something about her, she was a beautiful person." The staff liked her, and tried to prolong her life by getting her admitted to the Kidney Dialysis Program. But in the end, after a series of mishaps, she was turned down. She had run the entire gamut of hope — hope that her ailment was not serious, that treatment would make her well, that she would be accepted for dialysis . . .

One day she said to Dr. Ross: "My time is very near now, doctor. What is your concept of death?"

The psychiatrist was caught by surprise. She had asked 400 patients this same question, but no one had ever put it to her. She started to mumble some evasion, then stopped. "Peace," she replied, truthfully.

The patient nodded. "I'm going very peacefully from this garden into the next one." She fell asleep, and died about three hours later.

"This is acceptance," Dr. Ross stated.

28. The Logistics of Dying*

DAVID SUDNOW**

*Plan now to die during the night shift,
with your eyes closed and your relatives
nowhere in sight*

Most deaths in the U.S.A. take place in the hospital. The facts
reported here, then, are limited to those institutions and are based on
the extensive comparative study of two typical hospitals — a large,
urban, charity institution (referred to as "County") and a comparable-
sized, private, general hospital (called "Cohen"). Most of the observations concern County.

When a patient's condition is considered such that he is "dying," or
"terminally ill," his name is "posted" on the "critical patients' list." Once
"posted," a patient has the theoretical right to receive visitors throughout the day and night rather than only at the appointed visiting hours.
Posting also serves as an internally relevant message, notifying certain
key hospital personnel that a death may be forthcoming, and that
appropriate preparations are tentatively warranted. In the hospital
morgue, scheduling is an important requirement. Rough first drafts of
the week's expected work load are made, with the number of possible
autopsies anticipated and planned for. In making such estimates the
morgue attendant consults "posted lists" from which he makes a guess
as to the work load of the coming week. The "posted list" is also
consulted by various medical personnel who have some special interest
in various anatomical regions. County's morgue attendant made it a
practice to alert the ward physician that Doctor S., a research ophthal-
mologist, wanted to get all the eyes he could. To provide Dr. S. with the
needed eyes, the morgue attendant habitually checked the "posted list"
and tried, in informal talk with the nurses about the patient's family, to
assess the chances of getting the family's permission to relinquish the
eyes of the patient for research. When the attendant located a likely
candidate, he informed the pathologist, who made an effort, via a
resident physician, to have special attention given to the request for an
eye donation. At several places in the hospital, in doctor's lounges and

*Reprinted from *Esquire*, Aug. 1967, pages 102-103 and 130-133 with permission of
Prentice-Hall, Inc. This selection from *Esquire* was adapted from *Passing On: The Social
Organization of Dying*, by David Sudnow, Englewood Cliffs, N. J.: Prentice-Hall,© 1967.
**Mr Sudnow is a professional writer, presently living in New York City.

322

elsewhere, there were periodic signs which read, "Dr. S. needs eyes," "Dr. Y. needs kidneys," etc.

At County there is a Catholic chaplain whose responsibility is to administer the last rites. Each morning he makes his rounds through the various wards of the hospital. At each ward he consults a master schedule, which is an index file containing patients' names, religions, sex and diagnoses. All patients who have been posted are identified with a red plastic border which is placed on their cards. The chaplain goes through this file daily and writes down the names of all known Catholic patients who have been posted, whereupon he enters these patients' rooms and administers Extreme Unction. After completing his round on each ward, he stamps the index card of the patient with a rubber stamp which reads,

Last Rites Administered

Date . . . . Clergyman . . . .

Each day he consults the files to see if new patients have been put on the critical list. His stamps serve to prevent him from performing the rites twice on the same patient.

In fact, many "posted patients" do not die, as "posting" is often done well before obvious impending death is noted. Therefore, quite a few people have the dubious honor of having left County alive, yet having received rites of the dying. (The priest reported that such rites are not permanent: upon readmission to the hospital one must, before one properly dies, receive them again.)

It is significant that some "posted patients" at County can be properly regarded as candidates for autopsies before their deaths, a conception which is not properly entertained at Cohen Hospital. Indicative of the general stance taken toward some dying patients at County is the following conversation that occurred between two resident physicians at the bedside of a "terminally ill patient" in the first stages of a coma from uremic poisoning:

A: "Do you think, really, that both kidneys are as bad?"

B: "I know they're both bad because the output is so damned low. Let's put it this way, neither one is good."

A: "Well, we'll find out for sure at autopsy."

B: "Right."

To discuss a patient's forthcoming autopsy, while the patient is still a patient, would be severely censured at Cohen, without respect for the fact that the patient might be considered "comatose" and not aware of conversation in his presence. At County, there is a decided phasing out of attention given to "dying" patients, to the extent that the possibility of death within the period of a given work shift is taken to warrant instituting certain forms of postdeath treatment.

A tentative distinction can be made between "clinical death," the appearance of "death signs" upon physical examination; "biological death," the cessation of cellular activity; and "social death," which, within the hospital setting, is marked by that point at which a patient is accorded treatment essentially as a corpse, though perhaps still "biologically" and "clinically" alive. The following example is illustrative of what is intended by the term "social death": A nurse on duty with a woman who, she explained, was "dying" was observed to spend some two or three minutes trying to close the woman's eyelids. This involved slowly but somewhat forcefully pushing the two lids together to get them to adhere in a closed position. After several unsuccessful moments she managed to get them to stay shut and said, with a sigh of accomplishment, "Now they're right." When questioned about what she had been doing, she reported that a patient's eyelids are always closed after death, so that the body will resemble a sleeping person. After death, she reported, it was more difficult to accomplish a complete lid closure, especially after the body muscles have begun to tighten and the eyelids become less pliable, more resistant, and have a tendency to move apart. She always tried, she reported, to close them before death, while the eyes were still elastic and more easily manipulated. This allowed ward personnel to more quickly wrap the body upon death (if death indeed occurred) without having to attend to cosmetic matters, and was considerate, she pointed out, of those who preferred to handle dead bodies as little as possible.

"Social death" can be said to be marked by that point at which socially relevant attributes of the patient cease to be operative as conditions for treating him, and when he is, essentially, regarded as already dead.

A clear instance is seen in the circumstance where autopsy permits are filled out prior to death. For an autopsy to be performed, permission of the closest surviving relatives must be obtained. At County two forms of permission constitute legally actionable documents: 1) a signature on a prepared "autopsy permission form"; 2) a telegram from the surviving relative to the hospital, authorizing an autopsy. Obtaining an autopsy permit is regarded as a very important administrative necessity at the time of death. In order to qualify for the A.M.A. Internship Approval Program, and thus be able to offer internships and residencies, a hospital must perform autopsies on twenty-five percent or more of its deceased patients. The minimum rate is not considered sufficient and most hospitals strive for as high a rate as possible. It is apparently a relevant question for a prospective resident to ask of the hospital, "What is your autopsy rate?" then to partially base his decision on where to do a residency on the basis of these rates.

County's doctors attempt to obtain autopsy permission whenever possible, especially when they expect that they will lose contact with a relative. They will sometimes approach the relative of a patient who is considered to be "dying" and tactfully request that, "under the circumstances," a form be signed at the present time. At County this practice was employed only in cases where an autopsy was especially desired and then only if the relative had been made well aware that the patient was expected to die shortly. There is the feeling that one can risk the possible censure which such a proposal might incur only with either the very uneducated relative or the very sophisticated and emotionally cool one.

An instance of "social death" outside the hospital involved a male patient who was admitted to the Emergency Unit with a sudden perforation of a duodenal ulcer. He was operated upon, and for a period of six days remained in critical condition. His wife was informed that his chances of surivival were poor, whereupon she stopped her visits to the hospital. After two weeks, the man's condition improved markedly and he was discharged in ambulatory condition. The next day he was readmitted to the hospital with a severe coronary. Before he died, he recounted his experience upon returning home. His wife had removed all of his clothing and personal effects from the house, had made preliminary arrangements for his burial with the mortuary establishment (she had written a letter, which he discovered on his bureau, requesting a brochure on their rates), she no longer wore his wedding ring, and was found with another man, no doubt quite shocked at her husband's return. He reported that he left the house, began to drink heavily and had a heart attack.

A very common example of "social death" before "actual" death involves the assignment of patients to beds. A patient who is admitted to the hospital in what is considered to be a near-death state, with extremely low blood pressure, very erratic heartbeats and a nonpalpable or very weak pulse, is frequently left on the stretcher on which he is admitted, and put in the laboratory room, or large supply room. In such cases, a nurse explained, they don't want to mess a bed up, and since the patient would soon die, there was no need to assign a bed (upon death, the complete bedding must be stripped, the room thoroughly cleansed, disinfected). In several cases, patients were left throughout the night to die in the supply room, and in the morning, if they were still alive, nurses quickly assigned them beds, before the arrival of physicians or relatives. Here we see instances of movement back and forth between the statuses of life and death, with social life, at least as represented by a bona fide admission to the hospital bed, reinstituted after a night of treatment as a corpse. During a "death watch," the phrase used by nursing personnel to refer to guarding a dying patient in anticipation of his death, the patient is treated as in a transitory state, the relevant facts about him being the gradual decline of clinical life signs. As death approaches, his status as a *body* becomes more evident in the manner in which he is discussed, treated, moved about. Attention shifts from caring for his possible discomforts, and instituting medically advised treatments, to the sheer activity of "timing" his biological events. With a pre-death-coma patient, suctioning of the nasal passages, propping up pillows, changing bed sheets and the like routinely occur as part of the normal nursing routine. As blood pressure drops and signs of imminent death are taken to be apparent, these traditional nursing practices, at least at County, become regarded as less important, and the major interest becomes the number of his heartbeats and the changing condition of his eyes. Suctioning activity diminishes in frequency, his position is not as regularly altered to insure more comfort, and the surroundings are not kept in any particular state of cleanliness. On many occasions, nurses' aides were observed to cease administering standing order oral medications when death was expected to take place within the hour.

At County, relatives are infrequently present at the time of the death. After a death occurs, the family is occasionally asked, by the physician who announces the death, if they wish to view the deceased. Very few relatives request to do so, but should they, the procedure is that the body is to be wrapped completely, with the exception of the head, which is to be propped up on a pillow for display. On such occasions, the hospital stages a miniature ritual. An aide combs the hair, fluffs the pillow and otherwise tries to simulate that state of restful "repose" which morticians pride themselves in accomplishing. For at least one such aide, the hospital experience in this and related tasks served as a practical introduction to the mortuary profession.

Before death, with relatives continuously present in the "dying" patient's room, a more constant vigilance over the patient's condition must be maintained, requiring in effect the removal of a nurse from other activities to spend her exclusive time at the bedside. The routine handling of death, as it occurs in a matter-of-fact fashion in the medical wards at County, requires that the wards be kept relatively free of

outsiders, whose mere presence exacts greater demands on the behavior of staff than the likelihood of a death would normally warrant.
Discovery or even simultaneous discovery of the death by relative and
physician, or relative and nurse, is considered something to be avoided.
While the justification for shielding off dying patients from relatives is
made in terms of the "unpleasantness of seeing someone die," the fact
that such shielding does not always occur in other kinds of hospitals
(like Cohen, where relatives are considered specially entitled to be
present at the bedside when the patient "expires"), seems to point to
the character of hospital routines in these different settings and the
organization of "death-care" as the crucial basis for this practice. At
County, pre-death body treatment can occur as it does only if family
members are kept away, and a phasing out of attention is allowable so
long as the family is not able to witness or infer it.

The physician, too, at County prefers that relatives be kept away
from the bedside of a dying patient, so that he is freer to leave the
bedside himself and attend to other matters. This concern operates
particularly during late evening hours, when the sheer fact of a dying
patient on his service ordinarily would not be taken to require his
continuous presence. With respect to most of his "dying" patients, the
physician regards the forthcoming death matter-of-factly, and feels no
special discomfort in what takes place. The absence of relatives in the
ward, and especially at the bedside, allows him to wait until a more
reasonable hour to come to the ward to pronounce a patient dead and
then inform the relatives of the death. In many instances a patient is
discovered dead in the midst of the night and the doctor is not informed of the death until the morning. County physicians often express anger at nurses who awaken them at night because of the death of
one of their patients. It routinely happens that a patient will die while a
doctor is not on the ward, and remain "unpronounced" until the
physician finds it suitable and convenient to come in. The absence of
relatives at close proximity to the bedside further allows nurses to avoid
calling the doctor in charge until they themselves are about to leave the
shift. This way they can assist their aide staff in passing on the body for
the next shift. One of the disadvantages of the day-time shift, from the
perspective of nurses and aides, is the greater likelihood of having to
remove several bodies upon their arrival at work. They themselves find
it less easy to pass a body on to the evening shift, due to the great activity
of the day-time shift, the movement back and forth of patients and
doctors, the need for bed space for new admissions, and thus the
greater likelihood of discovering a body and the greater difficulty of

concealing one. Of course, the night shift cannot pass every body on to the day shift, because it becomes quickly obvious that not all nighttime deaths occur after six-thirty a.m. Some effort is made to randomize the recorded death times, but the night shift always manages to get away with fewer bodies to wrap than any other shift.

Discovery of a dead patient typically occurs in the course of ongoing ward activity. As nurses make their rounds, they periodically check up on "dying patients." This check involves a long stare from the door to see if the patient is breathing. The nurse's chief concern is to detect death shortly after it occurs so as to institute proper preparations to remove the body from the ward quickly and insure that her subordinate personnel do not neglect their responsibilities. While aides seek to avoid making such discoveries, in part because of the fact that they are the ones directly implicated in the body's care, most nurses, with the exception of a few alienated ones, are concerned to insure that such discoveries are promptly made. It is considered relatively disastrous for a young student nurse to unwittingly treat a dead person as though he were still alive, yet on several occasions newer personnel have had such experiences. In one case a man was being attended who had been severely burned and was nearly totally wrapped in gauze, with the exception of his eyes. A young student spent several minutes trying to get him to drink some juice through a straw and, having no success, reported to her instructor for help. The instructor said, "well, honey, of course he won't respond, he's been dead for twenty minutes."

While such occurrences are uncommon, their possibility seems somewhat enhanced by the fact that the general notion of "being in a coma" operates as it does. So-called "comatose" patients are treated as essentially dead. Considering a person in a coma is warrant for talking about him in his "presence" in ways which would not be permissible were he awake.

There is apparently some question as to whether a verbal interchange is accessible or not to the "comatose" patient, for some patients, those who live through the "coma," are known to have reported scattered details of things said in their presence. In County, however, the "coma" is considered equivalent to general anesthesia in its effects, and patients' conditions and prospects are freely discussed in their presence when they are felt to be "comatose." Such an assessment is made when the patient does not respond to verbal or physical stimuli, and the possibility that non-responsiveness may be an inability to respond to rather than receive stimulation, is not seriously entertained.

The non-comatose patient, who is expected to die on the current hospital admission, cannot be the object of pre-death treatment as a corpse until the coma itself is entered. In these patients' presence, talk about their prospects is camouflaged by the use of a special descriptive language which, it is taken, the patient cannot decipher. In the presence of a woman who was expected to die within a week of uremic poisoning, one physician said to a nurse, "She'll probably terminate this week." The patient, a very anxious woman who may have detected the relative somberness of the physician's mood and the general seriousness of her state, nervously asked, "Am I all right, doctor?" The physician answered, "Yes, Mrs. K., you're doing just fine."

From the physician's standpoint, a case ceases to be "medically interesting" in the comatose, pre-death stage. Once "palliative care" is instituted, diagnostic enthusiasm becomes less sustainable. The care of such patients is considered as essentially a matter for nursing personnel. When that point is reached and the likelihood of an improvement of condition is considered negligible, the activities of diagnosis and consequent treatment lose, for the intern and resident in training, one of their key functions, namely, their ability to allow him to demonstrate his technical competencies and engage in semi-experimental learning ventures.

A central concern of the physician is to attempt to minimize the likelihood of accusations of his own incompetence by providing, wherever possible, that others will regard death as always possible, even though no specific basis for its possibility, such as a disease or another causally adequate and appropriate category, is located. While seeking to introduce something of a general air of pessimism, at the same time the physician must be careful not to convey to others the sense that he is adopting a seemingly fatalistic stance toward recovery and the success of treatment. An important category for him to establish as a way in which others will regard his activities by way of the patient's performance is "possibly dying." The character of the language of medical prognosis can be analyzed as partially structured to establish the relevance of that category.

Physicians at County are always concerned that their prognostic conversations with patients' relatives convey a proper degree of solemnity. The general problem can be posed as follows: the physician must attempt to present a description of the patient's condition so that, in the event of a death, the family will retrospectively regard his own activities and attitude as having been warranted. The physician who tells the members of his patient's family that there is likely to be a death can find himself in the uncomfortable situation of having to re-encounter them on each of a series of successive days with much the same news, despite the fact that the patient continues to live. Unless the doctor is fairly certain that death is immediately forthcoming, he will not employ "dying" as a way of describing the patient's condition, out of a concern that the patient, in living for a longer period of time than he expects, will provide relatives with a basis for saying the doctor made and acted upon a premature estimation of forthcoming and inevitable death and, had he treated the patient with an eye toward effecting a cure, death might not have occurred, proclamations of inevitable death must thus be made at a well-timed point, unless "dying" could be proposed as a reversible process. It seems to be the case that persons regard the notion "dying," in County at least, as a description of a state of affairs which is non-preventable. Once personnel use the term, they intend by it to point to the expectation that death will occur within the course of the present admission. If they intend to point to a situation of possible death, they employ other terms.

On several occasions, premature proclamations of inevitable death resulted in embarrassing situations. An intern informed the members of a family that the father was "dying" and the father continued to live for more than a week. Each day, sons, daughters and grandchildren came to visit the patient and each member of the family took turns going into his room to have a last look at "papa." A son served as a ritual leader each evening, standing outside the door to the room and scheduling the visits so that each member of the family would have his turn. This went on for several days, and as time progressed the finality of their visits became questionable. Those relatives, who had made what they thought to be a final farewell, found themselves returning to the hospital and reentering the room again and again. Soon the ritual seemed to degenerate through a lack of closure. On the sixth such day, the son requested to see another physician and, it was reported, offered a cautiously voiced complaint because it seemed to him that his father was indeed not dying, yet being apparently treated as though he were. The intern was advised by his superiors of the tactlessness of his premature announcement to the family. Things had stretched out a bit too long so that he had provided for the relevance of pre-death bereavement when it wasn't apparently relevant. Fortunately perhaps, for the intern, the man died on the seventh night in the hospital.

Just as proclamations of inevitable death must not be made too prematurely, they must neither be made too close to the point of the death, for then, with death following quickly after the expectation of it, the physician has less time in which to transfer the patient's fate from the world of medicine and his own hands to those of "God." Death must be made to seem an outcome of "dying," as an inevitable transitory status, for without such a transition, death loses its apparent naturalness and becomes open to interpretation as a wrongly caused affair. A striking instance of planned sequencing was reported to have occurred in the operating room. A patient was operated upon for a gunshot wound, which apparently was not considered serious enough to warrant preparing the family for the prospect of possible death. He died on the operating table, and rather than deliver the news of the death forthrightly, the operating team was reported to have decided to create a sense that "dying" preceded death by filtering out news of progressive deterioration in the patient's condition, after he had already died. On each of several occasions, a member of the team encountered awaiting family members with increasingly poorer news of the operation's progress and the patient's health. After several progressively more solemn prognostications, the occurrence of death was announced, now placed within a history of "dying."

A woman was admitted to the hospital in a very weak condition with what were described as complaints of listlessness, nausea, fever and severe loss of weight. She was seventy-seven years old and had a history of recurrent diabetic difficulties and one previous heart attack. It was suspected, on the basis of a preliminary blood test, that she had developed a lymphosarcoma which may have been involved in a more extended cancerous development. In the course of the conference a decision had to be made as to whether or not to perform an extended series of tests to solve this rather ambiguous diagnostic situation. One physician argued that he was convinced a diagnosis of "leukemia" was warranted, and was prepared to make a prognosis of forthcoming death on that basis. Another felt less secure about that diagnosis and argued for a more complete series of tests and the temporary suspension of further treatment until a more specific diagnosis was obtained. The family's stake in learning of the illness was then discussed. After learning that the woman's husband visited her only once during the period of the week in which she had been hospitalized, and that he had been drunk at the time, it was agreed that, since she was so "sick," and that her diabetes was acting up again, it "didn't pay," as one of them put it, to bother with the additional tests. They decided to wait for several days and see what happened, to see if she became markedly worse, and if nothing happened then to order more tests. The fact of her husband's absence was stated to be a chief consideration for not rushing to make a diagnosis. His lack of concern was admittedly taken to warrant theirs, at least to the extent that she be allowed to deteriorate further, if she would, before more extensive diagnostic work was pursued. If she got worse and approached death, they agreed, there would be no point in worrying more about the diagnosis. If she didn't become more ill, they would wait to see that development, and then attempt to uncover a more secure diagnostic basis for initiating treatment.

The situation of choice, whether or not to make full efforts to treat quickly or adopt a wait-and-see attitude, is extremely common in the care of patients who are regarded as potential candidates for the week's tally of deceased patients. The wait-and-see attitude is deemed legitimate by County's interns and residents when there is reason to believe that death is a distinct possibility. It prolongs the need for extensive diagnostic attention which, with these patients, is considered warranted only if they are so located in the age and social structure that life is considered especially worth preserving.

In County, there is a clear division of labor and a clear difference in work styles with bodies. Physicians do not handle dead bodies except when they are pronouncing patients dead and conducting autopsies, and here their handling is limited strictly to the kinds of touch necessary for accomplishing these tasks. Gross body handling, movement of an entire body from one stretcher to another, from the morgue refrigerator to the autopsy table, is considered dirty work for doctors, and is exclusively the province of the aides and orderlies. This differentiation of touching is common in handling live bodies as well, though not as markedly so as in the case of dead ones. When performing a physical examination on a patient a doctor will, if necessary, assist in turning a patient over to place him in a better position for the examination. If several physicians of differing statuses are jointly conducting an examination, as in "rounds," senior doctors will characteristically step back and allow the junior men access to the body to aid in turning it into position. With dead bodies, interns themselves maintain a generally aloof position. Once they pronounce a patient dead, they leave the room. In the morgue, an attendant himself positions the body on the autopsy table, and if he has difficulty in doing so physicians do not offer assistance. Here physicians limit their physical contact with the body to that which is required for doing the postmortem as a technical activity.

On the wards, should a nurse have need to get something from the room of a recently deceased patient, she will generally send an aide or orderly in to secure what she needs rather than enter herself. Apparently a nurse feels he has a right to keep his distance from involvement in such activities as he might witness there. In witnessing body work which occurs on a gross level, there is a sense in which the witness thereby can become committed to the grossness of the task, particularly so if witnessing involves one in informal talk with the workers. If one witnesses such activities silently, he can assume the status of a mere witness, but in engaging in talk in the same genre of that of the workers, he gives others the impression that he is not being sufficiently concerned about what his higher status should require in the way of detachment.

A standard death procedure in nearly all American hospitals is the practice of body wrapping. When a patient dies, the hospital death-procedures manual instructs, his body is to be wrapped in a specially provided "Morgue Sheet." The body-wrapping activity is apparently done nearly everywhere in United States hospitals in essentially the same fashion.

At County, body wrapping is the work of aides and orderlies, more than ninety-five percent of whom are Negroes. There is a legal regulation, purportedly instituted to protect the corpse from sexual attention, which requires that nurses' aides wrap female bodies and orderlies wrap male bodies.

On any given ward there is usually a team that works together in wrapping a body. The aides do the task systematically, with a certain degree of finesse, and prefer to work on it with those with whom they have done it before. When a new aide or orderly is introduced to the wrapping task, he is asked to stand by and watch, as a narrative account of the procedure is given by one of the experienced members of the team. The procedure involves the removal of the deceased's clothing, including jewelry, and the folding of a muslin sheet completely around the body, pinning it down the front with large safety pins, in mummy style. Before the body is wrapped it is occasionally cleansed with a wet cloth, not thoroughly but only to remove any particularly noticeable dirt. A diaper-like sheet is wrapped around the genital area, the hands and feet are crossed and bound together with a special cotton-covered string. Two precut gauze pads are placed over the eyes, after the lids have been closed. Before the body is finally wrapped in the outside sheet, it is checked to make sure no paraphernalia is affixed to it. All intravenous tubes are removed. nasal suctioning equipment detached and catheters taken out.

In performing this task, aides or orderlies start at one end of the body and work step by step until the procedure is finished. Typically, there is a division of labor, whereby one woman turns the body as the other spreads the sheet. This practice is institutionalized so that the same aide will typically do the same parts when working with her teammate.

In all this routinization of death, however, it should be noted that on certain critical occasions (as when a child has died, or when a successful, middle-class person has been brought into the Emergency Unit as "Dead On Arrival") ordinary procedures of treatment are not instituted. Members of the staff, on such occasions, lose something of their grasp on matters which they otherwise would treat in the most perfunctory ways.

Nowhere is this disruption clearer than with the deaths of children. Nurses are observed to break down in tears when a child dies, and in such cases "dying" and "death" temporarily lose their routinized meanings, activities and consequences. When an intoxicated, suicidal or "criminal" patient is treated, these persons' moral characters are prevalent considerations for staff members. Rather than "just another patient," the attitudes toward such persons range from vehemence, disgust and horror to dismay. It can be noted as a general sociological observation, that no matter how routinized an institution's methods for handling its daily tasks, those routines remain vulnerable at certain key points. At County, no matter how nonchalantly staff members managed to wrap a patient's body for discharge to the morgue, taper off in the administration of drugs and the care to the "dying," or pronounce death and return to other tasks, the special cases — the morally "imperfect" and the especially "tragic" — upset those routines, make them more difficult to carry off, more interestedly attended or substantially revised. Thus Death, even to those who meet it as a matter of course during their working day, can occasionally appear as it does to the rest of us — as a fearful and unsupportable event.

IV
MEETING THE NEEDS
OF THE AGED

HOUSING, SOCIAL SERVICES, AND TREATMENT APPROACHES

Many of the services discussed in this section relate to problems mentioned in earlier readings. Major problems include housing, institutional care, social services, and various psychological treatment approaches. In singling out these areas for special attention, we do not mean to deemphasize other important areas — nutrition, health, etc.

The reader should be constantly aware of the interrelationship and interdependence of all of these problem areas and their solutions. An elderly person's economic resources influence his need for social services, for specific kinds of housing, and for a great many other aids. The physical and mental health of an older person will also limit and determine to a great extent what kind of living arrangements are possible for him, what kind of social services he will need, etc. Although we look at them and talk about them separately in order to comprehend their complexity more easily, the interrelationship and interdependence of all of these areas cannot be overemphasized. It is recognized that we need at some point to consider the total individual and all of his interrelated needs and problems.

A. HOUSING AND INSTITUTIONAL CARE

All of us are greatly influenced by the kind of living arrangements we occupy. Each person, young and old, needs some individual life-space which he can arrange to express his own individuality. Perhaps this is even truer for an elderly person who may spend a larger portion of his time at home, or wherever he lives. This section contains readings which describe alternative living arrangements, and their advantages and disadvantages for various groups of older people.

In the first reading, Ruth Weber discusses the contribution of the social worker in reconstituting the environment of the older person. This paper has direct relevance to the concerns of housing authorities for improving the living space of older persons residing in the community. Dr. Weber describes the application of new knowledge from the social sciences to the design of "behavior facilitating environments" for the aged. Case histories are used to illustrate ways of maintaining the older person in the community.

In the next reading, Robert Wray emphasizes the great variation in housing needs among the aged and reminds us of some of the essential social aspects of "good" housing which are so often overlooked in our preoccupation with physical and aesthetic qualities. He describes briefly different kinds of housing and the degree to which they meet the different personal needs of the elderly. Dr. Wray stresses that the elderly person be consulted about his wishes and needs.

The question of age-segregated housing is dealt with in some detail by Donald Grant. Some older people prefer to live only with other elderly persons, whereas others miss the contact with people of different ages. Dr. Grant feels that the central issue is how to deal with increased dependency and declining health without traumatically upsetting and removing the older person. Dr. Grant concludes that different elderly people adjust most happily to different kinds of housing arrangements. Again it is emphasized that there is no one arrangement appropriate for all of the aged.

The history of nursing homes is reviewed in the next reading by Herman Gruber. Whereas our widespread concern with nursing homes is a relatively recent thing, Dr. Gruber shows that nursing homes have been with us for a number of years. He describes briefly the relationships between hospitals and nursing homes and the impact of the health maintenance laws, particularly as they relate to the aged. Dr. Gruber discusses the different kinds of nursing homes and the current lack of good ways to distinguish among them.

The final reading in this section reviews alternative environmental strategies for the adjustment of the aged person both within and outside of nursing homes. Marian MacDonald points to inadequacies in the environmental conditions currently provided for the aged as a social group which seem to help to produce and perpetuate some of the unpleasant aspects of becoming old. Several suggestions for improvement are made.

29. Individualizing Natural Environments for the Community-Dwelling Aged*

RUTH E. WEBER**

Paper prepared for The Third Annual Institute on Man's Adjustment in a Complex Environment. Veterans Administration Hospital, Brecksville, Ohio, June 20, 1968. (Paper not previously published)

Crucial to the formulation of strategies for developing optimal environments for the community-dwelling aged is the question of what are our objectives? In my view, the aim of the therapist is to maximize and accelerate the adaptive capacities of the individual and not to emphasize conformity to the external environment. The goals of the therapist should reflect a dual commitment to the human need for inner fulfillment as well as accommodation to external pressures. The term *adaptation* is most appropriately used when there is a successful compromise between the demands of self and those of society *within the context of a specific situation.* The capacity to meet the expectations of a *variety of situations* and still maintain the integrity of self is more properly termed *adaptability.*[1] This conceptualization of adaptation is akin to Lois Barclay Murphy's[2] notion of coping behavior when she speaks of coping as being defensive or creative in nature with a mutual accommodation between the self and environmental stresses and supports. The ability to cope with a *wide variety* of environmental demands or adaptability then becomes the criterion of therapeutic success.

In a recently published paper, Roy Hamlin[3] postulates that the prevailing model in gerontological research is the *physiological* model. The physiological model, Hamlin suggests, emphasizes "pessimism, unutility and disintegration."[4] The physiological model promulgates a maintenance philosophy of care and reduced expectations for the elderly. Strategies are directed towards preserving residuals rather than developing the kind of environment which would provide incen-

*Unpublished summary of remarks presented at the Third Annual Meeting of the American Association of Housing Educators, Georgia Center for Continuing Education, the University of Georgia, 1968.
**Dr. Webber is Associate Professor of Social Work at the University of Georgia.

tive for what Hamlin calls "task-oriented" rather than "task-avoidance" behavior. Hamlin's utility model is consistent with the view that growth and learning as well as expansion of the personality are possible in the aged.

Existing literature on designing optimal environmental conditions for the aged stresses the physical environment, particularly the immediate or proximal environment.[5] There is less written on the interpersonal environment or the larger life space of the aged. Ogden Lindsley's paper[6] on the development of prosthetic environments for the aged is frequently quoted. Lindsley distinguishes the prosthetic environment from the therapeutic environment. The prosthetic environment compensates for the specific behavioral deficits of the aged and makes the deficits less debilitating. Therapeutic environments in contrast, generate behavior which is maintained when the patient is returned to the normal or general social environment. Prosthetic environments, according to Lindsley are permanent and operate continually.[7]

Lindsley's orientation impresses me as reflecting the physiological, decline model. Perhaps he is also generalizing from clinical, pathological populations of the aged found in institutional settings. The possibility of developing therapeutic environments for the reversal of defects and promoting growth in the aged through prosthetic devices will not become a reality if we continue to be blinded by a pessimistic view of the aged.

In this same vein, it is well to be mindful that less than 5 percent of persons 65 years of age or over in the United States are in any kind of institution and a high majority of the community-dwelling aged, about eight out of ten, function well and are not restricted to their immediate physical environment.[8] Over six out of ten aged heads of households are homeowners.[9] Homeownership can have a great symbolic meaning. Boundaries are clear, "territoriality" is established and there is freedom from the need to conform to group living. Recent surveys of aged persons suggest that only a small proportion of the aged report that they have any serious housing problems, and the majority do not consider especially designed housing as their greatest need.[10] Rather, community-dwelling older people are more likely to be concerned about limited income, possible failing health, boredom, and loneliness. If they complain about the environment, they are more likely to complain about their neighborhood than their housing.[11] The amount of research and clinical publication devoted to the development of special housing and institutional care of the aged far exceeds the literature bearing on what is needed to maintain older persons in their own homes, and I think regrettably so since most older people prefer to live independently in their own homes. There are dangers inherent in social policy and practice geared largely to institutionalization of the aged. Rosow, for example, warns that the preoccupation of social planners with developing special physical environments for the aged can distract from the more fundamental problem, that of inadequate income.[12]

It is also true that it is largely the very old who are most in need of environmental prosthetics, especially when independent functioning breaks down. Contributions to a growing body of knowledge of prosthetic devices for the aged will hopefully have the effect of contributing substantially to the ability of older people to remain in the community and in familiar surroundings as long as possible. The aged, like other age groups, will benefit from those labor-saving devices and other products of our scientific age that insure safety, hygiene, comfort and security.

To be sure, there is need for knowledge of the special requirements of the handicapped aged. However, contributors to this body of knowledge sometimes are not in agreement, especially concerning the *application* of knowledge. For example, in the instance of hearing losses, it has been suggested that extraneous sounds and noises should be suppressed so that the aged can converse, hear door bells, etc.[13] Others, for example, Busse, [14] maintain that the level of background noises, such as street noises and the hum of air conditioners, should be increased rather than reduced for the aged on the grounds that perception of background stimuli provides a basis for integration with the environment which is consistent with the observation that older people often hear better in a noisy room.

Having stressed the need to provide for continued, meaningful self-fulfillment as well as the use of prosthetics to maximize physical functioning in designing environments for the aged, I should like to draw upon my experiences at the Benjamin Rose Institute to illustrate the importance of individualizing the community environment for the aged.

The Benjamin Rose Institute is a non-sectarian, privately endowed multi-service agency for the aged in Cleveland, Ohio. Services provided by the Institute include professional casework and group services as well as medical, financial and legal assistance. The average age of the Benjamin Rose client is 82 with the high majority being over 75 years of age. Approximately 20 percent of the clients reside at the

Agency's nursing home, The Margaret Wagner House, 30 percent are patients in some 35 proprietary nursing homes in the Cleveland area, and another 50 percent live in the community. A high proportion of the community-dwelling clients live in their own homes or apartments. A few reside in the homes of relatives or friends and about 8 percent are in family care homes.

The Benjamin Rose Institute provides brief counseling services to the aged and their families, but a high majority of the clients require on-going services over the long term, most until death. Stated simply, basic to the program of services is the objective of maintaining the older person in the community as long as possible. Services are modeled after the three c's of care for the aged and chronically ill, viz., comprehensive, continued and coordinated care.

In discussing social services provided by the Institute, I would like to focus on the caseworker's role, especially that aspect of casework which Scott Briar and others have described as the "social broker role."[15] Time does not permit an adequate discussion of the many variables in the multiplicity of settings required to maintain old people in the community, and I have opted to focus on the broker role because it is crucial to successful implementation of a system of delivery of services to the aged living in the community. Brief case examples will be offered to illustrate the application of the social broker role with the aged.

At The Benjamin Rose Institute, the caseworker is the agent who has the initial contact with the older person and his family, and he usually carries the major responsibility for developing the strategies to deliver environmental supports. If the older person or his family cannot pay for the needed environmental supports, the caseworker may arrange for the Agency to purchase whatever is needed. Thus, the caseworker is limited in the implementation of a therapeutic environmental program only by 1) the willingness and capacity of the older person and his family to utilize the services; 2) the knowledge available, and the skill and creativity with which such knowledge is applied in reconstituting the environment; and, 3) the scarcity of community resources for the community-dwelling aged.

As has been well documented by research,[16] the existence of services does not guarantee their use by the aged. Experience has also taught us that special programs and beautiful settings for the aged often are not used by those who appear to need them the most. Fundamental to the success of maximizing environments then is the involvement and mobilization of the older person to use the services and the matching of resources to individual needs. Once services are introduced and accepted it is still necessary for an agent to coordinate the multiple services often required because of the multi-dimensional nature of the aged's problems. Finally, there must be someone to "pick up the pieces," as it were, when and if the service system should break down. Elaine Cumming[17] has written that the British system of health services, notable for its emphasis on central government planning, depends to a great extent on the effectiveness of the "traffic agent," a term similar to the social broker role. Because of the absence of central planning, service delivery systems in the United States are even more complex than the systems of Great Britain since the American service delivery systems depend more on criteria of acceptance for service by agencies.

Sometimes the cures proposed are perceived as worse than the sickness itself, or as Descartes is quoted as saying, "Defects are always more tolerable than the change necessary for their removal."[18] The aged are aware that our health and welfare systems are becoming more efficiently organized. Especially notable is the tendency to centralize care in institutions. Community agents are often all too quick to recommend institutional care. The aged know how difficult it is to get physicians to make home calls. They know as Goffman has noted[19] that professionals do not want to leave their well-equipped institutional "workshops." Thus, it is not surprising to find that the community-dwelling aged are often fearful of professionals and that they are tremendously reassured when a social worker comes to their home and talks with them about ways of making it possible for them to remain in their home and familiar surroundings.

An astute caseworker will quickly identify some specific reinforcer that will serve to make the services and the caseworker attractive and credible. One powerful reinforcer may be the provision of money to meet emergency expenses or it may be another type of gratification specific to the individual. For instance, in the case of Miss A who was isolated in her apartment because of increasing disability from an arthritic condition, the caseworker learned that Miss A had recently been advised to stop driving. For her, the loss of her car was the greatest of all deprivations. The worker was able to utilize trips in the worker's car as the occasion for facilitating substitutions for losses in the environment. Subsequently, Miss A was able to accept transportation provided by local volunteers to a center which, in addition to transportation, offered low cost lunches and recreational and diversional activities. In this case, the caseworker was successful in 1) extending the older person's environment, and 2) lifting the client's depression following a decline in functioning.

The social worker's expertise in the knowledge of environmental resources can also serve to reinforce the attraction of the worker. For example, the aged are sometimes confused about Medicare coverage and how to secure benefits. The social worker's specialized knowledge and skill in this area can serve to increase credibility of the potential value of services from the worker and the agency.

The use of money in the early stages of the contact to purchase items especially meaningful to the client may also be a powerful means of increasing motivation for working on solutions to problems. For some aged, it is highly effective to include in the budget that which the client perceives as a luxury. The result is that the client may feel over-compensated, and in return, develop an attitude of reciprocity such as wanting to repay the caseworker by working towards positive goals. It is important in early contacts to clarify both the health status and the physical functioning of the older person. A careful medical examination cannot be overestimated. The aged have a tendency to under-report their health problems and deficiencies and sometimes are very adroit at covering up for failing functional capacities. It is not unusual to find physical conditions that can easily be corrected with preventive medical services. Tunstall reports that in a special clinic developed for preventive health care for the aged in West London, it was found that older persons examined in the clinic had a median of 11 disabilities, most of which were considerably improved with treatment.[20] For example, 77 percent had "incorrect glasses," 70 percent had wax in their ears, 65 percent had foot defects, 52 percent had diseases of the stomach and digestive system, 34 percent suffered from anemia, 33 percent from thyroid deficiencies, and 27 percent from defective artificial teeth.

In reconstituting the environment of old people, clinicians often place heavy emphasis on activity as the key to increasing the older person's mastery over his environment. It is sometimes assumed that the lack of stimulation resulting from isolation has led to demoralization and often mental illness. Surveys of the community-dwelling aged in the United States and Great Britain offer evidence that socially isolated people are not necessarily desolate or demoralized.[21] Many isolated elderly have always lived this way and do not wish to have more social contacts. Yet, as a general principle it is better to err in the direction of trying to increase environmental stimulation and work toward moving the older person back into the mainstream of community life, except in cases where it is clear the client freely chooses to remain in social isolation. I am reminded of the example of Miss X, a 72-year-old spinster who was living as a recluse following the death of her sister some ten years previous to her contact with The Benjamin Rose Institute. Her sister was a teacher who provided her with financial support and made all major decisions. Miss X was never known to have a friend of her own. The agency caseworker was her only social contact except those business people necessary to the maintenance of life. The caseworker utilized her positive relationship with the client to persuade her to come to the meeting of a new group of older persons being formed in the agency's downtown central office. Miss X did so with great reluctance. Mrs. B, a new member of the group who had a sister similar to Miss X's quickly sensed Miss X's fears. It became Mrs. B's project to encourage Miss X's involvement in the group. Mrs. B telephoned Miss X persistently until Miss X agreed to return for group meetings. Mrs. B learned in her telephone conversations that Miss X spent most of her time reading and writing poetry. Mrs. B and the group worker joined forces to capitalize on Miss X's talent for writing. She became the "poet laureate" of the group. Miss X now regularly attends group sessions; her appearance has improved; she has gained confidence in her ability to negotiate with business people, and she has recently decided to move to a retirement hotel where she can eat her meals with other aged people.

Bandura[22] has proposed the use of the therapist as a model to increase the client's "behavioral repertoires" to maximize imitative learning. However, I am of the opinion that the use of the therapist in imitative learning is only marginally successful with the aged. Rather, another aged person who has mastered problems in his environment provides a more realistic model and a much more potent force for maximizing imitative learning than the worker. The result is a kind of imitative learning that is not only adaptive but is age appropriate. The use of the successfully aging older person as a role model in the interpersonal environment of the aged has not been sufficiently exploited by clinicians.

Occasionally, the clinician encounters an older person living in a physical environment that is remarkably replete with prosthetics, yet almost totally free from stimulus. One such unusual case is that of a 70-year-old unmarried former chemist who, over a period of years, had secluded himself in a completely soundproof apartment with numerous gadgets to provide a dustproof, perfectly humidified environment which he only left to do his shopping, visit his physician, and to be hospitalized on occasion for bleeding ulcers. His physician referred him to the Benjamin Rose Institute because an annuity, which had supported him over the years, would terminate in a period of some six months. He had no other income, and rental for the apartment was well beyond the maximum allowable in public assistance budgets. Calhoun,[23] writing of the role of space in molding the evolution and maturation of social behavior, has collected considerable data on the ecology of animal behavior, especially concerning what he calls "behavioral vacuums." He describes, for example, the instance of a mole indigenous to Australia which constructs its own subterranean network of tunnels with no connection with neighbors. These moles spend their lives in tunnels, each alone, buffered from sight, sound, smells, and social stimuli. Their only contact with others of the species is the minimum required for copulation.

For some aged, the physical environment is highly cathected. Others seem to be relatively unconcerned about physical convenience, aesthetics, etc., and place a much higher value upon the interpersonal environment. The possibility of loss of significant personal contacts often represents a great threat, yet these same aged may be relatively undisturbed by the possibility of moving from their physical surroundings. For some aged, isolation seems to increase their susceptibility to influence, even to the point of exploitation of others. For other aged, isolation is the result of suspiciousness and resistance to normative standards or societal controls. While it may be convenient to say that life-long patterns and life styles determine reactions to isolation and the ability to accept help from others there is need for more research on the precise manner in which physical and social isolation affects older people.

There is an interesting clinical phenomena in some aged referred to by a Benjamin Rose Institute psychoanalytic consultant, Dr. Herbert Weiss, as "loss of anxiety signal." Illustrative is the isolated person who is seemingly unconcerned about the dangers around him and apparently unable to perceive the connection between his failure to act and the consequences of his behavior. Often such persons evidence an extreme degree of self-neglect and, though resistant to changes in the environment, some have the capacity to relate to others. Such persons may be in such extreme danger that removal from the home to a protective environment may be necessary, but removal is often at great risk to the survival of the older person. In practice one must weigh the risk of alternatives.

Research in psychotherapy offers convincing evidence of the importance of expectations as a major determinant of behavior.[24] Rotter declares that "behavior is a function of the expectations of the subject and the role of the reinforcer is only to change, that is, to increase or decrease the expectations or to verify or negate the subject's hypotheses regarding the situation."[25] To illustrate, a 68-year-old recently-widowed woman confined in her apartment referred herself to the Benjamin Rose Institute and asked for help in finding a nursing home, saying she could barely walk. A thorough physical examination failed to reveal a physical cause for difficulty in ambulation. History suggested a previous pattern of high affiliation with others and enjoyment of group situations. The alternative of family care placement was offered and accepted. The client "blossomed" with the attention of the family caretaker's two teenage children and through socialization with three other elderly residents in the family care home. In this case it was important that the worker not reinforce the client's low level of aspiration which initially resembled what Raimy[26] calls "phrenophobia," frequently seen in institutionalized aged who have no expectation for recovery. Interventions that reduce the severity of "phrenophobia" may well account, in part, for the success reported by behavioral therapists. Patients recover from symptomatic attacks because they are expected to. Because of an adherence to a disease model, and because they may share with the general public an overprotective attitude, some clinicians fail to exploit the use of expectations in working with the aged. Social workers have, likewise, been criticized for developing programs in which older people are "over-serviced." Nevertheless, theory and research are still imprecise as to the specification of the optimal level of activity or stimulation beneficial for the aged.

Clinicians working with the community-dwelling aged are also handicapped by the lack of knowledge of the effects of the neighborhood on those who live in their own homes and apartments. There has been an upsurge of research on the adjustment of the aged to institutions and to special group living situations, the effects of relocation from community to institutions, and from institution to institution, but very little research has been done on how older people manage in their own homes or how the life space, including the neighborhood, affects older people living in the community. We do know that some 2 percent of the aged living in the community are bedfast and that an additional 6 percent are housebound. Another 6 percent have difficulty getting out of their homes for shopping, etc. Thus, some 14 percent, or more than three times the number of aged in institutions, are highly dependent upon their immediate physical and social environment, including the neighborhood for sources of care and stimulation.[27] As Marcelle Levy of the New York State Office on Aging has noted,[28] we do not have enough reliable data on who is taking care of the bedfast and housebound aged, and we do not know enough about the services they need or what supports are required by the people who are taking care of them. We have given relatively little of our time and attention to the prevention of the breakdown of these caretakers. Communities and professionals in general have allocated disproportionately little of their resources to the community-dwelling aged. Typically, health and welfare agencies learn of the needs of these bedfast and homebound aged when the caretaker's resources are exhausted and when they say they can go on no longer or when the older person's capacity for independent functioning results in serious and desperate situations. By this time, the odds of reversing the process of deterioration are often very poor. In general, clinicians are very much in need of epidemeological data on the needs of the homebound aged as well as data on how home ownership, for example, affects the aged as compared to living in rented or especially designed retirement housing for the aged. Increased knowledge of the variations in response of the aged to their natural environments would contribute toward our capacity to individualize planned environmental change. Much of what clinicians do to maintain older people in the community is still dependent upon their creativity and their ingenuity rather than a verified body of knowledge.

FOOTNOTES

[1] Melvin E. Allerhand, Ruth E. Weber, Marie Haug, *Adaptation and Adaptability: The Bellefaire Follow-up Study*, New York, Child Welfare League of America, 1966, pp. 1-16.

[2] Lois Barcley Murphy, et al., *The Widening World of Childhood*, New York: Basic Books, 1962, p. 6.

[3] Roy M. Hamlin, "A Utility Theory of Old Age," *The Gerontologist*, 7:2, June 1967, pp. 37-45.

[4] *Ibid.*, p. 37.

[5] Joseph Cautela, "Behavior Therapy and Geriatrics," *Journal of Genetic Psychology*, 108, 1966, pp. 9-17.

[6] Ogden R. Lindsley, "Geriatric Behavioral Prosthetics," in Robert Kastenbaum (ed.), *New Thoughts on Old Age*, New York: Springer Publishing Company, 1964, pp. 41-60.

[7] *Ibid.*, p. 46.

[8] Ethel Shanas, *The Health of Older People*, Cambridge, Mass.: Harvard University Press, 1962.

[9] D. M. Wilner and R. P. Walkley, "Some Special Problems and Alternatives in Housing for Older People," in J. McKinney and F. D. ViVeyer (eds.), *Aging and Social Policy*, New York: Appleton-Century-Crofts, 1966.

[10] Irving Rosow, *Social Integration of the Aged*, New York: Free Press, 1967, p. 333.

[11] *Ibid.*, pp. 336-337.

[12] *Ibid.*, pp. 333-336.

[13] Alfred H. Lawton, Gordon J. Azar, "Consequences of Physical and Physiological Change with Age in the Patterns of Living and Housing for the Middle-Aged and Aged," in Frances M. Carp (ed.), *Patterns of Living and Housing of Middle-Aged and*

Older People, Washington, D.C.: Department of Health, Education, and Welfare, Public Health Services Publication No. 1496, 1966, p. 23.

[14] Ewald W. Busse, "Therapeutic Implications of Basic Research with the Aged," *Strecker Monograph Series IV*, Institute of Pennsylvania Hospital, 1967.

[15] Scott Briar, "The Current Crises in Social Casework," *Social Work Practice Papers, 1967*, New York: National Conference on Social Welfare, Columbia University Press, 1967, p. 26.

[16] Margaret Blenkner, Julius Jahn, Edna Wasser, *Serving the Aged: An Experiment in Social Work and Public Health Nursing*, New York: Community Service Society, Institute for Welfare Research, 1964.

[17] Elaine Cumming, "Allocation of Care to the Mentally Ill, American Style," in Mayer N. Zald (ed.), *Organizing for Community Welfare*, Chicago: Quadrangle Books, 1967, pp. 128-129.

[18] As quoted in Jerome D. Frank, "Galloping Technology, A New Social Disease," *Journal of Social Issues*, 22:4, 1966, p. 10.

[19] Erving Goffman, *Asylums*, Garden City, New York: Anchor Books, 1961, p. 332.

[20] Jeremy Tunstall, *Old and Alone, A Sociological Study of Old People*, London: Rutledge and Kegan Paul, 1966, pp. 274-275.

[21] Marjorie Fiske Lowenthal, et al., *Aging and Mental Disorder in San Francisco*, San Francisco: Jossey-Bass, 1967. Ethel Shanas, "A Note on Restriction of the Life Space, Attitudes of Aged Cohorts," *Journal Health and Social Behavior*, March 1968. Jeremy Tunstall, *Old and Alone, A Sociological Study of Old People*, op. cit.

[22] A. Bandura, "Social Learning Through Imitation," in M. R. Jones (ed.). *Nebraska Symposium on Motivation*, 1962, Lincoln: U. of Nebraska Press, 1962. A. Bandura and R. H. Walters, *Social Learning and Personality Development*, New York: Holt, Rinehart, and Winston. 1963.

[23] John B. Calhoun, "The Role of Space in Animal Sociology," *Journal of Social Issues*, 22:4, 1966, p. 56.

[24] Arnold P. Goldstein, *Therapist-Patient Expectancies in Psychotherapy*, New York: MacMillan Company, Pergamon Press Book, 1962.

[25] J. B. Rotter, *Social Learning and Clinical Psychology*, New York: Prentice Hall, 1954, p. 102.

[26] D. C. Raimy, "How Strong is a Conviction?", *Journal of Arkansas Medical Society*, 1963, pp. 60, 181-187, as quoted in Peter Weiss, "The Custodial Hospital as a Community Resource for Psychiatric Treatment," *Community Mental Health Journal*, 3:2, 1967, p. 176.

[27] Ethel Shanas, *The Health of Older People*, op. cit.

[28] Marcelle G. Levy, "The Direction of the Aging Curve," *Proceedings of the Sixth Annual Governors Conference on Aging*, New York State Office For the Aging, April 1964. pp. 19-20.

30. Design for the Elderly: People and Places*

ROBERT P. WRAY**

The theme for today's meetings is "Quality in a Place to Live." Quality of what? Structure? Then build with the best bricks, mortar and steel available. Safety? Then build with non-combustible materials and provide ample exits, ramps, handrails, warning systems, and the like. Scenery? Then build amid nature's green, with trees, shrubs, and flowers that serve as home to the birds that complement the scenery itself with color and song.

The point of these illustrations is to suggest that we can't talk about quality in a place to live until we define the place itself. My assignment is to talk about housing design for the elderly in terms of *people* and places — not just places.

In a paper presented at the 1961 White House Conference on Aging, Dr. Abraham J. Herschel said, "Ours is a twin-problem: the attitude of society toward the old and old age, as well as the attitude of the old to being old." In his paper, "The Older Person and the Family in the Perspective of Jewish Tradition," Dr. Herschel then asked and discussed a question basic to a housing design for elderly people in its fullest sense:

> By what standards do we measure culture? It is customary to evaluate a nation by the magnitude of its scientific contributions or the quality of its artistic achievements. However, the true standard by which to gauge a culture is the extent to which reverence, compassion, justice are to be found in the daily lives of a whole people, not only individuals. . . .
>
> It is marvelous indeed that for the first time in history, our society is ready and able to provide for the material needs of its senior citizens. Yet in addition to the problem of material security we must face the problem of psychological and spiritual security.
>
> How to save the old from despondency, despair? How to lend beauty to being old? How to regain the authenticity of old age? . . .

*Summary of Remarks presented at the Third Annual Meeting of the American Association of Housing Educators, Georgia Center for Continuing Education, University of Georgia, Athens, Georgia.

**At the time this paper was presented Dr. Wray was Chairman of the Council of Gerontology at The University of Georgia. Currently Dr. Wray is Consultant on Retirement and Gerontology at the Georgia Center for Continuing Education of the University of Georgia.

While we do not officially define old age as a second childhood, some of the programs we devise are highly effective in helping the aged to become children. The preoccupation with games, hobbies, the overemphasis upon recreation, while certainly conducive to eliminating boredom temporarily, hardly contribute to inner strength. The effect is rather a pickled existence, preserved in brine with spices. . . .

Our work for the aged is handicapped by our clinging to the dogmatic belief in the immutability of man. We conceive of his inner life as a closed system, as an automatic, unilinear, irreversible process which cannot be altered, and of old age as a stage of stagnation into which a person enters with his habits, follies, and prejudices. To be good to the old is to cater to their prejudices and eccentricities.

At this point I must retort to Dr. Herschel and ask, "By whose standards do you say that old people have prejudices and eccentricities?" Obviously he is speaking for himself and others who are from one to three generations younger than those he classifies as "old."

But the important lesson to be learned from Dr. Herschel's question is that the younger generations are behind the times in their concepts of old age. A recent UPI column in the daily press, based on some research by Dr. Carl Eisdorfer at Duke University, carried the headline, "Over 35's Told To Act Age To Save Image." Yes, I stated it correctly; 35, not 65. The article states that if all of us over 35 don't start acting our age, the young folks of college years will stop thinking of us as kind, wise, trustworthy and good. Instead, they will see us as strange, cold, even dangerous, and decidedly embarrassing.

Here are a few quotes from the column based on the Duke University research report:

> As long as oldsters fit snugly into the pigeonhole allotted them by their juniors, . . . fine. But when Gramps persists in behaving as though he were still physically and mentally young — dancing from time to time or deftly clipping his own coupons — he gets the arched eyebrow of disapproving youth. . . .
>
> Men from 35 to 45 are "slowing down" but otherwise unchanged. Those 45 to 55 are "significantly" declining in health, activities, effectiveness, and happiness. The 65-year-olds are "declining in intelligence."
>
> It is precisely these signs of decline that endear the elderly to the young. If a 65-year-old is foolish, then he is "understandable,

predictable, poor, valuable and sad." If, on the other hand, he is strong, rugged, active, rich, effective, he must be "bad, dangerous, strange, tense and cold."

So much for the 65-year-old. Pity the 75-year-old. If he is weak, sick, slow, and ineffective, he is considered by the youngsters to be "safe, trustworthy, good, and familiar." But if he still has all his marbles and buttons and is "rich, clean, happy, warm, relaxed" and so on, "then he becomes completely untrustworthy."

Although we know something about the attitude of the younger society toward old age, and we don't like what we know in this respect, we know even less about the attitude of the society of the old toward themselves. I have made some related observations and suggestions in an article published in the July 1968 issue of *Dynamic Maturity* on the subject, "WANTED: Constructive Retirement Centers." In that article I pointed out that old age and retirement in today's terms did not exist at the time when our present day "over 65-year-olds" were born. In addition to the "developmental" and "employment" phases of life we now have a "retirement" phase. But, unfortunately, the image of retirement as a phase of life lacks the clarity of its predecessors.

Studies in which retired persons and those approaching retirement have participated indicate that there is no "Mr. Typical," but they do indicate at least a partial description of the desirable retirement image. One of the elements is appropriate housing. Now we know a great deal about housing, but we are not very clear on what is "appropriate" for a variety of persons in a variety of situations. And if we get clear on what is appropriate, we still have the ample problem of enabling persons to learn that housing appropriate to their needs and desires is available or could be made available. This is a very subtle problem since a person cannot make a decision for or against adequate housing unless he is fully informed on the subject. For example, if you ask me whether I would like to live in the community of "XYZ," I couldn't make a valid judgment unless I had seen the community or one like it, or had read or been told about it in great detail with plenty of visual aids. Thus, without knowing that there is a possibility of a better life for me in the XYZ community, I may continue to live less happily in a less adequate environment. (See Weber above)

Pioneering efforts should continue in developing what the experts think is adequate housing and an optimal community environment, but more needs to be done to involve older persons themselves in defining what they want to do in their old age, where they want to do it, and the housing they prefer *after they have learned what can be available to them*. Very little has been done to determine what motivates older persons to seek better housing. A good learning experience might include trial vacations in new surroundings as well as what can be learned through observation, reading and conversation.

In order to give academic respectability to this paper and deal in some specific aspects of adequate housing, I shall now refer to what the experts are saying, based on the best information available.

Writing on the subject, "The Impact of Living Arrangements on Ego Development in the Elderly," (presented at a conference on Patterns of Living and Housing for the Middle-aged and Aged, Bethesda, Maryland, March 21-24, 1965) Dr. Wilma Donahue made some very succinct remarks based on early observations of tenants in Lurie Terrace, a non-profit apartment house built under the direct loan provisions of the National Housing Act.

The basic emphasis was on *independent and active living* to promote social interaction and good adjustment. The site itself, near the center of Ann Arbor, facing a public park and next door to a community senior activity center, was chosen deliberately to facilitate continuing interrelationships of the tenants with the community as a whole. Dr. Donahue listed other attributes of Lurie Terrace, as well as other desirable housing for older adults, that facilitate social interaction and good adjustment:

Status housing — handsome building, carpeting, attractive furnishing, an art studio, music rooms, and a library;

High age density — one of the desirable characteristics reported by Rosow in 1964;

Homogeneous population along economic, occupational, and educational lines; residents living at essentially the same level with the same rights and privileges;

Role models as standards of expectations;

Autonomy — tenants are free to have pets, receive visitors at any time, have personal celebrations, and decorate their apartments to their own tastes;

Security — guaranteed by individual keys, and encouraged by architectural safety features and a sympathetic management;

Privacy — available to whatever degree the tenant wishes.

A number of pertinent observations have been included in the Proceedings of a Research Conference on Patterns of Living and Housing of Middle-Aged and Older People, 1965 (Public Health Service Publications No. 1496).

Lawton and Azar have reported in interesting fashion the reaction of three married couples between the ages of 68 and 78 years to a retirement community being developed in the Tampa Bay area of Florida:

> These couples reported that not one of them would of his own accord live in such a community, since they all resented the segregation by age. Furthermore, they voiced displeasure with the subtle socioeconomic distinction enforced by the initial costs of the housing and by the higher cost of living at least partially imposed by the relative isolation of this community from population centers and large shopping areas. They stated that they would have some anxiety about the distances to hospitals and other personal protective and care services.
>
> They also pointed out that people who had certain personalities, however, might be happy in such a retirement community. Their analyses indicated that if a person were to be satisfied in this environment, he would have to admit to full retirement and to being old. He would have to be content to associate only with his close peers in age and socioeconomic class and he would need to enjoy either virtual solitude or constant small group activity or a type characterized by incessant card playing. (*Ibid.*, p. 19.)

A study by Rosenmayer and Kockeis of housing in the City of Vienna led them to suggest the following principles as the basis for planning old-age housing:

    a. Every aged person should retain a maximum amount of independence.
    b. Accommodation, service, and help should be in accordance with individual physical and mental needs.
    c. The individual should decide how much organized aid he or she demands and accepts.
    d. Planning should aim at maximizing opportunities for help from the family and personal friends (to be supplemented by public schemes). (*Ibid.*, p. 41.)

So much is written about housing in urban areas, that it is refreshing to read a report about living in a rural community. Britton noted that older people in rural areas and small towns have strong ties with their geographical areas; that they believe in independence and self-sufficiency and staying in their own homes as long as possible; that very few would even think of emigrating permanently to a different place to live; and that the few who came to a small town to retire had a less satisfactory time than those who had lived there all of their adult lives. (*Ibid.*, p. 99.)

The two elements of friendship and accessibility work together to make the continuance of an independent life possible. Niebank states that:

> While no absolutes can be applied to the elderly, it does appear that most of the friends of elderly persons are also elderly. They share the same interests, needs, roles, and abilities. They are complementary rather than threatening to each other. As with younger persons, when grouped together, any given member is likely to have more friends and to be more creatively involved in community life than when age peers are less proximate.

> The other major implication for housing policy is that a variety of facilities should be provided within a very short distance from the housing unit. It is desirable, for instance, to have convenience stores within one block. Bus stops should also be close. Secondary facilities (library, bank, church) should be within easy walking distance. All other necessities should be provided either on site or within the distance of a short bus ride. Thus, it is further implied that, while most urban elderly thrive best in enclaves dominated by others of the same age group, they also require proximity to life-sustaining facilities and access to the world at large, which allow them to interact with the workaday world as they choose. (*Ibid.*, pp. 109-110.)

It was my good fortune to receive a copy of the Proceedings of a recent Institute on Rehabilitation of the Aging that was held at the University of Tennessee, October 1967. Here the emphasis was primarily on people. The following observations were made by Leon A. Pastalon who is Coordinator of Training and Research Sociologist at the University of Michigan. Dr. Pastalan states that (p. 43):

> The need for adequate housing takes on increased significance because the character of the older person's immediate living environment plays a large part in determining the extent to which facilities and services will be available and, consequently, the degree to which his needs may be satisfied. Further in retirement, the home tends to become the principal locus of his activity. . . .

> Environmental needs of the elderly can be viewed in terms of two basic categories: a) the physiological and b) the psychosocial.

> The physiological category includes such considerations as

temperature and climate control; illumination; sounds and noise levels; safety and energy conservation. . . .

Ventilation is also a significant factor in climate control. . . . one complete air exchange is equivalent in terms of its lethal effect on airborne bacteria to continuous glycol treatments of ultraviolet irradiation. . . . vertical temperature gradients in a given space can influence bacteria concentration, e.g., more bacteria in upper portions of rooms than in cooler lower portions. . . .

All safety planning for housing environments of the elderly seem to call for the provision of adaptive mechanisms to help [the elderly] cope with the sensory and motor losses of waning vision, hearing, strength and speeds of reaction.

Turning now to the psychosocial aspects of environmental needs of housing the elderly, . . . Irving Rosow in his famous Cleveland study found first that despite important differences between his working class and middle class subjects, *the number of old people's friends vary with the proportion of older neighbors* and *second, regardless of the number, these friends consist disproportionately of older rather than younger neighbors.* This expresses the general principle that friendships are formed between persons not only of similar status, notably of age, but also of sex, marital status, social class, beliefs and life style.

According to Rosow the active social life of the working class centers on the place of residence, while that of the middle class covers a larger sphere with less focus on the immediate environment. . . .

The various forms of housing for the elderly cover a broad spectrum — from the type of facility in which an older person may live in an independent fashion, fully responsible for the management of his own household and personal needs, to one in which his daily activities are closely supervised or regulated by an outside source.

At another point in the Proceedings mentioned earlier, Dr. Pastalon reported a study of the environmental needs of the physically disabled elderly (p. 124):

Frequency of use of "downtown" services, such as shopping, banking, health, and vocational rehabilitation was low. There are many reasons why the respondents did not utilize specialized downtown services more frequently. For instance, people often indicated that they thought busses were too difficult to get into and out of, expensive and inconvenient. Some are discouraged

because when they get downtown, they find it impossible to gain
access into the necessary buildings since most have "architectural
barriers": i.e., such formidable obstacles as long steep stairs, lack
of elevators, or find they can't cross streets because of high curbs,
and the like. However, in contrast to the findings of Professor
Nugent at the University of Illinois, fewer than 5 percent of the
respondents specifically mentioned such obstacles as the reason
for not going downtown. It seems just as feasible to entertain the
possibility that some individuals may be so withdrawn they avoid
going downtown for any reason. Further, it is quite possible that
others may not be able to spare the sheer physical energy it takes
to attain needed services because of the distance and difficulties
involved.

We can safely conclude that there is no one design of appropriate
housing for all of the elderly, and it is equally obvious that it is impossible to have as many designs as there are individuals. Practical com-
promises are essential.

At the risk of oversimplification, I suggest housing for older adults
without a categorical age qualification to avoid unreasonable age density and social homogeneity; that such housing be located in the midst
of activity in close proximity to a large variety of community facilities
and services; and that there be a wide range in the size of communities
in which such housing is located to accommodate those who prefer the
large city.

Having dared to make these summary recommendations, I conclude
by returning to an observation I made earlier; namely, that more needs
to be done in involving older persons in defining what *they* consider as
adequate housing, and in determining what motivates *them* to seek such
housing.[1]

[1] For a more complete analysis of housing conditions and Federal Programs related to
the area, see vol. 9, No. 1 (Spring, 1969), *The Gerontologist.*

31. An Architect Discovers the Aged*

DONALD P. GRANT**

The question of age-homogeneity versus age-heterogeneity in housing for the elderly is suggested to be peripheral to the central issue: the provision for dealing with increased dependency and declining health without traumatic uprooting and removal. A review of pertinent literature relating aging to housing practices also seemed to contradict a basic assumption of many architects that age-heterogeneous rather than homogeneous housing yields greater living arrangement satisfaction for most old people. These findings suggest that many architects work with assumptions that do not reflect current data from the behavioral sciences.

The topic of this review is the proper relation between housing for the elderly and housing for other age groups. The specific question of interest is whether housing for elderly people should be built in age-homogeneous projects, and thereby segregated from the surrounding community to some extent, or integrated into the community in the sense of being physically dispersed among housing for all age groups. A popular supposition in both Europe and America has been that it is preferable for housing for the elderly to be integrated into age-heterogeneous communities, and in cases where social goals have been the dominant factors in decision making this has usually been the practice. However, economy in providing services and facilities unique to the needs of elderly people seems to call for concentration of housing for the elderly into age-homogeneous groupings.

My interest in this topic arose in connection with a public housing program in which I participated as an architect. My initial opinion was based on a view that seems to be held by many architects, that age-heterogeneous housing for the elderly is preferable both from the viewpoints of the elderly and of the whole community. This project was undertaken with the intent of checking this opinion against current

*Reprinted from *The Gerontologist*, Vol. 10, 1970, pages 275-281, with permission of the author and the Gerontological Society.
**Dr. Grant is Associate Professor in the School of Architecture and Environmental Design, California Polytechnic State University.

views in the behavioral sciences. The project was approached by stating a hypothesis, reviewing the literature of the behavioral sciences, and then interviewing administrators of housing programs for the elderly in the San Francisco Bay area. In general, the survey of the literature did not bear out the hypothesis, and the interviews suggested that the question of integration versus segregation was the wrong question to be asking with regard to the location of housing for the elderly. The bulk of opinion in the behavioral science sources consulted either contradicted the hypothesis or argued that the positions of age-heterogeneity were too simplistic to explain all the needs of the elderly. The administrators interviewed felt on the basis of their experiences that the relationship of housing to facilities for increasingly needed medical care was the prime consideration with regard to location.

The initial hypothesis was that it is undesirable both from the standpoints of the elderly and of the communities in which they live to isolate the elderly from other age groups by locating their houses in age-homogeneous groupings, whether at a face-to-face level or on a larger scale. This is especially so in the case of low income elderly people who require public housing assistance, for whom the range of choice in dwellings is very small. Further, this hypothesis was limited to the elderly who are well and capable of independent living, as most housing programs are tailored to this group.

As population increases, the number of elderly people in a society can be expected to become very large. Since the nature of our society and economy insures that at least for the foreseeable future a large percentage of low income Americans will be elderly people, the question of how to relate their housing to the community becomes very important. This importance stems both from the side of the elderly, whose interests as people must be considered, and that of the whole community, an increasing part of which is affected in dealing with housing for the elderly. On the basis of human decency alone, decisions determinant of the life pattern of any group of people should not be taken lightly or made purely on the basis of administrative convenience or short-term economics. This is especially so with regard to groups who have limited alternatives available to them, and limited alternatives in housing are certainly conditions that apply to many if not most of the elderly in our society and in most western industrial societies. In both England and Sweden the bulk of substandard housing is reported to be inhabited by old people (Donahue, 1960).

The Place of the Aged in Society

In addition to considerations of decency due elderly people simply because they are people, consideration of the importance of their place in society is more than justified on the basis of the contributions they can make to the life of a whole society. One of the traditional roles of the elderly in the three-generation family was to care for the young, and in the process to pass on traditional values and culture through stories, songs, games, and speech patterns. This might be viewed as having both good and bad features, since while it might provide one key to an individual's personal identity through identification with his culture and a way to learn his culture's way of life and values, it might also serve to perpetuate conservative world views, resistance to change, stereotype prejudices, and disfunctionally outdated values.

Status, Role, and the Extended Family

Many authors writing on the problems of the elderly have characterized the mid-twentieth century as a time in which the position of the elderly in society has undergone drastic changes for the worse. Mumford (1956) writes that the elderly have never previously gone through a period of such rejection and attributes this to the breakup of the three-generation household. Burgess (1960) states that the main sources of satisfaction in life for elderly people in pre-industrial societies were experienced within the extended family and describes the breakup of the extended family as a process which left the elderly adrift and without psychological and economic support.

The popular image of the position of the elderly in society seems to envision earlier generations in which elderly people enjoyed a secure position in the extended multi-generation family, filling useful roles in family life, and enjoying a respected status, followed by industrialization and urbanization and the fading away of formerly satisfying position and status.

The role of the elderly as a segment of society capable of important contributions to the quality of human life includes service as models to the young, as repositories and transmitters of traditional human values, and as humanizing agents. Breen (1962) holds that segregation of the elderly from other age groups would make them unavailable to fill their social roles as models for the young and that this would be a serious loss to society. Berwick (1967) states that the wisdom and experience of the elderly are a potential counterweight to the dehumanization of modern life and that the elderly serve to maintain and transmit traditional human values that might otherwise be lost in the confusion of rapid change.

In Alton Estates housing development at Roehampton, a suburb of London, the London County Council's Architects' Department positioned one-story row houses for the elderly along paths to and from a school. One critic's assessment of the reasons for doing this holds that it was done in order to provide a likely setting for frequent contact between the very old and the very young, which if not mutually enjoyed, would at least help to keep both sides a bit more human (Canadian Film Board). Bengtson and Smith (1968) carried out a study comparing the status of the elderly in modern industrial societies with their status in more traditional societies. Interested in investigating the widely held assumption that the elderly enjoyed much higher status in traditional societies, they found that the status accorded the elderly in some of the more traditional societies of the present day is not substantially higher than in industrialized, or non-traditional societies.

Tibbitts (1968) reports that his research indicated that the popular picture of the past as some sort of golden age in terms of family arrangements and financial responsibility was a myth. He further states that the nuclear, two-generation family has always been the model in the USA, and that the three generation household has always been rare. He cites the dilemma posed by long-lived, retired parents for younger families who have children to raise and the fact that cases are now beginning to appear where children reach retirement age and suffer the resultant economic loss while their retired parents are still living.

One final observation on the status of the elderly is that there is at least a possibility that three-generation families in the past were cemented together only by basic necessity and that sufficient friction was generated within them to outweigh any positive intangible benefits derived from the three-generation household.

THE THREE-GENERATION FAMILY

Several studies have indicated that a large percentage of elderly people living in age-homogeneous housing do not have families, or have small families and that for these people, living in dwellings for the aged is probably not replacing any past situation in which they would have lived with their families. Tibbitts (1968) asserts that the three-generation household was never as common in America as popularly held images of the past would indicate. However, as Mathiasen (1962) reminds us, the three-generation household is not necessarily synonymous with the three-generation family. The general impression gained from several studies is that living in age-homogeneous groups does not necessarily imply isolation from one's family and, that perhaps three-generation family relationships can be maintained despite the fact that three-generation households will probably never again be common in this country, if indeed they ever were (Shanas, 1961; Sherman, Mangum, Dodds, Walkley, & Wilner, 1968; Tibbitts, 1968; Wilner, Sherman, Walkley, Dodds, & Mangum, 1968).

An interesting variation on the three-generation household versus the three-generation family is reported by Ginzberg et al. (1954). In rural Iowa it is customary for an elderly widow or widower to be accommodated in a small cottage on the same site with a younger relative's house. Such "granny cottages" were found to range from one-room 8' × 10' shacks to comfortable three-room houses. All degrees of satisfaction and dissatisfaction with these arrangements were reported, but in the cases where the greatest discontent was expressed, the reasons seemed to lie in family relationships and attitudes rather than in the nature of the physical setting. In one case, a retired European-born farmworker, who had moved into his son's household, soon became involved in friction and tension with his grandchildren. The son built him a small but comfortable cottage on the same lot with the family house. The father enjoyed the privacy provided by his own cottage, especially the freedom to get up and putter at odd hours, and became so contented with life that some previously rigid prejudices mellowed with the passing years (Donahue, 1960).

Mumford (1956) suggests that if groups of dwellings for elderly people are integrated into neighborhoods of all age groups, this might provide an opportunity for some of the activities of three-generation family arrangements, like baby-sitting, but still maintain an elderly person's independence and freedom from more contact with other age groups than he desires.

CONFLICTING THEORIES OF SUCCESSFUL AGING

Successful aging is the term used to describe a state wherein advancing age is accompanied by high morale and general feelings of satisfaction with life. Two conflicting theories of the social relations accompanying successful aging are the disengagement and activity hypotheses. The disengagement hypothesis was developed by Cumming and Henry (1961), who theorized that progressive social disengagement and inner or intrinsic disengagement were an inevitable part of aging and that an aged individual would generally exhibit high morale as he demonstrated these natural changes in his life. This implied a progressive disengagement from much of the social interaction of middle age, providing a source of possible tensions, since middle-age values generally stress social involvement and activity. If the disengagement hypothesis is accurate in its view of aging, then these arguments point toward age-homogeneous living arrangements as an aid to natural disengagements, since it might shelter the inhabitants from the involvement demands of middle-age communities and ease the role transitions of aging (Eisenstadt, 1956; Messer, 1967). Lipman and Smith (1968) criticize Cumming and Henry's study for its deliberate exclusion of people with poor health and low incomes. Their study would indicate that the matter of engagement-disengagement is not an isolated variable but is intertwined with other aspects of life organization and history and, in fact, that it was engagement rather than disengagement that they found to be a factor in high morale. In view of the factor that our socioeconomic scheme of things virtually guarantees that many of our older people will suffer from inadequate incomes and partially income-related poor health, Cumming and Henry's disregard of low income and poor health greatly weakens their theory as a frame of reference for considering the general population.

Activity theorists (Maddox, 1963; Maddox & Eisdorfer, 1962) hold that successful aging involves maintaining the activities and attitudes of middle age for as long as possible. Whereas the disengagement theorists assume that progressive severance of social ties will lead to high morale, and the activity theorists assume that successful aging depends on maintenance of the activities of middle age with little or no reduction, Havighurst (1968) holds that successful aging equals successful adaptation and that this varies with different people; differences in personality and life expectations can be expected to bring high morale and life satisfaction to some in an active role and to others in a passive role. The wide variety of life experiences of old people will, if anything, make them more varied as a group and less subject to explanation by any single theory.

RESIDENTIAL PROXIMITY AND SOCIAL LIFE

A key issue in the discussion of residential integration versus segregation for old people is the probable effect of spatial proximity on social life. Many studies have documented strong correlations between physical relations and friendship formation, or at least social interaction, in a variety of settings (Caplow & Forman, 1950, Festinger, Schachter, & Back, 1950; Hall, 1961; Osmond, 1959; Osmond & Izume, 1957; Sommer, 1960; Sommer & Gilliland, 1962; Sommer & Ross, 1958; Whyte, 1956). Dealing specifically with the aged, Lawton and Simon (1968) found that casual contacts are important in leading to exploratory conversations as the basis for viable friendships, even after the newness of a facility had passed. Their findings are also borne out by Carp (1967) and Friedman (1966). Rupp, Duffy, and Danish (1967) found that useful activity that brought elderly people in contact with others was an important factor in successful adaptation to aging. Proppe (1968) found evidence that physical layout was very important for a form of vicarious social activity enjoyed by the aged. In one home for the aged he observed that a comfortable, spacious lounge with no view of outside activities was virtually unused while residents crowded into a cramped, narrow lobby looking out onto the street.

The importance of spatial proximity to social relations is probably increased in the case of the aged, who experience progressively reduced mobility as they grow older. Lawton and Simon (1968) report that one major factor in friendship formation was residence on the same floor of a building and another was physical proximity on that floor.

AGE-HOMOGENEOUS VERSUS AGE-HETEROGENEOUS HOUSING

In a mental hospital setting, Kahana and Kahana (1967) found that elderly residents of age-heterogeneous wards displayed marked improvement in awareness and performance over elderly people in age-homogeneous wards. This fits well with the popular image of age-heterogeneity as a means of keeping old people socially alive and involved. Mumford (1956) calls for neighborhoods that include elderly people in the same proportion as in the general population. He suggests that perhaps elderly people should be included in heterogeneous neighborhoods in groups of 6 to 12 dwellings. Jacobs (1958) says that housing for the elderly should not be on an isolated site, as has been common in the past, and cites Donahue's comment (1960) that whereas old people want privacy without isolation, what they get is isolation without privacy. Loring (1961) notes a welcome trend away from the past practice of isolating elderly people in supposedly idyllic, peaceful settings in the country, which probably created a situation analogous to that observed by Proppe (1968) wherein a comfortable, spacious sitting room with no view of activities was shunned for a crowded streetside lobby, except that in an isolated country project there could be no such thing as a street-side lobby with a view of a lively human scene.

The argument of those who favor age-heterogeneous communities is that old people's dwellings should be finely interspersed in housing for all ages. The opposite position, which finds more support in current behavioral science literature, is that old people often express greater satisfaction in the company of their age-peers and that, in fact, contact with younger people does not necessarily lead to cross-age friendships. Tibbitts (1968) holds that today's circumstances call for the provision of age-homogeneous housing for old people that allows them to satisfy their social as well as material needs.

Many convincing arguments are set forth as to the social satisfactions provided by age-homogeneous housing. Rosow (1961, 1964) lists preference for increased opportunity for age-peer friendships in age-homogeneous housing as an important factor in the social integration of the aged. Eisenstadt (1956) holds that age-grouping is essential in easing role transition. Carp (1967) reports that in Victoria Plaza in San Antonio, a spectacularly successful project in terms of inhabitant satisfaction, the improved social and physical environment increased satisfaction with life situations in general, improved attitudes to self and others, improved physical and mental health generally, and provided more active and sociable patterns of life.

Jacobs (1958) describes a housing project in Cleveland where an attempt was made to integrate age groups on what was evidently too intimate a scale. Here, some buildings were strictly for younger families with children and others were for mixed occupancy, with both family dwellings and dwellings for the elderly on each floor. Both sides found this unsatisfactory. The elderly were bothered by the noise and the young were bothered by the inhibitions they felt, although relations between the elderly and young children living in other buildings were fine. This is perhaps supportive of Mathiasen's (62) contention that what is desired is peer group association, but not isolation. Europeans, who have at various times concentrated housing for the aged at many different scales, are now moving away from large projects, having found large age-homogeneous concentrations unsatisfactory (Beyer & Nierstrasza, 1967; Cleverly, 1960). In the USA, where it least needs to be so, economic factors generally prevail and the trend is toward larger developments.

Wilson (1962) suggests small, relatively protected clusters of old peoples' dwellings within larger, age-heterogeneous neighborhoods. Mathiasen (1956) suggests one-bedroom "granny" flats, built adjacent to three-bedroom family houses. At any given time, both units might be occupied by parts of the same family or one might be rented. Loring (1961) describes a very large project in East Harlem, New York, where

248 elderly dwellings are combined with a community center for all ages. Various outdoor spaces in the center allow the elderly residents to mix or not as they desire at any given time.

Caution is in order in viewing the matter of homogeneity versus heterogeneity solely through self-reported inhabitant satisfaction. In a study in the Boston area, Frieden (1960) found that self-reports of satisfaction with age-homogeneous housing correlated chiefly with socioeconomic and ethnic background. There is also the strong possibility that inquiries into user satisfaction yield only evidence of an extreme "halo" or "Hawthorne" effect; in this society, where the lot of the aged is all too often one of insecurity and deprivation, any security in the form of stable, comfortable housing may well overwhelm all other considerations by a huge margin. In cases where this is so, any attempt to isolate out the matter of age-segregation versus age-integration as a meaningful variable in morale is probably futile. That such a thing could be so in the wealthiest nation in history is a sad reflection on the way in which we have ordered our affairs.

THE PROBLEM OF HEALTH CARE

Interviews with administrators of housing and homes for the aged in northern California brought forth the following observation. As people grow older, they inevitably approach a time of great or even dire need for medical care. Well-meaning groups that undertake the provision of housing for the well and independent elderly are overlooking a vital aspect of their needs, the inevitable coming of medical problems. In attempting to restrict housing for the elderly to houses for independent living, it is being insured that a time will come when the aged person must be told that he will have to move out and go to a place where care facilities are available. Thus an uprooting is insured at the worst possible time for it. What is needed to meet the true needs of the elderly is a facility that can care for them through all stages of the increasing dependency that comes with advancing age. A truly humane approach to planning should not let a time come when the aged person must be sent away to another facility, especially during a time of stress and illness. Thus it can be seen that to argue purely on a social integration-segregation basis is to neglect the more important matter of health that is the major factor in aging.

Loring (1961) cites the sobering fact of the inevitable need for medical care. The San Antonio Housing Authority views health as the number one problem and holds that all housing should take it into consideration. Donahue (1960) described one of the major disadvantages of isolated sites in the country as being the inevitably second-rate health care available. Mathiasen (1962) states that no adequate consideration of housing for the elderly can be made without considering health problems.

An answer to problems of health care is the three-phase facility that provides accommodation for independent living, accommodations for necessary care once cooking and housekeeping become troublesome, and accommodation for medical care when it becomes necessary. A comprehensive three-phase development avoids the trauma of removal from familiar surroundings when medical problems arise.

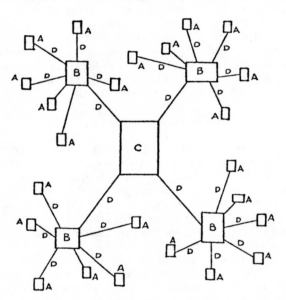

Fig. 1. A Tree-like Morphology of Housing Accommodations.

A — Clusters of 12 to 20 houses for people capable of living independently, as well as for those who require housekeeping aid and meals.

B — Residential care center combined with a home service center for housekeeping aid and meal delivery.

C — Nursing home and extended care facility.

D — Visually shared open space and easy walking distance. Age-homogeneous facilities A and B would be located in neighborhoods for all age groups.

Perhaps a profitable direction of inquiry would be to investigate a tree-like morphology of accommodations for the elderly, with independent living units at the outermost branches, in contact with housing for all age groups, but connected to and related to accommodations for persons in increasing states of dependence (Fig. 1). Once the sequence from independence toward dependence begins, the trauma of physical removal could be minimized by minimizing the distance moved at each step and maintaining at least visual contact with the previous environment by physical proximity. The tree-morphology might be manifested in the form of small, independent units at the outer branches and a large intensive care facility at the trunk. The matter of retaining physical proximity or at least visual contact with a familiar environment when the inevitable failure of health comes might be a fruitful area for research as a guide to design decision making.

CONCLUSION

This inquiry was undertaken to test the author's hypothesis that housing for the elderly should be thoroughly integrated into the community by dispersal among housing for all age groups. Considering the problem at this level, the hypothesis was not supported by the literature on the topic and in fact the author is now convinced that a generally age-homogeneous environment that still provides available contacts with other groups is preferable.

However, a more important conclusion drawn from this study is that to argue homogeneity versus heterogeneity in housing for the well and independent elderly is to argue on the wrong level, disregarding as it does the inevitability of declining health and the inevitable trauma of a move when illness and increased dependency come.

The popular concept that housing for the elderly should be integrated for involvement and interaction is a view that attempts to be humanistic in providing for the needs of the elderly. But the evidence seems to point toward age-homogeneous housing as contributing to high morale and life satisfaction for elderly people. Further, the truly humane position would seem to be one that views the process of aging as a continuum, in which the period of well, self-sufficient retirement living is but a part and which provides for easing the transitions along the course of failing health and increasing dependency.

REFERENCES

Bengtson, V. L., & Smith, D. H. Social modernity and attitudes toward aging: a cross-cultural survey. *Gerontologist,* 1968, 8 (Pt. II), 26 (abstract).

Berwick, K. The "senior citizen" in America; study in unplanned obsolescence. *Gerontologist,* 1967, 7, 257-260.

Byer, G. H., & Nierstasz, F. H. J. *Housing the aged in western countries.* New York: Elsevier Publishing Co., 1967.

Bean, L. Z. Housing the aging; some social and psychological considerations. In G. W. Grier (Ed.), *Housing the aging.* Washington: Brookings Institute, 1962.

Burgess, E. W. *Aging in western societies.* Chicago: University of Chicago, 1960.

Canadian Film Board. *Suburban living: Six solutions.* (film).

Caplow, T., & Forman, R. Neighborhood interaction in a homogeneous community. *American Sociological Review,* 1950, 15, 357-366.

Carp, F. The impact of environment on old people. *Gerontologist,* 1967, 7, 106-108, 135.

Cloverly, M. *An informal survey of housing for the elderly in nine European countries.* US Public Housing Aministration, 1960.

Cumming, E., & Henry, W. E. *Growing old.* New York: Basic Books, 1961.

Donahue, W. Housing and community services. In E. W. Burgess (Ed.), *Aging in western societies.* Chicago: University of Chicago, 1960.

Eisenstadt, S. N. *From generation to generation.* Glencoe, Ill.: Free Press, 1956.

Festinger, L., Schachter, S., & Back, K. *Social pressures in informal groups: Human factors in housing.* New York: Harpers, 1950.

Frieden, E. Social differences and their consequences for housing the aged. *Journal of American Institute of Planners.* 1960, 26, 119-124.

Friedman, E. P. Spatial proximity and social interaction in a home for the aged. *Journal of Gerontology,* 1966, 21, 556-570.

Ginzberg, R. *Rural improvisations in rural Iowa.* In W. Donahue (Ed.), *Housing the aging.* Ann Arbor: University of Michigan Press, 1954.

Grier, G. W. *Housing the aging. Research needs.* Washington: Brookings Institute, 1962.

Hall, E. T. The language of space. *Journal of American Institute of Architects,* 1961, 35, 71-74.

Havighurst, R. J. Successful aging. *Gerontologist,* 1961, 1, 8-13.

Havighurst, R. J. A social-psychological perspective on aging. *Gerontologist,* 1968, 8, 67-71.

Jacobs, J. Housing the independent aged. *Architectural Forum,* 1968, 109, 86-91.

Kahana, B., & Kahana, E. The effects of age segregation on the mental status of aged psychiatric patients. *Gerontologist,* 1967, 7, 37. (abstract)

Lawton, M. P., & Simon, B. The economy of social relationships in housing for the elderly. *Gerontologist,* 1968, 8, 108-115.

Lipman, A., & Smith, K. J. Disengagement, poor health, and poverty. *Gerontologist,* 1968, 8, (Pt. II), 26. (abstract)

Loring, W. C. Housing of the elderly. *Architectural Forum,* 1961, 114, 101-109.

Maddox, G. Activity and morale; a longitudinal study of selected elderly subjects. *Social Forces,* 1962, 42, 295-304.

Maddox, G., & Eisdorfer, C. Some correlates of activity and morale among the elderly. *Social Forces,* 1962, 40;, 254-260.

Mathiasen, G. Some current attempts at better buildings for the aging. *Architectural Record,* 1956, 119, 196-202.

Mathiasen, G. Trends in housing for older people. *Architectural Record,* 1962, 132, 109-116.

Messer, M. The possibility of an age-concentrated environment becoming a normative system. *Gerontologist,* 1967, 7, 247-251.

Mumford, L. For older people — not segregation but integration. *Architectural Record,* 1956, 119; 191-194.

Osmond, H. The history and social development of the mental hospital and the relationship between architecture and psychiatry. In C. Goshen (Ed.), *Psychiatric architecture,* Washington: American Psychiatric Association, 1959.

Osmond, H., & Izumi, K. Function as the basis of psychiatric ward design. *Mental Hospitals,* April 1957, 23-31.

Proppe, H. Housing for the retired and aged in Southern California; an architectural commentary. *Gerontologist,* 1968, 8, 176-179.

Rosow, I. Retirement housing and social integration. *Gerontologist,* 1961, 1, 85-91.

Rosow, I. Local concentrations of the aged and inter-generational relations. In P. F. Hansen (Ed.), *Age with a future.* Philadelphia: F. A. Davis Co., 1964.

Rupp, C., Duffy, E. L., & Danish, M M. Successful adaptation to aging: I. Psychological, social and psychiatric aspects. *Journal of American Geriatrics Society,* 1967, 15, 1137-1143.

Shanas, E. Living arrangements of older people in the U.S. *Gerontologist,* 1961, 1, 27-29.

Sherman, S. R., Mangum, W. P., Jr. Dodds, S., Walkley, R. P., & Wilner, D. M. Psychological effects of retirement housing. *Gerontologist,* 1968, 8, 170-175.

Sommer, R. Personal space. *Journal of the American Institute of Architects,* 1962, 38, 81-83.

Sommer, R., & Gilliland, C. W. Design for friendship. *Journal of the American Institute of Architects,* 1962, 38, 84-86.

Sommer, R., & Ross, H. Social interaction on a geriatrics ward. *International Journal of Social Psychology,* 1968, 4, 128-133.

Tibbitts, C. Some social aspects of gerontology. *Gerontologists,* 1968, 8, 131-134.

Whyte, W. H., Jr. *The organization man,* Garden City, N.Y.: Doubleday, 1956.

Wilner, D. M., Sherman, S. R., Walkley, R. P., Dodds, S., & Mangum, W. P., Jr. Demographic characteristics of residents of planned retirement housing sites. *Gerontologist,* 1968, 8, 164-169.

Wilson, R. L. Urban planning considerations in housing and related facilities. In G. W. Grier (Ed.), *Housing the aging; Research needs.* Washington: Brookings Institute, 1962.

32. History of Nursing Homes – A Review*

HERMAN W. GRUBER**

The term, "nursing home" refers to a varied group of nonhospital facilities with widely different functions. Some homes provide only custodial care; others furnish varying degrees of nursing and personal care; and still others are physician-oriented facilities providing continuous skilled nursing and rehabilitative care under close medical supervision. The absence of a logical classification of nursing homes, according to level of service provided, has impeded the development of standards and has created problems in licensure and accreditation and in financing the health care these facilities provide.

Recently the situation was partly clarified when the federal government and major voluntary health organizations in separate actions, identified the physician-oriented nursing home as an "extended care institution." This review has been prepared to explain the distinction between these and other nursing homes.

ALMSHOUSE CARE AND OLD-AGE ASSISTANCE

In the 1926 Modern Hospital Year Book, Dr. Haven Emerson, professor of public health at Columbia University, predicted:

"The day of the so-called county hospital or poor farm with its mixture of unclassified infirm, aged, and chronically ill is doomed. It is inevitable, in view of the tremendous efforts being exerted by other health and social agencies for the more advanced and humane purpose of reconstructing individuals and returning them to lives of usefulness and happiness, that communities will cease to tolerate the glaring inadequacies of mere domiciliary and custodial care."

Until the mid-thirties, the aged, who could not provide for themselves and were without family who could help, generally lived in county almshouses or "poor farms."

To help the aged leave the poor farm, some states began programs of direct cash assistance. All states sponsored such old-age assistance programs (OAA) for persons 65 and over after the Social Security Act of 1935 initiated a system of Federal grants-in-aid for them. The Act,

*Reprinted from *The Extended Care Facility: A Handbook for the Medical Society,* edited and published by the American Medical Association, Chicago, 1967, pages 115-126, with permission of the author and the American Medical Association. Copyright. American Medical Association, 1967.
**Mr. Gruber is Secretary of the Committee on Aging, Council on Medical Service, of the American Medical Association.

of course, also established the federal old-age insurance program
(OAI) with provisions for monetary benefits to retired workers.

For aged persons who otherwise would have had to live on the
county poor farm, another solution was now available. As long as they
lived on the poor farm, they could not qualify for OAA because federal
funds during the 30's and 40's could not be used by the states to make
OAA payments to residents of public facilities. Some aged preferred to
have a regular monthly income under OAA and live in family homes or
places of their own choice.[1]

To take care of the aged who had OAA or other income to pay for
services, private boarding homes began to spring up throughout the
country. Most of these were large, old multi-story family structures, not
fully occupied, with several bedrooms which could be used for guests.
Some boarding homes gave promise of providing a satisfactory environment for the aged, who required, most of all, understanding,
respect as individuals and friendship.

The aged were better able to survive such traditional killers as
"pneumonia, the old folks' friend" with the discovery of sulfa drugs
and penicillin. As a result, more of the residents lived into their 80's
and 90's. As the residents became older, sick, and less able to take care
of themselves, many boarding homes found themselves forced to provide nursing care.

Although some nursing-boarding home operators had nursing experience, most were without special training. But they had an opportunity to provide service to people needing care, and at the same time,
earn a livelihood for themselves.

Local welfare departments had to distribute their limited funds as
equitably and extensively as possible. With the funds available, they
could afford to pay only minimal fees for nursing home care. Shortages of funds and limits on the amount that could be paid for an
individual made it impossible for welfare agencies to place many clients
in nursing homes with good care, or to provide nursing home care of
any kind for some patients. Some welfare departments paid higher
rates for bed patients, thereby discouraging any attempt to promote
more patient self-care.

Patients in nursing homes had little or no opportunity to do anything
about their situation or even to make their objections known. The
public apparently accepted the nursing home as a custodial facility
providing limited amounts of nursing and personal care to the chronic

---

1. *Almshouse Care and the Old-Age Assistance Program.* Social Security Bulletin, March,
   1938.

elderly patient who could not be taken care of in his own home. The public generally did not even think of the nursing home as a medical facility where, after a period of acute illness or disability, a patient could convalesce, receive specialized care, and return to independent life in the community or remain there at a higher level of self-care.

LICENSURE

State licensing programs for nursing homes developed slowly. In the early days, the licensing function usually was left in the hands of a local agency. The first state program was adopted in 1941 and it was not until 1950 that every state had a program.

At best, the standards of licensing are set at a minimum level. Since licensing requirements at first dealt largely with "bricks and mortar," the background of the consulting staff was primarily in environmental health, architecture or engineering. These consultants could seldom be of assistance with patient care problems, but gradually, the need was recognized for a licensing staff with a nursing or medical background.

In almost all states, the agency responsible for licensure was the health department. These departments had difficulty in establishing and enforcing quality standards in nursing homes, when the welfare departments were making minimal payments for a large portion of their patients. Therefore, many licensing agencies did not fully enforce their own regulations. The agencies, already concerned about bed shortages, believed that strict enforcement of the regulations would close too many homes. It was the general policy to give operators ample time to comply with the regulations.

Because of insufficient funds, some licensing agencies found it impossible to have a field staff qualified to enforce regulations even had they wished to. It was also difficult to provide appropriate consultation to nursing homes on many important aspects of their operations.

NURSING HOME OPERATORS

Most nursing home operators saw the need for physical improvement in their homes and for more and better qualified staff. They also knew that most residents had limited funds and could not afford the rate increases that would be necessary if the licensing agencies made substantial efforts to raise their requirements. Some operators were concerned that licensing standards would be raised and require a substantial increase in rates. Higher charges would force the homes to discharge some patients who most needed care.

The operators recognized that the low level of assistance payments was the biggest roadblock to the improvement of care. This concern was shared by a U.S. Senate subcommittee, which in 1960 reported:

"It is inherently impossible for even the most altruistic nursing home proprietor (at the rates he charges) to provide registered nursing service, routine medical care, rehabilitative and recreational activity and still make even a small profit."[2]

To gain allies in improving nursing home conditions, some operators, through their organization, the American Nursing Home Association, tried to establish liaison with other health and welfare groups. At first the efforts were ignored or rebuffed. Traditionally, institutional health and welfare services had been provided under public or nonprofit auspices. Members of the other professions frequently looked down on the nursing home operators as "profit-motivated."

NATIONAL COMMITTEE ON THE AGING

Many professional groups did recognize the need for considerable improvement in nursing homes and other institutions for the aged. In 1954, the National Committee on the Aging of the National Social Welfare Assembly reported that "fire and other hazards still exist in many homes; that in many homes there is insufficient trained personnel, particularly nurses; that shocking evidences of inhumane treatment are known to exist in homes located in all parts of the country; that reports of local and state governmental and voluntary personnel reveal that residents in many homes receive grossly inadequate nutrition; that poor health and medical care practices exist in many homes under every type of auspice; that relatively few homes provide preventive and rehabilitation services; that the majority of homes provide no planned facilities for constructive recreation of any kind; that unrealistic restrictive rules exist in many philanthropic and commercial homes, limiting the freedom of residents and making it difficult for them to feel at home."[3]

These findings provided the basis on which the National Committee on the Aging developed a set of standards applicable to nursing homes and a suggested procedure for establishing and maintaining them.

2. "The Aged and the Aging in the United States: A National Problem," report to the Committee on Labor and Public Welfare, U.S. Senate Report No. 1121, p. 141, 1960.
3. National Committee on the Aging, National Social Welfare Assembly. *Standards of Care for Older People in Institutions.* 1953.

The standards and procedures were subsequently endorsed by the Commission on Chronic Illness, an independent voluntary organization sponsored by the American Hospital Association, American Medical Association, American Public Health Association, and the American Public Welfare Association.

COMMISSION ON CHRONIC ILLNESS

The Commission, in its 1956 report, stated that "there is still no general recognition that these (nursing) homes are medical care institutions. They are still thought of as residences for older people or for people whose needs can be adequately met by nurses or attendants . . . generally deleterious conditions exist in many nursing homes, and bedridden patients are not seen by a physician for months or years."

The Commission also reported, in regard to nursing home operators — public, nonprofit, and proprietary — that "by far the most of them are conscientious people, and some among them are truly dedicated. . . . Although a few charge rates which appear to be exorbitant, for most the monetary rewards are small. . . ."[4]

The reports of the National Committee on the Aging, the Commission on Chronic Illness, and numerous other organizations called on the health and welfare professions to accept increased responsibility for improving nursing home conditions. All of the professions were urged to recognize the potential value of the nursing home and to help bring about reforms needed to turn it into a real medical care facility.

GUIDES FOR MEDICAL CARE

In view of the lack of medical, skilled nursing, and restorative services in most nursing homes during the 1940's and 1950's, many physicians were reluctant to send their patients to them. Most physicians preferred that their patients convalesce in the hospital, if at all possible. At the same time, physicians realized that many long-term care patients in general hospitals did not require hospital services and should have less expensive care.

To help improve patient care in nursing homes and to help doctors make better use of them, the American Medical Association, American Hospital Association, and the American Nursing Home Association

---

4. Commission on Chronic Illness. *Care of Long-Term Patient.* Chronic Illness in the United States. Volume II. 1956.

collaborated in developing a set of guides for medical care.[5] Included were recommendations that the nursing home have policies and practices designed to maintain a continuing relationship between the patient and his personal physician; assure adequate medical supervision at all times; and help patients achieve their maximum potential for self-care.

HOSPITAL-NURSING HOME RELATIONSHIPS

Professional groups advocated close ties between hospitals and nursing homes. It was felt that such ties would help hospitals limit their beds to acute care by facilitating the transfer of patients to nursing homes, and assure better continuity between the hospital and post-hospital phases of treatment. Correspondingly, nursing homes would get better medical supervision of patient care, an opportunity to upgrade their services with the help of hospital staffs, and ready access to the hospital's diagnostic services. The results would demonstrate the concern of both institutions for the best use of the community's health care dollars in the interest of the patient.

On the other hand, many hospital administrators, preferring to ignore the potential of the proprietary nursing home, believed that the development of similar units as parts of general hospitals would be the only way to assure continuity of care for the long-term patient. The nursing home administrator, too, hesitated to develop a working agreement with a hospital because he feared it would threaten his independence. In time, some hospitals and nursing homes did develop agreements, but they were primarily between nonprofit insitutions.

In addition to the American Nursing Home Association, American Medical Association, and the American Hospital Association, many other professional groups, some in cooperation with the federal government, developed materials designed to improve nursing home operation, such as standards to which the homes could aspire, guides or manuals for improving the skill and services of staff, and statements of principle indicating necessary changes. These materials dealt with such subjects as nursing care, safety control, pharmacy services, recreation programs, and cost accounting. Many state agencies published similar materials.

5. American Medical Association, American Nursing Home Association, and American Hospital Association. *Guides for Medical Care in Nursing Homes and Related Facilities,* June 1960.

Many different programs were instituted to further the training of nursing home staff. Numerous groups — voluntary and government — sponsored training institutes, conferences, workshops and on-the-job training programs. Vocational schools and colleges offered courses. More consultants, especially from the licensing agencies, became available for assistance to help with patient care problems. Nursing home operators were encouraged to develop a sense of professional responsibility, not only to upgrade their own facilities, but to work with other health facilities in the community.

PUBLIC INTEREST

The public slowly began to realize that it had a vital stake in helping to improve the quality of care in nursing homes. The public became more knowledgeable because more people had to face the problem of finding a suitable nursing home for a sick relative. The nursing home population kept mushrooming — a rise of a third between 1954 and 1961 — because of the steady rise in the number of aged, particularly of those 75 and over, and changes in the nation's social and economic environment. Urban growth reduced the number of family homes available for older people with prolonged illness. Smaller homes and apartments did not have a spare room. In many homes, all adult family members worked and no one was available to care for someone in a time of illness.

The public tended increasingly to rely upon physicians for advice about nursing homes. The physician guided his patients to those homes where he had confidence that his orders would be carried out accurately and professionally and where he could better continue his medical supervision. These homes provided skilled nursing care and usually had a program of restorative services.

Charges doubtless were higher in these medically oriented homes. Most patients paid their own way either by themselves or with the help of relatives. Few were welfare recipients. As the public grew more willing to pay for medical care, shortages of beds in skilled nursing homes developed.

IMPACT OF CONSTRUCTION

To help alleviate the shortages, a number of federal programs were initiated to help finance new construction: the 1954 amendments to the Hospital Survey and Construction Act (Hill-Burton program), Small Business Administration Construction Program in 1956 and the

Federal Housing Administration Program in 1959. Applicants for assistance under these programs agreed to build skilled nursing care facilities which would meet substantially higher requirements than those of licensure.

The greatest volume of money for construction of new homes, however, came from private capital. A few entrepreneurs were motivated by the hope of quick profits. Most were attracted to the growing nursing home field as an area for business investment.

The growing demand for skilled nursing home beds attracted many newcomers into the field. They brought new ideas and sound business methods, both in construction and operation. They also brought more competition into the community, thereby upgrading levels of service in existing homes and helping to eliminate many poor ones. According to the American Nursing Home Association, about half of the nursing home beds as of January 1966 had been built in the preceding 5 years.[6] Since the total number of beds (500,000-600,000) had not changed significantly, many beds in use in 1961 (possibly half) were no longer operating 5 years later.

Even though the average size of the projects increased, the building cost per bed also rose steadily. Many new homes were carefully designed to provide a wide range of health and social services. The more services a nursing home planned to provide, the more costly its construction became.

PAYMENTS FOR NURSING HOME CARE

Many of the newer homes with their additional services and their higher rates did not have welfare patients. Competition among them forced their administrators to offer the best patient care for the rates their residents were paying because the resident could always move from one nursing home to another.

The majority of nursing homes, however, continued to have a significant proportion of assistance patients. A 1963 report on institutions for the aged and chronically ill indicated that 90% of them accepted persons on public assistance, and about half the beds were occupied by such residents.[7]

Consequently, nursing homes have long been engaged in efforts to raise the level of assistance payments. In the early days, the lack of

6. ANHA Fact Sheet No. 1, American Nursing Home Association, July 15, 1966.
7. U.S. National Center for Health Statistics. Utilization of Institutions for the Aged and Chronically Ill, United States, April-June 1963, Series 12, No. 4.

adequate financial information made it difficult for nursing homes to get appropriate reimbursement for their services.

The practice of welfare agencies of paying flat rates tended to keep levels of care low in homes with welfare patients, since the owner had no financial incentive to improve care. In time, however, many welfare agencies established several categories of nursing homes with different rates of pay based on the level of care offered. For example, some states provided a financial bonus to nursing homes offering physical and occupational therapy.

In some states, nursing home operators learned that they could obtain higher payments by showing the true costs of operation in relation to the services provided. Sound accounting practices enabled them to justify the rates they had to charge in order to finance their costs and realize a reasonable return on their capital investment.

ACCREDITATION

Both government and the health professions increasingly recognized the importance of identifying the medically oriented nursing homes as distinct from other facilities. For a number of years, the health professions had used hospital accreditation by the Joint Commission on Accreditation of Hospitals as a means of informing physicians, third-party payers, and the public where the best conditions existed for medical, nursing and hospital care.

By the early 60's there was general agreement on the need for similar accreditation for nursing homes but opinion differed as to how the program should be organized.

In 1965, the JCAH took over responsibility for accrediting "extended care facilities," the medically oriented nursing homes. In addition to the Joint Commission sponsors — the American College of Physicians, American College of Surgeons, American Hospital Association, and the American Medical Association — two other national organizations — the American Association of Homes for Aging and the American Nursing Home Association — assumed responsibility through the JCAH for initiation and development of the program.

To achieve accreditation as an extended care facility, the home is required to provide a "continuing program of medical and nursing care in accordance with the total needs of the patient and rendered in a physical and social environment that provides for the safety of the patient and the achievement and maintenance of an optimum level of restoration."

The home must provide such services as continuing medical supervision and a planned program of nursing care for each patient; physician guidance on medical-administrative and clinical matters; and laboratory, radiology and diagnostic services. It must also have a transfer agreement with a hospital, full-time RN supervision and an active program of restorative nursing care.

MEDICARE

The passage of the "Medicare" law (P.L. 89-97) provided further impetus to move nursing homes into the continuum of medical care in the community. The law provides for federal reimbursement of all "reasonable costs" incurred by an "extended care facility" for patients qualified for "extended care services." These services are provided to a Medicare patient, who has received care in an acute general hospital, where his medical condition and needs have been adequately appraised, and who is then moved to an "extended care facility" for high quality convalescent and rehabilitative care. The care is intended primarily to help the patient bridge the gap from hospital to home.

To become certified as an extended care institution under Medicare, a home must meet substantially the same requirements as those for accreditation by the Joint Commission.

As of March 1967, certification has been granted to 3,374 facilities with 250,000 beds. Included are 2,589 skilled nursing homes, 488 ECFs operated by hospitals, with a remainder of 289 extended care units which are distinct parts of other types of facilities. Most of the medically oriented nursing homes probably have been certified.

It is estimated that the number of Medicare patients needing extended care at any one time in the near future will range between 50,000 and 65,000. This figure is low in relation to the 500,000-600,000 nursing home beds, because "extended care" does not include the long-term care provided in most nursing homes.[8]

CONCLUSION

In 1967, Dr. Haven Emerson would see that the nation is well along toward realizing his prediction that "communities will cease to tolerate the glaring inadequacies of mere domiciliary and custodial care."

8. Robert M. Ball, 1966 Year-End Report: *Social Security and Medicare*. Medicare Newsletter, January 13, 1967.

The nursing home has become a major institution in the health field. There has been notable success in improving the level of medical, nursing and personal care and in financing the care. Many administrators of proprietary homes have become sensitive about their responsibility for meeting high standards of service. They are working to improve their own facilities, both in scope of services and in the competence of their staffs; to raise standards for all nursing homes by negotiations with professional organizations and government agencies; and, with areawide planning councils, to help meet overall health care needs of the community.

A decade ago, the nursing home was in an evolutionary stage. Today, it still is without specific identity. The term, "nursing home" still refers to many different kinds of facilities with a wide range of functions, and therefore, is a continuous source of confusion.

The health and welfare professions should welcome a recommendation made recently by a national conference convened to develop "a logical and integrated system of nomenclature, definitions and classification for health care institutions." The conference recommended that the term " 'nursing home' be dropped, on the basis that if the term were perpetuated, it would never achieve a single meaning generally acceptable to all its users including the general public." [9]

9. American Hospital Association, *Classification of Health Care Institutions.* 1966.

33. The Forgotten Americans: A Sociopsychological Analysis of Aging and Nursing Homes*

MARIAN L. MacDONALD**

The problems of the institutionalized aged are compounded by the passivity-inducing nature of nursing homes, but are rooted more deeply in contemporary cultural myths surrounding aging. A sociopsychological analysis of aging as a role label suggests that many of the assumed components of aging, such as disease, senility, and social withdrawal, are more a function of self-fulfilling social expectations than they are of natural, unavoidable processes. In many ways, environmental conditions currently provided for the aged as a social group help produce and perpetuate the unpleasant aspects of becoming old.

There is a minority group in our country today that is growing stronger in number, but weaker in voice. There is no legislated oppression explicitly imposed on this minority by any state or Federal agency; on the contrary, the members of this group enjoy the same constitutional protections as the members of the majority of American society. Yet these people have been victims of discrimination, both job (President's Council on Aging, 1963) and housing (Butler, 1969); they are continually derided in the mass media (Palmore, 1971); and, most egregiously, they virtually have been sentenced to life incarceration without due process of law.

Eighteeen and a half million people — nearly 10% of the American populace — are over the age of 65 (Brotman, 1968). Of this number, 4.3% of the women and 3.5% of the men (Boyd & Oakes, 1969) are currently residing in one of the nation's 25,000 nursing homes (U.S. Department of Health, Education, and Welfare, hereafter referred to as U.S. DHEW, 1960). Statistical summaries of America's nursing

*Reprinted from *The American Journal of Community Psychology*, Vol. 1, No. 3, 1973, pages 272-294 with permission of the author and Plenum Publishing Corporation.
**Dr. MacDonald was a Clinical Counselor at the Psychological and Counseling Center at the University of Illinios in Urbana when this article was written. She is now Assistant Professor, Department of Psychology, State University of New York at Stonybrook.

homes reveal that 91% are privately owned and have an average of 18 beds apiece, while 3% are publicly owned and average 60 beds apiece. The median age of the nursing home resident is 80 years (U.S. DHEW, 1960).

Qualitative summaries of facilities for the aged are not so common as quantitative ones; the only attempt at national evaluation was collated by the President's Council on Aging (1963). The Council found that (a) 60% of the licensed nursing homes failed to meet the Hill-Burton levels of acceptability, minimal standards concerned primarily with safety and building maintenance (U.S. DHEW, 1961); (b) 50% of the institutions claiming skilled nursing care did not have a registered professional nurse on their staffs; and (c) there were serious deficits in medical provisions and hygiene precautions. The sampling technique and the method of data collection render these results somewhat suspect; but because there is no bureaucratic superstructure enveloping nursing homes nationally (Morris, 1967), there have been no other comprehensive governmental efforts to evaluate them qualitatively.

Attempting to determine whether state legislators had heeded the findings of the Senate subcommittee, Braverman (1970) examined the regulations requisite for state licensure across the nation. His perusal of these requirements alone — not the degree to which they were actually met — resulted in a report entitled "Nursing Home Standards — A Tragic Dilemma in American Health." He found, among other things: only 14 states require inservice training programs for nurses; only 15 states require nurses' procedure manuals; only six states require that there be an emergency medication kit in the facility; 35 states do not require even an annual physical examination of patients; and 34 states permit the use of one patient's drugs for another patient. He evaluated his findings by noting:

> Nearly a decade since the 1960 U.S. Senate subcommittee on the problems of the aged and aging labeled the lack of medical care and restorative services the number one issue in the nursing home field, very little progress, if any, has been made by the states to solve this problem. . . . The rationales that allow unsanitary, overcrowded, and unsafe nursing homes to operate are no longer excusable. [Braverman, 1970, p. 5].

Furthermore, there is no evidence that even the inadequate standards reviewed by Braverman (1970) are actually met. "The fact that some states require certain standards is no guarantee that a home abides by the regulations [Larson, 1969, p. 1037]." In fact, there are numerous indications that nursing home practices are generally substandard. Tomlinson (1972) reported a host of observations: patient care is primarily the responsibility of poorly trained and poorly paid aides and orderlies, whose job satisfaction is reflected in their annual turnover rate — 75%; violence against patients erupts shockingly often; poor hygiene precautions have resulted in such tragedies as 25 deaths in one east coast institution from a single incident of salmonella food poisoning. McKnight (1971), in a survey of 14 midwestern nursing homes, found that the average daily time devoted to rehabilitative and recreational care was 3.69 minutes per patient. McKnight's methodology lends additional impact to the results, given that the observations were made by the treatment staff, a situation conducive to favorable overestimation. Ralph Nader (1971) reported observations of widespread substandard practices, while newspaper articles have documented appalling inhumanities (U.S. Senate, 1971b).

That laxity in care is the general rule rather than the rare exception was revealed in an evaluation conducted by the Associated Press (Pryor, 1970), which released a series of articles containing the following data concerning nursing homes: one-seventh of the drugs administered to patients are given incorrectly; most drugs are given to make patients easier to handle; the average food expenditure is less than one dollar per patient per day; in Minnesota, a sampling of 100 facilities revealed that the amount of physician care per patient averages 2.5 minutes per week; and the National Fire Prevention Association lists nursing homes as the most unsafe place to live.

Assuming only partial validity of these assertions reveals a disappointing picture of what Americans provide for their aged citizens. It is puzzling why such conditions not only would be tolerated, but indirectly would be encouraged economically by Federal funding in the form of allocations (Pryor, 1970). Part of the answer may be afforded by attention to the general historical evolution of nursing homes and consideration of the social status currently ascribed to aged Americans.

THE EVOLUTION OF AGED INSTITUTIONS AND THE AGED ROLE

Institutional care for the aged was provided in the Eastern hemisphere as early as the third century (Townsend, 1964). Western Europe, the major cultural ancestor of the United States, did not provide such care until Medieval times; during this era various monasteries established "Houses of Pity" to minister to a heterogeneous group including the aged, the destitute, the sick, and the disabled. These repositories were indirectly eradicated by the Reformation Parliament with its dissolution of the English monastic structure. Subsequently, institutional care of the aged, as well as other socially rejected groups, was relegated to Poor Houses established under the Poor Relief Act of 1601 (Townsend, 1964).

In the United States an awareness of the need for community involvement with the problems of the aging emerged around the middle of the 19th century as a minor part of the general "charity organization movement" (Field, 1970). Individuals such as Jane Addams made pioneering, but isolated, contributions by educating their communities to the issue, by encouraging the construction of appropriately modified living facilities, and by establishing medical care with a convenient, house-call style of service delivery. Between 1920 and 1930, other sporadic, small-scale innovations appeared including sheltered workshops for retired workers and cash allowances to encourage continued community residence.

Political leaders became involved in developing provisions for the aged when the elderly population increased sufficiently in size to attract public attention (Field, 1970). The Social Security Act, passed in 1935, allocated Federal funds to retirees and other financially disabled older persons. The number of nursing homes, retirement homes, and homes for the aged — which was diminutive prior to 1935 — increased dramatically to accommodate the newly monied aged population (Morris, 1967).

These early living accommodations were organized as private boarding homes. With the passage of time, several concurrent social developments converged to transform their original home-like milieu into a nursing home atmosphere. The resident population in these private facilities swelled, since Old Age Assistance was withheld from residents of public institutions. There was an increase in average resident age. Finally, there was an increase in incidence of illness producing a greater demand for medical services (Morris, 1967).

In 1950 amendments to the Social Security Act extended its coverage to include residents of public institutions. There was a subsequent increase in the number of governmental facilities, most of which followed the "nursing home" precedent set earlier by private institutions.

Historically, the current American aged role as a discrete entity may be traced to the emergence of the era of technocracy: "many of the responsibilities formerly allotted to older people became irrelevant in a mechanized economic system and a fast-changing society. . . . [White House Conference on Aging, 1971, p. 16]." Since the prestige or status of the aged in a given society is unequivocally dependent on the number of important functions they perform in that society (Simmons, 1964), the aged person became in our contemporary culture a low-status deviant in two senses. First, he was in a statistical minority, at the socially devalued end of the age distribution. But second, and more important, he was a functionless person, an onus on the majority. Consequently, a societal solution to the problem he created was found by labeling him "old," attributing the cause of his difficulties to natural biological deterioration (thus exonerating the rest of the populace), and eliminating him as a visible problem by relegation to an institutional setting.

Two concurrent factors in our society have contributed to the current explosion of the social problem posed by the aged to near-crisis proportions. First, the number of people in the over-65 age bracket has increased dramatically over the past seven decades. Since the turn of the century, the proportion of persons 65 years of age and older has increased by 8% (U.S. Senate, 1961). This increase, generally attributed to progress in public health, nutrition, and living standards (Mensh, 1969), but more correctly attributed to the decrease in infant mortality (Field, 1970), has had the unfortunate corollary of producing large numbers of people for whom society has not yet developed a satisfactory role; and these increasing numbers produced a magnification of the problem. Second, there is no single profession charged exclusively with the care of the aged. Consequently, there have been no concentrated efforts to develop, research, and publicize specific treatment programs for these people. These circumstances leave our society in the uncomfortable position of recognizing that a problem exists, but having no one responsible for ameliorating it.

The precise nature of the American aged stereotype, and consequently the aged role, has been studied by a number of investigators. Their results indicate that the role involves dressing more conservatively (Phillips, 1962), confining one's friendships to members of one's own age group (Phillips, 1962), withdrawing from social involvements (Turner, 1967), being in poor health (Boyd & Oakes, 1969), being unable to work and therefore financially dependent (Kastenbaum, 1964), and generally being in a markedly different and predominantly negative period of life (Kastenbaum, 1964; Palmore, 1971).

This role is obviously low in status and presumably aversive. That it is, in fact, unpleasant is indicated by two sets of data: the older person's resistance to labeling himself as aged and the younger public's negative attitudes toward aging. Kastenbaum and Durkee (1964) found that people over 70 years of age consistently classify themselves as middle aged. Similarly, Phillips (1962), using a sample of 342 persons aged 60 and over, found that 61% classified themselves as middle aged (compared with only 15% who classified themselves as old); 67% believed that other people thought they were middle aged; and 62% thought they felt younger than most people their age. As for the younger public's attitude toward aging, Aaronson (1966) found that older people are generally perceived as constricted and socially inept. Young women hold less unfavorable attitudes toward the elderly than do young men (Silverman, 1963), although both sexes have negative attitudes (Tuckman, 1965).

Because the aged role is so aversive to persons over 65 as well as to the younger public, one would expect a person to be hesitant to adopt it, even if society ascribed the role to him on the basis of an arbitrary age boundary. In fact, however, the nature of the aged role and the mechanisms of American culture interact to virtually impose the role of the aged on senior citizens, particularly senior citizens who have been confined to an institutional setting. The veracity of this statement may be demonstrated by an analysis of the components of the cultural stereotype of becoming aged.

FACTORS INFLUENCING ROLE ADOPTION

Physical health is the most important component of the aged role since it has been identified as the primary index used by a person to denote either another (Kastenbaum, 1964) or himself (Phillips, 1962) as aged. "The concept of 'old' is inextricably intermingled with the concept of 'sick' [Eisdorfer, 1969, p. 73]." It has long been thought that increasing age in and of itself naturally produced physical deterioration. While the human body may well become more susceptible to various disease processes with age, research indicates that there are no natural disease processes of aging (U.S. DHEW, 1970).

The contention that illness will accompany and indicate the onset of old age is a demonstrably powerful self-fulfilling social prophecy. The person over 65 expects sickness or physical discomfort to accompany aging naturally. Because discomfort is expected and appropriate, he accepts it as indicative of aging itself, rather than of a reversible or arrestable disease (Boyd & Oakes, 1969). Therefore, there is subtle but pernicious role encouragement to overlook health precautions and forego treatment. There is also likely to be a genuine hesitation to consult a physician, since the pronouncement of illness would be equivalent, given the cultural context, to the pronouncement of being aged.

The myth of a natural disease process of aging also affects what happens to those persons over 65 who do consult physicians. Most medical practitioners dislike working with the aged (Field, 1970), have usually received training that stressed the futility of treating this population (Hazell, 1960), and have only minimal motivation toward curing them (Boyd & Oakes, 1969). Barrow (1971) found that one-third of this nation's practicing physicians have a negative stereotype of the aged and expect aged patients to be both uncooperative and frustrating. This belief is likely to affect the physician's reaction to the elderly patient and consequently whether that patient continues treatment; it would most certainly affect whether these physicians would seek out aged patients. Barrow (1971) also found that half the practicing physicians regard aging as a non-disease-related and irreversible deteriorative process. As might be expected, these physicians employ fewer preventive medical procedures with the aged.

The deleterious effects of absent or improper medical care born of misconceptions is exacerbated by economic considerations, as medical costs in this inflationary era far outstrip funds available to the aged. Persons over 65 spend less than $311 annually on medical care (Brotman, 1968) — only $25 a year more than the average American (U.S. Bureau of Census, 1971). In addition, there are indications that more than one-third of this $311 is spent on tranquilizers (Tomlinson, 1972) rather than ameliorative drugs.

Friedsom and Martin (1963) found that older people rate their health more negatively than do their attending physicians. These results are difficult to interpret: probable biases on the parts of both the physicians and the patients render the assignment of either rating as a veridical standard arbitrary. Denney, Kole, and Matarazzo (1965) found that the aged person's negative health rating was an habitual pattern of rating perceived illness unrelated to prior illness; Desroches, Kaiman, and Ballard (1967) found that the number of physical complaints was unrelated to actual physical health. All these findings suggest again that illness is expected to accompany aging and, therefore, is permitted to do so. For the person over 65, the sick-aged role and its stoic acceptance become socially appropriate and consequently encouraged. It is clear and not surprising that aging and illness do correlate. What is less obvious is the intricate network of social misconceptions and consequent customs that unnecessarily inflate this correlation.

Employment status is a second index used by a person to judge whether he is aged (Kastenbaum, 1964). One of the first indications that a person is being socially classified as aged comes when he experiences job discrimination on the basis of age (President's Council on Aging, 1963). The designation of specific age limits beyond which an employer will not consider a worker for a vacant job, regardless of ability, has become a characteristic pattern in the 30 states that do not prohibit this practice. As a result, over 50% of the job openings developing in these states' private economy are closed to applicants over 55 years of age (U.S. Congress, 1965).

Employers generally contend that decreasing physical capability with advancing age is the rationale for imposing upper age limits. However, in 70% of 1965 cases in which employers made such a claim, no supporting evidence was presented. Moreover, upper age limits vary across different employers between 25 and 60 years of age for jobs involving comparable physical exertion and demands for strength (U.S. Congress, 1965). Despite the fact that the competence and work performance of workers over 60 are, by any general measures, at least equal to those of younger workers (U.S. Congress, 1965), employers continue perfunctorily to exclude them from consideration.

It would appear that this nonworking status is imposed forcefully primarily on the basis of socioeconomic policy rather than biological fact. In 1968 only 27.3% of males over the age of 65 were employed, usually in self-employed or part-time positions (U.S. DHEW, 1970) — less than half the number who wanted to be employed (Boyd & Oakes, 1969). Yet in 1890, during an era of hard labor conditions and rudimentary medical knowledge, nearly 70% of American males aged 65 and over were employed (U.S. Congress, 1965).

Job discrimination and forced retirement naturally result in a decrement in financial resources. For most of the elderly, social security benefits represent the major source of income (U.S. DHEW, 1970). Because the vast majority of older persons have virtually no financial assets to supplement their pensions, many are barely outside the poverty border; almost 15% of the nation's poverty problem involves the aged 10% of the population (U.S. Congress, 1965).

This financial status has several effects, not the least of which is the degradation befalling any impoverished member of a generally affluent society (Kalish, 1971). The person becomes, by definition, financially dependent and therefore in a devalued position that is associated with age (Kastenbaum, 1964). Limited financial resources discourage the aged individual from becoming involved in recreational activities; less than $40 per year is typically spent on recreation (Brotman, 1968). This economically induced social withdrawal not only additionally indicates the onset of old age (Turner, 1967), but directly contributes to psychological deterioration (Giordano, J. L., & Giordano, G., 1969). Finally, decreased financial resources encourage the aged individual to accept supplementary Federal aid provided only if the person is sick (U.S. Senate, 1971a), thus further forcing the person to adopt the sick-aged role.

The discrimination-retirement practice, an ingrained custom with little or no justification in fact, has far-reaching ramifications affecting more than the financial status of the older American. Perhaps more important, it also removes a central social role without providing a socially valued alternative and thus initiates a negative self-image and self-label (Lehr & Dreher, 1969). The older person is required to stop working in a society whose value system degrades the nonworker (Kalish, 1971).

As a final factor, the attitudes of friends and relatives have been shown to be an important determinant of whether a person adopts the aged role (Phillips, 1962). It is clear, however, that friends and relatives function primarily as transmitters of society's attitudes in general: social expectations converge at the age of 65 to produce a status change, a consequent role change, and a difference in how the individual is perceived and treated by others and by himself.

The Effects of Institutionalization

Once a person has been ascribed the role-label "aged," some decision must be made about what changes, if any, will be made in the disposition of that person. Early in this century, the home of adult children was the customary residence for aging parents (Lowenthal & Zilli, 1969). This extended family structure was conducive to the retention of social relationships and a meaningful role. Later in the century, however, social trends toward smaller houses, fewer children, longer life spans (necessitating a greater time commitment from the child), and increased mobility produced a shift from familial responsibility to societal responsibility for housing and caring for the aged (Morris, 1967). Institutions became the socially sanctioned and appropriate residence for the aged; as might be anticipated, the single most influential factor in the decision to enter a nursing home has been shown to be the advice of friends and relatives and the advice of professionals (U.S. DHEW, 1966).

This sanction of nursing homes is generally based on the premise that such facilities provide medical services vital to their aged residents (Dick, Friedsam, & Martin, 1964) — services whose necessity is implied by the mythical aged-sick role synonymity. In fact, however, statistics indicate that only a small minority of nursing home residents require more than minimal care, such as proper diets or pill medication (Tomlinson, 1972). In addition, evidence clearly indicates that actual medical provisions in homes for the aged are usually inadequate (Tomlinson, 1972). Nursing homes, traditionally conceptualized as medical facilities, appear to be in actuality more like business enterprises, with over 50 national nursing home corporations marketing stock that has been known to sell at 100 times its per-share earning (U.S. Senate, 1970). The result of such institutions' lucrative nature beneath a socially legitimate façade has been a proliferation of substandard facilities which "have too often been designated as a final resting place for the elderly, the infirm, and those members of society no longer supported by the community [Morris, 1967, p. 73]."

When a person is relegated to a nursing home, the full weight of the aged role is brought to bear on him and his behaviors. Nursing home staffs, adopting the societal conception of nursing homes, are medically oriented; hence, they tend to treat the resident as if he were sick, paying attention to him only if he requires medical assistance and, in some cases, actually encouraging the person to unnecessarily adopt the sick role (MacDonald & Butler, 1973; Turner, 1967). The residents are socially isolated without opportunities for community interaction, contact with younger persons, or exposure to stimulating and meaningful activities (Turner, 1967) so that behavioral alternatives to aged- and sick-role behaviors are at a minimum. Like other institutions (Paul, 1969), nursing homes have been shown to actively hasten deterioration (Lowenthal & Zilli, 1969) and induce passivity. More than in other institutions, there is a morbid sense of finality signified by incarceration in a nursing home; the remission rate is well known to the public as well as to the residents.

Senility is one of the most striking examples of institution-induced deterioration in the elderly. Estimates of the incidence of "confusion" or senility in nursing home residents vary from 21% (Derrick, 1967; Morris, 1967) to 80% (Miller, Keller, Liebel, & Meirowitz, 1966). For many years, senility (like other organic diseases) was considered to be a normal concomitant of growing older. While brain deterioration does occur more frequently in later life, it is severe enough to require institutionalization in only 1% or 2% of the aged population. Senility is more properly described as a social label, differentially applied, that produces a status change, a consequent expectancy and treatment change, and a resulting behavioral change in the person so labeled (Baizerman & Ellison, 1971).

There are at least three influences unrelated to organic cortical deterioration which may result in senile-like "symptoms" and precipitate the spurious ascription of the social label "senile." All these influences are operative both within and without institutions, although it is likely that their effects are exacerbated in institutional settings. The first influence is the general cultural expectancy for senility to accompany aging, an expectancy producing the same pernicious effects as the expectancy of physical discomfort: labeling (or, in this case, mislabeling) and consequent role fulfillment. The second influence is a group of preventable and reversible somatic illnesses with senile-like confusion as a symptomatic side effect. These illnesses frequently remain untreated because of myth-produced misdiagnosis of senility rather than diagnoses of the actual underlying and treatable disease processes (U.S. DHEW, 1970). Third, senile-like confusion may be produced by reduced environmental input or stimulus deprivation (Euster, 1971), a state of affairs very likely to exist within an institutional setting.

Because senility is expected eventually to accompany old age and is considered to be organically irreversible, only one study investigating the possibility of eradicating senile-like "symptoms" has been reported (Cosin, Mort, Post, Westropp, & Williams, 1958). The treatment, which involved active environmental programing, was significantly effective as long as the programing was maintained. Removal of provided activities, of course, resulted in an increase in senile-like symptoms; but when activity programs were reinstituted, confusion decreased.

With recognition of the interactions between the various aspects of the aged role, the impact of social expectations associated with that role, and the environmental reduction of role alternatives, the traditional view of the aged as inherently helpless seems unwarranted. There has been no definitive research to indicate that aging alone is responsible for any of its assumed effects (Birren, Butler, Greenhouse, Sokoloff, & Yarrow, 1971). On the contrary, there have been indications that cultural expectations are the most powerful influences in the development of phenomena associated with aging (Baizerman & Ellison, 1971; Kaplan, 1956; Maddox, 1970).

A SOCIOPSYCHOLOGICAL FORMULATION OF AGING

The thesis from which the present interactional formulation of aging is derived is known more generally as the sociopsychological model of behavior (Ullmann & Krasner, 1969). There are several important premises underlying this formulation. The first premise is that the content of a category or label grouping such as the aged is evanescent, depending for its meaning on the social context surrounding its specific use; as a culture changes, so does its definition of a category (Benedict, 1934; Louden, 1965; Mead, 1935; Murphy &

Leighton, 1965; Rosen & Gregory, 1965; Ullmann & Krasner, 1965). This premise has been illustrated in particular with the label "aged," a category whose definition at present appears to rest primarily on socioeconomic policy.

The second premise of the sociopsychological formulation is that the tendency to assign an individual to a particular category is an act that is perpetuated by its consequences. As Pronko (1963) explains:

> Classification is, first of all, a human activity. It always involves a person observing phenomena in which he can perceive similarities and differences. There is always another essential but easily overlooked point: the observer has a *purpose* or *aim* in ordering those same data [p. 34].

The social rationale for categorizing a person as aged has already been discussed: application of the label legitimizes the labeller's perfunctory dismissal of a person who has become societally functionless and therefore burdensome.

A third premise of the sociopsychological model is that once a category label is assigned, social expectations coerce the individual, both subtly and overtly, into acting in accordance with the entirety of that stereotype.

> Being labelled in itself has an enormous effect. The crux of the matter conceptually is that while some specific aspect of the person's *behavior* leads to labelling, in practice it is the total *person* who is labelled and who is then reacted to in terms of his label [Ullmann & Krasner, 1969, p. 207].

Thus, label application leads to a difference in the behavior of other people toward the labelled individual. He is expected and encouraged to fulfill his label role, and he is not expected to and discouraged from behaving out of accordance with his socially stipulated role (Ayllon & Azrin, 1968).

Considerable evidence has been cited to illustrate the tenability of these premises for the "aged." Recent geropsychological research lends additional support. One of the most popular areas in geropsychological literature has been disengagement, defined as the increasing tendency to disassociate oneself from people and activities with increasing age (Bell, 1967; Carp, 1968; Havighurst, 1968; Lipman & Smith, 1968; Roman & Faietz, 1967; Youmans, 1966). "As originally propounded, disengagement was presumed to be a natural or normal attribute of old age, and by implication, at least, a desirable one [Botwinik, 1970, p. 251]." Most current investigators, however, have rejected the notion that disengagement is inevitable, and have suggested instead that cultural patterns are rejecting of the older person and push dissociation on him (Botwinik, 1970; Davis & Obrist, 1966; Maddox, 1970; Strauss, 1963; Youmans, 1969).

Other repeated findings in the geropsychological literature are confounded by culturally derived misassumptions of inevitability similar to the misassumption in the original notion of disengagement. Memory, usually considered inherently deficient with advancing age (Davis & Obrist, 1966), has been shown to be as adequate as memory during younger years, provided original level of learning is equated (Hulicka & Weiss, 1965). Reaction time is also considered to deteriorate naturally as a function of increasing age (Botwinik & Thompson, 1966; Weiss, 1965). There is some doubt, however, as to whether it is age per se which slows the individual, or whether it is the lack of exercise, a frequent but not necessary concomitant of old age, which at least in part produces the slowing (Botwinik & Thompson, 1968). Participation in physical activity over a period of time has been shown to improve speed of response in the elderly (Barry, Steinmetz, Page & Rodahl, 1966; Clement, 1966).

Most of the geropsychological research of the last decade (Botwinik, 1970) has been directed toward discovering what was different about being aged; and discovered differences were almost invariably attributed to aging alone as the causal agent. There are two responses to this state of affairs. First, strong support is offered that most reported conclusions have been incorrect at the inferential level. That is, the causal connection between aging and its presumed effects is at least unwarranted and probably erroneous. But second, and on a different level, the primary issue in geropsychological research has been "What are the effects of aging?" It is clear that, on a variety of dimensions, persons over 65 are, for whatever reasons, generally different. At this point, social necessity demands that research be directed toward discovering methods for eradicating those differences that are myth-produced and avoidable (for example, social withdrawal), thwarting unpleasant differences which do, in fact, exist (for example, increased susceptibility to illness), and compensating for unpleasant differences that exist as a consequence of our current cultural atmosphere (for example, exclusion from employment and family roles) by providing meaningful alternatives.

Kastenbaum (1965) accepts as general knowledge the thesis that death occurs with substantial frequency within one month following admission to an institution for the aged. Since continued interest and activity (Chebotaryov & Sachuk, 1964) and a sense of continued usefulness (Butler, 1967) are significantly related to survival and since admission to current institutions usually results in "institutionalization" — a state of apathy and lack of motivation (Ayllon & Azrin, 1968), Kastenbaum's (1965) conclusion is tenable. To concede that such is presently the case, however, is not to agree that it must necessarily be so.

A SOCIOPSYCHOLOGICAL TREATMENT MODEL

There is evidence to suggest what sort of treatment programs would be effective for treating the institutionalized aged. Several reports of successful individually tailored procedures have appeared. Fowler, Fordyce, and Berni (1969) made staff attention contingent on appropriate but previously deficient behavior for three of their ward's residents. This manipulation was effective in increasing one person's toleration of elevation on a tilt-table to the level requisite for ambulation. It produced an increased fluid intake critical to the rehabilitation of a second resident. And finally, it resulted in the third resident's wearing a back brace for adequate periods of time to become sufficiently ambulatory for discharge. Chamings (1969) scheduled staff attention to discourage one person's incessant sick-role behaviors; following the institution of this procedure, the person's behavior became much more appropriate and self-directed.

Encouraging descriptions of ward-wide programs have also appeared. Lipscomb (1971) reports that his community-based agency's emphasis on early referral, coupled with a treatment rather than custodial orientation, resulted in continued community residence for the majority of the persons over 65 referred for "psychiatric evaluations." Moody, Baron, and Monk (1970) introduced daily discussion sessions for a nine-person group on their geriatric ward; mean gain on the Life Satisfaction Index after one week was 2.5 scale points. Giordano, J.L., and Giordano, G., (1969) introduced a comprehensive program including both recreational and rehabilitative activities; informal observations of the results of their procedure indicated that their environmental programing transformed the nursing home atmosphere into an active, involving one for its residents. Informal observations made by a second observer after the program had been in effect for more than a year corroborated the conclusions of the original report (Harsanyi, 1970). A similar procedure whose effectiveness was documented with more controlled observations was reported by Cosin et al. (1958). More recently, McClannahan and Risley (1972) have begun to investigate manipulable parameters which influence the degree to which aged persons participate in provided activities. And Martin and Shaughnessy's (1970) results suggest that a very powerful incentive for encouraging such participation can be informing the residents that they are preparing for a return to the community. In short, successful programs for the aged have consistently included considerable emphasis on keeping residents active (Smith, 1965). To accomplish this, the environment has been structured so that the resident can continue activity and social involvement to improve present functioning or maintain optimal functioning (Martin & Shaughnessy, 1970).

Structured environmental programs in general (Atthowe & Krasner, 1968; Ayllon & Azrin, 1968; Schaefer & Martin, 1966) are fashioned in three stages. First, the current functional levels of the individuals in the target population are assessed. Second, certain behaviors such as social interaction and participation in activities are established as desirable or beneficial. Third, both the physical (Lindsley, 1964) and the social (Hall & Broden, 1967) environments are structured to foster the development and maintenance of these desirable behaviors.

There is evidence to suggest that the application of environmental programing to the aged population would eradicate some of the most unpleasant effects of our present institutional system. For example, studies have repeatedly shown that increased age tends to be associated with increased isolation and introversion (Cameron, 1967a, 1967b; Walton & Hope, 1967). Structured environmental or remotivation programs, however, have as one of their primary goals the redevelopment of participation in social interaction and communication (Atthowe & Krasner, 1968); the anticipated beneficial effect of such programing for the aged is suggested by the findings that reminiscing in social groups is correlated with a high survival rate (McMahon & Rhudick, 1964). As a second example, it has been suggested that feelings of inferiority and loss of self-esteem are among the major causes of depression in the elderly (Zung, 1967). But, as Atthowe and Krasner (1968) point out, "the [environmental] program's most notable contribution to patient life is . . . putting the burden of responsibility, and thus, more self-respect on the patient himself [p. 42]."

Improvement in patient morale has not been related to the number of activities available, but rather the amount of actual participation in those available activities (Maddox, 1963). Thus, it is not sufficient simply to supply behavioral alternatives to inactivity; residents must be encouraged to participate in them. Such encouragement is the explicit task of remotivation programs. In fact, there is evidence to indicate that extrinsic factors (such as programed reinforcement) are more important to some oldsters than intrinsic rewards provided by various activities (Saleh, 1964). Being reinforced for activity following retirement has been shown to have a powerful positive impact on happiness, self-esteem, and relationships with other people (Carp, 1968).

The available activities should not only be interesting, but should also be of some social value to provide meaningful social roles (U.S. DHEW, 1970). Communities can, in fact, usefully engage the services of the elderly. Hickey, T., Hickey, L. A., and Kalish (1968) and Hickey and Kalish (1968) found that children regard old people somewhat favorably; thus, they can interact with the elderly absenting communication of the usual social stigma directed toward advancing age. Johnson (1967), capitalizing on this tendency, established a "foster grand-parent" program for emotionally disturbed youngsters. Gray and Kasteler (1970) established a parallel program and demonstrated that it did, in fact, improve the aged participants' sense of well-being. Similar community involvements could reduce the sense of isolation and obliterate the feeling of being, in the words of one resident, "no longer needed, [with] nothing to do [Hudson, 1970, p. 769]."

SUMMARY AND CONCLUSIONS

Many of the problems in both community and institutional treatments of the elderly developed because of the unplanned and unsystematic emergence of provisions for the aged and remained because of widely held cultural misassumptions about aging. The social sciences have progressed sufficiently at this point, however, to permit the strategic introduction of treatment practices based on documented effectiveness with either similar target problems or similar target populations.

Successful intervention will require multilevel changes. The dilemma of nursing home residents does not arise solely because of poor institutional management; it is produced in part by inadequate and misdirected national social legislation, insufficient local outpatient community facilities, and pernicious self-fulfilling cultural myths. Evaluative research must be considered a crucial concomitant of innovation at all levels, to insure that anticipated effects are in fact produced, and to prevent stagnation in once-effective methods rendered obsolete by changes over time.

On the National Level

(1) There should be stricter enforcement of the Civil Rights Act proscription against age discrimination, particularly in employment and housing.

(2) Financial aid to elderly individuals must not be made dependent on sickness, nor should aid be increased because of sickness. Health care — both preventive and ameliorative — should be provided, but remuneration should be given directly to the physicians and facilities involved.

(3) A realistic and enforceable system of national accreditation for elderly care facilities should be devised. Accreditation standards should be more comprehensive than current state license requirements, including rehabilitation program and psychosocial treatment requisites as well as health and safety standards.

(4) Accreditation inspections should be frequent, at irregular intervals, and unannounced. The results of these inspections should be made public, and facilities should be required to post a copy in the admissions office.

(5) Federal subsidies to institutions should be granted on the basis of a dual index incorporating both adequacy of provisions and effectiveness of treatment. High standards, rather than low standards, should be perpetuated by monetary support.

On the Community Level

(1) Multiservice, outpatient senior citizen facilities should be organized in the community to provide consultation as well as home-centered services. These facilities should have the dual functions of preventing unnecessary institutionalization by providing minor services and identifying persons who do need institutional rehabilitation before their conditions have drastically deteriorated.

(2) Low-cost senior citizen independent housing complexes should be constructed within the community. They should be built with appropriate physical adaptations in a convenient geographical location (near transit systems, recreational facilities, and shopping centers). Medical and psychological consultants should be available on a regularly scheduled basis to provide services within the housing complex.

On the Institutional Level

(1) Institutions should be located within the community so that residents may remain in familiar surroundings and retain community relationships. To facilitate retention of relationships, transportation systems should be both convenient and provided. Residents should be encouraged to make use of these provisions for independently arranged community visitations and visitors.

(2) The facility should be constructed with reasonable and appropriate physical adaptations.

(3) Facilities should have a small resident capacity. This guideline is a reversal of the present trend toward larger institutions (Morris, 1967), but is important for two reasons. First, it would encourage the provision of more facilities, enabling residents to remain closer to their original communities. Second, it would prevent the displacement of goals frequently associated with the development of bureaucracies in large institutions (Ullmann, 1967).

(4) Administrative procedures should clearly reflect the priorities of the institution. Care should be taken to insure that recordkeeping enhances rather than inhibits treatment effectiveness. A comprehensive handbook describing systematic and efficient procedures has been prepared by Miller (1969).

(5) Inservice training programs should be provided by consultants for the regular staff. These programs should be designed to provide current and specific information about treatment procedures specifically suited for problems of the aging. Such training programs would serve the dual functions of improving staff morale and upgrading staff quality.

(6) Staff members should be given feedback regularly concerning the degree to which their actual performance corresponds to the performance practices outlined in their training programs.

(7) Social workers should be included as a necessary staff position to promote community placement of residents who no longer need the supportive environment of a restorative residential facility. Residents should be evaluated by the social worker as soon as they are admitted to estimate probable length of residence and location of postinstitutional placement. If the family appears to be a desirable and reasonable placement target, the social worker should provide training in maintenance techniques for the family and generally promote continued family involvement with the resident to prevent his being gradually excluded by the family structure. If the family does not appear to be an appropriate placement target, the social worker should locate alterna-

tive placements, such as senior citizen housing complexes or community halfway houses. Near discharge, the social worker should ease the transition from institution to community by providing resident visits to the target placement locaion.

(8) Nursing homes should provide a variety of individual and group activities that are recreational and have social value. The activities should be recurrent and scheduled, visible to a social audience, and foster the formation of new roles and integration into social networks.

(9) The recreational activities in particular should be diversions considered attractive not only by residents, but also by guests and volunteers. The guests and volunteers should be encouraged to participate in these activities, providing additional community contact for the residents.

(10) The nursing home as a community agency should be interwoven administratively and functionally with other community agencies so that residents could perform socially valued functions and so that the facility itself would be conceptualized as a community facility rather than a facility exclusively for the aging. The community function served would depend on the needs of the particular community in which the facility was located; possible alternatives include day-care centers, apprenticeship training centers for semi-skilled labor, adult education centers, and community information telephone services. Remuneration should be provided to the residents for their participation.

(11) The atmosphere of the nursing home should be changed from a medical-custodial one to an active, homelike atmosphere. To accomplish this transformation:

(a) Residents should be allowed and encouraged to retain personal belongings and decorate their rooms.
(b) Staff members should not wear uniforms.
(c) Furniture should be arranged to resemble a residential facility rather than a hospital.
(d) Residents should be encouraged to actively participate in all aspects of program planning.
(e) The staff should convey an expectancy for activity and improvement rather than passivity and deterioration.
(f) Resident participation in activities should be encouraged by staff expectations, contingent staff social approval, and, if appropriate, social-learning procedures (Atthowe & Krasner, 1968) depending on the individual resident's particular level of functioning.

(g) Most important, persons who require primarily medical treatment should be tranferred to hospitals. It is unreasonable to expect nursing homes to become actual medical treatment facilities or to presume that they will be appealing if they continue to pretend to serve this function.

On the Cultural Level

(1) Both blatant and subtle castigations of aged persons in the mass media should be discontinued.

(2) Reeducation through advertisements and other informational channels should be instituted to correct misconceptions about aging.

That some measures must be taken to improve the lot of the elderly is hardly debatable. Projectionists estimate that by the year 2000 there will be over 32 million persons aged 65 or over — more than the total United States population in 1860 (Mensh, 1969). There will be increasingly greater numbers of people in the aged category, and there are no indices suggesting that the aged role left unattended will become any less unpleasant.

There is dramatic evidence to show that the contemporary dilemma of the aging is horrendous. A higher percentage of older people than younger people take their own lives (Botwinik, 1970). This high suicide rate tends to stem from perceived illness — which may or may not be illusory (Gardner, Bahn, & Mack, 1964), from loneliness (McCullough, Philip, & Carstairs, 1967), and very often from depression (Gardner et al., 1964; Hedri, 1967; Krupinski, Stoller & Polke, 1967; Walsh & McCarthy, 1965). "In this era when we are called upon to be 'relevant,' there are few areas of investigation which are more necessary [Botwinik, 1970, p. 257]." Alternatives to the existing situation must be provided.

REFERENCES

Aaronson, B. S. Personality stereotypes of aging. *Journal of Gerontology,* 1966, **21, 458-462.**

Atthowe, J., & Krasner, L. Preliminary report on the application of contingent reinforcement procedures (token economy) on a "chronic" psychiatric ward. *Journal of Abnormal Psychology,* 1968. **73(1), 37-43.**

Ayllon, T., & Azrin, N. H. *The token economy: A motivational system for therapy and rehabilitation*. New York: Appleton-Century-Crofts, 1968.

Baizerman, M., & Ellison, D. L. A social role analysis of senility. *Gerontologist*, 1971, **11(2, Part 1), 163-169.**

Barrow, G. M. Physician's attitudes toward aging and the aging process. *Dissertation Abstracts International*, 1971, **32(4-A), 2205.**

Barry, A. J., Steinmetz, J. R., Page, H. F., & Rodahl, K. The effects of physical conditioning on older individuals. II. Motor performance and cognitive functioning. *Journal of Gerontology*, 1966, **21, 192-199.**

Bell, T. The relationship between social involvements and feeling old among residents in homes for the aged. *Journal of Gerontology*, 1967, **22, 17-22.**

Benedict, R. Anthropology and the abnormal. *Journal of General Psychology*, 1934, **10, 59-82.**

Birren, J. B., Butler, R. N., Greenhouse, S. W., Sokoloff, J., & Yarrow, M. R. (Eds.) *Human aging: A biological and behavioral study*. (USPHS Pub. No. 986) U.S. Department of Health, Education and Welfare. Washington, D.C.: U.S. Government Printing Office, 1971.

Botwinik, J. Geropsychology. *Psychological Bulletin*, 1970, 150-272.

Botwinik, J., & Thompson, L. W. Age difference in reaction time: An artifact? *Gerontologist*, 1968, 25-38.

Botwinik, J., & Thompson, L. W. Components of reaction time in relation to age and sex. *Journal of Genetic Psychology*, 1966, **108, 175-183.**

Boyd, R., & Oakes, C. (Eds.) *Foundations of Practical Gerontology*. Columbia: University of South Carolina Press, 1969.

Braverman, J. Report on state licensure regulations: Codes contribute to low standards of care. *Modern Nursing Home*, 1970, **24(6), 5-9.**

Brotman, H. B. *Who are the aged: A demographic view*. Occasional papers in gerontology number 1 of the Institute of Gerontology. Ann Arbor: The University of Michigan, 1968.

Butler, R. N. Aspects of survival and adaptation in human aging. *American Journal of Psychiatry*, 1967, 123, 1233-1243.

Butler, R. N. "Age-ism: Another form of bigotry." *Gerontologist*, 1969, **9(4), 243-246.**

Cameron, P. Age as a determinant of differences in nonintellective psychological dimensions. *Dissertation Abstracts*, 1967, **28B, 1157.(a)**

Cameron, P. Introversion and egocentricity among the aged. *Journal of Gerontology*, 1967, **22, 465-468.(b)**

Carp, F. M. Some components of disengagement. *Journal of Gerontology*, 1968, **23, 382-386.**

Chamings, P. Need a little help. *American Journal of Nursing*, 1969, **69(9), 1918-1920.**

Chebotaryov, D. F., & Sachuk, N. N. Sociomedical examination of longevous people in the U.S.S.R. *Journal of Gerontology*, 1964, **19,** 435-439.

Clement, F. Effect of physical activity on the maintenance of intellectual capacities. *Gerontologist*, 1966, **6(126), 91-92.**

Cosin, L. Z., Mort, M., Post, F., Westropp, C., & Williams, M. Experimental treatment of persistent senile confusion. *International Journal of Social Psychiatry*, 1958, **4,** 24-42.

Davis, S. H., & Obrist, W. D. Age differences in learning and retention of verbal material. *Cornell Journal of Social Relations*, 1966, **1, 95-103.**

Denney, D., Kole, D. M., & Matarazzo, R. G. The relationship between age and the number of symptoms reported by patients. *Journal of Gerontology*, 1965, **20, 50-53.**

Derrick, W. P. Social behavior of state hospital nursing home patients. *Gerontologist*, 1967, **7, 283-285.**

Desroches, H. F., Kaiman, B. D., & Ballard, H. T. Factors influencing reporting of physical symptoms by the aged patient. *Geriatrics*, 1967, **22, 169-175.**

Dick, H., Friedsam, H., & Martin, C. Residential patterns of aged persons prior to institutionalization. *Journal of Marriage and the Family*, 1964, **26, 96-98.**

Eisendorfer, R. As cited in R. Boyd & C. Oakes (Eds.), *Foundations of practical gerontology.* Columbia: University of South Carolina Press, 1969.

Euster, G. L. A system of groups in institutions for the aged. *Social Casework*, 1971, **52(B), 523-529.**

Field, M. *Depth and extent of the geriatric problem.* Springfield, Ill.: Charles C. Thomas, 1970.

Fowler, R. W., Fordyce, W. E., & Berni, R. Operant conditioning in chronic illness. *American Journal of Nursing*, 1969, **69(6), 1226-1228.**

Friedsom, H. J., & Martin, H. W. A comparison of self and physician's health ratings in an older population. *Journal of Health and Human Behavior*, 1963, **4, 179-183.**

Gardner, E. A., Bahn, A. K., & Mack, M. Suicide and psychiatric care in the aging. *Archives of General Psychiatry*, 1964, **10, 547-553.**

Giordano, J. L., & Giordano, G. An activities program in a home for the aged in the Virgin Islands. *Social Work*, 1969, **14(2), 61-66.**

Gray, R. M., & Kasteler, J. M. An evaluation of the effectiveness of a foster grandparent project. *Sociology and Social Research*, 1970, **54(2), 181-189.**

Hall, R. V., & Broden, M. Behavior changes in brain-injured children through social reinforcement. *Journal of Experimental Child Psychology*, 1967, **5, 463-479.**

Harsanyi, S. L. Social attitudes regarding aging as a disability. *Journal of Rehabilitation*, 1970, **36(6), 24-27.**

Havighurst, R. J. Personality and patterns of aging. *Gerontologist*, 1968, **8, 20-23.**

Hazell, K. *Social and medical problems of the elderly.* London: Hutchinson Medical Publications, Ltd., 1960.

Hedri, A. Suicide in advanced ages. *Schweitzer Archives of Neurological Psychiatry*, 1967, **100, 179-202.**

Hickey, T., Hickey, L. A., & Kalish, R. A. Children's perceptions of the elderly. *Journal of Genetic Psychology*, 1968, **112, 227-235.**

Hickey, T., & Kalish, R.. A. Young people's perceptions of adults. *Journal of Gerontology*, 1968, **23, 1215-1219.**

Hudson, J. H. Decision. *American Journal of Nursing*, Apr. 1970, **760-769.**

Hulicka, I. M., & Weiss, R. L. Age differences in retention as a function of learning. *Journal of Consulting Psychology*. 1965, **29, 125-129.**

Johnson, R. Foster grandparents for emotionally disturbed children. *Children*, 1967, **14, 46-52.**

Jones, H. E. (Ed.) *Research on aging.* New York: Social Science Research Council, 1956.

Kalish, R. A. Social values and the elderly. *Mental Hygiene*, 1971, **55(1), 51-54.**

Kaplan, O. J. (Ed.) *Mental disorders in later life.* Stanford: Stanford University Press, 1956.

Kastenbaum, R. (Ed.) *Contributions to the psychobiology of aging.* New York: Springer, 1965.

Kastenbaum, R. (Ed.) *New thoughts on old age.* New York: Springer, 1964.

Kastenbaum, R., & Durkee, S. Elderly people view old age. In R. Kastenbaum (Ed.), *New thoughts on old age.* New York: Springer, 1964, 250-264.

Krupinshi, J., Stoller, A., & Polke, P. Attempted suicides admitted to the Mental Health Department, Victoria, Australia: A socio-epidemiological study.

Larson, L. G. How to select a nursing home. *American Journal of Nursing*, 1969, **69(5), 1034-1037.**

Lehr, U., & Dreher, G. Determinants of attitudes toward retirement. In R. J. Havighurst, J. M. A. Munnichs, B. Neugarten, & H. Thomae (Eds.), *Adjustment to retirement: A cross-national study.* Assen, The Netherlands: Royal VanGorcum, Ltd., 1969.

Lindsley, O. R. Geriatric behavioral prosthetics. In R. Kastenbaum (Ed.), *New thoughts on old age.* New York: Springer, 1964.

Lipman, A., & Smith, K. J. Functionality of disengagement in old age. *Journal of Gerontology,* 1968, **23, 517-521.**

Lipscomb, C. F. The care of the psychiatrically disturbed elderly patient in the community. *American Journal of Psychiatry,* 1971, **127(8), 107-110.**

Louden, J. B. Social aspects of ideas about treatment. In A. V. S. Deleuck & R. Porter (Eds.), *Transcultural psychiatry.* Boston: Little, Brown, 1965.

Lowenthal, M. F., & Zilli, A. *Colloquium on health and aging of the population.* Basel, Switzerland: S. Karger AG, 1969.

MacDonald, M. L. & Butler, A. K. Reversal of helplessness: The production of walking behavior in nursing home wheelchair residents using behavior modification procedures. *Journal of Gerontology,* 1974, *29,* **97-101.**

Maddox, G. L. Activity and morale: A longitudinal study of selected elderly subjects. *Social Forces,* 1963, **42, 195-204.**

Maddox, G. L. Themes and issues in sociological theories of human aging. *Human Development,* 1970, **13(1), 17-27.**

Martin, M. W., & Shaughnessy, F. D. Country club life eases burdens of aging. *Modern Nursing Home,* 1970, **25(1), 46-47.**

McClannahan, L. E., & Risley, T. R. The organization of group care environments: Living environments for nursing home residents. Paper presented at the Convention of the American Psychological Association, Honolulu, 1972.

McCullough, J. W., Philip, A. E., & Carstairs, G. M. The ecology of suicidal behavior. *British Journal of Psychiatry,* 1967, **113, 313-319.**

McKnight, E. M. *Nursing home research study: Quantitative measurement on nursing services.* U. S. Department of Health, Education and Welfare. Washington, D. C.: U. S. Government Printing Office, 1971.

McMahon, A. W., & Rhudick, P. J. Reminiscing, adaptational significance in the aged. *Archives of General Psychiatry,* 1964, **10, 292-298.**

Mead, M. *Sex and temperament in three primitive societies.* New York: Morrow, 1935.

Mensh, I. N. The aging population and mental health. In S. C. Plog & R. B. Edgerton (Eds.), *Changing perspectives in mental illness.* New York: Holt, Rinehart & Winston, 1969.

Miller, D. B. *The extended care facility: A guide to organization and operation.* New York: McGraw-Hill, 1969.

Miller, M. B., Keller, D., Liebel, E., & Meirowitz, I. Nursing in a skilled nursing home. *American Journal of Nursing,* 1966, 66(2), 321-325.

Moody, L., Baron, V., & Monk, G. Moving the past into the present. *American Journal of Nursing,* 1970, **70(11), 2353-2356.**

Morris, W. W. *Mental health of the older adult.* Proceedings of the University of Iowa's 11th Conference on Gerontology. Iowa City: The Institute of Gerontology, 1967.

Murphy, J. M., & Leighton, A. H. Native conceptions of psychiatric disorder. In J. M. Murphy & A. H. Leighton (Eds.), *Approaches to cross-cultural psychiatry.* Ithaca, N.Y.: Cornell University Press, 1965.

Nader, R. *Old age: The last segregation.* New York: Grossman, 1971.

Palmore, E. Attitudes toward aging as shown by humor. *Gerontologist,* 1971, **11 (3, Part 1), 181-186.**

Paul, G. L. The chronic mental patient: Current status — Future directions. *Psychological Bulletin,* 1969, **71, 81-94.**

Philips, B. S. *The aging in a central Illinois community.* Unpublished doctoral dissertation, University of Illinois, 1962.

President's Council on Aging. *Report to the President.* Washington, D.C.: U.S. Government Printing Office, 1963.

Pronko, N. H. *Textbook of abnormal psychology.* Baltimore: Williams & Wilkins, 1963.

Pryor, D. H. Somewhere between society and the cemetery: Where we put the aged. *The New Republic,* April 15, 1970, 15-17.

Roman, P., & Faietz, P. Organizational structure and disengagement: The emeritus professor. *Gerontologist,* 1967, **7, 147-152.**

Rosen, E., & Gregory, I. *Abnormal psychology.* Philadelphia: Saunders, 1965.

Saleh, S. D. A study of attitude change in the preretirement period. *Journal of Applied Psychology,* 1964, 40, 310-312.

Schaefer, H. H., & Martin, P. L. Behavioral therapy for "apathy" of hospitalized schizophrenics. *Psychological reports,* 1966, **17, 1147-1158.**

Silverman, I. Age and the tendency to withhold response. *Journal of Gerontology,* 1963, **18, 372-375.**

Simmons, L. As cited in Slater, P. E. Cross-cultural views of the aged. In R. Kastenbaum (Ed.), *New thoughts on old age.* New York: Springer, 1964, 229-236.

Smith, E. Nursing services for the aged in housing projects and day centers. *American Journal of Nursing,* 1965, **65(12), 72-74.**

Strauss, D. The relationship between perception of the environment and the retrenchment syndrome in a geriatric population. *Dissertation Abstracts,* 1963, **24, 1275-1276.**

Tomlinson, K. Y. Our shameful nursing homes. *Reader's Digest,* October 1972.

Townsend, P. *The last refuge: A survey of residential institutions and homes for the aged in England and Wales.* London: Routledge and Kegan Paul, 1964.

Turner, H. (Ed.) *Psychological functioning of older people in institutions and in the community.* New York: National Council on Aging, 1967.

Tuckman, J. College students' judgement of the passage of time over the life span. *Journal of Genetic Psychology,* 1965, **107, 43-48.**

Ullmann, L. P. *Institution and outcome: A comparative study of psychiatric hospitals.* New York: Pergamon Press, 1967.

Ullmann, L. P., & Krasner, L. (Eds.) *Case studies in behavior modification.* New York: Holt, Reinhart & Winston, 1965.

Ullmann, L. P., & Krasner, L. *A psychological approach to abnormal behavior.* Englewood Cliffs, N.J.: Prentice-Hall, 1969.

U.S. Bureau of the Census, U.S. Department of Commerce. *Statistical abstract of the United States,* 92nd annual ed., Washington, D.C.: GPO, 1971.

U.S. Congress. *The older American worker: Age discrimination in employment.* Report of the Secretary of Labor under section 715 of the Civil Rights Act of 1964, June, 1965.

U.S. Department of Health, Education, and Welfare. *Nursing home standards guide* (USPHS Pub. No. 827). Washington, D.C.: GPO, 1961.

U. S. Department of Health, Education, and Welfare. *Patterns of living and housing of middle-aged and older people* (USPHS Pub. No. 1496). Washington, D.C.: U.S. Government Printing Office, 1960.

U.S. Department of Health, Education, and Welfare. *Selected articles on nursing homes* (USPHS Pub. No. 732). Washington, D.C.: U.S. Printing Office, 1966.

U.S. Department of Health, Education, and Welfare. *Working with older people: A guide to practice,* Vol. II (USPHS Pub. No. 1459). Washington, D.C.: GPO, 1970.

U.S. Senate. *New population facts on older Americans, 1960.* Staff report to the Special 1961 Committee on Aging. Washington, D.C.: GPO, 1961.

U.S. Senate. *Trends in long-time care.* Pts. 2, 7, 12. Hearing before the Special Committee on Aging, subcommittee on long-term care. Washington, D.C.: GPO, 1970, 1971. (a) (b).

Walsh, D., & McCarthy, P. D. Suicide in Dublin's elderly. *Acta Psychiatrica Scandinavica,* 1965, 41, 227-235.

Walton, H. J., & Hope, K. The 1967 effect of age and personality on doctor's clinical preferences. *British Journal of Social and Clinical Psychology,* 1967, **6, 43-51.**

Weiss, A. D. The locus of reaction time change with set, motivation, and age. *Journal of Gerontology,* 1965, **20, 60-64.**

White House Conference on Aging. *Aging in the states.* Washington, D.C.: U.S. Government Printing Office, 1971.

Youmans, E. G. Objective and subjective economic disengagement among older rural and urban men. *Journal of Gerontology,* 1966, **21,** **439-441.**

Youmans. E. G. Some perspectives on disengagement theory. *Gerontologist,* 1969, **9(4, Part 1), 254-258.**

Zung, W. W. K. Depression in the normal aged. *Psychosomatics,* 1967, **8, 287-292.**

B. SOCIAL SERVICES

Our use of the term "Social Services" here is meant to be somewhat broader than the usual meaning of the phrase in the helping professions. In this section, we designate as social services the wide variety of public services needed by and helpful to the elderly person.

In the first reading, Mark Riesenfeld and his colleagues report on the variety of needs perceived by the helpers and the agency personnel who are responsible for providing this help. It is particularly interesting to contrast the importance and priority of the needs perceived by the professionals and by those who seek the help. It is important here to caution that social services should reflect the life styles decided upon by those being helped rather than an isolated set of values held by the helpers. Riesenfeld concludes that the differences in the perceptions are not irreconcilable.

In the next paper, Bruce Terris discusses the legal services needed by, but not always available to, the elderly poor. He points out how lawyers can protect the elderly from injustices and develop new kinds of affirmative programs to benefit them. After describing and illustrating several forms of legal assistance to the elderly, he suggests alternative ways in which the elderly poor can obtain legal help. While there have been several specific advances in this area, a great deal of work remains.

Elizabeth Nichols outlines the referral process and the resource agencies to whom referrals of the elderly may be made. With some specificity, Ms. Nichols describes the kinds of agencies in most communities and the types of information they solicit, as well as the problems which they attempt to alleviate.

In the next reading, the importance of the community worker and the services available in most communities are outlined. Various kinds of support services, personal and family adjustment services, health services and other services are briefly described.

Finally, Carl Eisdorfer gives a broad summary of how community services should enable the aged person to help himself. He emphasizes the importance of continued learning in later years and the need for our attention to potential sources of satisfaction among those whose lives are prolonged by advances in health care. He points out that psychological health for the aged has never received the same attention as has physiological health.

411

34. Perceptions of Public Service Needs: The Urban Elderly and the Public Agency*

Mark J. Riesenfeld, Robert J. Newcomer,
Paul V. Berland, and William A. Dempsey**

The perceptions of priority service needs of public agency personnel and a sample population of elderly urban poor are identified and compared.

Older persons in deteriorating urban ghettos are an important segment of the elderly population. The problems of this group are unique to their position in life. They are characteristically representative of a minority group; their resources are at low ebb both socially and financially and consequently they are often dependent on whatever public services are available to them. In the spring of 1970, the Los Angeles County Model Neighborhood agency requested that a group at the University of Southern California Gerontology Center develop a community plan to meet service and facility needs for older persons in south central Los Angeles. This report focuses on a small but significant portion of the material accumulated in the formulation of that plan (Gelwicks, Feldman, & Newcomer, 1971).

An important strategy in creating this plan was to determine how current public services were perceived and what alternative or additional services would be considered desirable. In order to gain a balanced perspective on how services were perceived, a sample of older people was administered an extensive conventional questionnaire and a small sample of agency personnel was guided through a Delphi experiment. The major purpose of this paper is to discuss the differences and similarities of perception found between elderly consumers of public services and the line agency personnel who develop and deliver these services. A primary hypothesis is that some wide discrepancies exist between policy formulators and poor elderly consumers in their perceptions of public service needs. Secondarily this paper will attempt to illustrate the usefulness of a qualitative Delphi method

*Reprinted from *The Gerontologist,* Vol. 12, 1972, pages 185-190, with the permission of the authors and the Gerontological Society.
**At the time the paper was published, Mr. Riesenfeld was a Planner for the Model Cities program in Compton, Calif. Presently he is the Senior Planner in the Marion County Planning Department, San Rafael, Calif. Dr. Newcomer was Preceptor at the University of Southern California Gerontology Center when the paper was published. He is presently Senior Social Planner in the Office of Senior Citizens Affairs in San Diego County, Calif. At the time the paper was published, Mr. Berlant was Associate Planner for the City of Fullerton, Calif., and Mr. Dempsey was City Planning Director in West Springfield, Mass.

of interview. In the first portion of this paper, the Delphi experiment will be explained in terms of its methodology and significance of operation.

DELPHI METHODOLOGY

The Delphi method utilizes a sequence of questionnaires and feedback from them to elicit opinions from a number of individual experts and specialists (Bender, Strack, Ebright, & Von Havnalter, 1969). In this method, an interdisciplinary group of specialists is asked to respond to several rounds of specific questions which are carefully designed to relate to a specific problem area. It should be noted that the expertise required in answering these questions is not likely to be provided by any one individual. Rather, each individual is bringing in a small piece of specialized experience or knowledge and is fitting it to a larger mosaic. Accompanying these questions, preliminary information must be carefully organized in order to create a common reference point upon which they can base their responses.

Participants are kept separate and respond to all phases of the experiment without any intercommunication. This type of incommunicado response assures a consistent and controlled base of information regarding questions and summaries of answers. The primary objective is to combine responses of the experts on such a panel into a single position — that is, to achieve a consensus. Consensus in the context of this experiment was determined as agreement among at least 55% of the respondents.

Generally, a Delphi experiment operates as follows: individual panel members are asked to state opinions or make estimates based on available background information. Then, with these opinions and estimates as new inputs to the original information, a new data base is computed and given to the participants to start another round of deliberations. The experts may be asked to state reasons for previously expressed opinions. A collection of such reasons may be presented anonymously to the participants so that they may reconsider and possibly revise their earlier estimate. The recycling tends to stimulate the experts to take into account considerations they might have neglected and to give due weight to factors they dismissed as unimportant.

This Delphi technique has significant practical applications. It can and should be used advantageously by agency personnel in many different contexts. Delphi methods are especially useful in situations where groups are required to make policy recommendations and submit priority rankings. In addition, it provides direct access to an important body of expert knowledge.

In its most elementary application, the Delphi technique is a basic tool for monitoring group perceptions of specific issues. Its use is important in removing the element of group interaction from group consideration of problems or issues. The Delphi process removes the intervening variables of confrontation and personal influence which occur when a group attempts to negotiate a set of priorities on a person-to-person basis.

This method of group decision-making can be used effectively by public agency personnel in their relationships with formal and informal groups. In situations where agency decision-makers must work with citizen task forces or citizen advisory boards, the Delphi method can be useful. With it, agency members can help committees to systematically review problem areas and obtain an objective measure of a group's priorities. This is helpful in all organizations where citizen participation has become institutionalized. In a similar way, Delphi methods are especially helpful where interagency coordination and participation is required. With the use of a Delphi polling device, the expertise of an interagency group can be exploited at the same time their relative status and power is minimized.

Findings of Delphi experiments with various groups can be utilized by political leaders to monitor opinions. Delphi presents a twofold benefit to the politician: (1) the findings yield a balanced, undistorted view of group perceptions of policy and issue areas, and (2) these findings present a measure against which subjective information (opinion and hearsay) can be compared.

MODEL NEIGHBORHOOD EXPERIMENT

As applied to our study, the Delphi method of collecting information generally followed the procedure outlined above. However, the format used for this particular experiment was designed to achieve several specific objectives. This format consisted of several detailed questions preceded by an explanation of their importance and followed by examples of the expected type of responses. The objectives of this method of interview were: (1) to produce a listing of perceived service needs and program priorities, (2) to discover what a representative group of local agency personnel viewed as high-priority needs of the Model Neighborhood communities, and (3) to use this information to compare it with responses from the residential questionnaire.

Questions in the Delphi experiment, and some of those asked of the area residents, closely correspond with regard to the kind of information which can be abstracted. In using this method, the panel served as a vehicle by which agency values and ideas could be transmitted effectively and in the context of the residential questionnaire. Procedurally, the experiment took this form: nine participants were selected from diverse fields representing public and private agencies. These panel members were contacted by mail for each round of the experiment (which lasted four rounds) and did not communicate with each other with respect to questionnaire responses. Thus, the only information which each participant received was from the group controlling the experiment. Figure I indicates the progression of question and feedback.

DELPHI EXPERIMENT

ROUND ONE

Experts list 20 facilities and services. ——————— Control group constructs composite list indicating frequencies.

ROUND TWO

Experts review composite list, then list and rank order 20 facilities and services. ——————— Control group constructs new composite with rank and rank score and requests experts to defend minor facility and service choices in Round Three.

ROUND THREE

Experts rethink ranking and construct new rank order list of 20 services and facilities. Defend previous minor selections. ——————— Control group constructs new composite of rank order distribution. Aggregation of defenses with input into Round Four.

ROUND FOUR

Experts construct final rank ordering of 20 facilities and services. ——————— Control group compiles final rank ordering of facility and service priorities.

Fig. 1. Progression of question and feedback.

DELPHI RESULTS

Four rounds of questions interspersed with feedback derived from the respondents were completed in the course of this Delphi experiment, which lasted approximately 1 month. Questions posed in the experiment deal with the listing and rank-ordering of facilities and services thought to be priority needs of older persons in the study area.

Three rounds of the questionnaire requested a listing and ranking of 20 important facilities and services (f/s). In one or more rounds, 43 facilities or services were submitted and ranked by the 9 participants. Thus, the participants had varied and diverse views as to which f/s were needed.

TABLE 1.
Facility and Service Needs Comparison of Preferences:
Agency Experts and Community Residents

Rank	Delphi Experts	(f)		(f)
1	Low income housing	(5)	Discount card	(183)
2	Senior citizen health clinic	(5)	Check on safety inside/	
3	Reduced property taxes	(6)	outside home	(171)
4	Public housing	(5)	Telephone reassurance	(164)
5	Minibuses	(5)	Consumer protection (complaints)	(160)
6	Full-service hospital	(6)	Transportation (special rates)	(160)
7	Food stamp delivery service	(5)	Reduced property tax	(159)
8	Multi-purpose service center	(6)	Transportation to hospital/clinic	(149)
9	Rent supplement	(7)	Telephone food orders/	
10	Loans & Grants for home repair	(6)	home deliver	(143)
11	Meals-on-wheels	(6)	Low-interest loans	(141)
12	Home care services	(6)	Retirement counseling	(134)
13	Telephone reassurance		Home health care/visiting/	
	programs	(6)	nurses	(130)
14	Law enforcement services	(7)	Information/referral services	(130)
15	Social & recreational services	(7)	Senior citizens' clubs	(125)
16	Legal aid	(5)	Interpreter services	(124)
17	Income and property		Consumer protection (credit)	(124)
	management	(5)	Legal aid	(123)
18	Continuing education	(5)	Transportation (special buses)	(121)
19			Multipurpose center	(119)
20			Food stamps	(119)
			Family health clinics	(115)
	Total N=9		Total N=278	

One of the major objectives of the Delphi study was to create a priority listing of recommended facilities and services which reflected the consensus of the expert participants. By Round Four, 18 services emerged as consensus recommendations (Table 1).

It is significant that the number of consensus services changed over time from Round One to Round Four. Results of Round One indicate only 13 recommendations which a majority of the participants could agree upon. In Rounds Two, Three and Four, the number changed from 15 to 16 to 18 different services respectively. Given that a fixed number of choices (20) were allocated to each participant, this increase in the number of "consensus" services indicates that the participants narrowed their focus of concern through the course of the experiment.

A distinct pattern of consensus can be observed among the 18 priority-ranked services. The first 5 and the last 4 recommended services enjoy agreement among 58% of the respondents. However, the services which were ranked in the middle range were indicated by nearly 68% of the experts. This difference in the degree of consensus, while not large, is significant. These 9 middle-range priorities were selected with a greater degree of consensus than any other group of services.

METHODOLOGY: RESIDENTIAL QUESTIONNAIRE

The older residents (55 years and older) of the Model Neighborhood area were surveyed on several aspects of their residential environment. A personal interview questionnaire was utilized, designed to elicit responses concerning need, awareness and use of social services. Analysis included 35 general service types covering such areas as health, transportation, and supportive, protective, and recreational services. It is this set of responses which relates most closely to services which are or could be provided to the elderly urban poor.

In the absence of extensive funds and information on the household location of older residents in the Model Neighborhood Area (MNA), an area probability sample was chosen. One hundred (100) randomly selected city blocks from a total of 648 blocks served as the interview source. With the exclusion of blocks having no residential structures, the sample size became 95 blocks. Interviewers attempted to contact all residents 55 years and over in each of the 95 blocks.

Interviewers for this study were chosen from among MNA residents over the age of 55 years. The utilization of elderly residents as interviewers was considered essential in order to gain access to and confidence of the sample population.

The resulting sample population of 278 older persons can be described by the following characteristics: age-sex distribution, ethnic distribution, and income level. The age-sex distribution of the survey sample follows the general shape of the area's elderly population pyramid. Approximately 44% of the survey respondents were under the age of 65, with the balance being older than 65. Females outnumbered males in the sample — 164 to 100.

The ethnic breakdown of the sample population largely reflects the distribution of the population at large. Nearly 63% of the sample were black and 26% were Mexican-American, with the remainder being white.

Reported income levels of the sample are low. Total income as reported by respondents ranges from less than $100 per month to more than $400 per month. Most of the sample (72.6%) receive less than $200 per month and all but 10% are receiving less than $300.

RESIDENTIAL SAMPLE RESULTS

As mentioned above, a sample of older residents of the Model Neighborhood Area (MNA) were interviewed in their homes. The major questions attempted to determine the sample's perceived need for services. It was a multi-tiered question which asked if the respondent had heard of, used, and/or needed a particular service. This question was utilized in reference to 35 different services or facilities. From this method of questioning, it was possible to determine not only need, but need which was heretofore unfulfilled. Table I indicates the 18 most needed services in comparison with the agency experts' priorities.

All services show an unfulfilled need of greater than 23%. Twenty-eight of the 35 services have an unfulfilled need greater than 49%. In general then, it can be seen that a high degree of unfulfilled service need exists among the older people living in the MNA. Although mere recording of unfulfilled need tells little about either the cause or consequences of the situation, it will be possible to gauge better the magnitude and seriousness of this need.

OBSERVATIONS

Perceptions of public service needs by both samples can be usefully compared on the basis of similarity and genre of services recommended.

A great similarity exists in the way that agency personnel and older people view public service needs. This similarity is manifested by the lists of priority recommendations which evolved from the extensive interviews conducted. Both public agency personnel and older persons cite the need for remedies to the same basic kinds of problems: good mobility, accessible health care, economic considerations in the purchase of housing, consumer goods, and protective services. Thus, no major gap exists between these two groups in their perception of problems.

However, the remedies to these general problems were expressed by each group in different ways. The diverse spectrum of service needs which was indicated can be divided into two well-defined categories. They are: (1) services which are direct and generally physical-facility oriented, and (2) supportive services which allow the individual maximum choice and flexibility. Low-income housing, minibuses, and health clinics can be considered in the first category of place-oriented, direct services. Discount cards, consumer protection, and telephone assurance programs fall into the second category of dispersed individual supportive services. Public agency participants usually opted for recommendations which solved problems with direct services. Respondents from the residential sample heavily favored supportive services. Reasons why the respective samples selected services in these different manners cannot be demonstrated by the data collected and thus is left to speculation.

Public agency people are most likely reflecting values generated by their respective administrative organizations. Direct-service, facility-based approaches to the solving of social problems is wholly consistent with a tradition which offers continuity and expansion to the organization. Organizational strength would be a major outcome of this approach to service provision.

The older persons responding are probably reflecting a non-institutional bias in that their needs are served through devices which will allow them to adapt better to their current city environment. This bias is set in the context of a history of failures in attempts to procure needed services. Economic problems are solved by non-specific discount cards while transportation difficulties are eased through special routes and better rates. Health service problems are not viewed in terms of a local facility, but rather in terms of a method of being transported to the health facility of their choice. In a sense, they are asking for aids to help them better adapt to their current environment instead of having it changed or being moved away from it.

In viewing the apparent dichotomy of problem-solving approaches, an interesting contradiction appears in the Delphi priority listing of needed services. As mentioned before, the recommendations of highest consensus for these participants are those in the middle priority range of 6-14. These recommendations are the services in which the agency participants are most agreed. It is interesting to note, however, that these particular services are mainly supportive services. This suggests that the Delphi respondents are maintaining a split image of the needs of older people. On the one hand, they set their highest priorities for direct services. On the other, they can most agree on environmental support services. However, the rankings or comments received throughout the experiment give no indication of a desire for integration of these approaches. It would seem that for the public agency personnel, pragmatism dictates the conventional, while speculation reveals insight and departure.

Another implication of the data is that services which are now currently offered may be lacking in relevance to the elderly urban poor. The major focus of the perceived needs of the older sample was not on services in their currently available format. These services, which the elderly desired, attack similar problems but in a different manner. Thus, with the current status of public services, policy makers may be overlooking potential services which are necessary for helping the older person adapt to the environment in which he now lives. Criteria for relevance must include choice and individual acceptance. It appears that the older sample is suggesting that these are values not well supported by current services.

The data which have been presented and the ensuing reflections imply that a chasm exists between what the urban elderly poor perceive as necessary in services and what the public agency representatives perceive as desirable. The remote dialogue on services between these two groups fostered by this comparison of data can give us important insights:

1. The elderly ghetto residents appear to perceive their physical life space as a given. In order to optimize that life space, they have indicated needs which will give them maximum flexibility and choice. They want services which will help them adapt to what their current physical environment offers.

2. Public administrators do not perceive the current physical environment as a given. They want to alter the physical environment in order to provide services. In doing so they would, to some extent, circumscribe an environment of choice and opportunity which characterizes an optimum life space.

An integration of these approaches is clearly called for. Behavioral factors must be weighed with structural ones in the design and distribution of public services. Choice and mobility must become integral parts of basic, place-oriented direct services.

A further implication of this paper is the potential use of the Delphi method which can be developed and utilized as a significant research tool for studies in policy formulation. Much of the information associated with policy decision-making is difficult to collect from groups of individuals in other than a subjective format. It has been a purpose of this paper to show that the Delphi method allows analysts to evaluate subjective data systematically and in a logical manner. Elements of a policy-making process which tend to be largely internalized and intuitive can be isolated and held up for a systematic review by policy makers with this Delphi procedure.

Another quality of the Delphi technique is its use as a systematic method of examining the exercise of policy choices among a series of alternatives. Not only can the acts of choice be analyzed, but dialogues can be established which can offer explanations and motives for choice thus permitting a close view at the policy decision-making process. Delphi interviews can also be used as a testing vehicle to plot shifts in policy priorities among groups over a given period of time.

It remains to be said here that, although the data suggest differences do exist in the perceptions of the agency representatives and the older persons they serve, they are not irreconcilable. Services must begin to reflect desired life styles instead of imposing an isolated set of values. This is particularly true for the urban elderly poor. The city and its servants must provide the largest possible life space for its older residents, a life space that contains many options and the opportunity to express individual differences in needs and desires — or they will fall short of success in their purpose.

REFERENCES

Bender, A. D., Strack, A. E., Ebright, G. W., & Von Havnalter, G. Delphi study examines developments in medicine. *Futures*, June 1969, 298-303.

Gelwicks, L. E., Feldman, A. G., & Newcomer, R. J. *Report on older population: Needs, resources, and services in Los Angeles County Model Neighborhood.* Los Angeles: Los Angeles County Model Neighborhood Program, Oct., 1971.

35. Legal Service for the Elderly*

BRUCE J. TERRIS**

INTRODUCTION

This monograph draws heavily upon the experiences of Legal Research and Services for the Elderly begun in 1968 by the National Council of Senior Citizens with funds granted by the O.E.O.

It has sponsored projects for providing legal assistance to the elderly all across the country from Boston to Los Angeles, in rural areas of Appalachia, in the resort city of Miami Beach, and in the congested urban center of San Francisco. Its programs have dealt with blacks in Massachusetts, with whites in Kentucky, with Jewish residents in Florida, with the Spanish-speaking in New Mexico, and with Oriental-Americans in San Francisco.

It has provided services through neighborhood legal service offices in San Francisco, through a legal aid society in Atlanta, through a university in New York, through a private law firm in Massachusetts, and through elderly community residents who have been trained as "lay advocates" in several cities.

The legal assistance has included providing representation in hundreds of lawsuits for individual clients, bringing test cases vitally important to thousands of the elderly, drafting and lobbying for legislation and administrative regulations, providing representation before welfare agencies, HEW, city and other administrative bodies, initiating housing and economic development projects, and preparing booklets and other methods of educating the elderly about their rights.

Not all these projects have been successful. Some have been terminated because they did not work. LRSE deliberately broke new ground, tried new ideas, developed new information. The projects sponsored by LRSE now provide the experience upon which other communities and other groups can, with some confidence, plan their own programs of legal service for the elderly.

*Abstracted from a monograph, *Legal services for the elderly,* published by the National Council on Aging, Washington, D.C. 1972, with permission of the author and the National Council on Aging.
**Mr. Terris is a member of the Washington law firm of Terris, Needham, Keiner, Black and Hostetler.

The Need for Lawyers for the Elderly Poor. The existing CAA legal service programs offer legal assistance to the elderly, as well as to all other agency groups among the poor. Nevertheless, at least two factors have seriously interfered with providing effective legal assistance to older people.

First, the elderly themselves have not responded to the invitation of legal service programs as readily as the younger poor. Some of them are physically incapacitated and have difficulty in getting to an office. Others live in out-of-the-way valleys or in back rooms and shacks hidden from view even in our cities. A considerable number have sight, speech, hearing or other difficulties in communication so they do not learn of the availability of legal service. And there are those who are even suspicious of help offered.

Some of the old people lack knowledge about programs available to them and many, who have been self-sufficient all their lives, are too proud to accept free assistance readily.

Second, legal service programs have been directed to middle-aged or younger people rather than to the elderly. Families and children undoubtedly are more attractive and easy to deal with for almost anyone. They have the appeal of having most of their lives yet to live if their problems can be alleviated. Since most of the lawyers of the legal service programs are young themselves, they have special difficulty in understanding the needs and problems of the elderly.

In any event, regardless of the reason, the experience of legal service programs is that they serve a disproportionately small number of the elderly poor.

Just as community action agencies have been most concerned with families (such as large-family housing) and with children (such as Headstart and Followthrough), legal service programs have emphasized issues relating to these same people. For example, Aid for Dependent Children has received far more attention than Old Age, Survivors, and Disability Insurance, although both are part of the same Social Security Act. The housing code enforcement and property tax difficulties of elderly home owners have been neglected in favor of landlord-tenant problems. Racial discrimination in employment is stressed rather than discrimination against the elderly or requirements of early retirement. Educational and juvenile issues are now receiving increasing attention in contrast to questions relating to pension rights and wills.

At the same time that legal service programs have emphasized the problems of families and younger people, they have been overburdened with handling even these problems alone. Frequently, legal service programs have turned away clients because of lack of attorneys to handle new cases adequately. With already too heavy caseloads and with no demands from the elderly for services, legal service programs have rarely attempted to develop special methods to expand services to the elderly.

All this does not mean that the elderly poor have not benefited from the success of legal service programs. When a legal service program establishes new consumer rights, it benefits all buyers regardless of age. When it establishes new rights for tenants of public or private housing, all tenants benefit. When legal action results in improved health care in public or private hospitals, all patients receive better treatment.

Even when the particular issue involves specifically the young, the effect may be far broader. For example, the Supreme Court decided that residency requirements for aid to families with dependent children were unconstitutional. While this decision directly benefited mothers and children, the principle of this decision is now being extended to Old Age Assistance recipients. Similarly, the Supreme Court held that AFDC could not be cut off from a welfare recipient without first providing a hearing. Efforts are now being made to impose this same requirement to the Old Age Assistance program.

Even though the elderly have significantly benefited from existing legal service programs, they have not received help to the same extent as if lawyers had been assigned to serve them. While occasional Social Security, Old Age Assistance, pension and similar cases have been handled, activity in these areas has not been pushed creatively and aggressively.

Moreover, in some instances, the interests of the elderly may even be inconsistent with those of the rest of the poor. Housing programs for the elderly, both public and moderate income, have often been neglected by poverty programs which emphasized housing for large families. The interest of older people in security and quiet is frequently sacrificed in the interest of young people's freedom from curfews, loitering laws, and various kinds of public action. The law in areas of peculiar importance to the elderly is still largely underdeveloped from the standpoint of protecting them. Consequently, there are great opportunities to help the elderly poor through a reasonable commitment of legal resources.

Legal service programs for the elderly should be specifically geared to their needs. They should concentrate on issues in which the interest of the elderly is either unique (Social Security, Old Age Assistance, pension rights, Medicare, and special housing) or significantly greater than for the rest of the poor (probate matters, workmen's compensation and other problems of disability). And they must include methods for reaching out to the elderly and attracting them to use legal service programs.

ESSENTIALS OF LEGAL SERVICE TO THE ELDERLY

Present CAA legal service programs do not provide the elderly with legal assistance in proportion to their numbers. This is caused by the physical and psychological difficulties of the elderly in using available services, and by special problems of old people. This section will suggest methods for dealing with both these issues so as to enable legal service programs to serve the elderly poor.

A. Outreach. The problem of getting the poor — particularly the elderly poor — to participate in, or to obtain the benefit of, various programs designed to assist them is an old one.

Legal assistance offices should be easily accessible to the elderly, located in or near places where old people often come for other purposes, such as senior centers, welfare offices or a store often patronized by the elderly. They should be in neighborhoods with high concentrations of older persons and near public transportation. Mobile units with regular schedules may be needed in rural areas; and for the bed-ridden or handicapped, legal assistance may have to be brought into their homes.

Every available means of mass communication, including newspapers, television, radio, posters and fliers in places which the elderly frequent, and newsletters to organizations of the elderly should be used. But such impersonal methods are clearly not enough for a large proportion of the elderly. The use of posters is not very effective because old people do not appear frequently in public places due to physical infirmity or fear. Often, too, they have difficulty in reading, especially fine print, and are suspicious of what they do read. This also means that distribution of written material from door to door may not work. And experience has shown that radio and television do not bring very good response.

Direct personal communication is essential to allay the suspicion, fear, pride or other characteristics which inhibit the elderly from responding; and to discover when physical infirmity, lack of transportation and other problems make a response without assistance impossible.

Perhaps the two best models for this kind of program are Operation Medicare Alert and Project FIND. In Medicare Alert, conducted by the National Council on the Aging, approximately 14,500 persons, mostly poor and elderly themselves, went door-to-door in communities across the country. They signed up over 4 million senior citizens for Medicare within six months.

Project FIND, also a program of the National Council on the Aging, paid for with OEO funds, involved 400 black, brown, and white workers in 12 rural and urban communities. Again, largely poor and elderly workers themselves went door-to-door to find the old people. Instead of simply signing them up for a single program as in Medicare Alert, the workers in Project FIND attempted to identify all their needs and to obtain the variety of services needed to meet them — Social Security benefits, Old Age Assistance, part-time employment, and health services, and recreation. This program appears to have been extremely successful in finding the totally neglected elderly poor in our society and in obtaining at least some of the assistance to overcome their most severe difficulties.

An outreach program for legal services could focus exclusively on trying to provide legal assistance for the elderly contacted, but this seems wasteful since they have many needs demanding attention. It would be more desirable to include legal assistance as one of the services in a general outreach program.

The outreach worker could be of great help in explaining the legal services the lawyers can provide in terms the elderly can understand. Outreach workers who are themselves old and come from the same background of culture and language, may do a far better job of continuing communication with elderly clients and maintaining their confidence.

It is, of course, important that outreach workers be able to identify problems with which lawyers can be of assistance. Initial and in-service training by lawyers and continuing contact with them can give the workers both the knowledge and confidence they need. Simple checklists can be useful so that workers keep in mind factual situations for which they are looking.

B. *Forms of Legal Assistance.* Legal service for the elderly poor must provide many kinds of assistance to have maximum effectiveness. It should include legal advice; educational materials; preparation of legal documents to help clients avoid getting into difficulty; legal representation on routine, but important, matters of individual clients: litigation in the courts or before administrative agencies in test cases designed to produce significant reform; drafting and lobbying for changes in statutes and administrative regulations or policies; packaging economic development, housing and other programs for the elderly and working with community organizations to put them into effect.

1. *Legal Advice.* Legal service programs for the elderly should provide advice on housing leases, credit arrangements, and consumer contracts.

Since a large proportion of the elderly own their own homes, these programs should also include information regarding second mortgages, repair home contracts, and property taxes.

A legal service program for the elderly should emphasize preparation of wills and handling probate matters. The homes and other possessions of the poor, while of modest financial value, are often of greater importance to them than larger amounts of resources to the more affluent. The lack of a will may mean that these assets do not go to the persons whom the decedent would have wanted to benefit — such as a common law wife, illegitimate children or a close friend who has lived for years with him. It may also mean that the assets are tied up in lengthy and costly probate proceedings which prevents persons who desperately need them from using them or which seriously reduce already limited resources for a widow or other relative.

Other legal advice particularly needed by the elderly would relate to special provisions in the income tax laws favoring the elderly; housing leases in federally subsidized housing for the elderly; and procedures and eligibility for Social Security, private pensions, Medicare and Medicaid.

Educational materials which are easily understood should be part of a legal services program to inform the elderly of their rights. Examples which have been, or are being prepared, include booklets describing Social Security benefits, the rights of New York residents to Medicaid (in both English and Spanish), and a similar booklet for Georgia residents including information regarding pension rights, veterans' benefits and consumer and housing problems.

2. *Routine Litigation.* The elderly poor, like the poor generally, need lawyers to defend them against eviction from their housing, against repossession of goods by stores, against suits for payment on unfair consumer contracts. They need lawyers to bring their

own suits in some cases to establish their eligibility for government benefits, food stamps, public assistance, public housing, Social Security, Medicare, and Medicaid. While such cases usually establish no major new rules of law helpful to many other poor people, they are of great importance to the individual.

Hearings and judicial review can also be arranged by lawyers when necessary. Administrative hearings can be obtained from HEW by a patient under the Hospital Insurance portion (Part A) of Medicare if the intermediary determines that certain care is not covered and the amount in controversy exceeds $100. Judicial review can be obtained if the contested amount is $1,000 or more. A fair hearing can be obtained before the carrier if the carrier determines that the Supplemental Medical Insurance portion (Part B) of Medicare does not cover particular medical service. HEW regulations provide for administrative hearings before the state agency administering Old Age Assistance, Aid to the Blind, and Aid to the Permanently and Totally Disabled concerning denial of eligibility or the amount of the grants. Judicial review can also generally be obtained.

Legal representation is also important when infirmity or death occur. Counsel is important in contesting an involuntary commitment to a mental hospital of an elderly person who is not dangerous and who could live more appropriately at home or in a nursing home. Similarly, a lawyer can contest attempts to appoint a guardian or conservator to manage the property of an elderly person who is purportedly incompetent. When a spouse or relative dies, an attorney can help in probating and settling the estate so that the property passes to the heirs as quickly and with as little expense as possible.

3. *Test Litigation.* The elderly poor need counsel not just for individual matters but to bring broader cases affecting thousands or even millions of people. While these efforts involve far fewer cases, they generally require elaborate factual investigation, research into the law, briefing and trial. It is essential to have far better than average counsel both because of the complexity of these cases and the far greater impact they have.

It is impossible even to begin to list the suits which could be brought to protect the interests of the elderly poor. Test litigation, by its nature, is innovative and imaginative. Any list therefore necessarily omits promising ideas which would be discovered if able lawyers had a full-time professional commitment to serve the elderly poor.

However, the kinds of test cases which have been brought in the last few years and which are now being considered by the handful of lawyers serving the elderly poor are at least suggestive.

Social Security. Actions have been filed challenging HEW's practice of suspending social security benefits without a prior hearing when HEW believes that the recipient has earned sums in excess of the amount allowed or has some other ground for suspending payment.

Old Age Assistance. Suits have been successfully brought challenging the constitutionality of denying Old Age Assistance to all aliens or those aliens who have not resided within the state for excessively long periods of time.

A suit has been brought in Ohio challenging denial of Old Age Assistance if an applicant has a burial contract in excess of $400 and insurance in excess of $500 which she would not assign to the state.

Pensions. A federal district court has held that the stringent rules of the United Mine Workers Welfare and Retirement Fund could not bar paying pensions to the plaintiffs.

Suits are possible contesting the lack of fair procedures before pensions can be denied.

Medicare and Medicaid. Suits can be brought challenging policies narrowing the scope of medical service paid for by Medicare and Medicaid. Examples might include particular kinds of care in nursing homes and transportation for medical treatment.

California court has ordered the state not to narrow eligibility for Medicaid by reducing the amount of money which can be earned. As a result, 50,000 poor persons continued to be eligible.

An injunction has been issued against a New York statute requiring the medically indigent not on welfare to pay 20 percent of the costs of outpatient care under Medicaid.

Hospitals and Mental Hospitals. A suit has been brought to compel a municipal hospital heavily used by the elderly poor to bring its treatment up to accepted medical standards. In large part because of the litigation, substantial improvements have been made in the emergency room. Similar suits involving the "right to treatment" are possible against mental hospitals.

A suit is being considered against a mental hospital for confining allegedly senile patients involuntarily who are not dangerous to themselves or society.

Federal district courts have held that patients involuntarily committed in mental hospitals cannot be transferred to the state where they used to live.

Nursing Homes. Suits can be brought to compel nursing homes to provide adequate food, shelter, and treatment particularly when they receive local or federal funds to care for patients.

Protective Services and Commitment. A federal court has held unconstitutional a New York statute allowing the appointment of a committee, without a hearing, to manage the financial affairs of a person involuntarily committed to a state mental hospital.

Suits are possible challenging the lack of procedural rights such as a hearing and free, appointed counsel before a person can be involuntarily committed.

Housing. Complaints can be filed with HUD and litigation brought in court challenging the lack of participation afforded the elderly in preparation of a community's workable program, in urban renewal, and in model cities planning.

Consumers. Hearings can be sought before state or local administrative bodies which regulate public transportation or utilities concerning lower fares and charges for the elderly. For example, lower bus fares have been approved in the District of Columbia and Miami.

The results in several of these cases already decided demonstrate the potential for test litigation. While some cases have been and doubtless will be lost, the possibility for substantial steps from test litigation to assist the elderly poor has been clearly shown.

   4. Legislative and Regulatory Reform. In every situation where test litigation offers promise of reform, the same results could be obtained if legislative or administrative agencies could be persuaded to act. Administrative agencies frequently have considerable power to establish policies under broad legislative grants of authority. For example, they could, if they desire, enforce nursing home regulations aggressively and strictly. Municipal hospitals can reorganize themselves to provide better medical treatment. Mental hospitals can release patients who are not dangerous to themselves or society.

   Similarly, statutes often give administrative agencies authority to issue regulations which have the force of law as long as they are not inconsistent with the language and intent of the statute. HEW could issue regulations allowing the suspension of Social Security benefits only after a hearing and make more flexible the standards for proving disability. HUD could adopt specific regulations requiring participation of the elderly in workable programs, urban renewal and model cities programs.

Where a rule is clearly embodied in a statute, it can, of course, be changed only by the legislature and not by an administrative body. A state statute denying Old Age Assistance to all aliens or those not residing in the state for a particular period of time could be amended by the state legislature to remove this restriction. Similarly, state legislation could remove or relax the requirements of many states that the elderly can not qualify for Old Age Assistance if they have burial contracts or insurance with a value above an extremely modest amount. Congress can broaden the kinds of medical treatment covered by Medicare and Medicaid and, as long as it is consistent with federal legislation, state legislatures can broaden both eligibility and coverage of Medicaid.

Legislatures can also pass statutes relating to private action. They can forbid unfair eligibility requirements for pensions and can require fair procedures before pensions are denied. They can require private bus lines and utilities to charge lower fares and rates to the elderly.

Any strategy designed to change the law with regard to the elderly poor therefore must consider going directly to the legislative or administrative agency. However, even though legislative or administrative changes could remedy a problem, this does not demonstrate that litigation is inappropriate. Litigation is sometimes easier and quicker than attempting a major campaign to get a statute or regulation adopted. More important, legislative and administrative bodies are all too often unsympathetic and refuse to act on behalf of the poor generally or the elderly poor in particular. The courts then are the only recourse to obtain vitally needed reform. Just as the courts provided leadership concerning racial segregation, reapportionment, and criminal procedures, they are now sometimes the best opportunity with relation to problems of poverty.

In addition to all the issues which are susceptible both to litigation and to statutory or administrative changes, there are other problems as to which statutory or administrative reform is the only, or clearly the best, remedy. This includes most obviously the level of benefits for Social Security and Old Age Assistance and the amount of federal and state funds available for housing for the elderly. In addition, statutes often so clearly exclude persons from Social Security, Medicare, Medicaid, food stamps, or some other benefit programs that there is no realistic possibility of any other interpretation of the statute by a court. And the elderly may need new statutory remedies to protect them from being exploited by unscrupulous landlords (such as rent control) or businessmen (such as deceptive practices).

There can be little doubt that attorneys for the elderly can have considerable success in obtaining legislative changes. In Massachusetts, attorneys for the Council of Elders helped pass a bill to create a cabinet-level Executive Office of Elder Affairs in the state government and appropriations for a Special Legislative Commission Relative to the Major Needs and Problems of Elderly Persons. The same Massachusetts attorneys helped obtain passage of a bill to disregard $12 in Social Security payments in computing Old Age Assistance; to have common kitchen and dining areas to be built in all state-aided public housing for the elderly; and to expand the state lunch program for the elderly. More recently, they have succeeded in persuading the Massachusetts legislature to pass both a significant increase in Old Age Assistance and a comprehensive home-care bill providing social services for the elderly which will allow thousands of the elderly to escape institutionalization.

In Miami Beach, attorneys for the elderly obtained passage of a rent-control ordinance which would protect the large number of elderly tenants in the city from rent increases. Fifteen senior citizens' organizations joined together in this effort and asked an attorney of the Legal Services Senior Citizens' Center in Miami Beach to represent them. Over 350 persons marched on City Hall and presented a petition to the Mayor supporting rent control. After three days of hearings, the City Council passed an ordinance drafted by the attorney. While the ordinance has been tied up in litigation concerning the power of the City Council to adopt it, its passage shows how organizations of the elderly and their attorneys can jointly be successful in obtaining needed legislation.

5. *Packaging Programs.* Two of the most important needs of the elderly are part-time employment and housing. Attorneys for the elderly can be extremely valuable in developing specific programs to deal with each of these fields.

Part-time employment can be created for the elderly by starting businesses which require the kind of abilities the elderly possess.

Child care, handicrafts, and repair services are possible examples. Some of the most useful businesses would allow the elderly to work in their own homes.

The development of businesses is an extremely complex undertaking. It requires obtaining both funds and technical assistance to ensure that the business can be financially successful. Money is often available for sound proposals through the Small Business Administration, Economic Development Administration, private financial institutions, and foundations. Technical assistance can frequently be obtained from SBA or foundation-funded programs to assist businesses with low income or minority owners. Attorneys for the elderly can help put together a package consisting of a sound economic proposal and the management, money and technical assistance needed to start it.

The Golden Age Legal Aid project in Atlanta, for example, started a nonprofit corporation to manufacture display cards and jewelry, a Senior Citizens' Sales Committee to market dashikis, and the Consumers Association for Self-Help which operates six cooperative retail outlets in public housing high-rise apartments for the elderly manned by paid senior workers. A consulting firm retained by Research and Services for the Elderly, sponsored by a legal service program, in Albuquerque, New Mexico, concluded that the elderly poor did not have the talent and experience needed to create successful business ventures and proposed a contract transportation service and landscaping business. That program also established the Senior Citizens' Employment Service to be a nonprofit self-sustaining corporation to obtain jobs for the elderly.

Housing for the elderly can also be built by elderly groups. Financing can be obtained, with substantial subsidies, by working through a maze of different programs of the federal government which provide housing for poor (public housing, leasing and rent supplement) and moderate-income (Section 221(d) (3) and (236) people. Similar state housing programs also exist in some states. In addition, conveniently financed housing, without government subsidies, can be built with funds from private financial institutions. As in the case of businesses, legal assistance is important. The packaging of a housing project requires a high degree of skill relating to finance, construction and other matters. A lawyer may have considerable knowledge of this field or he may at least be helpful in obtaining it.

For example, attorneys on the Housing and the Elderly Project in Santa Monica, California, have worked with local businessmen and others to create a nonprofit foundation to construct a 200-unit apartment for the elderly which is sponsored by a Jewish Community Center. They helped secure a $31,000 grant to provide seed money so that the project could be built.

Federal funds, both grants and loans, are also available for low-income homeowners whose houses need rehabiliation and who live in urban renewal or special code enforcement areas. Attorneys can help elderly homeowners benefit from these programs.

It cannot be stressed too much that economic development and housing programs must become financially self-sufficient. Unless they are economically feasible, their financial problems will become so severe that the project may well collapse. Some businesses designed to provide employment for the elderly have already experienced difficulty because of inadequate financing and economically unsound business ideas. Consequently, the highest level of technical assistance is essential in developing such a project.

The list of possible federal, state, local and foundation-funded programs which could be used to benefit the elderly is almost endless. Possibilities include community health centers funded by OEO, HUD grants for modernization of public housing for the elderly, Senior Centers using foundation or United Givers fund to provide a variety of services for the elderly, and the like. Buyers' clubs and perhaps other programs can be started without outside financial assistance.

While none of these programs require legal counsel to start them, attorneys would be of great assistance on numerous matters. They are more likely to know of and understand the incredibly complex statutes and regulations which relate to the numerous government programs. They can usually better understand the many legal documents involved in financing. And they can provide assistance concerning incorporating new organizations, obtaining tax exemptions and getting municipal licenses to operate.

6. *Assistance to Elderly Organizations.* Organizations of the elderly know better than probably anyone else the problems of old people and have the sense of urgency to want to do something about them. They often, however, need legal assistance to develop a strategy through which these needs can begin to be met.

The strategy of a senior citizens' organization might include litigation, legislative or administrative reform, or the initiation of economic development, housing, or other projects. In addition to helping the senior organization actually carry out such a program once decided upon, a lawyer can be of great assistance in planning the program. He can give valuable advice on the likelihood of success, the time involved, and the numerous difficulties to be encountered.

For example, two organizations of the elderly in Washington, D.C., decided to formulate a program for obtaining more housing for the elderly both through public housing and federally subsidized moderate income programs. They wanted to ensure that this housing would be suitable for old people by providing sound, decent homes easily accessible to commercial services and transportation and having health and recreational facilities whenever possible. Assisted by attorneys from the headquarters of Legal Research and Services for the Elderly, the groups went to city officials to demand that a housing program for the elderly be developed. The attorneys drafted, at the direction of the organizations, a specific program for presentation. A tour of existing public housing projects for old people was arranged for city officials and leaders of the elderly organizations. After numerous meetings with a variety of officials, the Mayor agreed to appoint a special Committee on Housing for the Elderly to assist him, the public housing authority and other city agencies to develop a program. As a result, the city has committed itself to a program significantly increasing housing for the aged and is not only allowing but insisting on the intensive participation of the Committee in formulating this program.

The Committee is composed almost entirely of older people and representatives chosen by the elderly. The Committee visits and evaluates all sites being considered for this housing and is negotiating to ensure that all urban renewal areas have their fair share of new or rehabilitated housing specifically for the elderly. Safety and security standards specifically for the aged are being developed. The Committee is also visiting all existing old people's public housing projects to find out from tenants if maintenance is adequate and if all necessary services are being provided. While decisions have been made by the organizations, they have had constant advice and other assistance from their attorneys.

ORGANIZATION OF LEGAL SERVICES FOR THE ELDERLY

The varied legal services needed by the aged have been discussed. This section will consider how to organize a program and obtain the resources to meet these needs.

The crucial resource is trained legal manpower — lawyers, law students, and laymen working as aides to lawyers. It can be volunteer or paid. The amount and kind of trained manpower obtained will directly affect the organization of the program. For example, even if a legal services program of five full-time attorneys is desirable, lack of funds may require the program to be conducted in part by law students or even entirely by volunteer attorneys. In some rural areas the problem of attracting full-time attorneys, even if paid, may require greater reliance on lay aides working with lawyers.

Each community will have to develop its own program tailored to its own problems and opportunities. Among the factors which should be considered are:

> Whether the community is urban or rural and where the elderly are located. If the aged are scattered and transportation is difficult, serious problems are obviously presented in reaching them.
>
> Whether existing senior membership or service organizations can utilize legal services as an integral part of their program.
>
> What are the most serious problems faced by the elderly and what kinds of legal assistance can be useful to meet them.
>
> Whether multi-generational social services programs such as community action programs, public welfare and voluntary family agencies can be utilized to provide outreach and referral to a legal service program.
>
> Whether there is an existing legal services program and what interest it has in setting up a program for the elderly through its own funds or whether other funds are available for this purpose.
>
> Whether a local law school or local private attorneys can be interested in helping provide legal services to the elderly.

A. Utilizing Existing Legal Service Programs. In most cities and many rural areas, legal service programs which have one or more paid full-time attorneys, now exist to help the poor. It would usually make little sense in such communities to establish new, separate legal service programs for the elderly. Duplication of legal service programs would be wasteful financially since programs can be operated more economically if a number of attorneys use the same library, bookkeeping, and other services. Moreover, proliferation of agencies serving the poor is confusing both to the poor and to the rest of the community.

Where legal service programs exist, the appropriate course will generally be to persuade that program to devote a reasonable portion of its resources in money and manpower to serve the elderly poor. An appropriate portion might well correspond to the percentage of the poor in the community which is elderly.

Legal service programs have found that complex problems require specialization. Whenever programs are of sufficient size to allow it, they generally have specialists for particular issues — welfare, housing, consumer rights, or for particular groups of people — juveniles, Spanish-speaking or tenants of public housing — who spend all or most of their time in their fields of expertise. The attorneys acquire in this way both the knowledge and the aggressiveness to create new litigative or legislative strategies to obtain greater benefits for their clients. Their energies and creativity are not dissipated by having too many different interests and demands on their time. And they are most likely to conceive and carry out such nonlegal strategies as developing housing and economic development projects.

Many larger legal service programs are now organized into a central headquarters staff — often in the downtown area of a city — and a number of offices in neighborhoods where the poor are concentrated. The central office often has a law reform unit which concentrates on test litigation and sometimes on statutory and administrative reform.

In such legal services programs, the law reform unit might have an attorney with full-time (or, in a smaller program, half-time) responsibility to do test litigation and statutory work for the elderly. He works directly with communitywide organizations of the elderly. He also trains all other attorneys in the program to be sensitive to the needs of the elderly so they can communicate effectively with these clients, handle their routine problems, and send particularly important cases involving the aged to the specialist on this subject. Another part of his job is to keep the other attorneys informed about new developments in law affecting old people and to suggest new legal methods for helping elderly clients.

Neighborhood offices with a particularly large number of elderly poor in their areas should have a specialist devoting all or a large proportion of his time to old people. Such specialization is necessary because of difficulties in dealing with elderly clients and the special legal problems which old people often have. This attorney would work with neighborhood organizations of the elderly.

Funding for these efforts should be at least partially available from existing legal services funds. An ideal program for the elderly will, however, usually require additional funds. Most legal service programs are already overburdened with a seemingly almost inexhaustible demand both to provide routine assistance and to develop test litigation and legislation. Therefore, if the elderly are to receive a larger quantity of services, not merely better organized and more knowledgeable services, additional resources must be obtained.

Most local programs will therefore have to rely in substantial part on local resources. The development of new legal programs to assist the elderly may be attractive to foundations, including those which are leery of many other kinds of social action programs. The local bar association or large law firms could be approached for funds. And, as we will discuss more fully below, the volunteer services of private lawyers and law students can be utilized to extend significantly the work of the paid legal service attorneys.

Such federal agencies as the Office of Economic Opportunity, the Administration on Aging and the Community Services Administration in HEW could also provide funding for legal services programs.

B. Working with Organizations of the Elderly. Another possible model for providing legal services to the elderly is to have a local senior citizens' organization, a senior center or some similar organization of the elderly have its own attorney or attorneys to serve the organization and its members. Many labor unions have attorneys who serve them not only as organizations but also serve individual members. There is no reason why senior citizens' organizations cannot do likewise.

Such a connection with a senior organization can help the attorneys serve the poor in several ways. The organization can often provide excellent outreach to the elderly poor so that knowledge of and trust in the services of attorneys will be established. Instead of attorneys in test litigation and legislation units determining their own priorities and interests, the senior organization can help establish them so they will best meet the needs of the elderly. The senior organization or its members can also often become the plaintiffs in test litigation and can be invaluable in lobbying for bills drafted by attorneys.

Conversely, attorneys can be of great assistance to senior organizations. Organizations grow and prosper when they can produce for their members. Attorneys can provide assistance to individual members which can even produce financial benefits. Attorneys can help bring suits and develop legislative strategies which can make major changes in how the elderly are treated. And they can formulate housing, economic development and other programs for the senior organization.

The attorney for a senior organization has a heavy responsibility to serve the needs of his client and not his own interests. He should subordinate himself to the priorities of his client. And he should keep the organization regularly informed of developments during what is frequently long drawn out litigation.

Senior organizations might obtain attorneys in several different ways. An attorney attached to a legal services program could be loaned full- or part-time to work for the senior organization or he could simply have the organization as one of its clients. A senior organization could use existing funds or seek foundation assistance to employ an attorney full- or part-time for its own staff. Alternatively, the senior organization could use such funds to retain a private attorney or law firm as the Council of Elders has done in Boston; or the senior organization could use one or more private attorneys as its volunteer counsel. Such private counsel, whether paid or not, may obtain for the elderly greater respect from the agencies, other attorneys, judges and legislators with whom they deal and greater self-respect among the elderly themselves.

C. *Using Volunteer Attorneys and Law Schools.* Many rural areas of the country do not have any CAA legal service programs funded by the Office of Economic Opportunity or any others. Consequently, in these areas, legal service for the elderly cannot be built into established programs but must be set up anew.

One excellent method of providing more legal assistance to the elderly is to use the volunteer services of private lawyers and law students. Over the last few years, private lawyers have increasingly devoted time to serving the poor and other groups needing legal assistance who do not have the money to pay for it. Sometimes this service has simply been the contribution of time by an individual attorney to serve clients who cannot pay. However, large law firms are beginning to assign one or more attorneys on a full-time basis to provide such legal services and to coordinate the efforts of other attorneys in their firm who are providing assistance on a more limited part-time basis. A few law firms have also established special offices in poverty areas to carry out this work.*

*Additional information on the work of local bar associations, law firms and individual attorneys can be obtained from the Pro Bono Project of the American Bar Association, 1705 DeSales Street, N.W., Washington, D.C.

Law schools, often as a result of the demands of their students, have similarly expanded their services to the poor. Large numbers of law students provide legal service to the poor in conjunction with courses given for credit, through student organizations like legal aid societies, or simply on their own time. As interest in poverty law has increased, law professors have similarly expanded their work in this field.

Law schools can be of particularly great assistance in the formulation of new theories and strategies to help the elderly. Law professors may be induced to give special courses on legal assistance to the elderly, just as such courses on other specialized poverty fields like welfare and housing law have been started. The students can be assigned a variety of different topics to investigate. The legal services program for the aged can then make excellent use of the papers and ideas developed.

Private attorneys, law firms, and law students are more available in middle and large cities. In such areas, the legal services program is probably already working with private attorneys and law firms. This effort could appropriately be expanded to legal services for the elderly by working through the local bar association, contracting other organizations of lawyers if they exist, and approaching law firms directly.

Unfortunately, those rural areas without legal service will rarely have either substantial sized private law firms or law schools. In such situations, law firms and law schools in nearby cities may still be persuaded to provide assistance outside their immediate community. Law schools are often interested in the entire state.

All areas of the country have attorneys in private practice. In a number of communities, senior centers and senior programs have obtained the services of attorneys on a volunteer basis. The county bar association may be persuaded to coordinate such an effort.

Particularly good sources of volunteer assistance are retired or semi-retired lawyers. Such lawyers, who are themselves older, have better ability to communicate with elderly clients and to understand their problems. They may also be more interested in helping the aged than are younger attorneys.

One senior center in a small town contacted a local 4-partner law firm, each of whose members agreed to donate 3 hours per week to serving the elderly.

The Small Business Administration has organized through SCORE retired businessmen to help minority and other poor people considering going into business. A similar organization of retired lawyers to serve the elderly might well be organized through the local bar association, community action agency or similar group.

Any volunteer effort, whether by private attorneys, law professors, or law students, is likely to work better if coordinated by full-time personnel. In places with legal service programs, such coordination should probably be the responsibility of the attorney specially serving the elderly. In places without such a legal service program, the volunteer efforts might be coordinated by the community action agency or similar group. Alternatively, a volunteer private attorney or law professor willing to spend considerable time may be willing to coordinate the effort.

Finally, there is a need for attorneys to provide counsel to the elderly in cases involving a fair fee. For example, the elderly are represented by counsel in less than one quarter of Social Security hearings even though successful attorneys are entitled to a fee from the payment due. Local bar associations can run programs to acquaint the elderly with their right to counsel and to train lawyers to carry out such representation.

D.   Using Legal Aides. Lawyers alone cannot provide all the legal services required for the elderly or for the rest of the poor. Lawyers are expensive and legal service programs are almost uniformly short of funds to serve their clients adequately. But even if far more money were available, it is doubtful that there are enough lawyers to serve all the poor and moderate -income citizens who need assistance. In any event, there are some functions relating to law that laymen can perform better than lawyers.

Consequently, a number of efforts have been made in the last few years to have laymen serve as legal aides to attorneys. These legal aides can perform a variety of different functions.

They can act as advocates for elderly clients. They can listen to the elders' problems and work with local welfare, Social Security or other agencies to obtain additional benefits for them. If the aides' efforts fail, they can call in an attorney to bring legal action.

For example, a blind man living only on Social Security benefits sought assistance from the Council of Elders in Boston. With the help of a legal aide, he was certified under Aid to the Blind and the aide successfully contended that the man was owed $4,600 in back payments. When an elderly welfare recipient was denied his request for false teeth, the aide pointed out to welfare officials that denial of teeth could result in a large public expenditure by harming the man's health and forcing him into a nursing home. The aide not only obtained the money for the false teeth but also for a special telephone allotment.

California Rural Legal Assistance aides have similarly worked on health benefit programs in San Francisco. A client received over $5,000 from Medicare when an advocate sought reconsideration after benefits were denied. These aides have also represented the elderly at hearings relating to Aid to the Totally Disabled.

Aides performing the role of advocates for the elderly can be located within institutions with whom the elderly deal. They can work for, or at least within, hospitals to assure adequate treatment, payment for Medicare, Medicaid, and private insurance benefits, and the like. The Council of Elders has negotiated with the Boston City Hospital to hire advocates to protect the rights of patients and California Rural Legal Assistance is training aides as in-hospital advocates. They can also represent the aged with welfare agencies, Social Security offices and public housing authorities.

Such advocacy requires thorough training. It also probably necessitates that the aides specialize in one or two areas, such as health or welfare. In this way, they can become experts on the basic legal framework and the procedures of the agency with which they deal.

Aides can also be used to handle routine legal matters. For example, with thorough training, armed with detailed checklists of what to look for and given model legal documents, they can write wills and handle probate matters. This is probably the only way all of the old people can get the legal services they need. The Council of Elders is planning to train lay aides as conservators for elderly persons who cannot manage their own property, which would include finding those who need this assistance, providing them with the legal and social services required, and obtaining for them other community resources.

Aides can assist lawyers by investigating facts and interviewing witnesses. This can be done both in individual cases and broader problems. An aide in California Rural Legal Assistance, together with a social welfare student, is investigating all nursing homes in San Francisco as preparation for litigation or legislative reform. The aides' knowledge of the community and the trust they can engender may often make them superior in these functions to attorneys.

Aides can also participate in lobbying and other legislative activities. The aides of the Council of Elders have worked on a legislative program lobbying for bills drafted by a private law firm retained by the Council.

Similarly, an aide in the California Rural Legal Assistance program in San Francisco has helped organize a statewide Committee Against Medi-Cal cutbacks and has coordinated a turnout of some 500 older persons from San Francisco at hearings on the cutbacks in Sacramento at which legal service attorneys represented the aged. An aide in the program in Rowan County, Kentucky developed community support for a new water line so residents would not have to use contaminated well water, and successfully persuaded the county water board and state to build it.

Aides can help educate the elderly concerning their legal rights. This can be done door-to-door as part of outreach to bring the old people who need the help of an attorney to the legal service office. It can also be done by speaking at community meetings or developing special meetings for this purpose. The aides of Small Estates Administration for the Bronx Aging set up meetings attended by 4,000 elderly persons concerning will and probate matters. If questionnaires are distributed at such meetings, legal problems can be discovered and aides and attorneys can later provide necessary legal services.

Finally, aides can work with legal service clients, both individuals and organizations. They can keep them informed about efforts being made in their behalf. They can speak regularly to organizations about the progress of litigation and legislative reform. After the lawyers are finished with their work, aides can provide follow-up with the client to ensure that the benefits of any legal successes are maximized.

It is vital that any legal aide program not lead to second-rate legal services just because money and attorneys are in short supply. Constant effort therefore must be made to assure high-quality service. Aides must receive considerable initial and in-service training. The aides of the California Rural Legal Assistance program in San Francisco received three months of initial training, including field trips, role playing and other educational devices described in a model training manual for lay advocates. Aides shall receive checklists and other materials prepared by attorneys and be closely supervised by them. Attorneys should review all cases to ensure that legal issues beyond aides' knowledge and experience are not overlooked.

Besides their contribution to the legal services program, the use of aides has another important benefit. Since the aides should be recruited from the ranks of the elderly poor, when possible, this can provide employment for old people. A legal services program should be able to design such a project to allow part-time employment at flexible hours which would spread the work and income and best meet the needs of the elderly.

Legal aid programs can be developed by using persons loaned from other agencies. A community action agency, settlement house or senior center might train some of its existing aides to assist attorneys working on behalf of the poor. Alternatively, such organizations might seek funds from local or state units of OEO, AoA, HEW, or from the local United Givers Fund or its equivalent, to finance a legal aide program.

Private foundations might find a legal aide program attractive as an innovative way of using community people to assist professionals.

E. Setting Up Statewide Legal Services. Legal services for the elderly are needed on a statewide as well as local basis. Such an office can carry out test litigation in areas of the state that do not have any legal services program or do not have a program devoting significant attention to the elderly. It can provide training, information, and continuing assistance to legal service attorneys who are concentrating on the aged and can circulate model legal documents prepared by one attorney to others.

Perhaps most important, a statewide office is needed to draft and lobby for state legislation to benefit the aged. State legislatures determine many of the most important issues affecting old people, such as eligibility and level of benefits for Old Age Assistance, eligibility and scope of benefits for Medicaid, development of special housing programs for the elderly, and tax measures. Besides drafting bills, the attorneys should develop the factual and legal basis for the legislation in the form of memoranda, testimony at hearings, and speeches for friendly legislators. The attorneys should work with senior organizations and business, labor, poverty and other groups to get persons to support the legislation at hearings and otherwise demonstrate broad support for the legislation.

A statewide office should generally be located in the state capital, which is usually reasonably accessible to the rest of the state. It is generally the headquarters of the state bar association with which the state legal assistance office for the elderly should work. And it is the obvious place to be most effective in obtaining passage of state legislation as well as changes in state administrative regulations to benefit old people.

A state legal office for the elderly might well be combined with a general state office of legal assistance for all the poor, since it would make available more and varied legal talent.

A state office could probably not be financed with foundation money because foundations cannot provide funds for lobbying which would be a central function of a state office. It may be possible to persuade existing, large legal service programs to loan attorneys for this purpose. Alternatively, all existing programs in a state might contribute fixed proportions of their budgets for a state office. The Office of Economic Opportunity, which has funded state legal services in Massachusetts and Ohio, might be willing to provide funds. Paid attorneys could be supplemented by volunteer private attorneys, who often have considerable experience in obtaining legislation from the legislature, and by law students who frequently have a considerable interest in researching and drafting legislation.

CONCLUSION

There can be little doubt that the elderly poor urgently need and can significantly benefit from a substantially greater degree of legal assistance than is now available. Legal assistance for them is even more scarce than for the younger poor. While lawyers cannot perform miracles, they can protect the elderly from injustices and can develop new kinds of affirmative programs to benefit them. The elderly, and most especially those who work with the elderly, have a responsibility to develop new legal service programs and obtain the resources to implement them. Only in this way can the aged be guaranteed that most basic of human and American rights, equal justice.

36. How to Make an Effective Referral*

Elizabeth Nicholds**

A person who has found himself in trouble, financial, emotional, or legal, is likely to turn to a friend or professional acquaintance, or to an agency about which he has heard. If this is his first experience, the troubled one may by chance turn to an agency that cannot meet his particular problem, but the caseworker to whom he tells his story must hear him out. Anyone who has accepted a profession that claims to be a helping profession has accepted the obligation to listen to a person who comes to him in trouble. It may be evident fairly early in the interview that the troubled one has come to the wrong place for the special help he needs, and if that is the situation, then the worker must direct him to an agency where help is available. The caseworker will listen to him, ask questions, and through this initial interview diagnose as far as possible.

This initial interview and the resulting diagnosis are known in most agencies as the "intake process." In a large organization the whole job of one or more persons consists of seeing new applicants when they first come in for help. In smaller agencies the intake is usually done by staff members who have other responsibilities as well. Either way, it is important that anyone who undertakes an intake interview should be skillful in creating an atmosphere in which the client can open up and talk freely. The intake worker should also have a thorough knowledge not only of the resources and limitations of his own agency but also of other resources in the community. If the agency can help with this particular problem, the intake worker will start at once formulating some sort of plan.

The intake worker may close the case, his agency at the point of intake transferring the whole problem, lock, stock, and barrel, to another agency. This might happen, for example, if a boy should go to a school nurse for help in finding a summer job. The nurse would probably send the boy and his request to the school guidance director, or to an employment agency, along with any information about the boy and abilities that she might have. Or, if a man worried about his sick

*Reprinted from A primer of social casework, Chapter 9, pages 66-77, published by Columbia University Press in 1960 with permission of the author and Columbia University Press.
**Ms. Nicholds wrote this book while teaching a summer course on casework in the New York State University. She is currently living in Gales Ferry, Conn.

447

child should go to his pastor, the minister might call in a doctor, or send the man to a clinic, or possibly, if there was also a problem of money to meet the medical bills, to a public welfare agency.

At times, however, the one who sees the client at intake may hold open the case, giving through his own agency what his agency is equipped to give, and applying to resources in the community for additional help in areas beyond the scope of his organization. This would happen, for instance, if a man applied to a public welfare agency for help in placing a mentally retarded child in an appropriate state school. An agency worker would refer the child to a psychologist for accurate diagnosis, and if placement were recommended by this source, he would make a further referral to the institution selected and help the family through the legal procedures for admission.

It is impossible that any one agency should be equipped to meet unaided all the varieties of problems that may be presented to its intake worker during the course of a year, or even, perhaps, during a day. Let us look, for example, at the situations met in the intake office of a large family-serving agency.

A mother comes in with a spastic child. Authorities have told her that he needs some sort of education, but clearly he cannot get along in the rough-and-tumble of public school, she cannot possibly pay for a tutor, so what can she do, she asks. Or perhaps the child is blind, or deaf, or epileptic, or mentally retarded, or hampered by any of the handicaps that make public school life intolerable and pointless for a youngster. The mother needs help in planning for him.

A shiftless-looking man lounges in. He has lost his job, the unemployment insurance has not started yet, he has no savings, rent is due, and there is no food in the house. He needs help right away, he says, or his furniture will be put on the street.

A hesitant seventeen-year-old girl comes to the agency. She is pregnant, and terrified that her father will find out. Her mother knows, but she too is afraid of the father. The girl has six months to wait before the baby will be born, and where can she go? She does not know what to do about the baby, either. The man was a cross-country truck driver, she does not know where he is now, and she does not want anything to do with him any more even if she finds him.

The judge of the Children's Court phones to refer a fifteen-year-old boy who has been taking joy rides with other kids in stolen cars. The judge feels that this boy was never a leader in the gang, that he is far from incorrigible, but that his family is quite incapable of coping with him. The boy would probably straighten out with a little help. Is there any place for him to go, not quite so rugged as a state correctional school?

A seventy-year-old man fumbles his way into the office. He assures the worker that he is just as smart as he ever was, but it seems that nobody wants to give him a job any more, so how can he earn an honest living? He has always done odd jobs, so he does not have any Social Security, but he cannot get odd jobs now because he cannot work fast enough to suit people. His daughter-in-law will not have him in her home. She claims he scatters tobacco in the bed, and he likes to sit in the living room where the television is but her daughters want to entertain their dates there and do not want him around. Nobody wants him around. So where can he go?

An exhausted-looking man collapses in the client's chair. He has hitchhiked from a city 300 miles away because he heard there was work here, but he has looked all day and cannot find anything. He needs a place to flop for the night, and he needs help to get back to his family.

A school nurse telephones. A high school girl badly needs dental work. Her teeth are in shocking condition, a menace to her health and an embarrassment to her because of their appearance. Both her social life and her schoolwork are suffering. Her family are not on relief, but they cannot afford the extensive work required. Can the agency do anything for her?

A distracted mother comes in carrying a small baby and dragging three other preschoolers behind her. Her husband has walked out. The electricity is turned off because the bill has not been paid, and there is not much food in the house. She would work if she could, but how can she leave the kids alone? And she could never make enough to pay a baby sitter. Cannot somebody make her husband do what he ought to, and cannot somebody help her with the bills meantime? She does not want to "put the kids away" if she does not have to.

The hospital telephones. A migratory worker has been brought in by ambulance with a bad knife wound in his side. Who will pay the medical bills?

A farmer calls up. Does the agency know any husky boy who could help with chores in return for his keep? There would be no wages, but the boy could go to school, and there would be plenty of food.

A harried man comes in. His wife is going to have another baby pretty soon, and he does not see how he can take care of the two kids already at home. There is no relative who can help, and although he has looked around for a woman to stay with the children there does not seem to be anybody. If he stayed home with them himself he would lose time from his job and he might even be fired. The boss does not like men who do not appear regularly. Is there anything the agency can do, just for a week or so, until his wife gets back on her feet? The children are four and two, good youngsters, but too little to be left alone.

With some of these situations a family agency can help directly. With others, it cannot. Clearly, the intake worker must have at his finger tips information about educational resources for handicapped, and medical resources for those who are afflicted by all sorts of physical and mental disabilities. He must know the employment possibilities in his community, and how to help the unemployed by referral to employment agencies or with information concerning applications for unemployment assistance or retirement benefits or survivor's benefits, or for home relief if none of the other resources is applicable. He must know about service clubs, neighborhood clubs, Travelers' Aid, court resources. He must know about foster homes, visiting housekeeping services, visiting nurses. He must know all the social agencies, public and private, both their potentialities and their limitations.

The list of resources that follows can do no more than suggest, since resources vary from state to state, from county to county, from city to city. However, from this list the person who hopes to help a client can select whatever is both suitable and available.

HEALTH PROBLEMS

Clinics
Cancer
Cardiac
General medical
Pediatrics
Tuberculosis
Loan closets for invalid equipment such as crutches,
wheel chairs, and hospital beds
Nurses
Insurance company
Private
Public health
Visiting
Private medical or dental practitioners
Public health officers
Special committees
Cancer
Heart
Muscular dystrophy
Tuberculosis

Special hospitals
    Cancer
    Epileptic
    Mental
    Tuberculosis

HANDICAPPED

Associations for the blind, state and private
Itinerant teachers
Private schools for special handicaps
    Cardiac
    Mentally retarded
    Spastic
Rehabilitation programs and training centers
State aid for the handicapped child
State schools for special handicaps
    Blind
    Deaf
    Mentally retarded

FINANCIAL NEED

Fraternal organizations
Private relief organizations
    Church-related
    Secular
Public welfare agencies
    Child welfare
    Public assistance for adults or family groups
Special need
    American Legion
    American Red Cross
    Legal Aid
    Travelers' Aid
    Visiting homemakers

LAW ENFORCEMENT

Courts
    Children's

County
Domestic relations
Supreme
Surrogate
Police department
Probation and parole officers

CHARACTER-BUILDING GROUPS

Boy Scouts and Girl Scouts
Campfire Girls
Church groups
Community houses
Future Farmers and Four H
Home and Farm Bureau
Neighborhood clubs
Y.M. and Y.W. Christian Associations and Hebrew Associations

MENTAL HEALTH

Clinics
    Child guidance
    Mental health
Psychiatrists
Psychologists
Public or private schools offering therapy

EMOTIONAL PROBLEMS

Agencies offering casework and marriage counseling
Psychiatrists
Religious leaders

It is of the utmost importance that the person who makes the referral should know exactly what he is talking about. In addition to a pretty clear picture of the client's situation, the worker should have a thorough acquaintance with the resources, and the regulations of the agency to which he is referring his client. Imagine the frustration of some unhappy individual who is shunted from agency to agency, only to be informed by each one that he is not eligible for the type of help provided there. Repeated rejection is certain to aggravate any problem in the mind of the sufferer.

Many institutions, both state and private, can accept applicants from only a limited geographical area. There are often age limits, or requirements concerning the intelligence quotient of an acceptable client. Private organizations sometimes accept clients of only a specified religious faith. Most of the state schools and private institutions offer brochures which outline their services and their regulations. Many of them give explicit directions which should be followed in making a written referral before sending a client on to them.

A referral may be made to an agency or an institution at some distance, but more often it will be to a resource in the community. It is wise for anyone working with troubled people to acquaint himself not only with the resource agencies but also with the personalities of the staff members of those agencies. No organization is more helpful than the people who run it want it to be, and the special slant of any agency is determined by the director and the staff. In one community a pastor or a priest may keep himself available to anyone in trouble, while in another the leaders of those same denominations may limit their activities to their own people. In one area a public agency may do adoption work; in another, it does not. Some school vocational guidance directors serve also as counselors in personality problems; in other schools they limit their work to advice on employment. Some Salvation Army Corps operate shelters for transients; some maintain workrooms where second-hand furniture is refinished and sold for very little; some specialize in collecting inexpensive clothing; some, in serving hot soup to the indigent. It all depends on the special interests or skills of the personnel, the funds of the Corps, the greatest need of the vicinity. As the worker gains experience and puts down roots in his own community he will learn which individuals and which organizations can be called on for the particular type of help needed in any situation. The wider and more personal his knowledge of area resources and organizations, the greater his value to his own agency and to his clients.

When a worker refers a client to another individual or another agency, whether for complete care or for help to supplement that which is already being given, he should first get in touch with the person to whom the client is referred. Sometimes this can appropriately be done by phone; more often it should be done in writing; possibly it may be done by a telephone call that is followed by the detailed written referral. This is one of the many times when a caseworker benefits from the kind of imagination which enables him to put himself in the other fellow's place. What sort of information does the intake worker of the second agency need in order to make this interview as easy as possible for the client? What should the referring worker say that will lead the other worker to ask just the right questions that will put the client at ease and prompt him to tell his whole story?

There are three questions, the answers to which the intake worker of the second agency should always be given:

1. What is the problem as the first worker understands it?
2. What is expected or hoped for from the second agency?
3. How does the client feel about the referral? In other words: how has it been interpreted to him by the first worker?

If the case has been closed by the first agency at point of intake and the client referred at once to a second agency, these questions may be the only ones which the written referral can cover. But if the client has been known for some time to one agency and is referred to another organization for supplementary service, a great deal more information will be available and as much of this should be given to the second worker as could be considered helpful toward quick interpretation of client or of problem.

By way of illustration, suppose we outline the information which might profitably go with a child referred by a school to a child guidance clinic from whom psychological testing, psychiatric diagnosis, and recommendation are expected:

1. Description of the present problem
2. Present school life
   a. Scholastic record
   b. Scores of mental or aptitude tests
3. Physical condition
   a. Defects of hearing, seeing, breathing, coordination
   b. Known permanent effects of old illnesses, operations, or accidents
   c. Tendencies toward colds, sore throat, indigestion, nervousness, constipation
   d. Marked physical weaknesses
4. Social record in school
   a. Participation in school activities
   b. Friends: Number? Age? Type?
   c. Adjustment to fellow students: — Is child a leader or a follower?
5. Life outside school
   a. Meals: Regular? Adequate? Quality?
   b. Sleep: Regular? Adequate?
   c. Exercise: Type? Effect (stimulating; enervating)?

6. Home
   a. Housing
   b. Cultural facilities and standards
   c. Religion
   d. Number of children
   e. Outsiders in the home: Relatives? Boarders? Servants?
   f. Attitude of child toward other members of the household
7. Family background
   a. Father
      1) Age
      2) Health
      3) Personality
      4) Occupation
      5) Education
      6) Religion
      7) Interests outside the home
   b. Mother (same information as for father)
   c. Siblings (same information as for parents, where applicable)
   d. Attitude of members of the family toward child
8. Early history of child
   a. Physical history
      1) Duration of mother's pregnancy
      2) Health of mother during pregnancy
      3) Birth history: instrument used; any difficulties; weight
      4) Method of feeding: breast or bottle; feeding difficulties
   b. Early childhood
      1) At what age did he walk? Talk? Teethe?
      2) Toilet training: At what age? How accomplished?
      3) General health
      4) Childhood diseases
      5) Shots and immunizations
   c. Emotional history
      1) Fears and anxieties
      2) Tantrums
      3) Shyness
      4) Delinquencies
9. Attitude of parents toward present problem
10. Attitude of child toward present problem

This may seem to be an unnecessarily detailed outline, but every item in it would help the psychologist and the psychiatrist to a deeper, truer understanding of the child, thereby enabling them to make a recommendation based on an accurate diagnosis. All of the facts needed to complete such an outline could be obtained through interviews with the child's family, his teachers, school nurse, school doctor, family physician and guidance director.

In other situations, less information would be required in order to make an efficient referral. A person sent by an agency to apply for a job, for example, might be accompanied or preceded by an outline that gives:

> Name
> Sex
> Age
> Education
> Medical record
> Previous work history
> References from previous employers
> Anything that has transpired since the last employment which
>   might affect present employability
> Special skills
> Special handicaps
> Attitude of the employee toward this referral

Each referral must necessarily be different, each outline adjusted to the individual circumstances of the special referral. But the two included here are sufficient to show that what every worker needs in making a referral to another agency or another worker is: (1) knowledge of his client and the client's need; (2) knowledge of the other agency's rules, requirements, and limitations; and (3) an imaginative awareness of what the worker in the other agency needs to know so that he may help the client promptly and efficiently.

Nor should the client himself be forgotten in the process of referral. He must never be left with the impression that he is being shunted from spot to spot without being consulted and without explanation. Any referral from one caseworker to another carries with it some slight implication of rejection, and this must be minimized as much as possible. The rejection may be very slight indeed. A man perhaps goes to a social agency quite well aware that this organization is not equipped to help him but hopeful that he can obtain information about other resources: "I know you're not the ones that find people, but my boy left home last week. He's nineteen and probably all right, but I just wish I could hear about where he is." "My old father is getting very queer in the head, and I just don't know how to go about getting him put where he can't do himself an injury. Can you tell me what I have to do?" In such cases straight factual information is all that is needed. But often an applicant comes in hoping for help, expecting it, unaware that he has come to the wrong agency for his purpose. Then it may disturb him very much indeed to be sent elsewhere, the depth of the hurt depending on the seriousness of his trouble and on his own temperament. An insecure person might give up and not seek help again even if another address were given him.

Perhaps the client is to be sent to another agency, or he may be transferred from one division to another within the same agency, or perhaps he is transferred from one caseworker to another because the first one is leaving the agency or taking a holiday. Then the referral must be carefully and tactfully made, with complete explanation to the client of the reasons, whether due to agency organization or more personal matters concerned with an individual worker. Even when reasons are given and all explanations supplied, the client may still have a nagging suspicion that the first agency, the first division, the first caseworker, really wanted to get rid of him. There are three practical suggestions for helping a client overcome this feeling: Explain the transfer in terms he can understand. Give him a chance to say how he feels about the referral, which will help him express any resentment or hurt he may feel. And see to it that he has a definite appointment with the second agency or the second worker, an appointment explicit as to day, hour, and place. In fact, the first worker should accompany him and make the introduction, if that is at all practicable.

37. Creating Opportunities For The Aging*

In the small town of Earlham, Iowa, John R. Carson has a job that is quite unusual in America, as illustrated by a typical day in his life. On his way to the office from his home at 7:30 a.m., he stopped at the apartment of an elderly man, Nitus Slaven, who had been ill. Slaven said he was feeling much better and would start eating at the local cafe again. The elderly man had been receiving his food through a service which Carson has developed in Earlham. Called "meals on wheels," it is designed to bring well-prepared, reasonably priced food to the homes of elderly people who can no longer cook or go out to eat.

At 7:50, Carson arrived at his office, which is in the front of a sizable recreation hall and is headquarters for the "Earlham Care Program." As program director, he has the task of developing a self-sustaining program to help the many older citizens of the small rural town. A grant of Federal and State funds administered by the State of Iowa, which has the Nation's highest per capita count of older people, is helping the program get started.

The young program director, previously a schoolteacher, was hanging up his coat when the telephone rang. An elderly lady who had a doctor's appointment at the local clinic requested that the program's taxi be sent around to her house. Carson agreed, asked the caller how she was feeling this morning, and politely ended the call. Immediately he dialed the special taxi service operated by a retired man who for 25 cents will transport an older citizen anywhere in town.

Before 8:30 A.M., when his secretary arrived, Carson had little time for anything but answering the telephone and filling requests for various services that he has established for Earlham's older people. The secretary took over most of the requests, giving the director an opportunity to read some information forwarded from Kansas City. He was particularly interested in the explanation of some new Federal legislation for the elderly.

*Reprinted from *On growing older*, by the President's Council on Aging, chapter 8, pages 133-141, published by the U. S. Government Printing Office, 1964.

This book was written for the President's Council by L. A. Stevens of Bridgewater, Conn.

During the morning he held several meetings with individuals, including town officials, interested in the care program's success. One meeting was with a lady who heads Carson's program called "Telephone Visitations," for which each of a group of Earlham women agrees to call a certain number of older citizens every day to check upon their needs, see that they are in good health, and provide them with the comfort of knowing that someone is concerned with their welfare. Another care program, "Friendly Visitations," augments the organized telephone calls. In this case, people of the town, through church-organized committees, pay regular visits to their less able elders.

About noon Carson checked with a local nursing home whose cook prepares the meals on wheels and learned that several were to go out that day. The retired taxi man makes the deliveries for 25 cents per meal. The elderly customer is charged the delivery fee in addition to the price of $1 per meal.

After a quick lunch at home, Carson stopped by the house of John and Della Prior, one of Earlham's oldest couples. John Prior, 90 years old, was waiting with a Chinese checkerboard because every Friday after lunch Carson drops by for a game. This time Prior won.

Back at his office about 1:30, Carson found one of his part-time employees, a "homemaker," waiting by his desk. The lady, a member of the Earlham program's "Homemaker Service," spent a few minutes discussing the problems of an elderly woman under her care. Carson's homemakers, who work for a minimum hourly wage, take care of several elderly citizens, doing their shopping, cleaning, and any other required chores.

After the homemaker left, Carson closed his office door, saying to his secretary that he needed privacy for a half hour. He then wrote a short article for the local weekly newspaper, carefully describing some recent rate changes in a nonprofit health insurance plan that interests many older people.

When the office door was opened, a local businessman was waiting to discuss hiring an older person for part-time work. Carson also has an elderly citizens employment service. The prospective employer left, and a widow, perhaps 68 or 70 years old, came in. She was upset by a plumbing problem that had plagued her for some time, and Carson promised to bring a plumber over to her house. He was deeply concerned about this widow, whose husband had died 3 years before. He had obviously taken care of everything for her, and now the elderly woman seemed completely lost in the world. Whenever Carson visits her, she cries, as she thinks of an unending series of problems that confuse her.

When she departed, the program director reviewed the requests for his newly formed "Handyman Service," which is always busy on Saturdays because it is staffed by high school boys. For a small hourly fee, these youngsters do all sorts of chores for Earlham's older citizens. Those who are good with tools take care of minor home repairs. Others rake leaves, mow lawns, wash windows, and do a hundred other jobs which crop up around any home.

As the business hours ended, Carson's telephone was still ringing, and he and his secretary were filling a half dozen more requests that could help the elderly of Earlham. Around 6:15 he went home and relaxed on the living room sofa while his wife prepared the evening meal. But then the telephone rang, and the widow asked when she could expect the plumber.

A Little Means a Lot

Many of America's institutions associated with the elderly, from nursing homes to mental hospitals, house thousands of older citizens who need not be there. A large percentage are relatively able and mentally capable but are institutionalized because no other place seems available and not because of the older people's choosing. In their institutional setting — even in the clothing they wear — they become people who have reached the end of the road. Life is then a burden devoid of the joys that are possible even in its latest decades. The tragedy is heightened by a look at the reasons why many of these people have been taken from their homes. Here are but a few:

> They can no longer go shopping.
> Meal preparation is difficult and frequently neglected.
> Housecleaning is too taxing.
> Home maintenance cannot be properly handled.
> A son or daughter fears leaving an elderly parent alone and
>   unchecked upon.
> The simplest of medical care cannot be afforded.

But assistance, either publicly or privately sponsored, in any of these areas or combination of them, is not too difficult to render. Furthermore, the comparative cost for keeping someone in his own home where he wants to be against the expenses he incurs at an institution provides an additional motive for assisting the elderly to remain on their own.

In years past, the term "care for the aged" brought certain stereotypes to people's minds. They thought of old people's homes, nursing homes, county farms, or other institutions where the elderly sat out their few remaining days. Such images are still widely held, but they are changing, as the Earlham story may indicate. With our increasing concern for the older American, a great deal of thought and action is going into the problems of aging. One major result is an important change in emphasis concerning how we look at the elderly citizen. Instead of asking: "Where can we put him?" authorities are asking: "How can we help him stay independent?"

In this shift of emphasis, the older American's chances for continuing independence are rising rapidly. We are learning that assistance, well thought out and offered at the right time, does not rob an individual of his independence, but it gives him his only chance to continue on his own. Working from this point of view, the possibilities for helping older people are full of hope.

Such thinking is being implemented across the Nation in a general social movement that certainly will bring better living in old age. It is evident in different degrees and forms in many communities, reflecting the Nation's wide variety of customs, values, and leadership. It springs from growing national recognition that older people in our society are important, that *the problems of aging solved today will enrich our own tomorrows.*

At the forefront of the movement many different groups are creating opportunities and services for the elderly. Among the public agencies, local welfare and health departments have been most active. Public schools, libraries, and recreation departments are recognizing their responsibilities to older people. Local housing authorities are looking beyond the mere provision of shelter to programs for later life, such as health maintenance activities.

Citizens' committees for the aging have been appointed in many municipalities and counties. Community health and welfare councils often spark community action. Church groups, service clubs, and local affiliates of national organizations are sponsoring special activities. And older people are organizing to help themselves.

State government offices are examining their responsibilities to the aged as health, education, employment, recreation, and welfare departments coordinate efforts in behalf of older citizens. Forty-three States have commissions or Governor's committees on aging, and a substantial number of State welfare agencies have staff specialists on the problems of growing old.

All these people are seeking knowledge and training. It is being provided more and more through research and educational programs in aging financed by foundations and government and conducted by universities. Seventeen universities already have established institutes of gerontology. Educational efforts on the subject are also moving down into grade and high schools.

Concern at the national level is extensive. More than 300 national organizations signed up to participate in the White House Conference on Aging in 1961, because of their concerns and activities for older people. They include the National Council on the Aging, the United Auto Workers Department of Older and Retired Workers, and the Gerontological Society, Inc.

The best known of the Federal Government's programs for the aging is social security, which for many older beneficiaries makes continuing independence possible. However, a total of 10 agencies administer over 40 different programs in health, housing, welfare, income maintenance, research, and other areas. In 1 year the Government is spending some $19 billion for benefits and services to older people.

The President's Council on Aging was created in May 1962 by Presidential Order. Among its tasks are the development of recommendations to the President to meet Federal responsibilities related to the problems of the aging and assistance in coordination of Federal programs serving older people. Its membership includes the Secretary of Health, Education, and Welfare (Chairman); the Secretaries of Agriculture, Commerce, Labor, and Treasury; the Chairman of the Civil Service Commission; and the Administrators of Veterans Affairs and the Housing and Home Finance Agency.

The Senate Special Committee on Aging, one of the largest Senate Committees, was established in February 1961. It has held numerous hearings throughout the Nation on the problems of age and has issued a variety of reports and legislative recommendations.

In the Executive Branch the Public Health Service created a Gerontology Branch concerned with the many programs of health maintenance and chronic diseases. The Office of Housing for Senior Citizens in the Housing and Home Finance Agency is directed by an Assistant Administrator of HHFA to give special emphasis to the range of elderly housing programs in that agency.

The Office of Aging in the Welfare Administration of the U.S. Department of Health, Education, and Welfare provides information and consultation through a central staff and regional representatives and cooperates with public and private organizations in the development of programs for the older people.

When all these efforts, public and private, are added together, one finds a considerable list of varied services available to the older American.

Some of the services are widespread, while others are offered in but a few places across the Nation. They can usually be found, when available, through health and welfare departments, or other organizations, such as a visiting nurse association.

Four areas are briefly mentioned and described as follows:

FINANCIAL SUPPORT SERVICES

Financial counseling helps people who may be eligible for benefits or pensions but don't know it. It also helps people take an objective, beneficial look at financial assets and responsibilities.

Employment counseling and job placement offices found in many communities are strengthening programs to place older individuals in suitable part-time jobs to help the large numbers of elderly seeking gainful employment.

Vocational rehabilitation helps disabled older people overcome employment handicaps, through skilled counseling, corrective physical therapy, and guided job placement.

Sheltered workshops open opportunities to older workers who, because of some disability, such as deafness or blindness, are unable to engage in productive jobs except in a unique, protected situation where production pressures are reduced, specially designed equipment is available, ramps replace steps, hours are adjusted to transportation problems, and other compensations are made. A workshop is usually sponsored by a rehabilitation or health agency, but one could be operated by volunteers guided by health and employment specialists.

PERSONAL AND FAMILY ADJUSTMENT SERVICES

Counseling social casework extends help on personal problems, living arrangements, retirement adjustments, and health problems of the older individual. A social worker is often able to restore, reinforce, or strengthen the effective performance of a troubled person in his daily life.

Family counseling copes with problems related to how the older person functions as part of his family.

Protective services provide the social, medical, and legal assistance needed to safeguard the rights and well-being of physically or mentally handicapped older people unable to deal with life's practical problems;

for example, the man in his 80's who becomes confused on a trip downtown and can't find his way home, or the old lady who in the face of almost insurmountable difficulties, insists on staying alone in her 10-room house, subsisting chiefly on toast and tea.

Information-referral services give older people a chance to talk with specialists who can advise on what is available to the elderly in the community and how to take advantage of it.

Homemaker services are designed to help preserve or create wholesome family living and prevent family disruption in times of stress. Homemakers are trained, professionally supervised women who furnish housekeeping and other home help to the aged. They are especially useful to the convalescent, acutely or chronically ill, or disabled.

Home-delivered meals (meals on wheels or portable meals) bring hot, nutritious food to the homes of the elderly unable to shop and cook or obtain help to do so. A hot meal may be delivered with a cold snack for later in the day. Many people who otherwise might require nursing home or other such living arrangements can often remain at home with delivered meals.

Shopping services, usually provided by volunteers, insure that older people unable to leave their homes receive what they need from local stores.

Friendly visiting (in person or by telephone) is also likely to be a volunteer service. It offers a regular, perhaps daily, human contact to old people who otherwise would suffer from unbroken stretches of loneliness. It also gives a systematic check upon a person's well-being which, in some cases, may bring help to an elderly person for a minor problem that could become a serious difficulty if left unattended. But most of all, the visiting services have the psychological benefit of saying in effect: "Someone cares for you." One older person has described it as "a judicial surveillance that feels mighty good when you live alone."

Night sitting, well known in England, provides a competent person to give a night off to another adult who takes care of an elderly invalid. It is particularly important when an older person requires round-the-clock help and his helper badly needs a night or two of unbroken sleep.

Transportation services are twofold. First is one where volunteers use their personal cars or drive an agency's vehicle to provide taxi service to the elderly, as described above in the case of Earlham, Iowa. The second is an escort service which sends out people to accompany elderly citizens on public or other forms of transportation to insure their safety and comfort.

Foster and personal-care homes are carefully selected, continually supervised private homes willing to take in older people no longer able to live on their own but not requiring the care of a nursing home. Social welfare agencies, which make the selections and do the supervision, recommend these homes to older people. Social workers help the homes, and the older tenants adjust to one another.

EDUCATION AND ACTIVITY SERVICES

Adult education for many older people in retirement permits a return to formal learning — arts and crafts, health, physical fitness, vocational skills, and general education from the study of literature to acquiring new languages. Recent Federal legislation is helping States expand adult educational programs, like the extension of library services to small communities with no public library. Retired teachers and professional people from many walks of life have much to contribute to these expanding programs.

Senior citizen centers and clubs are increasing to fill the social needs of older people. Some open only once or twice a week, but many now function all the time to offer a list of activities for all kinds of people. The director is usually paid, but members often elect officers and promote new programs. Health clinics in some centers fill the badly needed preventive medical services for the elderly. A number of centers also have social caseworkers for counseling. But more important is the opportunity for meaningful activity among other people of a like age. More centers are needed in addition to those already operating. Some of the most successful are under the direction of older, retired people.

Volunteer services using older people themselves are on the increase. Thousands of retired people, still able and active, find they can be useful to their communities and to themselves by volunteering for work in hospitals, nursing homes, children's institutions, senior citizen centers, schools, and settlement houses. The Veterans Administration Voluntary Service is making good use of many older people. Children especially can use the warmth and concern, as well as the experience and knowledge, of our older citizens, through such efforts as "proxy grandparents" established by a few churches.

HEALTH SERVICES

Preventive maintenance services, which are especially important to the elderly and are on the increase, have been discussed in chapter IV.

Coordinated home-care programs, developing in a number of communities, allow the elderly suffering a long-term illness to stay at home when ordinarily they would be hospitalized. The programs, usually administered by public health departments and visiting nurse associations, bring necessary hospital services, equipment, and personnel to a patient's home as opposed to keeping him in a hospital. While he receives required medical attention, he simultaneously experiences his family's love and care. Furthermore, such a service can release valuable hospital space to patients who definitely need to be there.

38. The Impact of Scientific Advances On Independent Living*

CARL EISDORFER**

If you break society up, using the old socio-economic bit of high, middle, and low, "low" is usually blue collar or productive assembly kind of work. It may not be low economically, but it's low in socio-economic status breakdown. It turns out that three studies I know indicate that retired workers get better after retirement, for at least the year or so following retirement. For the blue-collar workers, health gets better after retirement. The reason for this is that many people are hanging on till age sixty-five in order to retire at slightly higher Social Security. So they're working when they are sick and really don't want to work. If they were able to retire at 62 at the higher base, they probably would have retired at 62 or 63. There are many arguments for a flexible retirement age.

Consider the high socio-economic group. People in this group seem, just before or immediately after retirement, to show signs of emotional upset. After about six months, though, these people seem to make a new and pretty effective adjustment. They find new activities to replace their work activities. They find retirement activities, volunteer activities, travel, and so on. This group has an advantage in that these are the people who are maneuvering in communities anyway. They are the ones who have been rich enough, strong enough, powerful enough, well-fed and healthy enough to know how a community runs. In fact, in many cases they have run it. Even if they stop running the factory or the plant or the business, they find that the same kinds of skills are effective in the new community, and they make a good adaptation. Some have six months of problems; some don't even have that. They take a trip, work at their problems away from home, come back, and make the readjustment. This has also been confirmed in a couple of studies.

If there is a retirement crisis per se, it's at the middle-level group.

*Reprinted from *Action Now, Conference Proceedings*, edited by James Thorson, 1973, pages 44-51, with permission of the author and Dr. Thorson.
**Dr. Eisdorfer is Professor and Chairman of the Department of Psychiatry and Behavioral Sciences at the University of Washington in Seattle.

Here the evidence is elusive at best. For example, you find it most clearly in the military, where people retire at middle officer's rank after twenty years because they didn't make bird colonel. They have another problem, in effect, in that this is a forced retirement, not an automatic retirement. If they had been promoted they could have been kept on for a longer period. One of the things you know about these people as well as a lot of people who expected to get higher up in their own job — and these are typically white collar semi-professionals — is that they retire with a sense of failure. Your blue-collar worker doesn't retire with a sense of failure. He has already locked into his job and has not been particularly interested in the product he was making. His interest seems to be more with his union than with his employer. The middle income individual, on the other hand, typically has the responsibility of signing his name to something. If you are identified with something, if you put your signature on a piece of paper, it belongs to you. I think this is very important.

Now you have to decide whether you wanted to be head of the agency or not. If you never expected to be head, then there is no great problem. If you wanted to be the head, at some point you have to work that desire out of your system, for retirement signals the end of a possibility.

Now I've given you the first year following retirement. If you look about two or three years later, you have another set of problems. The middle income person does have continuing problems, and the low income person now begins to have problems, problems related to money. This relates to another study that was done in the Pacific Northwest, Oregon and Washington, using several thousand upper-middle income technicians. These are bright people, high school and college graduates by and large. This goes back four years ago to an AoA study in the aerospace industry. The intriguing things were, first, that nobody seemed to prepare for retirement and, second, that when they asked people how much money they were making they got a reasonable dollar figure. When they asked then whether this was enough to support them, though, about 85 percent of them said "no." They needed much more money to be able to live effectively. These were people fifty-five to sixty-two who were from three to ten years away from retirement, who were saying that they didn't have enough money to make ends meet. Then they asked these people whether they would have enough money in retirement, and about 85-90 percent said "yes," they thought they would have enough money in retirement. These workers who said they would have enough money were going to get a reduction in income of roughly 55 percent. Let me explain what I just said. A man who's making a salary, whatever it is, and saying he can't make ends meet but that when he retires at a 55 percent reduction he will be able to manage. I think we need a saner approach to the whole business of money handling.

I bring this up to show that bright people are obviously using some form of what the psychiatrist likes to call "denial," in this case denial of reality. When people deny reality, it's not a simple matter of telling them that they are denying reality, because these people are bright enough to know they get a reduction in income. They all know it's a fact. We're dealing with an emotional issue, and it requires a much more subtle way of handling the problem. I have repeatedly suggested, for example, that retirement planning has to start in the early forties, not in the fifties, because by the time you get into the late fifties, when most people start worrying about retirement, it's so traumatic that it begins to look too frightening when you hear the data — and you turn it off.

People in their forties aren't interested particularly, but they can be made interested. I think it's to the advantage of all of us to begin to think about, if not other people's retirement, then our own personal retirement sometime pretty soon. I think also it implies something about the nature of people working in the field of aging. We have to broaden our mandate. You can't wait until a person is sixty-five before you worry about aging. We will talk about that in a minute. The great advances in health, keeping people alive, have not been in curative medicine. They have been in public health. It's the prevention of illness that really counts, and I am talking about the disabilities in aging. So I think we need to broaden our mandate. I think we need to sell this argument. Any of you working in the field of aging should see yourself as beginning to work with people at the age of forty.

Let's talk about health and its importance to you. If we are talking about alternatives to institutional care, it turns out that physical health may be one of the most important areas we can worry about. Most of you ought to know about the data coming out of the Langley Porter Institute in San Francisco, where essentially they set up a screening service to look at roughly 600 people a year in the San Francisco General Hospital, people who would have been slated for institutionalization. The study was done very simply. They dealt with roughly 600 people referred to San Francisco General who were above age 65, who were first psychiatric admissions, and who were referred because that hospital was the intake center for the state hospitals. They began the study for a couple of reasons: (1) because they are bright and sensitive people, and (2) because the state began to make noises like it was going to close down admissions to state hospitals. So they had to take a good look at what was going on. They brought in a psychiatrist, an internist, a social worker, a psychologist, some nursing help; and they decided that all patients who come into this thing for a psychiatric work-up would get a full-scale physical and social work-up at the same time, and the results were nothing short of incredible.

They found that three-quarters of the people who were referred into this system had an acute, undiagnosed, untreated physical illness. Within two years, using alternate placement, social work, and medical help, they were putting only two people a year into the state hospitals. That's a fact: from six hundred to two. State hospitals were cooperating because they could raise their admissions standard.

During that same period, about one hundred people wound up in nursing homes in the community. What they demonstrated, then, was that with a combination of health and social service they could in fact divert the vast majority of people from state hospitalization. Those data are there, and that's been going on, by the way, for about ten years. It's hardly a new and exciting project, but very few people know about it.

I'll raise another question, and then I would like to get some feedback in terms of how we can make these kinds of data available. I think they are profoundly important data. I did a study in a state hospital in North Carolina which I never published. All I did, very simply, was to pick up thirty serial admissions in one of our regional state hospitals and discover some absolutely incredible things, things which really were indictments against the medical community. I've said this repeatedly to the medical community. Six people were sent in in one variety or another of coma where the coma was because of medical and nursing care in hospitals. They come on weekends, by the way, because that's when people like to take a day off; and they don't want to be bothered with having a sick patient in the hospital. If the patient is sixty or seventy, or seventy-five, it's just easier to make a referral to a hospital, particularly if the patient is dehydrated, as were four of these patients, who had started to hallucinate. Hallucination is not an uncommon phenomenon in old people when they get ill.

It turned out that these people were not psychotic, however, but now were in a state hospital and couldn't get out. The state hospitals wanted them out, but there were no resources. It's always incredible to me how you have a pie, take out a slice, then decide you don't want it, and try to put it back — only to discover there's a whole pie there. You know, the older person has a role in the community, then he's taken out of the community, and suddenly — zap! — his world closes up and there is no place for him. That's in fact one of the things we have to worry about.

The way social services must operate in this arena may vary from state to state, but one of the things that's compelling is that you really have to operate in some kind of collaboration with the health resources available. Straight admissions from any physician to a state hospital must be subverted. I say this with my AMA and my American Psychiatric Association cards neatly tucked into my wallet. The medical community really has not been alert to the needs of the patient. So you have another role, which is an interpretive role; and that's really a very important one. It seems to me one of the key variables in keeping people out of hospitals. It is also true that families probably do not dump patients. Elaine Brody says unequivocally that families are very upset about having to dump their folks. They have to work on it long and hard, and as often as not the big problem is that they wait too long.

This leads me to the next general notion that we need to look at, the whole business of who gets hospitalized. The aged psychiatric patient has received a lot more attention than the aged nursing home patient until very recently, because of the stigma of psychiatry and because the National Institute for Mental Health has given very little to aging. Some of the people in psychiatry have looked at this problem. I think you ought to know, by the way, that up until a couple of years ago we were delivering to the state hospitals about a third of their intakes in the form of first-admission geriatric patients. Putting it in a different way, about a third of all state hospital first admissions were geriatric first admissions. On an out-patient basis, 2 percent of all out-patient mental health services throughout the country have been delivered to the aged mentally ill. So that's another area for work. We have to get to the community mental health community because, whatever they are doing, they aren't attacking one of the prime reasons for getting into state hositals, namely geriatric illness.

It is not clear, incidentally, that all of the people going into state hospitals don't need it, because just like everybody else they believe the stereotypes, and they act accordingly. State hospital patients are very adaptive. They are supposed to be crazy, so they act crazy. They are just like you. You're supposed to act like a professional, so you do — or try to. You may think I'm being facetious, but some superb studies have demonstrated that expectancy is the best predictor of what a patient will do. It has nothing to do with the state of the patient; it has to do with the state of the staff.

Let's talk about some research in this context, since this was an important piece of work. Lowenthal presented us with data, and there are a couple of books now — *Lives in Distress, Mental Health in San Francisco.* I think they really need to be understood by the social service community. First of all, what Marjorie has demonstrated is that one of the most important protectors of the aged person is what she calls the confidant. The confidant is the presence in the community of a person, an individual, with whom the aged person can talk. All other things being equal, it's typically the eldest daughter of a family. The roles of the confidant seem to be established and are very important. Rich and middle class people seem to establish them more than poorer people. Men seem to have less effectiveness at establishing this confidant relationship than do women. A woman takes a friend, very often a daughter, but maybe an older woman. A widow, for example, may turn to another widow. She will be somebody to talk with, someone to rely on, someone she can reach on the phone, someone who is relatively near by. Let me mention that a lot of older people do not have somebody nearby whom they can rely upon. One of the reasons that they don't is because of the feeling that they are imposing. I'm trying to let you know that in your work in the community you can typically find somebody and help foster a confidant relationship. This is a crucial element in maintaining people in the community.

The people who wind up in state hospitals — and Lowenthal showed it in the Michigan study — tend to be the aloners — not just the *loners,* but the *aloners.* In fact, Gottesman found that this was so dramatic that he almost aimed at making the state hospital play an important role in checking up on them, because these people were alone in the community, had no one to care for them, to look out for them. It's interesting that Ruth Bennett has found a very similar phenomenon in New York, where again many people are literally alone. Here the role of social services in providing some kind of personal contact is very important.

Lowenthal also shows, in her many years of long study, something that somehow puts us on the horns of dilemma; and I will let you think about it. She demonstrates fairly effectively that the aged psychiatric patient tends to have symptoms for a long time before he gets service. That is to say that in her case patients seemed to have symptoms that dated back at least six months or as long as five years. Many people had been showing psychiatric symptomatology for a long time, but nobody bothered hospitalizing them until they got sick physically. Then, since there was no one around to care for them, they started hallucinating; and they had the psychiatric symptomatology which made it seem like a good idea to hospitalize them. They were now eligible, eligible by virtue of having disease. The interesting thing is that they had the same psychiatric disease while they were living in the community, but the physical disease triggered off the admission. This is what I've been trying to tell you. It's a very important concept. You can't ignore physicians, even though they are tough people to work with. Certainly we can't ignore health, and I'm not sure we can ignore physicians any more.

Another aspect of this situation is that psychiatric help was turned off by a lot of these people and by their families. So now we have a very interesting dilemma. One of the greatest pushes in community mental health has been the acceptance of deviance in the community. You have to appreciate the fact that not everybody should be locked up. Every time somebody does a little something aberrant, you don't run and incarcerate him or institutionalize him. On the one hand, you have the notion of acceptance of deviance. On the other, you have this notion of people who are showing deviance and increasing psychiatric symptomatology for one to five years. Nobody is going in there to help them. One of the things that needs to be done, it seems to me, is to educate people in the social service community and begin to deliver a new kind of help — help in trying to get early psychiatric help and intervention on an out-patient basis for a lot of patients. Often by the time they come into the hospital you are dealing with somebody who has multiple systems disease. Then you've got all kinds of problems, because even if you divert them from the state hospitals, they wind up becoming long-term nursing home patients, which leads me to the other hassle.

We use the word "community" in very elusive terms. Only recently we have begun to figure out that a nursing home is no more a community than a state hospital. The data also show, very conclusively, I am afraid, that geriatric mentally ill patients do better in state hospitals than they do in nursing homes. The long-term studies of Simon and Epstein show, by virtually all criteria — walking, talking, bathing, the amount of flexibility that people have, you name it — that long -term patient care results in a better, more adaptive, person in a state hospital than in a nursing home. This study was done in twenty-six nursing homes in the Bay area, and they were by and large pretty good nursing homes. Patients were really deteriorating there at a faster rate than in the state hospitals. There may be some extra reason for this. In California nursing homes get more money for keeping the patient in bed than for having him walk around. That's not unique to California, by the way. That's a classic example of the psychosis of social service management. Everything you know about reinforcement theory says they ought to pay to make people better, buy we pay to keep people in bed. If you get an extra two to four dollars a day to keep people in bed and there's no bonus for getting them out of bed, where do you think the nursing home manager is going to keep his patient? I realize that there are problems the other way around, that it *should* cost more to keep patients in bed. You can almost make it cost less, though, if everybody is getting the same care in bed. Then it might in fact be cheaper to keep people in bed than to have them wander around the halls. Some of you are in positions to do something about this. It's a matter of thinking very carefully about the effects of fiscal policy.

I have to bring up the beer and wine studies of Kastenbaum. These studies happened to be done within the state hospital, but some of the issues raised there should apply to the care of people in the community. They are a variation of the theme. We are talking about the expectancy and the role relationships, and I talked about advocacy the other night. Kastenbaum became the research director of the Cushing State Hospital, which is in Massachusetts and is the hospital primarily devoted to geriatric psychiatric patients. If you have been to any state hospitals lately and looked at the way geriatric psychiatric patients are cared for, you know about how the Cushing State Hospital works. It's no better, no worse. Bob Kastenbaum was concerned about the models of care. We all know about the Medical model, and I think it's a bad term because it means too many different things. But basically the notion is that the aged mentally ill patient is somehow sick and is a patient, and all patients are targets. That's why I was coming on so heavy the other night. They were supposed to be crazy sick, so they were some kind of crazy targets — the helpless, hopeless syndrome. So he was looking for a way to break out of this deadlock, and he came up with an idea.

A lot of money is spent in tranquilizers. The use of pharmacologic straight jackets for geriatric patients is one of the great scandals of America today. A couple of years ago 250 million prescriptions for tranquilizers and psychotropic drugs were written by non-psychiatrists — 250 million. It's not clear how many are written on geriatric patients, but over and over again you run into this business of finding people who are totally wiped out. We don't use straight jackets anymore; we are using chemicals now. In this situation, Bob came up with a notion, and he sold it to the physician on the basis of alcohol's being a good tranquilizer. It is, in fact, and there's been some very good research data on that. His notion was to have a cocktail hour and serve wine, which he got free, to the patients. He sold it because it was a tranquilizer.

He was really trying to sell a different principle, though. The principle simply is that patients don't have cocktails, patients don't drink wine; and this sets up a conflicting social model. He was saying that the patients will get a very different message from getting wine than from getting pills. Some of you are sort of smiling at me, thinking that's kind of wild. Well, it is wild because it's dissonant, because it's not supposed to be what happens to patients; but that is exactly why he wanted it. He in fact did set up a system where they had a wine cart coming into the ward at 4:00. The results of this study were nothing short of phenomenal. The first thing he began to notice was that the patients got better oriented. He noticed that people who had been disoriented as to time, place, and person suddenly knew what time it was. Sounds funny, right? Do any of you know how important that is and how in state hospitals there are no clocks and no calendars? If you were there for seventy-two hours you probably wouldn't know what day it was. But if a patient doesn't know, we mark it on his chart; and that's an excuse to keep him in the hospital for another month. Under this program, though, patients who never talked began to talk, patients who couldn't shave themselves began to shave themselves, patients changed for cocktails. The staff couldn't believe what was happening. Patient management changed, and they saved incredible amounts of money on drug bills.

So they pushed it, and they went on to do the beer study. The wine study was successful, but the state wouldn't pay for wine, and the program had to be dropped when they ran out of free wine. It wasn't dropped because it was a failure; it was dropped because no one was ready to pay, even though it would be cheaper and more effective than any of the other techniques they were using. So they went on to the beer study. They got free beer from Boston. This time, though, they went to a ward which was called Death Valley. Patients went to that ward when they got deathly sick, and they were lying there in various states of near-death. They took the beer cart to Death Valley, and for the first time in the history of Death Valley they began to get returns. About 30 percent of the patients who were on this ward began to go back to their old wards. They didn't equate (a) being a patient and (b) the ambience of a ward change. The attendants in that ward had been studied and it was found that they never spent any extra time on that ward. They ate off the ward, took their coffee breaks off the ward, and were very willing to run messages for anybody. Nobody in the working group wanted to stay on that ward. After the beer started — and the attendants weren't getting any, by the way — the amount of time that the attendants stayed with the patients went up by an incredible amount.

The beer experiment was stopped in a very bizarre way, though. The daughter of one of the patients was on the ward when the cart came through, and the ward got very noisy. You know, the patients got very agitated and excited because the beer was coming. They were really pleased. They got only one glass of beer, by the way. She complained to the governor and the state hospital and all sorts of people, saying it wasn't appropriate to bring beer to these sick people. So it stopped.

I think this makes a great point. That point is that you get what you expect. If you victimize — and I'm using that word in a very special sense, but you can interpret it however you want — if you make somebody a victim, he becomes a permanent victim and becomes more and more and more dependent. If you make him a resource and a partner in his own care, he will respond accordingly. That point needs to be driven home again and again. It is not easy, because you see these people as being without resources.

I'll have to say something about health now just to point out that I know something about it. Maybe the following is appropriate. In the literature today, the curve for adult intelligence is called the bow-shaped curve. It goes to a peak, then down slowly. It used to peak at about age sixteen, but the guys who developed the intelligence test got a little older so it peaked at twenty-three, twenty-four, or twenty-five. This very classic curve you see describing the aging process goes down from this point. Everybody knew that's what happens when you get old. You get brighter up to one point, and then you begin to lose marbles slowly but inexorably. At some point you have no marbles left; you are just lying there like a demarbleized jellyfish, waiting for something to happen. It would be nice if this kind of information were usable because there's so much of it.

We now know that those data are wrong, though. Those data are wrong because they were done on a cross-sectional basis. What nobody bothered to think about was the fact that the average twenty year old has about nine and a half years of education, education that was roughly a nine-and-a-half-month-a-year proposition, whereas the average seventy year old has about four years of education of four months a year. Our attempts to compare intelligence have been sheer nonsense, as we've been comparing education. Nobody in his right mind would say that sixteen months of education is going to wind up having the same effect as eighty-one months of education. So the cross-sectional studies have problems. Longitudinal studies take time and they're expensive, but they're finally beginning to bear fruit.

Research in aging, in fact, is very, very new. The Duke study is one of two or three of the oldest in the country, and ours dates back only to about 1955. Taking a group of people between sixty and seventy and following them for ten years and then winding up ten years later with a group of people between seventy and eighty, we found that there was no intellectual decline in that group as a whole, whether intelligence was high, middle, or low. This is contrary to all the cross-sectional professional studies in this regard, but other people have found the same thing. So the concept of individual deterioration as a necessary part of aging has, I think, been knocked into a cocked hat. The evidence is so compelling now that the task force on aging of the American Psychological Association has said there is no evidence for intellectual decline at least until age seventy-six.

We do know that older people do have more trouble learning. This raises a very compelling problem. Why? If the pure psychology types are saying people aren't declining — though behaviorally they are changing — then we have to ask why. I think you know the answers. Look at the distance from education between a sixty-five, a forty-five and a twenty-five year old? What about the concepts of life-time education? I give you gratis the Eisdorfer self-destruct diploma plan. I think that all the diplomas on your wall ought to dissolve five years after you're awarded them. Then it's time to go back and get more education. It's very clear that the muscle between your ears deteriorates at a rate faster than the muscles in your arms and legs.

That's something we need to do in the community. We need to develop patterns of lifetime learning. That's no joke. Presently we are actively promoting deterioration. I think we have programmed the deterioration of older Americans, and that is a violent sin of omission.

The studies we did also proved that where people are physically ill (and here blood pressure is implicated) deterioration does occur. People with hypertension will deteriorate at a much faster rate than normal. Here's another thing we can do. We can make sure that the people we work with not only have health exams but also have some kind of on-going care. Where hypertension exists but where drugs are supplied to make subjects normal-tensive people don't decline. The older people we were working with, unfortunately, didn't have the resources, and they weren't getting the kind of drugs that would maintain their blood pressure, so I couldn't show this. We were not allowed by the nature of our support to provide any kind of medication.

I could go on to great lengths, but I think I've made the point. We're not just being nice guys. Expectancies, health care, the delivery of services to the community, the availability of a confidant, some kind of contact, changing the attitude and posture of the aged individual to be a partner rather than a target: all are very, very necessary components in maintaining people for independent living outside an institution.

Let me give you another bit of research data before I quit. It's worth repeating. Until this point we have had an increasing low-level problem in the field of aging. In the last sixty to seventy years, approximately, the population of the U.S. has gone up about two and one-half times. The population of people over sixty-five has gone up approximately seven times. It is true, however, that the longevity of individuals from about age sixteen, the predicted life span of individuals aged sixteen has not changed dramatically in the last fifty years. We are getting more older Americans because we're keeping more kids alive — not because we're extending life.

The prediction of 40 million older Americans by the turn of the century is based on the current projections, but now we've got a problem. President Nixon has launched a very impressive 400-million-dollar campaign to wipe out cancer. It happened last year, and this year he's talking about another one to wipe out cardiovascular illness. Those are diseases not of childhood but of advanced years. We now have to talk about a different set of problems. What about pro-longation of life? Why?

C. TREATMENT APPROACHES

For some individuals at any age the environmental supports referred to in earlier readings are not sufficient to help them meet all of life's problems. Many people at one time or another exhaust their own resources to deal with what appear to be overwhelming problems and are not able to carry on without some intensive aid. The differentiation between the kinds of help referred to in earlier sections of this book and those referred to here is not great. This section will describe a variety of approaches to psychological readjustment which fall in the broad area of mental health.

Eleanor Barns and her colleagues describe a range of mental health treatment approaches which are useful with different older persons in varied situations. The methods described include reality orientation, resocialization, remotivation, attitude therapy, reinforcement therapy, self-image therapy, sensory retraining, and milieu therapy. Each of these is discussed quite briefly and references are given for further information.

In the next reading, Mary Buckley describes the needs for counseling among the aged. She points out that personal growth and creative living do not end with the beginning of retirement. Older people, like adolescents, may have an identity crisis as they pass from one stage of life to another. Counseling can provide an atmosphere of understanding and sharing in order to foster growth in the retirement years.

In the final reading in this section, Sidney Pressey outlines the values of an older counselor as he works with the elderly. As a counselor and an elderly resident of a home for older persons, Pressey describes his experiences and the approaches which he has found to be helpful. He feels that the counselor should help reshape psychological, social, medical, and legal attitudes toward death, and give attention to the welfare of the dying and their families.

39. Guidelines to Treatment Approaches:

Modalities and Methods for Use with the Aged*

ELEANOR D. BARNS, ANN SACK, AND HERMIT SHORE**

Modern medical institutions have been faced with large and increasing numbers of aged individuals, particularly those with chronic and mental disabilities. Social and cultural attitudes toward the aged as a group have been principal obstacles to improving the care and rehabilitation of the aged person. The attitudes of the medical profession and of the lay public have differed little, although the rationale of the former has been somewhat better formulated. Physicians have noted the low level of effectiveness of the usual methods of treatment and rehabilitation of the aged and have admitted the limitations of ability to reverse the aging processes. The shortage of physicians and other skilled professionals specially prepared to cope with the problems of the aged has been evident, and the wisdom in allocating costly resources to patients who are unlikely to improve has been questioned.

Allison (1961) in *The Senile Brain* states that old age is a losing game. "We must therefore, focus attention upon the ways and means of ensuring that points in the game are not given away unnecessarily." There is a popular poster that says, "Not to decide is to decide." The absence of a treatment program is a treatment program, be it custodial, warehousing, or containment.

In working with the mentally impaired aged, three conditions are recognizable, although they may not always exist independently. There are: mind lack, mind twist, and mind loss. Mind lack is commonly characterized by the mentally retarded or mentally deficient. Mind twist covers those mental, psychological, or psychiatric disorders in the behavioral sphere commonly classified as neurosis and psychosis. Mind loss is that process of impaired functioning in which the individual may have functioned and behaved normally until the aging changes make the individual function less effectively.

*Reprinted from *The Gerontologist*, Vol. 13, 1973, pages 513-527, with permission of the authors and the Gerontological Society.
**Ms. Barns, OTR, MA, Ms. Sack, M.A., and Herbert Shore, Ed.D. are on the staff of Golden Acres, the Dallas Home for the Jewish Aged in Dallas, Texas. Dr. Shore is Executive Vice-President of the home and Director of Continuing Education of the Gerontological Society.

DICTIONARY OF SYMPTOMS

The majority of patients in long-term care institutions generally have three basic problems, regardless of diagnosis. These are: lack of self-confidence, social withdrawal, and difficulty in interpersonal relationships. In addition, older people in long-term care institutions have been observed to be suffering from cognitive, emotional, and physical impairments associated with senile mental deterioration. The symptoms associated with these conditions usually are (Sandoz, 1973):

Anorexia: Loss of appetite, disinclination for food, inadequate intake, necessity for dietary supplements, loss of weight, change in attitude toward eating.

Anxiety: Worry, apprehension, overconcern for present and future, fears, complaints of functional somatic symptoms including headaches, dry mouth, trembling, sighing, sweating.

Bothersome: Frequent unnecessary requests for advice or assistance, interference with others, restlessness.

Confusion: Lack of proper association for surroundings, person and time; "not with it." Slowing of thought processes and impaired comprehension, recognition and performance; disorganization. Inappropriate response and behavior, including perservation.

Depression: Dejected, despondent, helpless, hopeless, preoccupation with defeat or neglect by family and friends, hypochondriacal concern, persistent functional complaints, early waking.

Disorientation: Diminished awareness of place and time and identification of persons including self.

Dizziness: In addition to true vertigo, dizziness including spells of uncertainty of movement and balance, subjective sensations in the head, apart from pain as represented by light-headedness.

Emotional Lability: Instability and inappropriateness of emotional response as illustrated by laughing or crying or other undue positive or negative response to non-provoking situations.

Faulty recent memory: Reduction in ability to recall events and actions of significance to patient such as visits by family members, content of meals, environmental changes, personal activities.

Hostility: Verbal aggressiveness, animosity, contempt, mocking, threshold to aggravation, stress, or challenging situations.

Impaired judgment: Reduction of mental alertness and attentiveness, concentration, responsiveness, alacrity and clarity of thought and actions, impaired judgment and ability to make decisions.

Indifference: Lack of interest in everyday events, pastimes and environment or surroundings, where previously existed oftentimes in areas of news, TV, heat, cold, noise.

Irritability: Edgy, cantankerous, easily frustrated, low tolerance threshold to aggravation, stress or challenging situations.

Motivation-initiative: Lack of spontaneous interest in initiating or completing tasks, routine duties and attending to individual needs.

Self-care: Impairment of ability to attend to personal hygiene; dressing, grooming, eating and getting about, bathing, toileting.

Uncooperativeness: Poor compliance with instructions or requests for participation. Performance with ill grace, resentment, or lack of concern and consideration for others.

Undue fatigue: Sluggish, listless, tired, weary, worn out, "bushed."

Unsociability: Poor interpersonal relationships, unfriendly negative reaction to social and communal recreational activities. Indifferent and aloof.

A variety of treatment techniques, modalities, methods, and therapies have been developed and used to assist the older person who exhibits mind loss and cognitive emotional impairment to break the Spiral of Senility (Fig. 1). Some are more effective than others. Some are easier to learn and some appear easier to use. The success or failure of any given approach is dependent upon a number of variables which include administrative philosophy, team concepts, and degree of pathology in the population. No single variable can be considered the determining factor.

Fig. 1
THE SPIRAL OF SENILITY

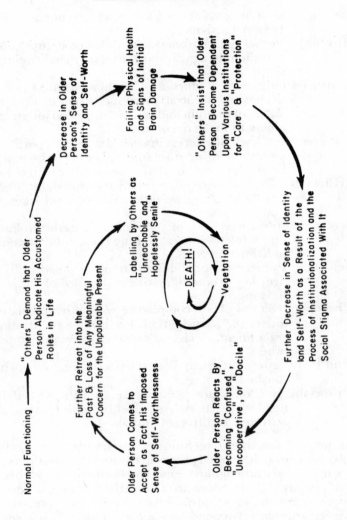

It will be observed that "failing physical health" and "brain damage" may occur in varying degrees at any point along the spiral. Should these occur, it only hastens the spiraling process which, if continued unabated, leads to vegetation and death, although death itself may intervene at any point.

The desire to bring about improvement in patient care is an essential catalyst for change as it stimulates interest in the patient, better communication by staff, and increased interpersonal relationships. The label of the modality is less important than the ingredients. However, in the supermarket of social and psychological approaches, one may wander the aisles and select a wide variety of treatments: behavior modifications, operant conditionings, milieu therapy, remotivation, reality orientation, reality therapy, token economy, to name a few.

What are the aims of these approaches? What are the differences? What materials and resources do you need? How does it work? Who can do it? — are questions often asked. It is the aim of this paper to present in a brief, useful form, a review of the major treatment approaches used in long-term care facilities, and, in doing so, to encourage centers to select and use a therapeutic model as an umbrella approach.

In long-term care facilities, emphasis in the past has been placed on meeting the basic physical needs of the patient. Providing clothing, food, shelter, and religious services had been considered adequate in the total treatment program, with the philosophy geared to the concept of custodial care. In recent years a new concept or philosophy has begun to emerge. New theories have been formulated about the aging process and the social and emotional problem of the older person. Changes in the health field concerning the older person have presented new and greater challenges to the field of medical rehabilitation. Attention focused on the traditional therapy processes has increased dramatically over the last few years. The evidence supporting the value of the different therapies has been increasingly impressive, and the thoughts and practice of many professionals are being affected by them. However, new models of treatment for the aged chronically ill and mentally impaired are needed. To help meet this need this material has been prepared.

REFERENCES

Allison, R. S. *The senile brain, a clinical study.* London: E. T. Arnold, 1961.
Sandoz Pharmaceuticals. Assessment of clinical status scale, 1973.

REALITY ORIENTATION

Reality Orientation is a basic technique effective in the rehabilitation of elderly persons having a moderate to severe degree of memory loss, confusion, and time-place-person disorientation. This technique was initiated in 1958 at Winter Veterans Administration Hospital in To-peka, Kansas, by Dr. James Folsom and was refined in 1965 at the Veteran's Administration Hospital in Tuscaloosa, Alabama.

Reality Orientation is suitable for use in homes for aged, nursing homes, and psychiatric hospitals. It should be used at all times by everyone who has contact with elderly patients, including nursing assistants, housekeepers and porters, dietary workers, professionals from all disciplines, volunteers, and family members. Reality Orientation should begin to be used as soon as the first signs of confusion are noticed following a stroke or any major loss or change.

The backbone of Reality Orientation is the repetition and learning of basic information such as the patient's name, the place, the time of day, day of the week and date, the next meal, time of bath. This essential repetition and relearning is conducted both formally and informally.

Formal Reality Orientation classes should be conducted at the same time every day by a nursing assistant, housekeeper, or other person having close, frequent contact with the patients. During the class the instructor should drill the patients on the essential information — name, date, place, time.

Informal Reality Orientation is conducted on a 24-hour basis and is crucial to the success of the program. Here, too, it is important that all persons having contact with the patients constantly stimulate them by repeating the essential information. Comments such as, "It's 3:00 in the morning, Mrs. Jones. Are you having trouble sleeping?" or "It's 11:30, Mrs. Smith, It's time to get ready for lunch." are not only polite, but also critical in reorienting the individual. These statements tell who he is, where he is, and what the appropriate activity should be.

Two additional techniques, Attitude Therapy and Remotivation, are also employed. Attitude Therapy is often used in conjunction with Reality Orientation, while Remotivation should begin as soon as the patient has successfully completed Reality Orientation. Both are dis-cussed later as separate entities and are compared in Table 1.

EQUIPMENT

The following audio-visual aids are useful for both Reality Orienta-tion classes and 24-hour Reality Orientation.

(1) *Reality Board* (Fig. 2). Reality Boards should be prominently displayed at nursing stations, dining areas, day rooms, and wherever patients spend their time. The boards should be changed as often as necessary and the day of the week and date, the place, the weather, the

next meal, the next holiday, the next activity, the next bath, should be maintained.

(2) Large-face clocks or mock-up clocks for instruction telling time are useful.

(3) Brightly colored pictures of food are conducive to reorientation.

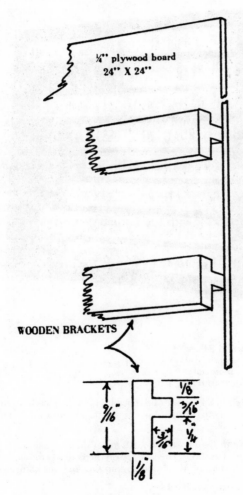

Fig. 2. Reality board

Reality Orientation Board

LELAND C. BOWLES, *OCCUPATIONAL THERAPIST*

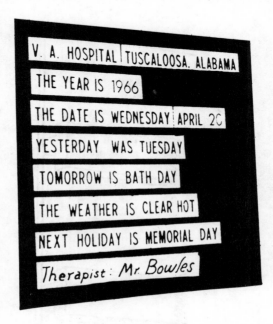

Materials needed:
    1 pc. ¼" plywood 24" X 24"
    8 or 10 pc. wooden bracket material, as described
    4 pc. framing material 30" X 1½" X ¾"
    Pebble board cut into 2½" strips.

ASSEMBLY: Wooden brackets must be spaced (glued or nailed) on the plywood so the printed cards will slip in, top groove first, pushing upward and then resting in the bottom groove.

After all brackets are in the plywood board, it can then be painted and framed, using 1½"X¾" stock. No rabbet is neccessary on the framing material. The lettering on this board was done on the embossograph, colors black and white.

Designed and made in PMRS, VA.
Hospital, Tusculoosa, Alabama

488

Personnel and Training

Every person who has contact with the patients should know the basic techniques of Reality Orientation. Five-day seminars teaching these techniques are offered through the Veterans Administration Hospital in Tuscaloosa. For further information, contact Mrs. Dorothy Scarbrough, Reality Orientation Training Program, Veterans Administration Hospital, Tuscaloosa, 35401. Phone area code 205-553-3760, extension 295.

References

Barker, H. R. Jr., Smith, B. J. *Influence of a reality orientation training program on the attitudes of trainees toward the elderly.* Tuscaloosa: Alabama Regional Medical Program: Reality Orientation Training Project, VA Hospital, 1970.

Folsom, J.O. Reality orientation for the elderly mental patients. *Journal of Geriatric Psychiatry*, 1968, 1, 291-307.

Stephens, L. (compiler). *Reality orientation: A technique to rehabilitate elderly and brain-damaged patients with a moderate to severe degree of disorientation.* Washington: APA Hospital & Community Psychiatry Service, 1969.

Taulbee, L. R., & Folsom, J. O. Reality orientation for geriatric patients. *Hospital & Community Psychiatry*, 1966, 17, 133-135.

VA Hospital, Tuscaloosa. *Guide for attitude therapy.* June, 1970.

VA Hospital, Tuscaloosa. *Nursing service, guide for reality orientation*, rev. Feb., 1970.

Resocialization

Resocialization is a structured program involving patients in a geriatric setting, using group techniques to both expand consciousness and also broaden the recognition of available choices in their living community. The prime group goals are to: (1) stress interpersonal relations: (2) help the patient renew interest in the world he lives in by focusing attention on simple objective features of everyday life that are unrelated to emotional difficulties; (3) help the patient to reach into the past and give of himself once again.

The core of group resocialization is based on the premise that the principal obstacle in the development of acceptable socialization patterns is to be found in the orientation toward authority and intimacy which each member brings to the group. Patients can establish fresh relationships and form friendships: chronic complainers can find new interests; the agitated can be distracted. The program can help an older person retain or regain his desire to live by exposing him regularly to the kinds of experiences which give any person the feeling that life is worthwhile. Greater awareness of surroundings, values, and contributions can be realized, and an interest in the beauties of old age can be experienced. Resocialization is the catalyst to a shared experience which produces communication out of isolated individuals.

It is paramount for group members to begin to focus upon relationships to each other, the problems of living in a community, and the reliving of happy experiences. The leader provides a model for behavior by his activity in the group, his acceptance of the group members, his non-evaluative comments, his willingness to deviate from planned programs, and his ability to raise questions. By his own behavior, he aids in establishing an atmosphere of acceptance and freedom of expression whereby the group is enabled to discuss interpersonal problems that otherwise might be unsolved.

EQUIPMENT

Resocialization requires no special equipment. Refreshments are served in the group and the group leader is responsible for suggestions to supplement the activities of the group.

PERSONNEL AND TRAINING

All staff members should be made aware of the role of the patient in a resocialization program. Any staff member can be a group leader in resocialization. However, the group leader — if not a professionally trained person in the techniques of group dynamics — should be under such direction and supervision. For further information on Resocialization contact St. Joseph's Manor in Trumbull, Conn.

REFERENCES

Bion, W. R. Experiences in groups. 1. *Human Relations,* 1948, 1.

Cartwright, D., & Zander, A. *Group dynamics.* Evanston, Ill: Row Peterson, 1953; London: Tavistock, 1954.

Kunkel, S. Resocialization: A technique that combats loneliness. *Nursing Homes,* 1970, 19 (8), 12-13.

Kunkel S., & Sr. Brian (O.Carm.) Resocialization: A challenge in geriatric nursing. *Catholic Charities,* 1969, April, 4.

REMOTIVATION

Remotivation is a technique to encourage the moderately confused elderly patient to take a renewed interest in his surroundings by focusing his attention on the simple, objective features of everyday life that are unrelated to the patient's emotional difficulties. Remotivation is intended to augment the other therapies and not to replace them. Remotivation is begun following successful completion of Reality Orientation.

Remotivation was originated by an English teacher, Dorothy Hosking Smith, an experienced mental hospital volunteer who served in veterans' institutions. Remotivation was first consciously used in the Philadelphia State Hospital in 1956 and has since been used in over 200 homes for the aged, public and private mental hospitals, and schools for the retarded. When Remotivation began to develop, the thought was that the remotivators would be social workers, nurses, psychologists, and other professional therapists. Hospitals, however, began using non-professional workers. There was value in giving this responsibility to attendants, aides, and other non-professional people, since these people saw the patients more than the professionals and were, therefore, more aware of the ward climate.

Remotivation is essentially a technique of simple interaction between a remotivator and a group of patients. There are two important therapeutic aims: (1) to stimulate patients into thinking about and discussing topics associated with the real world; (2) to assist patients to relate to and communicate with other persons. A Remotivation meeting consists of a group of 5 to 12 patients, who meet once a week for about an hour to discuss a specific topic chosen to motivate the group's interest and participation. A Remotivation series consists of one meeting each week for 12 weeks. In turn, each meeting is conducted through five successive steps or stages geared to motivate group interaction and conversation. This procedure includes:

(1) *The climate of acceptance.* — The leader introduces himself and welcomes each group member individually by name. This climate of acceptance can be enhanced by comments about the weather, the nice appearance of some member, or any other appropriate, objective, pleasant topic. (5 min.).

(2) *A bridge to reality.* — This step starts the group thinking about a selected topic of the real world and helps the participants to externalize and focus their interests upon the world in which they live. Several approaches are used to accomplish this step. These include: (a) the bounce question, (b) poetry, (c) visual aids. Joyce Kilmer's *Trees*, for

example, is soothing for listening. It also leads easily into a discussion of Spring, birds building nests, and similar things the patients can observe from their windows. Well-known quotations, articles from newspapers and magazines, or similar items can also be used. The leader should encourage individual patients to read portions of the poem or story and to participate in the discussion. (15 min.).

(3) *Sharing the world we live in.* — The purpose of this step is to elaborate upon and promote discussion in a specific direction. This is accomplished by 10 to 12 objective questions prepared in advance by the remotivator to serve to keep the group on the track and eliminate the tendency to diverge from the topic. These questions may stem logically from the topic in the Bridge to Reality or may probe a totally different subject. Visual aids serve as important stimulants in this step, and at least two visual aids should be used during each meeting. Colorful photographs and pictures help to focus the members' attention upon the main idea being exhibited. Other types of visual aids, such as cloth, dress patterns, and tape measures, can be used in the discussion of sewing. As the visual aid is being examined, the remotivator stimulates discussion by asking questions about it. (15 min.).

(4) *Appreciation of the work of the world.* — This fourth step is aimed to stimulate the patient into thinking about work in relation to himself. A discussion of the jobs and tasks that patients used to perform is especially useful in working with older persons. Individually tailored crafts and work activities, like those produced in an Occupational Therapy Department, both as a group and within the group, are also helpful in creating a meaningful appreciation of the world for older patients. (15 min.).

(5) *The climate of acceptance.* — The fifth step has the main purpose for the remotivator to express his appreciation to the patients for attending and participating in the meeting. At this time, the remotivator summarizes the high points of the discussion and announces the time and date of the next meeting to provide a sense of continuity and expectation. (5 min.).

EQUIPMENT, PERSONNEL, AND TRAINING

Visual aids, colorful photographs and pictures pertaining to the subject, books of poetry and quotations, articles and anecdotes from magazines and newspapers, and any related items to subjects being discussed are useful.

A remotivator may be a nursing assistant or aide who has satisfactorily completed the basic program. In order to assume the role of remotivator, one must become a leader and be patient in manner. There are major responsibilities the remotivator must take. These include: (1) selection and structure of a group, (2) topic selection, (3) preparation for meeting (the meeting plan), (4) scheduling the meeting, (5) conducting the meeting, and (6) observation and evaluation.

For further information about the techniques of Remotivation, including a 30-hour course on the fundamentals of Remotivation, write to American Psychiatric Assn., Smith, Kline & French Remotivation Project, 700 18 St., NW, Washington 20009.

REFERENCES

Remotivation Training Centers
National Training Center, Philadelphia State Hospital, Philadelphia

Regional Centers
Patton State Hospital Patton, CA
Colorado State Hospital, Pueblo
Norwich Hospital, Norwich, CT
Milledgeville State Hospital, Milledgeville, GA
Moose Lake State Hospital, Moose Lake, MN
State Hospital North, Orofino, ID
Osawatomie State Hospital, Osawatomie, KS
Western State Hospital, Hopkinsville, KY
Marcy State Hospital, Marcy, NY
Rusk State Hospital, Rusk, TX
In addition, refer to:

Pullinger, W. F., & Sholly, E. M. Outline for a remotivation training course. American Psychiatric Assn., & Smith, Kline, & French Labs. Remotivation Project, no date.
Robinson, A. Remotivation techniques. American Psychiatric Assn. & Smith, Kline, & French Labs. Remotivation Project, no date.
Smith, Kline & French Labs. *Remotivation Directory*, 5th ed. American Psychiatric Assn. Mental Hospital Service, no date.

ATTITUDE THERAPY

Attitude Therapy is a form of behavior modification. It involves using certain prescribed attitudes in all dealings with elderly patients.

Table 1. Differences Between Remotivation, Resocialization, and Reality Orientation.

Classroom Reality Orientation	Resocialization	Remotivation
1. Correct position or relation with the existing situation in a community. Maximum use of assets	1. Continuation of reality living situation in a community	1. Orientation to reality for community living
2. Called Reality Orientation and Classroom Reality Orientation Program	2. Called discussion group or resocialization to differentiate between a social function instead of a therapeutic need	2. Called remotivation
3. Structured	3. Unstructured	3. Definite structure
4. Refreshments and/or food may be served for identification	4. Refreshments served	4. Refreshments not served
5. Appreciation of the work of the world. Constantly reminded of who he is, where he is, why he is here and what is expected of him	5. Appreciation of the work of the world. Reliving happy experiences. Encourages participation in home activities relating to subject	5. Appreciation of the work of the world; stimulates the desire to return and function in society
6. Class range from 3-5, depending on degree/level of confusion or disorientation from any cause	6. Group range from 5-17, depending on mental and physical capabilities	6. Group size: 5-12 patients
7. Class meets one-half hour daily at same time in same place	7. Group meets three times weekly for one-half to 1 hour	7. Group meets once to twice weekly for one-half to 1 hour
8. Planned procedures — Reality Centered Objects	8. No planned topic; group centered feelings	8. Preselected and Reality-Centered Objects
9. Consistence of approach response of resident is responsibility of teacher	9. Clarification and interpretation is responsibility of leader	9. No exploration of feelings
10. Periodic RO test pertaining to residents' level of confusion or disorientation	10. Periodic progress notes pertaining to residents' enjoyment and improvements	10. Progress ratings

494

Table 1 (Continued)

11. Emphasis placed on time, place, person orientation	11. Any topic freely discussed	11. Topic: Cannot discuss religion, politics, or death
12. Use portion of mind function still intact	12. Vast stockpile of memories and experiences	12. Untouched area of the mind
13. Greet resident by name, thank him for coming, and extend hand and/or physical contact according to attitude approach in group	13. Greet resident on coming, thank him, and extend handshake upon leaving	13. No physical contact permitted
14. Conducted by trained aids, activity assistants	14. Conducted by RN, LPN/LVN, aides, and program assistants	14. Conducted by trained psychiatric aides

495

The twin goals of Attitude Therapy are to reinforce desirable behavior and eliminate undesirable behavior.

There are five major attitudes to be used with five major identifiable behavior patterns (Fig. 3). A psychiatrist, psychiatric social worker, or other similarly trained professional should select the appropriate attitude to be used with the individual patient, but it is important that everyone coming into contact with the patient — including all staff members, volunteers, visitors, and other patients — participate in the therapy by using the designated attitude.

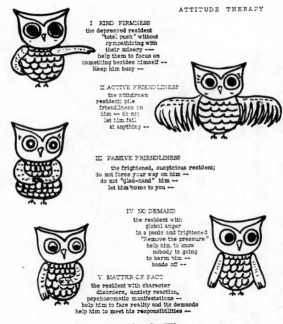

ATTITUDE THERAPY

I KIND FIRMNESS
the depressed resident
"total push" without
sympathizing with
their misery ---
help them to focus on
something besides himself --
Keep him busy ---

II ACTIVE FRIENDLINESS
the withdrawn
resident; pile
friendliness on
him -- do not
let him fall
at anything --

III PASSIVE FRIENDLINESS
the frightened, suspicious resident;
do not force your way on him --
do not "glad-hand" him --
let him come to you --

IV NO DEMAND
the resident with
global anger
in a panic and frightened
"Remove the pressure"
help him to know
nobody is going
to harm him --
hands off --

V MATTER OF FACT
the resident with character
disorders, anxiety reaction,
psychosomatic manifestations --
help him to face reality and its demands
help him to meet his responsibilities --

Fig. 3. Attitude Therapy

These behavior attitudes include:

(1) *Kind firmness.* — Kind firmness is prescribed for depressed elderly patients. Depressed patients have turned their hostilities inward. It is here where tasks should be structured to be menial, monotonous, and patient nongratifying. When using kind firmness one must be careful to criticize the job or task but not the patient. It is important the

patient knows that you know exactly what is to be done and that you expect your requests to be carried out to the letter. One should not sympathize with the patient's misery or attempt to sympathize with his feelings of worthlessness.

(2) *Active friendliness.* — Active friendliness is used with withdrawn, apathetic old people, particularly those who have had few successes in relationships with people. The basic principle with active friendliness is to give the patient attention before he requests it. One should seek this patient out and spend extra time with him, give him sincere praise for accomplishments which show progress, and — insofar as possible — make certain the patient never fails. Active friendliness is the attitude most typically prescribed for patients in Reality Orientation.

(3) *Passive friendliness.* — Passive friendliness is prescribed for the old who are distrustful and frightened by active friendliness and closeness. It is important that the worker show his interest in and concern for the patient without pushing. One should wait for the patient to make the first move and then respond accordingly.

(4) *No demand.* — No demand is the attitude prescribed for aging/aged residents who are suspicious, frightened, or in an uncontrollable rage. Friendship and activities should be offered but one should not appear eager for him to participate. He should know the only thing you expect of him is that he not hurt himself or others.

(5) *Matter-of-fact.* — Matter-of-fact is the attitude prescribed for manipulative and seductive old people, as well as for those approaching normal behavior. Responses to the patient's pleas, complaints, and maneuvers should be consistent, casual, and calm.

EQUIPMENT

No particular equipment is needed for attitude therapy. It is helpful, however, to have some obvious means of identifying which attitude has been prescribed for individual patients. Green name cards on the door could be used for active friendliness, blue for passive friendliness, as illustrative techniques.

PERSONNEL AND TRAINING

Every person who has contact with the patient should know and apply the prescribed attitude to be used with the individual patient. Four day seminars teaching Attitude Therapy are offered through the VA Hospital, Tuscaloosa. Contact Attitude Therapy Training Program, VA Hospital, Tuscaloosa 35401.

498   *Meeting The Needs of the Aged*

REFERENCE

Folsom, J., Attitude therapy workshop. *American Archives of Rehabilitation Therapy*, June, 1966, 21-34.
Treatment Team. VA Hospital, Tuscaloosa. Attitude Therapy and the team approach. *Mental Hospitals,* Nov., 1965, 307-323.

REINFORCEMENT THERAPY

Behavior Modification and Reinforcement Therapy have become synonymous in the realms of therapy and rehabilitation in many leading institutions. Behaviorism is the objective of human and animal behavior in which reinforcement is one of various techniques for modifying interrelationships between response and action. Mental concepts such as emotion and sensation are replaced by concepts of stimulus, response, learning, habit, receptor, effector function.

The basic theory is that a person learns to behave in a way which allows him to experience a pleasant or rewarding stimulus. The general breakdown of the theory is as follows; (1) behavior is repeated if it is followed by a pleasant or rewarding experience or by a token reward; (2) behavior tends to disappear when no experience occurs, thus undesired acts should be ignored; the only time negative reward is used is when the behavior is so intent that there is a potential danger to self or others; (3) behavior is repeated or discontinued to whatever degree it is or is not rewarded.

It is of maximum importance to be careful in selecting the behavior to be altered. The selective behavior should be sufficiently broken down to be able to be generalized for aid in forming other desirable acts. The rewards should be given as soon after the desired act as possible. The *token* exchange is one starting point to be replaced eventually with a verbal reward, then to be phased out.

Tokens may be money, metal slugs that can be exchanged for privileges and/or items, candy, or any object items of value. The token reinforcement is especially beneficial when working in a home for the aged with regressed, disoriented residents. This is beneficial when working with groups of residents in a reality orientation class and when reinforcement is used as a motivator for memory retention, increasing attention span, and encouraging a response.

There can also be an immediate decrease in the frequency of bizarre or unusual behaviors and incidents of incontinence when positive behavior is reinforced by the use of tokens. Tokens can be used to increase interpersonal communication, taking of responsibility, decrease loss of early memories, and to increase eye contact and physical contact.

Programs can be maintained on the units in the home for the aged when the desired goal is to establish a more independent role for the resident. Areas that may be considered are: social behavior, self-care, unit work. Social behavior would include helping another resident, talking to another resident, starting an activity by oneself, and both the starting and the activity with others. Self-care might include bathing self, washing one's hair, dressing self, combing hair and brushing teeth, both with little help or without help, with the degree of self-help to determine the amount of reward, shaving self, and dressing especially neatly in the morning. Unit work might include making one's bed, cleaning one's room, cleaning the bathroom, dusting a dayroom, helping to distribute trays, washing ashtrays, or cleaning tables after meals.

A commitment on the part of the staff to this program can produce the desired results and develop and maintain the desire on the part of the resident to participate in this program to his fullest capabilities. From the first to the last day of therapy, good motivation is of prime importance. The staff, as therapist, must manipulate conditions to which behavior leads. Reinforcement may increase the likelihood that a desired response behavior may occur. It may be directed toward decreasing the likelihood that a response will occur because it is considered undesirable, maladaptive, or inappropriate. In this way, environmental interactions are synthesized in such a manner that therapist and resident are able to arrive at their mutually shared goals.

EQUIPMENT

There are many different objects/items useable for reinforcement. These should be chosen to meet the need of the individual and the group and limited only by the therapists' imagination. A detailed, but simple, bookkeeping system should be developed to keep track of all tokens. Tokens should be earned on a set scale established by the particular Home.

PERSONNEL AND TRAINING

Courses in behavior modification (Reinforcement Therapy) are offered by colleges and universities as well as in many special workshops and continuing education classes. In a Reinforcement Therapy program, the staff at all levels is trained in the mechanics of the project and is instructed that the program includes: (1) activities, social stimulation, and a more cheerful environment, (2) the residents are given more opportunities for self-direction, and (3) the staff becomes more aware of the benefit of the program to the patient.

REFERENCES

Ayllon, T., & Azrin, N. *The token economy, A motivational system for therapy and rehabilitation.* New York: Appleton-Century-Crofts, 1968.
Freedman, A. M., & Kaplan, H. I. (Eds.) *Comprehensive textbook of psychiatry.* Baltimore: Williams & Wilkins Co., 1967.
Goodall, K. Field report: Shapers at work. *Psychology Today,* 1972, 6, 53-58.
Goodall, K. Simple case of behavior engineering. *Psychology today.* 1972, 6, 132-138.
Goodal, K. Who's who and where in behavior shaping? *Psychology Today,* 1972, 6, 58-63.
Hall, C. S., & Lindzay, G. *Theories of personality.* New York: John Wiley & Sons, 1957.
Hawkins, R. P. Stimulus-Response. *Psychology Today,* 1972, 6, 28-30.
Hilgard, E. R. & Marquis, D. G. *Conditioning and Learning.* New York: Appleton-Century-Crofts, 1961.
Milton, O. *Behavior disorders.* New York: Lippincott, 1965.
Morgan, C. T. *Introduction to psychology.* New York: McGraw-Hill, 1961.
Ruch, F. L. *Psychology and life,* 7th ed. Glenview, Ill: Scott, Foresman, 1967.
Skinner, B. F. *Verbal behavior.* New York: Appleton-Century-Crofts, 1957.

INDIVIDUAL REINFORCEMENT THERAPY

Individual Reinforcement Therapy studies are planned programs of therapeutic care which are designed to modify the resident's behavior by specific therapeutic actions and an evaluation of results. The purpose of individual reinforcement therapy study is: (1) to modify the resident's behavior so that he may move toward a state of wellness and (2) to learn through systematic evaluation better methods of therapy. How this is undertaken is as follows:

STEPS IN THE PROCESS

(1) Choose a resident who has a particular need or one in whom you have a special interest.
(2) Obtain the resident's background, his age, former occupation, education, special talents or interests, illness record, length of hospitalization, and other data deemed pertinent.

(3) Review his pattern of behavior in the facility, especially reaction to assignments, general appearance, ability to express himself, general mood, contact with reality, and other viable documentation.
(4) Observe the resident's current behavior carefully for several days, and
    (a) describe in simple words the specific undesirable behavior you wish to modify, such as hitting, spitting, screaming.
    (b) obtain a baseline by recording the time and frequency of occurrence of the behavior and any factors that seem to precipitate or to increase or decrease it. Items to consider, among others, are amount of time, frequency, patterns.
    (c) list the desirable behaviors of the resident in terms of what is he doing right and what are appropriate behaviors, and
    (d) find out what is meaningful to this aged person that could be used conveniently and effectively as a reward or reinforcer for the behaviors to be encouraged.
(5) Set up one goal at a time and focus attention to adaptive behavior. One should pay as little attention as possible to maladaptive behavior.
(6) Identify the maladaptive behavior to be discouraged/ extinguished and the desirable behavior to be encouraged/reinforced. A plan of action should be designed to bring about the desired results.
(7) Set up goals achievable in a reasonable length of time.
(8) Inform team members and others involved for consistency of approach.
(9) Set dates for team conferences to discuss program and plans at least once a week.
(10) Observe and record the resident's behavior and summarize on a specially designed study form. If feasible, a separate sheet on which to record the frequency of behavior should be developed.
(11) Continue until the goal has been reached, or change the approach if the desired results are not observed after a reasonable length of time.
(12) Upon completion of the study, summarize the technique and include a summary of:
    (a) the resident's behavior at the beginning of the study and at the end, indicating what progress had been made in the particulars studied.
    (b) the specific treatment actions taken, and
    (c) your own evaluation of the study, particularly suggestions for improving the techniques employed.

REFERENCE

Cleino, Elizabeth. *A Guideline for Individual Clinical Nursing Studies,* Tuscaloosa, Ala.; Nursing Service, VA Hospital, June, 1968.

MILIEU THERAPY

The Therapeutic Community (Milieu) concept is based upon the assumption that the social milieu itself can be the instrument of treatment. The realization that people change, learn, and mature as a result of their interpersonal and social relationships and experiences is not new. It is interwoven within all theories of personality development.

Harry Stack Sullivan and the Menningers were among the first to use the concept of the Therapeutic Community. The Menningers set about to create a favorable array of interpersonal relationships for each patient by prescribing attitudes for staff adoption.

The Therapeutic Community is a very special kind of milieu therapy in which the total social structure of the treatment unit is involved as part of the helping process. It is organized and developed in order to make available for treatment purposes all relationships and activities in the life style of the patient. It differs from other kinds of therapy to the extent that it operates on the principle that all of the social interpersonal processes within the institutional environment are important and relevant to the treatment of the individual. No elements are left out of the treatment, and all transactions are considered potentially therapeutic.

Historically, the Therapeutic Community bears certain resemblances to other treatment modalities. For instance, it has much in common with the moral treatment of the early and middle 19th century. The respect for human rights, the family feeling of hospitals, the humane consideration for patients, and the recognition of the therapeutic effects of activities are all elements shared by moral treatment and the Therapeutic Community. However, while its roots have many connections, it seems clear that the Therapeutic Community represents a departure from previous treatment methods.

All facets of the life of the older resident/patient in the social milieu are seen as presenting opportunities for living-learning experience. The role of the staff is to use their various skills to realize these opportunities to the fullest. The environment then becomes one in which there is a favorable climate for helping the older resident/patient to gain an awareness of his feelings, thoughts, impulses, and behaviors. The aim is to help him to try new skills in a relatively safe environment, to help him achieve a realistic appraisal of his social and interpersonal relationships, and to help him to increase his self-esteem.

In such a treatment setting, a value is placed upon a greater sharing of responsibility with patients than is found in the usual hospital. The rationale is that by offering a great degree of meaningful participation in the decision-making functions of the community, trust and respect between patients and staff are developed.

Emphasis on patient responsibility has another value. The treatment process addresses itself to the intact ego function of each patient. It assumes that even the sickest person is not wholly sick, but that only part of his ego functioning is disturbed. Each person starts with what he has and builds from there. In the usual course of events one is not permitted to say, "I cannot participate in anything because I am too sick."

Most Therapeutic Communities discourage regression by patients. Ordinarily patients are not permitted to go to bed (stay in bed) during the day or to withdraw from all social contacts. Instead, there is an expectation by the community to participate, to assume responsibility, and to interact.

A Therapeutic Community may be the treatment method in a 24-hour hospital, a day hospital, a rehabilitation center, a halfway house, and most particularly, in a nursing home or a home for the aged. There have been, as yet, insufficient experiences to say what kinds of people are most or least likely to benefit from this kind of treatment, or in what kinds of settings this method may be effective.

Experience is, as yet, insufficient to determine the best type of training to prepare people for employment in these settings.

PROBLEMS OF A THERAPEUTIC COMMUNITY

There are at least seven major problems related to the Therapeutic Community:

(1) There is no clear, conceptual model underlying the Therapeutic Community. The problem lies in the fact that while there is both intrapsychic and social models, a super-ordinate model is required.

(2) While the gains, in terms of personal and professional satisfaction for the staff are sizeable, the lack of clear boundaries among the various professional identities is anxiety-provoking.

(3) Group responsibility, unless skillfully nurtured, can become distorted in practice to become no one's responsibility.

(4) There is a continuing possibility that the individual patient may become lost in the concern for the group. It seems clear that in a well-functioning community there is an increased concern

504 *Meeting The Needs of the Aged*

and respect for the individual. When patients are permitted to withdraw, to become isolated, this in itself is a problem which must be dealt with by the community.

(5) The Therapeutic Community may teach values that are appropriate to its own culture but that might lead to difficulties if the learner were to apply these elsewhere. For instance, while a patient may be encouraged to speak his mind in the Home, it may be more appropriate to hold his tongue when speaking to someone outside the Home (family, friends).

(6) Research and program evaluation are complex because of the proliferation of the factors leading to change.

(7) Since few centers in this country currently offer training especially suited to functioning in a therapeutic community, it remains the function of the setting itself to train its own staff.

EQUIPMENT

Milieu therapy requires no special equipment. However, the physical structure must invariably be modified to meet the needs of the group. The furnishings should reflect the needs and aspirations of the community. It should be livable and comfortable. Brightly colored bedspreads and draperies give the rooms brightness and individuality. Pictures on the walls add much to the rooms and the Home in general.

PERSONNEL AND TRAINING

Because milieu therapy is an all-inclusive way of treating the individual patient, it requires the cooperation and support of the entire staff. All staff members should be made aware of their role in the rehabilitation process. For members of the treatment team, work in a Therapeutic Community requires a reexamination of the roles for which they have been trained. Previous training frequently has not prepared them for the jobs in which they find themselves. Fortunately, the Therapeutic Community lends itself especially well to a continuing process of in-service training.

Staff training programs in Milieu Therapy are now available through the Institute of Gerontology, University of Michigan-Wayne State University. For futher information contact Ypsilanti State Hospital, 3501 Willis Rd., Box A, Ypsilanti, MI 45197.

REFERENCES

Buck R. E. A large milieu therapy group. *American Journal of Psychotherapy*, 1972, 26.

Cumming, J., & Cumming, E. *Ego and milieu theory and practice of environmental therapy.* New York: Atherton Press, 1963.

Fidler, G. S., & Fidler, J. *A communication process in psychiatry occupational therapy.* New York: McMillan, 1963.

Gottesman, L. E. Milieu therapy of the aged in institutions. *Gerontologist,* 1973, 13, 23-26.

Herz, M. I. The therapeutic milieu: A necessity. *International Journal of Psychiatry,* 1969, 7.

PREVLAB

The PREVLAB program (Prevention of Loneliness, Anxiety, and Boredom) asks the question,

> Is the sensory input of older people in nursing homes and homes for aged adequate to prevent or alleviate problems of loneliness, anxiety, boredom and frustration, or are there important benefits which would accrue by examining the problems and by making constructive changes?

PREVLAB is based on the concept that sensory input can be altered in a positive direction for most subacute or chronically ill patients by introducing high-interest items into their immediate environment and by altering or modifying the design and decor of the facility itself. These changes also help to improve the quantity and quality of conversations that patients have with other patients, visitors, volunteers, or with Home staff.

Multi-high interest items can be introduced by development of multi-item kits or by designing or modifying Homes so that display cases are available for exhibits and demonstrations. By providing multi-item kits, patients may have the possibility of self-stimulation and have available a variety of useful diversional activities. It is difficult to know what past interest patients have had or predict what will prove of interest to them while in the nursing home. For this reason a variety of interest items should be made available to increase the probability of stimulating and diverting interest in a positive way.

The basic plan for a PREVLAB program in a Home requires that multi-item kits be developed, distributed, and periodically serviced: that resources capable of making cultural and diversional contributions to the nursing home be identified and mobilized; and that personnel develop and survey nursing homes to determine the needs of the patients.

The multi-item kit program is developed by following certain steps: (1) Planning Phase, (2) Collection Phase, (3) Assemblage Phase, (4) Distribution Phase, (5) Utilization Phase, (6) Evaluation-follow-up Phase. Attention is called to the reference for more special detail on how to develop a multiitem kit and how to undertake each of the six phases.

EQUIPMENT

It is possible to make up interesting multiitem kits from inexpensive items or surplus items found in homes or in most communities. Items should be chosen on the basis of having: appeal to vision, tactile, or odor senses; humorous or gimicky aspect, cultural or historical interest; active involvement (handling) by the patient; a potential long-range patient interest time; and being relatively inexpensive, compact, light, and not perishable.

PERSONNEL AND TRAINING

Anyone can be responsible for a PREVLAB program. For training materials and design for the kit contact F. R. Mark, MD, 18-34 Parklawn Bldg., 5600 Fisher's Lane, Rockville, MD 20852, for the publication, "A Project for Nursing Homes or Hospitals." It has been suggested that volunteers could be utilized to put together new kits or refurbishing older kits.

REFERENCES

Mark, F. R. A project for nursing homes to combat loneliness, anxiety, and boredom. *Nursing Homes, 1973, 22,* 32-33.

SENSORY RETRAINING

Sensory Retraining (also know as Sensory Training) is a technique that is used effectively with the regressed older person who shows an inability to interact with his environment. The goal of Sensory Retraining is to bring this type individual back into touch literally with his surroundings.

Sensory Retraining is a structured group-individual experience involving all five senses. The aim is to provide the older person with differentiated stimuli to improve his perception of, and response to, both the physical and human environments.

Members of a Sensory Retraining group sit in a circle. The leader introduces himself to the group and the participants to each other. He then explains the purpose of the meeting, e.g., to exercise the senses through which the world is known. Following the introduction, the leader discusses each sense separately and provides some type of activity, using a particular sense. At the end of the session the leader thanks the participants for their cooperation and reminds them when the next meeting will be held.

Because Sensory Retraining is an elementary technique, it is important that the therapist recognize he is working with adults and should conduct the session on an appropriately adult level.

EQUIPMENT

There is an infinite variety of objects useful in stimulating the senses; mirrors and colorful objects stimulate use of the eyes; sharp or acrid-smelling substances contrasted with sweet, pleasant-smelling things exercise the sense of smell; records, whistles, tambourines, clapping, singing, humming, and whispering provide a variety of sounds; candy, pickles, potato chips show different types of tastes; soft, hard, smooth, rough, hot, and cold items offer tactile stimulation. To avoid monotony, it is important to vary the materials used and to contrast as much as possible day-to-day activities.

PERSONNEL AND TRAINING

Any staff member may serve as a sensory-retraining therapist. Patience is an important requirement.

For information on staff training for sensory retraining, contact Leona Richman, OTR, Bronx State Hospital, Bronx, NY.

REFERENCES

Huber, R. Sensory training for a fuller life. *Nursing Homes,* July, 1973, *22*, 14-15.
Richman, L. Sensory training for geriatric patients. *American Journal of Occupational Therapy,* 1969, *22*, 254-257.

SELF-IMAGE THERAPY

The conceptual theory of Self-Image Therapy is based on the work of Maxwell Maltz. The self-concept contains all the descriptions of the objective "me." This includes not only the portraits rendered by the individual but also his impressions of his portraits done by himself or someone else. Once an idea or belief about himself goes into this picture it becomes true as far as he personally is concerned and is added to the mental blueprint each person carries of himself.

The use of group reading with physically disabled geriatric patients is a successful way of organizing and maintaining a cohesive group. The development of a group seems to provide the patients with a greater sense of security and belongingness. The use of group reading as a tool helps the handicapped, institutionalized geriatric patient reach his maximum level of adjustment and enhances his self-image. This technique can be used with a variety of disabilities and has been of benefit when working with residents with Parkinson's Disease, multiple sclerosis, rheumatoid arthritis, and with others who have had amputations or have been severely burned.

Self-Image Therapy is based upon the rationale that as a person grows older he experiences feelings and reactions in terms of self and their impact upon self. He becomes what he thinks he is. If the environmental factors distort reality, then a poor self-image may be formed. This awareness of his environment, plus age and physical condition of the individual, are factors which determine the particular kind of relearning involved. His view of his environment and of his place in this environment determines his reactions and his behavior. Social interaction within this environment is of importance, for without adequate interpersonal relationships a concept of self cannot be maintained. Man defines and perceives himself as he believes others percieve and define him, thus, giving him a reflected or "looking-glass self."

An older person who has a physical disability may have a distorted concept of self. He is not like other people; he cannot do certain things others can; he has often been laughed at, chilled, or ignored because of his disability. This may cause an individual to feel that he is not as good as a normal person and that he is just a freak. This attitude about self leads to failure and unhappiness. The nightmare of failure tends to be compensated through the creation of a rigid and/or idealized self-image, that is, a much distorted image of the self. The staff needs to work closely to help the patient maintain and/or change his concept to a more realistic one.

The purpose of Self-Image Therapy, utilizing reading groups as its tool, gives the therapist the opportunity to help the patient/resident clarify his identity, to increase his self-esteem and his acceptance of self and others, to assist in developing group cohesiveness and a feeling of belonging; to assist in adjusting to the disability by providing an opportunity to explore and discuss similarities and differences in abilities and limitations, to explore feelings and attitudes concerning disabilities, to provide an opportunity to share experiences and frustrations resulting from disability; to realistically assess strengths and assist the person in becoming aware of his assets, and to establish an environment in which the person is genuinely respected.

Only by helping a person gain a sense of a respect for self and a willingness to accept the self for what he is will he be able to live a fuller, happier, more successful life.

Equipment

The book to be read is the choice of the group; however, suggestions are made by the leader. Film strips, pictures, posters, and/or items pertaining to the book may be used to supplement the readings.

Personnel and Training

Any staff member may serve as a leader in a Self-Image Therapy group. An observer in the group is also necessary to report pertinent observation about problems and difficulties of group operation and reactions, both verbal and non-verbal, of each group member. The leader may have more experience with groups, but the observer should have skills in working with people. The leader and observer work together on behalf of the group, one helping to guide the group and the other watching how it works.

For further information on Self-Image Therapy and training using the reading group technique contact Occupational Therapy Dept., Dallas Home for Jewish Aged, 2525 Centerville Rd., Dallas 75228.

REFERENCES

Johnston, N. Group reading as a treatment tool with geriatrics, *American Journal Occupational Therapy*. 1965, 19, 4.
Maltz, M. *Psycho cybernetics*. New York: Essandess Special Editions, 1960.
Burnside, I. Group work among the aged. *Nursing Outlook*. 1969, 17, (6), 68-71.

Reality Therapy

Reality Therapy is a technique developed by William Glasser which attempts to lead emotionally disturbed patients of all ages away from denying the world and helps them to recognize that reality not only exists, but that they must fulfill their needs within its framework. The fundamental principle of Reality Therapy is that all human beings satisfy their basic needs through involvements with other people.

Glasser feels that there are two basic psychological needs: the need to love and be loved, and the need to feel worthwhile both to oneself and to others. Reality Therapy is particularly important for the institutionalized older person who feels worthless and rejected. Reality Therapy teaches patients better ways to fulfill their needs. Interpersonal relationships will not be maintained unless the patient develops more satisfactory patterns of behavior.

Reality Therapy consists of five separate but interwoven procedures. The first step is involvement. The primary therapist, as well as all concerned team members, must pierce the patient's wall of loneliness and self-involvement and convince him of his sincere interest in him as a human being. The second step is "current behavior." In this step the patient becomes consciously aware of his behavior at the present time. The third step is evaluation of behavior. The patient must look critically at his behavior and judge it on the basis of whether it is responsible and beneficial to himself and others. The decision to change or alter behavior is a rational decision made by the patient himself, not the therapist. In the fourth step the patient and the therapist formulate a realistic plan to follow in changing the patient's behavior. The plan should be sufficiently ambitious to produce noticeable, recognizable change, but not so grand that failure is likely. A failing person, after all, needs success. He needs small steps to attain it. The fifth step is the implementation of the plan. The therapist helps the patient gain the experience of fulfilling a commitment to a responsible plan. The patient is held responsible for his behavior, something is expected of him, and somebody cares about him. If one plan does not succeed, another should be developed and tried until one works.

EQUIPMENT

Reality Therapy requires no special equipment.

PERSONNEL AND TRAINING

Courses in Reality Therapy are taught in colleges and universities and are often offered as one-day institutes and special workshops. Reality Therapy should be conducted only under the direction of a psychiatrist, psychologist, psychiatric social worker, or some other professional specifically trained in the theories and techniques of Reality Therapy.

REFERENCE

Glasser, W. *Reality therapy.* New York: Harper & Row, 1965.

SUMMARY

Appropriate care of the aged requires the acceptance and implementation of a treatment model which is essentially built on the determination that sick older people can improve function. The modalities presented are based upon the following assumptions:

(1) If the normal patterns of living could be restored, senility could be reversed.
(2) Senile symptoms, or at least some senile symptoms, could be substituted for frustrated impulses due to inner conflict, or a protest against inner conflict.
(3) Memory losses may be selective.
(4) Disorientation and confusion could be reversed by relearning the skill of thinking and remembering.
(5) Mental ability that has deteriorated through disuse could be restored.
(6) Stimulation of all kinds (sensory, emotional, occupational) could be curative for the disorientated and confused person.

If a treatment model modality is selected and used, it is believed that such intervention can break the cycle of senility which is described in the Spiral of Senility Chart (Fig. 1). The result is a richer and rewarding life for the elderly, their families, and their caretakers.

Bibliography on Treatment Models and Their Relationship to Measures of Program Effectiveness.

Becker, W. C. *Parents are teachers.* Champaign, Ill: Research Press, 1971.

Contingency Management in Education. Kalamazoo (POB 1044): Behaviordelia, 1971.

Diebert, A. M., & Harmon, A. J. *New tools for changing behavior.* Champaign, Ill: Research Press, 1970.

Glasser, W. *Reality therapy, a new approach to psychiatry.* New York: Harper & Row, 1965.

Harris, T. A. *I'm OK – You're OK, a practical guide to transactional analysis.* New York: Harper & Row, 1967.

Holland, J. C. Ethical considerations in behavior modification. *In Current Ethical Issues in Mental Health.* Washington: NIMH, HEW Publ. No. HSM 73-9029, 1973.

Kiresuck, T., & Sherman, R. E. Goal attainment scaling: A general method for evaluating comprehensive community mental health programs. *Community Mental Health Journal,* 1968, 4 (6).

Programmed Instruction in Goal Attainment Scaling. Minneapolis (50 Park Ave. S.): Program Evaluating Project, 1971.

40. Counseling the Aging*

MARY BUCKLEY**

In a culture preoccupied with youth, the aged are often relegated to a secondary and neglected status. Mary Buckley's article asks us to take another look at the aged and realize that, contrary to our prejudices, personal growth and creative living do not end with the beginning of retirement. She describes her counseling style with the aging, which is designed to provide an atmosphere of understanding and sharing in order to foster their growth.

In this age of crisis and change, the aged have been devalued culturally and physically and have become forgotten parts of the whole in American society. Too often they are seen as victims of sad deterioration to be filed away in retirement villages, in their own homes living on public assistance, and in nursing homes.

American society draws a line at age 65 and says, "Now you're old." This labeling and enforced separation of most of the aged from the activities and responsibilities of youth is the result of our society's failure to understand the special needs of the elderly as a group or to appreciate their individuality.

IDENTITY CRISIS

When old people come for counseling, they have the same needs that we find among youth and the middle aged: the need to be loved, to feel self-worth, to have the practical matters of life made clear or easier, to be understood by someone who cares, to find a way to cope and carry on when problems seem insurmountable, and to find acceptance and support. The challenge for the counselor, however, is to help the aged client find ways to satisy these needs in the face of the fact that so much of their unhappiness is a response to objective, irreversible circumstances.

*Reprinted from the *Personnel and Guidance Journal*, Vol. 50, No. 9, 1972, pages 755-758 with permission of the author and the American Personnel and Guidance Association. Copyright 1972, American Personnel and Guidance Association.
**Ms. Buckley is Director of Social Services at the DePaul and Mount St. Vincent Nursing Home in Seattle, Wash.

Elderly people in America suffer from a complex of identity crises caused by the diminishment of their physical abilities and changes in their social roles, status, and relationships. "Who am I and what am I doing here when I've just retired? . . . when I've lost my mate? . . . when I've had to move from my home of many years? . . . when my health has failed? . . . when I find myself in an institution?" Often an elderly person has to face more than one of these major changes at a time when both his strength and resilience seem to be failing him.

One of the major obstacles to satisfying their needs that these clients face is their accumulation of losses as they age. This problem is compounded because any one loss of health, work, mate, or money often necessitates other major life changes, such as an entire restructuring of life style or finding a new place to live. Husband or wife, job, home, community, friends, family, health — one by one these may slip away with nothing in sight to fill the vacancies. Not only do old people suffer from a lack of opportunity to replace meaningful attachments but also many are reluctant to risk new involvements. They find it easy to capitulate to what might seem to them an unavoidable fate: "Nothing much is going to last very long anyway."

The nearness of death — and, frequently, fear of it — is another problem the aged must face without any prospect of being able to change the objective source of their unhappiness. The inevitability of death, and death itself, must be faced alone. We can only go so far along that path with another, but still a person needs to know that someone cares enough to support him along his journey as long as anyone can, to empathize with him as deeply as anyone can.

Each individual has his own needs and his own variations of the problems I am describing. But perhaps the most severe crisis of identity for aged people, and the one I have found to be most common among the old clients I have counseled, is a feeling of *separateness*. So many of them feel that they have been put aside, discarded as useless to society. They cry out with the desire to be brought back to participate in the giving and taking that other age groups take for granted. The aged want to be included in the mainstream, not rejected; they want equality rather than sympathy, to be able to give as well as to receive. They ask that society see not only what they have lost and how much they have deteriorated but that it also recognize the aged as persons with something to contribute, persons of whom others have high regard and expectations.

Our present attitudes about and definitions of age lock people into categories of relative usefulness and function, demoralize those in the socially less attractive category (the aged), and waste precious human potential.

UNDERSTANDING THE NEEDS OF THE AGED

To meet the needs of the aged, counselors need a counseling model based on the recognition that the unique problems of these persons militate against their seeking help. The sense of separateness so many of them suffer is most often kept hidden or denied. For some, admission of this feeling about themselves would shake their last remnants of a sense of dignity and self-worth (which have already been pretty well shattered by a society that as a whole does not look on old years as good years).

Only 1 percent of the contacts made by a local mental health center in a recent year were with people over 65. This statistic is not surprising, because the elderly need to see themselves as strong and don't want to acknowledge weakness. Self-sufficiency was an important value in the culture of their younger days, so they tend to deny that they need the help of others, to keep their fears and feelings in the privacy of their own families — if not in their own hearts. They are caught by a cultural lag between their behavior patterns learned in the past and the problems presented to them by the world of today.

In another generation, this situation may well change. We have come to recognize that it is part of the human condition to need the support of others and that there is a very healthy side to seeking help — a recognition not shared by many born in the last century or the early years of this one.

Both the reluctance of the aged to seek counseling and the nature of their problems preclude the usefulness of a counseling model based on adjustment. It would hardly be psychologically healthy for a man of 65 who has had a fulfilling career as either an executive or a laborer and who still wants to be active, suddenly to try to conform his life style to the socially imposed image of a rocking chair grandfather or leisurely golfer. Neither is it economically feasible for many to do so. Second, although adjustment to the role society tries to dicate for the elderly is not desirable, many of the conditions that cause them unhappiness or anxieties are not things that they can change. What, then, can counseling offer them?

A MODEL BASED ON SHARING

I have found that most frequently, although not always, elderly persons find it easier to accept help from a person who has himself lived a good number of years, at least into middle age. In such a relationship, they can feel assured that the helping person has also been faced with the experiences and problems they find so overwhelming. They know that the counselor has also known some of the losses, fears, joys, and privileges of growing old. This comfort elderly people feel in a counseling situation with someone close to their own age gives the key, I feel, to the steps that counselors — regardless of their age — can take to respond in new ways to the needs of their old clients.

Elderly people's greatest need is to be known and understood in their life situation, to experience a healing touch of the genuine regard of one human being for another. An older counselor partakes of his client's life situation, but a younger counselor can also take on the life issues of an aged client as his own, encouraging his client as an individual rather than trying to change him to meet the expectations of the social structure.

As a social worker, I was taught that the helper can use sharing of himself in a counseling relationship with a client as a part of therapy. I find this to be essential in counseling the aged. The willingness to enter into the situation with my clients as much as I can, to compare and share similar situations and accompanying emotions I have experienced can yield a fruitful benefit that goes beyond practical solutions to what the elderly client needs most — the strength to continue on his own, knowing that he's not alone. As does anybody suffering from feelings of rejection, the aged especially need to receive understanding and caring. A counselor doesn't have to be old to be able to empathize and enter into the life of old folks by examining and sharing his own similar patterns of needs for love and self-worth.

The best counseling of the aged will not be noticed as such, because it consists more of asking questions than giving answers. This idea may be considered heresy by some, and I'll grant that there are times when a clearly competent counselor who reaches down to give advice is what a fearful person needs most, or what a proud client needs for formal cover. But in the majority of cases, I find that the slow and subtle, even disguised, ways of supporting the old are the best for meeting their needs. The idea of counseling is an unknown, a threat, and seeking it is an admittance of weakness for them. Support of their very real strengths is what they need — support received through the casual but continuing relationship with a counselor.

To establish this kind of relationship, the counselor will often find that he must use an outreach approach, initiating an encounter with the old who are so hesitant to impose. The counseling that ensues will of necessity be slowly paced, because it takes time for the old to learn to trust the counselor. A more practical concern is that it also takes a longer time for them to move, speak, think, and respond.

Frequently, the helping relationship with an old person can be initiated when he is seeking an answer to a practical problem dealing with the mechanics of everyday life. The aged person usually can say comfortably that he needs help dealing with the complications of Social Security and Medicare. The counselor in such a situation can help his client achieve his goals within the limitations of the client's economic alternatives, his individual situation and the social structure.

CONCLUSION

Although I have tried to sketch roughly the techniques I find most beneficial in counseling the aged, in general I follow my feelings and senses in deciding what will bring out the best in an individual client. Formal or informal, businesslike or at ease, weak or strong, competent or confused, speaking or listening, verbal or silent, actively moving in or staying away — what each seems to need I try to provide. Whatever each has to offer, I try to receive thankfully. My purpose and intention is always to relate slowly and gently with the aged in order to foster their growth, to establish an atmosphere in which both the old person and I can give and receive from each other.

41. Age Counseling: Crises, Services, Potentials*

Sidney L. Pressey**

This final of two papers regarding the values of the older counselor in dealing with the elderly stresses the distinctive contributions that he may make if he himself is resident in an institution of the old. Such values are illustrated by problems met and help given the writer in connection with the long illness and death of his wife. Detailed diaries kept over a 4-year period, and sample days recorded by another resident-counselor, illustrate the great variety of problems and counseling.

A previous paper (S. L. Pressey and Alice D. Pressey, 1972) argued that counseling regarding problems of age was a major need of both the old and their families and that the older counselor, himself experiencing age and its exigencies, might be especially competent in such work. The authors argued that the best modern institutions for the old, with their apartments and other facilities for those still active and with medical units for those needing nursing care, had potentials not recognized even by many gerontologists and that an older resident counselor might render many services. We lived in such an institution and we did somewhat so serve as well as were so served. Since that paper was written, Alice has died — after a long cardiac illness. Further material has been gathered in two institutions.

Crisis Counseling — And Experiencing!

First, as counselors ourselves in crises, what counsel did we need and receive? We were helped more than we anticipated when other residents, whom we met in corridors, lounges, or dining rooms, were solicitous and understanding; it was supportive to be thus in this little society of the old. Especially helpful were two resident women, also retired

*Reprinted from the *Journal of Counseling Psychology*, Vol. 20, 1973, pages 356-360, with permission of the author and the American Psychological Association. Copyright, 1973 by the American Psychological Association.
**Dr. Pressey is Emeritus Professor of Psychology at Ohio State University. He has lived and worked as a counselor in several settings for the aged.

faculty with long practical experience in counseling and themselves acquainted with illness and bereavement. While Alice was able to continue with me in our apartment, they were cheery, helpful neighbors. When she was moved to the nearby nursing facility, they visited her there when her condition permitted, sent her clever notes, and were often my sympathetic companions in the dining room. When the end came, they were at once with me understandingly to help, in many ways, in the trying days following. When one evening the loneliness seemed unbearable, a visit down the corridor to see them helped much. In this fine insititution, the physician, nurses, chaplain, all were helpful, but they were busy people. The two neighbor-counselors were understanding friends, living right there with us. Several other residents with somewhat similar competence have so served others, all as volunteers. In a church-sponsored retirement community in California, a vigorous kindly resident is a paid staff member for such work.

Counseling resources are available to those who would so counsel and to those who would so be counseled. Both may find help pithily put by a newspaper columnist (in Collins, 1970). All concerned with age will find valuable a volume by a team of experts — medical, psychiatric, psychological, sociological, and economic — connected with the Duke Center for the Study of Aging (Busse & Pfeiffer, 1969). Specifically on the psychological management of loss and grief, again by a team of experts, mostly from Columbia University, is another recent book (Schoenberg, Carr, Peretz, & Kutscher, 1970). Insightful is a book just out by (Weisman, 1972). Two older volumes also have been helpful, one consisting of poignant accounts by physicians of their own critical illnesses (Pinner & Miller, 1952) and the other by a wide-ranging panel of theologians, physicians, and psychologists on *The Meaning of Death* (Feifel, 1959), which ends with an outstanding commentary by my old friend Gardner Murphy, then of the Menninger Foundation. Sundry helpful material may be readily accumulated.

By being thus somewhat informed, and by living there, the neighbor-counselor can be watchful for crises and often be the first to know of them, as in the case of a midnight cardiac attack or a stroke. In such a time, often of confusion, he should know whom to call (nurse, what physician, what neighbor to watch for him, any relative or friend to be phoned) and any possible first aid to render. In crises, a calm knowledgeable friend can help so much. During the time of bereavement, the bereaved may be somewhat helped and the counselor may help more, if both know how various may be the effects of this state; that is, of the whole psychological and physical self which, being pervasively disturbed, can exhibit an illness that is perhaps at least partly caused by grief.

Everyday Counseling — And Therapy

The resident-counselor has special opportunities to note impending crises in such things as a senile's increasing forgetfulness and fretting, perhaps with delusions, or a cardiac's increasing need to rest on the way to the dining room. Auditory loss may be especially evidenced in conversational difficulties; the need may be stressed that soft-voiced old people learn to speak loudly and clearly (perhaps more important than learning lip-reading!) and the need stressed also of dining-room soundproofing. Not any hearing-aid salesman but an adequate expert should be consulted. An upset glass of water, container and content both translucent, may suggest need for a visual checkup (Stone, 1969, p. 315). If difficulty in reading is mentioned, the neighbor-counselor can stop by and see whether a brighter bulb in a better placed lamp might help. The oldster with a car should understand how variously handicapped for night driving he may be, since he has less accommodation to distance, dark adaptation, color discrimination, and recovery from glare (Geist, 1968, pp. 60-67). The active old may need warning how easily a fracture may now occur with a fall.

As the earlier paper emphasized, detailed diaries kept by old people may strikingly reveal problems, helpfulnesses, or total life-styles. Thus on a recent Saturday an 83-year-old man, depressed by his wife's death, prepared his doctor-prescribed breakfast of milk-toast, worked on this paper, lunched with three sympathetic other residents in the dining room, rested, then worked, then to supper with an ailing 90-year-old friend and his wife and daughter whom he tried to cheer, finally back to his apartment for a newscast and bed. That was his day, all in the residency, chatting with six people, working, and perforce resting.

How different that same day for an ebullient resident neighbor 10 years younger, one of the two already mentioned as so helpful. Breakfast bound, she shoved any morning paper that was outside a door under it so as to make it easy to reach. In the informality of the buffet breakfast room she waved, nodded, or said good morning to everyone there, helped an almost blind resident prepare her menu, advised another how most tactfully to make a complaint: in the total breakfast period she made some 50 friendly contacts all with people she knew by name. Back in her apartment she phoned a breakfast absentee to be sure she was not ill, went to the service room to press a dress and chatted there with two neighbors, took yet another friend to the residency clinic and while waiting there chatted with some dozen passersby, and then went to another apartment to meet a guest. At lunch she gaily chatted with several friends. Then a bus trip to a movie she had arranged for 10 other residents was followed by a cafeteria supper with them. Finally she visited a sick friend. Total: some 90 social contacts all with people she knew by name and 18 kindly acts — from helping the poorly sighted one at breakfast to the evening visit!

Much of the above might be called simply friendliness, but an abundance of that is needed in an "old folks home." The afternoon trip, also a picnic and several all-day trips, were managed with the deftness of the long-experienced teacher and counselor: the lonely and shy were enticed out of their rooms to go, seated with friendly companions, visited with as circumstance permitted, and noted as needing help if so it seemed to be. Thus the trip was used to acquaint people with one another and to help in sundry ways. The wise counselor also will keep such records that those who do *not* go on trips are noted. Be they those physically handicapped, isolated, or odd, the devoted counselor will seek them out. And dining room records of who is there *and* sits with whom may show (as stressed in the earlier paper) cliques desirably broken up and may be exhibits of social relations. The resident-counselor eating there has many opportunities to affect those relations. He may help those on diets, gently josh the merely hypochondriacal, seek out the lonely, or know what to do if illness occurs, as not infrequently happens.

Cases — And Their Courses

So much primarily about an old man, the death of his wife, and a helpful neighbor. Notably and tragically helpful was a man who was also a former teacher, counselor, and a somewhat similar cardiac case. He also watched for and tried to help lonely residents, sometimes led chapel services humbly but with the understanding of a fellow oldster for religious needs in age. One bright October day he drove some feeble old women into hill country, gorgeous with autumn color; came back exhausted: and died that night. Some who knew him thought it all intended (though doubtless subconsciously), that he wanted to go without further lingering, after a day of beauty, serving friends. A clergyman's widow was almost compulsive in her many kindnesses, helped much in the nursing facility, finally became exhausted, and then needed care herself. A counselor will watch lest some overdo.

A few residents continued somewhat in career, a lawyer and a physician some practice, a teacher some substituting. All this seems good mental hygiene — not disengagement and withdrawal but activity and participation seem most healthy. Further, it is predicted that

> American society will develop new roles for the aged and expand their present useful roles . . . There is an unlimited amount of counseling, . . . therapy, tutoring, and training that could helpfully be done . . . And one of the greatest resources . . . is the

experience, skill, and devotion of millions of aged persons [Palmore, 1967, pp. 63-64].

Since a variety of volunteer work in the residency, nearby churches, or welfare organizations is usually needed and it gives healthy social contacts, a counselor can foster such undertakings.

In a residency we have the helpful and the busy, also we have the lonely needing to be drawn into things, the fretful complainers needing perspective on themselves, and the increasingly odd needing psychiatric attention. There are those who are haggard from helping care for a relative or close friend in a nursing facility who is perhaps senile, demanding, or incontinent. All these a councelor may help. Also there are those complacent with bridge, visits from relatives, and small talk. But there is another topic not to be forgotten.

WHEN AND HOW DIE?

A recent survey reported that of those entering homes for the aged, 58% died within 4 years as compared to 71% of those entering nursing homes (Goldfarb, 1969, p. 308). Further, an individual "in irreversible coma . . . may be sustained on this level for years with respirators, cardiac stimulators . . . draining the emotional and financial resources of family members [Schoenberg et al., 1970, p. 255]." Surely such a sustaining of minimal existance is not desirable. But how long should measures be maintained to continue life, perhaps with great pain, as from a cancer? If such a person desires that his misery not be continued, might he even be helped in fulfilling his wish — as in the case where a physician left an oldster with three pills, saying that if taken once every 4 hours they would ease his misery but taken all at once they would kill him. Gratefully, the patient took the latter alternative. Under certain such circumstances might the "right to die become another generally accepted civil right," as suggested in a report from the American Medical Association? Perhaps "the science and art for the preservation of life needs, as a counterpart, a science and art for the closure of life [Palmore, 1969, p. 62]." Psychologists have been leaders in programs for suicide prevention. Might not counseling psychologists be especially competent to present the above point of view?

As already mentioned, the back rooms of nursing homes are full of persons who are senile, many incontinent, disturbed, or almost in coma, some remaining so for years (Goldfarb, 1969, p. 302). If earlier they might have foreseen such a terminal condition, might they then have authorized euthanasia, if that could legally be done? Shouldn't it be made possible? There is now much discussion of the matter

(Church, 1972; *The Right to Die with Dignity,* 1971), and support by older people. Might a resident-counselor be helpful in considerations of the topic? There is also an increasing recognition, as in the hearings of the Church Senate Committee and in a recent psychiatric study (Weisman, 1972), that the usual hospital or nursing facility, concerned with physical care, neglects the needs of the still-integrated dying person for understanding, companionship, and facing up to death. A "hospice" with psychiatrist, chaplain, or counselor may then be especially needed by both patient and family. Such an institution can give "a new useful experience in community living [Goldfarb, 1969, p. 305]." Such care may lengthen life and make its ending more of a fulfillment (Church, 1972, p. 136), as indeed may occur in the best church-sponsored residencies.

PLANT, COMMUNITY — LABORATORY?

Counseling from diets to dying — how the issues do range! Institution planners may need age counselors! What is to them a gentle rise in a walkway may be exhausting for many oldsters. For their visitors, or for physicians or ambulances hurrying to them perhaps in the night, are the drives clearly marked and buildings and rooms clearly numbered for old eyes? Are doors hard for old arms to open, corridors too long without rest places, the edges of outside steps in need of clear markings as with yellow paint? Are help-calling cords or buttons in fact readily reached? In the nursing facility, may the beds be so high that even an old person who is well might have trouble getting in? And "side-rails generally cause more falls and fractures than they prevent, in addition to being personally humiliating [Goldfarb, 1969, p. 306]," as almost any old person who has been so penned up will agree. An age counselor who has at least visited about a little will be aware of such matters.

But now two last broad issues. Traditionally, institutions for the old are avoided by them as poorhouse tainted and viewed askance by their neighborhoods as repositories for the tottery or querulous or queer. But as such places get better, some even luxurious, and entered earlier by oldsters still active and attractive, may such "residencies" be viewed with pride and so mentioned by the chamber of commerce! A kindly resident-counselor, perhaps retired from relevant experience in a local college, school, or welfare program, might foster such a view. Such a person also might envision and develop special institutional roles benefiting the community. Thus one long-established residency became known over a wide area for its Thanksgiving Festival, with residents in Pilgrim costume.

Finally, if managed carefully, what opportunities for helpful research — old people known intimately, as fellow residents and as counseled, in joy and sorrow, and even into their dying, the resources of the institution to help. Surely valuable contributions thus might be made to gerontology, counseling, and institutional management.

The most understanding, humane, and courageously realistic of gerontological counselors might join those of similar understanding and courage in the clergy, medicine, and law in urging a "bill of rights" for the old which, with adequate legal and medical safeguards against abuse, should provide those who so desire, with assurance that *(a)* their dying should not be prolonged beyond all hope of value by intravenous feeding or other artifacts of modern medicine, *(b)* if in great pain or for other good reason they desire to die they should be helped to do so, and *(c)* if long hopeless senility becomes their condition, they should have life ended. There should be courageous discussion of the question put by Sir George Thompson, Nobel Laureate and leading British advocate of euthanasia, "Why should people be obliged to live unwillingly for an indefinite period in a state which is a travesty of humanity, retaining only its most sordid elements [Thompson, 1971, p. 24]?" Yet perhaps a majority of those who now live to be old, so end. Surely it should not so be. As one hospital chaplain has declared, "We have perverted the Judeo-Christian tradition into a belief that biological existence *per se* is of supreme value . . . and been sidetracked into an ethical dilemma of ghastly proportions [Reeves, 1971, p. 11]." Even the gerontologists, busy with their research, mostly have not faced up to it. Might not some elderly counselors so do?

REFERENCES

Busse, E. W., & Pfeiffer, E. (Eds.) *Behavior and adaptation in late life*. Boston: Little, Brown, 1969.

Church, F. (Chm.) Death with dignity. Hearing before the Special Committee on Aging, U.S. Senate, August 7-9, 1972. Washington, D.C.: U.S. Government Printing Office, 1972.

Collins, T. *The complete guide to retirement*. Englewood Cliffs, N.J.: Prentice-Hall, 1970.

Feifel, H. (Ed.) *The meaning of death*. New York: McGraw-Hill, 1959.

Geist, H. *Psychological aspects of the aging process*. St. Louis: Warren H. Green, 1968.

Goldfarb, A. I. Institutional care of the aged. In E. W. Busse & F. Pfeiffer (Eds.), *Behavior and adaptation in late life*. Boston: Little, Brown, 1969.

Palmore, E. Sociological aspects of aging. In E. W. Busse & E. Pfeiffer (Eds.), *Behavior and adaptation in late life*. Boston: Little, Brown, 1969.

Pinner, M., & Miller, B. F. (Eds.) *When doctors are patients*. New York: Norton, 1952.

Pressey, S. L., & Pressey, A. D., Major neglected need opportunity: Old-age counseling. *Journal of Counseling Psychology*, 1972, 19, 362-366.

Reeves, R. B. Recognizing the death of the individual. In *The right to die with dignity*. New York: Euthanasia Educational Fund, 1971.

The right to die with dignity. New York: Euthanasia Educational Fund, 1971.

Schoenberg, B., Carr, A. C., Peretz, D., & Kutscher, A. H., (Eds.) *Loss and grief; psychological management in medical practice*. New York: Columbia University Press, 1970.

Stone, V. Nursing of older people. In E. W. Busse & E. Pfeiffer (Eds.), *Behavior and adaptation in late life*. Boston: Little, Brown, 1969.

Thompson, G. An old problem in a new form. In *The right to die with dignity*. New York: Euthanasia Educational Fund, 1971.

Weisman, A. D. *On dying and denying*. New York: Behavioral Publications, 1972.

V
Summary and Overview

JOHN R. BARRY AND C. RAY WINGROVE

As the readings in this volume suggest, interest in the field of aging has burgeoned in recent years. From a relatively small number of people who wrote about and researched the problems of the aged, the field has expanded more rapidly each succeeding year. The reasons for this rapid expansion of interest and activity in gerontology are many. Primary among them is the rapidly increasing numbers and proportion of elderly people in our society today. This rate of growth is well described in our introductory reading by Hanns Pieper.

While a disproportionate number of aged persons are still found between the ages of 65 and 75, more and more are living longer at all ages. Thirty-eight percent of the aged population was 75 or over in 1970 compared to 33 percent in 1960. It is estimated that by the year 2000, 44 percent of all those over 65 will be over 75. This means greater heterogeneity among the aged than ever and necessitates more interest in treating the different groups of elderly people *differently* rather than as a single group of old people. The person who is 65 may be as different (e.g., in his needs, ideas, hopes, and health) from the person of 85 as from the person of 45. The increasing diversity among the subgroups of aged persons regarding characteristics such as educational and socioeconomic backgrounds, makes many of our former ideas about the aged out-of-date.

This relatively recent growth in the numbers of elderly has resulted in needs for more manpower in all aspects of service and care for the aged. More personnel and specialists are needed in social work, housing, counseling, medicine, nutrition, and a host of other helping and maintenance fields. Many of these people have only recently come into the field of aging and are eager for information about the older person. Thus, educational and training programs at very basic levels, as well as at college and university levels, have developed. Graduate research centers in gerontology have been developed at Duke University, the University of Michigan, the University of Southern California, and in a few other institutions. Undergraduate education is just now becoming available, often through personnel trained at one of these centers. Introductory adult education and programming about the aged is also being developed through state and Federal assistance programs. This book was developed as an aid in meeting the training and educational needs of people entering the developing field of gerontology.

A major characteristic of gerontology is its interdisciplinary nature. Knowledge about the aged person is drawn from a variety of disciplines, for example, physiology, sociology, psychology, economics, and many others. This interdisciplinary nature is reflected in the readings of this volume. The field of gerontology has drawn upon approaches, knowledge, and services from these disciplines as they might be applied to the problems faced by the aging person. Ideas, hypotheses, research and practices from a variety of fields have been applied in settings where the aged live and are served. The selections in this book reflect this interdisciplinary focus and the interdependence of information in the different areas.

False stereotypes about the aged developed partly because early reasearch concentrated upon institutionalized aged persons, the most available groups for study. Now that more "normal" non-institutionalized groups of aged persons have been described through research, stereotypes have been broadened and in some cases negated. For example, the decline of intellectual functioning is no longer seen as inevitable (see the Baltes and Schaie readings) as once believed. Likewise, sexual interests and sexual behavior are no longer denied (see the Rubin and Wingrove papers) and viewed as inappropriate for the aged. These are but a few examples of changing stereotypes pointed out in selections in this reader.

The readings in this volume uncover many other misconceptions and biases in the field of aging and offer in their place new knowledge based upon recent studies employing improved research methodology. Whether the research is as basic as physiological and psychological processes of aging, as mundane as housing and retirement, as personal as sex and religion, or as taboo as death and dying, the findings are presented with the hope that the knowledge will contribute toward a better understanding of and service to the elderly.

Hopefully the papers reprinted in this book will facilitate a more complete understanding of and respect for the uniqueness and individuality of each older person. We must enlist the strengths and resources of the aged, and we must encourage their participation in the planning and conduct of whatever help is provided to them. To whatever extent is possible for them, the aged should participate in and be responsible for their own destiny.

If the reader is challenged by these readings to question some of the myths and stereotypes about the aged, if he is encouraged to work more hopefully and more creatively with the elderly, the goals of the editors will have been met.